A HISTORY OF CHRISTIANITY IN AFRICA

D1488353

A HISTORY OF
CHRISTIANITY
IN AFRICA

From Antiquity to the Present

Elizabeth Isichei

WILLIAM B. EERDMANS PUBLISHING COMPANY
GRAND RAPIDS, MICHIGAN

AFRICA WORLD PRESS INC.
LAWRENCEVILLE, NEW JERSEY

© 1995 Elizabeth Isichei

First published 1995 in Great Britain by
Society for Promoting Christian Knowledge
Holy Trinity Church
Marylebone Road
London NW1 4DU

This edition published jointly 1995, through special arrangement with SPCK, by
Wm. B. Eerdmans Publishing Co.
255 Jefferson Ave. S.E., Grand Rapids, Michigan 49503
and Africa World Press, Inc.
11-D Princess Road, Lawrenceville, New Jersey 08648

Printed in the United States of America

02 01 00 99 98 97 96   7 6 5 4 3 2

Library of Congress Cataloging-in-Publication Data

Isichei, Elizabeth Allo.
A history of Christianity in Africa / Elizabeth Isichei.
p.   cm.
Includes bibliographical references and index.
ISBN 0-8028-0843-3 (pbk.)
1. Christianity — Africa. 2. Africa — Church history.
I. Title.
BR1360.I75   1995
276 — dc20   94-46617
CIP

Africa World Press ISBN
0-86543-442-5 (cloth)
0-86543-443-3 (paper)

If you will listen, I shall tell you a mystery of simplicity.

Speratus (one of the Scilli martyrs, in AD 180, at his
trial at Carthage).

CONTENTS

Acknowledgements

This is my first book since taking up a foundation Chair in Religious Studies at the University of Otago, and will appear in the year when it celebrates the 125th anniversary of its foundation. Many of the books and articles cited here were not available in Dunedin. A research grant from the University not only paid for international interloans but enabled me to employ a succession of helpers who, by tracking down the books I needed, gave me more time to read them. My thanks to Juliet Robinson, Marinus La Rooij, and Chrystal Jaye, and to Judith Brown who compiled the index. The patience and helpfulness of the staff of the University Library's reference department are beyond all praise. My indebtedness to the University goes far beyond this, and the vote of confidence which my appointment represented has lent wings to my work.

My colleagues Malcolm McLean and John Omer-Cooper generously found time to read part of it, as did my son Uche Isichei, an architect now engaged in his own research on Africa. Jenny Murray, one of my oldest friends, read it all. Scholars too numerous to list individually corresponded with me on points of detail.

If the department did not have, in Sandra Lindsay, a wonderfully helpful and efficient secretary, I would not even try to write books while running a university department, and carrying a demanding teaching load.

My father and stepmother, Albert and Jeanne Allo, now well into their eighties, read the manuscript sentence by sentence, and eliminated both infelicities of style and my typing errors. Shirley and Al Bain continue to be endlessly supportive and hospitable.

My five children, Uche, Katherine, Ben, Caroline, and Frank have been the sunshine of my New Zealand years. The oldest four have grown up and left home. This book is, accordingly, dedicated to my youngest, Frank, who put up with me while I wrote it.

A Note on Terminology and Chapter Arrangement

In early drafts of this study, I punctiliously used Bantu prefixes (luGanda, buGanda, baGanda, muGanda). Some who read it felt that it added an unnecessary dimension of complexity for those unfamiliar with the subject matter. I have accordingly adopted the practice of using the root only (Ganda), though occasionally I have retained a prefix. I have, on the whole, used the geographic terminology appropriate for the era I am writing about (German Kamerun, French Cameroun, modern Cameroon). Sometimes I use the more familiar modern place name to refer to an earlier period—Malawi, rather than Nyasaland, for example. Cameroon is part of West Central Africa, but I have also cited some Cameroon material in the chapter on twentieth-century West Africa. There is a note on Kongo/Congo/Zaire in chapter 7, n. 2. Because of the length and complexity of the book and its predominantly regional organisation, I have chosen to repeat a few facts and themes, rather than assume they are remembered from several hundred pages earlier!

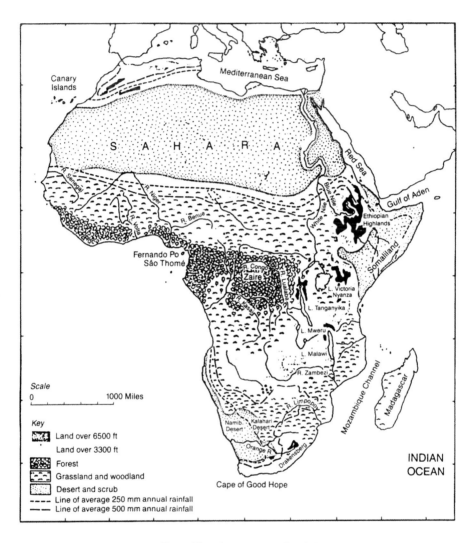

Map 1. Africa the environment. Frontispiece

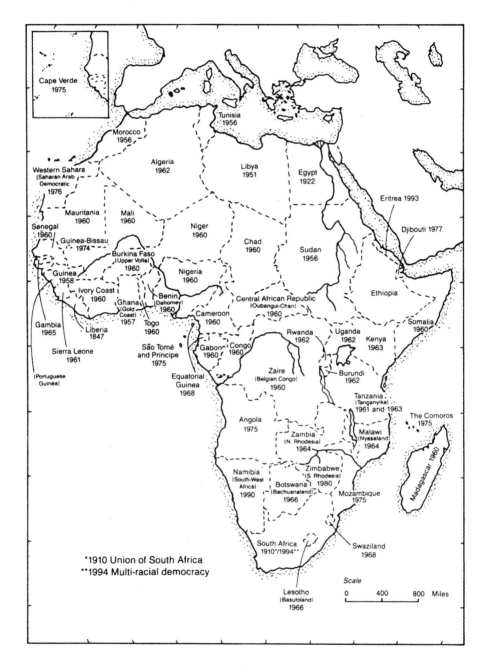

Map 2. Modern Africa

xi

Prelude

> While every day in the West, roughly 7500 people in effect
> stop being Christians every day in Africa roughly double that
> number become Christians . . .[1]

The expansion of Christianity in twentieth-century Africa has been so dramatic that it has been called 'the fourth great age of Christian expansion.'[2] According to much-quoted, if somewhat unreliable, statistics, there were 10 million African Christians in 1900, 143 million in 1970, and there will be 393 million in the year 2000, which would mean that 1 in 5 of all Christians would be an African.[3] There are other estimates and the range of variation reflects the ambiguity and incompleteness of the raw data on which they are based. Much depends on how one defines a Christian, and Africa is full of small, independent churches that have never filed a statistical return.[4] Kenya has the largest Yearly Meeting of Quakers in the world, outside the United States,[5] and more Anglicans attend church in Uganda than in England.

It is clear that, in the words of one thoughtful scholar,

> perhaps one of the two or three most important events in the whole of
> Church history has occurred . . . a complete change in the centre of gravity
> of Christianity, so that the heartlands of the Church are no longer in
> Europe, decreasingly in North America, but in Latin America, in certain
> parts of Asia, and . . . in Africa.[6]

Ahafo, in Ghana, has been called 'a much more predominantly and vigorously Christian area than, for example, the United Kingdom', and the site of a 'Christian ideological triumph'.[7] There is nothing, in the African context, peculiarly religious about Ahafo. Christianity in Africa is of global significance, and the directions it takes are of importance to Christians everywhere. At the 1974 Roman Synod, Cardinal Joseph-Albert Malula of Zaire said, 'In the past, foreign missionaries Christianized Africa. Today the Christians of Africa are invited to Africanize Christianity'.[8]

In the first Christian centuries, northern Africa provided some of the keenest intellects and most influential apologists in Christendom. Origen was an Egyptian from Alexandria, and Tertullian and Augustine came from the

1

Maghrib. Egypt's gnostics and North Africa's Donatists grappled with fundamental problems that still perplex the Christian. How do we explain evil and suffering? Is the Church a gathered remnant of the Just, or are the wheats and tares separable only in eternity? At the end of the third century AD, the eastern Maghrib was one of perhaps three places in the world where Christians were in a majority; the others were Armenia and modern Turkey.

The African Christianity of antiquity was largely, but not wholly, lost. The flourishing churches of North Africa and Nubia, at different points in time, gave way to Islam. Christianity in Egypt survived, though as the faith of a minority. Ethiopia preserved its national adherence to Christianity, in a highly distinctive form, through many centuries of peril and threat, though the Christian kingdom was much smaller than the modern state of the same name. To twentieth-century African Christians, its history seemed a fulfilment of the promise of the psalmist, 'Princes shall come out of Egypt, Ethiopia shall stretch forth her hands to God'.[9]

The next phase of encounter with Christianity—if we exclude the fruitless attempts to convert the Muslims of northern Africa—extends from the sixteenth to the eighteenth centuries. A few African societies were introduced to Christianity, usually in a Catholic and Portuguese form. Christian court civilizations were established in the Kongo Kingdom, and in Warri in the western Niger Delta. The former survived, in a deeply laicized and indigenized form. The latter endured for two centuries and ultimately died out.

There were other enclaves of Christian influence at various points on the West African coast and in the Zambezi valley. It transformed individual lives, but remained marginal to mainstream African cultures. In the atypical context of originally uninhabited islands, the Cape Verdes and São Thomé, Christianity was part of a new Luso-African culture.

The Reformation churches showed curiously little interest in the missionary enterprise. All this changed in the late eighteenth century, as a result of the Evangelical revival. There was a great proliferation of Protestant missionary societies; the Catholics followed later, and on a smaller scale.

The majority of African Christians have remained in the older churches, gradually creating their own maps of reality, interpreting their religion in terms of their own Old Testament of inherited culture. It has been said that the true encounter between Christianity and traditional religion takes place in the heart of African Christians. For many years, it has been common for movements of vigorous autonomy to develop within mission churches. The Revival in East Africa and Zaire, from the 1930s on, is a well-known example of this, as are the powerful women's movements called Rukwadzano in Zimbabwe, and Manyano in South Africa. Since independence, there has been a rapid Africanization of leadership, and of many dimensions of Church praxis. The Zaire Rite, submitted for the approval of Rome in 1983, is a well-known example of a much more extensive process.[10] Once, missionaries insisted on biblical or saints' names for converts; it is now common for African Christians to give their children traditional names, chosen for their congruity with their beliefs, such as Uchechukwuka, God's Wisdom is supreme, Olisaemeka, the Lord has done well, Chinye, God gives, or Chukwubuike, God is my strength.[11]

The so-called African or Ethiopian churches, founded between 1880 and 1920, established new religious organizations that were run by Africans, but differed only in detail from the mission churches from which they had separated themselves. In several instances, they sought and obtained affiliation either to black American churches, or to Greek Orthodoxy. Generally, they are in a state of relative, and sometimes absolute, decline, overtaken by an immense proliferation of 'prophetic' or Zionist churches. It is not easy to explain the geographic distribution of the prophetic churches. They proliferate in Kenya, but are of minor importance in Tanzania.[12] They abound in South Africa, where their appeal especially is to the poor and dispossessed, and in Nigeria, where their members include lawyers, doctors, and university teachers. Some of their founding prophets, such as Harris and Kimbangu, have had a success in winning converts that no mission church in Africa has ever equalled. The Apostles of John Maranke have branches in seven countries, but many prophetic churches are limited to a single congregation. Small churches, like small ethnic groups, tend to slip through the cracks of academic analysis.

With a few exceptions, such as Buganda and the Creole community in Sierra Leone, only a handful of people became Christians in the nineteenth century. Their numbers expanded vastly in the twentieth, largely through the impact of mission schools and the economic benefits of education in the colonial situation. In many areas, such as central Nigeria, Christianity has expanded still more vigorously since independence.

Contemporary Christian intellectuals in Africa are much preoccupied with inculturation and the search for identity. This, in part, is a reaction against white racism in the past, but it is likely that inculturation from above is less effective than the prophetic churches' inculturation from below.

The quest for autonomy has many practical implications. Often, the older churches are torn between the exigencies of their members' poverty and their desire for real independence. In theory, but not in practice, they supported a call for a moratorium on external aid. The prophetic churches are self-supporting, and always have been. To some, the quest for inculturation has become a form of false consciousness. It is always easier to fight yesterday's battles, and the most urgent and acute challenge to the Christian conscience lies in poverty. In South Africa, being poor is largely, though not entirely, synonymous with being black. The division between rich and poor Christians though is, on the one hand, global, and, on the other, mirrored in the microcosm of many independent African states. A radicalized liberation or 'contextual' theology is strongly developed in South Africa, but conspicuous by its absence elsewhere. Critics have expressed anxiety about the spread of a very different response to poverty, that of a cult of prosperity, associated with American tele-evangelism,[13] which seems very far removed from the Sermon on the Mount.

Wherever Christianity is professed, there is a constant dialectic arising from its relationship with the cultural presuppositions and practices of the cultures where it is located. Christianity came to sub-Saharan Africa in European cultural packaging, and contextualization, as we have seen, has been a major concern of Africa's theologians. However, clearly there is a point where contextualization becomes syncretism, and Christian content is eroded, losing 'the conforming of a Church's life to standards outside itself, standards which may cut across everyone's culture pattern. . . .'[14] In 1961, the World Council of Churches defined a criterion for Christian churches seeking membership: if they accept 'Our Lord Jesus Christ as God and Saviour' and are ready 'to fulfil together their common calling to the glory of one God, Father, Son and Holy Spirit'.[15] It is a definition that would exclude the incumbents of many pulpits in the Western world.

When Jesus or Mary join the pantheon of spirits in Cwezi possession cults, or peasants turn Mulele into a saviour/magician, we have clearly moved a long way from mainstream Christianity. One obvious line of demarcation is to exclude cults where the African prophet becomes a saviour, similar to Jesus. However, if Christianity centres on belief in a resurrected Lord, Kimbangu was much more orthodox than Schweitzer.

A number of distinguished Africanists have reflected on the nature of syncretism, and its meaning in the African situation. Shorter suggests that it is radically different from dialogue. 'Syncretism is the absence of dialogue, or perhaps, the failure of dialogue; to avoid it there must be a continuous and consistent exchange of meanings.'[16] Peel points out the ambiguity of the word itself:

> if it means 'a mixing of ideas and practices from different sources' it is by no means peculiarly African. For no adherent of the world religions anywhere derives all the furniture of his mind from his religion. Man's [sic] beliefs are nearly always syncretistic, in that their content shifts in response to new experiences, and that some attempt is made to harmonize old and new . . .[17]

'Syncretism occurs', writes the Cameroonian Eboussi Boulaga, 'where collections of objects, rites or institutions are transmitted—where the future is rejected in the name of a settled acquisition, which one has no desire to modify or lose.'[18]

Many of the prophetic churches have a profoundly biblical religion, differing from the older churches in that they reclaim many aspects of Christianity that have become eroded or forgotten in much western praxis, such as guidance through dreams and visions, miraculous healings, prayer that expects immediate and concrete answers, and often, Old Testament taboos.

4

Even the most fundamentalist Christians, in the West and elsewhere, are selective in the biblical texts they regard as important. A Zambian Anglican, who became a Seventh Day Adventist, said:

> When I asked them about the Bible they would not give me true answers. I was very much puzzled about Daniel and Revelation. But they said, 'These are only dreams. You need not read those books. They are very hard and nobody can understand those books. It is better to read the Gospel'. But there was a great demand in my mind to understand these.[19]

Most observers, including Christians as orthodox as Harold Turner, applaud the Zionist and Aladura churches as deeply inculturated authentic forms of African Christianity. Not all African Christians agree. 'There has been a tendency to glorify the Independent Churches', writes Ogbu Kalu. 'Most of them are neo-pagan, engaged in non-Christian rituals.'[20] All this can best be understood in terms of a wider debate, which seeks to reconcile the historically exclusivist claims of Christianity with the desire to show equal deference to other faith traditions. 'There seems no consistent theological way to relativise and yet to assert our own symbols.'[21] To its critics, religious pluralism erodes the basic content of faith traditions, for it is the essence of the Religions of the Book, though not of 'traditional' religions, that they make exclusive truth claims.[22]

Religious meanings are changed, nuanced, eroded by journeys through time as well as by journeys through cultures. Here, again, there is a division, between those who believe that there is an essential core of Christian beliefs, unchanged by historical circumstance, and those who hold that, ' "the world" is constructed by human perceptions, concerns and interests. "Reality" therefore, differs from society to society and from age to age. This applies to Christianity too.'[23] This division is made wider by the fact that a great deal which is apparently extraneous tends to be added to the essential core of religious meaning. Religious systems are conservative, creating a fossilized ideal of a time that never was, but is often located in an imaginary early church. Twentieth-century Anglicans using the 1662 Prayer Book continued to pray for the Queen, and her Privy Council, rather than the real institutions of later government, Cabinet, Parliament, and Prime Minister. The Vatican is notorious for policies justified and motivated by the desire for consistency with a recent and/or largely invented past.

Sykes, in a thoughtful reflection on these issues writes, 'the contestants are held together by the conviction that the contest has a single origin in a single albeit internally complex performance . . . the life, death and resurrection of Jesus Christ'.[24]

'Where world religions become social frameworks, two things must have happened to the old ethnic religion. Firstly it must be eliminated . . . Secondly elements of the old religion are incorporated . . . A third possibility is that the ethnic religion may survive, attenuated . . .'[25] African Christians have often chosen the first option, burning the images of traditional gods and tearing the masks from cult dancers. However, there is an underlying problem, which greatly complicated relationships between foreign missionaries and African Christians, and it lies in the question – are traditional divinities an illusion, or are they real, but evil? To nineteenth-century missionaries, the spirits of traditional religion were very often real demons. To modern Africanists, this is a good example of white racism, but they did take the spiritual world of the Other seriously, even while condemning it. Modern clerical enthusiasts for spirit possession take it for granted that the spirits have no objective existence and that, therefore, their cults are a form of gestalt therapy.

The great strength of the modern prophetic churches is that they offer deliverance from evil, perceived as witchcraft, and specific spiritual remedies for the multiple afflictions to which we are all heir, but poor Africans more than most. Emmanuel Milingo, Catholic Archbishop of Lusaka from 1969 to 1982, fully accepted the world of witches and *mashave* spirits and offered a ministry of healing and exorcism to those so afflicted. He was critical of foreign Christian experts on Africa who did not accept the reality of this spirit world. But, while clearly meeting the needs of many Zambians, he was unacceptable to the authorities in his own church, which removed him from his see.

Milingo attempted to integrate elements of traditional belief with mainstream Catholicism. It is much more common for these beliefs to lead a parallel existence in the same individual. The Nigerian radical, Tai Solarin, makes this point, citing his mother, who, in an electrical storm, would call on the spirit of her grandfather more often than Jesus.[26] 'Where world religions become social frameworks, two things must have happened to the old ethnic religion. Firstly it must be eliminated . . . Secondly elements of the old religion are incorporated . . . A third possibility is that the ethnic religion may survive, attenuated. . . .'[27] This kind of inconsistency is not peculiar to Africa. The banking system of the western world would collapse if we all followed the precepts of Jesus about laying up treasure on Earth.

A history of the growth of Christianity easily slides into a form of triumphalism, where local cultures are passive and static. This tendency was for long reinforced by the tendency of anthropologists to seek out cultures as little westernized as possible, and to focus on the 'traditional', even where it was in the process of disappearing. Some twenty-five years ago, there was an energetic reaction against all this, in which the innovation in 'traditional' religions were emphasized, and anthropologists have become much more aware of their assumptions about time.[28] In a sense, the changing forms of traditional religion lie outside the scope of this book. However, the increasing importance of the High God in 'traditional' religion, the tendency to identify Chukwu (in Igboland), or Mwari (among the Shona and their neighbours) with the Christian God is apparent. Among the Nyakusa, a Supreme God was introduced into 'traditional' religion between the 1930s and 1950s.[29] To

Horton, this is one aspect of the transition from the village world, where local nature or ancestral spirits flourish, to a larger community, where 'universal' religions seem more appropriate. However, it is clear that just as Christianity has been influenced by insights from African cultures, African religions have absorbed intimations from Christianity. This is seen not only in concepts of God, but in the rise of 'regional cults' that transcend ethnic boundaries and are organized on congregational lines.[30] The process of translation, where 'God' becomes 'Mwari' or 'Chukwu' has contributed to this, but, in Yorubaland, the worship of the Supreme God, Oludumare, is in decline, while that of divinities such as Ogun, god of iron, flourishes. To modern African Christians, it is self-evident that the God they now worship is the same as that of the past. The Fipa say, 'Where the elders pray, there is the God of the Door and the God of the Door is the Christian God also'.[31]

The idea of western scholars sitting in judgement on African churches and deciding on their orthodoxy or otherwise is not an appealing one. Such judgements are unavoidable, if one is writing on Christianity in Africa, because one has to decide what falls within one's study's scope. Thus, Gray specifically excludes the Bwiti cult from his valuable collection of essays on the subject.[32] The present study includes it, but, as several anthropologists have pointed out, whether a given church is 'orthodox' or 'syncretistic' is not a usual academic question, unless, perhaps, in theology. 'The invidiousness often presented in such discriminations could not interest anthropologists'.[33] They 'could only', writes MacGaffey, 'acquire interest and validity if we were to apply them to churches everywhere'. His alternative is to employ Kongo categories of thought, such as *kingunza*, which are clearly not appropriate to 'churches everywhere'.[34]

The underlying critique is that all western analysis, however sympathetically intentioned, is, in Mudimbe's words, an 'invention' of Africa. It utilizes categories of thought, including 'religion' that African cultures do not recognize. Far from encountering traditional religions with mutuality, it describes them from outside, in works to which most Africans have no access. One of the most eloquent statements of this viewpoint was made in a document which grew out of discussions and interviews in Zulu and Sotho among a group of South African Independent Church leaders in 1984. 'Anthropologists, sociologists and theologians from foreign Churches have been studying us for many years . . . We have become a fertile field for the kind of research that will enable a person to write an "interesting" thesis and obtain an academic degree. . . . It is therefore not surprising that we do not recognise ourselves in their writings.'[35] This makes sober reading for the western scholar. It sheds a precious and invaluable light on the limitations of our scholarship, and reminds us that the sympathetic Africanist creates the Other, whether working from oral sources or archives, just as the Victorian missionary or colonial administrator did. Every book must be read, as it were, in inverted commas, and historians and anthropologists write 'true fictions'.

The problem, though, is much more fundamental than the question of the limitations of the western scholar writing on African cultures. Where African academics write on the history of sociology of their own cultures, or, indeed, on faith traditions to which they themselves belong, their work is not obviously different from that of their western counterparts. There is a real sense in which Peel has grown so close to the Yoruba, or MacGaffey to the baKongo that their work has become a voice 'from within'. I was encouraged by many to think of myself in this way when I lived and wrote in Igboland.

In a book published in 1982, I pointed out 'that what religious people see as centrally important—that dimension of inner experience and search . . . should also be of central importance to a historian of religion'.[36] I was concerned at a tendency to subsume the study of Christianity in Africa under other categories, to focus on the role of missionaries in spreading imperialism, or interpret the independent churches as forms of proto-nationalism.[37] The questions we ask of a body of historical material reflect our own priorities and values. There was a profound, if unconscious, secularity in the way in which the history of Christianity was made a subordinate ingredient in the rise and decline of empire.

My critique was based on the assumption that the history of religion should focus on what is central to religion: belief, ritual, the religious community. Much the same point was made in *Speaking for Ourselves*, the document issued by black South African leaders of independent churches.

> . . . there is one enormous omission throughout the whole history that has been written by outsiders. The work of the Holy Spirit throughout our history has simply been left out. The events of our history have been recorded as if everything could be accounted for simply by sociology and anthropology . . . We would like to write our own history from the point of view of the Holy Spirit.[38]

They were not primarily concerned with an imperfect knowledge of African languages, or an incomplete understanding of African cultures, though such issues are indeed discussed. They are complaining about the failure to make God the core of church history. However, faith cannot be a prerequisite for writing on church history or the anthropology of religion. Agnostics have done so with notable sensitivity and insight, and those who share the same general beliefs often disagree in their application to specific instances (this is as true of neo-Marxists, as it is of Presbyterians). The solution is not for prophetic church members to embark on academic exegesis, and those who have done so[39] find themselves using the techniques and approaches of the work Ngada condemns.

No one now studies prophetic churches primarily as a form of proto-nationalism. In a sense, this approach has been disproved by events, the battles between the Lumpa church and newly independent Zambia, the hostility of a Mobutu or a Banda to sectarianism, but it is clear that they often embodied and enhanced forms of political consciousness, and empowered protests of various kinds against colonial or post-colonial oppression. There are many variations on this theme in the pages that follow.

To some Marxist scholars writing on Africa, religion is an illusion. The prophetic churches concentrate on healing, and the composition and performance of hymns and liturgies rather than on the understanding of the society in which they live, and ways in which to effect its transformation. However, it is self-evident that religion is of central importance to contemporary world history, whether it takes the form of Islamic fundament-alism or the New American Right, whether it foments civil conflict in Northern Ireland, former Yugoslavia or the Lebanon. Scholars, including those on the Left, have come to give ever-increasing emphasis to the ways in which people understand the world in which they find themselves. An important collection of essays on South African history is subtitled, 'African class formation, culture and consciousness'.[40] It is evident that an analysis which excludes religion leaves out an important dimension of what those who are the subject of such a study regard as being of central importance. 'If a people's behaviour is in part shaped by their own images and concepts, to the degree that these images and concepts are ignored and alien ones imposed or applied, that behaviour will be misunderstood and faultily explained.'[41] There is a deepening understanding that religious sensibility is often expressed in non-analytical ways, such as hymns and liturgies, and in non-verbal ways, the elaborate uniforms, the chosen Holy Place. Evans-Pritchard epitomized it all long ago when, speaking of the Azande, he said, 'their ideas are imprisoned in action . . . The web [of belief] is not an external structure in which he is enclosed. It is the texture of his thought and he cannot think that his thought is wrong'.[42] African religion is embodied in ritual and symbol. Fernandez contrasts its 'embeddedness' with the 'imageless thought' of academic analysis.[43] The incorporation of African words into an academic text, which, taken to a logical conclusion, would limit it to an ethnically specific audience, is a cosmetic change that does nothing to bridge this gap.

Christianity is a religion of the Book, and the transition to literacy was an important part of the transformations it engendered. Much has been written on its implications for religious understanding:

> . . . religions of the Book . . . emphasize the 'true interpretation' of things and the condemnation of heresies . . . They are exclusive religions to which one is 'converted' . . . Literate religions are less tolerant of change, once their fixed point of reference has been determined to be a sacred text . . . literate religions are individualizing and salvationistic . . .[44]

The fascination of literacy runs through the chapters that follow. Some African prophets, such as Simon Mpadi, in Zaire, wrote voluminously. Some, such as Josiah Ositelu, or the founders of the Oberi Okaine church, both in Nigeria, wrote in a new revealed script. Often frustrations at the injustices of the

9

colonial era found symbolic expression in the myth of the true Bible, the secret of their power, that the whites had withheld from Africans.

Elaborate typologies of African Christian movements have been invented and found wanting, or irrelevant.[45] Are new religious movements vehicles of protest, or are they alternative communities offering, in symbolic and ritual terms, an alternative explanation of reality? Scholars have conducted impassioned debates about these issues—some of them, oddly enough, focused on a tiny Kenyan religious movement[46]—but the points of difference are more apparent than real. The creation of an alternative community and framework of discourse *is* a form of protest. Both old and new churches have many dimensions of meaning: they create new communities, they challenge the hegemony of colonialism and of its successors, they offer healing and protection against evil. A Zionist prophet once said that his church was a hospital. The prophetic churches have always known what the West is painfully rediscovering—that healing must be a holistic process, involving mind and spirit, as well as the body.

In a much-cited book published in 1963, Lanternari listed the Zionist churches among *Religions of the Oppressed*. Some twenty years later, he had moved on from the specifics of his interpretation (based on the land question in South Africa). He still understands the prophetic churches as communities of affliction, but affliction is understood in more complex ways. They may include poverty, but they also include other forms of suffering and deprivation.[47] Comaroff, in a justly acclaimed study, suggests that the Zionist churches do offer an appropriate ideology for the oppressed and marginal: 'Zionism is part of a second global culture, a culture lying in the shadow of the first, whose distinct but similar symbolic orders are the imaginative constructions of the resistant periphery of the world system'.[48] This and other recent studies, are more nuanced than their predecessors and, accordingly, expressed in more complicated language, but the passage I have just cited is essentially *Religions of the Oppressed* writ large.

To an ever-increasing extent, African intellectuals are reconstructing the text of Christianity's encounters with African cultures. While black South African Christians such as Boesak or Tutu have often welcomed Liberation Theology, Francophone scholars such as Eboussi Boulaga regard it as just another form of triumphant secularity. Boulaga tries western Christianity in the balance and finds it wanting. He finds dominance intrinsic in all missionary situations ('. . . the language of derision, the language of refutation . . .) and critiques a 'middle-class Christianity' where faith has become divorced from love.[49]

The account that follows uses expressions such as 'the Yoruba'. These are useful, but not particularly true fictions. More precisely, if they bear some relationship to external reality, it is a recent one. These monolithic ethnic entities were inventions of the colonial period. The ethonym 'Luhyia' was invented in 1939 by Bantu speakers in North Nyanza, to distinguish themselves from the Nilotic Luo. These ethnic labels are used for convenience, but they are a shorthand for a complicated and changing reality.

I lived for sixteen years in Africa, and have been a part of certain African worlds. The study of Christianity in Africa has been a central concern for much longer. My understanding of Africa and of Christianity, and, indeed, of the whole academic enterprise has changed very considerably in recent years. What seemed so clear to me in the 1970s and early 1980s is now riddled with complexities and contradictions that probably come closer to the obdurate and ever-changing nature of reality. The pages that follow distil it all, as I have now come to understand it.

✌ ONE ßß

North African Christianity in Antiquity

There cannot be only one path to such a great secret.

Symmachus, a supporter of the old gods,
in the late Roman empire[1]

Christians in a landscape

North Africa is part of the Mediterranean world, and it is, in a sense, artificial to analyse the growth of Christianity there in isolation from developments elsewhere. The man whom history remembers as Clement of Alexandria (to distinguish him from Clement of Rome) was born in Greece, reached Alexandria in 180, and left it forever twenty-two years later. The Alexandrian Gnostic, Valentine, spent many years in Rome and ended his days in Cyprus.

Greeks have lived in Egypt from the seventh century BC, and their history there had a great influence on the development of Christianity. In 331 BC, Alexander the Great founded the city that bears his name, and when, after his death, his three generals divided his empire, Egypt fell to Ptolemy, who turned Alexandria into one of the great cities of the ancient world. Its lighthouse was regarded as one of the seven wonders of the world, but the title was perhaps more appropriate for the scholars of the Museum, one of whom accurately calculated the circumference of the world.

Egypt became part of the Roman Empire in 30 BC when Cleopatra, the last of the Ptolemies, and the only one to speak Egyptian, committed suicide by embracing a cobra, the symbol of the ancient Pharaohs. Greek remained the language of scholarship and of the great cities, 'Egyptian' (or Coptic) the language of the countryside. It is generally agreed that Roman rule brought increasing impoverishment and desperation. Egypt provided a third of the corn consumed by the Roman populace, and the weight of taxation, in time, became so great that peasants fled their land to escape it and many even settled in Palestine. Tax collection was not a sinecure but an appalling burden as the tax collector had to make up any shortfall from his own resources. A poll tax from which Greeks and Romans were exempt, but which Jews and Egyptians had to pay, left these latter peoples with a strong sense of relative deprivation. It is against this background of suffering that most historians interpret the appeal of mystery religions in general, and of Christianity and gnosticism in particular. But perhaps this is to oversimplify. Most ages have seemed epochs of crisis and threat to those who lived in them and a golden age appears only in restrospect, the perspective of a Gibbon reflecting on the Antonines.

Nubia, South of Egypt, has been called a country 200 miles long and 5 yards wide. Lower Nubia is virtually desert, for the Nile cuts deep into soft sandstone and the flood plain is narrow or non-existent. The Nile moves in a great sweep so that for a time it flows away from, rather than towards, the sea, and is joined by a series of great tributaries. To the South, there is sufficient winter rainfall for farming. This was the setting for the civilization of Meroe, which flourished from about 300 BC to about AD 300. Christianity came late

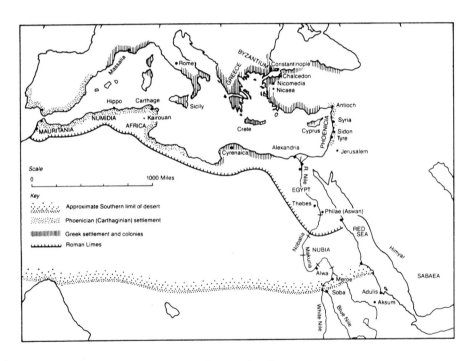

Map 3. Places mentioned in Chapter One.

to Nubia, introduced in the sixth century by missionaries not, as one might have expected from Egypt, but from Byzantium.

Cyrenaica lies West of Egypt, in what is now eastern Libya. The Arabs were to call it 'the Green Mountain', for its hills attracted sufficient rain for pastoral farming. Greek colonists settled among the Berbers; tradition dates this to 639 BC when the Delphic oracle directed a youth who sought help for a stammer to go to Cyrenaica.

> O Battos for a voice you come
> But the lord Apollo
> Sends you to Libya nurse of flocks
> To build cities.[2]

Its exports included sylphion, valued both as a food and as a medicine, but sadly, it was over-exploited and became extinct. Ethiopia and south-east Arabia, the Yemen, have much in common, geographically and historically. Their altitude means that they are relatively well-watered, though surrounded by desert. Settlers from south-east Arabia, Sabaea, the biblical Sheba, settled in northern Ethiopia in about 600 BC, bringing with them their semitic language and their script, ancestral to Ge'ez, and modern Ethio-semitic languages such as Amharic. In medieval Ethiopia, the legend of the marriage of Solomon and the Queen of Sheba and of their princely child, Menelik, became a founding charter of Ethiopian national identity. Like most myths, it contains a grain of truth, an ancient memory of immigrants from Sabaea.

Roman North Africa

West of Cyrenaica the sea bites deep into the land, forming the Gulf of Sidra. Here, where the desert comes close to the sea, the Greeks and Carthaginians built pillars to mark their respective spheres of influence. Carthage began as a Phoenician colony, founded, tradition tells us, by a Phoenician princess in about 800 BC. The Carthaginians fought a series of bitter wars, first with the Greeks and then with the Romans, until Carthage was finally razed to the ground in 146 BC. Cyprian's and Augustine's Carthage was a later, Roman city. In due course, North Africa became part of the Roman empire. The Maghrib exported vast quantities of wine, olive oil, and wheat to Rome, and aqueducts, the ruins of which can still be seen, carried water to many areas that are now desert. Great cities were built on Roman lines, and an urban, Latin-speaking élite developed that became part of the cosmopolitan Roman world. The great playwright, Terence, first came to Rome as a Berber slave. Victor, in the late second century, the first Pope, whose native speech was Latin, was a North African, and so was the Emperor Septimius Severus (reigned 193–211) and Apuleius, whose novel *The Golden Ass* is one of the few masterpieces of the ancient world that the ordinary reader can still peruse with pleasure.

The Jewish Diaspora

In Asia Minor, and the Mediterranean world, Diaspora Jews often provided Christianity with its first converts and with its most bitter opponents. Isaiah, in the eighth century BC, lists Upper and Lower Egypt and Kush among Diaspora communities: 'Beyond the rivers of Kush there is a land where the sound of wings is heard. From that land ambassadors come down the Nile in boats made of reeds.' Jeremiah, who lived in the late seventh and early sixth centuries, castigated the Jews of Egypt for their syncretism.[3] Judaism, like Christianity, was a missionary faith that found many converts in the ancient world. Many Greeks were attracted to its pure monotheism, though alienated by the requirement of circumcision. Such people often became sympathetic supporters, though not full members, of the Jewish community. It was for such that the Alexandrian Jew, Philo (20 BC–AD 50), wrote his monumental attempt to synthesize the tradition of the Hebrew Bible with Greek philosophy, a synthesis that profoundly influenced the Christian intellectuals of Alexandria. Many Jews settled in Egypt under the Ptolemies. According to one estimate, they formed 10–15 per cent of the population of Egypt in the first century AD. Like other Jewish Diaspora communities, in time they lost the knowledge of Hebrew. In 280 BC, the Old Testament was translated into Greek, the Septuagint—the first translation of any part of the Bible into a foreign language. It was later used by Christians who, in response to Jewish taunts that they had no access to the Hebrew original, developed a myth that the Septuagint was divinely inspired, the work of seventy translators in seventy days, working independently and producing miraculously identical texts. It was the Septuagint that was read by the black eunuch in a chariot, whom Philip met on the road from Jerusalem to Gaza, in one of the most famous encounters of the ancient world.

The Jews dominated two of the five quarters of Alexandria, and had their own treasury and court of justice. Tragically, they were repeatedly involved in ethnic violence. There was a pogrom in AD 58, and a Jewish rising in 73. In 115, they were involved in a very widespread Jewish revolt that began in Cyrenaica and ended in tragic loss of life. It may have been these disasters, as well as the two successive destructions of Jerusalem, that created a state of angst and anomie, conducive to conversion.[4]

These cosmopolitan, Greek-speaking Jews of Egypt and Cyrene were present at Pentecost. Simon of Cyrene carried Jesus' cross, and the fact that his sons, Rufus and Alexander, are mentioned by name suggests that they became Christians. Apollos was an Alexandrian Jew, a religious enthusiast who 'knew only the baptism of John' and was brought to a more complete knowledge of Christianity by the missionary couple Priscilla and Aquila. Jewish Christians from Cyrene preached to Gentiles in Antioch: 'the Lord's power was with them and a great number of people believed and turned to the Lord'. The teachers at Antioch included Lucius from Cyrene and 'Simeon called the black'.[5] It is a good example of the essential unity of the Mediterranean world.

Many Arabs were converted to either Judaism or Christianity. From the fourth to the sixth century, the Himyar kingdom in the Yemen was ruled by converts to Judaism. Himyarite persecution of Christians led an Ethiopian emperor to invade the Yemen and briefly transform it into an Ethiopian colony. The last Jewish king of Himyar, in despair, rode his horse into the sea in 525. Christianity vanished in the Yemen, but Judaism survived. In modern times, there were still 150 thousand Jews in the Yemen, who migrated to Israel between 1948 and 1962.[6]

The Falashas are a community of black Jews who are clearly Ethiopians, and call themselves the House of Israel. They know only the Pentateuch, not the Talmud, and do not speak Hebrew. Their liturgy is in Agaw, an ancient Cushitic tongue; their daily speech, Amharic; their history, in the centuries following their conquest by the Christian kingdom, a tragic one of persecution. It seems likely that they are descended from Agaw, who absorbed Jewish teachings via South Arabian influences.[7] In the 1970s, when Ethiopia was ravaged by famine, the Jews of Israel had to decide whether Falashas were acceptable to them as Jews, or not. They decided that they were, and many migrated to Israel.[8]

The dawn of Egyptian Christianity

The story of the Flight into Egypt has never ceased to glow in the Coptic imagination. In the words of the Coptic liturgy, 'Be glad and rejoice, O Egypt, and her sons and all her borders, for there hath come to Thee the Lord of Man. . . .'[9] Modern African Christians cherish the same tradition: 'When Jesus was persecuted by the European Herod, God sent him into Africa; by this we know that Africans have naturally a true spirit of Christianity'.[10] The Copts have never ceased to believe an ancient tradition that St Mark was the first apostle of Egypt and was martyred in Alexandria. Eusebius, in his *Church History* (written in 324), mentions this,[11] and a much earlier fragment from Clement refers to Mark's presence in Alexandria. The *Acts of Mark* were written in Greek in the late fourth or early fifth century, claiming that Mark first preached in Cyrene, and was a Cyrenian Jew. Whether Mark was, indeed, the apostle of Alexandria we cannot know.

There are similar difficulties in interpreting the tradition of St Thomas' apostolate in India. The name of the king at whose court he preached has been found on inscriptions, and the Christians of south India believe that his tomb survives eight miles from Madras. But scholarly consensus is that the *Acts of Thomas* were written in the early third century in Edessa. Like the tradition of Mark in Alexandria, the story of Thomas in India is unprovable, and, perhaps, improbable, but not necessarily untrue.

Alexandria was one of the three great sees of the ancient world—the others were Rome and Antioch[12]—but we know curiously little about its early history, or, indeed, about the early history of Christianity in Egypt in general.

The churches of Egypt, Nubia, and Ethiopia had close links with the rest of eastern Christendom. There is a great unity of spirit between Egyptian and Syriac Christianity. The Syrian churches rejoice in the fact that their language is the closest to the Aramaic spoken by Jesus. Syrian Christians converted Aksum, and later strengthened its faith by their missionary presence. A beautiful legend is told of the dawn of Syrian Christianity, how King Abgar of Edessa wrote to Jesus, seeking to be cured of his leprosy, and with an invitation: 'I have a very little city, but comely, which is sufficient for us both'. After Chalcedon, the spiritual unity of Ethiopian, Nubian, Egyptian and Jacobite Syrian Christians was cemented by their adoption of a Monophysite Christology (see pages 29–30).

The Egyptian gnostics

In 1945, an Egyptian peasant made a remarkable discovery at a place called Nag Hammadi. He discovered a library of forty-eight books that had been translated from Greek into Coptic. The texts were gnostic, and they had been concealed because, by the time the manuscripts were written, in the late fourth century, gnosticism had become a heresy.

The existence of this large library is one indication among many of the importance of Egypt in the history of gnosticism. Alexandria was probably the world's leading gnostic centre in the second century AD, and it is the names of gnostic teachers that emerge from what are otherwise almost hidden Christian years before 180. Although, ultimately, gnosticism was condemned as a heresy, many gnostics lived, taught, and died peacefully within the Catholic Church. '*Gnosis*' means intuitive knowledge, the knowledge of the heart. The gnostics' emphasis on individual religious experience and quest, and the importance of the feminine in both theology and praxis, make them immensely attractive today. They never formed a unified school of thought; each gnostic teacher had her or his own teachings. The orthodox, such as Irenaeus, mocked them for this diversity. Simon Magus of Samaria was often seen as a gnostic.[13] They believed that they had inherited a secret tradition within the Church, quoting texts such as Mark 4.11.

The gnostics believed that the different religious traditions of mankind were distant echoes of the same ultimate truth. Alexandria and Asia Minor were closely linked by trade to India, and there is an eastern ring in the often-quoted words of the gnostic Theodotus, concerning one 'who seeks to know who we were, and what we have become; where we were and whither we are hastening; from what we are being released; what birth is, and what is rebirth'.[14]

Basilides (*flor.* 125–155) was the earliest Alexandrian gnostic known to us.

He was a prolific writer, as was his son and disciple, Isidore, but his works, as with so many gnostics, survive only in fragments in the hostile polemic of his enemies. Basilides believed that he was the heir to a secret tradition that went back to either Peter or Matthias. His starting point was the utter transcendence of God. He thought that God is so utterly other that we cannot, even by analogy, say anything about him at all. In this, he anticipates some contemporary theologians, such as Tillich. God created a series of powers, beginning with Thought (*Nous*) and Word (*Logos*), which created the 'principalities and angels', which created the first heaven. Further powers created the second heaven, and our world was the work of the powers of the lowest, 365th world. Irenaeus states that, 'These men practise magic, and use images, incantations, invocations. . . .'[15] The gnostics believed that magic charms would enable them to pass through the intervening levels to God.

Valentine was the shining star of Alexandrian gnosticism. Jerome, who was savage in his condemnation of those he considered heterodox, said, 'No one can bring heresy into being unless he is possessed by nature of an outstanding intellect and has gifts provided by God. Such a person was Valentinus'.[16] He claimed that he inherited a secret tradition, received from Theudas, a disciple of Paul, and endorsed by mystical experience.[17] 'He saw a newborn infant and when he asked who he might be, the child answered "I am the Logos" and then went on to expound the secrets of the gnostic way.'[18]

Valentine's fundamental insight was a sense of the utter otherness of God, the inadequacy of all our analyses and descriptions. He begins with the Father who is the Deep (*Bythos*).[19] The Deep produces Silence (*Sige*), who becomes his bride, and, together, they give birth to Thought (*Nous*). Silence produces knowledge from the depths of the subconscious.

In this way, twenty-eight spiritual beings, called Aeons, ('everlasting ones') were produced. The youngest of these was Sophia; the Fall was hers. She tried to attain a direct knowledge of the Deep, which was forbidden to her, and then transgressed the natural order by giving birth alone, but produced only a formless monster, the origin of material being. The Aeons pleaded with the Father on Sophia's behalf, and he expelled the monster, sending *Huros* the Boundary, and then Christ and the Holy Spirit, to complete the number of Aeons. Sophia's spiritual being lived among the Aeons, but her fallen being was excluded. The material world, all living souls and the Demiurge, grew from her fear, grief, and desire. The Demiurge, in his ignorance, knows nothing of the worlds of spiritual beings and thinks he created the visible world alone.

A female Aeon is at the centre of Valentine's cosmic vision. This sensitivity to the feminine element in spirituality was typical of the gnostics, and is perhaps linked with the emphasis on individual experience, rather than authority. One of the manuscripts discovered in Upper Egypt, at Nag Hammadi, is a poem called *Thunder Perfect Mind*, in which a female divinity speaks:

I am the barren one
and many are her sons.
I am the silence that is incomprehensible
I am the utterance of my name.[20]

Women were prominent in the daily life of gnostic churches. One of Valentine's disciples, Marcus, settled in Lyons. His congregations included many women, one of whom celebrated the Eucharist[21] and divinity appeared to him as a woman.[22] Tertullian raged against gnostic women who led congregations in North Africa: 'The very women of these heretics . . . bold enough to teach, to dispute, to enact exorcisms, to undertake cures, may be, even to baptize'.[23]

Gnosticism developed out of two traditions: philosophic Platonism and Ptolemaic astronomy. To Plato, the spiritual world is separate from and infinitely superior to the material, and the eternal soul is imprisoned in the body. The history of Christian thought has been profoundly influenced by this tradition, but many neo-Platonists could not accept the Incarnation. Neo-Platonism was the preferred ideology of the educated opponents of Christianity, as the latter gradually became a majority creed. Its seminal intellect, Plotinus, was an Egyptian.

The catechetical school of Alexandria

The catechetical school of Alexandria was probably founded as a reaction against gnosticism. Its first teacher was a converted Stoic called Pantaenus, who was probably a Sicilian,[24] and who left Alexandria after a time to work as a missionary in India.[25] His place was taken by another convert, Clement, an Athenian whose avid search for truth led him on a restless quest from one spiritual teacher to the next: 'When I came upon the last (he was the first in power), having traced him out concealed in Egypt, I found rest'. The Samarian Greek, Justin Martyr, after a similar search, was brought to Christianity by a conversation on the beach at Ephesus.

Clement came to Alexandria to learn, and remained to teach. He was immensely learned, and one of his works cites 360 classical texts, many of which do not survive in any other form. Influenced by Philo, he attempted to make Christianity acceptable to those educated in Greek philosophy: 'For God is the cause of all good things. . . . The way of truth is therefore one. But into it, as in a perennial river, streams flow from all sides'.[26] Clement compared Christians who were afraid to study Greek philosophy with children frightened by actors' masks.[27]

He tempered the rigours of the Gospel imperative for his prosperous clientele. Thus, in his sermon, 'Who is the rich man that shall be saved?', which, significantly, has been read and cited more than any of his other works, he says: 'We must not fling away riches that benefit our neighbours as well as ourselves'.[28] In 202, there was a savage persecution in Alexandria, and Clement fled, never to return.

His successor as head of the catechetical school was a teenage genius, Origen (185–253). Born of mixed Egyptian and Alexandrian Greek parentage, he grew up in a fervently devout Christian family. As his name means born of Horus, it has sometimes been suggested that his parents were converted after his birth. He was immensely learned, both in Scripture and in the classics; a hostile critic, centuries after his death, suggested that he took a memory drug! One of the most prolific writers of the ancient world, he worked for some forty years with collaborators on the Hexapla, a remarkable pioneering attempt to establish an accurate text of the Bible, consisting of six (in some cases eight) parallel columns of different Greek translations. His wealthy patron, the Alexandrian, Ambrose, employed a whole team of shorthand writers and scribes to take down texts as he dictated them and make copies of the results. He attempted to learn Hebrew as a young man, but never mastered it. He wrote a refutation of pagan polemic, *Against Celsus*, which was to be read for many centuries, and a large number of voluminous scriptural commentaries, many of which have been lost. Like Philo and Clement before him, he interpreted Scripture in an allegorical way. Unlike Clement, he was a theologian of genius.[29]

Origen was the first major thinker of the early Church seriously to tackle the intractable problems of Christology. Sabellius the Libyan, another thinker from the African continent, attempted to define the Trinity as three modes, or aspects, of one God, so that God has one substance, and three energies. This led to problems—the posing of questions like 'Did God the Father die on the cross?'—but other attempts to define the Trinity sometimes led to tritheism. Origen, like other thinkers of his time, gave little thought to the Holy Spirit's role in the Trinity. (The Nicene Creed states simply, '. . . and we believe in the Holy Ghost', without stating the Paraclete's divinity or defining a role within the Trinity.) He was mainly concerned with the relationship between the Father and the Son. He speaks of the eternal generation of the Son, that the Father is truly God and the Son only so by participation in the Father. This subordinationism was not criticized by his contemporaries, most of whom shared it, but it was to be of critical importance in bringing his theology into later disrepute.

Origen had a bold, cosmic vision. He believed that as revealed religion tells us nothing about the universe before this world existed, or what will happen when it ceases to exist, these are legitimate spheres for speculation. Before all ages, God created spiritual beings, souls, angels, spheres and what later became the powers of darkness. The Fall was not that of Eve and Adam, but of these spiritual beings who wearied of the adoration of God. They fell from God in varying degrees, the angels least, the powers of darkness most. Human bodies were given to souls, both as a punishment and as a remedy for their fall. Souls exist before the moment of conception and go, not through one, but many lives. This is how he interprets, 'Jacob I have loved and Esau I have hated', not as a harsh predestinarianism, but in terms of the quality of their previous lives. Just as souls go through many incarnations, so there have been and will be many worlds. Origen was a universalist. He believed that even the beings furthest from God still have a capacity for repentance and a return to God. One of the elements in his thought that caused most scandal was his insistence that even Satan could, and one day would, be saved. However, his insistence on the freedom of will meant that even the blessed in heaven still had the capacity to reject God.

His interpretation of the spheres (perspex-like layers, thought to surround each planet) as spiritual beings was rooted in classical astrology. He believed that the planets' orderly paths reflected their rationality, and even found biblical texts to describe both *their* spiritual life and *their* fall in the infinitely remote past!

Origen's adult life was lived largely between Alexandria and Palestine. In 215, Egyptians were ordered out of Alexandria and Origen left with them. He later returned to Alexandria for ten years, and then spent some twenty years in Caesarea, the Roman capital of Palestine. He became an international celebrity, on one occasion summoned to meet the Emperor's mother at Antioch, and brought there with a military escort. On another, he was invited to discuss theology with the wife of the then Emperor, Philip the Arabian. He influenced history not only through his writings, but through his work as a teacher, most spectacularly through his pupil Gregory the Wonderworker, who came from Cappadocia (in what is now central Turkey) to Caesarea intending to study law. He fell under Origen's spell, and returned to Cappadocia as a missionary. Legend tells us that there were seventeen Christians in Cappadocia when he was young and seventeen pagans there when he died.

Among Origen's pupils were a number of women, among them the martyr, Herais. Another student was a former soldier who was converted by the heroism of a woman martyr, Potamiaena, who was slowly covered with boiling pitch.[30]

Origen, like many Christians of his time, longed for martyrdom. He was an enthusiast. As a young man, he castrated himself for the Kingdom of Heaven's sake, in a literal following of Matthew 19.12, an act that was less bizarre then than it appears now.[31] In 249, he was imprisoned during the Decian persecution. He was tortured on the rack and threatened with death, but did not recant. He died four years later in Tyre, at the age of sixty-nine.

Origen is the tragic star of the early Church. After successive Councils defined trinitarian orthodoxy, he became regarded as a heretic. The impassioned enmity of two Wise Men from the West, Rufinus and Jerome, both of whom settled in Palestine, centred on Origen. In the Middle Ages, he was esteemed, but suspect. A classic of mystic spirituality, St Bernard of Clairvaux's commentary on the *Song of Songs* owes much to Origen, and he influenced the brilliant and subtle thought of John Scotus Erigena and William of St Thierry, but, generally speaking, he was regarded as heterodox and a popular subject of scholastic debate was whether Origen (or Trajan, or Solomon) could be saved. Reformation thinkers, with their emphasis on faith rather than works, abhorred him. Luther said, with typical exaggeration, that the name of Christ was not mentioned in any of his works. But Erasmus, who wrote a treatise on the freedom of the will, sought inspiration from Origen. His affirmation of human freedom rings down the centuries: 'Let us take up eternal life. Let us take up that which depends on our decision. God does not give it to us. He sets it before us. "Behold, I have set life before thy face" '.[32]

The achievements of the Alexandrian catechetical school did not end with Origen. In the fourth century, it was headed by the extraordinarily interesting figure of Didymus the Blind (313–98). An Alexandrian, Didymus was blind from infancy. Credited with the invention of a script for the blind, he was the teacher of Jerome and Gregory of Nazianzus and wrote many books.

Arius and Athanasius

From about 320 to about 450, the Christian churches of the East were deeply divided by what now appeared to be rather obscure theological controversies, first about the Trinity and later about the nature of Christ. These controversies did not begin with Arius, nor did they end with Chalcedon. So complicated is their history that one sometimes remembers the words of Gibbon, that it is interesting to study a particular plant: 'but the tedious detail of leaves without flowers, and of branches without fruit, would soon exhaust the patience and disappoint the curiosity'.[33] However, as the subtle intellects of the East fully realized, these basic questions were at the heart of the Christian faith. They said that Christians of the West numbered the Trinity without understanding it. The questions they asked are of lasting importance. How can one define the Trinity without falling into tritheism on the one hand or unitarianism on the other? Did Jesus pray, and why, and who did he pray to? There is a limit as to how largely these controversies can figure in what is, after all, a history of Christianity in Africa, yet, throughout these stormy years, Alexandria dominated the thought of eastern Christendom.

Arius lived from 250 to 336, so he was already old when his theological views first became subject to scrutiny. The Meletians were Egyptian rigorists, who believed that those who lapsed during persecution should be excluded from the Church. Arius began as a Meletian sympathizer and changed sides. The Meletians never forgave him and scrutinized his later theology mercilessly. In 318, he was charged with heresy and a local synod condemned and excommunicated him. Arius was an accomplished musician and poet, and put his theological views into a series of folk songs called the 'Thalia' or 'Banquet', in order to popularize his views. They were sung in bars, and a modern scholar has expressed mild surprise at their popularity![34]

23

Arius' thought was rooted in a sense of the utter transcendence of God. Influenced by neo-Platonism, he believed that the Word is subordinate to the Father, and, as it was begotten, it must have had a beginning, even if that beginning was inconceivably remote. He did not accept his condemnation and rallied support abroad.

In 324, the Emperor Constantine won a final victory over his rival. The empire was now officially Christian and Constantine did not want Christendom divided by obscure theological disputes. He summoned a Council to solve all the problems of the Church at once, including the date of Easter. It was held at Nicaea, near the imperial capital of Nicomedia, in what is now northern Turkey. In 325, 230 bishops, nearly all from the East, met together. It seems that Constantine was personally responsible for the formula *homoousios* (that the Father and the Son are consubstantial). The familiar Nicene Creed was followed by a series of anathemas that condemn those who say, 'there was when He was not and before He was begotten He was not . . .'.

Few supported the full Arian position, but many eastern thinkers in the tradition of Origen were deeply troubled by the implications of the Nicene Creed. In particular, they were concerned by *homoousios*, which seemed to them to be close to the Monarchian heresy that saw the three persons of the Trinity as three aspects or activities of the one God. They thought that if the Father is known by the Son, the Son must, in some sense, be distinct from him. Arius died in Constantinople in 336, a broken, and largely forgotten man.

Athanasius was only a deacon at the Council of Nicaea, but played a dominating role there. He became the Patriarch of Alexandria in 328, and, from then to his death in 373, led a life of turbulent controversy, immutable in his steely adherence to the truth as he saw it. He was exiled from his See no less than five times, beginning with a sojourn in Trier in distant Gaul. One of the most significant aspects of his life was his close relationship with the Desert People. He was deeply attached to St Antony and wrote his life. When the old hermit died, he left his few possessions—his cloak and his sheepskin—to his dear friend, Athanasius. Nicaea did not put an end to trinitarian and christological speculation, but, despite the accession of two emperors with Arian sympathies, the Nicene party was ultimately victorious. The Second Ecumenical Council, held at Constantinople in 381, reaffirmed the identical essence of the Father and the Son, and also declared that the Bishop of Constantinople ranked second after Rome, a direct challenge to the ancient Sees of Alexandria and Antioch. This was, except in one respect, the effectual end of Arianism. The Goths had been converted by an Arian missionary, Ulfila, himself of Visigothic descent, the translator of the Gothic Bible. The Vandals, who invaded North Africa in 430, had been converted to Christianity in its Arian form and looked on Catholics as their enemies.

One cannot readily separate events in Egypt from the rest of Eastern Christendom. A classic case of this can be found in the tragic last years of John

Chrysostom ('the golden tongued'). The chain of events that led to his fall began with a conflict among Egyptian monks. A small, educated minority of these were Origenists, and attacked anthropomorphic concepts of God. This deeply distressed their less learned counterparts who were accustomed to think of God as an old man in the sky. The Origenists, the Tall Brothers, fled to Constantinople and sought the support of John Chrysostom. The Patriarch of Alexandria, angry at being thus bypassed, began the chain of events that led to John's death in lonely exile, in Armenia.

As time went by, western and eastern Christendom drifted apart, partly because of the language barrier (Latin, or Greek), and partly because of more profound differences in intellectual emphasis. The immensely learned Augustine disliked the study of Greek.[35]

A later Patriarch of Alexandria was destined to play a dominant role in theological controversy. Cyril the Great succeeded his uncle as Patriarch of Alexandria from 412 until his death in 444. He shared the anti-semitic tendencies that disfigured the spirituality of John Chrysostom, and, in his time, both Jews and a few remaining pagan neo-Platonists were persecuted in Alexandria. His major controversy was with Nestorius, a monk from Antioch who became the Patriarch of Constantinople. Nestorius rejected the description of Mary as Mother of God, and emphasized that the human and divine natures of Christ were entirely distinct. He thought it blasphemous to say, for instance, that the Eternal Word was once a little child. The Third Ecumenical Council, held at Ephesus in 441, convened by the Emperor Theodosius and his wife, Eudokia, condemned Nestorius. Eudokia is an interesting figure. A highly educated Greek convert to Christianity, she is one of four women writers in the early Church whose works survive.[36]

Nestorius died in Africa, on the eve of the Council of Chalcedon. He was exiled to the Libyan oases and spent his last years in Cyrenaica. There he wrote a defence of his tragic life under a *nom de plume*, as if he had written it under his own name it would have been condemned, unread. After his death, those who accepted his theology formed a separate church, based in Persia, with branches in Arabia and throughout Asia. The Nestorians were to provide one of the most remarkable phases of the history of Christian missionary endeavour. They taught in India and in China, and Nestorian churches survived in China and Central Asia until extinguished in the fourteenth century by the persecutions of the Ming Dynasty and of Timur the Great. A minuscule Nestorian ('Assyrian') Church still survives.

The Council of Chalcedon was held, with momentous consequences for Christendom, in 451. In 450, Theodosius died of a fall from his horse. He was succeeded by his sister Pulcheria, who took as her consort the soldier, Marcian. They summoned a council, hoping, as Constantine had done, that divisive theological disputes would finally be ended. At Chalcedon, 520 bishops met, across the Bosphorus from Constantinople. No gathering of Christians has had more momentous consequences.

According to the definition agreed on at Chalcedon, Christ has two natures: human and divine, distinct and indivisible. It was profoundly unacceptable to Coptic Christians who felt that this was to divide Christ, and diminish the glory of his divinity. The word Monophysite was not used at the time, but, in due course, the definition of Chalcedon was to lead to the foundation of five Monophysite churches, three of them in Africa, the Coptic Church in Egypt, the Nubian, Ethiopian, and Armenian Churches and the Jacobite Church of Syria.[37] It is difficult now to enter into these ancient controversies that were fought then with such passion. From the point of view of Christian life and devotion, there was little difference between the warring parties. There were, however, important implications in the rival formulations. Chalcedon gave a more positive value to humanity and to the created world and laid a greater emphasis on human freedom.

The Coptic dimension

The word Coptic can refer to a people, a language, or a Church. Both 'Copt' and 'Egypt' come from a Greek word, *Aigyptos*, which, in turn, comes from the ancient Egyptian name for Memphis, 'the house of Ptah'. The history of ancient Egyptian literacy falls into three phases, each progressively less formal: the hieroglyphs used on inscriptions, hieratic used in official documents, and the more popular cursive script, demotic. One consequence of the Greek presence was that it became increasingly the custom to write the Egyptian language in the Greek alphabet, with seven letters added. The earliest surviving exemplar dates from 150 BC. Coptic was used in writing much Christian literature, demotic gradually dying out entirely. In its turn, Coptic was supplanted by Arabic. It survived until the thirteenth century, but, after that, even Christian Copts spoke Arabic and Coptic survived only in liturgy, as Latin did in the Catholic Church until recent times.

Coptic Christianity was forged in persecution and its most distinctive expression was in the lives of the Desert People. In Egypt, as in North Africa, a mass turning away from the old religion towards Christianity seems to have begun in the middle of the third century and to have been virtually complete by 400, with the exception of a few neo-pagan aristocrats. It is not easy to know why the Egyptian people accepted Christianity with such enthusiasm. The move has been associated with the sufferings of the Egyptian peasantry and with the relative deprivation of Jewish and Egyptian élites. It has been pointed out that temples were associated with tax collection and that people were alienated from synthetic Graeco-Roman cults, such as that of Serapis, but, even if the hardships of Egyptian life did attract them towards salvation religions, why did they turn to Christ rather than Osiris?

To many Christian apologists, the spread of Christianity, the inability of traditional gods to halt its spread, were the most convincing proof of its truth. Many individuals were converted by the courage of the martyrs, and women often played a key role in converting households to Christianity. Christianity empowered the disinherited, though some women came to feel alienated from Christianity and identified with 'heretical' cults.

In an enormously influential hypothesis, Horton has suggested that peoples are attracted to world religions when they come into contact with a wider world, that the traditional religions are profoundly rooted in a particular locality and when individuals find themselves in a cosmopolitan environment, these local divinities seem less appropriate.[38] This model has been used internationally, and, within Africa, it suggests a convincing reason for many conversions, both to Christianity and to Islam. At the same time, we should realize that other salvation religions were also truly international. There was for instance, a temple of Isis in London.

Persecution became most severe towards its close, in the last years of Diocletian and under Maximin in late 311 and early 312. Eusebius describes the atrocious sufferings of the martyrs of the Thebais, in upper Egypt, torn to pieces by sharp shards, or dismembered, or burned alive, executions so numerous that the executioners were exhausted and the axes worn out.[39]

Sadly, the experience of persecution divided those who suffered from it. The point of division was the policy to be adopted towards backsliders. Were Christians who recanted during persecution to be readmitted after penance, or should they be permanently excluded from the Church? Peter, the Patriarch of Alexandria, who himself died a martyr's death, took the more generous line; Meletius and his followers the harsher one. The Christians in prisons in Alexandria in 304 hung a curtain between the factions, so sharp were their divisions. The followers of Meletius came to form a schismatic church. It was strongly rooted in some areas, but did not enjoy the almost national support that Donatus was to have in Numidia. So deeply ingrained were these events in Coptic sensibility that the Church calendar is dated from the Era of the Martyrs, beginning with the accession of Diocletian in 284.

The story has a sad sequel. In time, Christians became the persecutors. The Patriarch Theophilus, in the late fourth and early fifth centuries, led riots against the Temple of Serapis, during which much of the Museum and its priceless library were destroyed. In 415, Christian mobs put to death Hypatia, a woman neo-Platonist philosopher and mathematician returning from a lecture. Charles Kingsley wrote a novel about this almost forgotten martyr to intellectual integrity. She was thirty years old.

The Desert People

Perhaps the most distinctive contribution of the Coptic Church to world Christianity lay in its virtual invention of both the eremitical and the monastic way. Scholars write conventionally of the Desert Fathers. It is a sad case of unconscious sexism in language that Helen Waddell called her study of the women and men of the Egyptian desert, *The Desert Fathers*, though many of the passages in the book refer to women saints, such as Sarah or Syncletica.[40] The Desert People invented a way of life in which the world was totally given up in pursuit of God. Paul of Thebes left his native city at a time of persecution. Having moved into the desert, he came to discover the treasures within its silence and never returned. When he was a very old man, he met St Antony, a more celebrated pioneer of the desert way.

Antony inherited a substantial smallholding from his parents. When he was twenty, he heard a text in church that changed his life: 'If thou wouldst be perfect, sell all that thou hast, give to the poor and follow me'. He sold his land, gave the proceeds to the poor, making provision for his sister, and went to live on the desert's edge. Many followed his example. It was as if literal obedience to the Gospel had just been invented. The contrast with Clement's wise words on the spiritual value of prosperity is dramatic.

The beginning of western monasticism, as well as of eremiticism, is written in Coptic. Pakhom (290–346), was an Egyptian, born of pagan parents in upper Egypt. He spent some years as a soldier, and, it is said, was converted by his experiences of Christian charity. After his discharge, he lived for a time as a solitary, and then established a large monastery in the Thebaid. When he died, he ruled over nine monasteries for men and two for women. His rule survives in Latin translation and influenced Basil the Great, John Cassian and Benedict. His great innovation was the recognition that a life of moderate austerity, lived in community, suited most would-be saints much better than solitude and ferocious asceticism.

It was said at a later date, with pardonable exaggeration, that there were more Egyptians in the desert than in the cities. The Desert People emphasized work and self-sufficiency, weaving palm fronds into mats and baskets, and working as harvesters. It is said that with their earnings, they fed not only the local poor, but sent shiploads of grain to the prisons and poor of Alexandria.[41] Most, but not all, came from a poor background, which doubtless made the privations of the desert easier to endure.[42] On one occasion, a monk returned to his cell to find robbers carrying his possessions away. He helped them load his own goods on to a donkey and said, 'Look, here is a little bag which you have forgotten'. On another, a hippopotamus was causing havoc in the Nile delta and one of the Desert Fathers reproved her; she went away at his word.

Beyond the savage austerities, and the extravagant fear of the opposite sex, there is sometimes a limpid wisdom that speaks to us still:

> Certain men once asked the abbot Silvanus, saying, 'Under what discipline of life hast thou laboured to have come at this wisdom of thine?' And he answering, said, 'Never have I suffered to remain in my heart a thought that angered me'.[43]

Some tried the life and found that they could not endure it. Jerome spent some time in the Syrian desert, learned Hebrew to rid his imagination of dancing girls and discovered, in the end, that his calling lay elsewhere. St John

Chrysostom ruined his digestion when a desert ascetic and, as a result, he later gained a reputation for being inhospitable.

Athanasius' *Life of Antony* was translated into Latin and had a great influence in western Europe. John Cassian was a monk at Bethlehem. He visited the Egyptian monks, and spent some time in Constantinople, and in Rome before settling in southern Gaul, where he founded monasteries and wrote the *Institutes* for their guidance, closely modelled on the work of Pakhom, but tempering Egyptian austerity for a different environment. In 286, Augustine was living in Milan. He was visited by a North African imperial official, Pontician, who told him he had gone walking one afternoon in Treves with friends, and they had come to a little Christian community practising the common life. One of them picked up from a table the *Life of Antony*. He and a companion were so deeply moved that they joined the community on the spot. This conversation led Augustine directly to the great moment of conflict and decision in the garden that changed his life.[44]

Not everyone admired the Desert People. Rutilius in the early fifth century, wrote of:

> a credulous exile skulking in the dark,
> Thinking, poor fool, that heaven feeds on filth,
> Himself to himself more harsh than the outraged gods.[45]

Gibbon condemned ascetics 'inspired by the savage enthusiasm which represents man as a criminal and God as a tyrant',[46] but, in our own times, when western Christians have rediscovered the spirituality of the Eastern churches, when the Jesus prayer is popular, and Americans build *poustinias*,[47] the Desert People speak to many hearts. Thomas Merton devoted a book to them.

The growth of Monophysite churches

The growth of the independent Monophysite churches was the ultimate consequence of Chalcedon, but it was a consequence that was long delayed. Egyptian views on Christology were so passionately held that the Egyptian bishops present at Chalcedon said that if they agreed to its statement of faith, they were signing their own death warrants. Six years later, the Chalcedonian Patriarch of Alexandria was actually lynched. The Western Church and the Papacy were unalterably committed to Chalcedon and the doctrine of Christ's two natures. In the late fifth century, an attempt was made to effect a compromise, but without success.[48]

Justinian was emperor of Byzantium from 527 until his death in 565. He was incomparably the greatest emperor of late antiquity, remembered especially for his bold and temporarily successful attempt to regain the lost western provinces. He was also a gifted theologian, deeply involved in the controversies of his time and concerned, above all, to win the theological unity that was seen as a necessary support of empire. Justinian supported Chalcedon, but his wife, Theodora, whose fearless spirit saved his throne at a time of crisis, was a convinced Monophysite.

Ironically, it was under a Chalcedonian emperor that the foundations of a separate Monophysite church organization were laid. The leading role was played by Severus, who was Patriarch of Antioch until 518, and died in exile in Egypt twenty years later. He was a devout Monophysite, and began to ordain Monophysite clergy because he feared for the souls of the faithful if their sacraments were mediated to them through clergy who lacked the true faith. He was deluged by huge numbers of candidates for ordination. It was, in the words of a contemporary, '. . . like a river that had burst its banks'. The creation of a Monophysite church organization was completed by a remarkable Syrian, Jacob Baradaeus, who was appointed Bishop of Edessa in 542 as a result of Theodora's influence.

Egyptian Christianity was divided between a vast majority of fervent Monophysites and a small group of Melkites, king's men, headed by a Chalcedonian Patriarch of Alexandria, who owed his position to Byzantine support. The divisions of Egyptian Christians paved the way for Arab conquest, which, later, Coptic historians interpreted as a just punishment for the transgression of Chalcedon.

Nubia[49]

Christianity came curiously late to Nubia, when one considers the fervour of its Egyptian neighbours.

Despite much detailed research, the history of Nubia still has many question marks. The kingdom of Meroe flourished from about 300 BC to about AD 300. Its people invented their own alphabetic script, and some were also literate in Greek. The sounds of Meroitic words are known, but little is understood of their meaning; the same is true of ancient Etruscan. The eunuch whom Philip encountered and converted was a high official from Meroe, in the employ of the Candace, the Queen Mother.

In the fourth century AD, the growing kingdom of Aksum conquered Meroe, which was already in decline. The next phase is called the Ballana culture. There was virtually no evidence of literacy, nor of the palaces and monumental architecture of a former day. This change was not the result of poverty as Ballana princes were buried with rich grave goods, including elaborate crowns of silver. It was a culture where Christianity was known, though not adopted. In one grave, for instance, a cross was found next to charms of gold and of lead. Three separate states developed in Nubia: from North to South, Nobatia, Makouria, and Alwa, or Alodia.

In 543, Theodora sent the Monophysite monk, Julian, to Nubia, instructing the Governor of the Thebaid to stop any other mission. Julian converted Nobatia to Christianity, beginning with the court. So rapid and complete was the process, that it suggests either that the King wielded great power, or that a considerable degree of prior Christian influence existed.

Makouria was converted by Chalcedonian emissaries in about 569, and Alwa to Monophysite Christianity in 580 by Longinus, the Bishop of Philae, who made a great detour through the desert to avoid Makouria. Nubian Christianity developed in great isolation. Between 639 and 641, the Arabs conquered Egypt, and, from then on, Coptic Christians were a diminishing minority in a country under Muslim rule. Despite this isolation, Nubian Christianity was to survive and, indeed, flourish for centuries.

The Arabs did not conquer Nubia. They were repelled by Nubia's brilliant archers in two battles at Dongola, a setback they doubtless accepted the more readily because of the poverty of the country. They recognized the independence of Nubia in a *baqt*, the only treaty in which the Arabs recognized the independence of a non-Muslim state; Aswan was their only officially accepted frontier.

Nubia was one of the few countries in the ancient world that was converted to Christianity without a prior experience of Roman rule; Ethiopia was another. Culturally, its Christianity was greatly influenced by Byzantium. The Nubians used the liturgy of St Mark, and decorated the walls of their churches with murals that showed their royals dressed in Byzantine style. In 1961, Polish archaeologists excavated what appeared to be a mound of sand, and, within it, found Faras Cathedral, its walls decorated with 169 magnificent paintings of dark-skinned Nubian kings, queens and bishops, and biblical figures, and saints. To Frend, Nubia was a tiny Byzantine court, far away from Constantinople.[50] Adams, a Nubian specialist, saw the Byzantine dimension as a superficial veneer.[51]

Literacy revived and took many forms: Greek, old Nubian, written in Greek characters, and Arabic. Christian Nubia at its height was a land of great cultural vitality. This was reflected not only in its churches and paintings, but also in a new tradition of brightly decorated pottery, characterized by realistic designs from the natural world, an idiom that owes nothing to outside influences, and which has been described as the most distinguished pottery tradition in Africa.

Pre-Christian religious buildings were often situated far from centres of population, but there were up to six Christian churches in each village. The practice of burying the dead with grave goods died out at once. Every pre-Christian Nubian king is known by his grave, but not a single Christian one. In time, Nobatia was absorbed by Makouria. The enlarged state adhered to the Monophysite faith, probably because of the overwhelming influence of Coptic Egypt.

Written records from Christian Nubia include inscriptions, and fragments of religious texts, usually Gospels, lives of the saints, or liturgical documents. Ibn Selim was an Egyptian visitor to Nubia in 969, and he speaks with sympathy of 'lovely islands and at a distance of less than two days' journey about thirty villages with beautiful buildings, churches, monasteries and many palm trees, vines, gardens, fields and large pastures . . .'.[52] Near Faras, archaeologists found a cave that was inhabited by an eighth-century hermit: 'Theophilus this least of monks who wrote these writings on my dwelling', in 739. The texts he chose to write on his whitewashed walls over a period of years shed a vivid light on the religious sensibility of an eighth-century Nubian. They include the Nicene Creed, stories from the lives of the saints, and various amuletic texts, including the beginnings of the four Gospels, written in circular form; also the apocryphal letter to Jesus from King Abgar of Edessa, mentioned above, and the famous palindrome,

SATOR
AREPO
TENET
OPERA
ROTAS.[53]

Thus did Theophilus protect and inspire his chosen solitude.

Changing styles of church architecture reflect an increasing distance from the people. The churches became smaller so that the congregation stayed outside, a pattern familiar from village Greece. However, the decline of Christianity in Nubia seems to have been mainly caused by a gradual process of Arab Muslim immigration. As time went on, the Nubian population became increasingly dominated by Arabs or Arabized Nubians. In 1315, the Muslim government of Egypt imposed a Nubian Muslim as the King of Makouria, and, in 1317, Dongola Cathedral officially became a mosque. However, the tiny Christian splinter kingdom of Dotawo survived in lower Nubia until the late fifteenth century. Further South, the Christian kingdom of Alwa seems to have survived to about 1500. In 1523, a gallant Jewish traveller, David Reubeni, visited its capital, Soba, and found it in ruins. As recently as 1930, local Arabs still swore an oath in the name of, 'Soba the home of my grandfathers and grandmothers, which can make the stone float and the cotton boll sink'.[54]

Aksum

There were undoubtedly Christian and Jewish merchants in the cosmopolitan cities of Adulis and Aksum, but the Christianization of king and people came with dramatic suddenness in the early fourth century, as a result of a romantically unlikely chain of events. A Christian philosopher from Tyre called Meropius travelled to India[55] with his wards, Frumentius and Aedesius. In the Red Sea, they fell prey to pirates and were shipwrecked. Meropius lost his life, but the people of Aksum found the two boys sitting under a tree, studying. They were welcomed at the court of the king, Ella Amida; Aedesius became his cupbearer, and Frumentius his treasurer and secretary. When the

King died, leaving an infant son, the future King, Ezana, Frumentius acted as regent. When Ezana grew up and took over his inheritance, Aedesius returned to Tyre. Frumentius went to Alexandria, met the great Athanasius and informed him of the needs of the Christians of Aksum. Athanasius sent him back to Aksum as its first Bishop. Ethiopian traditions written down much later call Frumentius 'Abba Salama', Father of Light; the Christian kings are remembered as two brothers, with the symbolic names of 'Abreha', he who has made light, and 'Asbeha', he who has brought the dawn. The story has independent corroboration for we have a letter from the Arian Emperor, Constantius, to the King of Aksum urging him to obtain his Bishop from Arian sources rather than from Athanasius, 'who is guilty of ten thousand crimes'.[56]

Ezana's monuments and coins provide a fascinating mirror of his gradual adoption of Christianity. His earliest inscriptions are dedicated to the South Arabian gods, Astar, Baher and Meder; later, they invoke 'The Lord of Heaven', and, finally, the Trinity. Ezana's conversion has been explained in different ways, most cynically by suggestions that he knew of Constantine and had come to consider Christianity an appropriate ideology for great kings. A recent thoughtful reconsideration of the question interprets it in terms of the theories of Robin Horton, referred to earlier in this chapter,[57] suggesting that when one breaks free from the microcosm, as Ezana did in his conquests of Meroe, a universal religion comes to seem appropriate.

Ethiopia was converted by Syrians, and the connection was to be of enduring importance. The Syrian missionaries whom Ethiopia remembers as the Nine Saints arrived in the fifth century. They founded monasteries, and translated the Bible into Ge'ez from a version of the Septuagint in use in the Patriarchate of Antioch. It is possible, but not certain, that they were Monophysites, fleeing from the aftermath of Chalcedon. Certainly, from that day to this, the Ethiopian Church has espoused the Monophysite cause with passionate conviction. The sixth-century King of Ethiopia, Kaleb, invaded the Himyarite kingdom when Dhu Nawas was persecuting Christians. For a short time, Ethiopia ruled the Yemen, but it was displaced, first by the Persian conquest of Arabia, and later by the advent of Islam.

The Maghrib

The churches of the Maghrib, like their counterparts in Nubia, are long since dead. In their heyday, they produced some of the most brilliant intellects of Christendom, and their memory endures, not only in the writings of the famous, and the ruins of Roman cities, but also in the remains of innumerable village churches, both Catholic and Donatist.

The growth of North African Christianity can only be understood against the background of Roman rule, which began with the sack of Carthage in 146 BC, and was completed with the conquest of Mauretania (northern Morocco) in AD 40. The Maghrib underwent a process of Romanization that had no parallel in Egypt. Roman cities were founded, most notably Carthage, on the site of its predecessor, razed to the ground. New provinces were founded, Mauretania, Numidia (northern Algeria) and Africa, in Tunisia, which, taking its name from the local Afri, gave its name to a continent. Many former Roman soldiers were given land grants and became colonists; local notables and whole townships, were given Roman citizenship (which was granted to all the freeborn in the empire in AD 212). Many North Africans took the path of social mobility in the Roman world, most notably the emperor Septimius Severus, who, throughout his life, spoke Latin with an accent,[58] married a Syrian princess, and died at York, a symbol of an empire that had ceased to be Roman. Augustine grew up 200 miles from the sea and was of Berber descent, but spoke no language other than Latin.

According to Josephus, Africa supplied Rome with corn for eight months a year, the rest coming from Egypt.[59] Great groves of olive trees were planted, often in areas that are now virtually desert. 'Here lies Dion . . . he lived 80 years and planted 4000 trees'.[60] It is an enviable memorial. This productivity was largely due to Roman canals and viaducts.

The known Christian history of the Maghrib begins dramatically in 180, with the martyrdom of five women and seven men from the little village of Scilli, near Carthage. One of them carried in his bag, 'books and letters of Paul, a just man'. The kindly Roman proconsul who presided at their trial did not desire their deaths. He pointed out that he, too, was a religious man, and suggested they take 30 days to think things over, but the Scilli martyrs needed no time for reflection: 'Today we are martyrs in heaven. Thanks be to God'. The words resound through a North African Christian history dominated by a passion for martyrdom.

The *Passion of Saints Perpetua and Felicity* is one of the most moving documents left us from the first centuries of the Church. Perpetua is one of four early woman Christians in the ancient world whose writings have survived. Most of the text in her prison journal was, '. . . written in her own hand and according to her own perceptions'. She was a member of a prosperous family, aged twenty-two, married, with a baby boy. Her father was a pagan; the journal describes his despairing attempts to save his beloved child from the death she embraced. She was martyred with others, among them Saturus, and her friend, the slave, Felicity, also the mother of a new baby.[61]

Perpetua had a number of visions. In the first, she ascends a bronze ladder to heaven, treading on the head of a dragon to do so. The edges of the ladder are instruments of war. She avoids them, and is unharmed. At the top of the ladder she finds a nurturing father figure, who gives her cheese to eat. In another vision, she becomes a male gladiator, and, after a successful fight, is rewarded with apples from another nurturing father (we cannot here explore the psychological and other implications of these visions).[62] Saturus had a vision in which he saw a priest and bishop excluded from heaven, '. . . severed and sad. And they cast themselves at our feet, and said,

"Make peace between us . . ." '. The rival claims of bishops and confessors was to be a major theme of North African Christian history.

Perpetua, Felicity, and their companions were martyred in the arena at Carthage, in March 203. Perpetua guided the executioner's sword to her own throat. 'Perhaps so great a woman . . . could not otherwise be slain except she willed it . . . '

Tertullian (*c.* 160–240) was a convert to Christianity. Like Perpetua, he was part of the Latin-speaking élite of Carthage, and probably a lawyer. Jerome states that his father was a centurion.[63] His voluminous writings, like his life, are full of contradictions. He praised martyrdom, but died a natural death at an advanced age. Widely read himself, he denounced classical learning: 'What has Athens to do with Jerusalem?' Happily married, he praised virginity. *Ad Uxorem*, addressed to 'my best beloved fellow-servant in the Lord', gives her detailed instructions about her way of life if she is widowed. It concludes with the warmest description of Christian married life in the ancient world.[64] A denouncer of heretical sects, he joined the Montanists, a sect founded in Phrygia (central Turkey), given to fasting and ecstatic experiences. Augustine tells us that in his old age he founded a little group, Tertullianistae, a sect whose existence is well attested in the late fourth century.

Tertullian was a Puritan. He believed that Christians should be a gathered remnant, avoiding all the corruption of a tainted world.[65] Women should avoid cosmetics, elaborate hairstyles, and fine clothing: 'That which He Himself has not produced is not pleasing to God, unless he was unable to order sheep to be born with purple and sky-blue fleeces'.[66] In his writings we see, although through a flawed glass, the growth of North African Christianity in his time. His denunciations of heretical sects, with their women leaders, reflect the strength of gnosticism. He describes, perhaps with exaggeration, the contemporary growth of Christianity: 'We are but of yesterday, and we have filled every place among you—cities, islands, fortresses, towns, market-places, the very camp, tribes, companies, palace, senate, forum . . .'.[67]

The *Passion of Saints Perpetua and Felicity* has many Montanist overtones, and it is possible that Tertullian was the editor.

After decades of obscurity, the Carthaginian Church emerges into the light of day again in the writings of St Cyprian. In 246, when in his mid forties, Cyprian went through a dramatic conversion experience, finding in Christian baptism a miraculous release from the vices that enchained him. He was a wealthy man, a lawyer, skilled in magical arts.

> I myself was held in bonds by the innumerable errors of my previous life. . . . I was disposed to acquiesce in my clinging vices, and because I despaired of better things, I used to indulge my sins as if they were actually parts of me. . . . But after that, by the help of the water of new birth . . . a second birth had restored me to a new man.[68]

In 248, he was chosen as Bishop of Carthage. He died a martyr's death ten years later, greeting his death with the words of the Scilli martyrs, 'Thanks be to God'. In the approaching divisions of the North African Church, both Catholics and Donatists believed that they stood in his tradition.

Cyprian affirmed the authority of the Church *vis-à-vis* the schismatic rigorist movement that followed the Roman presbyter, Novatian. He successfully established the authority of bishops, rather than confessors, in determining policy to be followed towards those who lapsed and repented, but, like the Donatists after him, he believed in the rebaptism of heretics and schismatics, defying the current Pope (Stephen) to do so. Accordingly to Jerome, he read Tertullian daily, and he had similar views on purple sheep.[69]

The poor were often the most enthusiastic martyrs. Tertullian realized this. 'I fear the neck, beset with pearl and emerald nooses, will give no room to the broadsword'.[70] Cyprian, an exception, like Perpetua, gave his wealth to the poor on his conversion, 'dispensing the purchase money of entire estates'.[71] He described the worldliness of some at least of his co-religionists: 'Very many bishops . . . became agents in secular business, forsook their throne . . . hunted the markets for gainful merchandise, while brethren were starving in the church'.[72] However, the Christian community was still capable of idealism and self-sacrifice. When plague struck Carthage, and many died, the Christians, led by Cyprian, devoted themselves to the afflicted.

Traditional religion declined in the third century, a change that is easier to document than to explain. North Africa had many traditional divinities, but none more feared than Saturn, who was closer to the Punic Baal than to the Italian Saturnus. He communicated with believers in dreams, and they honoured him with human sacrifice, only later substituting offerings of lambs. Even Christians found him so alarming that they referred to him indirectly as *Senex*, old man. Tertullian wrote, '. . . children were openly sacrificed in Africa to Saturn as lately as the proconsulship of Tiberius . . .'.[73] The last dated inscription to Saturn in Numidia and Mauretania is AD 272, the last in Tunisia, 323. As the appeal of Christianity became more popular, paganism became the preserve of an aristocratic and/or highly educated minority: 'There may be a direct connection, in the Late Roman period, between the narrowing of Latin culture in its pagan form—its "aristocratisation"—and its widening—its "democratisation"—in its Christian form'.[74] Augustine's teachers at Madaura were pagans, and there were riots in 399 when traditional shrines were suppressed at Carthage.[75]

The Donatist Church

There is a profound irony in the fact that just when Christianity became official and respectable, North African Christians were torn apart by what was to prove a permanent division. The Novatian schism grew out of the Decian

persecution, the Donatist out of Diocletian's, from 303 to 313. This broke out suddenly after some 40 years of peace that had undoubtedly undermined the enthusiasm for martyrdom. Christians were ordered to hand over copies of the scriptures and their churches were burned. It was a situation that lent itself to evasion, and some handed over heretical texts or books on secular subjects. As before, the problem arose, what policy should the Church follow towards the *traditores*.

In 304, the conflict between confessor and Church authority broke out once more. Forty-seven Christians from the village of Abitina were tried and imprisoned in Carthage. They declared that no one who associated with the *traditores* would enjoy paradise. They were challenged by the Archdeacon of Carthage, Caecilian, who cut them off from visitors and supplies, a classic clash between the authority of the confessor and the organizational structure of the Church. There was an element of class hostility in this as the poor had been more prominent among the martyrs, partly because, perhaps, they had less to lose. In 311, Caecilian was chosen as Bishop of Carthage. The election was hurried through before the arrival of the Bishop of Numidia, who traditionally played a prominent role in his consecration. He then appointed an alternative Bishop of Carthage, Majorinus, an obscure figure who soon fades from the scene and is replaced by the much more formidable Donatus. He gave his name to a major North African church that was to endure until Christianity in the Maghrib came to an end.

Donatus came from southern Numidia near the desert's edge. He was a charismatic figure; 'Men swore by his "white hairs" . . . Like some Jewish High Priest, he celebrated the mysteries alone'.[76] By a sad irony, persecution divided Christians just when persecution was coming to an end.

Constantine became the Emperor of Rome after the battle of the Milvian Bridge in 312. This sincere, but far from exemplary, convert, baptized on his deathbed, saw Christian unity as a concomitant of a united empire, and, as we have seen, summoned the Council of Nicaea. He threw the full weight of imperial authority on the Catholic side in North Africa. In Donatist eyes, imperial persecution was not a disadvantage: 'You come with edicts of emperors, we hold nothing in our hands but volumes of scriptures'.[77] Constantine built a new capital on the Bosphorus, which long bore his name. The gradual separation of an eastern and western empire, formalized in 395, had profound effects on Christendom. In the end, the original Roman empire disappeared, swallowed up by barbarian invasions. Byzantium survived, despite the attacks of Muslims and of (western) Christian crusaders, until 1453.

The great church historian, Frend, interpreted Donatism as a vehicle for Berber patriotism and for socio-economic protest, the protest of the urban poor and the rural peasants against a Church increasingly closely identified with the landowning classes and imperial authority.[78] That it embodied such elements is beyond doubt. The Donatists claimed Simon of Cyrene as an *Afer*

(African) like themselves, and Augustine had to use an interpreter in the countryside around Hippo, where local people spoke *lingua punica*, probably Berber rather than Punic.

The Circumcellions were an extremist wing of the Donatists, who seem to have first appeared in about 340 (the name was invented by their enemies; they called themselves Champions, *agonistici*). This was clearly a Peasants' Revolt; they lived in community near the tombs of rural martyrs, carrying clubs called Israel, attacking their propertied opponents with the war cry *Deo Laudes*. They had women associates whom Augustine called nuns: (*sanctimoniales*):

> . . . no man could rest secure in his possessions . . . At that time, no creditor was free to press his claim, and all were terrified by the letters of these fellows who boasted that they were "Captains of the Saints". . . . Even journeys could not be made with perfect safety, for masters were often thrown out of their own chariots and forced to run, in servile fashion, in front of their own slaves. . . .[79]

Augustine described their defence of 'any debtor whatever that sought their assistance or protection'.[80] At the bottom of cliffs in Numidia are boulders marked with a name, a date, and *nat(alis)* (anniversary) or *r* (*redditio*), where Circumcellions plunged to their deaths in pursuit of a kind of martyrdom.

Frend's critics have pointed out that Augustine differed little from the Donatist bishops in his education and economic circumstances, that Donatist apologists apparently wrote only in Latin, that Donatism was as much an urban as a rural phenomenon (the great basilica at Timgad covered five acres), and that not only Donatist literature, but even their war cry was in Latin.

Many Donatists were converts from paganism, their church affiliation determined by geographical accident. What distinguished the Donatists above all was an ideology, a concept of the Church as a small body of the chosen. Augustine, on the other hand, believed that tares and wheat could be distinguished only in eternity. Donatists described the Church in texts beloved of Cyprian: '. . . a garden locked, a fountain sealed',[81] or as an Ark, caulked to prevent leakage in or out. The journal of a modern New Zealand conservative Catholic group is called *Hortus Conclusus*.

Donatism was not confined to Africa. Donatus' gifted successor was a Spaniard or Gaul, and there was, for a time, a Donatist Pope in Rome, but they cherished texts that could be construed to mean God's special predilection for Africa, such as a version of the *Song of Solomon* 1:6 ('My beloved is from the South'). To the much travelled Augustine, it was bizarre to suggest that God's Church was primarily located in Numidia. He compared the Donatists with frogs in a pond, who thought they were the universal Church: *Securus adindicat orbis terrarum*, The whole world is secure in its judgement. The words troubled Newman, in his Anglican days.

'Heretics, Jews and pagans—they have come to form a unity over against our Unity', said Augustine, in words that anticipate much that was sinister in the future. Augustine's views on Donatists were used to justify the persecution of the Huguenots,[82] and no biblical text has been used more oppressively than *Compelle intrare*. Laws imposed fines and legal disabilities on Donatists, but were often not strictly enforced.[83] However, it is a sombre thought that, in the empire as a whole, more Christians were persecuted by Christian emperors than by pagan ones.

Donatists and African Catholics had much in common. They shared a fundamental austerity, a separateness from 'the world', to which Christians elsewhere were increasingly accommodated. It was, perhaps, their essential orthodoxy that exasperated Augustine, their creation of a separate church on the basis of an obscure ecclesiastical quarrel.

Augustine (354–430)[84]

No Christian in the world of late antiquity is as well known to us as Augustine. Thanks largely to his *Confessions*, we know him better than many people we meet every day. We know about his dislike of travel, especially by sea, his childhood theft of pears, which he remembered as an instance of human depravity. His literary output was prodigious, an inscription in a Spanish library says that anyone who claims to have read it all is a liar! His *Confessions* was written in what he believed to be his old age—he was 43! Many commentators have dwelt on his attachment to his mother, Monica, and his alienation from his father. Like Perpetua's narrative, it has its own silences. He does not mention the name of the mother of his son, with whom he lived for many years, sending her away disconsolate when he planned to marry an heiress (Perpetua similarly, says nothing of her husband).

Until his final conversion, Augustine was a restless seeker after truth. It is interesting that he never seems to have considered Donatism or paganism to be viable alternatives.

For nine years, he was a Manichee. In North Africa, as in Egypt, Manicheism largely replaced gnosticism. Mani was a Persian who died in 260; he attempted to synthesize the various faiths known to him. The religion he founded lasted a thousand years, won converts from Rome to China, and has left a great literary inheritance in a variety of languages, including Coptic.

> Be like a jar of wine
> Firmly set on its stand,
> Outside, it is pottery and pitch
> But inside it is fragrant wine.[85]

Its world view was dualist, its great attraction, which it shared with other dualist systems, is that by making evil an independent principle, it avoids the problem of the compatibility of sin and suffering with a good and omnipotent God.

Manicheism was one of many religious alternatives confronting North Africans. Another was the well-established and long-continued tradition of Judaism.[86] We have noted the Tertullianistae, and Augustine tells us of another splinter group, a village that emulated the continence of Abel, despite the problems this posed for sectarian survival!

For a time, Augustine was attracted by neo-Platonism. In August 386, after his famous conversion experience in a garden in Milan, he turned from ambition and the prospect of an advantageous marriage. He reverted to the orthodox Catholicism of his mother and returned to Africa, soon to become Bishop of Hippo and the implacable opponent of Donatism. He attacked the Donatists in public debates and learned treatises, placed posters on the walls of their basilicas and wrote popular songs, like 'The ABC against Donatists'.

There is a sense in which Augustine never left the Manichees. Their influence is clear in his ideas on sin and salvation, that only a few are predestined for salvation, most of humanity ending up in Hell. No ideological encounter has had more momentous consequences than his long debate with Pelagius. Pelagius, who may have come from Britain (the only heresiarch from the British Isles in the early Church), had a long and distinguished career as a teacher in Rome. When one of his disciples sought ordination in Carthage, he incurred the unrelenting hostility of Augustine. Pelagius, like the Reformation leaders after him, attacked the idea of a two-tier spirituality, where sanctity was only to be expected of monks and nuns. It was obligatory for all—God had commanded it ('Be ye therefore perfect'), and he would not demand the impossible. It was not only possible, but mandatory to create a just society. The idea that all humanity would suffer for Adam's sin was intolerable. In the words of Julian of Eclanum, one of the most gifted Pelagian controversialists, the idea of Original Sin 'is improbable, it is untrue; it is unjust and impious'.[87] Most modern Christians would agree with Pelagius, but his humane and optimistic theology was condemned by successive Popes in 417 and 418, with incalculable consequences for medieval and later history.

It is difficult for us to enter into the passion that underlay these long-dead debates on doctrine. A famous description of Constantinople during the Arian controversy reflects how they touched the lives of everyone: 'If you ask for your change, the shopkeeper philosophizes to you about the Begotten and the Unbegotten'. In northern Africa, as elsewhere, religious differences sometimes led to bloodshed. A Greek historian of the fifth century, reflected disapprovingly, 'surely nothing can be further from the spirit of Christianity than massacres, fights and transactions of that sort'.[88]

Christianity and political events

North Africans lived on the edge of the empire, and of *Romanitas*, yet, as we have seen, they often identified closely with both. They brooded over the relationship between religious change and temporal fortunes; the issue was far from academic. Tertullian complained that if the Tiber flooded, or the Nile failed to flood, there was a cry of 'Christians to the lion!'[89] Arnobius Afer (*flor.* 290–303) was a pagan polemicist in the Roman province of Africa who became a Christian, and wrote *Against Pagans* during Diocletian's persecution to attack this kind of thinking. Another African, Lactantius, (*flor.* 290–320), Arnobius' pupil, and also a convert, wrote a pamphlet on *The Death of Persecutors*, claiming that they were punished for their cruelty to Christians.[90] His life's work was to make Christianity acceptable to cultured pagans, but he denounces the injustices by which empires are created. Rome's boundaries spread '. . . by inflicting injustices according to legal forms', and he asks a question that has not lost its relevance, 'What are the interests of our country, but the inconveniences of another state or nation?'[91]

When Constantine became Roman emperor, most Christians had no difficulty in seeing his success as evidence of divine approval. The most famous example is Eusebius' *Ecclesiastical History*. Like many Greek Christians after him, he saw the Christian empire as the mirror image of the heavenly kingdom. However, in 410, Rome fell to the barbarians. Rome had already ceased to be the capital of the empire by then, but the symbolic and psychological impact of the fall of the 'Eternal City' was tremendous. Pagans blamed it on the spread of Christianity (Gibbon agreed with them, and perhaps, he was not wholly wrong). Augustine's response to this was his *City of God*, which took him fifteen years to write. His two cities cannot be identified with any earthly polity; their inhabitants are divided by the ultimate direction of their will and the membership of each can be known only in eternity: 'Two loves therefore have given origin to these two cities, self-love in contempt of God unto the earthly, love of God in contempt of one's self to the heavenly'. Rome, and other earthly states are not, and cannot be, the counterpart of the heavenly city 'and yet have those a kind of allowable peace . . . during our admixture with Babylon we ourselves make use of her peace . . .'.[92]

Commodian was a Latin poet, widely, but not universally, believed to be a fifth-century African. He welcomed the barbarians as agents of God's wrath against the pride of Rome, and the avarice of the rich, who, in the millenium, will be the slaves of the saints.

The fall of Roman Africa

One of the mysteries of church history lies in the way in which some Christian communities but not others feel a strong commitment to evangelization. Despite a gloomy view of the eternal fate of the unbaptized, Augustine and his compatriots seem to have felt no duty to preach Christianity beyond the Roman boundaries, unlike the Nestorians, Byzantines, and Syrian Monophysites who did so much to spread Christianity further east. The inward focus of the North African Church is reflected in the striking density of ecclesiastical administration in 411: no less than 286 Catholic bishops, and 284 Donatist ones held a debate.

In 426, 'barbarians' living outside the charmed circle of African Romanitas invaded and plundered it: Augustine wrote of 'hordes of African barbarians, plundering and destroying without resistance'. The Church was weakened both by sectarian and class divisions: 'The clergy were hated because of their possessions'.[93] Augustine described the dissatisfaction of the poor: 'They alone [the rich] really live'.

In 429, the Vandal king, Gaiseric, in one of the great gambles of history, brought his entire people, some 80 thousand of them, to North Africa. They settled in Tunisia, the old Carthaginian heartland, after 'the fourth Punic war'. The Vandals were Gothic in language, and Arian in religion, and persecuted Catholics and Donatists impartially. The only extant Donatist document from the period identifies the Vandal King with the Beast of Revelations. Gradually, the Vandals mellowed. Thrasamund, a later king, enjoyed theological debate; his successor was a Catholic. There was even a resurgence of Latin poetry, associated with the now obscure names of Luxorius and Dracontius.

The Vandals were too few to modify local society, or speech patterns. Their regime was overthrown by the forces of the Byzantine Emperor, Justinian, in 533; not a single Gothic word survived. The most enduring consequence of their regime was a still more profound weakening of Romanitas. In western Numidia and Mauretania, independent Berber kingdoms re-emerged, Christian in faith, and Latin in their official language (much earlier Berber kingdoms had been swallowed up by Roman imperialism). The peoples of the desert's edge, to the South, the Lawata, worshipped Hammon-Baal, the ancient god of the Libyans and Carthaginians. Byzantine Africa was larger than the Vandal kingdom, smaller than Roman Africa, which had included western Algeria and northern Morocco; the Romans' monuments were plundered to fortify its frontiers. By the seventh century, however, Christianity in Byzantine Africa seems to have been in decline, the small size and inferior construction of its churches reflect this.[94]

Where most Egyptians were passionately Monophysite, North African Christianity was vehemently Chalcedonian. Indeed, in 550, the Council of Carthage excommunicated the Pope for his hesitations in this area! There was a resurgence of Donatism; the correspondence of Pope Gregory (590–604) is full of references to their 'execrable wickedness'.[95]

The Arab invasions

The prophet Muhammad died in 632. Seven years later, an Arab force invaded Egypt. Its success was greatly aided by the collaboration of several highly placed men, notably Cyrus, the 'Melkite' Patriarch of Alexandria, and the Byzantine Governor, who surrendered both the fortress of Babylon and

Alexandria, and the Coptic 'Duke' Sanutius, who handed over the Egyptian fleet. All this shows the bitterness of the divisions between the Christian parties. It was not clear at the time that Islam was a new religion; the 'Ishmaelites' were initially widely regarded as a Christian sect. The Arab victors recognized the Monophysite church and the Copts received the religious toleration accorded 'Peoples of the Book' in return for poll tax. The Byzantines withdrew, and with them the hated Chalcedonian church.

The Arabs valued the Copts as taxpayers and as civil servants. They were even, initially, prohibited from conversion, and the army was replenished by clients, *mawali*, initially from Libya. Coptic Christians could not bear arms or serve as soldiers until the nineteenth century. The survival of the Coptic church is sometimes explained by economic factors, such as the church's rich endowments and the Copts' dominance in the civil service. Christians formed a majority in Egypt until the tenth century. They declined to their present minority position as a result of successive waves of Arab immigration, and persecution under the Mamluks, from the mid thirteenth to the early sixteenth centuries. The worsening of the Copts' position was, in part, due to the aggression of the Crusaders, who, at various times, proposed blockading the Red Sea, or diverting the Nile. Historians cite the marriages of Arabs to Coptic women whose children became Muslims. However, the influence of Christian wives is one of the main causes adduced as originally spreading Christianity. Copt, originally meaning 'Egyptian', now meant 'Christian'.

Religious adherence and language choice were quite distinct. At the end of the tenth century, most Egyptian Christians spoke Coptic; by the end of the twelfth, most spoke Arabic, and Christian literature was translated into it. The thirteenth century was the golden age of Coptic literature in Arabic.[96] Coptic remained the language of liturgy, like Latin in the West. The Coptic church supplied the head of the Ethiopian church, the Abuna, until 1951, 'which must surely constitute an ecclesiastical record for dilatory indigenization'.[97] Today, there are roughly 4 million Copts in a population of 48 million.

The Arabs conquered Byzantine Africa between 670 and 705, with the aid of the *mawali*, one of whom was later to give his name to Gibraltar, the Rock of Tariq. They called north-west Africa 'the Maghrib', which means 'the West'; Africa became Ifriqiya, and Carthage, Tunis. The opposition they encountered came mainly from the independent Berbers, rather than from Byzantine Africa. The names of two Berber leaders are preserved, Kasila, who founded a short-lived state at Kairouan, and died in 686, and al-Kahina, the Prophetess. Tradition depicts her as a Jewish queen, who waged a long struggle against the Arabs, but urged her sons to go over to their side. She was killed in *c.* 698 at a place called Kahina's well. An eleventh-century source calls her a Christian, and the whole story may be a legend based on a corruption of the male name, Kahya.[98]

The extinction of Christianity in the Maghrib is one of the great mysteries of African history. It was a gradual process. Though the evidence is fragmentary, it is clear that the Arab invaders encountered a Christian culture largely confined to the towns and weakened both by sectarian divisions and by the invasions of, first, Arian Vandals, and then of Berber nomads, Lawata, 'ignorant of the Christian god'.[99]

Gradually, the Berbers of the north-west became, first *mawali*, then Muslims. There were economic inducements to conversion: the chance of joining the armies that conquered Spain, and freedom from poll tax. The Maghrib lacked the monastic tradition that did so much to preserve Christianity in Egypt and Ethiopia. There was a process of desertification, the causes of which are debated, and the vast olive groves of inland Numidia gradually gave way to steppe, the natural habitat of Arab and Berber pastoralists.

By the ninth century, the Cyrene Cathedral had been converted to residential use.[100] Until the twelfth century, Arab writers refer to the *Afariqa*, whom they distinguish from the *Barbar*, and seem to have been Christians. Latin was used in inscriptions until the eleventh century and al-Bakri found a Christian community at Tlemcen in 1068, as well as numerous ruined and empty churches in Algeria and Tunisia. Jewish communities survived, and were reinforced by those expelled from Spain. Rabbis in Algiers guided the Jews of Tuat on issues such as how to keep the sabbath when crossing the Sahara.[101] As in Egypt, Arabization was distinct from Christianization, and many Maghribi Muslims speak Berber to this day. Some have discerned continuities between the Puritanism and separatism of the Donatists, and North Africa's Kharijites, the cult of local saints and the shrines of dead sufis. Herodotus, in *c.* 430 BC, related how the Libyans would sleep on their ancestors' graves, and Augustine, writing in AD 397–8, observed, 'it had been my mother's custom in Africa to take meal-cakes and bread and wine to the shrines of saints'. *Plus ça change.*

Muslim and Christian saints in the Maghrib shared the same passion for truth, the same combativeness. Carthage was a centre of Christian scholarship. Its Muslim counterpart was Kairouan, the 'caravan', or resting place, founded in 670. A traveller asked what the people of Kairouan were discussing, and was told, 'the names and attributes of God'. Dhu'l Nun al Misri ('the Egyptian'), of Nubian parentage, died in 860. He was one of the founders of Sufism. A pleasant legend states that when he died, words appeared on his forehead, 'This is the friend of God, he died in love of God, slain by God'. Much the same could have been said of the Desert People. Muslims succeeded, where Christians failed, in spreading their faith far to the South, across the Saharan trade routes, and into the western Sudan. In the Roman ruins of Hippo, Arab visitors looked for the cathedral of 'Augodjin, a great doctor of the Christian religion'.[102]

❧ TWO ❧

The Churches of the Middle Years,
c. 1500 to c. 1800

They are possess'd with a strange notion, that they are the
only true Christians in the world.

Jeronimo Lobo on seventeenth-century Ethiopia[1]

Introduction

The Christianity of the Maghrib had virtually disappeared by the eleventh
century, and, in 1317, Dongola Cathedral, in Nubia, became a mosque. The
modern phase of missionary activity in Africa, and elsewhere, began with the
foundation of the Baptist Missionary Society in 1792. Christianity in Africa, in
the centuries between the Church of Clement and Augustine, and that of the
nineteenth century, has three main themes: the continuing life of the Coptic
and Ethiopian churches, some strikingly unsuccessful attempts to 'convert'
Muslim North Africa, and the history of the Catholic churches founded in
black Africa, initially by the Portuguese.

The first Portuguese ships anchored off the coast of the west-central
African kingdom of Kongo in 1483. Catholicism survived, in an indigenized
form, until the late nineteenth century, when a new wave of missionary
activity began. It was introduced into the Niger Delta kingdom of Warri in the
1570s; despite long periods without missionaries, it endured until the mid
eighteenth century. In Benin, it proved ephemeral. On the once-uninhabited
Atlantic islands of São Thomé and the Cape Verdes, Christianity became part
of the dominant Luso-African culture. There were comparable enclaves in the
Senegambia, in Guinea-Bissau, and elsewhere in West Africa. Not all African
converts were Catholics, some joined the various Protestant churches
represented in the fort cultures on the Gold Coast, where several protégés of
European merchants acquired a university education abroad. However, when
they returned home they were, almost without exception, unhappy and
marginalized. Sometimes, they could no longer speak an African language. In
southern Africa, several Mutapa princes became friars, and when Livingstone

45

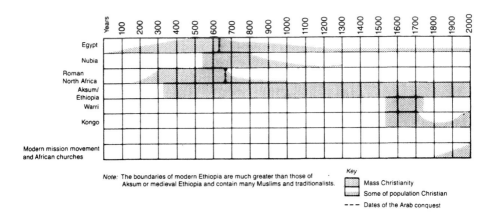

Christianity in Africa, a chronological perspective

travelled on the Zambezi, he encountered a Catholicism that had never entirely died out.

The history of all Christian missions is a theme in counterpoint, the intricate and ever-changing relationship between Christianity, the cultural packaging in which it is presented, and the culture of the host community. To the missionaries, Christianity was inseparable from their own cultural inheritance, and their converts acquired many cultural traits that had nothing to do with religion, so that the nobility of the Kongo became counts or marquises, with family names such as da Silva. Despite this, African Christians inevitably understood Christianity in terms of their own culture, and incorporated many of its insights. As we have seen, scholarly opinion is sharply divided as to when this becomes inculturation, and when syncretism.

Ethiopia

The spread of Islam in Arabia, Egypt, Nubia, and throughout the near East, meant that Christian Ethiopia became increasingly isolated. The early relationships between Muslims and Christians were amiable, not least because a king of Aksum gave sanctuary to some of the first Muslims, fleeing from the then hostile city of Mecca. Gradually, Muslim merchants settled on the coastal plains.

In the tenth century, the Aksumite kingdom went through a crisis, created by Muslim pressure from the North and attacks from a traditionalist from the

46

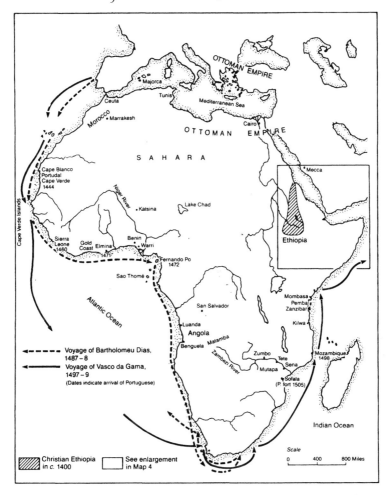

Map 4. Peoples and places mentioned in Chapter Two

South, an Agaw queen, who is remembered for her passionate hostility to Christianity.

Aksum declined, and the centre of political gravity moved further South. From 1150 to 1270, the kingdom was ruled by the Zagwe dynasty, based in Lasta (see Map 5), its name reflecting its Agaw origin. It was a classic case of the vanquished taking the victor captive. Lalibela (reg. *c.* 1205–25) is remembered as one of the greatest of the Zagwe kings. It was in his time that the miraculous rock-hewn churches were created, in an attempt to recreate the Holy Places in his own land. Perhaps he was seeking to sacralize the new dynasty, but, if so, the attempt was ultimately a failure for the Zagwe dynasty was overthrown by an Amharic one that could lay claim to Solomonic descent.

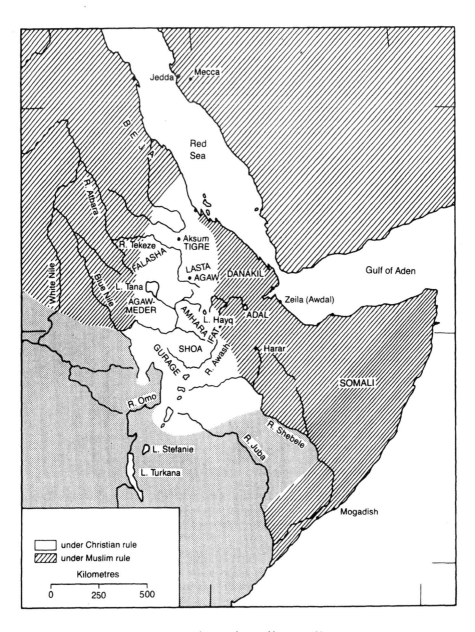

Map 5. Ethiopia and its neighbours *c.* 1400

Ethiopia's new rulers no longer built in stone. The Solomonic tradition became the core symbol of Christian Ethiopia, the cornerstone of its sense of national identity. It was first recorded in the *Kebra Negast*, *The Glory of Kings*, written early in the fourteenth century, but it had lived in Ethiopian hearts long before. The Coptic chronicle of the life of the Alexandrian Patriarch, Cosmas, (*b.* 920) refers to, 'Abyssinia which is a vast country, namely the kingdom of Saba from which the Queen of the South came to Solomon'.[2] The Solomonic legend, as related in the *Kebra Negast*, tells how the Queen of Sheba visited Solomon, and, after her return home, bore his child, who grew up to become Menelik I of Aksum. When he grew up, he went to Jerusalem and took the Ark of the Covenant back to his own people. From then on, the Ethiopians considered themselves, rather than the Jews, to be the chosen people of God. The Ethiopians called their homeland Siyon (Zion) which is still the promised land of black spirituals and of reggae music.

The Ethiopian Church's strong Hebraic elements give it a unique role in Christian/Jewish dialogue. It has grown directly from Christianity's Jewish roots, without the admixture of Hellenism.

The Hebraic practices in Ethiopian Christianity are generally thought to have been adopted gradually, rather than being ancient survivals—an identification with Israel seemed especially appropriate for an isolated people with a sense of peril and encirclement. In the same way, nineteenth-century Maori prophets in New Zealand repeatedly described their people as Jews. The world of the Hebrew Bible clearly has much in common with African cultures, in the importance placed on dreams and visions, and the felt need to establish boundaries with ritual prohibitions. Many modern African prophetic churches keep the sabbath holy, and adopt dietary and other prohibitions similar to those laid down in Leviticus, as the Ethiopians do.

Only the head of the Church, the Abuna, could ordain clergy or consecrate the *tabot* (Ark), which is essential in every Ethiopian church. The need to obtain every Abuna from Muslim-ruled Egypt often created difficulties, and sometimes the post was vacant for years after the death of an incumbent.

The sabbath was kept holy as well as Sunday, a situation achieved after conflict: two great monastic orders disputed the issue to the brink of schism, until it was resolved in the mid fifteenth century. Jewish dietary taboos were strictly observed, as were the laws regulating ritual cleanness, and baby boys were circumcized on the eighth day after their birth. The Church's year was full of festivals and fast days. No Christian church has fasted with the resolution of the Ethiopians: there are 180 fast days in the year for the laity, and 250 for the clergy, with every Wednesday and Friday being fast days. On a fast day, one meal is eaten, after noon, and there is total abstention from meat, fat, eggs, and all dairy products. In the nineteenth century, Ethiopians exported coffee, but the Church forbade them to drink it.

There are large numbers of priests, who support themselves, and may marry before, but not after, their ordination. They have often been of limited education. On one occasion, for example, a group of priests were confounded when Lalibela told them to read the ritual of baptism.[3] Each church, even the smallest, is divided into three sections. These include a Holy of Holies, where the Ark is kept, and where only priests and the king might enter. The Ethiopian liturgy, with its drumming, dancing, scriptural readings, and antiphonal singing is a powerful amalgam of Jewish and African elements.

The monks were the cutting edge of Ethiopian spirituality. They were celibates and ascetics, a foreign missionary describing one who lived (like some modern diet gurus) on raw vegetables and beansprouts, saying, with a shudder, that it was 'the most dismal food in the world'.[4] The monks were healers and missionaries; they did battle with the forces of Satan, whom Kaplan calls 'the forgotten "man" of Ethiopian history'.[5] The saints of Ethiopian Christianity are almost unknown in the West. They include Gebre Christos, a king's son who prayed for leprosy in order to share the sufferings of Christ. His prayer was answered.[6]

The Church, especially the monastic element, was often riven by controversies, the intensity of which reflects the Ethiopians' passionate absorption with religion. We have mentioned the fifteenth-century conflict over the Saturday Sabbath, between the followers of Teka Haymanot, based in Shoa, and those of Ewostatewos, based in Tigre, but there were many others. Monks denounced the royal practice of polygamy, and some representatives of both monastic groups, including Ewostatewos himself, died in exile. A late fifteenth-century monastic movement, the Stephanites, refused to prostate themselves before images of Mary or the Cross. In the early seventeenth century, a monk called zä-Krestos departed much further from orthodoxy; he claimed to be the Christ of the Gentiles, and was executed. Until they were eliminated by persecution, his followers believed he rose from the dead: 'On the basis of this faith of theirs they founded a false church. . . . They ordained priests and deacons. The priests even gave them communion, saying, "The body of zä-Krestos, our God, which he took from Amätä Wängel, the lady of us all" '.[7] The movement took the inculturation of the faith in Ethiopia, and the reconstruction of its Holy Places, to an extreme conclusion.

Recent scholarship reminds us that we should not idealize the Ethiopian Church and some have condemned its endowments. A more fundamental criticism is that it underpinned a monarchy and nobility that were often rapacious and oppressive, and which were closely identified with an Amharic culture that despised both Oromo and 'Shankilla', 'blacks who lived in the lowland wilderness . . .'.[8] It also strengthened the dominance of the husband/father in the family. The word for fasting, so central to Ethiopian Christianity, is the same as the word for a field worked for a lord's benefit by compulsory labour.[9]

The Falasha were feared and despised as the Other, in a situation similar to that of European Jewry. From the fifteenth century on, they were forbidden to own land, and, by the nineteenth century, they were shunned and despised as buda ('evil eye'), 'wizards and cannibals eating men by some secret process of sorcery'.[10] Christianity was spread largely by force of arms. The warrior king, Amda-Siyon (1314–44), was the architect of the Ethiopian State, and its cultural hegemony was extended and consolidated by missionary monks. In the late seventeenth century, Yohannes devastated the Agaw countryside: 'Then every Agaw who lives in the middle of Sikut . . . was terrified, took refuge at a church . . . and said . . . 'I shall become Christian and submit to the king and pay tribute and I shall do whatever the king orders me to do" '.[11] Ironically, the Agaw now venerate the memory of Yohannes the Saint. All this is not, of course, peculiar to Ethiopia; it is exactly paralleled in medieval Europe.

Christian Ethiopia, like the Coptic community, was not a mission field at all; it was an ancient and thoroughly Africanized church that would have provided most valuable precedents for other African Christians, had they come into contact with it. To Catholics, the Ethiopian Orthodox Church was heretical (because Monophysite), and schismatic, although they were not blind to its strengths: '. . . notwithstanding their separation from the Roman Church, and the corruptions which have crept into their faith, yet [they] retain in a great measure the devout fervour of the primitive Christians'.[12]

Peaceful coexistence gave way to war, as Muslims created powerful new states, such as Ifat and Adal, to the East of the Christian kingdom. Ethiopia extended much further South than Aksum had done, but was still confined, in the main, to Ethio-semitic-speaking peoples of the highlands.

In the early sixteenth century, a dynamic Muslim leader arose in Adal, the Imam Ahmad, who came close to overthrowing the Christian kingdom. It was just at this time that Ethiopia came into direct contact with emissaries from Europe. Pero de Covilha reached Ethiopia in 1494, but was not allowed to leave, and died there thirty years later. Later delegations fared better, and a Portuguese contingent assisted in the defeat of Ahmad's forces in 1543. Ethiopia's kings were torn by the desire for European assistance on the one hand, and fear of the threat to their religion and independence on the other.

Pedro Paez was a Jesuit who was sent to Ethiopia in 1589. Captured by pirates, he served in the galleys for seven years, finally reaching his destination in 1603. A remarkable linguist who soon learned to read and write Ge'ez and Amharic, he converted the king, Susenyos, and some of his kinsmen and courtiers. Susenyos openly declared himself a Catholic in 1622. Paez died in the same year, and his successors, lacking his tact and wisdom, opposed cultural practices that were, from a religious viewpoint, neutral, such as the pork tabu and circumcision, while insisting on the Latin calendar and liturgy. The popular opposition was enormous, and Susenyos abdicated in 1632: '. . . even the ignorant peasants of Lasta have died fighting against it. Now therefore we restore to you the Faith of your ancestors . . .'. His heir, Fasilidas, expelled the Jesuits two years later. The episode left a heritage of mistrust of the western churches and of western culture, which long endured.

Missionary attacks on Monophysitism led to impassioned christological controversies within the Ethiopian Church, which profoundly weakened and divided it.

In the 1790s, an Ethiopian convert to Catholicism, Tobias Gabra Egzi'abeher, titular bishop of Adulis, worked as a missionary, but he had no more success than his West African contemporaries, such as Quaque and Amo.

The Jesuits paid tribute to the quality of Ethiopian religious life, although they tried to change it:

> No country in the world is so full of churches, monastries, and ecclesiasticks as Abyssinia; it is not possible to sing in one church or monastry without being heard by another, and perhaps by several. . . . The instruments of musick made use of in their rites of worship, are little drums, which they hang about their necks and beat with both their hands . . . They have sticks likewise with which they strike the ground . . . when they have heated themselves by degrees, they leave off druming and fall to leaping, dancing and clapping their hands . . . They are possess'd with a strange notion, that they are the only true Christians in the world. . . .[13]

It was the accretion of custom that separated the churches, rather than the obscure mystery of the Nature of Christ (the editor of a Hakluyt text notes, with unconscious condescension: '. . . it need hardly be said that Ethiopic is not a satisfactory language in which to discuss a problem of this kind'[14]).

The next major visitor to Ethiopia was James Bruce, an eighteenth-century Scottish laird equally hostile to Jesuits and Monophysites. He wrote, 'The two natures in Christ, the two persons, their unity . . . are all wrapped up in tenfold darkness'. Precisely, but not only for Ethiopians!

Portugal in Africa

In comparison with the Ethiopian and Coptic churches, the Christian communities established through western, and especially Portuguese, influence during the Middle Years were fragile, exotic plants, which did not always survive in African soil.

Christianity did not always flourish in Portuguese soil either: Isabella's church reforms, in the late fifteenth century, led 400 friars to go to Africa and become Muslims![15] The factors that shaped Portuguese national and religious sensibilities are to be found in the history of the Iberian peninsula, which was, for centuries, largely under Muslim rule. The process of Christian Reconquista was complete by 1492. Portugal gained its independence in 1143, and retained it in part through the accidents of dynastic marriage.[16]

Granada Muslims were promised toleration, but, ten years later, they were offered a choice between conversion and exile, the choice that had been given to Spanish Jews not long before. In 1609, some half a million *Moriscos*, who accepted Christianity but retained Arabic speech and Moorish dress, were also expelled. Cruelty and ethnic chauvinism in Christianity's name were not peculiar to the Iberian peninsula, as the history of the Crusades reminds us. They were not only directed against peoples of different faiths either. When a Spanish interloper challenged Portugal's commercial monopoly in Guinea, he was burned alive.[17]

Much mission history is explicable only against this background, the identification of national identity with Catholicism, and the hostility to Islam. Portugal was a small country with a population of perhaps a million and a half. It created an empire that spanned the world, but which it lacked the resources to sustain.

Spain and Portugal carried the Reconquista to North Africa. In 1415, Portugal obtained a foothold in Morocco, at Ceuta, which still retains a separate political identity. Spain established a chain of coastal garrisons in the Maghrib, the last of which was relinquished in 1791. Their main impact, perhaps, was to enrage Muslim sensibilities.

Prince Henry, whom history knows as the Navigator, took part in the expedition to Ceuta. On his return, he established a school of navigation in southern Portugal, sending annual expeditions down the Atlantic coast of Africa, 'being desirous to learn new things, particularly of the peoples dwelling in those lands, and to cause injury to the Moors'.[18]

When Vasco da Gama reached Calicut, in May 1498, he said that he came in search of Christians and spices. A sea route to India would enable the Portuguese to bypass the Muslim middlemen who controlled the routes through the near East, and, perhaps, to find a new ally in Prester John. The legend of this mysterious Christian potentate may have had its origins in medieval encounters with Ethiopian pilgrims and monks in Jerusalem. It has been suggested that it was deliberately elaborated as propaganda, to encourage the Crusaders.[19] The quest for Prester John survived long after contacts were established with Ethiopia. In the 1620s, a Jesuit working on the Zambezi hoped that he would be found north-east of Lake Malawi.[20] In 1469, the trade of Guinea was leased for five years to Fernando Gomes, a condition that his ships explored a hundred leagues further each year; his vessels reached the Gold Coast, often referred to simply as Elmina, the Mine.

Portuguese claims to exclusive control of the Guinea trade did not go unchallenged. Spanish ships, in particular, challenged this monopoly until the Treaty of Tordessillas (1494), which divided the newly discovered world between the two, at a point 370 leagues west of the Canaries, Africa and Brazil going to Portugal, and the rest of the New World to Spain. (See Map 4) However, this did not preserve Portugal's hegemony in Africa. From 1530, French, English, and, later, Dutch merchants, for the most part with little interest in religion, became involved in its trade.

The world views prevalent in western Europe and in black Africa in about 1500 had a great deal in common: 'No difference can be perceived between the practices of the Christians and those of the heathen', said a Jesuit in Sierra Leone at the beginning of the seventeenth century.[21] Religion was part of the continuum of life, not compartmentalized on its margins, and it was supernatural interventions that made rain fall, and determined the outcome of battle. The belief in witchcraft and magic was as characteristic of Europe as of Africa, and a study of seventeenth-century Brittany suggests 'that the majority of the inhabitants of medieval Europe were sunk in animist worship of trees, stones and springs and that Christianity was the thinnest of veneers on top of this'.[22] In Portugal, the dead were thought to return on All Souls' Day and the statues of saints were mutilated if they failed to provide expected benefits.[23] In modern times, among the Kalabari of the Niger Delta, the same fate befel sculptures of dangerous spirits.

Missionaries were professionally concerned with religion; European traders had other priorities. In the words of a visitor to the Gold Coast in the late seventeenth century, 'The great concern of the *Dutch* on this coast, as well as of all other *Europeans* settled or trading there, is the gold, and not the welfare of those souls: for by their leud loose lives, many who live among these poor wretches rather harden them in their wickedness than turn them from it'.[24] A Jesuit described the Portuguese in Guinea at the beginning of the seventeenth century as 'men turned wild whose way of life is more heathen than Christian'.[25]

Portuguese missions were organized within a structure called the *padroado*, created in a series of papal bulls and briefs between 1452 and 1514, which gave the Portuguese crown power of appointment to all benefices in its overseas possessions, in return for financial support. The Kongo kings fought against this close association of church and state, and the introduction of (Italian) Capuchins from 1645 on was a result. As Portugal became weaker, and its colonial possessions shrank, it lacked the resources to sustain the *padroado*. The Catholic missionary enterprise was linked to a small and declining imperial power, and this was a continuing source of weakness.

Northern Africa

Christian mission activity in North Africa and Egypt was sporadic, and had no lasting impact, which is not surprising as it took place against a background of endemic hostility. Various forays by the early Franciscans were essentially symbolic gestures, seeking martyrdom and Paradise, rather than conversions. In 1219, the year in which he himself went to Egypt and Palestine, St Francis sent five friars to convert the Moors. After adventures in Seville, they went to Marrakesh and preached in the streets, though only one of them, Berard, knew Arabic. They coveted death, and obtained the martyrdom they desired, as did another group of Italian Franciscans, Daniel and his companions, seven years later. Much later, in 1710–11, two Franciscans crossed the Sahara, dying of sickness in the city of Katsina, in what is now Northern Nigeria.[26]

The Majorcan, Ramon Llull[27] (1232–1316), was an extraordinary genius, comparable in some ways with Augustine. His output, in Arabic, Latin and Catalan was prolific: 256 works survive, ranging from pamphlets to tomes of 150 thousand words. He wrote novels, and treatises on theology, philosophy and science, and was one of the architects of Catalan as a literary language. He was married with two children, 'reasonably well off, licentious and worldly' when, in 1263, his life was transformed by a series of visions of Christ. He decided he was to serve Him 'by carrying out the task of converting to his worship and service the Saracens who in such numbers surrounded the Christians on all sides'.[28] He felt called 'to write a book, the best in the world against the errors of unbelievers'; he learned Arabic from a Muslim slave, so effectively that he wrote books in it, and worked for the creation of centres of learning where it could be studied by prospective missionaries. He had some success, as the ruler of Majorca endowed a monastery for this purpose, but successive Popes were less responsive: '. . . this petition was of little interest to the Pope and to the cardinals'.[29] He made several missionary journeys to North Africa: to Tunis in 1293, when he was over 60, and to Bougie, when he was about 75. His last works were written at the age of 83, in 1315, during a final trip to Tunis. It is uncertain whether or not he died there or in Majorca soon after his return.

There is a touching humanity about the converted Llull. He abandoned his first projected journey to North Africa when still in Genoa, 'fearing for his skin . . . held back by a kind of paralysing fear', and afterwards, for a time, doubted his own salvation,[30] but, for all his exertions and learning, he made, as far as we know, no impact on North Africa. He did not even convert his Muslim slave, who remained hostile to Christianity, and finally hanged himself.

African clergy

West Africa produced a number of indigenous priests and brothers, often from the Cape Verde islands or São Tomé. A Portuguese expedition of 1444 brought back 235 captives. With the myopia of the time, some were given to a church, as revenue, 'and another little Moor, who afterwards became a friar of St Francis, they sent to St Vincent do Cabo, where he lived ever after as a Catholic Christian'.[31] In 1494, a German visitor to Portugal saw many black young men being educated in Latin and theology as a prelude to returning to Africa, and reflected, 'It seems likely that in the course of time, the greater part of Ethiopia will be converted to Christianity'.[32]

African and Eur-African clergy, like their Portuguese counterparts, produced examples of holiness and devotion, but black and white alike were often reluctant to exchange the relative comfort and security of São Thomé and the Cape Verdes for life on the African mainland. Some deserved the harsh strictures of a French abbé in Kongo in 1776, who urged Christian rulers not 'to destroy with one hand what he builds with the other by sending on the track of missionaries a set of men who have nothing of the Christian but the name they dishonour; whose worse than pagan conduct makes the idolaters doubt whether the gods whom they worship are not preferable to that of the Christian'.[33]

Eur-Africans were disproportionately prominent in Africa's Christian communities and among the clergy. Atkins described a family on the Gold Coast, where a British trader was a 'kind husband and father', who educated his four children in England, and shared in his wife's traditional religion: 'He cannot persuade this Woman to leave the Country'.[34]

Often, however, Europeans were savagely hostile to those of mixed descent, anticipating the attitude so often shown by colonial officials to the educated and westernized. There are only too many parallels to the words of a French visitor to the Gold Coast in the late seventeenth century: 'They are generally profligate villains, a bastard race . . . and tho' they assume the name of Christians, are as superstitious idolators as any of the *Blacks* can be'.[35] Often they clung tenaciously to Christianity to establish the perimeters of an otherwise ambiguous identity.

A chronicler of the Dominican missions in Zambezia and on the Zimbabwe plateau noted that women and children were the easiest to convert,[36] but all the missionaries were men, until a group of Cluny sisters settled on Goree island in 1819. The records of those years are overwhelmingly preoccupied with their relationships with men and, especially, the ruling class. However, the first of African Christianity's prophetic churches, the Antonine movement in Kongo, was founded by a young mother, Vita Kimpa.

The Atlantic islands

The Atlantic islands, São Thomé and the Cape Verdes, played a role disproportionate to their small size. Originally uninhabited, their very isolation made them more accessible to external influences. The population of the Cape Verdes came to be overwhelmingly Luso-African, its identity symbolized by its language, *Crioulo*, which combined Portuguese and African elements, ('*Affinal: Africa? Europa? Cabo Verde*',[37]). A black priest from Cape Verde, João Pinto, was a devoted missionary in the region of 'the rivers of Guinea' in the late sixteenth and early seventeenth centuries.[38] In 1652, a Jesuit visitor gave a glowing picture of the indigenous priests, though some later observers were more critical.

> Here there are clerics and canons as black as coal, but so grave, so respectable, so learned, such great musicians, so discreet and so temperate that they could arouse the envy of those we see there in our own cathedrals.[39]

São Thomé was an important centre of sugar production, until repeated revolts by enslaved Angolans, the Angolares, undermined the viability of its plantations. For a time, it was an entrepôt in Atlantic trade, but it soon became an economic backwater. Both São Thomé and the Cape Verdes became independent dioceses in the 1530s, and for centuries they provided priests, albeit irregularly, for Lower and Upper Guinea, respectively. On the small island of Annobon, an unsympathetic Protestant described religious practice as he perceived it in the late seventeenth century.

> The Inhabitants of the Island are black, and but a sort of half Christian . . . for if they can but read a *Pater Noster* and *Ave Maria*, confess to the Priest, and bring some Offerings with them, they pass for good Christians. . . . I found here also two White Priests, who were endowed with no other Qualities than the profound ignorance and Stupidity of the meanest of their neighbours. . . . They invited us to come and see their Churches, which we did, and found them very handsome, and large enough for four times the Number of inhabitants on the island.[40]

The Senegambia

As they struck ever further down the Atlantic coastline of Africa, the Portuguese were impressed by the contrast between the arid sands of the Sahara (Cape Blanco), and the green vegetation that lay South of the Senegal (Cape Verde).

The Wolof people, who lived between the Senegal and Gambia, formed a loose confederation, under the overlordship of the Burba Jolof. Here, as elsewhere in Africa, the Portuguese supported one of the protagonists in a civil war, in return for his baptism. This prince, Jelen, visited Lisbon, returning home with a substantial Portuguese force, only to meet his death at Portuguese hands in *c.* 1486.[41]

In general, Islamic influence was much stronger than Christianity in the Senegambia, and remained so. There was a community of 'Black Portuguese' at a few coastal settlements, including Rufisque, Joal, and Portudal, and on the Gambia. Essentially indistinguishable from their Wolof and Serer neighbours, they clung to vestiges of Christianity as symbols of a distinct identity, the concomitant of their broker role in Atlantic trade.

The French coastal settlements at St Louis and Gorée dated from 1659 and 1678 respectively. A similar social pattern developed, where a small Eur-African class cherished a French and Catholic social identity, while speaking Wolof. European residents were sometimes converted to African religions, rather than vice versa: it was noted in the seventeenth century that they 'have begun to believe in witchcraft and are convinced that African sorcerers can prevent their firearms from working or kill them by placing charms in their drinking water'.[42] The Luso-Africans of Guinea-Bissau, further south, were described in much the same way.[43]

Sierra Leone

The Jesuit mission in the Cape Verdes was founded in 1604, in part at the urging of a Luso-African layman. Balthasar Barreira was a Jesuit who had worked for thirteen years in Angola. He left Portugal again, at the age of sixty for the Cape Verdes but concentrated especially on the Sierra Leone peninsula. A Bullom ruler was baptized as Philip Leonis, with other family members. He was converted by one of his wives, 'who was already a Christian, having been reared by the Portuguese',[44] an interesting testimony to the enduring faith of the Luso-African enclaves. Barreira came close to converting a Susu king, in the Bena country to the North, but was foiled by a rival missionary, a Muslim.[45] A Capuchin mission that arrived in 1669 found that the Susu still remembered Barreira, who died in 1612, and the image of the Infant Jesus he carried, but its members soon left or died. They baptized thousands, like their counterparts in Kongo, but the continuity was lacking to create enduring Christian communities. Seraphim was a Capuchin from Castile, who arrived in Port Loko in 1647, and stayed there, enduring poverty and illness, until his death some ten years later:

> Seraph in name, looks and works . . . The poor life he led brought about his death. . . . He made the Church his home and was so careless of human comforts that if any devout persons . . . sent him any he kept them only to share with the sick.[46]

After the Capuchins left, there were no more resident missionaries until the arrival in about 1714 of an extraordinary black Christian, Signor Joseph. He seems to have been an indigene of the Sierra Leone peninsula, and various visitors to the area paid him warm tribute:

> He has been in *England* and *Portugal*; at the last place he was baptized, and took in that Christian Erudition that he endeavours to propagate. He has built a little Oratory for his People's Devotions; erected a Cross; taught several of his Kindred Letters, dispersing among them little Romish Prayer-Books, and many of them are known by Christian Names.[47]

Joseph founded a model town, first on the future site of Granville, then at what became Kissy.

> Their Huts are mostly orbicular, forming a spacious square Area in the middle, and *in this*, the doors paved with Cockle-Shells; two or three Crosses erected, and round about, Lime-trees, Papais, Plantanes, Pine-apples, and a few bee-hives. . . . This Christian *Negro*, by the Advantage of

Trade, has in some measure removed the Wants of his own Family (his Town). . . .[48]

The Gold Coast

São Jorge da Mina was built in 1482, on the boundary of two African states, Komenda and Efutu, in disregard of the wishes of the local ruler, who asked the Portuguese to leave, with the words, 'Friends who met occasionally remained better friends than if they were neighbours'.[49] Such was the lure of the gold, and, later, the slaves, to be obtained on the Gold Coast that other European nations set up land establishments: English, Dutch, Danes and for a time, Swedes and Brandenburgers. By the mid eighteenth century, there were thirty forts along 300 miles of coast, each of which made appropriate payments to the local African ruler. This settled European presence contrasted with the state of affairs in the Niger Delta and elsewhere where foreign merchants traded from their ships, and had no permanent land establishment. São Jorge da Mina was captured by the Dutch in 1637.

The chaplains at the forts were primarily concerned, not with the conversion of African peoples, but with the spiritual welfare of the European and Eur-African enclaves. In the late seventeenth century, the Portuguese fort included, 'a chappel in the fort, where mass is said by a black priest, ordained by the bishop of *St Thome*'.[50]

There was little impact on surrounding peoples. Thus, in Elmina:

> . . . if there are any among them that shew some sense of christianity; they are only the *Mulattos* of *Portuguese* descent whereof there are near two hundred families in the town; . . . their religion being mixed with much pagan superstition.[51]

There were two Protestant missionary initiatives there in the eighteenth century. The Moravians sent nine missionaries between 1737 and 1770; they died almost at once, except for Christian Protten: 'The Lord had so clearly closed up the road to the country with thorns. . . .'

In 1752, Reverend Thomas Thompson, Africa's first Anglican missionary, went to the Gold Coast. He was in the employ of the Society for the Propagation of the Gospel (SPG), founded in 1701 for the benefit of Britons abroad, whose spiritual welfare was endangered by 'atheism, infidelity, popish superstition and idolatry'. He had worked among the enslaved in America, and went to West Africa at his own request. He concentrated on the local people, rather than the expatriate enclaves. When he left after four years because of ill health, he was accompanied by three Fante boys to be educated by the SPG. Two died; Europe, it has been said, often proved the Black Man's Grave. The survivor was Philip Quaque, the son of Birempon Kojo of Cape Coast. He was ordained an Anglican clergyman, returned to Cape Coast in 1766, and worked there until his death in 1816. When he returned, he had forgotten much of his

native Fante, and, later in life, he was criticized for his involvement in trade—
the chronic ambiguity of one who stood between two worlds—but he worked
in Cape Coast for fifty years, and the school he ran laid the foundation for later
educational initiatives.[52]

Ambiguity and marginality characterised other eighteenth-century Gold
Coast men who acquired an education abroad. Frederick Svane, the son of a
Danish father and a Ga mother, studied at the University of Copenhagen and,
in 1735, returned briefly to the Gold Coast with a Danish wife, before
returning to Denmark.

Jacobus Elia Johannes Capitein (1717–47) was taken to Holland as a child
by a Dutch trader and received an excellent education, studying at the
University of Leiden. With profound irony, he published a defence of the slave
trade, in Latin, as being consistent with Christianity (Thompson, despite his
genuine concern for Africa, also published a defence of the slave trade). He
was ordained as a minister of the Dutch Reformed Church, and worked in
Elmina from 1742 until his death, five years later, translating some texts, such
as the Lord's Prayer, into Fante. His life in Africa seems to have been isolated
and unhappy—not least, perhaps, because the Church prevented him from
marrying the African wife of his choice.

William Amo of Axim was also taken to Europe as a child and obtained a
doctorate at Wittenberg. He was a protégé of the Princess of Brunswick, and,
when she died, he returned to Axim, after thirty years in Europe, living as a
recluse.

Christian Protten's father was a Danish soldier, and his mother a cousin of
the King of Popo.[53] He was educated in Denmark, returning to Accra as one of
the first two Moravian missionaries in sub-Saharan Africa, in 1737. His work
there was interspersed with two long sojourns in Europe, but he died on the
Gold Coast in 1769.

These lonely, brilliant men were the precursors of later distinguished 'been
tos'. Their achievements involved a degree of alienation from the society that
had produced them, symbolized, in some cases, by their loss of fluency in their
mother tongue, and they lacked the organizational support and infrastructure
that might have enabled them to effect major, enduring change. Like the
chaplains before them, they tended to concentrate on the European and Eur-
African enclaves.

The Slave Coast

East of modern Ghana lie Togo and Benin, the region known, sadly, in the
eighteenth century, as the Slave Coast. Whydah, in particular, became a great
slave exporting centre from the 1670s on. French Capuchins founded a
mission there in 1644. They were expelled by a populace incited by English
and Dutch traders, 'for they feared that the conversion of the people and their
chiefs would spoil their trade'.[54] There was an abortive Castilian Capuchin

60

mission in 1660, significant chiefly for a translation of the catechism into Ewe, 'the earliest publication in any Guinea coast language'.[55] There were other short-lived missions, their impact limited by lack of personnel and high mortality rates. A few individuals, such as the interpreter Matteo Lopez or a Whydah chief called Assou or a king of Allada had Catholic sympathies.[56]

Warri

The Itsekiri kingdom of Warri was a tiny state (there were fewer than 33 thousand Itsekiri in the 1950s) in the mangrove swamps of the western Niger Delta. There is some evidence that it was founded shortly before the Portuguese advent, and this may have made it easier for its rulers to embrace new ideas.

At the time with which we are concerned, it consisted of the capital, Ode Itsekiri, and a few small outlying settlements. Livelihood depended on fishing, salt making, and trade. Tradition speaks of a founder from Benin, but Itsekiri is a dialect of Yoruba, and the legend may simply reflect the symbolic importance of a powerful neighbour.[57]

The history of Christianity in Warri began in the 1570s, when Augustinian monks were sent there from São Thomé. They converted, not the king (the *Olu*), but his heir, who became Sebastian, an ardent supporter of Catholicism for the rest of his long life. The major difficulty he faced was the lack of clergy. In the words of the Bishop of São Thomé, 'this kingdom is very poor and clergy would be unable to live there in reasonable comfort; moreover their health and their lives would be in very grave danger from the great unhealthiness of the climate'.[58] In the early eighteenth century, two Capuchins in Warri supported themselves by trading in locally made pots! Sebastian attempted to solve the problem by sending his own eldest son, Domingos, to Portugal, with the hope that he would be ordained. In the event, he returned with a noble Portuguese bride, the mother of the next king, Antonio Domingos. She died in the next few years; life must have been extraordinarily difficult for her in an area too poor and unhealthy for missionary priests. Meanwhile, Sebastian, 'worn out with extreme old age', instructed his people in Christian doctrine, and organized processions. There were to be some Itsekiri clergy, but they seem to have lacked the fervour of the King, and some preferred benefices in São Thomé.

In 1620, Catholicism in Warri was described as a court religion:

> Outside the small town of Santo Agostinho there are no other Christians; and even in the town only a minority are of the Catholic faith. Although very many of them are nominally Christian, true Christianity is almost wholly confined to the King and the Prince; the rest only call themselves Christians in order to please the King. . . .[59]

In 1644, when Antonio Domingos was on the throne, quite a different picture was given of the Warri Church: 'And the Negroes enter this church with paternosters in their hands all the while, like true Portuguese people, and they read these, as well as other Popish prayers. They appear to be most godly, and can also read and write, and are eager for Portuguese books, pens, ink and paper'. Christianity also modified traditional religion: the offerings of human and animal sacrifices were abhorred, and no *feticeros* (traditional religious specialists) were permitted.[60]

The strong attachment of the crown to Catholicism continued, despite long periods without priests, until the middle of the eighteenth century. The Olu who came to power in 1733 seems to have reverted to traditional religion. A statue of Christ was smashed because it failed to end a drought, for example. There were parallels in Europe at much the same time: 'The people of Castelo Branco were so enraged at S. Antonio for allowing the Spaniards to plunder their town, contrary, as they affirmed, to his express agreement with them, that they broke many of his statues to pieces . . .'[61] An English sailor visited Warri at the end of the eighteenth century; he states that the Olu of the day had sixty wives, and described in the palace the decaying ritual apparatus of a faith in deep decline:

> . . . we were much surprised to see, placed on a rude kind of tablet, several emblems of the Catholic religion, consisting of crucifixes, mutilated saints, and other trumpery . . . A large wooden cross, which had withstood the tooth of time, was remaining in a very perfect state, in one of the angles formed by two roads intersecting each other . . . King Otoo's subjects appeared to trouble themselves very little about religion of any kind.[62]

In 1840, another Englishman recorded the sequel: 'I observed the Church or Catholic Chapel had disappeared and the streets were covered with grass'.[63]

That Christianity survived so long was due to the devotion of its kings. Its ultimate extinction was caused by the lack of priests, compounded, on occasion, by the shortcomings of those who actually reached Warri.

Benin

Warri's great neighbour, the kingdom of Benin, grew out of a number of small principalities, probably in the thirteenth century. When the first Christian missionaries reached the capital, in 1515, they found a walled city and a splendid court with highly developed artistic traditions of working in bronze and ivory. They learned of a distant, sacred monarch to the East, called the Ogane—'held in as great veneration as is the Supreme Pontiff with us'—who sent a newly crowned king a cross to wear,[64] crosses which are depicted on some Benin statuary. Not surprisingly, they believed they had found Prester John.

The King's, [*Oba's*], initial response was sympathetic. In 1516, he sent his son to be baptized, and learn to read, but he died soon afterwards. Nearly forty years later, it was said 'the king could speak the Portugall tongue, which he had learned as a child'.[65] It is possible that human sacrifice was introduced into Benin by this baptized Oba.[66]

There was a tiny handful of Bini converts in the early sixteenth century, the first Nigerian Christians. Like their counterparts in Whydah and Allada, they seem to have acted as interpreters and brokers for the Portuguese. One of them, Afonso Ames, ran the school where a prince became literate in Portuguese. They stood between two worlds and had a freedom of choice denied to ordinary Benin people, of whom it was said, 'They consider themselves slaves of their King and would not dare to become Christians until the King himself is converted'.[67] However, the King himself often had little freedom of choice. In the seventeenth century, when a succession of weak Obas were kept virtual prisoners by their great officials, it was said of one of them, 'he showed himself well disposed to hear the arguments for our Holy Faith, but he lacks the liberty to follow his laudable inclinations because he is hemmed in on all sides by certain ministers . . .'[68] In 1710, a later Benin King was sympathetic to Christianity, provided land for a church, and avoided human sacrifice, but was exiled after a brief and troubled reign.

Formal Christianity had no lasting impact in Benin, partly because, as in Warri, the missionary enterprise was sporadic, and partly because traditional religion was deeply entwined with the sacred monarchy. There was no attempt to understand Benin religion and society: 'The way of life of these people is full of abuses and witchcraft and idolatry, which for brevity's sake I omit'.[69]

Elements of Portuguese Christianity were incorporated into Aruosa, a royal cult to which outsiders have had little access. A British colonial administrator caught a glimpse of it.

Following the Oba I went through a heavy Iroko door, which opened into a long, narrow corridor-like room, with a tall window at the other end. He showed me a brass crucifix which was attached to a cord round his neck, and said that every morning at dawn he entered this place alone and waited for the first rays of day to illumine the window, when he pressed the crucifix to his forehead and prayed for the Oni of Ife, the Alafin of Oyo and the Oba of Benin (that is himself); after which he prayed for all the other Yoruba kings. This had for long been the custom, he said, whether the Oba was a Christian or not. . . .[70]

The kingdom of Kongo

Today, the Kongo people number 3 million and are to be found in Angola, (including Cabinda), Zaire, and the Democratic Republic of Congo.

The first Portuguese vessel anchored off the Zaire river in 1483. As in West Africa, it was a tragedy that the Europeans brought not only Christianity but the slave trade. In time, the European presence was to destroy the Kongo kingdom, inaugurating a brutal era of warlordism,[71] but all that lay in the future.

There is a rich literature on Kongo history, and a corresponding variety of interpretations, though the differences are sometimes more apparent than real. To some, Christianity was a superficial façade, maintained for political reasons: 'The Christian commitment of Kongo kings was in all probability less a matter of personal belief than one of diplomatic status'.[72] Gray has cast much light on the fervour and devotion of the late seventeenth century Soyo court, (advocates of economic determinism would do well to note that much of its external trade was with the Dutch, but its people evinced no attraction to Calvinism). To Axelson, Christianity was strong at the beginning, followed by a period of decline; there was a resurgence when the Capuchins arrived in 1645, followed by its gradual extinction. Both Hilton and Thornton emphasize the way in which the Kongo understood Christianity in terms of earlier religious concepts.

Thornton questions the widely accepted pattern of decline, and makes the interesting suggestion that the change was in the eye of the beholder. Foreign visitors in the sixteenth and seventeenth century always regarded Kongo as a Christian state—'They might denounce Kongo customs as sinful, even superstitious, but not pagan'[73]—as they were using a more inclusive definition of Christianity, which required, essentially, self-identification, but this was replaced, in the nineteenth century, by a Eurocentric attitude that condemned Kongo Christianity as syncretism.

The Kongo court welcomed Christianity. Perhaps this was linked with the fact that, in traditional cosmology, white was the colour of the spirit world, and the supernatural origins of the strangers were confirmed by their exotic speech, rich gifts, and links with the sea. However, the association of whiteness and the sea with the spirit world was true of other African peoples, including the Bini, who did *not* turn to Christianity in this way.

The history of Christianity in the Kongo will always be linked with the name of Mbemba Nzinga, baptized as Afonso. He became king after a civil war, after the death of João I in 1506, and ruled until his death in 1543. In a 1516 description, he is a saintly apostle, preaching and teaching, falling asleep over his books late at night.[74] His extant correspondence, much of it dictated to a Kongo secretary, is full of pleas for what we would now call development aid: stone masons, 'two physicians and two apothecaries and one surgeon'. At first, he was prepared to pay for imports with slaves. In time, he came to realize that the price was too high: '. . . our country is being completely depopulated, and Your Highness should not agree with this nor accept it as in your service. And to avoid it we need from these [your] Kingdoms no more than some priests and a few people to teach in schools, and no other goods except wine and flour for the holy sacrament'.[75]

There has, perhaps, in the past been a tendency to idealize Afonso. A recent study, reacting against this, points out that he had no traditional right to the throne at all, and that this may well explain his enthusiasm for a new dispensation.[76] Afonso followed the traditional Kongo pattern of forming marriage alliances with different parts of the kingdom, and his opposition to the slave trade has a hollow ring in the light of his own willingness to export slaves. What he most objected to was that, 'they kidnap even noblemen and the sons of noblemen and our relatives'. None of this, though, impugns Afonso's sincerity in his new faith, and his desire for technological development, or his gradual recognition that the Atlantic slave trade was a source of depopulation and disorder, and that the price paid for exotic imports was too high. A group of Portuguese, at the instigation of a friar, attempted to assassinate him at the Easter service in 1540. However, he remained a Christian despite his many experiences of Portuguese violence, rapacity, and duplicity.

In these early encounters, two symbolic universes meet. In a sense, the world views of the Portuguese and the Kongo had much in common. Both took the irruption of the supernatural world into daily life for granted, in visions, significant dreams, the ending of drought. Naturally enough, both interpreted events in terms of their own cultural history. In a Portuguese narrative, Afonso wins a battle when a bright light appears, which echoes the vision claimed for Constantine.[77] In an account of events in the Mutapa kingdom, this precedent is explicit: 'As the army was setting out, raising his eyes to heaven, he saw there a resplendent light, and beautiful cross, in the same form (but without letters) in which it before appeared to the Emperor Constantine the Great'.[78]

The Kongo people, inevitably, located the new teaching within their own world view—a process made easier by the fact that the missionaries translated 'priest' as *nganga* (a traditional religious specialist), and used the word *nkisi* (traditional religious object) to refer to crucifixes or rosaries, the Bible becoming *mukanda nkisi*, and the church, *nzo a nkisi*. Converts reluctant to embrace monogamy defined one spouse as a wife, and the rest as concubines.

The ruler had traditionally maintained his power by his control of tribute from different ecological zones. The rich goods brought by the strangers greatly increased the amount of patronage at his disposal. Luxuries, though, become necessities, so, when trade shifted North, to the Loango coast, or South, to the new Portuguese settlement of Angola, the monarchy was weakened. So great was the disorder of the years that followed, that fathers would brand their own sons to protect them from enslavement (the implication being that they were someone's slave already). In 1568, the kingdom was invaded by a mysterious and ferocious people called the Jaga; it may well have been a jacquerie, a desperate uprising of potential victims of enslavement or actual victims of a society apparently in dissolution. They destroyed the capital, now called San Salvador, and burned its churches, and the king regained his capital only with Portuguese aid.

To some, the Kongo nobility formed a comprador class, collaborating with the foreign exploiter to prey on the masses. Their foreign titles—dukes and marquises—seem exotic and inappropriate imports. Others are profoundly moved by these pioneers of Christianity and Western education, who corresponded on banana leaves because of paper shortages, and whose records were preserved in local archives into the late nineteenth century.

The progress of Christianity was impeded by the unworthiness of many clergy, who were often involved in trade, including the slave trade, and often at odds with each other. Afonso's son, Henrique, after thirteen years of study in Portugal, returned to the Kongo as a bishop (not of Kongo, but as titular Bishop of a Muslim province in North Africa). He was marginalized by the Portuguese clergy, and the situation made him depressed and ill. Henrique went to Europe in 1529, and died on a return voyage in the 1530s. The next black bishop in West Central Africa was appointed in 1970. When Kongo became a see in 1596, the King of Portugal appointed a Portuguese bishop, and ever-fewer Kongo were ordained. What became the Portuguese colony, Angola, began as a private proprietary colony, similar to Virginia, created in 1571 under the grandson of Bartholemeu Dias. Many Kongo clergy ended their careers in Luanda, where a distinctive Luso-African culture evolved.

In 1645, the first Capuchins arrived in West Central Africa. They were more fervent than most of their predecessors, and were destined to have a transforming effect, especially on the coastal province of Soyo. Their social role varied at different times and places. They were often closely identified with the court, but their conflict with Garcia II (1641–61) reflects something of a 'preferential option for the poor'.[79]

At the battle of Ambuila, in 1665, the king and many of his courtiers were killed by invading Angolan forces, led by a Luso-African general. Among the dead was another Luso-African, Manuel Roboredo, co-author of several language manuals. He was a Capuchin of royal blood, who, having opposed the war, died at the king's side.

The Kongo kingdom never recovered from Ambuila, and, for a long period, the capital was deserted. It is difficult to better the words of the soldier historian, Cadornega, in 1681: 'we will say how our lord punished this kingdom which was so Catholic. [It] is a pity and heartache to see how this new Christianity of the Kongo was retarded'.[80]

In this situation of crisis, several women prophets emerged: Appolonia Mafuta and Vita Kimpa, baptized as Beatrice, who claimed to be the medium of St Antony. A member of the nobility, she had been an *nganga*, and absorbed the idea of spirit possession from traditional religion. She destroyed both crucifixes and traditional *nkisi* as powerless to save, and taught that Jesus was black, born in the Kongo capital. Both nobles and poor responded to her teaching, and Mbanza Kongo was reoccupied. She was burnt at the stake for heresy in 1706, at the age of twenty, her baby son narrowly escaping the same fate.[81]

The king's wife, Hipolita, left him to join the movement. The king himself, on one occasion, refused to make war on a rebel.

> in no way would he make war, as it was the continual warfare which had already destroyed the kingdom, and also the Faith. Nor did the Kongolese want any more troubles. They were already tired of being like beasts in the fields and wastelands: outraged, murdered, robbed and sold.[82]

The conventional view is that Christianity declined in West Central Africa during the eighteenth century. Nineteenth-century visitors were unanimous in painting a picture of syncretism. An English ship anchored at Soyo in 1816; its personnel met a local priest with a wife and five concubines, who could write his name and that of St Antony, and read the Roman liturgy in Latin.[83] In 1857, a German geographer visited the ruins of San Salvador, and recorded a stereotype, common in West and Central Africa, that the slaves sold abroad were eaten by cannibals, and their bodies processed into oil. He found crosses everywhere, and was told 'that the Portuguese Desu was a far too powerful fetiche for the common man and could be assigned only to the king'.[84]

However, Catholicism in some sense endured, even in the absence of priests, sustained largely by the efforts of the noble laity, who often held additional titles such as 'Master of the Church'. An account from the 1780s described well-kept chapels and schools, run by laity literate in Portuguese.[85]

Matamba's Queens[86]

Vita Kimpa was a late seventeenth-century woman who responded to the needs of an age of traumatic change and violence with prophecy. Nzinga, who died in 1663, responded to crisis in a different way. She was the sister of the last effective ruler of the west-central African state of Ndongo, whose kings, the *ngola a kiluanje*, gave their title to Angola. She seized power by murdering her nephew and ward, but was forced to leave a state in dissolution and founded a new kingdom further inland at Matamba. In 1623, she was baptized as Doña Ana da Souza, but, for many years, had little to do with Christianity, allying herself instead with the ferocious Imbangala.[87] Her return to Christianity from the 1640s onwards was, like her initial baptism in Luanda, clearly politically motivated; it enabled her to repudiate the Imbangala and ally with the Portuguese of Angola. She had a Kongo confessor, Calisto Zelotes dos Reis Magros.[88] She was succeeded by her sister, Barbara, and there were further regnant queens in the eighteenth century, whose names, Veronica or Ana, reflect a continuing identification, in some sense, with Christianity. Nzinga's life can most plausibly be understood as the struggle of a woman ruler, lacking precedents in a male-dominated world, to obtain political support and legitimation wherever possible.

The Zambezi, and the Zimbabwe Plateau

No monument in sub-Saharan Africa is more famous than the ruins of Great Zimbabwe, which was abandoned by 1500, perhaps because of ecological changes, perhaps because of the exhaustion of local gold, which was the chief commodity foreign visitors were to seek.[89] The Mutapa state, sometimes called Monomutapa after its ruler's title, *Mwene Mutapa*,[90] grew up on the northern plateau in the fifteenth century or earlier.

The first Portuguese settlements on the coast, Mozambique Island and Sofala, were founded in 1505 and 1508, respectively. The former developed as a halting place on the long journey to Goa, and its Dominican community was long supported by a rich Javanese woman, Violante.

The Zambezi was the gateway to the interior, and the Portuguese established trading posts at Sena and Tete, 160 and 320 miles upstream, respectively. Missions in Zambezia suffered from a chronic lack of personnel and resources. They counted their baptisms in hundreds, but were not able to instruct such numbers adequately: 'And he affirms that by the numbers entered in the books, up to the year 1591 more than twenty thousand souls were baptised by them in that district of the rivers of Cuama [Zambezi]'.[91]

They suffered, too, from the inextricable intermingling of their role with Portuguese military, political, and economic goals. Friar Nicolas do Rosario lost his life in 1592 during a Portuguese expedition against the 'Zimba'. To a pious chronicler, he was a composite of St Sebastian and St Ignatius of Antioch,[92] but he was essentially a military chaplain.

In 1561, there was a Jesuit mission to the Mutapa court. The Mwene agreed to accept baptism, but the missionary was put to death soon afterwards, at the instigation of Muslim traders anxious about their economic future. In 1569–72, the Portuguese attempted to conquer Mutapa by force of arms and two Jesuits accompanied the expedition, which failed, both because of disease and the strength of opposition it encountered. The Jesuits returned to Mozambique in 1610, and remained there until expelled by the Portuguese crown in 1759. The Dominicans worked in the area from 1577 on.[93]

We cannot here explore the tortuous role the Portuguese played in the Mutapa kingdom's fortunes in the decades that followed, but suffice to say that they exploited internal divisions and permanently weakened it, but never acquired real and lasting control. A Mwene Mutapa complained of the Dominicans that they spent nine months a year trading: 'I have never come across one who called my children or my vassals and asked them whether they would like to become Christians'.[94] Like the comparable involvement of many Angola and Kongo clergy, this reflects less the iniquity of those concerned than problems of sustenance, compounded by the difficulty of retaining religious values in an environment that does not share them, a perennial problem for missionaries and other Christians who live in the midst of alien religious traditions.

In 1607, a Mwene, Gatsi Rusere, weakened by internal opposition and other factors,[95] ceded the Portuguese all his mines (a concession that existed largely on paper), and entrusted them with his four sons to be educated as Catholics. When he died in 1624, civil war followed. Mavura won the contest with Portuguese help, and at a great cost—a treaty accepting vassalage to the Portuguese state. He was baptized as Philip. When he died in 1652, he was succeeded by his son, who was baptized as Domingos with his sons and other palace officials, but was soon overthrown and killed in a rising of the Portuguese prazeiros.

As we have seen, women and children were more readily converted than men.[96] In 1560, André Fernandes noted: 'The women are very devout and frequently visit the church to see the pictures, which they are very fond of, especially that of our Lady'.[97] Some Shona men entered religious life. Like their Kongo counterparts, they were drawn from the ruling class, a fact that reflects the focus of missionary energies. Friar Luiz do Espirito Santo, put to death by Mavura's rival, was 'a native of Mozambique', and probably a scion of the royal house. Father Damião do Espirito Santo was another Shona Dominican, involved in the same tumults. Domingos' eldest son, baptized as Miguel, became a Dominican and Master of Theology, and died in Goa in 1670 as the Vicar of Santa Barbara. An Italian Theatine said of him: 'Although he is a model priest, leading a very exemplary life, saying Mass daily, yet not even the habit which he wears secures him any consideration there, just because he has a black face. If I had not seen it, I would not have believed it'.[98]

Two other Mutapa princes (the sons of Pedro Mhande, who reigned briefly in the 1690s) also became friars, ending their days in Goa.[99] That they preferred a marginalized life in a foreign land to a return home sheds much light on the violence and disorder that had come to prevail there.

Portuguese names conceal the ethnic variety of the clergy. Many of those who worked in Zambezia, then and later, were Goans. Criticized by European visitors, but struggling equally with the stresses imposed by an alien environment, they merit more attention from scholars than they have hitherto received.

The *prazos* were great estates in the Zambezi valley, granted by the Portuguese crown in return for tribute and the support of the *prazeiros'* slave armies. The system began in the late sixteenth century, and expanded greatly in the seventeenth. The *prazeiros'* insatiable demand for slaves, cattle and gold, their attacks on the Shona kingdoms and each other, caused immense suffering: 'It was the insolences of our people [the Portuguese] that caused these wars, because those who possess many Kaffirs and have power are guilty of such excesses'.[100]

In 1692, a southern Shona state, under the Rozvi, succeeded in driving the Portuguese from the plateau. A Jesuit reflected:

Thus came to an end all the fairs of gold in consequence of the injuries and injustices, which from our side were committed against the Emperors of Mwene Mutapa, who always received and treated us as if we were their sons. . . .[101]

The *prazeiros* survived. Like the Creoles of Angola or Cape Verde, they saw themselves as 'white', Christian and Portuguese. They became, in fact, African warlords, hostile to all external authority, including that of Portugal. In a 'group of twenty *prazeiros* each one has nineteen enemies, but all are the enemy of the Governor'.[102] They had large harems, and it was found necessary to pass an edict in Goa in 1771 prohibiting ritual intercourse after Catholic funerals.[103]

Some of the largest *prazos* were controlled by Jesuits. A Dominican friar at Zumbo, who died in 1751, was, in the nineteenth century, the subject of a spirit possession cult. He left an estate worth 100 thousand cruzados in gold, copper, and slaves.[104] Livingstone visited Tete and Sena in 1856:

None of the natives here can read, and though the Jesuits are said to have translated some of the prayers into the language of the country, I was unable to obtain a copy. The only religious teachers now in this part of the country are two . . . natives of Goa . . . During the period of my stay a kind of theatrical representation of our Saviour's passion and resurrection was performed.[105]

One of the most interesting aspects of religious changes in the Zambezi valley was the absorption of Christian practices by neighbouring African peoples. In many cases, these were first described in the late nineteenth and early twentieth centuries, and it is not always easy to ascertain their antiquity. A rowing song was recorded among the Tonga of Lake Malawi and the Shire river that they said they had learned long ago from the Jesuits:

I have no Mother.
I have no Father.
Who will take care of me but our Mother, Maria?[106]

The Swahili Coast

The Portuguese undermined the trade on which the prosperity of the Swahili city states relied, and repeatedly attacked them. The much-travelled ibn Battuta had called Kilwa 'one of the most beautiful and well-constructed towns in the world'.

These societies had been Muslim for centuries, and the Portuguese tactic of enforcing Christianity on a contender in a succession dispute led only to disorder. A claimant to the sultanate of Pemba reluctantly accepted baptism as the price of the Portuguese backing, but lost his throne and his life.[107]

Yusuf was the son of Sultan Husain of Mombasa. He spent some time in Goa, becoming a Christian and taking the name of Don Jeronimo Chingulia.

He served as a soldier in the Portuguese fleet, returning to Mombasa in 1623. Despised by his people, and marginalized by the Portuguese, he reverted to Islam, and led a revolt in 1631. He held Mombasa against the attack of a Portuguese fleet, then withdrew to Arabia in search of reinforcements. He was killed by Arab pirates in the Red Sea in 1638.[108]

Christianity and the Atlantic slave trade

The great weakness of the Christian enterprise in black Africa in the Middle Years was its close association with the slave trade. There was a basic contradiction between converting Africans and purchasing them as slaves. Captain William Snelgrave, in 1719, told a Dahomey official of the Golden Rule, 'And that our God had enjoined this to us on pain of very severe Punishments', and yet he was there to buy slaves.[109]

Some priests traded in slaves. The Church in Angola derived much of its income by instructing and baptizing the enslaved, and the end of the slave trade caused a financial crisis for the Luanda see. Exported slaves were branded as proofs of ownership *and* of baptism. It was a peculiar irony that only Christians could be sold, and that they could be sold only to Christians. Catholic debates about the slave trade tended to focus not on its intrinsic evils, but on matters such as whether or not slaves should be sold to heretics. Protestants shared this myopia. John Newton made three slaving voyages after his conversion: 'I never knew sweeter or more frequent hours of divine communion than in my last two voyages to Guinea'.[110]

For the most part, the enslaved move beyond African history. Some were, and remained, devout Muslims, while those from a traditional religion often became Christians. One of the most notable was Olaudah Equiano (1745–97). Kidnapped as a boy in Igboland, he went to sea for some years, learning English, acquiring an education, and saving up enough to buy his freedom. He went on expeditions to the Arctic and to central America, became involved in the abolitionist movement and in the proposed Sierra Leone settlement, and wrote an autobiography which went through many editions. He married an Englishwoman, and died in England. He was a devout Christian, concluding his narrative with the question, 'what makes any event important, unless by its observation we become better and wiser, and learn "to do justly, to love mercy, and to walk humbly before God?"'[111]

In the late seventeenth century, a black Catholic layman launched an attack on slavery, which was considered by the Vatican and led to an important policy statement, albeit one honoured more in the breach than in the observance. The source of the petition was a Luso-African from Luanda, Lourenço da Silva, who claimed to be of 'the royal blood of the kings of Congo and Angola', and was 'the competent procurator of all the Mulattos throughout this kingdom, as in Castile and Brazil, so that he might obtain a papal brief concerning a certain matter for which they are petitioning'.[112] Da

Silva petitioned against perpetual slavery, and against the cruelty that often accompanied it. In 1686, the Holy Office accepted a series of propositions that would have made the slave trade unworkable, but this was not enforced in practice because, in the words of an anonymous Vatican official, of 'America's great need for Negroes'. Like his kinsmen, the Angolares of São Thomé, da Silva struck a blow for freedom. He appealed, on the basis of Christianity, 'in the name of all the oppressed'—a distant forerunner of black and liberation theology.

Conclusion

African Christians, including the Luso-African communities, developed various forms of synthesis between Christianity and local religions. In a sense, this was syncretism, which sometimes, as among the *prazeiros*, clearly eroded much of the content of the new Evangel, but their stubborn attachment to Christianity as they understood it was manifested in many ways, such as their hunger for baptism. They encountered a Christianity in Western packaging. Each generation of African Christians has tackled the task of disentangling the message from foreign contexts, and inculturating it in African worlds. Their attempts to do so form a central theme of this book.

Many of the themes of later mission history are first adumbrated in the Middle Years, such as the obstacle placed to evangelization by the Church's insistence on monogamy: 'the Confinement to one Wife is an insuperable Difficulty'.[113]

There was also the profound attachment to the traditions of the past. Bosman recorded a dialogue at Whydah between an Augustinian from São Thomé and 'one of the King's Grandees':

> This Priest . . . said in a menacing manner, *That if the* Fidafians *continu'd their old Course of Life, without Repentance, they would unavoidably go to Hell, in order to burn with the Devil*: to which the sharp *Fidafian* reply'd, *Our fathers, Grandfathers, to an endless Number, liv'd as we do, and Worship'd the same Gods as we do; and if they must burn therefore, Patience, we are not better than our Ancestors, and shall comfort our selves with them.*[114]

Missionaries tended to concentrate on kings, and some royal conversions were politically motivated and superficial. Even where they were sincere, the lack of missionary personnel tended to mean that the masses had no real instruction in Christian belief, even if they welcomed baptism.

The shortage of missionaries was an endemic problem, intensified by the high mortality rates caused by a new disease environment. Europeans' ethnocentricity sometimes led them to believe that the most inadequate white clergy were preferable to the local product. In 1644, João IV of Portugal 'circulated the prelates in Portugal that they should dispatch thither their unwanted, unruly, or even convicted criminal clergy'.[115] Not all were unsatisfactory, though, Seraphim, the Castilian Capuchin who died in Sierra Leone in 1657, was devoted to the point of self-immolation, and so were others, but they were exceptions.

Christianity's impact was limited by the vitality of traditional culture, by the shortage of clergy, and by a long-continued experience of European 'injuries and injustices'.

The new religion was brought by men with a relative abundance of novel material goods. In traditional religious systems that emphasized this-worldly blessings, this gave a prima-facie indication of its probable truth. However, a Wolof ruler in close contact with Islam had a different perspective: '. . . he considered it reasonable that they would be better able to gain salvation than we Christians, for God was a just lord, who had granted us in this world many benefits of various kinds, but to the negroes, in comparison with us, almost nothing. Since he had not given them paradise here, he would give it to them hereafter'.[116]

THREE

Mission Renewed

Selection is either random or invidious. But if the Epistle to
the Romans is not in fact complete without an addendum of
. . . names, otherwise unknown, this chapter is improperly
without one.

K. Cragg[1]

Much writing on Christianity in Africa—my own included—has been shaped
by a reaction against a tradition of missionary biography, where the foreign
Christian is the heroic actor, and African communities merely the backdrop
for her or his good deeds. Often, Africans are depicted as savage and
degenerate to highlight the beneficial impact of Christianity.

The response to this, pioneered by the Nigerian historians Ajayi and
Ayandele,[2] was to emphasize the African role in the spread of Christianity, and
indigenous responses and initiative. Where attention has focused on the
expatriate missionary, the evaluation has tended to be critical.[3] The stress on
African Christian initiatives was part of a wider historiography that
emphasized the positive aspects of the African past, in a salutary reaction
against the racism that deforms so many older accounts.[4] However, clearly
one cannot do justice to African encounters with Christianity without some
understanding of those who brought it. Christianity has never existed in an
abstract form; it is always incarnated in a particular milieu. The age,
nationality, gender, church affiliation, and theological bent of the missionary
had a decisive impact on the message transmitted. Flemish Franciscans, Anglo-
Catholics from Oxbridge, Dutch Reformed Church missionaries from South
Africa, black Presbyterians from the southern United States, Mill Hill Fathers
from the Tyrol, and the Wurttenbergers, who comprised 80 per cent of the
personnel of the Basel Mission were among them. This chapter analyses these
agents of change.

At the beginning of this book, we touched on the much-debated question of
Christianity's relationship with historical and cultural relativism. A nine-
teenth-century European traveller in what is now the southern Republic of
Sudan said of its people, 'Without any exception they are without a belief in a

Supreme Being, neither have they any form of worship. . . .'[5] Such passages are now cited only to condemn them, and they are contrasted with classics of modern anthropology by Evans-Pritchard, and Lienhardt. However, these studies have also been criticized for their silences.[6] Both the actors in historical events and scholars see Africa through particular 'I-glasses'.[7] There is no other way it can be seen. This is the problem of relativism in a different form. In a sense, missionaries understood African societies most imperfectly, but, as a body, they probably came closer to Africa, especially a knowledge of its languages, than most other foreigners have done. Some of them, such as Henri Junod, wrote ethnographic studies of enduring value.

Evangelicals and mission

Christians have not always looked on missionary work as a self-evident duty and, for centuries, it was not a priority of Protestant churches, as Cotton Mather lamented.[8] The Catholic mission enterprise in Africa was overly closely linked with the Portuguese crown, and shrank as Portugal's power dwindled. The Society for the Propagation of the Gospel (SPG), founded in 1701, provided clergy for the colonies,[9] and was financed by Parliament. In the 1830s, it was transformed into a missionary society, under the impetus of the Oxford Movement. The Universities' Mission to Central Africa (UMCA) (1859) was, likewise, founded by High Churchmen. With these two exceptions, the new Protestant mission societies formed from 1792 on were overwhelmingly Evangelical.

As so often seems to happen, there was, in the late eighteenth century, a climate of opinion that found expression in a number of independent publications and initiatives. In 1784, Melvill Horne, a chaplain in Freetown, published a *Letter on Missions*, appealing for an interdenominational missionary society, supported by 'liberal Churchmen and conscientious Dissenters, pious Calvinists and pious Arminians'.[10] The London Missionary Society was founded on these lines in 1795, though in practice it was less ecumenical than Congregational.

It was often the achievements of explorers that attracted potential missionaries to Africa, the Pacific or Asia. 'Shall the Christian missionary be surpassed by a Park or Lander?', asked the Honourable Baptist Noel, who was, and remained, minister of St John's Chapel in Bedford Row.

The Baptist Missionary Society was founded in 1792 as a result of the initiative of a shoemaker, Thomas Carey, who later became a missionary in India. He first thought of foreign missions when he read of Cook's journeys in the Pacific (soon, missionary work was to seem a self-evident duty to Evangelicals; that it was not so then is seen in the famous reproof Carey received: 'Sit down young man, when it pleases God to convert the Heathen, he'll do it without your help, or mine'.[11]) The London Missionary Society (LMS), as we have seen, dates from 1795; the Church Missionary Society

(CMS) was established by Evangelical Anglicans four years later. The process continued with the foundation of the British and Foreign Bible Society in 1804, the American Board of Commissioners for Foreign Missions (dominated by Boston Congregationalists) in 1810, and many more. The Leeds Methodist Missionary Society was founded in 1813, and the national Wesleyan Methodist Missionary Society several years later.

They differed considerably in their forms of organization. The CMS was a voluntary association, while the WMMS was an official part of the Methodist Church. The divisions of Christendom were writ large on missionary maps. Established, Free and United Presbyterians, and Wesleyan and Primitive Methodists maintained separate missions, though the latter united, in 1932, as the Methodist Missionary Society.

The Basel Mission was founded in 1815. At first, it supplied recruits for the Church Missionary Society; from 1828, it also had its own mission field on the Gold Coast. A French auxiliary led to the creation, in 1822, of the *Société des Missions Evangéliques*, under whose auspices Coillard worked, first among the Sotho, and later, the Lozi. A Berlin auxiliary became a separate mission in 1824, a Bremen one did likewise in 1836, and worked in Togo until the First World War. The Saxony branch became a confessional mission—the *Lutherische Leipzig Mission*—but in both the Basel and Bremen Missions,[12] Lutherans and Reformed churches worked together, believing that 'the standpoint of missions as a work of faith and love, is neither in Wittenberg nor in Geneva . . . but in Jerusalem on the Mount of Olives'.[13]

The concerns of these bodies were world-wide. Africa was only one of their mission fields, and they combined fundraising with actual mission work. Each developed a particular regional focus: the LMS in Southern Africa and Madagascar (and the Pacific), the CMS in West and East Africa, the Universities' Mission to Central Africa, as its name states, in Central Africa, the Baptists in the Congo basin, the Basel Mission in what is now southern Ghana.

There were also smaller missionary societies, one of the most interesting being the Hermannsburg Missionary Society, founded by Louis Harms. He believed that the Church in Europe was doomed, and wanted to create new Christian communities in Africa, untainted by Modernism. He drew on the resources of a single village, his missionaries were to be celibate, and his model was the conversion of the Saxons. His goal was the conversion of the Oromo, but circumstances made the Hermannsburg mission field Natal.[14]

Who became missionaries?

Missionaries have always been self-selected. Two twentieth-century comments—one from a sympathetic outsider in Kenya, the other from a woman who worked for the Worldwide Evangelisation Crusade in Zaire—are instructive:

76

. . . missionaries are chosen, not by the Church . . . but by themselves. Such men and women go out to Africa in intense enthusiasm, regarded by their friends and sometimes by themselves, as heroes . . .[15]

Someone, possibly deeply stirred at a missionary meeting . . . feels constrained to offer for overseas service. Almost inevitably this 'offering' comes to be regarded as a 'holy call' to a sacrificial vocation. The whole idea becomes wrapped in a veil of romantic splendour . . . many may know that, mentally, physically or spiritually, the candidate is unsuitable for missionary service.[16]

There was, at first, a considerable social dividing line between the prosperous advocates and patrons of foreign missions, and those who actually reached Africa: 'It has been the custom to think of missionaries as an inferior set of men, sent out, paid and governed by a superior set of men formed into a committee in London'.[17] The first English CMS missionaries included a joiner, a blanket maker, and two shoemakers.[18] Until 1830, 34 per cent of the LMS's missionaries, and 31 per cent of the CMS's were artisans or retailers. Most missionaries, wrote an East African big game hunter, were 'manufactured out of traders, clerks and mechanics'.[19]

The wealthy and eminent dominated meetings and committees, but much mission funding came from the many small donations of the poor: 'You will find enclosed half a sovereign; it is all we have in the world, and it is for the [Baptist] Congo mission. I am a crippled widow, and have been in bed with a bad spinal complaint for five years'.[20]

British-based missionary societies, in their early years, recruited a third of their missionaries abroad, mainly in Germany, because of the shortage of English recruits.[21] In most cases, lack of education reflected a lack of opportunity, and some artisan missionaries, including Carey, were remarkable autodidacts. In a sense, the mission field gave them careers that England would have denied them. Both Robert Moffat and Thomas Birch Freeman for instance, were gardener's sons, and started life as gardeners. By becoming missionaries they became community leaders, authors, and figures of international eminence: 'The missionary movement was an expression of a far wider development—the social emancipation of the underprivileged classes'.[22] The facile identification of Christianity with material progress, which they so often saw as a panacea for Africans, was an extrapolation from the realities of their own lives.

Not all missionaries were of humble origins, however. The Universities' Mission to Central Africa, as its name implies, recruited its missionaries from Oxbridge graduates. Bishop Mackenzie had been a Cambridge don in Mathematics; other missionary societies, in the later nineteenth century, had an increasing proportion of graduates among their candidates. One of the two leaders of the CMS's Sudan Party in 1890, G. W. Brooke, was a former public schoolboy of independent means, and the other, J. A. Robinson, had a First in

Theology from Cambridge. Recruitment in the CMS rose steadily between the 1870s and 1900, less because more candidates offered than because more were graduates, and, hence, were readily accepted.[23]

Some missionaries felt a call to mission work in general, and others to a particular work and field. They accepted a degree of control over their lives, especially over their marriages, which seems bizarre to a later age, although the members of the home committees had not been missionaries, nor even, in most cases, visited the mission field.[24] A missionary in southern Tanganyika complained in 1903:

> The one thing the fathers lack is practical knowledge. Men who are born in Germany, live there and never do continuous practical work as real missionaries, can have no clear insight into the requirements of this work. . . . In my conception, we missionaries stand to the Committee neither as mercenaries to their employers nor as German soldiers to their com- mander-in-chief . . . Rather, we stand . . . as individual shareholders in a corporation to one another.[25]

Like their Italian and Portuguese predecessors, nineteenth-century missionar- ies inevitably tended to identify Christianity with the world from which they came. They often experienced a profound isolation, and cultural dislocation when they reached Africa. In 1796, a party of Methodists reached Freetown, bound for the inland centre of Timbo.

> This morning there was nothing to be heard among the Missionary ladies but doleful lamentations or bitter complaints. To their astonishment Freetown resembled neither London nor Portsmouth; they could find no pastry cooks' shop, or any gingerbread to buy for their children. Dr Coke had deceived them; if this was Africa they would go no further.[26]

These people were not members of a missionary society, and most who came to Africa were not so naive or ill-prepared, but complaints of depression and loneliness thread their way through missionary letters and journals. In 1886, a Catholic missionary from Alsace wrote:

> One can hardly understand the trouble one experiences, arriving in a savage land, unknown and inhospitable, and being there without what one could call a home—one can't understand what I'm saying, unless one has been there. A thousand worries and a thousand anxieties pursue one daily. No bread, no wine, no eggs. . . .[27]

Christina Coillard's marriage was childless and her husband, François, was often away. She had spent twenty-six years in Africa when she wrote, in Bulozi, in 1886, that there was 'a wall of brass between me and the people . . . I don't live here, I languish'.[28] She died there, five years later.

All missionaries experienced deprivation and illness, and, for many, the call

78

to Africa was a death sentence. Minnie Comber reached San Salvador in 1879. Newly wed to a Baptist missionary, 'she had regarded the journey up country as one long picnic'.[29] Within a few weeks, she was dead. Her husband, Thomas Comber, was also to die in the Congo, as did Percy Comber and his wife Annie and a third brother, Harold; a sister, Mrs Wright Hay, died in Cameroun.[30]

It was understandable, in the light of mortality rates, that male missionaries, especially those with families, devoted much of their energy to matters such as housebuilding and vegetable growing, their wives to baking, jam-making or sewing, or, more precisely, to training Africans to perform these tasks for them. Much of their time and strength was devoted to the maintenance of a quasi-western lifestyle. This is very evident in, for instance, the household of the Moffats, at Kuruman.

Some missionaries did adopt African lifestyles, the preferential option for the poor that is more often advocated than practised. An example is the lifestyle of the first Plymouth Brethren in Shaba. Paradoxically, they were often not particularly successful. One of the Brethren pioneers lamented the later process of embourgoisement: 'Missionaries get too proverbially snug in all their stations. As long as we keep to the jungle and the rough life of itinerating, only the good old things can befall us'.[31] Yet, it was in the later period that the Brethren attracted converts.

Women

The first Protestant missionaries were male, like their Catholic predecessors, and wives were only grudgingly allowed. The word 'missionary', like 'actor', referred to males. When the door was opened to single, women missionaries, women were soon in a majority, though their preponderance is partly masked by the fact that wives were not listed separately: 'Their work in the mission has always been gratefully recognised. But they are, of course, not separately accepted; their entry on the roll is automatic along with their husbands'.[32]

Some who wished to marry were unable to do so, because of the isolation of their lives and the imbalance of women and men, or because a suitor was unable, or unwilling to be a missionary. Mary Slessor's engagement ended when her fiancé was invalided home. Many years later, when she died, two books he had given her were among her few possessions.[33] A twentieth-century autobiography, with unusual candour, described the unfulfilled desire to marry, and also a bonding to another woman candidate so close that the missionary society concerned sent the two to different continents.[34]

Some women married men they scarcely knew, out of a desire for a missionary life. Rosine Dietrich was engaged to a missionary who died. She travelled to Ethiopia to marry Johann Ludwig Krapf, the pioneer of Protestant missions in East Africa, who wrote in his memoirs, 'In leaving Europe I had not harboured the slightest idea of marriage, but my experiences in Abessinia convinced me that an unmarried missionary could not prosper'.[35] She buried a new baby in Shoa, and died soon after bearing a second; both lie in a grave near Mombasa. Krapf did not remarry until his return to Europe.

Other women felt differently. Mary Livingstone was the daughter and the wife of famous missionaries. She brought up her children alone in poverty in England, and died on the banks of the Zambezi. It is not surprising that she came to loathe the missionary enterprise, and was accused of a fondness for drink. Livingstone grieved deeply when she died, but he said of MacKenzie, who brought his middle-aged, invalid sister to the Zambezi: '. . . he is a muff to lean on a wife or a sister. I would as soon lean on a policeman'.[36]

Charles and Priscilla Studd worked together as missionaries in China and India. When he was fifty-two, Charles left his wife, who was in poor health, in England, and went to Africa. He stayed there continuously for the last thirteen years of his life, Priscilla visiting him once. Before he left, she wrote, 'I sat down by the fire, and as I thought of all that was going to happen to me, I began to weep. I do not often weep . . . '.[37]

All this was not peculiar to Africa. Dorothy Carey followed her husband to India with great reluctance; her mind failed when her five-year-old son died. She was not the last missionary wife to come home insane from India.

Between 1804 and 1880, 87 women and 902 men were separately accepted by the CMS. In 1915, of a total of 1354 CMS missionaries in the field, 444 were single women and 378 were wives.[38] The change was due partly to the example of the China Inland Mission, which accepted single women enthusiastically, and partly to the gradual widening of vocational opportunities for women in the metropolitan countries.

Unrepresented on the local decision-making body, women in the field met in a separate conference, the recommendations of which were often disregarded: 'Our position is intolerable', wrote a woman missionary in Kenya in 1920.[39] The ablest and most highly educated women tended not to become missionaries, perhaps because the mainstream missionary societies were so male-dominated.[40]

The central organization was also originally a male preserve. In the CMS, 'Men only attended and the presence of ladies was not expected'. When some women *did* attend a provincial SPG meeting, they were concealed behind the organ![41] Women first sat on the LMS Central Board in 1891, and on the CMS General Committee in 1917. R. Cust resigned from his post in the CMS in 1892, in protest when they were not allowed to do this: 'Concede in time what is inevitable . . . they will have equal rights because they are fit for them: what fools some men, old and young, are'.[42]

There were other forms of inequality: ordained clergymen, whose work was 'spiritual', were more highly esteemed than laymen, a fact which often led the latter to seek ordination. It was, to some extent, the social insecurity of upwardly mobile individuals that made them hostile to the aspirations of educated Africans, and insistent on retaining their own leadership roles.

Evangelicalism and perceptions of Africa

The Earl of Shaftesbury observed in later life, 'I know what constituted an Evangelical in former times. I have no clear notion what constitutes one now.[43] Evangelicals, whether Anglicans or Dissenters, were distinguished less by their doctrines than by characteristic emphases, such as the necessity of conversion, the Atonement, and 'the vital operation of Christian Doctrines upon the heart and conduct'.[44] The Evangelical stress on action contributed to the Anti-slavery movement, to a myriad philanthropies, and to missions at home and abroad (the Wesleyans maintained a Worn-Out Ministers Fund). 'Action is the life of virtue and the world is the theatre of action', wrote Hannah More.[45]

There were divisions among Evangelicals, notably the split between Wesleyans and others regarding whether or not Christ died for all, or only for the elect. This was the issue that divided General and Particular Baptists, and, when the two bodies reunited in 1891, their action reflected a world in which the debate had become less important.

Catholics and Protestants tended to regard each other as little better than 'heathen', and we saw earlier how the founders of the SPG regarded 'atheism, popish superstition and idolatry' as equivalent evils! However, they had more in common than either would have been willing to admit. Were all non-Christians, including those who had never heard the Gospel, really destined for Hell? Catholics and Evangelicals often wrote as if they believed so.[46] Moffat spoke of:

> . . . the teeming millions that are . . . moving every day like some vast funeral procession; onward and downward, sadly and slowly, but certainly to the regions of woe. 'Oh, you are a hard man', some might say; 'do you think they will go to hell?' Where do they go to? Do they go to heaven? All idolators, we are told, have their portion in the lake that burneth with fire and brimstone.[47]

To many, this was unacceptable: '. . . the wisest and safest course . . . is to leave the question of his manner of dealing with those who never hear the Gospel message, as one among his "secret things" '.[48] Actual first-hand contact with non-Christians led some to agonize over their eternal fate. Livingstone admired Sebitwane, who led his people on a great migration and founded the Kololo state on the Zambezi. He grieved when he died of a lung infection in his mid forties:

> He was decidedly the best specimen of native chief I ever met . . . it was impossible not to follow him in thought into the other world. . . . The dark question of what is to become of such as he, must, however, be left where we find it. The 'Judge of all the earth will do right'.[49]

The belief that the heathen were eternally lost declined, among missionaries as among others, towards the end of the nineteenth century. It was noted in 1882 that: 'The ghastly argument drawn from *the appalling picture of the future misery of the heathen*, which once roused missionary assemblies, has been abandoned'.[50] However, as late as 1957, the White Fathers prayed daily for the Muslims 'and other infidels of Africa', 'Have mercy on these unfortunate creatures who are continually falling into Hell in spite of the merits of your Son Jesus Christ'.[51]

But it was, in a sense, this polarized view of the world that strengthened missionary resolution. It is no coincidence that expatriate missionary commitment declines where liberal theology flourishes, and flourishes among fundamentalists, but it fostered a hostile, even racist, view of other cultures:

> In vain with lavish kindness
> The gifts of God are shown,
> The heathen in his blindness
> Bows down to wood and stone.

In 1884, a CMS missionary in East Africa, Charles Stokes, a widower, married an African woman and was expelled.[52] He became an arms dealer.

There was a natural tendency for those writing in missionary periodicals to stress the darker side of African society, such as human sacrifice, though the evils that they described were often recent developments, directly attributable to the Atlantic slave trade. Sometimes they misinterpreted what they saw. For example, the Igbo left the corpses of those who died 'bad deaths' in a grove called *ajo afia* (evil forest), and some central Nigerian peoples exhumed the skulls of their loved ones and preserved them in ossuaries. European observers tended to assume, wrongly, that these various visible remains were human sacrifices.

Some, both Catholic and Protestant, described African society as demonic. For example, the first CMS missionary to the Igbo, the Sierra Leonian son of Igbo parents, wrote, 'May many come willingly to labour in pulling down the strongholds of Satan's kingdom, for the whole of the Ibo district is his citadel'.[53] Similarly, the founder of the Spiritan mission to Igboland wrote to his nephew, 'All those who go to Africa as missionaries must be thoroughly penetrated with the thought that the Dark Continent is a cursed land, almost entirely in the power of the devil'.[54]

Modern scholars have often condemned expatriate missionaries for their Eurocentricity, their condemnation of indigenous culture. In a sense, though, this was inevitable. The newly-arrived missionary could not be an instant expert on African languages and cultures, and the incarnation of Christianity in different African cultures involved a great multiplicity of choices that, ultimately, could be made only by Africans themselves. However, in their identification of Christianity with western culture, missionaries often opposed practices that were morally neutral. The long list of missionary prohibitions among the Kaguru of Tanganyika in 1911 included wearing discs in the ears or numerous chains on the neck, removing the incisors and braiding men's hair with fibre.[55] In 1902, a CMS representative condemned Ganda domestic architecture:

> There was no home life among them and their houses were an outward symbol of that sad fact. They were round, very dark inside, having only one opening; there were no partitions beyond those made by hanging bark-cloths. . . . It could not be a wholesome life. . . .[56]

Persistently, missionaries condemned circular houses, and advocated rectangular ones! Such stereotypes were ethnocentric, but they were correct in perceiving that house design mirrored social values: 'The African house did not cut off nuclear families from one another . . . it did not manifest the owner's industriousness'.[57] Africans reflected on the symbolic meanings of house design: 'A chief argued with me for a week that by making a square house I had at once created four points of near or remote breakage'.[58]

Robert Moffat's daughter even tried to impose on a Tswana woman aristocrat the tyranny of Victorian stereotypes of the ideal female form: 'Bantsan . . . is very stout. . . . I told her that in civilized and especially Christian countries, it was a great dishonor to be thought to eat, drink or sleep too much, and consequently to grow fat'.[59]

Christianity and commerce

Humanitarians were sometimes accused of a 'Telescopic Philanthropy',[60] more sensitive to the plight of Africans than to that of the English poor. On one occasion, O'Connell said, 'If the Irish people were but black, we should have the honourable member for Weymouth coming down as large as life . . . to advocate their cause'.[61] John Campbell White (Lord Overtoun), who died in 1908, gave £50,000 to Livingstonia, but 'did nothing to rectify the appalling conditions of work in his own factory at Rutherglen until Keir Hardie publicly exposed them in 1899'.[62]

In the middle years of the nineteenth century, British Evangelicals tended to believe that Christianity and Commerce went hand in hand. They envisaged an Africa producing raw materials, such as cotton, for British industry, and purchasing the products that resulted. They believed that the development of alternative forms of commerce was the surest way to eliminate the slave trade: 'The mills of Manchester . . . will yet shout for joy through the cotton wealth of the Niger districts'.[63] Krapf recorded a conversation with the Queen Mother of Shoa:

> She asked me . . . how my countrymen had come to be able to invent and manufacture such wonderful things? I replied, that God had promised in His Word not only spiritual but temporal rewards to those who obeyed his

commandments; that the English, Germans, and Europeans in general, had once been as rude and ignorant as the Gallas, but after their acceptance of the Gospel, God had given them with science and arts wondrous blessings of an earthly kind.[64]

Missionaries and traders in Africa often co-operated, with the former relying heavily on commercial transport and other resources. However, they were often at odds, especially over the liquor trade. A Xhosa aristocrat pointed out that material prosperity and spiritual wisdom were not necessarily found together: 'Why should you English set down the Kaffirs as fools?', he asked, 'You certainly have great skill in arts and manufactures but may not we surpass you in our knowledge of other things?'[65]

A Catholic missionary resurgence

Contemporary Catholic religious orders are, internationally, in a state of crisis and decline. Their members sometimes take comfort from the fact that religious orders experienced a still more traumatic crisis in the late eighteenth century, which was followed by a period of revival, when new orders were founded on an unprecedented scale.

The Jesuits were expelled from Portugal in 1759, an event which reflected the continuing power of the *padroado*. France and Spain followed suit, and, in 1773, the Pope suppressed the order in Europe. During the French Revolution, religious orders were suppressed *en masse*. There were 15 000 Benedictines in 1775, and 2500 in 1850; the figures for the Dominicans were 20 000, and 4560 respectively, while many other orders entirely ceased to exist.[66]

Propaganda Fide was re-established in 1816, and successive popes succeeded in asserting their control of foreign missions. This was achieved by the control of funds, and by the creation of some seventy new dioceses, filled with members of the new orders, and answerable to Rome.[67] An important source of revenue was the Association for the Propagation of the Faith, founded in 1819 by a working-class woman from Lyons. It collected small weekly sums from large numbers of subscribers, and was destined to become, 'the one chief source of support for the whole of our foreign missions'.[68] The days when African sees were in the gift of the King of Portugal had gone for ever.

The growth and work of the new congregations can be understood only in terms of the changing relations of Church and State on the Continent.[69] Anti-clerical politicians in France were less hostile to Catholic missionary congregations than might have been expected, because they recognized their contribution to the spread and maintenance of French power abroad. Lavigerie, for example, worked for France's acquisition of Tunisia, as did the

Spiritans, under Augouard, in French Equatorial Africa. When the French Government separated Church and State in 1905, the aristocratic prioress of the Algiers Carmel pleaded successfully for the exemption of the White Fathers' and Sisters' schools. In the Belgian Congo, the Concordat of 1906 provided subsidies for Catholic schools in return for a measure of state control. The Protestants were not included until forty years later. In the coalitions that were the norm in twentieth-century Belgian politics, the Catholics tended to win control of the Ministry for Colonies, in return for trade-offs elsewhere.[70]

Italy seized the Papal States in 1870, and successive Popes felt that the Church was endangered both by the loss of this territorial principality, and by modernism. They looked for allies in the missionary congregations, and in their converts. To Pio Nono, as to Louis Harms, Africa promised new Christians, free from the taint of theological liberalism.

Many missionary congregations were created in the middle years of the nineteenth century, and some, like the White Fathers or the Society of African Missions, were specifically for Africa. The Holy Ghost Fathers, founded in 1703, were reduced to a single man during the French Revolution. The order survived, but in an enfeebled state, providing clergy for the colonies, much like the SPG. In 1848, it acquired a new lease of life by amalgamation with a newly founded missionary order, the Society of the Sacred Heart of Mary. The latter was founded by a fervent convert from Judaism, a Rabbi's son who became a priest, Francis Mary Paul Libermann. Many Spiritans died in West Africa, but the order survived; those who joined in the early years, did so in the spirit of *morituri te salutant*.[71] In 1904, there were 696 Spiritan priests and 667 brothers in missions in Senegal, Nigeria, Gabon, Angola, and East Africa.[72]

The Society of St Joseph (usually called the Mill Hill Fathers, after their base in North London) was founded by Cardinal Herbert Vaughan in 1866. Members of this society reached Uganda in 1895, and later founded missions in Kenya, the Congo, Cameroun, and the Sudan. They recruited members from Britain, the Netherlands, and the Tyrol.[73]

The Society of African Missions (SMA) was founded in 1856 by a former missionary bishop in India, Melchior de Marion Bresillac. Although he and his fellow missionaries died soon after their arrival in Sierra Leone, the Society survived. It was estimated that, in Dahomey, a male missionary survived for three years, a missionary nun for four. In 1905, the SMA had 330 members, and there were 150 sisters in an associated order. Its administrative centre was in Lyons, and all but one of its missions were in West Africa.[74] It was noted that, 'The Society of African Missions has lost two hundred and eighty three of its members, almost all cut down in the flower of their age by a deadly climate'.[75] Many of these missionaries were recruited from peasant families[76] in Brittany or Alsace.[77] In time, French missionary orders made a conscious attempt to recruit Irishmen to work in English-speaking areas.

One of the most important African missions was the Society of Missionaries of Africa, founded in 1868 by Charles Lavigerie, and generally known as the White Fathers. Lavigerie began his work in Algiers but like many before and after him, he found it impossible to convert Muslims. Later, the White Fathers were entrusted with vast expanses of East Africa, including the interlacustrine kingdoms.

The Oblates of Mary Immaculate, yet another nineteenth-century French society, founded by Eugene de Mazenod, worked in Natal and Lesotho. They 'were drawn mainly from small villages in Provence and the Jura: they brought with them . . . an emphasis on hell-fire beside which all but the most extreme Protestant sermons seemed mild'.[78]

Many other orders, old and new, came to work in Africa. The first Catholic missionaries reached Khartoum in 1846. They saw the Nile as the gateway to Africa, and pushed South. However, the mission was decimated by disease, forty-four out of ninety-five dying between 1846 and 1863; many of the rest were forced to leave as a result of sickness. A survivor, Daniele Comboni, founded the predominantly Italian Verona Fathers.[79] German Benedictines worked in Tanganyika, and German Pallotins in Kamerun.

A community of Cistercians came to Mariannhill in Natal in 1882 (it is pleasant to note that the name was chosen as a tribute to the Abbot's generous and supportive stepmother!) They were, of course, contemplatives, bound to a life of silence and solitude in the community. The Bishop who originally invited them had hoped, it seems, less for their prayers than for the dissemination of their agricultural techniques! Mariannhill was soon the largest Cistercian monastery in the world. However, the monks did not take long to turn to educational and missionary work, which was incompatible with their contemplative calling, so, in 1909, the Mariannhill missions of Natal, Cape Province, and Rhodesia became a new Missionary Institute.[80]

Among the prosperous, missionary vocations were '*d'une singulière, d'une affligeante rareté*'.[81] In 1919, an Irish study noted that, 'In the popular estimate, the "foreign mission" usually implies only a very modest grade in the scale of ecclesiastical respectability',[82] but there were exceptions, such as Father Henry Kerr, Superior of the Jesuit Zambezi mission in the late nineteenth century, who was the second son of the sixth Marquis of Lothian.[83]

Commitment to foreign missions often became a family tradition, among both Protestants and Catholics. Joseph Lutz (1853–95) was an Alsatian Spiritan who worked in Sierra Leone and on the Niger. One of his brothers was also a Spiritan, and two sisters were religious of Saint Joseph of Cluny. A number of nieces, nephews, and cousins followed in their footsteps, making a total of eight priests (five of them Spiritans), and eleven nuns (seven of them Josephites).[84]

Often, these missionaries were attracted by a romantic dream of martyrdom. A French missionary, who died aged 26 on the Ivory Coast, said '. . . from afar, to die in Africa is the most beautiful dream, but once here, the instinct for life asserts itself and one would wish to live as long as in France'.[85]

Religious orders were often reluctant to admit African members. African seminarians were encouraged to become diocesan priests rather than join a missionary congregation, and expatriate nuns tended to form separate orders for African sisters. In modern Africa, many prefer to join local congregations, which have offered fewer obstacles to indigenization in leadership and praxis, but their foundation often reflected a reluctance to admit Africans into the close-knit family of religious life. A Sotho, Benjamin Makhaba, worked as a catechist in the early days of Mariannhill. He wanted to join the community, but 'it was considered that the Natives of South Africa, at their stage of development at the time, were unsuitable candidates for this kind of rigorous life'. He attempted to enter a contemplative monastery in England, but was turned down. In 1923, Mariannhill founded a separate (Franciscan) congregation for African priests and brothers.[86]

In 1949, an Irish bishop wrote to the Cistercian monastery at Roscrea, seeking admission for an exemplary Nigerian priest, but in vain: 'The "admiratio" that would be caused by coloured men in our Community and the strong objection of the members to same was a big factor in deciding the issue'.[87]

Hundreds of missionary nuns worked in Africa, but, as yet, their history has been little studied, and their records little used, so that the literature emphasizes men's congregations. 'For the sake of completeness, some mention must be made of the many female religious congregations', notes a study published in 1969, but adds 'Since lack of space makes it impossible to describe them in as much detail as the male congregations, only their names will be given'.[88] In addition to their own work—often teaching—they were expected to perform various services for missionary priests: 'The sisters at Kisantu [in Zaire, in 1906] do at the Mission all the wash, ironing, mending and sewing for the priests and brothers of all the mission posts of the region.'[89]

Often, they were not members of a specifically missionary congregation. The sisters of Notre Dame de Namur, who went to the Lower Zaire in 1894 at the invitation of the Jesuits, were founded after the French Revolution for the education of poor girls. Most of their early members in the Congo were the daughters of Belgian farmers; some were Dutch, German or Irish. From the 1920s, Kongo women tried unsuccessfully to join them, but it was not until the late 1930s that the Jesuit bishop agreed.[90]

A Franciscan convent at Mill Hill in London supplied sisters to work among North American blacks. In 1903, it agreed to supply them for Uganda. In time, the Uganda province became larger than the parent body, and, in 1952, the Franciscan Missionary Sisters for Africa became an independent congregation. Their first Superior-General was seventy-seven-year-old Mother Kevin, who first reached Uganda in 1903, and founded 15 convents there. In 1923, she had established a society of African nuns, the Little Sisters of St Francis, which, by 1948, had over 200 members. Both congregations worked in education, in leprosariums, and in hospitals (although, until the 1930s, canon law prevented nuns from practising midwifery!) In her old age she said, 'Everything is darkness and dryness, and sometimes I am tempted to despair'.[91]

There was, and still is, a vast number of African women's congregations, many of which exist only at the diocesan level. The oldest of these, which still flourishes, is the Congregation of the Daughters of the Sacred Heart of Mary, founded in Senegal in 1858.[92] The majority were founded during the colonial period. Thus, in Zaire, one was founded before 1930, thirteen between 1930 and 1945, three between 1945 and 1960, and seven between 1960 and 1975.[93] As we have seen, they experienced fewer obstacles in inculturation than their international counterparts, but, instead of control by expatriate nuns, they often suffered from domination by a local expatriate or African bishop. They were, and still are, isolated—some congregations speak only an African language—with less access to international funding and education abroad.

There were many Christianities, as there were many African host societies. The rural Catholicism of peasant Europe had a good deal in common with the religions of rural Africa. In the 1930s, the records of Triashill in Rhodesia included the following entry: 'A big swarm of locusts (8 miles long) is quite near. All the church bells are sounded and Fr. Schmitz applies the exorcism. Soon after, the beasts disappear'.[94] Pilgrimages to Lourdes grottos or other local shrines fitted in well with a traditional emphasis on the sacred place. The feast days of peasant Catholicism, such as St Patrick's Day, corresponded with the annual festivals of traditional eco-religion.

Not all missionaries claimed power over drought, locusts, or disease, though. More typically, they endorsed a rationalist, scientific explanation of sickness, and had more confidence in hospitals than in healing by prayer. Even Pentecostals saw healings and miracles as a special gift, rather than an essential ingredient in daily life.[95] Many missionaries hovered uneasily between two worlds, like the White Fathers in Rwanda who offered both holy water *and* black coffee to a woman in labour![96]

Nineteenth-century missionaries, both Protestant and Catholic, were very often closer to African communities than their successors. Although they were often sweeping and extreme in their condemnation of African cultures, they were much more successful than most of their successors in learning African languages. The early French missionaries on the lower Niger seldom if ever went on leave, and acquired real fluency in Igbo, while assiduously cultivating coffee beans! Their Irish successors preached through interpreters.

Keswick and the Faith Missions

The belief that perfection is attainable in this life was an important part of early Methodism, but it was a teaching that easily exposed the devout to ridicule, and it was, to some extent, forgotten in the decades that followed. From 1870 onwards, there was a new Holiness movement in Evangelical spirituality, due largely to the teaching of Robert and Hannah Pearsall Smith. They taught that, beyond the gift of conversion, was a second gift, that of sanctification, though, in its practical application, this was often understood in terms of very selective criteria, such as teetotalism rather than kindness. From 1875 onwards, a series of conventions was held at Keswick, which became the focal point of the new spirituality. Keswick was middle-class—'a Convention for the rich alone'.[97] It produced recruits for the mission field well into the twentieth century, and contributed to the increasing proportion of middle-class and graduate missionary recruits, which we have noted in the older missionary movements described earlier.

The China Inland Mission was founded by J. Hudson Taylor in 1865. He emphasized complete dependence on God, and insisted on the wearing of Chinese dress. Missionaries did not receive a salary, and depended on offerings for their needs. His work was the model for a large number of Faith Missions in Africa, interdenominational, but strictly fundamentalist. They included the Sudan United Mission, the Sudan Interior Mission, the Africa Inland Mission, the Heart of Africa Mission, the Gospel Missionary Union, and the Christian and Missionary Alliance. Like Taylor, they accepted single women with enthusiasm.

The Faith Missions were romantic and anti-clerical; they emphasized the religion of the heart, and combat with the Devil.

> Christ's call is . . . not to build and furnish comfortable chapels, churches and cathedrals at home in which to rock Christian professors to sleep by means of clever essays, stereotyped prayers and artistic musical perfor-mances, but . . . to capture men from the Devil's clutches. . . . *But this can only be accomplished by a red-hot, unconventional, unfettered Holy Ghost religion*, where neither church nor State . . . are worshipped. Not to confess Christ by fancy collars, clothes, silver croziers or gold watch-chain crosses, church steeples or richly embroidered altar cloths . . .[98]

The history of most of these missions remains unwritten. There is a considerable body of pious biographies, but little academic research.

The Sudan United Mission was founded in 1904 by Karl Kumm with the aim of creating a chain of mission stations across Africa, at places of encounter between Islam and traditional religion. There were a number of national branches, each with a mission field—the South Africans, for instance, worked among the Tiv. Kumm made an exploratory journey from the Niger to the Nile, but never worked for any length of time in Africa. His views of Africans were paternalist, indeed, racist. The Aryan race 'is today in the full strength of its manhood, while in Africa and in the South Sea Islands we have the infants of our human family'.[99] He wrote of the Sudan, 'There is a land in this wonderful world, called "The Land of Darkness"; dark are the bodies of the people who live there, darker are their minds, and darker still their souls'.[100]

C. T. Studd captained the Cambridge cricket team; he was one of the

Cambridge Seven who joined the China Inland Mission, and inherited a fortune, which he gave to charity. In 1908, when he was 52 years old and a severe asthmatic, he was drawn to Africa by 'a strangely worded notice', emanating from Kumm: 'Cannibals want missionaries'.[101] After a visit to the southern Sudan, he travelled with a twenty-year-old companion to the Belgian Congo in an epic journey that began on the Kenya coast. He left for the Congo again in 1916, remaining until his death in 1931. This was the origin of the Heart of Africa Mission, which grew into the Worldwide Evangelism Crusade. When he lay dying, he said nothing but 'Hallelujah'.

Studd was a man of single-minded devotion, and some of his fellow workers found him difficult to live with. It is impossible not to admire the courage and tenacity that led him to work in China, India, and Africa, and not to feel for his wife, who spent her last years alone.

The Plymouth Brethren developed a separate corporate life from the 1830s on; they were very much like the Faith Missions, stressing the imminence of the Second Coming, and rejecting the rituals and organizations of the established churches. Frederick Arnot, drawn to Africa as a child, when he played with Livingstone's children, was a lonely pioneer in Bulozi and Shaba. Like the Faith Missions, they relied on offerings, and enjoyed even more individual freedom: 'Brethren of all kinds and persuasions were free to embark upon missionary adventures, to occupy new areas, or to join existing teams. There was no selection process'.[102] Brethren and Faith Mission personnel recognized that they spoke the same language, and Hudson Taylor bade the Brethren leaving for Shaba an affectionate farewell.[103]

The Africa Inland Mission was founded by Peter Cameron Scott (1867–1896).[104] He, too, had a dream of a chain of mission stations across Africa, but died within a few months of reaching Kenya. Charles Hurburt took over when Scott died, and worked in Kenya until 1926. By 1960, the AIM had over 600 missionaries in six African countries, but a study at the grassroots level in Kenya shows failures that are not always apparent in the hagiographies. Candidates were expected to be able to document conversion and a Call, but the emphasis on individual spirituality led to several schisms within the movement. More seriously, they failed to provide the efficient schooling for which their Christians hungered; they tended to regard education with impatience, preferring direct evangelization. Their schoolgirls worked as domestic servants for the missionaries, while schoolboys spent half of every day growing vegetables that the mission sold in Nairobi. There were separate church services for black and white, and the missionaries, whose views on the unimportance of education never extended to their own children, ran an élite school for their own progeny in Nairobi.[105] None of this was peculiar to the AIM or, indeed, to Kenya, but it reminds us that Holiness is not easy to acquire, or even understand.

A Holiness spirituality, whether in the older missions or in Faith Missions, often led to the condemnation of the Other, and an intolerant autocracy.

Missionaries habitually demanded higher standards from their African converts than were expected in English congregations: '. . . are we to settle down content with the miserable parody of Christianity which all too commonly passes muster in "Christian England"?',[106] asked a CMS missionary in Buganda. Perfectionism tended to lead to the destruction, rather than the furthering, of African aspirations. European missionaries rejected Tucker's suggested Church constitution in 1898 because it gave more authority to Africans: 'To me the greatest objection seems to be the proposed equality of European and native workers, thereby in some cases placing Europeans under native control'.[107]

The advocates of Christianity and Commerce had tended to believe in 'progress', by which they understood the gradual spread of Christianity, and Western civilization throughout the world. Wilmot Brooke of the Sudan Party said:

> . . . very much confusion is caused & very much nonsense talked by Evangelicals and Broadchurchmen both confusing the work of saving men from the power of Satan, and that of building up political, commercial and social civilisation. I believe these two to be very frequently opposed, & I know they are invariably distinct.[108]

Much mission work was justified by the Great Commission (Matt. 28. 19–20). An eschatology, propounded in different forms by the Irvingites and the Brethren, looked for the dramatic irruption of Christ in history, in the Second Coming. It was believed that this could not take place until the Gospel had been preached to all nations, and, for some, this became the dominant motive for mission work. In the words of Brooke, '. . . to hasten that time is, I believe, the function of foreign missions . . . I therefore should be inclined to frame any missionary plans with a view to giving the simple gospel message to the greatest number of ignorant heathen in the shortest possible time'.[109]

Robert Arthington was a wealthy, eccentric recluse, who gave large sums to missions, and often used his largesse to influence their strategies. He was a pre-millenarian, in favour of entering new fields, if necessary abandoning old ones '. . . that *all* his elect may be gathered speedily'. On one occasion, he offered a missionary ship, provided that the BMS withdrew from most of the Indian sub-continent![110]

These differences in theory, the strategy of the Bible and the Plough, or Keswick's more 'spiritual' emphasis on individual conversion, had important practical implications.

> I am entirely in favour of the Lay Evangelist, the Female Evangelist, the Medical Evangelist, whenever Gospel-preaching is the substantive work; but when it is proposed to have a pious Industrial Superintendent, or an Evangelical tile-manufacturer, or a Low Church breeder of cattle or raiser of turnips, I draw my line.[111]

The author of this passage was a member of the CMS's General Committee in the 1890s. The cherished CMS projects of the 1840s had included a model farm at Lokoja.

Missionaries and the extension of empire

The number of missionaries at work in Africa expanded dramatically between 1880 and 1920, the heyday of imperialism. Missionaries in the field often supported the imperial ambitions of their compatriots: the Ganda called Catholic missionaries *baFranza* (French), and Protestants, *baIngereeza* (English), as did many other African peoples. It has been suggested that both mission and imperialism rest on the same postulate: the superiority of one's own culture to that of the other. An Asian theologian has said that not only the missionary enterprise, but western theology has been 'a handmaid of western expansion . . .', and that the linkage of mission with western political, economic, and cultural dominance has been 'disastrous for Christianity itself',[112] Ludwig Krapf, the CMS pioneer in East Africa, warned his co-religionists to 'Expect nothing, or very little, from political changes in Eastern Africa . . . Whether Europeans take possession of Eastern Africa, or not, I care very little, if at all'.[113] In some instances (Kumm is an obvious example), the missionary enthusiasm for empire was based on the conviction that white cultures were superior, and that it was the duty of Europeans to be 'trustees' or 'guardians' of the supposedly less civilized. There was often an ingredient of national chauvinism—'. . . *Deutsche Christen mussen wir in Kamerun erziehen*'[114]—and missionaries were more critical of colonial administrations when they were, from their own perspective, foreign. In many cases, the extension of empire was welcomed because it was hoped it would lead to the end of abuses such as human sacrifice. Often, when they had been unsuccessful, they recognized that a change of government would break the cake of custom, and make other changes easier. After Mpande destroyed his mission in 1842, Aldin Grout always prayed for the overthrow of the Zulu state.[115]

No one became a missionary with the conscious intention of furthering imperialism, and often there were serious sources of friction between missionaries and colonial officials. Sometimes missionaries denounced various forms of oppression and injustice, and their representatives in the metropolis lobbied on humanitarian issues. An endemic source of friction between fundamentalist missionaries and white admininistrators, settlers and merchants lay in the former's sabbatarianism, and hostility to drink, gambling, and racing—very often the major sources of solace for colonial Europeans in tropical Africa. A Faith Mission did, however, succeed in converting one of the most prominent administrators in northern Nigeria.

Missionary conflict and co-operation

In their early days, the Evangelical missions showed a high level of mutual co-operation.[116] The LMS and the British and Foreign Bible Society were consciously ecumenical, the Anglican CMS obtained its first recruits from Germany, and Anglicans willingly played an active role at the annual meeting of the Methodist Missionary Society. In the field, however, there was often an element of rivalry, even between Faith Missions, or different Catholic congregations:

> . . . the departure of newly won converts to rival missions was invariably viewed with the same sense of loss and failure as that occasioned by the 'backsliding of local Christians into paganism'; and the possibility of rival missions establishing a presence in their field caused as much concern as the possible introduction of a new pagan shrine.[117]

Occasionally, a gleam of ecumenical charity shines through the records, as when Bishop Samuel Crowther gave the newly arrived Holy Ghost fathers in Onitsha a plot of CMS land: 'I acquired this land for God's cause, take it'.[118] However, the denominational hostility that deformed religious dialogue at the court of the Kabaka of Buganda was much more typical:

> M. Lourdel was spokesman. He became all at once very excited, and said, 'We do not join in that religion, because it is not true; . . . we do not know that book, because it is a book of lies. If we joined in that, it would mean that we were not Catholics, but Protestants, who have rejected the truth. For hundreds of years they were with us, but now they believe and teach only lies'.[119]

On a personal level, though, the rivals helped each other, and sometimes became close friends.

Christianity and culture

At the heart of the missionary enterprise lay a dilemma: to what extent should converts adopt western 'civilization'? Faith Missions, fearful that converts would be motivated by material factors, claimed that African culture should remain unchanged, but the social implications of conversion were far-reaching. One could not introduce Christianity without changing the host society. The crucial question was, by how much? To some missionaries, for example, western dress was anathema, and to others it was the *sine qua non* of being a Christian. Fundamentalists expected converts to read the Bible, but not to use their newly acquired literacy to earn a living.

In England, the established Church and Methodism tended to be socially conservative, accepting the social relations of master and servant. In Africa, missionaries were committed to a transformation of society, but often had little understanding of the long-term implications of their actions. They took it for granted that the plough was beneficial, and so, in a sense, it was, but its adoption also led to a growing social gap between richer and poorer farmers, and changed the relationship between work and gender.

The missionaries who embarked on these social transformations were often, paradoxically, hostile to westernization and education, believing that these fostered worldliness. The bizarre contradictions that these ideas could lead to were seen in an extreme form in the history of the CMS Sudan Party in the late nineteenth century. Its members, such as Brooke, had a romantic attachment to the language, dress, and culture of Hausaland, but attacked African missionaries with vitriolic prejudice and injustice.[120]

Not all Victorian missionaries were oblivious to these problems. In 1887, a missionary in Uganda wrote:

> I believe we shall gain a great point when Christianity ceases to be called the white man's religion. The foolish phrase, 'Kusoma Kizungu' (to read the English thing) creates needless suspicion. I am ever battling with it among our own people and trying to get them to use 'Soma Luganda' instead. When will they learn that Christianity is cosmopolitan and not Anglican?[121]

None had a more sophisticated awareness of these dilemmas than John Colenso, the embattled Bishop of Natal. He opposed the belief that non-Christians are doomed to Hell, defended polygamists, and respected the positive qualities in Nguni life, but he won no more converts than others. He reached Natal in 1853, and, by 1880, had a congregation of 86.[122] The most enduring consequence of his work was a divided South African Anglicanism.[123]

Where central mission boards advocated black pastors and catechists, it was largely because they were paid less. An occasional expatriate missionary, invariably criticized by his fellows, attempted to share the lifestyle of the poor. Van der Kemp married a Khoi wife, and lived on the edge of destitution in the Eastern Cape until his death in 1811. The Norwegian, Lutheran Hans Schreuder, worked among the Zulu from the 1840s on: 'His personal appearance is bad. . . . His food was chiefly pumpkins, eggs and milk'.[124] Few chose to share the sufferings of the poor, and none could do much to relieve it:

> I asked a man, 'Do you know that you have an undying soul?'.
> 'Yes, my soul tells me that I am hungry, and I want you to give me food.'
> 'You have heard that Jesus Christ came into the world to save sinners?'
> 'Yes; I go naked and I wish you would give me a blanket.'
> 'You have heard that the Bible says, God is angry with the wicked everyday?'
> 'Just see (pointing downwards) what a great sore I have on my foot?'[125]

A romantic ideal of rural life meant that missionaries tended to be suspicious of the new cities and to do too little to minister to the welfare of their inhabitants. In the words of a study of Zaire:

> Their own anti-intellectualism and anti-cosmopolitanism also led many many missionaries to become exponents and supporters of African provincialism. They idealized African village life and rejected such aspects of modernity as urbanization and industrialization. To them rural life was the epitome of virtue while the city was filled with evil and atheism.[126]

In the long run, the pattern of African Christian life, and its relationship with western education and technology were not for white missionaries to determine. African individuals explored a variety of options. Some sought western education and technology without Christianity, while others reacted against white hegemony by founding independent churches. In doing so, they not only enriched the African expression of Christianity and its global development, but also contributed to an ongoing process of emancipating Christian thought and praxis from the domination of European concepts and values.

As the nineteenth century neared its end, there was a growing hostility to educated Africans in their role as actual or potential church leaders. The destruction of the Niger mission is the most famous case of this. Where there was a white community, settler congregations held aloof from African ones. In 1846, the first Methodist Sunday school in Pietermaritzburg, taught black, white, and brown children. By 1880, black, and white Methodists worshipped apart.[127]

In the twentieth century, fundamentalism became less characteristic of the home churches, and foreign missions were very much a minority concern. In Britain, in the 1920s, 'contributions to missions amount to one eight-hundredth part of the national income, and probably less than a tenth of the population take any interest in them . . . most missionaries are adherents of the older theological ideas, now becoming less common in Europe'.[128] The missionary in Africa was marginal to other Europeans, unless he became their chaplain. Even then, he was divided from them by his lower income, and hostility to many of their most cherished recreations. In the home country, missions were more marginal still.

The host societies

Encounters with Christianity were, of course, as complicated and various as African cultures themselves. They varied with the political structure of the state, and the position of the individual within it. Missionary teaching encountered a world of cultural values and practices, of which 'religion' was a part. Traditional religious values were implicit in myth and ritual, rather than explicit.

The essential dilemma for the historian is to discern patterns of meaning in unique events. One is tempted to delineate the 'African religion' that missionaries encountered; but one of the central insights of scholarship in recent years has been that 'African traditional religion', as it has sometimes been described, did not exist.[129] There are clearly some recurring, though not universal, patterns: the invocation of ancestral shades, the cults of nature divinities, and of divinized heroes and kings, the prevalence of secret societies (sometimes, but not always male preserves, sometimes appearing in public as masked figures). There is a strong emphasis on temporal benefits, such as health, long life, prosperity, children. Many African peoples believed in witchcraft, and tended to attribute misfortunes, such as untimely death, to its malice. They invented various social mechanisms for discerning witches, and obtaining protection against them. Foreign missionaries who regarded witchcraft as a dangerous delusion could do little to meet these deep-seated needs.

Missionaries in general expected Christians to be monogamous, while aware of the cruelty and injustice involved in disrupting polygamous unions. Plural marriage was deeply rooted in the social fabric. Kings cemented good relations with subject provinces in this way, and the great value placed on children, and the contributions made by wives in farming[130] meant that the more prosperous had overwhelmingly strong motives to acquire more wives. Sometimes, pioneer Christians, such as the early Yoruba cocoa farmers, obtained the economic resources that made plural marriage possible to them for the first time. Missionaries familiar with the story of Jacob and Rachel were, for the most part, blind to the way in which love could flourish in a plural marriage:

'How many wives have you, Zatshuke?'
'Seven.'
'Have you ever put any away?'
'No.'
'How old is the eldest?'
'I married her when Dingane came into power. She is an old woman now.'
'Don't you think of putting her away, now that she is old and useless?'
'I would rather say, "Let us be killed together".'[131]

Postscript

Many things brought Europeans to Africa. The vision of the mystic, Emmanuel Swedenborg, attracted several of his followers to Sierra Leone. He believed that somewhere between the Nile and Lake Chad was a pure African church, the recipient of a special revelation. A Swedenborgian in Sierra Leone, the botanist Afzelius, 'met three persons of great spiritual beauty' in the interior. A later member of the sect wrote, 'Any exterior communication with the

African church I think very improbable in the present state of the Christian world, and until the life of heaven is more internally found, I do not see what use it would be'.[132]

In an age that has learned to appreciate the spiritual insights of traditional religion in Africa and elsewhere, Swedenborg's vision of an African revelation, and Afzelius' glimpses of spiritual beauty do not seem bizarre.

ৰঙ্গ FOUR ঙ্গ

Southern Africa to c. 1900

> . . . he became the more bewildered, especially when he thought of the spirit of the Gospel message, 'Good-will to man'. He often wondered whether the book he saw some of the farmers use said anything on the subject; and then he would conclude, that if they worshipped any such being he must be one of a very different character from that God of love to whom the missionaries directed the attention of the Namaquas.
>
> Afrikaner Jager (d. 1823)[1]

Africa 1800 to 1900: an overview

In 1800, the dominant form of monotheism in Africa was clearly Islam. Apart from the Copts and highland Ethiopia, Christianity was confined to small enclaves on the coast, in the Congo basin, and on the Zambezi. Even there, foreigners described it with disapproval, as a mélange of Catholicism and traditional practices. By 1900, new Christian communities had been created, among them the black American settlers of Liberia and the Creoles of Sierra Leone, some of whom carried their new faith back to their original homes. The courage of the Christians of Buganda and Madagascar astonished the world, and the African Christians of southern Africa had come to form a new, educated élite.

Both the Creoles and the Americo-Liberians were originally the victims of enslavement, which cut them off abruptly from their original environment. The latter had been uprooted for generations, so that they no longer spoke an African language, but elsewhere too, the first converts were often marginal to traditional cultures, whether as individuals or as entire communities, such as the displaced Mfengu of South Africa.

Often, however, decades of missionary endeavour produced only a small number of converts. It is a paradox that the most famous missionary names belong to the nineteenth century—Livingstone, the Moffats, the Hinderers, Mary Slessor—whereas the expansion of Christianity took place in the twentieth, and then largely through the work of African evangelists. A famous study of catechists is called 'Missionaries to Yourselves', and these words encapsulate the essential core of modern Africa's Christian history.

Wherever there were European settlers, the churches were forced to choose whether their primary ministry was to whites, or Africans. Different churches and individuals found different answers at different times. Some missionaries became pastors to colonial congregations, and some colonial chaplains were drawn to outreach among local people.

The dilemma is writ large on the history of Christianity in Algeria, Kenya, Mozambique, Angola, and the Rhodesias. Despite much additional immigration after the Second World War, these white communities were not large or

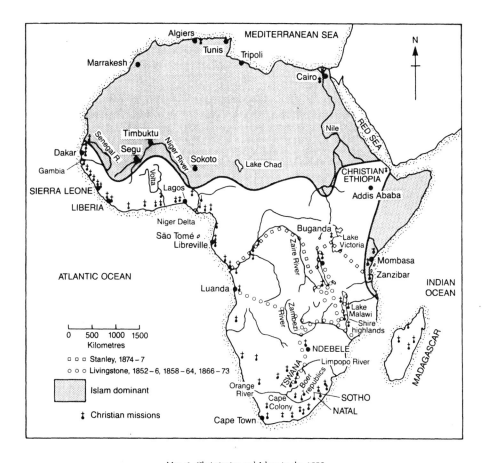

Map 6. Christianity and Islam in the 1880s

powerful enough to retain power permanently. However, in the modern Republic of South Africa, there are 4.9 million people of European descent. Although greatly outnumbered by a black population of 23.9 million (and 2.9 million 'Coloured'), they succeeded for generations in controlling resources and power. Race and class have been inextricably linked, and Christians have responded to this in very different ways.

South Africa 1800 to 1900: an overview

In 1911—when there were over 30 missionary societies and 1650 missionaries there—it was said that 'South Africa may well claim to being, with the possible exception of the South Sea Islands, the best occupied mission field in the world'.[2] However, for much of the nineteenth century, the missionaries often had curiously little success. Moffat admitted that he had fewer Christians than fruit trees, and Livingstone became an explorer largely because he was discouraged by the lack of converts in his southern Tswana mission station. Those who became Christians were often ostracized or punished, yet they also experienced discrimination from their white co-religionists. An African Methodist said in 1863, 'to the natives we are but despised believers—to the English we are no more than Kaffirs'.[3]

European missionaries shared a common culture, and, sometimes, a common language with white settlers, and the latter were an important potential source of funds. It was difficult, in these circumstances, to maintain a critical attitude to white injustice, but many did so. Some bodies, such as the LMS, maintained a primarily mission identity. This was more difficult for Methodists and Anglicans, who also needed to cater for white settler needs. In modern times, the liberal Christian tradition in South Africa has been tried in the balance and found wanting, but it spoke against oppression at a time when few other voices were to be heard.

The missionary enterprise in South Africa is often dated from the arrival of the first LMS representative, van der Kemp, in 1799, although a few Moravians did, in fact, precede him. Christianity took root most readily among the uprooted: the Griqua of the frontier, the Mfengu who fled from their homes during the Mfecane. In Natal and Zululand, Christians remained marginal. Warlike rulers, such as the Zulu or Ndebele kings, tended to tolerate missionaries, for diplomatic and other reasons, but prevented large-scale conversions. Moshoeshoe invited members of the Paris Evangelical Missionary Society to Lesotho in 1833, again, for largely economic and diplomatic reasons. A reformer who was well-disposed to Christianity, he sought baptism on his death bed. A number of Tswana rulers became Christians, of whom the most famous was Kgama, who ruled the Ngwato from 1875 to 1923. Even so, by the middle of the twentieth century, many Tswana were still traditionalists.

South Africa: the context

The Cape and Natal are well-watered, thanks to rainbearing winds from the sea, and it was the combination of adequate rainfall and a temperate climate that originally attracted white settlement. To the West of the Drakensberg mountains, and the highlands of Lesotho, lies the High Veld (see Map 5), grasslands suited to pastoralism. Rainfall diminishes as one travels West, towards the Kalahari and Namibia. The first inhabitants of southern Africa were the Khoi ('Hottentots'), and San ('Bushmen'), light-complexioned peoples, speaking related, but otherwise, unique click languages. The former were pastoralists, the latter hunter-gatherers. The San created South Africa's glorious heritage of rock art, and modern research has praised their lifestyle, their varied and ample diet, and their abundant leisure. In the seventeenth century, perhaps 20 thousand San, and between 100 thousand and 200 thousand Khoi lived south of the Orange River. By 1800, they were decimated, partly by violence, but, above all, by introduced diseases, especially smallpox. They were too few in numbers to resist white settlement effectively, and became its victims. As a white settler said in 1825, 'At present they have scarcely any choice but of predatory warfare and precarious existence, or servitude to the Boers. The only certainty they have is the desert and the best parts even of it are taken from them'.[4] A Khoi told Robert Moffat why he never visited the mission station:

> I have been taught from my infancy to look upon Hat men (hat-wearers) as the robbers and murderers of the Namaquas. Our friends and parents have been robbed of their cattle, and shot by the hat-wearers.[5]

It was once a cherished legend of the white South African community that the Bantu crossed the Limpopo at much the same time as the first white settlers reached the Cape. It was demolished by archaeological research, which established the arrival of iron-using Bantu in South Africa from at least AD 200, and, perhaps, earlier. Their striking terracotta sculptures, dating from the fifth and sixth centuries AD, have been found in the eastern Transvaal. By the late eighteenth century, there were three major Bantu subgroups in Africa South of the Zambezi: the Herero of Namibia were untypical in their lifestyle in that they practised pastoralism, but not agriculture, and did not work iron; the Nguni lived on the coastal plain between the Drakensberg mountains and the sea, and the Sotho-Tswana inland, in the mountains and on the High Veld. These were linguistic rather than social groupings, and they had much in common, including a passionate attachment to cattle.

Mfecane is a Zulu word that means grinding. It is conventionally used[6] for a great complex of migrations that had their origins in wars among the northern Nguni in the late eighteenth century. Their causes are disputed, and some emphasize the role of European trade in slaves and ivory, but it is clear that the background was, at least in part, ecological, the pressure of an expanding population hemmed in between the mountains and the sea. To the South, expansion was prevented by another group of pastoralists, hungry for cattle and land: the Afrikaners. The southernmost Nguni, the Xhosa, were driven back across the Fish River, which became a boundary between white and black pastoralists. The need both communities had for land led to a series of wars, which some have called a Hundred Years War.

The Zulu built up a powerful military state among the northern Nguni under Shaka, who met a violent end in 1828. Refugees fleeing South became the Mfengu (the name means 'beggars'), who enthusiastically adopted

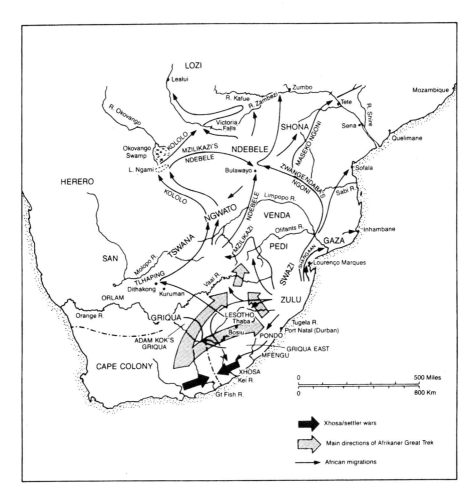

Map 7. Movements of peoples in Southern Africa c. 1820–1840

modernity in all its guises, including Christianity, education, and commercial agriculture.

The Ndebele were a Zulu-related group who fled to the High Veld in 1821, led by Mzilikazi (*d.* 1868). After wars with Griqua, Tswana, and *Voortrekkers*, they moved North to what is now the Republic of Zimbabwe..

The Kololo were a Sotho people who fled in 1822 from their war-stricken homeland, and settled in the fertile plains of the Upper Zambezi, conquering the Luyana kingdom. They were soon overthrown by their subjects, but their language survived.

Migrant Nguni warriors founded the Gaza kingdom in Mozambique, and smaller states in Malawi and southern Tanzania, the latter adopting the name Ngoni.

In the mountains of Lesotho, Moshoeshoe created a new social order on the ruins of a world in collapse. He became famous for his welcome to the various forces of modernity, including Christianity, as did the rulers of most of the Tswana states. Ngwane (later Swaziland) was also founded as a result of the Mfecane.

The genesis of the European presence

From 1600 on, ships sailing to India stopped at the Cape to replenish their stores and water. In 1652, the Dutch East India Company founded a permanent station there. At first it was a small enclave around Cape Town, but it later became a colony. Dutch settlers came and farmed in the vicinity. By 1710, there were about 2 thousand of them, and rather more slaves. The modern Afrikaners are descended from this quite small eighteenth-century population.

Slaves were first introduced in 1658. They were predominantly Malagasy or Malay. Indeed, the people who call themselves Cape Folk ('Cape Coloured') have Dutch, Khoi, and Malay/Malagasy forebears. Their owners often opposed their baptism as Christian slaves could not be sold, and had some claim to manumission. In 1772, a visitor to a farmhouse found the women slaves singing psalms:

> Their master . . . had prevailed with them to adopt this godly custom; but with the spirit of economy which universally prevails among these colonists, he had not permitted them to be initiated into the community of Christians by baptism; since by that means . . . they would have obtained their freedom.[7]

Not surprisingly, many slaves, especially in Cape Town, became Muslims instead.

By the early nineteenth century, the white population comprised the urban dwellers of Cape Town, the mixed farmers of the fertile western Cape, and the ranchers, *trekboers*, whose need for cattle and land brought them into conflict with African pastoralists, whose lifestyle was very similar to their own.

The Cape became a British colony in 1795, and, with a brief interlude, remained one. The first large influx of British settlers was in 1820; they were to be joined later by many other immigrants. The white population of twentieth-century South Africa was to consist of two distinct groups, the English-speaking people, and the Afrikaners.

During the nineteenth century, Dutch evolved into Afrikaans, the *Taal*, with African loan words and a simplified syntax. Christianity was an important dimension of Afrikaner identity, and, in the eighteenth century, it was often used as an ethnic term. It was said then that all Christians are called baas. They were Calvinists, though circumstances had differentiated their faith from its Dutch urban origins, and the religious life of the rural Afrikaner centred on the family. The circumstances of their nineteenth-century history forged a powerful myth of national identity, underpinned by religion.

Christianity and the Khoi

The first Christian missionary work took place among the victims of the Mfecane and of white settlement: the Khoi, the Mfengu, and the frontier Xhosa. Many Khoi died of imported diseases, were absorbed into the white community, or became its servants. The rigid Afrikaner emphasis on 'racial purity' came later; in the eighteenth century, many Europeans had Khoi partners, and it has been estimated that 7 per cent of the gene pool of modern Afrikaners originated outside Europe.[8]

Not all Khoi employed on Dutch farms were oppressed—almost as many Khoi servants as Afrikaner masters went on the Great Trek (see Map 8)—but they had exchanged freedom for servitude, and some suffered great cruelty. Some voted for freedom with their feet, and opted for the hardship and uncertainties of life on the frontier, where they developed a new identity as the Griqua.

When the slave trade was abolished, the settlers responded by formalizing the subjection of the Khoi. This was the so-called Hottentot Code, which compelled the Khoi to work on settler farms or join the Army, unless they were members of a mission village: 'Thus was poverty riveted in chains'.[9] Not the least of their sufferings was the way in which their culture was despised and marginalized. Van der Kemp once met a wandering Khoi 'who had heard from the Dutch colonists that God had not created him and therefore did not care about him'.[10] One writes of dialogue, and quotes fragments that seem to encapsulate different forms of encounter, but, very often, no true dialogue was possible because those concerned did not understand each other. A Xhosa elder said in the 1830s, 'He had gone once or twice [to hear the missionaries] but that he could not understand what they said, and he had therefore discontinued his visits, though he believed them to be a good kind of people who did him no harm'.[11] Only those who have attempted it can appreciate the difficulty of gaining fluency in a tonal language for which no textbooks exist.

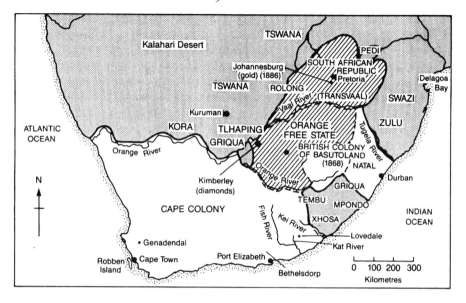

Map 8. European encroachment in Southern Africa, late 19th century

Some missionaries did this with great success, writing grammars and dictionaries, and translating the entire Bible, though not without blunders on the way. Moffat, translating 'the lilies of the field' invented a neologism, and wrote in Tswana, 'consider the tarantulas, which toil not'![12]

George Schmidt, a Moravian, was the first missionary to the Khoi.[13] He reached the Cape in 1737, and left seven years later, because of problems with the Dutch clergy over his right to baptize. Finding Khoi impossible to learn, he taught his people Dutch. In the evenings, he read them Zinzendorf's *Berlin Discourses*, and lectured on the theology of Paul's epistle to the Romans.[14] However bizarre his catechetics, the love and concern shone through. He died forty-one years later in Silesia, 'with a prayer for South Africa on his lips'.[15] When more Moravians arrived in 1792, they met one of his converts, an eighty-year-old Khoi woman called Helena, with a cherished Dutch New Testament.

Conversion to Christianity involved dislocation, a break from the traditions of the past, and it came more easily to those who had endured disruption already. The ethnically mixed communities of the South African frontier welcomed Christianity, a transition made more readily as the individuals that comprised these communities had already moved far from their original cultures.

The Orlam were a group of Khoi, and former slaves who escaped to the Orange River area in the late eighteenth century; their name is a Malay one. In the early nineteenth century, their leader was Afrikaner Jager,[16] who died in 1823, a Khoi who had once been a shepherd on a Cape farm, and driven to violence and flight by injustice. In colonists' eyes, he was an outlaw with a price on his head, and his people lived by cattle-raiding until he became a Christian. He became a devoted friend of the missionaries, and once embarked on an eight-week journey to transport the Moffats' possessions and stock.

Like so many African Christians, he was guided by a dream, where he climbed away from a chasm full of fire up a mountain, on the peak of which stood a shining figure: 'He at last reached the long-desired spot, which became increasingly bright, and when about to address the stranger, he awoke'.[17] His son, Jonker, went back to banditry.

The Griqua were another group of mixed descent who settled West of the junction of the Orange and Vaal rivers. The missionary, William Anderson, lived with them for twenty years from 1801.[18] The Griqua Republic, as it came to be called, had a written constitution and its own coinage. Its people at first relied on pastoralism and cattle-raiding, later turning to agriculture.

When Andries Waterboer, a mission teacher, became the elected leader of Griqua Town, he spent several evenings a week studying political science: 'Minos, Lycurgus and Solon', noted his mentor, 'were names unknown to him'.[19] To such communities, and people of mixed descent, Christianity offered a new mode of identity, a place on which to stand. In 1804, a man of mixed descent was asked to serve in the Army, and replied 'that he served Jesus Christ and none other'.[20]

The Griqua were Dutch-speaking Christians, essentially indistinguishable from the *trekboers* in everything but colour. Their small states were swallowed up by an advancing settler frontier.

The Moravians, who arrived in the late eighteenth century, were artisans, and founded a Christian village, which they called Genadendal, Valley of Grace. Settlers looked with approval on their teaching of practical skills. For decades, the missionaries continued to found such settlements, offering a sanctuary to the oppressed, the refugee, and the landless, but the price was a high one in that missionaries acquired vast tracts of land, and seemed indistinguishable from other settlers. They ruled their settlements autocratically, often excluding non-Christians from their land; because of the settlements' association with refugees and the marginal, Christianity seemed less attractive to surrounding peoples.

By 1850, on the Eastern Cape, 16 thousand Africans (in a population of some 400 thousand) lived at 32 mission stations.[21]

In 1799, Johannes Van der Kemp reached the Cape. A Dutchman in the service of the London Missionary Society, he was to earn the bitter hostility of the Afrikaners. He combined the Christian village tradition of the Moravians with a prophetic denunciation of settler injustice. Van der Kemp[22] was fifty when he arrived. A former Army officer, and physician, he led a wild life when young, and became a free thinker. However, a boating accident, where his wife and child were drowned, changed his life, and led him to become a missionary. He punctiliously informed the LMS of his chequered past.

Van der Kemp first worked among the Xhosa, but, because of the violence on the frontier, he soon devoted himself to the Khoi, establishing a Christian village at Bethelsdorp. It was often compared unfavourably with the Moravians' settlements; they may have had greater practical aptitudes, but they also had the merit, in settlers' eyes, that they were not outspoken critics of white injustice.

Van der Kemp seems to have welcomed privations, perhaps in a spirit of penance for his past. He was a man of great learning, who surrounded himself with recondite books, and gave a visiting missionary a Syriac New Testament! He suggested the holding of a world mission conference at the Cape, in 1810. It was eventually held a hundred years later, at Edinburgh.[23]

A number of early LMS missionaries, Van der Kemp among them, married Khoi or ex-slave wives, which earned them much obloquy at the time, and later. Inter-ethnic marriage is the litmus test of racial prejudice.[24] Van der Kemp's wife, Sarah, who was over forty years younger, bore him four children. She was part Malagasy, and, in his last years, he was torn between a new mission venture in Madagascar, or a shift to England for the sake of his children's education. He died in 1811.

The Christian community at Bethelsdorp was a small one, in which women predominated. Despite its size, its influence extended much further, through the agency of African missionaries. Cupido Kakkerlak was a Khoi who grew up on a Dutch farm, and was more at home in Dutch than in Khoi. He became a sawyer, achieving a modest prosperity. Converted at the age of forty, he moved to Bethelsdorp, and gradually became involved in full-time mission work. In 1817, he went to work among the nomadic Kora, then, six years later, the LMS dismissed him, at the age of sixty. Having paid him irregularly, or not at all, they condemned him to poverty.[25] A Xhosa ruler's son, Dyani (Jan Tshatshu), spent years at Bethelsdorp with his wife Noetha, and became a notable interpreter and preacher. 'Exhibited in London as the model convert',[26] he fell from missionary favour when he fought on his people's side in the 1846–7 war.

James Read was another LMS missionary who married a Khoi woman. His sons inherited their father's calling, and his daughters established an infant school on the Kat River. An artisan who was ordained in the mission field, Read earned the hostility of the settler community by his role in the Black Circuit of 1812, where Khoi servants were encouraged to bring cases against cruel and oppressive masters. Many, but not all, of the cases were thrown out. The Black Circuit has been debated by historians ever since, but the Khoi were not used to courts of law; neither were they among the judges. When, in 1829, the Cape Folk were given land at the Kat River, they chose James Read as their minister. It was the first independent black church, as distinct from mission, in South Africa. The Kat River settlers saw their move as an Exodus to a Promised Land, and named their schools after Wilberforce and Buxton. However, the settlement was destroyed three times in frontier wars, and from the last of these, in 1851, it did not recover.

John Philip (1777–1851), like Colenso after him, had achieved middle-class status before he came to Africa. The son of a handloom weaver, he became the popular minister of a Dissenting congregation in Scotland. In 1819, despite the protests of his flock, he went to South Africa at the request of the LMS to deal with a crisis. He remained there, 'the Protestant Pope', until his death. The problems he was sent to solve revolved around the conflict between the settler community and their missionary critics. Philip was destined to criticize oppression with much greater political effect. His starting point was an empirically-based belief in the equality of black and white:

> So far as my observation extends, it appears to me that the natural capacity of the African is nothing inferior to that of the European. At our schools, the children of Hottentots, of Bushmen, of Caffres, and of the Bechuanas, are in no respect behind the capacity of those of European parents; and the people at our missionary stations are in many instances superior in intelligence to those who look down on them as belonging to an inferior caste.[27]

Philip opposed both slavery and the Hottentot Code. As the former was under effective attack from abolitionists in England, he concentrated on the latter, which was repealed in 1828 by the celebrated Ordinance 50. In that year, he published his *Researches in South Africa*, an indictment of white settler oppression.[28] He won the enduring hostility of the settler community, which was intensified when he espoused the cause of the Xhosa.

Like other missionaries of his time, Philip believed that he had the right to change the lifestyles and beliefs of whole communities; but he advocated freedom of opportunity within the colonial situation, because: 'By locating them [tribes] on a particular place, getting them to build houses, enclose gardens, cultivate corn land, accumulate property, and by increasing their artificial wants, you increase their dependency on the colony. . . .'[29] To modern radicals, he leaves a great deal to be desired as a prophet of social justice, but he resolutely opposed the interests of his fellow Europeans, and fought against social oppression, as he understood it.

The Xhosa: prophets and improvers

The war with the British in 1811 was fought with a level of bloodshed and destructiveness that had no precedent in Xhosa experience. The British sought to expel Xhosa living west of the Fish River, and the expedition was deliberately timed to destroy standing crops. The Xhosa realized that the settlers could, and would advance further: '. . . only one river more, the Nxuba (Fish) and then they will be in our land. What will become of you then?'[30]

In this crisis, prophets took over effective leadership from chiefs. Nxele advocated war against the whites, and ended his life attempting to escape from Robben Island. Ntsikana was a mystic and hymn writer. They both foreshadowed the ways in which black South African Christians have responded to an unjust society. The prophetic churches retreat inwards, into a world of liturgical innovation and individual healing. The theologians of liberation say society must be radically changed, and some Christians take up arms.

Because Nxele grew up on a Boer farm, where he learned Dutch and acquired a knowledge of Christianity; he was well suited to being an intermediary between the two cultures.[31] At first, he preached orthodox Christianity, but, in 1812, he went through the ecstatic experiences of a Xhosa diviner. In time, he called himself the younger brother of Christ. He also summoned a crowd to witness the resurrection of the dead and the destruction of witches. Neither happened, but, as on so many comparable occasions, his standing was not affected. He drew closer to the model of diviner, abandoning monogamy, and wearing red ochre.

In 1819, after a further British invasion, he led his people to war. He had come to see the world as the scene of a battle between the God of the whites and the God of the blacks. The latter should be worshipped in dancing, the enjoyment of life and in love, so that blacks would fill the earth, and not 'to sit and sing M'de-e, M'de-e all day and pray with their faces to the ground and their backs to the Almighty'.

The Xhosa attack ended in disaster: Nxele was captured, and sent to Robben Island, like so many political prisoners after him. He drowned during an attempt to escape.

Nxele's rival, Ntsikana, moved towards Christianity instead of away from it. He began with a Xhosa mystical experience, which revolved round his favourite ox. Unlike Nxele, he was drawn to give up ochre and traditional dancing, and to send away all wives but one. He said that there were, indeed, two Gods, but they were Father and Son. He opposed the war of 1818, and wrote a magnificent hymn, which is still sung today:

He is the one who brings together herds which oppose each other,
He is the leader who has led us,
He is the great blanket which we put on.[32]

When death was near, in 1821, he asked his family to bury him in the Christian manner. When they were reluctant, he took a spade and turned the first sods. His memory is still cherished among the Xhosa as that of a saint to whom Christian teachings were independently revealed.[33]

In 1850, another warrior prophet led the Xhosa against the settlers,

Mlanjeni. He claimed that 'he had been to Heaven and had talked to God who was displeased with the white man for having killed his Son. . . . God would help the black man against the white'.[34] However, the Xhosa were defeated, and much of their land was alienated. To these afflictions was added the catastrophe of bovine pleuropneumonia, which killed many of their cherished cattle. In 1856, two Xhosa girls, sixteen-year-old Nongqawuse, and a companion, went out to chase the birds from the fields. They met two ancestors, who gave them a message for their people:

> Tell them that the whole nation will rise from the dead if all the living cattle are slaughtered because these have been reared with defiled hands, since there are people about who have been practising witchcraft.[35]

This vision, disseminated by Nongqawuse's uncle, a Christian convert, combined Christian and traditional Xhosa elements.[36] The sequel was catastrophic: some 400 thousand cattle were killed, and 40 thousand Xhosa starved to death. Many of the survivors were forced to look for work in the Cape Colony. Many widows urged their sons to kill their cattle in the vain hope that this act would retore their husbands to life: 'It is all very well for you, Sandile. You have your wives and children, but I am solitary'.[37] The Xhosa had inflicted on themselves the total defeat that the settlers had been unable to achieve.[38]

The Improvers recognized that it was hopeless to attempt to overthrow the whites by force of arms. They believed that by mastering western education, they would earn equality. Experience was to teach them, however, that equality would still be denied them.

Tiyo Soga (1829–71) is the prototype of South Africa's Improvers, a man whose devotion to Christianity was transparent. He was the son of one of Ntsikana's supporters, reputed to be the first Xhosa to use the plough and practise irrigation.[39] Soga studied at Glasgow University, and was ordained a minister of the United Presbyterian Church. He returned to South Africa in 1857 with his Scottish wife, Janet.

Although his health was undermined by tuberculosis contracted during his years in Scotland, he worked devotedly among the Xhosa until his premature death. He translated the first part of Bunyan's *Pilgrim's Progress*, a task that his son completed. There is a sad significance in the fact that the first-published work in Xhosa by a Xhosa was a translation of a foreign original. The Improvers had not yet discovered their own authentic voice. Bunyan's Christian, is the archetypal individualist, whose search for salvation leads him to forsake both family and community, the life situation of so many early African Christians.

Soga crystallizes the ambiguities and anguish of the first generation of educated black Christians. He was devoted to the (British) royal family, and spoke of Scotland as 'home', but he and Janet were rejected by many whites, and by many Xhosa. Also, when he sent his sons to Scotland, in an attempt to protect them from South African racial prejudice, he advised them. '. . . take your place in the world . . . as Kafirs, not as Englishmen'.[40] After his death, Janet remained at Mgwali mission station.

The Afrikaners

The Afrikaners, like so many other pastoralists in southern Africa, embarked on the series of migrations their descendants were to call the Great Trek in search of a new home. In the process, they forged a sense of national identity, where religion was a central component. They saw themselves as a *Volk* in exodus, a chosen people of God, who survived because of His special care for them. Some wanted to call the state they hoped to found, 'the new Eden'.

Before leaving, Piet Retief published a *Manifesto* in which he complained of vagrant Khoisan, the abolition of slavery, Xhosa conflict, and 'the unspeakable odium which has been cast upon us by interested and dishonest persons, under the cloak of religion. . . .'[41] Others felt the same way. Anna Steenkamp wrote of the slaves, 'It is not their freedom that drove us to such lengths, as their being placed on an equal footing with Christians, contrary to the laws of God and the natural distinction of race and religion . . . wherefore we withdrew in order to preserve our doctrines in purity'.[42]

In 1838, Afrikaners in Natal won a bloody victory over a Zulu army. It is of the essence of the nation's tragedy that the Battle of the Blood River (see Map 8) became not only part of the mythology of Afrikaner nationalism, but an annual celebration. Through conflict with powerful African states—the Zulu and the Ndebele—their racial attitudes hardened. Between 1846 and 1853, Livingstone worked among the southern Tswana, and there bore witness to the development of a violent and exploitative racism among the Afrikaner frontiersmen:

> In their own estimation, they are the chosen people of God, and all the coloured race are 'black property' or 'creatures'—heathen given to them for an inheritance . . . the boers feel themselves insecure . . . the direct vengeance appears to the most mildly disposed among them a simple measure of self-defence.[43]

Some of the Trekkers, the Doppers, were extremely conservative Puritanical Calvinists, and believed that their journeys were charted by the prophet Joel and would end in the discovery of a New Jerusalem, which is a dream strangely close to that of the *ama-Ziyoni*, the Zulu People of Zion. The Voortrekkers founded two new branches of the Dutch Reformed Church: the Hervormde Kerk in the Transvaal (1853), and a church established in 1859, in the Dopper tradition. It has been suggested that the ultimate wellsprings of apartheid are to be found in these frontier churches.

The Afrikaners founded two small states (the South African Republic), in the Transvaal and the Orange Free State. They were economically weak, and relied on pastoralism, much like their African neighbours. The history of South Africa was transformed by the discovery, first of diamonds in 1867, and then of gold in 1886. From being, in global terms, an economic backwater, South Africa became of crucial importance to industrial capitalism. The discoveries led to the growth of new cities, and of the railway network. The spread of British imperialism was to swallow up the Boer republics, and those African states that still remained independent.

Natal and the Mfengu

When the British annexed Natal in 1842, most of the Afrikaners left for the High Veld; the white settler population in Natal, which numbered 14 thousand in 1863, has been mainly British ever since. When the Afrikaners first moved into Natal, many of its original inhabitants had fled from its violence and insecurity. As they returned, they soon outnumbered the white settlers, this situation often producing racism as intransigent as that of the Afrikaners.

Theophilus Shepstone, in charge of 'native policy' from 1853 to 1875, maintained white hegemony by constructing a largely artificial mosaic of tribal jurisdictions, which were a forerunner of modern Bantustans.

Into this complicated situation came a great influx of missionaries: Methodists, German and Norwegian Lutherans, the French Oblates of Mary Immaculate (who made no converts in Natal at all), the Anglicans (destined to be riven by a spectacular schism), Scottish Presbyterians, and members of the American Board of Missions. Despite their efforts, relatively few Africans were converted. Indeed, in 1880, there were fewer than 10 thousand African Christians in Natal. Some were forced to live on mission stations as a result of their need for land, for many Natal Nguni, displaced by Shaka's wars, returned to find their homes swallowed up by settler farms. Others who were drawn to the missions were disabled by disease, or age, or accused of witchcraft. A Zulu diviner gave the missionaries his little son, and, with him, two cows for his support: '. . . his position is one of peril and it was that consideration made him give the boy to me. I wish, he said, to have at least one child in safety'.[44]

The Mfengu, as we have seen, were northern Nguni who, in the 1820s and 1830s, fled South from Zulu expansion, and lived among the Xhosa as clients. They were invited by the British to settle as peasant farmers West of the Kei river, as a buffer group between the Xhosa and the Colony. Uprooted from their homes, they turned willingly to Christianity and western ways, and fought for the Colony in frontier wars. They pioneered commercial agriculture, and many other African farmers followed, adopting the plough, cultivating wheat, selling wool, and competing successfully with white farmers at agricultural shows:[45] 'Man for man the Kafirs of these parts are better farmers than the Europeans.'[46] Missionaries encouraged this growth of peasant agriculture, indeed, the first missionary to the Ngqika took with him plough, harrow, and spades. Not all peasants were Christians, but the new technology (and also new diseases) spread in ever-widening ripples from mission settlements. Later, the position of the African peasantry was to decline, largely because of white demands for land and labour.

The implications of all this were far reaching. The introduction of the plough changed the traditional gender division of labour, for men did the ploughing, whereas women were previously responsible for hoe cultivation. Polygamy, therefore, became less important as a way of obtaining labour.[47] Also, education often produced divisions between parents and children. Henry Callaway spoke with a man who had sent his children to school: 'I took him into the schoolroom and showed him the children learning to read, write and cypher . . . he was much pleased, and went away very happy, but said, as he was departing, "my children will never come back to me"'.

The Mfengu's enthusiasm for Christianity is a good example of the way in which social disruption readily produced a change in religious beliefs, but there were also Christians who had nothing to gain by conversion, and lived their new faith with transparent devotion. In the 1870s, a Methodist woman at Mtwalume gathered a congregation of her own, while, in 1880, an old couple, also Methodists, went out on a preaching tour from Ladysmith, returning with twenty women converts.

Very often, Christianity and westernization came in the same package, so that Africans, like the Natal chief who said he 'should like to see practical industrial schools, more than the religious', were not allowed to select the elements they desired. Society was divided between the 'red people,' whose ochre symbolized their adherence to tradition, and the 'school people', whose life situation was symbolized by their western dress. One of the former said in 1848:

> I am a believer. I do not like others who profess to believe, come to the station, put on clothes, and deceive you by saying I am a Christian when I am not. But I live at my kraal, go without clothing and believe with my heart, my religion does not consist in clothing myself, for God does not take notice of these things . . . God looks at the heart.[48]

The Zulu and Ndebele kingdoms

As with warlike nations elsewhere, the Zulu and Ndebele sought to profit from the presence of missionaries, while limiting their impact. In a dangerous world, missionaries had much to offer. They often acted as scribes and go-betweens, and were thought to attract trade. They could act as advisers, explaining the powerful Other to African rulers faced with pressures that had no precedents. The first missionary endeavours among the Zulu were undermined by the latter's wars with the Afrikaners. Successive Zulu kings tried to benefit from the services missionaries could render them, while avoiding the creation of an *imperium in imperio*. In 1843, Mpande summed up the difficulties:

> The missionary came to me, and I welcomed him, and allowed him to select a location where he pleased. He built there. I told the people to go to meetings and attend to his instructions. But the people soon began to call themselves the people of the missionary, and refused to obey me.[49]

Very few Zulu became Christians, largely because converts were, in effect, excluded from Zulu citizenship as mission congregations consisted largely of Christians from Natal and mission employees.

The Ndebele originally fought in the Zulu army. In 1828, a regiment under Mzilikazi, which may have numbered only 300, fled to the Transvaal. The new state grew rapidly, absorbing both local people and further refugees from Zululand, but its survival was imperilled, not only by the Zulu, but by immigrant Griqua and *Voortrekkers*. In this situation, Mzilikazi sent diplomats to Robert Moffat at Kuruman. Moffat returned the visit, and a striking friendship developed between the two. In 1837, Mzilikazi led his people to a lasting home in what is now western Zimbabwe. Again, they absorbed many of the indigenous people, and a hierarchical, three-tiered social structure developed.

In a sense, the Ndebele were predisposed to religious change. They had left behind the sacred places of their original homeland, (including the royal graveyards where rain was made), and they showed a striking willingness to absorb the religious concepts of the African peoples they encountered. In 1829, Mzilikazi told Moffat that their High God was *Molimo* (a Tswana word).[50] Later, they absorbed the Mwari cult from the Shona of Zimbabwe, but they remained hostile to Christianity. In 1859, four LMS representatives, among them Robert Moffat's son and grandson, settled among the Ndebele. One of these four pioneers, Sykes, stayed there until he died in 1887, and never won a single convert. Coillard, who spent four months at Lobengula's court in 1878, called their obduracy the most perplexing problem in modern missions.[51]

Lobengula, like many other Africans, believed that God had given each people the culture he intended for them:

> . . . he believed God had made all things as he wanted them. He had made all people and that he had made every country and tribe just as he wished them to remain, he believed God made the Amandebele as he wished them to be and it was wrong for anyone to seek to alter them.

He attempted to correct missionary misunderstandings: 'We do not believe that the killing of an ox or burning particular herbs makes rain, but these are the means by which we ask it, just as you ask it by reading your book and saying prayers'.

When a missionary preached a sermon on human equality, an angry king told the interpreter to stop such lies. Ndebele were afraid of being accused of disloyalty, or being blamed for disasters, especially in the light of Lobengula's well-known predilection for executing his opponents as witches.

The arrival of the first missionaries in 1859 was followed by a series of afflictions, including bovine pleuropneumonia, and the Ndebele sang:

> This wind whence comes it?
> From Moffat from Kuruman.

In 1886, Ndebele said, 'We like to learn and hear about God and His Word but if we say openly that we belong to King Jesus, then we shall be accused of disloyalty to Lobengula and of Witchcraft and killed'.[52]

Most missionaries welcomed the overthrow of the Zulu and Ndebele kingdoms, and it was only after their conquest that their enterprise began to succeed. In 1898, it was said of the Ndebele, 'The impression I received from the old men was that if power were ever to come back to their scattered and conquered race it was not by way of guns or spears or shields, but through the channels of teaching and educating their children'.

Inja Mhlope, a former diviner, became an enthusiastic schoolmaster. He was not the only converted diviner; Sitjumi and his son prayed 'to God to give them something more durable and profitable than the wretched bones'. Muyengwa Khumalo, Lobengula's cousin, in her old age became 'the pillar of our Church' among the Methodists of Tegwani. Gambo (*d.* 1917), was a Ndebele chief who had been exiled among the Tswana, and was influenced by Kgama; his son became a pupil at Lovedale. He supported the whites in the 1896–7 rising, but never became a Christian. He said he was like an ox whose horns have long grown backwards, and cannot change direction.[53] Rachel Masinga was born in 1895; she grew up in Natal, the child of Christian Zulu parents, and became a schoolteacher. She came to work among the Ndebele with a conscious sense of missionary vocation, and, at the age of 21, was one of the founders of a girls' boarding school.

The Shona

Lobengula prevented the establishment of a mission among the Shona. Coillard, who worked among the Lozi after decades in Lesotho, had originally hoped to reach the Shona, but could not overcome Ndebele opposition: 'Where shall we go raiding if the Banyai [Shona] have missionaries?'[54]

The term 'Shona' was Ndebele in origin, and was first adopted by the Shona themselves from the 1890s onwards. Previously, they had had no sense of common identity, and identified themselves by local names, such as Karanga, Manyika, and Zezuru.

The Ndebele settled in the south west of the Zimbabwe plateau in 1840, exacting tribute from a clearly defined area. They absorbed many Shona people, who 'became Ndebele' in language and culture; the Nguni state of Gaza, in Mozambique did the same. An older historiography depicted the

Shona as hapless victims, and, in part, this was a justification for colonialism, which was seen as their 'rescue'. Some Shona paid the Ndebele tribute, and thus avoided raids, but many Shona communities remained untouched by Ndebele or Gaza.

In the great rising of 1896–7, some Shona communities fought the white invaders, and others took no part. Spirit mediums played a major role in the war, remembered as *chiMurenga*, after the praise name of one of them.[55]

The LMS, as we saw earlier in this chapter, pioneered missions among the Ndebele; Anglicans did likewise among the Shona. They arrived in 1891, although it was five years before they baptized their first convert. The pioneers included both Europeans and African volunteers from South Africa. Among the latter were the Mpondo priest, Hezekiah Mtobi, and the catechist, Bernard Mizeki. Mtobi became insane, and left Mashonaland in 1901, another victim of the acute stresses endured by one who stands between two worlds.[56]

Mizeki was killed in the 1896 rising, apparently for felling trees in a sacred grove. He came from Inhambane, and became a Christian when he worked in Cape Town. He acquired perfect fluency in Shona, and married a Shona woman. When he set out for the mission field, he said, 'Why should I be afraid? . . . Mashonaland is no further from heaven than Cape Town'.[57]

The Tswana

In the early nineteenth century, the major Tswana peoples were the Kwena, the Ngwato, the Ngwaketse, the Kgatla, and the Tawana. Like the Sotho, they suffered enormously as successive groups, displaced by the Mfecane, invaded their homeland, as did the *trekboers*. 'Mosilikatze was cruel to his enemies, and kind to those he conquered', said the Tswana, 'but . . . the Boers destroyed their enemies and made slaves of their friends'.[58]

Like many other African peoples, they hoped that a missionary presence would lead to secular advantages, such as increased trade.

Livingstone, who began his missionary career among the Kwena, said, 'Wherever a missionary lives, traders are sure to come; they are mutually dependent, and each aids the other'.[59] When the first missionary appeared, at the end of 1816, the Thlaping said that he could settle if '*he would not preach or teach*',[60] but that they did not want to be like the Griqua, 'who once wore a corrass, but now wear clothes, once had two wives, now one, this . . . the Boochuannas will never submit to'.[61]

Often, missionaries and Africans appeared to live in much the same intellectual universe. Missionaries criticized traditional rainmakers, but were not averse to praying for rain, and to taking credit when a drought broke. This kind of argument was a two-edged sword: the Kwena blamed Christianity for drought when Livingstone first worked among them, 'we never get rain, while those tribes who never pray as we do obtain abundance. This was a fact . . .'.[62]

Like the Khoi before them, many Tswana were alienated by the violence and racism of white Christians. In 1845, it was said, 'Formerly to be baptized was to be hated and despised by all men, but now it is an honour to be called a Christian'. However, when Christian *Voortrekkers* from the Transvaal invaded the area, attitudes changed, and Livingstone noted in 1851, 'There are no candidates, no conversions'.[63]

In the late nineteenth, and early twentieth century, Christian kings, such as Kgama, made Christianity a national religion, though Christians were still in a small minority. Rulers, Christian and non-Christian, made every effort to maintain their own control over the Church, hence their penchant for preaching sermons: 'The Chief [Kgama] thinks that one church brings the people together and binds them to one another and all to their Chief'.[64]

Robert Moffat (1795–1883) was originally a gardener. He reached Cape Town in the service of the LMS at 21, and worked in Africa until he was 74. He and his wife established a mission station at Kuruman, a site selected because of its springs. They created a flourishing oasis, abounding in fruit and vegetables, but it was not a major centre of population, and the Christian community was a small one. His life's work was the translation of the Bible into seTswana.

He met the young Livingstone during a visit to England, made to supervise the publication of his translation. Livingstone had already chosen a missionary career, and he now decided that it should lie in Africa rather than China. He married the Moffats' eldest daughter, and ran a mission station among the Kwena, until, frustrated by the lack of converts, he came to feel that his true vocation lay in exploration. The Kwena ruler, Sechele, was candid about the factors that attracted him to Christianity: 'his reasons were, a missionary could help him in sickness, mend his gun, teach him to read and 'nthuta botlale [teach me wisdom].'[65] Sechele turned to Christianity and modernization with single-minded enthusiasm:

> . . . he set himself to read with such close application that from being comparatively thin, the effect of being addicted to the chase, he became corpulent from want of exercise. He acquired the alphabet on the first day of my residence at Chonuane . . . he has since, I am informed, become the missionary to his own people.[66]

Sechele was baptized in 1848, sending away all his wives but one, and renouncing rainmaking in a time of drought. He was soon expelled from the Church for resuming sexual relations with a former wife,[67] but remained an enthusiastic Christian. He was readmitted to the fold shortly before his death in 1892.

Missionary influence went far beyond individual conversions; Christian and western ideas, as we have seen, caused major changes in the social fabric. Irrigation on the Kuruman pattern gradually made the rainmaking role of the ruler superfluous. Missionaries who spoke with enthusiasm of the Good Shepherd were hostile to herding, the traditional male occupation. They favoured commercial agriculture instead, and advocated private enterprise.

Kgama, who ruled the Ngwato from 1875 to 1923 (and for a brief period earlier), became, in European eyes, the very archetype of the Christian gentleman, and there were also Christian rulers in some other Tswana polities. The price paid, among the Tswana as elsewhere, was a people divided. In 1878, the Thlaping complained, 'We accepted the Word of God in our youth . . . but we did not know all that was coming behind it'.[68] The division between Kgama and his father was so bitter that it led to civil war.

The Tswana kings prudently avoided denominational conflict, allowing only one missionary society in each kingdom, and prohibiting the formation of independent churches. Thus, in 1879, when Jesuits wished to work in the same area as the LMS, Kgama turned them down: 'If the two religions, the Catholic and the Protestant, are the same, we clearly need only one of these two. If they are different, there will be constant conflict between them and they will cause division among my subjects'.[69] Until the twentieth century, the LMS reigned supreme in all the Tswana kingdoms but one; the Dutch Reformed Church had a monopoly among the Kgatla.

Observance of the Sabbath was compulsory. Kgama always wore western dress, and married only one wife. He encouraged monogamy, 'but my words seem to be unwelcome to the people'. He also tried, unsuccessfully, to prohibit the consumption of alcohol. In a time of famine, he ruled that none should be punished for killing another's sheep or goats. He prohibited the sale of cows, 'the fountain that yields a man wealth year after year'. Later, other Tswana rulers were to legislate against excessive woodcutting because 'the majority of green trees have been felled and used for wagons, etc., and our future generation will have no trees left'.

Traditional religion was modified by these events. We have noted the decline in rainmaking, one of the most important functions of a king. The initiation ceremonies, which had heralded the duration of new age grades, and which missionaries tended to condemn, were given up, beginning with the Ngwato in 1876, though age sets survived. Traditional planting and harvest festivals were readily given a Christian form. By the 1940s, the name and concept of the Christian God had replaced the traditional *Molimo*, and the ancestor cult had almost disappeared. Magic, which the churches condemned, still flourished, and only Kgama attempted to legislate against it.[70] By the early twentieth century, all the major Sotho and Tswana states had Christian kings; Christianity had become quasi-official, and various practices, such as the observance of Sunday, were legally enforced. However, the 1946 census showed that less than 20 per cent of the Ngwato and Tawana, and about 40% of the Kwena and Ngwaketse were Christians.[71]

Moshoeshoe of Lesotho (1786–1870)

In 1816, a diviner called Mohlomi died in Lesotho. During his initiation, he had a vision in which God told him, 'Go, rule by love, and look on thy people as men and brothers'. He urged the powerful to care for the poor, and to spare those accused of witchcraft. He said to the young Moshoeshoe, 'Let thy decisions be just. The law knows no one as a poor man'.[72] Other African societies have traditions of such figures; sometimes they foretell the shape of things to come, and sometimes they advocate a social ethic strikingly like that of Christianity. Are such stories examples of 'the invention of tradition', a way of inculturating novelty? Who can tell?

Mantsopa Makheta was a transitional figure, born in 1793, who lived to extreme old age. At the court of Moshoeshoe, she predicted events, made rain, and proclaimed both *Molimo* (the traditional Sotho high God) and a new intercessory divinity. At the end of her life she became a Christian.[73]

Moshoeshoe himself was not born to rule, but succeeded in creating a new state. He grew to adult life in a country destroyed by war. Lesotho was ravaged by the Ndebele, and other Nguni invaders: many of its people were killed, or starved to death, and some were reduced to cannibalism: 'Hunger . . . was the first cannibal, it' devoured us'.

Moshoeshoe established a capital on a flat-topped mountain and created a loosely structured kingdom, based largely on consent. Like many other nineteenth-century African rulers, he had a reforming vision that, in its origins, owed nothing to Christianity. He was totally opposed to cannibalism, and a lifelong foe of strong drink, cannabis, and even tobacco. He first restricted the death penalty, and then virtually abandoned it.[74]

In 1833, Moshoeshoe learned of the existence of missionaries from a visiting Griqua hunter, and invited them to visit him. Three Protestant Frenchmen, members of the Paris Evangelical Missionary Society, were already in Griqualand, seeking a mission field, so they responded promptly to this invitation. Like other African rulers, Moshoeshoe welcomed them, initially because of the Europeans' technological superiority, and because he needed allies against dangers that included not only the Nguni, but the advancing tide of Afrikaner settlement: 'It is enough for me to see your clothing, your arms, and the rolling houses in which you travel, to understand how much intelligence and strength you have. This country was full of inhabitants . . . wars have devastated it . . . I have been told that you can help us'.[75]

Like many other African rulers, he attended church, and added a sermon of his own. He encouraged the import of European goods, and, like many of his subjects, learned to ride and shoot. 'He is now', it was noted in 1843, 'particularly anxious to introduce the cultivation of all European vegetables and fruit trees.'[76] As among the Mfengu, there was a steady expansion of commercial agriculture. The Zulu and Ndebele kingdoms were military states, geared to conquest. Moshoeshoe, like Shaka, founded a kingdom, but, although he too fought wars on occasion, the political unity of Lesotho rested on consultation and diplomacy. 'Peace', he told a British governor of the Cape Colony, 'is like the rain which makes the grass grow, while war is like the wind which dries it up'.[77]

Moshoeshoe supported Christian burial practices, and, for a time, ended traditional initiation. He allowed two of his wives, who became Christians, to divorce him, and took a strong stand against the persecution of witches. Although many of his royal kinsmen took this step, he was never baptized, because, like so many African notables, he found monogamy impossible: he could not sustain the hospitality expected of him without the help of his wives, nor could he repudiate them without causing much individual hardship, and alienating their families.

Like the rulers of Buganda and of Zululand, he found that Christianity easily became a source of division. When a measles epidemic came, a diviner said, 'the children of Thaba Bosiu [his capital] die because Moshoeshoe is polluted and because the school of the *Moruti* [missionary] and the evening prayers offend the *barimo* [ancestral shades]'. In his last years, Catholic missionaries arrived, and he faced the complexities of their competing claims. He wished for baptism on his death bed, but died before it was administered.

Missions and imperialism

Recognizing that it was impossible to retain their independence, the Sotho and Tswana preferred British annexation to rule by white farmers or diamond magnates. A much-reduced Lesotho was taken over by the British in 1868, two years before the old King died; some of its best land, which the Sotho still mourn, was lost to the Afrikaner republic, the Orange Free State.

In the nineteenth century, free Sotho peasants experimented with technological improvements, and sold grain to Afrikaner pastoralists, and miners. Increasingly, the Sotho, like the Tswana, were forced to support themselves by working as migrant labourers on settler farms, or, in atrocious conditions, in the mines. In their eroding, and overcrowded homeland, the women, children, and old struggled on alone.

The diamond fields were in southern Tswana territory. The area became part of Cape Colony, and huge tracts of land were alienated to white farmers and mining magnates. Like the Sotho, the southern Tswana could survive only by working as migrant labourers. The northern Tswana fared better. Three Tswana kings, Kgama among them, travelled to London in 1895, and, largely as the result of their representations, the North became a British Protectorate, and, ultimately, modern Botswana.

Missionaries in general tended to support the extension of colonialism. They were motivated partly by the desire to eliminate abuses, such as the persecution of witches, and by the belief that when the cake of custom was cracked, people would be more readily converted, as proved to be the case.

In southern Africa, men such as John MacKenzie supported the extension of British rule because the alternative seemed to be the hegemony of Afrikaner farmers, or Cecil Rhodes' British South Africa Company. He believed that 'people who are living under English law are in a far more advantageous position as to the reception of the Gospel than when they were living in their own heathen towns . . .'.[78] 'We invite John [Bull]'s attention to this delicious morsel of a gold field; let him spread it like jelly over Transvaal and Free State and Bechuana countries and swallow the lot.'[79]

The tradition of missionary advocacy of African causes was not wholly lost. John William Colenso became Bishop of Natal in 1863, and stayed there until his death in 1883. Led to doubt Moses' authorship of the Pentateuch, partly by Zulu questions, he was excommunicated for heresy in 1863. He appealed to the Privy Council, and retained both the title of bishop and control of church property in Natal, but was cut off from the Anglican Church in Natal as a whole, and from the SPG. He spent his last years defending the Zulu people. His children continued the struggle, especially his daughter, Harriette, who spoke fluent Zulu, and referred to 'we Zulu' in her letters. When the old Bishop died, the Zulu King, Cetshwayo, wrote of his wish 'that a stone may be bought in my name, which shall be set up over the grave of my Father, to show that we loved him in return for his so great love to us, and his efforts to deliver us out of our distress'.[80]

In 1906, there was violence once more in Natal: this followed resistance to an unjust poll tax. It was repressed with a harshness mirroring the anxieties of a white settler community that knew itself to be a perpetual minority. Most educated Africans stood aloof, knowing it could not succeed. The Zulu King, Dinizulu, took no part, but was exiled anyway. When asked at his trial if he was a Christian, he replied, 'I do not know who is a Christian in this country. It was only Christ who was a Christian'.[81] Some of the rebels were members of independent 'Ethiopian' churches:

> They had been taught by native preachers and evangelists that the whole of the holy Scripture pointed to the fact that the curse on the black race which was to keep them under, was now to be removed. . . . the witness examined them in their knowledge of Scriptures at length and he found that they were exceptionally well acquainted with the main facts, more especially of the Old Testament. . . .[82]

Dialogues of the heart

We have seen how language problems often created barriers to a true meeting of minds. A further obstacle was the failure of most missionaries to enter deeply into African worlds. 'Satan', said Moffat, after twenty years in Africa, 'has employed his agency with fatal success in erasing every vestige of religious impression from the minds of the Bechuanas, Hottentots [Khoi] and Bushmen [San]; leaving them without a single ray to guide them from the dark and dread futurity . . .'.[83] All three peoples have profound and complicated religious systems. A century later, an anonymous Tswana Methodist, a woman replies: 'We have learnt nothing new about religion from the missionaries. All they have taught us is *tlhabologo* [western civilization]'.[84]

This is not to say that dialogue did not exist. It existed in the hearts of individual Africans. It led to decisions that missionary narratives call 'conversion', or 'backsliding', or syncretism, and, often, to all three, at different times, in the life of the same individual: 'One suddenly remembered that he had heard the missionary say "we are all travellers, we are all going to *some* place" and the question rushed into his mind, "am I not a traveller? Where is my soul bound?" '[85] This profoundly moved the missionary who heard it in 1852. It reads like the beginning of a conventional hagiography, but this man ceased to be a Christian two years later.

Was the name of God in missionary discourse to be that of the withdrawn Creator God so typical of African cosmologies? If so, how did this shape perceptions? 'God' was translated into seSotho as the name of the traditional High God *Molimo*. The Ganda martyrs in East Africa died with the local equivalent, *Katonda*, on their lips. Setiloane suggests, with conscious iconoclasm, that Christian influences have impoverished traditional concepts of God. Certainly, there is much evidence of an African spirituality centred on 'God', rather than Jesus.

At one level, the encounter that took place was between a written and an oral culture. Sermons were repeated almost verbatim by the people who had listened to them, and Moffat, deep in the bush, was astonished to be told recognizable Bible stories by those who had heard them at second or third hand.

Traditional religion was, typically, rich in visual symbolism, and this formed a bridge between African and Christian cultures. Catholics cherished rosaries, crucifixes, and medals. Protestants scored a similar success in Natal with the Blue Ribbon of Temperance.[86]

We have emphasized the social determinants of conversion, but some were influenced by purely religious considerations. Etherington, analysing the known life histories of those who joined Natal mission stations, puts such conversions at 12 per cent![87] Nevertheless there were some, in southern Africa and elsewhere, who found in Christianity the end of a journey on which they had already embarked. A Sotho said, 'Your news is what I need, what I was seeking before I knew you'.[88]

It seems to have been, above all, the teaching of eternal life that drew converts in this category, though pastoralists asked, 'Why should not cattle rise as well as human beings? They have spirits . . .'.[89] When James Read told the Xhosa 'that women and all mankind would rise again from the dead, it caused uncommon joy among the Caffres. They said they should like to see their grandfathers, and others whom they mentioned. Congo enquired when it would happen, and if it would be soon, but Mr Read could not gratify his wishes on that point'.[90]

Not all were intimidated by, or attracted to the Christian's polarized vision of eternity; the Zulu, it was said, neither feared Hell, nor desired Heaven.[91] Sechele asked Livingstone why western Christendom had developed an interest in their eternal welfare so belatedly: '. . . my forefathers were living at the same time-yours were, and how is it that they did not send them word about these terrible things sooner?'[92]

The concept of original sin was alien to African peoples, though the occasional individual was drawn to conversion by a sense of guilt.[93] The dying Moshoeshoe chided the daughter of his old friend Eugène Casalis: 'You bad child, who said I was a sinner?'[94] In coastal Kenya, Krapf received a similar reproof from an old Mijikenda woman, perhaps motivated by the fear of witchcraft accusations: 'Who has been slandering me to you? I have a good heart, and know of no sin'.[95]

Some displayed a critical sense that was not far distant from the questioning of contemporary Biblical scholarship: 'How did those words get in the book you tell us about?'[96] Colenso was driven to reconsider the verbal inspiration of the Pentateuch by the enquiries of his Zulu assistant, William Ngidi.[97] Meeting the Biblical narratives for the first time, Africans often perceived moral difficulties to which missionaries had been oblivious: 'If David was eminently a good man, how should he have had so many and such bitter enemies? . . . How can his goodness be reconciled with his prayer for the destruction of his enemies? . . . In view of the Gospel is war ever justifiable?'[98] Pondering on an all-powerful and good God, and the existence of evil, the Xhosa asked why God did not convert the Devil.[99] Defoe put much the same question into the mouth of Man Friday.[100] Because of their experience of suffering and privation, some also questioned a loving Providence. The Ndebele asked, 'how could I say Jesus did only good things to us? Was it not he who sent the sun to burn their corn and grass and because of that they and their cattle were likely to die out of hunger?'[101]

Traditional African religion was life-affirming—the benefits it sought were long life, health, good crops, children, and protection from evil—but it offered little solace in times of famine or disease, and even the longest life must end. People groped for explanations of misfortune, and sometimes found them in the malice of witches. They explained their pain in a way that caused more pain. For example, the Xhosa aristocrat Gcaleka (*d.* 1778), who founded the lineage that bore his name, was a sickly man who tried to restore his health by killing witches; he did not get better, so he killed more. In the 1850s, when Xhosa cattle were dying of bovine pleuropneumonia, more witches were killed, but still the cattle died. Some farmers turned to Christianity in search of a superior spiritual technology that might succeed where all else failed. The missionaries encouraged this, attributing rain to prayer, and drought to unbelief: ' "Jesus Christ . . . is Lord of Heaven. I will speak to Him and He will give rain; I cannot." . . . The next day the Lord sent "plentiful rain" lasting two days'.[102]

Christians and ambiguity

Missionaries presented Christianity, as we have seen, in a particular cultural packaging, closely identified with literacy, so that 'reader' was a synonym for 'Christian'. They were advocates of rectangular houses and the plough, of private enterprise, and the creation of 'artificial wants'. It was a vision that ever-growing numbers of African teachers, pastors, skilled artisans, commercial farmers, and clerks came to share. The last African to hold a private diamond claim at Dutoitspan was a Lovedale graduate and Free Church of Scotland minister.[103] The famous educational complex at Lovedale, founded in the Ciskei in 1841 by the Glasgow Missionary Society, played an incalculably important role. Its teaching staff and student body were drawn from both blacks and whites and, by 1887, it had taught over 2 thousand Africans, 538 of them women.[104] Equally, the Improvers published newspapers in English, and in African languages, they affirmed their loyalty to Britain (the alternative was local settler hegemony), and they believed in the persuasive power of petitions and delegations. John Tengo Jabavu (1859–1921), who founded a famous Xhosa newspaper, was a fervent Methodist. Walter Rubusana, the only African ever elected to the Cape Provincial Council, was a Congregational minister, and John Dube, the first President of the South African National Congress, was a Methodist.[105] Although the Cape Colony franchise was colour blind, they tended to support white liberals rather than seek office themselves. Dube, at the Ohlange Institute, tried to make 'Anglo-Saxons of Africa'.[106]

Whether they joined the Ethiopian or mission churches, the Improvers were destined to a lifetime of ambiguity and pain. They identified enthusiastically with Christianity and European culture, but were often rejected by European Christians. When the First World War broke out, Rubusana offered to raise 5 thousand men, but the offer was rejected.

The legal edifice of discrimination grew ever stronger after the passing of the Natives' Land Act in 1913. Davidson Don Jabavu was a third-generation Christian, named by his famous father after a missionary. In 1920, he described his fellow Africans as 'landless, voteless, helots, pariahs, social outcasts in their fatherland with no future in any path of life'.[107]

A nascent literature in English, and in African languages crystallizes their ambiguity and suffering. We have noted Tiyo Soga's translation of Bunyan's *Pilgrim's Progress*. Thomas Mofolo wrote a Sotho adaptation of the same work, entitled *East-bound Traveller*. Its hero, Fekisi, begins by attempting to reform a Sotho society 'clothed in great darkness'. He fails, and leaves leSotho on a pilgrimage. After many perils, he reaches the sea, where he learns of Christianity from men 'white in color, with hair like a horse's mane'.[108] It is a symbolic exodus from his own society to the culture of the Other. Many, though, found disillusion at the ends of their journeys.

Jonas Ntsiko, a blind catechist from the Transkei, speaks for them. His poem, published in Xhosa in 1884, appeared, significantly, under a *nom de plume*:

> Some thoughts till now ne'er spoken
> Make shreds of my innermost being;
> And the cares and fortunes of my kin
> Still journey with me to the grave.
> I turn my back on the many shams
> That I see from day to day;
> It seems we march to our very grave
> Encircled by a smiling Gospel.
> And what is this Gospel?
> And what salvation?
> The shade of a fabulous spirit
> That we try to embrace in vain.[109]

The Ethiopian churches

The Ethiopian churches were founded as a protest against white domination, and the ceiling it imposed on the aspirations of African church employees, against the readiness with which Africans were expelled, especially for plural marriage, and against the growing segregation of black and white congregations. The denominational differences of European Christianity empowered Africans to make new choices of their own. White Christians understood little of this. A book published in 1931 even attributed the growth of the independent churches to the desire for clerical concessions on the railway![110]

Independency in South Africa began in 1872, when 158 Sotho Christians left the Paris Evangelical Mission in Hemon. They returned, as did many seceders after them; it was 'the beginning of that pernicious revolt against European guidance, now known as the Ethiopian movement'.[111]

The Tembu National Church was founded by Nehemiah Tile in 1884.[112] Like many later Ethiopians and Zionists, he was originally a Methodist. He fell out with the white missionaries over activities that included 'taking part in political matters, stirring up a feeling of hostility against magistrates in Tembuland, addressing a public meeting on a Sunday . . .'.[113]

In 1892, Mangane Mokone and others founded the Ethiopian Church, estranged from the Methodists by the fact that black and white met separately at a missionary congress.

Ethiopia's victory over Italy at the battle of Adowa in 1896 had, at least for the educated, a profound symbolic meaning that strengthened the Ethiopian cause. The Tembu Church soon joined it, but it was not the only independent church to be founded on ethnic lines. For early church leaders, as for early nationalists, it was by no means obvious whether the appropriate unit of action was the ethnic group, the colony, or something still larger.

In 1898, Pambani Mzimba founded an independent African Presbyterian Church. He was the first ordained minister at Lovedale, and two thirds of his congregation followed him. This blow to one of the core missions and educational institutions in South Africa had major repercussions.[114]

The Ethiopian churches were modelled on those their leaders had left, and were often little different from them, though they sometimes accepted plural marriage. Both the churches, and their individual members experienced a desire for respectability, for acceptance in a white-dominated world. In a sense, this limited their cultural creativity, and it was an impossible goal, for they could never match the financial resources, and international standing of the older churches.

One path to funds and recognition seemed to lie in affiliation to a black American Church. James Dwane left the Wesleyans when money he had raised in England for an African college was put into general Church funds. He went to America in 1897 to negotiate the affiliation of the Ethiopian Church to the African Methodist Episcopal Church, with the result that Bishop Henry Turner visited South Africa the following year. Turner recommended Dwane as a bishop, but the Church in America did not concur, and Dwane led a large section of the Ethiopian clergy to Anglicanism, as members of a newly created Order of Ethiopia. Dwane hoped for a bishopric, but was disappointed, and waited eleven years before he was even ordained.

Insofar as their goals were political, they were superseded by the African National Congress. Churches that began with disputes over authority were intrinsically prone to divisions over power and resources. In 1904, two representatives of the Ethiopian Catholic Church in Zion were interviewed by government officials.

What were you belonging to before?
To the AME Church.
And before that?
We belonged to the Church of England . . .
Why did you leave that Church . . .
When we found that we could not get ahead, Makone and myself came together to raise the Church of Ethiopia, and later on we joined the AME Church of America . . . as they had education and other things better than we had . . . so that they could help us, being coloured people themselves . . . but we found they helped us down, and they took all the best positions without telling us a word, sending men from America.[115]

Despite their internal differences, as conditions for South African blacks worsened, the islands of autonomy these churches represented seemed increasingly important. Between 1900 and 1904, AMEC was carried by clerks and other migrants to Basutoland, Bechuanaland, Swaziland, and Southern Rhodesia. The first attempt to introduce AMEC in Bulozi failed, but its representatives later returned, and, in the 1970s, it was the third largest Church in Zambia.

The Ethiopian churches were founded by and for the urban and educated, and their heyday was between 1880 and 1920. The circumstances that had led to their formation did not end then, though. In 1942, Job Chiliza (1886–1963) founded the African Gospel Church, breaking away from the (Pentecostal) Full Gospel Church. Later, he explained it all:

> The sad thing is that a European missionary does not really like to see us being blessed in our work. Instead, they grow envy inside. . . . I spoke to Rev. Cooper. My pastor and I are grown-up people. We need a constitution. They want a say in the Church. Then he said, you can go away.[116]

There was a basic dilemma that these churches never satisfactorily resolved. Their main appeal was to the educated and urbanized, so they were spread by clerks, artisans, or teachers. However, their lack of financial resources meant that they could not meet the needs of their aspiring members. Their ministers were paid less than their counterparts in mission churches, their schools faltered for lack of funds. Johnson's picture of AMEC in Zambia in the 1970s has a much wider applicability: '. . . composed of middle-aged people. Its educational standard, rate of literacy in English, and income levels are low. It is no longer the church of Zambia's élite . . . a slowly dying church'.[117]

A South African woman explained both their attractions and their limitations:

> The people are flocking to the African churches. They say the Europeans did them wrong, and they are now much happier among themselves. They say the Europeans only pretend to be Christians-all-of-us and oppress us . . . But even if it may be like that, the Church of England does lots of good. They help with the education of our children.[118]

The churches that flourished, and now count their adherents in millions, were not founded to protest against white hegemony, or enhance the career opportunities of African church professionals. Their prophets began with visions of an unseen world, and the quest for healing of mind and body. Looking towards an eternal city, they called themselves *ama-Ziyoni*, People of Zion.

❧ FIVE ❧

East and East Central Africa to c. 1900[1]

> The hippopotamus is child of the herd. He dives to the
> deepest waters, [because] the white sands [of the shallows]
> betray him.
>
> Lozi proverb[2]

Introduction

Christianity in eastern Africa had two great nineteenth-century successes: in
Madagascar, and Buganda. LMS representatives first reached Madagascar in
1820, and, in the decades that followed, Christianity flourished despite, or,
perhaps, because of, persecution.

The mission enterprise on the East African mainland began near Mombasa
in 1844, but had singularly little success: 'I often prayed fervently for the
preservation of my life in Africa', remembered Krapf, the pioneer, 'at least
until one soul should be saved'.[3] The tide turned only when missions were
founded deep in the interior, in Buganda, north of Lake Victoria, from 1877
on. In the decades that followed, some Ganda Christians, and Muslims,
embraced dreadful martyrdoms, and others left their homes to carry the
Christian message far afield; a classic instance of 'missionaries to yourselves'.

In 1861, a UMCA mission party followed Livingstone to the Zambezi. Like
the Niger Mission twenty years earlier, it was a failure, and the UMCA soon
abandoned the Zambezi for the Muslim island of Zanzibar. From this base,
new missions would be founded on the mainland, at Masasi in 1876, near the
modern Tanzania–Mozambique border, and at Likoma Island in 1885 in Lake
Malawi.

Livingstone died near Lake Bangweulu in 1873 and this inspired a
resurgence of mission interest in eastern Africa, just at the time when the Suez
Canal made it more accessible. The Free Church of Scotland established the
first Livingstonia on the southern shores of Lake Malawi in 1875. After several
changes of site, Livingstonia was destined to have much success among the
Tonga, and form many of Nyasaland's educated élite. But, on the whole,
Christianity had made little headway by the end of the century. Whole peoples

128

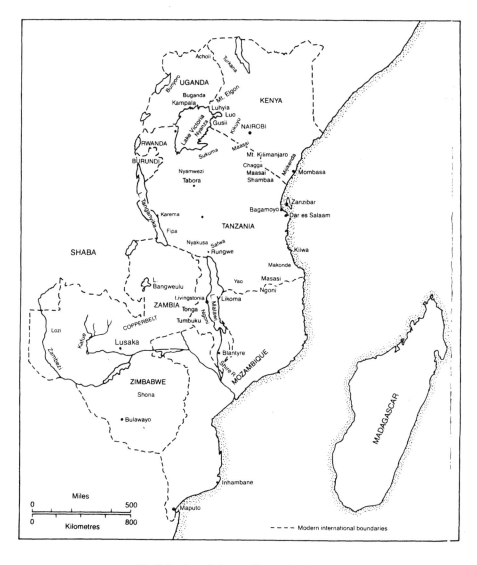

Map 9. Peoples and places in Chapters 5 and 9

129

had never heard the Christian message, and even in the areas of the most intensive evangelization, Christians were still in a minority. Buganda was an extraordinary success story, but less than half the Ganda were Christians in 1911. Often missions followed in the wake of colonialism, rather than preceding it, taking advantage of improvements in communications, and a widespread arousal of interest in western education. Here, as elsewhere, it was to be in the twentieth century, not the nineteenth, that Christianity became firmly established.

The background

Islam had been established since the fourteenth century, and probably longer, in the Swahili towns such as Kilwa, which stretched like jewels along the Indian Ocean's shore. Islam, literacy, houses of coral blocks, imported pottery and porcelain became core symbols of their identity. The Portuguese ruined the Swahili states, both by military aggression, and by usurping their trade. In the early nineteenth century, a poet from the island of Pate wrote lines that are both a reflection on mortality, and a lament for vanished glories.

> How many rich men have you seen
> who shone like the sun . . . ?
> their lighted houses were aglow
> with lamps of crystal and brass.[4]

Behind the coast lie hundreds of miles of barren scrub, *nyika*, where both tse tse and the malarial mosquito often flourished.

> I hunt in the waterless *nyika*
> and cook game
> in juice wrung from wild sisal leaves.[5]

In these circumstances, people lived in small, mobile communities, and rainmaking was a crucially important aspect of religion. Well-watered uplands sometimes rise from the plains like Pilgrim's Delectable Mountains: the Usamabaras, Kilimanjaro, the Kenya highlands. There was ample rain to the North and West of Lake Victoria, but not on its eastern shores. Far to the South, the Luyana (later Lozi) kingdom, exploited the resources of the fertile Zambezi flood plain, and every year its people migrated in a fleet of canoes to higher land as the waters rose.

The nineteenth century was a time of traumatic change in eastern Africa. It felt the impact of the Mfecane (see page 101) as highly militarized immigrants arrived: the Ndebele in Zimbabwe, the Kololo in Zambia, and the Ngoni in Malawi and southern Tanzania. Zanzibar was a fishing village at the beginning of the eighteenth century; by the middle of the nineteenth it was a wealthy Sultanate, its prosperity resting on the re-export of ivory, and slaves from the mainland, and on its clove plantations.

The Arab and Swahili merchants began to travel inland, and great caravan routes grew up. Inevitably, they were to be at loggerheads with Christian missionaries, less perhaps, because of religious differences than because of the latter's hostility to the slave trade. Like the missionaries, Muslims saw themselves as the bearers of a distinctive and superior civilization. They made many converts, and, in Buganda, Ahmed bin Ibrahim took his life in his hands, and reproved the ferocious Suna in the name of Allah the Compassionate.

At first, the merchants sought mainly ivory, but, as elephant populations were depleted, the ivory frontier moved ever further inland, and slaves were bought instead.

The slave trade in East Africa reached its peak in the nineteenth century. Its victims worked on Zanzibar's clove plantations, in the sugar fields of Mauritius and Reunion, or were exported to Brazil.

Some individuals and communities were enriched by the slave and ivory trades. A new entrepôt, Tabora, grew up in arid Ugogo, and the Nyamwezi and the Yao became bold entrepreneurs, sharing the profits and perils of the long-distance caravans. But Livingstone's *Last Journals* bear poignant witness to the social price the slave trade exacted. Traditional legal processes were distorted, and their punishments sometimes extended to entire families; a murderer's children were sold as slaves in Usamabara.[6] Ivory paid for firearms, which were used to collect slaves, as well as hunt elephants. Africans paid a heavy price for Europe's billiard balls and piano keys.

Africans had a real choice between two world religions, and the Ganda debated the rival merits of Islam and Christianity, and of Catholicism and Protestantism. The adoption of Islam, like that of Christianity, was often determined by socio-economic factors.

Presbyterians and High Church Anglicans tried in vain to convert the Yao, but they were already committed to a Muslim-dominated system of trade: 'Among the Yao on the lake shore it is becoming the natural thing to be a Mohammedan', noted a missionary in 1910.[7] But to those who had suffered from Muslim raids, Christianity was initially suspect because it seemed so much like Islam: 'I could not avoid seeing that the people were somewhat shy of me for fear that I should convert them to Mohammedanism; for they could not draw any distinction between Christianity and Islamism. Mothers removed their children as soon as they saw me in the streets of the village, a practice not uncommon among the Wanika [i.e. Mijikenda], arising out of the apprehension that strangers merely come to steal the children and sell them into slavery'.[8]

At the end of the century, the lives of pastoralists were ravaged by rinderpest, which decimated their cherished herds, and the crisis, in some cases, led to a resurgence of traditional cults. In others, natural disasters may have encouraged people to experiment with the supernatural powers of missionaries.

The ecological crisis was compounded by colonialism, often imposed and maintained with great brutality. The suppression of the Maji Maji rising in southern Tanzania in the early twentieth century was accompanied by a scorched earth policy, and the population of the region was permanently reduced.

The turbulence of the nineteenth century may have made the eternal safety the new religion promised more attractive. The martyr god Ryangombe, whose cult flourished West and South of Lake Victoria, offered his neophytes salvation, too, but usually, traditionalists could do little but rage against the dying of the light.

> If I could reach
> The homestead of Death's mother
> O! my daughter
> I would make a long grass torch . . .
> I would destroy everything utterly utterly . . .[9]

Choices

Some of East Africa's modern peoples claim that in the nineteenth century, prophets arose who foretold the shape of things to come. They were the intellectuals of their society and time, able to look beyond the confusing detail of particular events, and understand long-term historical processes. Later generations have reflected on their words, and perhaps added to them, because they seem to create a bridge between the modern world and their own past. A Safwa woman prophet in southern Tanganyika, for example, spoke of a spear to come from a distance, against which the fortresses of local warlords would have no power. Later this was interpreted as the Europeans, and the technology they brought with them.[10] Kaswa, in Ufipa, 'foretold how they would eventually forsake their ancient beliefs and become converts to new religions but that in the process a degeneration of the people would be seen'. In Shambaa, a prophet said that 'very white people . . . would bring the religion of the one who is above (Mulungu) whom he called "Kiumbe". He told them to go with him to the Umba River so that he would give them new names; but the people refused'. When the missionaries came, he encouraged his relatives to seek baptism, but said that he had been baptized already.[11]

We glimpse African responses to Christianity through a glass, darkly, because we have access to them, for the most part, only in the writings of Europeans. In the Lozi metaphor, the hippopotamus is invisible in the deep water. Missionaries realized this, at least some of the time: 'The more one knows of the natives, the more one finds consistently they keep on concealing from strangers what they really know'.[12]

We oversimplify the choices, as if it were either 'Christianity' or 'Tradition', but, in reality, every individual made his or her synthesis. They were not totally free in their choices, because the missions did not allow it.

They invented rigid stereotypes of what was acceptable to Christians, and, in doing so, lost much that was of value, much that was, from a religious standpoint, neutral. They opposed, for instance, a Ganda custom where a bride sits three times on the lap of each parent before she leaves their home, symbolizing the fact that she is always welcome there.

Here, as in South Africa, unfamiliar meanings were glimpsed through the medium of unknown, or largely unfamiliar languages. Not all missionaries succeeded in mastering an African language. Bishop Tucker, for example, despite his sympathy for African aspirations, did not. Many spoke a bowdlerized version, with English pronunciation and idioms, intelligible only to, 'Natives who being accustomed to Europeans, knew what was intended as well as the speakers themselves'.[13] The first Rwanda catechism was a composite of pidgin kinyaRwanda, Rundi, and Swahili, and the first Rwanda seminarians studied in Latin, conversed in Swahili, and corresponded with their European counterparts in German. The Primitive Methodists working among the Ila used seSotho, not ciLa; the Paris Missionary Society did the same in Bulozi. The first verse of St John's Gospel in Luo, reads, 'From long long ago there was News, News was with the Hunchback Spirit, News was the Hunchback Spirit'.[14]

Missionaries arbitrarily selected a traditional divinity to be 'Satan': the hero Mbasi filled this role in Rungwe, and the Berlin mission made war on his priest, though it was traditional forces that finally overthrew him. As all divinities were connected, the Nyakyusa complained that they were left without protection.[15]

Children were drawn to schools by the charm and power of the written word, and often became Christians with little conscious choice: 'I wanted to become a Christian, just because everybody was becoming a Christian'.[16]

However, here, as elsewhere in the world, the factors that led to a particular religious adherence often had little bearing on the subsequent quality of an individual's spiritual life.

The missionaries were perceived as magicians and diviners, workers of wonders, an image they deliberately reinforced with magic lanterns and fireworks. In August, 1886, there was a solar eclipse: '. . . the Chiefs of Sesheke had been in a plite on the Sunday of the Eclypse as they thought the Missionary had darkened the sun because they had not been to the morning service . . .'.[17] The Lozi arranged a deliberate trial of strength, giving missionaries land on the sinister sites where witches were executed. Literacy had its own magical power. Sebofo said, ' "Missionary, you haven't written for him." [the sick man] "What do you mean? I have given him some medicine", I replied, "Yes, yes, but you know you haven't written in your book, you haven't divined . . ." '.[18]

Sometimes, one hears the voice of Christianity's opponents. On one occasion when Coillard was preaching at a Sunday service, an elderly man began to recite the Lozi creation myth at the top of his voice.[19] The Mijikenda of the Kenya coast, it was said, 'never seriously exhort the young to come to school; fearing that the Ada or customs of the Wanika will be destroyed, that the young people will conform to the Ada of Europeans, and that the Koma or spirits of the dead will be angry, withhold the rain, and send diseases'.[20]

Age-based conflict, between the youths and the elderly men, was often characteristic of village society. The elders perceived, correctly, that western education would give the young an independent power base. An Ngoni elder said, towards the end of the nineteenth century:

> If we give you our children to teach, your words will steal their hearts; they will grow up cowards, and refuse to fight for us when we are old; and knowing more than we do, they will despise us.[21]

Some responded to a situation of religious pluralism with agnosticism: '. . . the chief of Kambe said openly, "There is no God since he is not to be seen" '.[22] Others expounded a kind of relativism, suggesting that each people has its own path to God, appropriate to its own culture: 'The foundation of our kingdom is the spear and the shield, God has given you the Book and cloth, and has given us the shield and spear, and each must live in his own way'.[23]

Christianity undermined the sacred office of the king (who was usually also a rainmaker), and the role of traditional religious specialists, and, in some societies, diviners were among its most outspoken opponents. Sometimes, however, they, or their children, were among the first converts. Ambilishye, a notable Moravian evangelist in late nineteenth-century southern Tanganyika, was an example. John Kapuye, the first Anglican convert in Mashonaland, was the son of a famous diviner.[24] One could not succeed in this field without considerable insight into human nature and social change, and diviners were sometimes among the first to perceive the crucial importance of western education and literacy. Some were alienated from their own arts when divination failed.

The first Christians were drawn from those to whom the traditional world offered little happiness. The first CMS convert in East Africa, Mrenge, of Rabai, was disabled, and the first Christians in Usambara were lepers, or mothers of twins. The first ordained Moravian pastor in Nyasa Province was a former slave, and so was the first baptized convert at the LMS station at Fwambo, at the southern end of Lake Tanganyika. The most extreme example was Swema, a Yao child born in 1855, who was enslaved, buried alive at Zanzibar when apparently dying, rescued, and taken to missionary nuns. She became a Sister of Mercy, Sister Marie Antoinette. There were exceptions, such as the Ganda and Malagasy aristocrats who suffered for their new faith, and sometimes died for it, or the High Church padres of southern Tanganyika, drawn from the Yao aristocracy, who struggled unsuccessfully to draw their people to Christianity, rather than Islam, and enjoyed a brief period of relative autonomy early this century.

Independent rulers often welcomed missionaries as allies in a situation of peril. They were valued go-betweens in their dealings with European powers, but often they found, as Mpande had done, that the missionary created what was, in effect, a rival state that weakened their own, and offered a haven to their enemies (see page 114). Sometimes missionaries could prevent a famine, not by superior rainmaking, but by a mission steamer carrying food from one end of Lake Tanganyika to the other. It was believed, correctly, that trade followed them. A group of Giriama villages, in coastal Kenya, asked for a CMS teacher in the 1870s: 'their predominant motive may be (as almost confessed by themselves) the desire that traders in cloth, knives, etc. may settle among them'.[25]

Forced into a wider world, villagers may have found that Christianity or Islam provided a more helpful cognitive map than local religions, which often centred on ancestral, or nature, spirits. Some traditional religions spread over large regions, but it was often true, as an early African priest put it, that 'there was no *special* religion in the area between Masasi and Makonde'.[26] Political institutions were in a ferment, and many new states were created. In this situation, some new communities chose to follow missionary leaders, who became, in effect, chiefs, or squires, as they sometimes liked to call themselves.

Missionary islands

We saw in the last chapter how Christian villages tended to grow up around mission stations in southern Africa. This was equally true of eastern, as it was of West and Central Africa. Sometimes it was unavoidable, when missionaries redeemed slaves, or harboured refugees. Ultimately, they were to give up the strategy of ransoming slaves in the belated recognition that this encouraged the slave trade by providing a convenient market, unique in its willingness to absorb the sick and the old.

The villagers obtained economic and social security in return for a control over every detail of their lives, including their marriages. They were not all redeemed slaves—freemen were often willing to exchange their liberty for security. Some of them were devout Christians, but there was little real impact on autonomous African societies. When Christian settlements were perceived as collections of former slaves, accused witches, and other undesirables, Christianity seemed less attractive.

The establishment of Christian villages often reflected the belief that Africans could not practise a Christian life in a traditional environment, that it was necessary to make a clean break. In the twentieth century, mission boarding schools embodied something of the same attitude. It was rooted in an understanding of Africa as, in the words François Coillard used of the Lozi, an 'unfathomable abyss of corruption and degradation'.[27] There was also the hope that redeemed slaves would become evangelists, carrying the gospel back to their own people, like the missionary Creoles of Sierra Leone.

The UMCA educated children obtained from slave ships in Zanzibar, some of whom, in due course, brought Christianity to their original homes, but they experienced many difficulties. Cecil Majaliwa had forgotten the Yao language and pined for Zanzibar: 'I am left alone in the midst of the heathen like a cottage in the middle of a forest.' Several experienced these tensions to such an extreme degree that they became insane.[28]

In practice, Christian villages tended to form permanent settlements under the rule of a white missionary, usually well-intentioned, sometimes harsh, even brutal, but always autocratic. It was said of the White Fathers in Rwanda, by one of their number:

> they have got their hands on 3000 hectares of land on which about 8000 people live; they exercise the authority of a king over this property, not only judging cases but conscripting labour, ordering fatigues for construction materials, chasing out polygamists, removing amulets, demolishing the little huts for sacrifices, replacing even a chief whom they have expelled, and imposing on the chiefs catechists . . .'[29]

The Church of Scotland established a mission in the Shire Hills in 1875, naming it Blantyre, after Livingstone's birth place. In its early years, missionaries practised such severity that it led in 1879 to an international scandal, when they flogged some Africans to the brink of death, and performed an execution. This was an extreme, though, sadly, not unique, case.

In 1898, a newly arrived recruit in Northern Rhodesia was horrified to find whips of weighted hippo hide 'being cured for the abominable practice in the hands of the missionaries of the London Missionary Society, of horsewhipping the natives'.[30] These abuses died out in the early twentieth century, and, in the colonial situation, the Christian villages declined. Often, their members voted against autocracy with their feet, but sometimes they were tied to the mission by their reliance on its land. The vast tracts of mission land were often deeply resented: *Gutiri mubea na muthungu*, 'There's no difference between a missionary and a settler', said twentieth-century Kikuyu.[31]

In the last quarter of the nineteenth century, the CMS ran two freed slave settlements near Mombasa that had, in their heyday, perhaps 2 thousand inhabitants. They were run by fewer than 20 Europeans, and 145 'Bombay Africans', who had been freed from slave ships and resettled, not in Africa, but in India. They were educated men who often spoke Indian languages as well as English, and one of them was picked as a future bishop, 'the Crowther of the East Coast'. However, they suffered from the same kind of white racism as that which destroyed Crowther's Niger Mission. They were forbidden to wear European dress (Muslim dress was encouraged!), and, as so often happened, were paid less than a labourer, but condemned for materialism.[32] William Jones worked in Rabai from 1865, and was ordained in 1895. When he died, in 1904, it was said, 'They called him their "big father" and looked to him as their great friend and adviser in all their troubles and difficulties. No other man can ever occupy the same place in their hearts and lives'. But Jones, once a prospective bishop, was forced to resign in 1897 by white racism, and the parsimony of the CMS.[33]

Geography often increased the division between the mission and Christian village, on the one hand, and the local community on the other. In an age that believed that disease was caused by river "miasma", Europeans preferred to build on hilltops. This often meant that water supplies, and local inhabitants, were far away, and so African Christians carried water, imported goods for mission use and sale, and sometimes, the missionaries themselves, up the steep paths to the mission house.

Beginnings

The modern missionary enterprise in East Africa began almost by accident. Johann Ludwig Krapf was one of the German recruits from the Basel seminary who played such an important role in the early history of the CMS. He began his missionary career in Ethiopia in 1837. Forbidden to return to Shoa, he started work in Mombasa in 1844. His aim was to convert the Oromo ('Galla'), who, because of their sheer size and rapid expansion, he saw as the key to the conversion of north-east Africa: 'To my mind, Ormania is the Germany of Africa. If the Gallas were not gathered into the Christian Church, it seemed to me they would fall into Islamism'.[34] The missionary strategy he advocated, a chain of mission stations stretching across Africa near the southern frontier of Islam, anticipated that of the SUM's founder, Karl Kumm. The post he founded at Rabai, near Mombasa, was intended to be the first link in the chain.

Rabai is a community of the Mijikenda ('Nine Towns'), a series of hilltop settlements, *Kaya*, immediately behind the Islamicized coast.[35] Because they lived in a number of independent settlements, it was not possible to convert them by winning the support of a single ruler. The first Christians, such as the crippled Mrenge, baptized near death, were often the disinherited.

Krapf was a notable linguist and explorer, visiting Kilimanjaro and Usambara, both of which, ironically, were to prove much more responsive mission fields than the Kenyan coast. He endured great hardships (once when travelling he was forced by hunger and thirst to sample ants, and even elephant dung), but he was unable to create a Christian community.

The missionary enterprise in East and East Central Africa began to succeed when stations were established deep in the interior. This was not part of the original CMS strategy; they had planned a gradual movement inland from the coast. The difficulty was that this led to regions that were arid and sparsely populated, except for fertile uplands, like the slopes of Kilimanjaro. The move deep into the interior was due to particular constellations of circumstances, which we shall now examine.

Livingstone (1813–73) and the Zambezi

The pattern of David Livingstone's life is well known.[36] He began as a worker in a Scottish textile factory, and, by iron determination, became a medical doctor. He decided to be a missionary, and a decisive meeting with the Moffats brought him to southern Africa, rather than China. He gradually became restive, deciding that it was oversupplied with missionaries: 'I do not believe that equal advantages are enjoyed by any town or village in the United Kingdom as those which are pressed upon the people of Algoa Bay, Uitenhage, Graaf Reinet & Colesburg. . . . I tell my Bakwains [Tswana] that if spared ten years I shall move on to the regions beyond them'.[37]

Deciding to embark on exploration, he sent his wife and children to England. They cannot have been cheered by his correspondence, 'If your sins and your naughtiness are not forgiven . . . you will go away into Hell when you die like the rich man of whom we read in the Bible'.[38]

Livingstone left his mission in November 1853, spent some time in the Zambezi valley, where he hired Kololo bearers, and then travelled across Africa to the coast of Angola. He then returned to the East, reaching the Zambezi delta in May 1856. This was a 'discovery' of routes already known to Africans, but it was an epic journey; Livingstone became a popular hero, and his *Missionary Travels and Researches* a best seller. It was not, however, conventional missionary work. He left the service of the LMS, and returned to the Zambezi in government employ. He said, and the unconscious ordering of his words is interesting, 'I go back to Africa to make an open path for commerce and Christianity'. 'The Book says you are to grow cotton, and the English are to come and buy it', explained his interpreter helpfully in the Lower Shire Valley.[39]

The Zambezi expedition had much in common with its ill-fated predecessor, the Niger expedition of 1840–1. Both enjoyed government support and substantial resources, both carried missionaries, both were intended to supplant the slave trade with legitimate commerce. Both began in a blaze of publicity, and both ended in disaster. Like the architects of the Niger expedition, Livingstone believed that river transport held the key to the development of legitimate trade, which would replace the slave trade. He saw the Zambezi as the gateway to the interior, believing that a flourishing commerce could be established, especially in cotton, and that the uplands of the interior were suited to white settlement, perhaps 'good Christian Scotch families'.[40]

However, in his enthusiasm, he exaggerated the commercial resources of the area, and socio-economic conditions had deteriorated gravely by the time the expedition arrived. The Mang'anja of the Shire valley were under constant attack from Yao and 'Portuguese' slave raiders, and, to the afflictions of war, were added the horrors of a famine caused by lack of rain. Mothers threw their starving children into the river, and hurled themselves after them.

The missionaries searched in vain for cotton, having imported a cotton gin with enormous difficulty. There was not, one of them complained, enough of it to fill his hat. James Stewart, destined for a long and distinguished missionary career, threw his copy of Livingstone's *Missionary Travels and Researches* into the Zambezi in his anger and despair.[41]

With the exception of Stewart, the Zambezi party consisted of High Church Anglicans. They had been looking for a mission field, and Livingstone's appeal proved the catalyst that led to the formation of the Universities Mission to Central Africa, though the pioneer party, led by a bishop who was a former Cambridge don, were notably short of the practical skills Livingstone had envisaged.

Soon after their arrival, in 1861, they freed some ninety recently captured slaves. Thenceforth, they devoted themselves to this miniscule community; they made no attempt to convert them, partly because of language problems. Because the slaves were liberated by force of arms, the affair, when it became known, exposed them to criticism in England, and the enthusiasm of financial supporters waned.

Bishop John MacKenzie died on the Zambezi, as did Livingstone's wife, confronted with a Hobson's choice between solitude in England, and her husband's company in Zambezia.

A new Bishop, William Tozer, fresh from a parish in Lincolnshire, was appointed. He made a short-lived attempt to relocate the mission on a mist-covered mountain top, finding, like his predecessors, that Livingstone's glowing descriptions bore little relationship to reality: 'Lemons certainly grow wild but oranges are unknown. Water is *scarce*, and the inhabitants very few and very poor'.[42]

He relocated the mission in Zanzibar. It was a stronghold of Islam, and, as an island, by no means the obvious starting point for the conversion of a continent. Livingstone said bitterly that 'the Mission, in fleeing from Morambala to an island in the Indian Ocean, acted as St Augustine would have done, had he located himself on one of the Channel Islands'.[43] Some of MacKenzie's freed slaves were settled in South Africa; others returned home. Some were to take part in a new venture on the Zambezi, in 1875.

The essential obstacle to Livingstone's scheme lay in the fact that the Zambezi was blocked by the Cabora Bassa rapids, and the Shire by the Murchison Falls. Both rivers were full of sandbanks, which meant that any vessel must be of shallow draft, and frequently unloaded. Livingstone had dreamed of a steamer on Lake Malawi, but the British government recalled him in 1864 before he could achieve this goal, his great reputation temporarily overshadowed by disaster: 'The Doctor is in bad odour at the Foreign Office . . . and they hate the name of the Expedition'.[44]

He returned to African exploration in 1866. Nothing was heard of him for years, and it was rumoured that he was dead. The journalist, Stanley, went to look for him, and, in 1871, they had their famous meeting on the shores of

Lake Tanganyika. Stanley described his emaciation, his grim endurance of pain. Livingstone refused to return with Stanley, and dreamed of discovering the source of the Nile. When he died, on the shores of Lake Bangweulu, his faithful servants buried his heart in Africa, and embalmed his body and carried it to the coast so that he might lie among his own people.

Livingstonia

After his adventures in Zambezia, Stewart went on to a notable career as Principal of Lovedale (see page 124). He still shared Livingstone's confidence in the transforming potential of commerce and water transport, and hoped that Livingstone would find a connection between Lake Tanganyika and the Nile, paving the way for an African Chicago.[45] Through his intervention, Livingstone's dream of a steamer on Lake Malawi was realized. The opening of the Suez Canal in 1869 caused a resurgence of interest in eastern Africa's economic potential, and Livingstone's death provided a valuable focus for fundraising. The great explorer was commemorated in two Presbyterian missions, on Lake Malawi and in the Shire hills, respectively: Livingstonia, run by the Free Church of Scotland, formed after the Great Disruption of 1843, and Blantyre, founded by the Church of Scotland. The cause of 'Commerce and Christianity' was upheld by the African Lakes Company.[46]

Longevity was one of the most important determinants of a successful missionary career. Robert Laws, 'the Bishop of Central Africa',[47] fulfilled this condition pre-eminently. He was one of the United Presbyterians, who joined the Free Church in 1900.[48] The son of a cabinet maker, he was typical of the self-made men whose careers were made possible by the structure of Scottish education, and was both an ordained minister and a physician. He was one of the pioneers who sang the 'Old Hundredth' as the first mission steamer sailed on Lake Malawi in 1875, and he remained at Livingstonia until 1927. The steamer was called *Ilala*, the place where Livingstone died.

Livingstonia fared better when it was relocated further North, among the Tonga and Ngoni. Under threat from Ngoni invaders, the Lake Tonga had been forced to retreat into stockaded villages, and to plant cassava, because it was more difficult to steal. They welcomed missionaries as allies in a situation of peril. Their traditional culture was geared to individual achievement, and its values served them well in a changing world.

The Ngoni, a pastoral people organized on military lines, invited the missionaries to settle among them, pointing out that one could not milk the fish of the lake! The Ngoni state was in crisis, due to the acquisition of firearms by peoples formerly raided, to problems in assimilating the conquered peoples, and to succession disputes. It may have been this that led the Ngoni aristocracy to seek allies and supporters. 'I showed them a Bible', noted a missionary, in words which echoed those of Krapf to the Queen of Shoa, 'and told them it was it that made our nation rich and powerful'.[49]

By 1898, there were some 5 thousand Tonga children, and some 4 thousand Ngoni in school. There was a vast structure of outstations, where most pupils taught someone in their turn. Livingstonia Christians were to provide clerks, teachers, interpreters, typists, foremen, and mechanics, not only in Nyasaland, but in South Africa and the Rhodesias.

The Overtoun Institution, founded in 1894, provided a higher level of education where, *inter alia*, students learned the names of the capes of the east coast of Scotland, and the right of James I to the throne of England. Its industrial training prepared bricklayers and telegraphists to play a role in the colonial economy, but fed no skills into the rural sector, where, as was repeatedly pointed out, the African peasant was more successful anyway.

Livingstonia was staffed by white and black missionaries, four of the latter from Lovedale. One of them, William Koyi, who died in the mission field in 1886, was fluent in chiNgoni, which was related to his mother tongue. Three were second-generation Christians, and they were paid at the same rate as Scottish artisans. As so often happened to African mission employees, they found their salaries gradually eroded, and their position challenged by the Europeans. It was decided 'that African evangelists have no advantage in health, economy of expenditure or efficiency over Scottish artisans'.[50] Local Christians endured similar difficulties. Qualified men waited for years for ordination: 'Let us be ordained before we die', said the Ngoni, Daniel Mtusu, during the First World War.

In 1905, a young Tonga Christian and his Tumbuka wife went from Livingstonia to work among the Bemba, a warlike people whom missionaries regarded as ferociously savage. When he was asked where he found the courage for his long, and dangerous journeys alone, he would say '*ni Leza*', 'It is because of God'. He died saying a prayer in Bemba, Tonga, Tumbuka, and English: 'Father God, let your Kingdom come in this land'. He is not mentioned in contemporary mission publications, and is remembered now because he was David Kaunda (*d.* 1932), father of a more famous son.[51]

Mission teachers were badly paid, and African clergy were forced to work under the supervision of Europeans, who were often younger, and less experienced. Charles Domingo was one of those who waited year after year for ordination, and his life encapsulated much of the history of his time. He was one of the marginalized who found an alternative social identity in Christianity. His father was a cook from Quelimane, so he had no ethnic roots in Malawi. After some years as a teacher, he left the mission, and became a Seventh Day Baptist pastor. After years of grinding poverty, he became a clerk in government service. In 1911, he penned a deservedly famous indictment. He had studied at both Lovedale and at Overtoun, and was one of the best-educated Africans in Malawi at the time. The imperfections of his English are eloquent in themselves:

There is too much failure among all Europeans in Nyassaland. The Three Combined Bodies: Missionaries, Government, and Companies or Gainers of money do form the same rule to look on a Native with mockery eyes. It sometimes startle us to see that the Three Combined Bodies are from Europe, and along with them there is a title 'CHRISTNDOM'. And to compare or make a comparison between the MASTER of the title and His Servants it pushes any African away from believing the Master of the title. If we had power enough to communicate ourselves to Europe, we would have advised them not to call themselfs 'CHRISTNDOM' but 'Europeandom'. We see that the title 'CHRISTNDOM' does not belong to Europe, but to future BRIDE. Therefore the life of The Three Combined Bodies is altogether too cheaty, too thefty, too mockery.[52]

So famous have these words become that in a book on African historiography, a chapter was entitled 'Still Too Cheaty, Too Thefty, Too Mockery', without a source cited, or further comment.[53]

Bulozi

The Lozi kingdom lies in the upper Zambezi flood plain. Its nineteenth-century history was particularly dramatic. In about 1820, the Sotho-speaking Fokeng, who came to be called Kololo, left their homeland to the South, and settled in Zambezia, in one of the many migrations of the Mfecane. The Kololo regime lasted only until 1864, but their language survived, becoming siLozi. Like Buganda, the Lozi state was a powerful monarchy, buttressed by the cult of royal graves, with an elaborate political structure, and an ambitious aristocracy.

The first missionary to Bulozi was Frederick Stanley Arnot, whose family were among the first Plymouth Brethren. Founded in 1830, the Brethren, in their dislike of ecclesiastical structures, and their expectation of the imminent End, had much in common with the Faith Missions. Drawn to Africa by his friendship with Livingstone's children, Arnot prepared elaborately for a missionary career, going on cross-country walks with a compass, and mastering trades that included joinery and watch repair. He worked in Bulozi in 1882–4, but made no converts. He went on to work in Shaba, and was instrumental in bringing other missionary societies to Northern Rhodesia. Later, the Brethren were to establish an important network of missions, in Shaba, Angola, and Northern Rhodesia.

A more lasting missionary presence was created by outreach from the Church in Lesotho, and will always be linked with the names of François and Christina Coillard. François Coillard was a Protestant Frenchman, in the employ of the Société des Missions Evangéliques de Paris, his wife a Scot, and they had worked for years among the Sotho. They came with Sotho co-workers, with the precious advantage that they knew a closely related language. Coillard's European colleagues soon came to see the Sotho as a threat, rather than as allies in a common cause: 'I do not subscribe to the evangelisation of Zambezia by Basutos, I would really be *frightened* to see them arrive in great numbers'.[54] Like the Bombay Africans, and the Yao padres, they fell victim to the racism of white missionaries.

The Lozi king, Lewanika, had recently survived a civil war, and was very much aware of the dangers from '. . . other nations such as the Portuguese and the Boers, the latter Khama was affraid [sic] of and now he has nothing to fear'.[55] Most of all, he feared the Ndebele, encroaching on his southern frontier. He welcomed the material, diplomatic, and magical resources of the strangers—'They think that all our wisdom and skill comes to us by taking medicine'[56]—while keeping them in a subordinate role, which he affirmed symbolically, by compelling Coillard to make an offering of cloth at a royal grave.[57]

Like the Ganda kings, he was anxious for the spread of literacy and technical skills. In 1891, it was said that he 'wants teachers to instruct his people to read and write but especially to train them as carpenters, blacksmiths, and other trades'.[58] In a particularly effective essay in modernization, he embarked on a very successful programme of canal construction. His priorities, and those of the Lozi aristocracy, were significantly different from those of the missionaries: 'Lewanika and the more important Barotse indunas have long cried out for education. They are not satisfied with that provided by the missionaries . . .'.[59] This led to an interesting 'Ethiopian' episode, when the Sotho, William Mokalapa, who had left Coillard's mission, joined the African Methodist Episcopal Church, with Lewanika's blessing. The experiment foundered on ill fortune: funds entrusted by the Lozi king to Mokalapa were given to South African auctioneers who went bankrupt, and the British South Africa Company forbade the recruiting of AMEC teachers, but it did lead to the creation of a secular school for the Lozi aristocracy, the Barotse National School, founded in 1906.

Lozi notables discussed the pros and cons of the missionary advent:

> First speaker . . . 'Don't we hear tell of all the black nations, all the chiefs having their missionaries to teach the young people and the kings the wisdom of the white nations?' Others said, 'No we do not need these teachers unless they know and teach us to make powder and such like things'. One man said the missionaries were bad . . . and not long ago they caused the sun to rot (meaning the eclipse [sic]) and they chased away the rain.[60]

Perhaps because his subjects were reluctant to become Christians unless the king did, the missionaries at first made few converts.

Lewanika's wife, Nolianga, was a notable exception; she became a Christian, with his permission, in 1895, perhaps in the (wrong) expectation that Lewanika would soon do likewise.[61]

Another royal woman, Lewanika's sister, the *Mulena Mukwae*, Matauka, had a long and interesting relationship with the mission.[62] She was virtually an associate monarch, with her own capital in the South, and, on one occasion, she slew a high official with whom she was displeased with her own hand. However, for years she attended church and, in 1916, she preached a sermon, which ran, in summary:

> I am not a Christian: I don't want to deceive the missionaries. And yet it seems to me that I am coming nearer and nearer to the things of God. . . . If our missionary left here, I should follow him hobbling.

In 1921, she became a Christian.

Both traditional rulers and colonial administrators were sometimes anxious about the subversive potential of Christian teachings on human brotherhood (Arnot infuriated Lewanika with a sermon on Nebuchadnezzar), but in both Buganda and Bulozi, the ruling class was to form an alliance with the colonial government, benefiting from élite schools, run by missions in the former case and government in the latter. When Lewanika died, he was succeeded by his Christian son, Litia.

New arrivals in Zambezia

Livingstonia and Blantyre were not the only missions founded in memory of the great explorer. Robert Arthington gave money to the Baptists to advance into Central Africa from the West, and to the LMS to do likewise from the East, founding a Livingstone Memorial Mission on the southern shores of Lake Tanganyika. In 1877, an LMS expedition reached Ujiji, where Stanley had met Livingstone, though, like so many other pioneer missions, it was soon relocated. The Primitive Methodists, who had broken with the Wesleyans in 1811, had worked in Cape Colony since 1872, and, in 1889, they reached Zambezia with the hope of working among the Ila. At first, Lewanika prevented them from going further, but, at the end of 1892, he relented. The White Fathers worked on the northern shores of Lake Tanganyika, and, in 1898, they established themselves among the Bemba. The Bemba king was dying, and Bishop Joseph Dupont, succeeded in having himself recognized as his successor—a move soon thwarted by the British South Africa company! The Dutch Reformed Church began work among the Ngoni in 1889. In 1905, both the Seventh Day Adventists and the Jesuits founded stations among the Plateau Tonga, soon followed by the American Brethren in Christ. This missionary struggle for territory did much to determine the future denominational allegiance of the peoples concerned.

A Primitive Methodist wrote anxiously, 'I dread lest this field so long regarded as our own, should be filled by other societies',[63] but the Missionary Conference of North-West Rhodesia in 1914, was attended by six missions, including the Jesuits, Plymouth Brethren and Primitive Methodists!

The greater geographic mobility of the colonial period made it easier for African Christians to break from the rigid denominational control of particular areas, but the Bemba are still predominantly Catholic.

Buganda

Livingstone and Arthington—the former unknowingly and indirectly—contributed to the inception of mission work in Buganda. After his meeting with Livingstone, Stanley was a celebrity. He was invited to embark on a new journey of discovery, during which he crossed Africa from Bagamoyo to Boma, in the estuary of the Zaire. In the course of this epic journey, which took from 1874 to 1877, he visited the Ganda court. With the help of an African Christian trained by the UMCA in Zanzibar, Dallington Scopion Maftaa, and a Muslim scribe, he prepared 'an abridged Protestant Bible' in Swahili, in Arabic script.[64]

Maftaa stayed behind, the first apostle to the Ganda, and Stanley reported the King's apparent enthusiasm for Christianity in the English press. Once more, Arthington's wealth determined the pattern of missionary advance—his anonymous donation forced the hand of the CMS, and they established a mission in Buganda.[65]

There is no more extraordinary chapter in the history of African Christianity than its growth in Buganda. The courage of its martyrs is reminiscent of the early Church, and Ganda Christianity, and Ganda society and history in general, have been the focus of much scholarly study.[66]

Buganda began as a small state on the northern edge of Lake Victoria, in what later became Busiro County. From the mid seventeenth century, it began to expand, until, by the nineteenth, it was the giant of the interlacustrine kingdoms. The king's power, which was often used with caprice and cruelty, is reflected in many proverbs: 'The king is the lake, which kills those who fish and those who do not fish alike'.[67] Mutesa's praise names included, 'Cause of Tears'.

The Buganda were divided into thirty totemic clans, each under a head, *Mutaka*. There was no royal clan, kings taking the totemic affiliation of their mothers. Superimposed on this, was a system of territorial lords, *Bakungu*, each ruling one of ten counties, and of regionally based military leaders, *Batongole*; both classes of office were in the king's gift. There were few hereditary offices, and the royal princes were excluded from them. In the absence of a clear principle of succession, the accession of a new *Kabaka* was often marked by a massacre of his rivals.

The Kabaka was the source of all advancement. The most powerful office holder was the *Kattikiro*, usually translated as prime minister. The risks, as well as the rewards, of life at court were so great that chiefs often sent protégés to court, rather than their own sons, and the Kattikiro, Mukasa, asked missionaries for laudanum, in case he should be tortured.

145

Religious change was perhaps easier for a Buganda king because his office was relatively distinct from religious structures: 'Ndaula, the nineteenth Kabaka, "stipulated on ascending the throne that he should not be made the medium of the God Mukasa" '.[68]

Islam was brought by the Zanzibari Arabs. They were expelled by Suna (*d.* 1856) after eight years' residence, but allowed to return by his successor, Mutesa (1856–84). Mutesa was never circumcised, perhaps because tradition forbade the shedding of royal blood, but kept Ramadan, and built mosques, and would sometimes expound the Qur'an.

The first CMS missionaries arrived two years later. As they were soon followed by the White Fathers, the Baganda were confronted with the claims of four mutually hostile religious systems. They embarked on 'the interminable debates which from 1879 onwards, week in week out, month in month out, year in year out, regularly took place at the open meetings of the Kabaka's court, for the most part in his presence':[69] 'Now, Stamlee, tell me and my chiefs what you know of the angels?'[70]

Mutesa's attachment to the faith of his ancestors weakened, and he dismissed the custodian of the royal tombs, but traditionalists did not give up easily, and, in his later years, afflicted by incurable disease, he accepted the demand of the medium of Mukasa, lord of the lake, that this and other changes be reversed.[71]

To Mutesa, and many other Ganda, the power and wealth of both Muslims and Christians gave an a priori indication of the validity of their religious claims, but whose? He was aware of the dangers inherent in Egypt's southern thrust, and welcomed European Christians as a political counterweight, and a source of technical aid: 'He said he wants us to make guns and gunpowder and seemed rather disappointed at first when we told him we had not come to teach such things, but afterwards he seemed satisfied and said what he wanted most was to be taught, he and his people, to read and write'.[72] The technological superiority of the Christians seemed to suggest that their religion was greater:

> The Arabs bring cloth, beads and wire, to buy ivory and slaves; they also bring powder and guns; but who made all these things . . . ? I have seen nothing yet of all they have brought that the white man did not make. Therefore, I say, give me the white men.[73]

Mutesa showed the same initial sympathetic interest in Christianity as he did in Islam: 'As soon as I had finished the King took it up and spoke most eloquently to them telling them to believe in Christ now saying that they could only do so in this life, when they were dead it would be too late'.[74]

Like the Tswana kings, he took it for granted that any religion would be a state religion, and that he would dominate it. His attitude made religious choice possible for his subjects, but, when religious choices had been made, he came to understand that, at his own court, some now owed a higher loyalty.

He was outraged, for example, when Muslim courtiers refused meat slaughtered by non-Muslim butchers. Mutesa's persecution of Muslims in 1875–6 claimed far more victims than his son's attack on Christians. According to one estimate, 70 Muslim chiefs and pages were burned at Namugongo, and 1 thousand killed throughout the country. Mwanga executed, perhaps, 100, some of them non-Christians.[75]

The Ganda were drawn to Christianity, in part, by their admiration for the technical achievements of western culture: they may have experienced revulsion against the bloodshed that so often marked Buganda life in the nineteenth century. Low makes the perceptive suggestion that, 'since Kiganda society was traditionally so bound up with the supremacy of the Kabaka, . . . once the boundaries of that society began to appear to have been incorrectly limited, it was perfectly logical to question the supremacy of its master and look for one beyond, who encompassed the whole of the new world which was beginning to appear'.[76] Indeed, one of the martyrs, Matthias Kalemba, said, 'My father had always believed that the Baganda had not the truth, and he sought it in his heart . . . he had often mentioned this to me, and before his death he told me that men would one day come to teach us the right way. These words made a profound impression on me'.[77]

Why did Mwanga persecute Christians in 1886? The occasion of this outbreak of violence was the refusal of some of his pages to participate in homosexual practices he had learned from the Arabs. Like his father before him, he may well have been disquieted by the realization that the primary loyalty of some of his subjects now lay elsewhere, and Christian Europe had come to seem more of a danger to his independence than Muslim Egypt. The converts were no ordinary subjects; there were many Christians in the new gun-bearing regiments and among the court pages, who were the future leaders of Buganda and the specialist craftsmen. Some of the latter were spared because their skills were irreplaceable. The pages were young and single, and so were spared the conflict of loyalty that confronted older men with more than one wife. They brought to their new religion the core values of the Ganda aristocracy: courage, and a loyalty that endured into the shadow of death—'No tears, no regrets, the Baganda know how to die'.[78]

Thirty-one Baganda were burned alive at Namugongo, on Ascension day in June, 1886. The martyrs met horrifying deaths with incredible heroism. One of them, Matthias Kalemba, was an aristocrat who disregarded the fact that most Ganda regarded agriculture as women's work, and helped his wife in her plantain garden.[79] His executioners cut off his arms and his legs, and pieces of flesh, while preventing him from bleeding to death, and left him to die, a process that took two days. While he was being dismembered, he said, *Katonda*, which means, God.[80] His friend, Noe Mawaggali, a potter, was wounded by a spear, and then eaten alive by dogs.[81]

Noe's sister, Munaku, still an unbaptized catechumen, pleaded in vain to share his fate. For a time, she was imprisoned, and finally sold to the mission.

When baptized, she took a vow of celibacy. She worked for the Church till her death in 1938, joining the Bannabikira, an order of nuns founded in 1910 in response to the generosity of Ganda women.[82]

Charles Lwanga was the leader of those who were burned to death. At first, the fire consumed his feet and legs, leaving him still alive. He said to his executioner, 'You are burning me, but it is as if you were pouring water over my body. I am dying for God's religion. But be warned in time, or God whom you insult will one day plunge you into real fire'.[83] His last word was *Katonda*.

Denis Kamyuka was to have been among the martyrs, but was saved, despite his protests, at the last moment. He was an eye witness to the deaths of the others: 'The flames blazed up like a burning house and, as they rose, I heard coming from the pyre the murmur of the Christians' voices as they died invoking God'.[84]

Women were exempt from capital punishment in traditional Buganda society, so they did not figure among the martyrs. In May 1886, Nalumansi, a daughter of Mutesa, married. This was in itself a breach with tradition, for Ganda princesses were forbidden to marry, in order to limit those with a claim to royal descent to the male line. She became a Catholic, baptized as Clara. She burned the ritual objects from the shrine of a former Kabaka, to which she had been appointed custodian, and destroyed her umbilical cord, an object, to Ganda, of the greatest ritual value. She was shot in 1888.[85]

Mwanga did not seek to wipe out the Christian community entirely. Some courted death, others went into hiding, protected, often enough, by non-Christian relatives and friends. Soon, the survivors were restored to favour. Honorat Nyonintono, who endured castration only to die in a later war, was given a high military command. The surviving Christian pages led a rumbustious life, reminiscent of the Crusaders. A future clergyman recalled his turbulent youth, 'We the young men indeed had freedom during this reign. . . . we would click at everyone with the tongue and say, "Let every peasant enter into his bag". Everyone ran away into the bush; he who did not was beaten to death'.[86]

Again, Mwanga became concerned about the potential danger from his subjects, and planned to maroon the Christian regiments on a deserted island in Lake Victoria. The plan failed, and, in self-preservation, Muslims, Catholics, and Protestants united in a successful coup. A month later, Muslims seized sole power, and many Christians went into exile. They regained power later, restoring a now-powerless Mwanga in 1889, such was the enduring strength of the monarchy. In 1892, the victorious Christians fought each other, and the maxim gun of the Imperial British East Africa Company, represented by Frederick Lugard and his forces, played a decisive role on the Protestant side at the battle of Mengo. Much later, an Anglican remembered:

> In the early days, especially during the persecution, there was no distinction of religion or denomination; we were all Christians. . . . All

148

Christian converts were one family, with two internal arbitrary divisions, as it were; we loved one another, and wished one another well. It was only at Kabula, during our exile, that trouble began. . . .[87]

The Catholic mission doctor, Francis Goge, was killed at Mengo. He had been born far from Buganda, in Hausaland. He could have had a career similar to that of Adrian Atiman (see page 222), but it was not to be.

In 1893, Uganda became a British Protectorate, and Buganda was divided into Protestant, Catholic, and Muslim counties. There followed 'one of the most remarkable and spontaneous movements for literacy and new knowledge that the world has ever seen', when missionaries were constantly waylaid by people anxious to know what a wine press was or the distance from Jerusalem to Jericho.[88]

Expatriate missionaries were not among the martyrs of 1886. They were much more likely to die from sickness than to be killed, though a few individuals, among them an Anglican bishop, Hannington, met a violent end. George Pilkington was a lay CMS missionary, translator of the Bible, and the leader of a major revival in 1893. He accompanied the British forces during a rising of Sudanese troops, and a bullet severed his femoral artery.

> Aloni said to him, 'My master you are dying; death has come'. to which he replied, 'Yes, my child, it is as you say'. Then Aloni said, 'Sebo, he that believeth in Christ, although he die yet shall he live'. To this Pilkington replied, 'Yes, my child, it is as you say, shall never die'.[89]

The Ganda soon began to bring their new faith to others. In 1894, eighty evangelists left Mengo, supporting themselves with banana cultivation, and a small stipend from their home church. By the end of the year, there were 200 rural churches, more than half of them run by unpaid volunteers.

By 1902, Ganda missionaries had spread far beyond Buganda, and were working in Busoga and Toro; the saintly Apolo Kivebulaya worked among the Pygmies of Zaire.[90] The same movement was evident among the Catholics, and new converts would appear who had never seen a European missionary, but knew both catechism and prayers. Ganda catechists worked in the far North of Uganda, and in the southern Sudan. The income that supported one European missionary could sustain 100 Ganda.[91] In June 1896, Tucker wrote of 'the noble band of 725 teachers from Busoga in the east to Toro in the west, and from Bunyoro in the north to Nasa in the south', who were instructing some 60 000 'Readers'.[92] There was a sense in which a European cultural packaging was replaced by a Ganda one and in Busoga and Bunyoro, the educated and progressive learned luGanda.[93] In time, their privileged role led to resentment and division.

The White Fathers reached Rwanda in 1900, with twelve Ganda auxiliaries. The survivors of more than a decade of violence, they were well-armed, and kept guard at night like sentries. Some of them were more like soldiers than missionaries, forcibly acquiring Hutu children for training as catechists; it was believed that they were destined for sacrifice to *Nyina'rupfu*, Mother Death, and families hid their children when they approached. Tobï Kibati was a Ganda catechist in Rwanda whose family had been killed in an attack on a Catholic settlement in 1895. He refused to remarry, and learned kinya-Rwanda. He was killed on the way to found a new mission.

By 1911, 155 thousand Ganda were Catholics, and 127 thousand Protestants; together, they comprised rather less than half of a population of some 660 thousand.

The Anglican Bishop Tucker, who reached Uganda in 1890, urged a constitution where missionaries should become part of a Ugandan church, but it was rejected, as we saw on page 91 because of 'the proposed equality of European and native workers'. European missionaries were increasingly critical of the Ganda. In 1904, much was said at a missionary conference 'on their unfitness, on the whole, for bearing responsibility . . . a considerable number . . . had become listless and inactive.'[94]

This was the year in which Rachel Sebulimba died. In 1901, the islands of Lake Victoria were ravaged with sleeping sickness, and, in 1903, four Ganda women evangelists went there. Rachel, who was one of them, returned for a second time, caught the disease, and died of it. She said, near the end of her life, 'my body hurts me very much, but my spirit rejoices'.[95]

Religious devotion could take many forms. Although Catholic priests were committed to celibacy, and needed eighteen years of training, the Ganda came to produce a uniquely large body of priests and nuns. In 1927, there were 31 Ganda priests, and 162 professed Bannabikira who concentrated on the religious instruction of children.[96]

In Buganda, as elsewhere, some Christians developed new churches. Joshua Mugema and Malachy Musajjalumbwa founded one in the early twentieth century, which emphasized healing by faith in God alone. Joshua was called 'Merciful to the poor'.[97]

Madagascar[98]

The Malagasy are descended from immigrants from south-east Asia, who arrived before *c.* AD 200, and their language is as closely related to those of Indonesia as French is to Italian.[99] Until the late eighteenth century, Madagascar was divided into a large number of mutually hostile polities. Much of the island was uninhabited, its population of perhaps 2 million living mainly in the interior, or the eastern coastlands. Nampoina, who reigned from 1783 to 1810, united the four Merina kingdoms, and much of the rest of the island, a task continued by his son Radama, 'the Napoleon of Madagascar'.

The LMS established a mission in Madagascar in 1820. Radama welcomed it as he had an avid enthusiasm for modernity, and a receptivity to new ideas. Some Malagasy were sent abroad for education, and the missionaries were a welcome source of new technology, including the making of unfired bricks, soap, and sulphur. Before the end of 1820, there were 23 local schools with 2300 pupils, a third of them girls.

It is noteworthy that southern Madagascar had an older tradition of literacy, writing Malagasy in Arabic characters. The missionaries embarked on the transcription of the Merina dialect in Roman characters, and, by 1827, 4 thousand Malagasy were literate in it.

Radama displayed the same sort of scepticism towards traditional belief that characterized the younger Mutesa, and, when asked to give red cloth to a traditional divinity, he asked why the spirit could not provide it for himself. He ended the poison ordeal, and the practice of abandoning infants, regarded as tabu. He died in 1828, the year when the first biblical text was printed in Malagasy.

One of his wives, Ranavalona, seized the throne, which she retained until her death in 1861. She showed ever greater hostility to Christians, whom she may have perceived as a subversive fifth column: 'They hold assemblies in the night and deliver speeches without permission from the Queen. The Christians are exhorted to serve Jehovah, the first King of the English, and then Jesus Christ, the second. These meetings are carried on by slaves'. Forbidden to preach, the missionaries concentrated on printing, and finally left Madagascar in 1836. Although she limited foreign contacts, Ranavalona did not turn her back on modernity; a Frenchman, Jean Laborde, who became a member of the Malagasy aristocracy, established an industrial town, which manufactured a great many products, including guns.

There seem to have been 1 to 2 thousand Christians at the beginning of the persecutions, 7 to 10 thousand when they ended in 1857, and 27 thousand eleven years later. Christianity was largely confined to the aristocracy, and the young. A noblewoman, Rafavavy, was the first Christian arrested. She was condemned to death, but escaped. The first martyr was another woman, Rasalama. The Malagasy scriptures were copied and recopied by hand during this time. In 1849, three noblemen and a noblewoman were burned to death, and fourteen hurled to death from a rock. Two thousand or more were punished in other ways, such as flogging or slavery. Those about to be burned sang '*hod' izahah Zanahary*', 'Going home are we to God'. They were fastened to stakes a little above the firewood, and, as the flames rose, they could be heard praying, and quoting scripture. One witness said, 'They prayed as long as they had any life'.

The old Queen died in 1861, and was succeeded by her son, who became Radama II. He proclaimed religious freedom, and freed the imprisoned Christians. The LMS returned, and was soon joined by Catholics, Anglicans, Norwegian Lutherans, and the Quakers. When an epidemic broke out, it was interpreted as the revenge of the ancestors, and, in 1863, Radama was overthrown, and put to death. His wife became queen, with the name of Rasoherina, the Chrysalis. Real power, though, was in the hands of the Prime

Minister, Rainilaiarivony, who ruled until 1895, in the name of three successive queens, whom he married in turn. Rasoherina died in 1868, and was replaced by a cousin, who became Ranavalona II. The new queen was a Protestant, and, as a result of her urging, the icons of traditional religion were destroyed, and, in 1869, the couple were married in church. The main concentration of mission work—and education—during this time was Merina. By 1875, the Protestants alone had 30 thousand pupils.

Christianity spread among the aristocracy, but traditional religion was still the dominant faith of the masses. In the mid 1970s, only 20 per cent of the population of 8 million was Protestant, and 21.3 per cent Catholic.[100] The history of Malagasy Christianity, for all the heroism of its martyrs, is one of a minority.

⋖ SIX ⋗

West Africa to c. 1900

There arrived at the station a white man from beyond the sea,
who brought with him six corpses—bodies of holy men—to
be buried here. The white man asking for the agent in charge
of this station, I presented myself; he then handed to me a
paper on which were written the names of the six holy ones
who are to be buried: with my own hand I wrote my name the
seventh.

A vision described by Jacob Akiwuli, a Yoruba
CMS catechist before his last illness, in 1905[1]

Introduction: contexts

The Atlantic coast of West Africa is sometimes a zone of pounding surf, and
sometimes of intricate swamps and waterways. A thousand years ago, it was
the remote frontier of human society, the home of a few scattered fishermen
and salt makers. Travelling North, one moves imperceptibly from the forest
zone—now largely cultivated—into the savanna. Trees become fewer and
settlement sparser; a landscape dominated by vegeculture and oil palms gives
way to orchard bush; yam barns are replaced by granaries. Imperceptibly, the
savanna becomes the sahel and then the desert.

Islam was dominant in the savanna and further North, and Muslim
merchants and scholars also penetrated deep into the forest zone; European
visitors met them at the courts of Asante and Dahomey (see Map 10). In the
first-recorded dialogue between a European Christian and a Nigerian Muslim,
in 1822, the latter had much the better of it: 'He continued to ask several
other theological questions, until I was obliged to confess myself not
sufficiently versed in religious subtleties to resolve these knotty points, having
always left that task to others more learned than myself'.[2]

Islam in West Africa was not a single monolithic entity; there were infinite
permutations in its relationship with traditional cultures, as there were in the
case of Christianity: 'To the question whether a certain chief was Muslim, the
answer was, "He was praying"'.[3]

Atlantic trade with visiting Europeans began in the late fifteenth century.

153

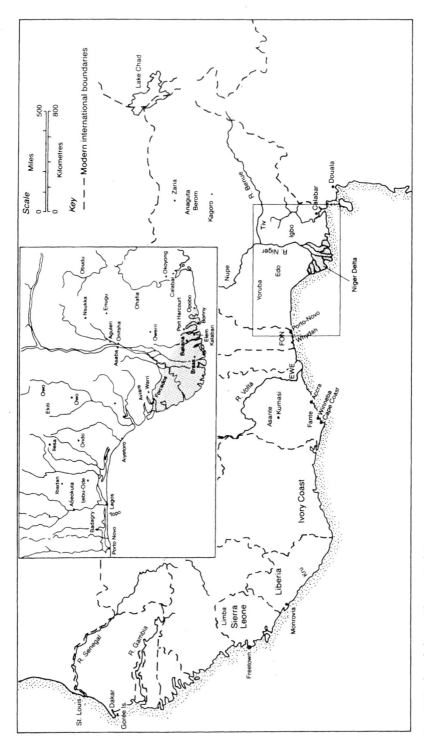

Map 10. Peoples and places in Chapters 6 and 10

Increasingly, it became a trade in slaves, the source of immense suffering to those who became its victims, and to their families. However, for some, the once desolate coastline became a frontier of opportunity. New commercial states grew up, notably in the Niger Delta. Perhaps because of dislocations caused by the European presence, they remained small, while larger, and more powerful kingdoms grew up inland: Asante, in modern Ghana, Dahomey in modern Benin. The northern Yoruba of Oyo created a great empire that collapsed in the early nineteenth century, soon after reaching its greatest extent. Further south, new states such as Ibadan, Ijaye, Abeokuta, and a relocated Oyo struggled for supremacy and survival. In the course of these wars, many were enslaved; some of them were destined to become pioneer Christians.

Despite the Atlantic slave trade, West Africa's populations remained dense. The Igbo, who were among its chief victims in the eighteenth century, now number perhaps 20 million.[4] They lived in a large number of village democracies (according to one estimate, there were 2240, excluding those west of the Niger). Peoples such as the Yoruba, Igbo, Fon, and Asante spoke Kwa languages, their deep differentiation reflecting the antiquity of settlement. Western scholars have been fascinated by the richness and vitality of these cultures. The Yoruba, for instance, are justly famous for: their large corpus of oral literature; their sculptures in bronze, terracotta, and iron; their elaborate mask costumes; the intricacies of their systems of government; the richness of their religious life.

By 1900, western and Christian influences had touched only the fringes of these cultures. Many peoples had never met a missionary, and, even in centres with a long-established mission presence, such as Lagos or Onitsha, Christians were in a minority. In 1897, the CMS had worked continuously and intensively on the lower Niger for nearly forty years, but one of their representatives there reported:

> In a small district we perhaps touch one per cent of the people, the remainder are indifferent or hostile to our work . . . progress is painfully slow and the great mass of heathenism around is still untouched. . . . At first they receive us gladly, but as soon as there are any converts & the inevitable collision between heathen customs & Christian principles takes place, this cordiality is replaced by coldness and suspicion which in many cases develops into active hostility.[5]

The Ijebu of southern Yorubaland turned to monotheism *en masse* in the 1890s, but many became Muslims rather than Christians. The Niger Delta (see Map 8) was an exceptionally successful mission field, but even there, Christianity proved bitterly divisive where it was strongest, and the converts of Brass reverted to their ancestral faith.

Among the black Americans who settled in Liberia, Christianity, like English and western dress, was an essential dimension of their identity. In

1807, the British slave trade was abolished; a number of other slaving nations followed suit, and others were coerced into signing anti-slave trade treaties. A British naval squadron on the coast of West Africa intercepted illegal slavers, and freed their living cargoes, not in their original homes, which was probably impossible, but in Sierra Leone. Some of these slaves had been Muslims and remained so; most eagerly embraced Christianity, and western culture.

Jacob Akiwuli's dying vision, with which this chapter begins, is a moving symbolic statement of the self-sacrifice of scores of European missionaries who came to nineteenth-century West Africa in the knowledge that they were likely to die there. When the Eur-African, Thomas Birch Freeman, went as a missionary to the Gold Coast, he said, echoing a hero of antiquity, 'It is necessary for me to go; but it may not be necessary for me to live'.[6] Freeman lived to be eighty-one, but few were so fortunate.

By far the most successful missionaries in nineteenth- and twentieth-century West Africa were Africans: 'As evangelists we are a failure', wrote an English missionary bishop, Herbert Tugwell, in Nigeria, in 1895; 'I do not know of one successful European evangelist'.[7]

Like their South African counterparts, West African missionaries often suffered from profound isolation. A white racism, which was largely unconscious, darkened countless lives, but the same African Christians were often ostracized, or even persecuted, by traditional rulers. Their self-immolation is reflected in Akiwuli's vision: 'With my own hand I wrote my name the seventh . . . to be buried'. When a catechumen in Bonny was asked if he had reflected on the consequences of his decision, he said, 'a man does not take only a single day to think about committing suicide'.[8]

Many active evangelists were not employed by missionary societies at all. Anna Peters worked as a trader in Ondo from 1880 until her death in 1892, and led a group of women on weekly preaching tours.[9] Bribrina was expelled from her home in Patani, a village in the Niger Delta, when she gave birth to twins. She was rescued, with her babies, by an Isoko trader who married her, and she pioneered Christianity among his people.[10]

Encounters

In West, as in South, East, and Central Africa, early converts were often drawn from the enslaved, the poor, the disabled, and the marginalized. There were exceptions, such as John Okenla, Balogun of Abeokuta, or Idigo, founder of a new dynasty of Aguleri kings, but it was generally true that 'most of the people attending the Church are *women* that have no *money* and the rest are the poorer class, very few of the *wealthy* Cheifs [sic]'.[11]

Often, a missionary presence created something like a class conflict, 'the chief cause of all these repeated and most annoying pesecutions since 1874 is *slavery*—the fear of some of the Chiefs is that, should Christianity progress more than it is now . . . civilised ideas naturally will follow & a revolution may take place. . . .[12] As the number of converts increased, rulers became increasingly anxious about the existence of a rival centre of authority, especially when enthusiasts deliberately flouted traditional customs. All this led to conflict and persecution.

The rulers of powerful military states, such as Asante and Dahomey, tended to believe, correctly, that Christianity would threaten both internal unity, and the kingdom's warlike ethos. For example, the overthrow of Agonglo, King of Dahomey, in 1797, may have been due to his stated willingness to become a Catholic.[13] As late as the 1960s it was observed that no Akan chief had become a full member of a church and retained his office.[14]

However, leading men often welcomed missionaries in the belief that their presence would encourage trade, and that they could contain their influence:

> This earnest desire for missionaries which many of the chiefs I visited showed was in great measure owing to a belief current that missionaries will bring merchants with them, or if they are there already they will not easily remove should missionaries be there also.[15]

In time, they were forced to grapple with the conflict of values and loyalties that the introduction of Christianity created. In 1868, the Onitsha King suggested that converts should attend church, but not catch sacred fish, or eat fowls offered in sacrifice, that they should wear the local dress, and 'That an agreement should be entered into for intermarriage between the children of the settlers and those of the natives of Onitsha that all may become one people'.[16]

Complaints were made that Christianity undermined the obedience children traditionally gave their parents, and the authority of chiefs and elders.

In the records of the time, one can glimpse, albeit through a glass darkly, debates much like those that we have outlined in other contexts. Like the Zulu, West Africans often criticized the fundamentalist Christianity presented to them. King William Dappa Pepple of Bonny said, 'He thought some people must have been fools to attempt to build a tower to heaven'. He rejected the Atonement as absurd, and, when he asked for proof, he was told, 'it was the almost universal belief among white men', and that the Bible said so. He was not convinced, 'Does lie never live for book?'[17]

Missionaries seem seldom, if ever, to have reflected on the intrinsic difficulty of presenting a religious system convincingly to one who stood outside its frame of reference, and did not accept its sacred texts. Recorded debates show a leap from what is common ground, such as the existence and attributes of a supreme God, to the alien and incomprehensible: 'I pointed to him that Jesus is the way, the truth, and the life'.[18] People were even exhorted to be washed in the blood of the Lamb![19] Language barriers compounded the problem: 'Is it possible a sensible man, like Mr Horne, can suppose it is in his power to imprint notions of Christianity . . . through the bare medium of a language they do not understand?'[20]

Those who rejected Christianity often expounded a sophisticated relativism, suggesting that different religions were appropriate for different cultures. It was said of Diali, the short-lived king of nineteenth-century Onitsha, that 'he regarded all religions as equally true'.[21] This kind of scepticism received external reinforcement when, in the 1880s, Herbert Jumbo of Bonny visited England, and discovered that 'one Bradlaugh, cleverer than any English Bishop or Clergy has opened the eyes of England that there is no God'. Returning home, he held rationalist meetings in a canoe shed.[22]

Christianity was exclusive; African religions were more fluid and adaptable. When Umon, a town on the Cross River, was visited by Presbyterians:

> Mr Goldie expounded the laws and exhibited the grace of God. At the close old *Asuqa* said that they would think of what had been told them, and we must return the next morning, and tell them again all things God liked and did not like; and then they would tell us what things they could agree to, and what not; and as far as they could keep them, they would take oath to that effect. . . . Their plan of choosing and rejecting among God's laws we could not sanction.[23]

Christian influence often raised community consciousness about repressive elements in local cultures, even among those who did not become Christians. One of the most dramatic and best-documented cases was in Calabar in 1850–1, when the sacrifice of slaves at the funerals of the affluent was abolished.[24] In 1893, 'a public spontaneous reaction against human sacrifice' was noted in Ondo.[25] Such reforms were not always due to outside influences,[26] but, in some cases, at least, Christianity seems to have been a source of new humanitarian insights.

To suggest that those who had least to lose were among the first Christians is not to say that all conversions were determined by socio-economic factors. Some were profoundly affected by the doctrine of eternal rewards and punishments: entering the subconscious, these teachings often produced visions or dreams, where the fear of suffering was frequently more evident than the hope of eternal happiness. Okwuose was an Obi of Asaba, holding the highest title in traditional society: 'The Chief saw, as it were, a very dark figure, with flowing hair, chained by the neck, while its body appeared as blazing fire. The Chief begged not to be punished as that figure'.[27] He was later baptized as Michael. The fear of Hell could also act as a deterrent: 'You could not possibly be good enough to satisfy the Christian God, and if you fail the hairs of your head will be burnt off one by one'.[28] Some elders, with stoic loyalty, said that if their ancestors were in Hell, they would join them.

Traditional religions offered protection and blessings. Those who suffered misfortunes, especially the loss of children, were often ready to try something different: 'We again and again, here in and around Onitsha, come across men and women who have paid sums of money, and offered sacrifices to their own gods, on account of some children of theirs whom they wished to keep alive, but who have forsaken heathenism and come to Christ on the death of the child'.[29]

Literacy was a powerful attraction, too. Some West African peoples, such as the Vai, invented new scripts in response to western stimuli, as did several independent churches in the twentieth century:

> A man living in Ijebu Ode was commissioned by one of the Christians to take a letter to a second Christian: on presenting the letter he saw that the receiver clearly understood its purport. This aroused his curiosity and he determined to join the Christians.[30]

Once converted, people grappled in various ways with the relationship between their new faith, their cultural inheritance, and the needs and obligations of their immediate environment. One of the most enduring, and complicated problems was plural marriage. Some new Christians renounced all their wives but one. For many, this was impossible. In the words of a certain Sade:

> I have long renounced idolatry . . . here are my two wives, from this I have got children, but she is poor; that one has no child, but she finds my daily bread. I have also suffered from a long sickness which has thus disabled me.[31]

A Yoruba clergyman, Emmanuel Moses Lijadu, told him to choose between children and bread. He died before he decided.

The mission embargo on plural marriages was fossilized for Anglicans by a ruling of the Lambeth Conference in 1888. Many factors made monogamy difficult, not least a sense of loyalty to existing wives, and Bible study revealed the existence of polygamous Old Testament patriarchs who walked with God. Some Christians evaded the prohibition by sending different wives, and their respective offspring to different churches. In 1917, ten leading laymen of a Lagos Methodist church were indicted for polygamy. At a crowded meeting, fifty-five others said that they were guilty as well. Their dismissal led to the creation of the United African Methodist Church.[32]

Some converts risked their lives by attacks on masqueraders, whose costume was an obvious physical manifestation of traditional belief. Others attempted to create a Christian form of Ogboni, the secret Yoruba cult of the sacred Earth. Some renounced traditional titles, while Idigo of Aguleri acquired a superannuated horse, with the help of the Holy Ghost Fathers, and took the rare and prestigious title *ogbu anyinya*, Horse Killer.

Some missionaries, Thomas Birch Freeman among them, always needed an interpreter; others, both black and white, entered deeply into the scholarly study of African languages and cultures. The great German linguist, Sigismund Koelle, collected language data from the Recaptives of Sierra Leone while working for the CMS, and recorded it in his *Polyglotta Africana*. Johann Gottlieb Christaller, of the Basel Mission translated the whole Bible into Twi

159

and wrote 'a dictionary in the first rank of dictionaries of African languages, or indeed of any languages'.[33] A Ga scholar-clergyman, Carl Christian Reindorf, wrote *The History of the Gold Coast and Asante* (1889) in Ga, and later in English, basing it on information from 200 informants. His Yoruba counterpart, Reverend Henry Johnson, wrote a monumental *History of the Yoruba*, which was lost by publishers in England; it was rewritten from the original notes after his death, by his brother, Obadiah.

In the selection of languages or particular dialects for translation and as a medium of instruction, the missions often unwittingly contributed to the growth of chosen languages as 'official', and to the decline of others. The CMS, in the early twentieth century, translated the Bible into Union Igbo, an artificial concoction of five dialects, based, in the main, on Owerri Igbo. But, Owerri Igbo is as different from Onitsha Igbo as Dutch is from German: the result was 'a dialect spoken and written easily by no Igbo district'.[34] In Efutu, the language of the Church and of public discourse became Twi, the language of the Akan, who are the majority in southern Ghana. The local language, Guan, became limited to use in the home.[35]

Traditional diviners or mediums sometimes perceived and articulated the shape of things to come. A mid nineteenth-century Igbo, Ewenihi of Aguinyi, foretold that most of the old gods would starve to death, and that any survivors would have hot oil poured in their eyes. In the early twentieth century, the medium of a Kalabari water spirit urged people to go to church, since the spirits were becoming weak.[36]

It is not easy to date the renewal of missionary work in West Africa. Perhaps it was in 1792, when a body of black Nova Scotians landed in Sierra Leone, singing hymns. In 1819 Mother Javouhey reached Senegal, but her sojourn in West Africa was a brief one. The first Basel missionary reached Ghana in 1828, and, in 1842, Thomas Birch Freeman preached in Badagry, the beginnings of modern missions in Nigeria. However, all these beginnings are, in a sense, artificial—the Catholic Luso-African culture of the past had not wholly died, and it had been reinforced by the lives of freed slaves returning from Brazil.

Catholicism and the Brazilians

In some coastal areas, Catholicism was sustained by black priests from São Thomé and the Cape Verdes. In the mid nineteenth century, a Protestant naval officer cited their activity at Whydah as an example of 'the extraordinary capacity of the African mind':

> The Black priests from the island of St Thomas preach to large flocks and converts are frequently made. . . . The island of St Thomas sends forth hundreds of black Roman Catholic priests to many parts of Africa, and

these sable fathers assist materially towards the great object, the civilisation of Africa.[37]

Other observers criticized the Christian cultures of the coast for syncretism: 'An appearance of Christianity, Mahomedan manners and fetishist superstition, that's all there is to religion in Senegal'.[38]

The black Brazilians who contributed to the growth of West African Christianity included Venossa de Jesus, a woman, who built a church at Agoué (in modern Benin) in 1835. The 'Brazilian' who exercised the greatest religious influence was a humble and obscure man, born in São Thomé[39] in 1800, called Antonio. He was enslaved at the age of ten, and taken to Brazil, where he was redeemed by the Bahia Carmelites, and became a fervent Catholic. He decided to return to West Africa when he was told that Brazilian repatriates were losing their faith, for lack of a pastor. He settled in Lagos,[40] and took upon himself the spiritual guidance of its Brazilian Catholic community, estimated at 6 thousand in 1868. They erected an eight-foot cross, built a church, and went through the streets at Epiphany, re-enacting the journey of the Magi. When European missionaries arrived in 1868, Antonio gladly surrendered his pastoral role. When old and ill, he continued to study his catechism, 'More than ever I need to study, to know the path to eternity'. His calm in the face of death affected all who saw it.

The modern phase of Catholic mission work in West Africa began with the arrival of the sisters of St Joseph of Cluny at Gorée in Senegal in 1819. Their foundress, Ann-Marie Javouhey, was invalided home from Sierra Leone in 1823. Like many other nineteenth-century foundresses, she influenced lives less by her own exertions than by her ability to recruit and organize large numbers of dedicated women. King Louis Philippe, intending a compliment, called her 'a great man'![41]

By the 1950s, there were at least fourteen women's congregations at work in West Africa.[42] Most of them were either twentieth-century foundations, or established their first African missions then. As well as the Cluny sisters, at work in the Gambia and Sierra Leone, they included the sisters of Our Lady of Apostles, who reached West Africa in the 1870s, and had convents in the Gold Coast, Ivory Coast, Nigeria, and Dahomey.

The main male Catholic congregations to work in nineteenth-century West Africa were the Holy Ghost Fathers, and the Society of African Missions (see page 85). Bresillac, the latter's founder, died in Sierra Leone soon after his arrival, but, like Mère Javouhey, he influenced African lives, not so much through his own efforts, but through the continuing work of his congregation.

In 1861, SMA Fathers came to Whydah. Like Lagos, where they settled seven years later, it already had a well-established Catholic presence. They relied heavily on the support of Brazilian Catholics, from whom they were separated by language barriers. They had little sympathy for their characteristic blend of religious fervour, plural marriage, and syncretism.

In 1864,.the Holy Ghost Fathers arrived in Freetown, to be joined two years later by the St Joseph of Cluny sisters. In 1884 and 1885, the SMA and the Holy Ghost Fathers settled on opposite banks of the lower Niger.

Catholic missionaries had little success in the nineteenth century, partly because of limited personnel and high mortality rates, partly because of a mistaken mission strategy. Like their counterparts elsewhere, they concentrated on redeeming slaves and founding Christian villages, such as Topo, a coastal settlement near Lagos, or Aguleri, near a tributary of the Niger. By concentrating on 'poor & castoff creatures',[43] they reduced the general acceptability of the new religion.

Protestants also tried the experiment of redeeming slaves. The Basel Mission in Togo ransomed 150 slave children between 1857 and 1867, when they gave up the practice, finding that they were considered responsible for their actions when they grew up, and that the children themselves, not surprisingly, had problems of identity.[44]

The most enduring consequences of Mère Javouhey's sojourn in Senegal was the education of twenty African seminarians in Europe. Some fell victim to an unfamiliar climate, and disease environment, with the result that others were recalled by their understandably anxious families. Three Senegalese, ordained in 1840, returned as priests: two Eur-Africans, David Boilat and Arsène Fridoil, as well as Pierra Moussa. Boilat was to prove a distinguished scholar and artist.[45]

Despite their outstanding gifts, their careers in their native land led only to unhappiness and frustration.[46] Boilat and Fridoil established a secondary school, which foundered because of lack of resources, and the rivalry of a European teaching order. Fridoil worked among newly freed slaves, and was blamed for inculcating fraternity and equality.

Province of freedom: Sierra Leone

In the late eighteenth and early nineteenth centuries, three separate groups of black settlers came to the peninsula where Freetown stands, and where a Portuguese visitor had seen a Lion Mountain. The resettlement of the London Black Poor was inspired, in part, by philanthropy, and, in part, by the desire to rid Britain of a social problem. The voices of the migrants, many of whom died, are not heard. They were joined by the Maroons of Jamaica, who had escaped from slavery, and maintained their freedom in the face of overwhelming odds, and by 'Nova Scotians' who had supported Britain in the American War of Independence, but were denied the farms they were promised, and sent to a bitterly cold environment. The Sierra Leone settlement offered them a new start. Much suffering and disappointment lay before them, and many died within a few months of their arrival: 'It is quite customary of a morning to ask "how many died last night?"'[47] They were, for the most part,

Dissenters—Methodists, Baptists, and members of the Countess of Huntingdon's Connection. They landed in 1792, Bibles in hand, singing a hymn:

> The Day of Jubilee is come;
> Return ye ransomed sinners home.[48]

Religion defined their identity, and the church congregation was the central focus of their loyalties:

> Among the Black Settlers are seven religious sects, and each sect has one or more preachers attached to it, who alternately preach throughout the whole night; indeed, I never met with, heard or read of, any set of people observing the same appearance of godliness.[49]

It was the Nova Scotians who were the role models of the Recaptives, rescued from the slave ships on the high seas, and resettled in Sierra Leone from 1808. At that time there were fewer than 2 thousand Settlers; 74 thousand Recaptives were to join them. Unlike the Settlers, they had recently been torn from their homes, and were still thoroughly conversant with their original language and culture. They had been through traumatic experiences, and were forced to make a new life for themselves far from home, in close proximity to people different in language and culture. They settled in mission-run villages, whose very names echoed a land they had never seen—Regent, Leicester. They adopted European names and western dress, learned English, and began to read and write.

Many prospered through trade, and, like so many West Africans after them, invested in their children's education. The Sierra Leone census of 1860 showed that 22 per cent of the population was at school (the figures for England and Prussia at the time were 13 and 16 per cent respectively).[50] Fourah Bay College was founded in 1827, and, from 1876, it awarded degrees of the University of Durham. James Horton was an Army doctor who wrote books on tropical medicine and politics; he adopted the name Africanus as a statement of identity. Another Creole physician, J. F. Easmon, was the first to isolate blackwater fever, and Samuel Lewis, a famous lawyer, became West Africa's first knight. There were many other brilliant Creole doctors, lawyers, and clergymen.

Not all the Recaptives became Christians. Those who were already Muslims often kept to their original faith, but, for many, as for their Victorian mentors, progress and Christianity seemed a package deal: 'We know that England and indeed Europe owes her prosperity, greatness and security mainly to Christianity'.[51]

The Creoles created a composite of African and imported culture, symbolized in their language, Krio, and masquerades of Yoruba origin are still performed in Freetown. In 1867, it was noted, 'amongst professing Christians

I have found those who take delight in "Oru", Last Burying and other such . . . relics of heathenism'.[52] White missionaries showed little sympathy for these attempts to integrate African culture, and new beliefs. In 1837, one of them was reproved by a Recaptive, 'We were born in another country, this fashion we learned from our fathers. What they did we do too'.

In 1861, the CMS Native Pastorate, later the Sierra Leone Church, was established. It was the first step towards a self-governing Church, the 'euthanasia' of missions, of which Henry Venn had dreamed. Still headed by white bishops—one of whom spent six out of ten years outside the country— it was, as was pointed out at the time, the closest approximation to an autonomous institution in colonial Sierra Leone.[53] Creole Muslims subscribed to the building of churches, and Christians to the building of mosques. They gave generously to causes far from Freetown, such as the Syrian Christians, and the widows of the Crimean war.

But Christianity did not spread far beyond the Creole community and those who became part of it, such as children who worked as servants in return for education. Mission societies concentrated their main energies in the Freetown area, though there were enclaves of Christian influence elsewhere. Creoles trading in the interior often built churches for their own use, but the main thrust of their missionary energies was directed to the societies from which they had originally come. The Creole Methodist pastor, Peter Hazeley, was an exception, and he was called the Apostle to the Limba.

The Creoles reached a pinnacle of success and prosperity in the mid nineteenth century. Their achievements were applauded, and their work encouraged by mission strategists, partly because of the high mortality rates among Europeans in tropical Africa. As the century progressed, the latter's life expectancy increased,[54] and there was an influx of whites into the missions, commercial firms, and expanding colonial administrators. They perceived the educated African as a threat rather than as a partner. The Royal Niger Company received a Charter in 1886 and used its new powers to drive Sierra Leonian merchants from the Niger. In 1881, a white Baptist missionary in Yorubaland wrote that no more black Americans were required. The last one died that year, and no more were sent.

> The upset of the Sierra Leonian began with the upset of thought of his white rulers concerning him. A day came when white thought began to be changed, white feeling began to be altered, and white action began to be fitted to the thought and feeling. . . . Segregation was the first blast of the trumpet; then other things and other things.[55]

'The missionary-made man is the curse of the coast', wrote the much applauded Mary Kingsley, 'The pagans despise him, the whites hate him . . .'[56]

Liberia

There are certain similarities between the histories of Liberia and Sierra Leone. The modern nations are quite small, their populations estimated at 2.5 and 3.9 million, respectively. Like Sierra Leone, nineteenth-century Liberia was the site of settlement by black Settlers and Recaptives. Despite their small numbers, they were destined to have a disproportionate share of the nation's power and resources.

The first Settlers arrived in 1822, former slaves, or their descendants, from America. At the time, there was a black population in America of 1.75 million, a seventh of whom were free. By 1866, when emigration had virtually ended, under 12 thousand had gone to Liberia; half of them had been freed on condition that they do so, and many died within a year of arrival. They were joined by 5700 Recaptives, freed on the high seas. The American Colonization Society was supported largely by white slave owners, who feared the existence of a free black population, while most blacks preferred to struggle for a place in the sun in America: 'America is more our country than it is the whites'—we have enriched it with our blood and tears . . . and will they drive us from our property and homes, which we have earned with our blood?'[57]

Liberia's independence was recognized in 1847, although it was dogged by economic and other problems that limited the extent of its true autonomy. In 1926, Firestone leased a million acres of land; in 1951, its after-tax profit was three times the total income of Liberia, which was sometimes called the Firestone Republic.[58] Some of the Settlers were fourth- or fifth-generation Americans. They no longer spoke an African language, and clung to American culture (and Christianity) as ways of defining their identity, duplicating the institutions of the society that had oppressed them—colonial-style mansions, a Frontier Force, and even a Capitol.

Like the Creoles, they held aloof from indigenous peoples. The latter are invisible in the national motto, 'The love of liberty brought us here'. The 1847 Declaration of Independence states, 'We the people of Liberia were originally the inhabitants of the United States of America', and makes no mention of the fact that they originally came from Africa. It was intended to call the capital Christopolis, but it was named after an American President instead.

Americo-Liberian hegemony was to last until 1980. The separation from local people was never total as many children were entrusted to Settler families, and Settler Americo-Liberians often married (additional) 'country wives', so that, by the 1950s, 'pure' Americo-Liberian descent was the exception. However, to the Settlers, the local African was the Other. Lott Carey was a black Baptist pastor from Virginia who played a leading role in the early days of Monrovia. With tragic irony, he blew himself up in 1828, while making ammunition to use against local Africans. A black Episcopalian priest wrote of a conflict between Americo-Liberians and local Africans, 'A few brave colonists were beset by hosts of infuriate savages'. A black American Baptist in Liberia called Africans 'servants and soldiers for hell'.[59]

Some indigenous peoples, notably the Grebo and Kru, showed an avid enthusiasm for Christianity, and westernization. In 1871, Christian converts founded a short-lived Grebo Reunited Kingdom at a meeting where the Gloria was sung. They fought for, but did not obtain, political independence. Much later, William Wade Harris, the Grebo who was incomparably West Africa's most successful Christian missionary, had the vision that changed his life while he was a political prisoner in a Monrovia gaol.

Edward Wilmot Blyden (1832–1912) was born in the West Indies and migrated to Liberia when he was denied the opportunity to study theology in the United States. He was a man of immense learning, who mastered numerous languages, including Hebrew and Arabic, and devoted himself to his adopted country with consuming passion. He became increasingly critical of Christian missions, and sympathetic to Islam. He moved away from Christianity to deism, and left the Presbyterian ministry. His immense erudition was an inspiration to many, but much of his great ability and energy was devoted to misplaced goals. He had an obsessive hatred of Eur-Africans, whom he tried to bar from Liberia.[60] His life, like that of many others, reflects an agonized quest for identity.

By 1848, there were four denominations in Monrovia: Baptist, Methodist Episcopalian, Protestant Episcopalian, and Presbyterian (the last of these has always been relatively small). By 1900, they had been joined by Lutherans, and the African Methodist Episcopal and African Methodist (Zion) churches; after three unsuccessful attempts, a Catholic mission was founded in 1906.

Black missionaries from the New World

In 1839, soon after the emancipation of the slaves in the West Indies, a man called Thomas Keith worked his passage back to Africa with the aim of spreading Christianity among his own people. Nothing more is known of his fate. Another, called James Keats, was reported to have reached Sierra Leone, and boarded a ship bound for the Congo river. Again, he drops out of history like a stone. At a Baptist meeting in Jamaica, 100 poor labourers offered a week's wages for missionary work in Africa.[61]

At least 115 black Americans are known to have served as missionaries in Africa in the last quarter of the nineteenth century. Many of them worked in Liberia, where the line between Settler church and mission is sometimes difficult to draw. Mrs Kelley Kemp went with her husband to the United Brethren for Christ mission in the Sherbro when she was already mortally ill, and worked for four years before she died there: 'I can teach the women to read the Bible and sew. The doctor says I cannot live many years. The road to heaven is as near from Africa as it is from here. Yes, I will go'.[62]

The United Presbyterian mission in Calabar was founded in 1846 by black and white Christians from Jamaica. From 1843, West Indians worked on the Gold Coast with the Basel Mission, and served on Baptist missions, as did black Americans, in Fernando Po, Cameroun, and the Congo.

Some West Indians, like some Europeans, left the mission field; others laboured for decades, like Mrs Waller, in Calabar. But racial prejudice is blind to what it will not see. Whites, said Mary Kingsley, are 'more devoted to the evangelisation of the African' than Jamaican Christians.[63] Fifty black Americans were sponsored by white, and sixty-five by black denominations, such as the African Methodist Episcopal Church.

White churches tended to recruit black missionaries for work in West and West Central Africa, where the health conditions were worst. Black churches lacked financial resources, which made it difficult for them to maintain staff abroad, 'the poverty of the people who had so recently been slaves'.[64] Often, their leaders believed that their true calling lay in America, and one warned of the danger of African Methodist Imperialism. Individuals with a strong missionary calling sometimes persuaded their churches to back them. Thus, Andrew Cartwright, born a slave, persuaded the African Methodist Episcopal Zion Church (AMEZ) to support him in Liberia. In both West and South Africa, black churches made an important contribution by bringing young Africans to study in America. AMEZ supported four Gold Coast students, among them the future internationally famous educationalist, James E. K. Aggrey. In twentieth-century Kenya, white missionaries supported the colonial government in excluding their black American counterparts.[65]

The Gold Coast

Continuities are apparent in the Gold Coast, where, as we saw earlier in this book, small Christian enclaves had clustered round the European forts for centuries. The Methodist Church in Ghana began with a Christian study group, which owed its genesis to Philip Quaque's school (see pages 59–60).

Four Basel missionaries reached the Gold Coast in 1828. The Basel Mission was to work in the Gold Coast for almost a century until their missions were taken over by the United Free Church of Scotland during the First World War. They came in response to African invitations, and three of the four soon died. The survivor, Andreas Riis, a former glass-blower, was saved by the ministrations of an African herbalist. In 1835, he moved eighteen miles inland to the healthier environment of the Akwapim ridge. In time, others joined him, but for decades they had relatively little impact on local people:

> The three fronts of heathenism are fetish worship, polygamy and the power of chiefs, funerals are a great hindrance . . .[66]

Missionaries and Christians lived in western-style houses in separate villages, called Salems. Tradition remembers Riis as a 'builder of houses'. Without realizing the full implications of their policies, missionaries were to catapult their converts into the cash economy: 'In the early days, when a man was converted he was obliged to settle on mission ground, so he needed doors and window shutters, a table, chairs and bed, all of which he had not required before'.[67]

The first converts were drawn largely from the marginal, ex-slaves; the widowed; the childless; and those with some kind of physical abnormality. A small, but influential category of converts were drawn from princes, who, in a matrilineal society, could not succeed to their father's office; the first catechists and pastors were often drawn from their number.[68] David Asante, for example, was the son of Nana Owusu Akyem, and one of the first mission schoolboys, who became a Basel pastor. He was a man of transparent devotion, who at first refused baptism, on the grounds that he was not good enough, but changed his mind when he heard the hymn that begins, 'Come ye sinners, poor and needy, weak and wounded, sick and sore'.[69]

Sometimes, both missionaries and local Christians outraged local suscepti-bilities, as when one of the former collected earth from a sacred grave for his garden.[70] Converts were often attracted by the belief that Christianity was stronger than evil:

> In the Christian village, there are no witches, and the witches have no power there; the pagans say, that as soon as a witch becomes a Christian, her witchcraft is extinguished.[71]

But the afflictions attributed to witchcraft, such as sterility, illness, and premature death did not go away. The attraction of the twentieth-century prophetic churches was the power they claimed over evil.

Paul Mohenu was the priest of a traditional divinity; he was baptized in 1857, at the age of sixty. He lived for another twenty years, learned to read, and worked as an evangelist in the villages of the Accra plain.

The Methodist Church in Ghana developed from a Christian study group formed in 1831. Its members decided that they needed no regulations, 'as the word of God is the best rule a Christian ought to observe'.[72] One member was imprisoned for a time, because of the energy with which he urged sinners to flee from the wrath to come. They petitioned the Bishop of London for a teacher, but it was the Methodists who responded, sending a former tea dealer in his twenties, who lived only six months. The infant church survived: 'They said they would remain in the profession; for though the missionary was dead, God lives'.

Fante Christians, travelling inland to trade, carried their new faith with them. Like the Creoles of Freetown, they had a generosity that stretched far beyond their immediate environment. They not only contributed £60 for a mission among the Asante, their traditional enemies, but, in 1839 raised over £35 for the British Methodist Centenary Fund.

Thomas Birch Freeman (1809–90)[73] was born in England, the son of an

English mother and a black father, a gardener. He was a gardener, too, until his enthusiasm for Methodism cost him his job. He was to spend over fifty-two years in Africa, outliving two wives, perhaps through inherited immunity, perhaps because of his liking for mosquito nets. Paradoxically, he never learned an African language, and was regarded as a European.

Freeman had an enthusiasm and energy that neither misfortune nor the passing years diminished. He paid missionary visits to Dahomey, Asante, and Yorubaland, resigning in 1855 because the mission authorities had become critical of the expense of his work: 'One single passion has absorbed my life— namely the extension of our work, and in the midst thereof I have overlooked and neglected matters of expenditure'. He remained on the Gold Coast, where he worked for the Government, returning to the ministry at the age of sixty-four. On his death bed he said, 'I feel like a little bird with wing ready raised for flight'.

Elizabeth Waldron was another Eur-African. Like Jean Slessor, Mary's adopted daughter, she was childless, and her marriage failed. Like her, she poured her affections and energies into Christian work, concentrating on girls' education.

Women were often the first to respond to Christianity, and, in the Basel Mission, they outnumbered men to such an extent that it was almost impossible for them to find Christian husbands. Converts composed new hymns in Twi: 'Let us sing a song to our Saviour, who makes us dwell in quietness and blesses us daily'.[74]

By 1848, the Basel Mission had 40 Christians in Akwapim. Two years later in 1850, the Methodists had 857, scattered in small congregations throughout the Fante area. Christianity spread more rapidly after the Gold Coast became a colony in 1874 (and especially after the annexation of Asante in 1901).

Riis visited Kumasi in 1839, and 'came back with the impression that we had to wait for better hints from the Lord'. Freeman made several visits, and had an acceptability in Asante that no other missionary enjoyed. But the Methodist mission founded there in 1843 languished 'from the circumstance of the people being afraid to expose themselves to the ire of the king, whose frown is indeed death for people becoming christians'.[75] Among the Asante, as among the Zulu and Ndebele, colonial conquest broke the cake of custom. Many churches were sacked during the Asante rising of 1900, but, in the long run, the way was open to the spread of Christianity. Yet, by the mid twentieth century, it was still true that no Akan chief was a communicating Christian.

The spread of Christianity was furthered by improvements in communications, the new value placed on western education, and the missionary efforts of Fante and Akwapim traders, and clerks in the interior. There were over 12 thousand Basel Christians in 1894 and two years later, 7600 Methodists.

In the early twentieth century, Catholic and Anglican missions expanded, and were joined by Pentecostal missions from America.[76] The prophet, Harris, drew thousands to Christianity in the coastal area West of Axim in 1914, and, in 1920, an illiterate lay preacher, Sampson Opon, led a revival that transformed Asante Methodism, so that in two years, 10 thousand were baptized, and the number of mission stations jumped from nine to seventy-two.[77]

The Saro

The Yoruba were by far the largest of the Seventeen Nations of Sierra Leone. The need for greater economic opportunities and the love of an unforgotten home impelled some of them to brave the dangers of return. Many settled in Badagry, Lagos or Abeokuta, where there were 3 thousand returnees. They were called Aku in Sierra Leone, and Saro in Yorubaland, symbolic of a divided identity. When Christians were persecuted in Abeokuta in 1849, 'Sierra Leone emigrants were permitted to do as they pleased, it being the religion of the country whence they came'.[78]

The Saro formed the nucleus of new Christian communities, and were important role models for new Christians. They struggled to synthesize their inherited culture with the imperatives of Christianity. In Abeokuta, many opted for plural marriage, and joined Ogboni, a powerful secret society dedicated to the sacred Earth[79] (some white missionaries, including Henry Townsend and J. B. Wood, are said to have done the same).[80] In each generation, African Christians have reinvented their culture. Perhaps all Christians must do so.

In 1861, the little island state of Lagos became a British colony. By 1868, it had a population of 27 thousand, of whom just under 4 thousand were Christians. They were outnumbered both by Muslims and traditionalists, and half of them were repatriates.[81] Victorian Lagos, like Freetown, looked on the expression, 'Black Englishmen' as a term of praise rather than reproach. The Saro of Lagos went to fancy dress balls, and played cricket, celebrating Christmas with turkeys, plum puddings, and Christmas trees. Like the Americo-Liberians, most relied on Christianity to define the perimeters of their group identity.

They were not oblivious to the need to synthesize their acquired culture with their African inheritance. Some adopted African names, and there was much discussion of the merits and demerits of western and African dress. Their sense of self-esteem, imperilled by white racism, was sometimes fragile. An editorial in the *Lagos Weekly Record* in 1896, said that, 'The Europeanised African is a nondescript, a.libel on his country, and a blot on civilisation'.[82] These doubts sometimes extended to Christianity itself. In 1902, that passionately devout Baptist, Mojola Agbebi, said bitterly, 'The Gospel may be good news indeed; but it has ceased to be good news to many of our people'.[83]

Mission renewed

The modern missionary enterprise in Nigeria began in 1842, when Thomas Birch Freeman and a Fante Christian, William de Graft, founded a Methodist mission in Badagry. Four years later, an Englishman, Henry Townshend, and Samuel Ajayi Crowther established a CMS post at Abeokuta, soon to acquire symbolic significance for English readers as a Sunrise within the Tropics.[84]

In the same year, a group of black and white Presbyterians from Jamaica settled in the Efik city state of Calabar. In 1850, an American Baptist, Thomas J. Bowen, reached Badagry, inspired by de Graft's account of a conversion in Igboho. Baptists established several stations, among them Ogbomoso, founded in 1855, but soon abandoned as a result of war. In 1872, visitors found twenty Christians there who had endured, despite persecution, 'in the very ruins of their missionary station'.[85]

The Niger Mission

The Niger expedition of 1841 was intended to undermine the slave trade by developing alternative exports and to open up the African interior to Christianity and Commerce. In the 1840s, it seemed self-evident that the two went together, and mission strategists and European merchants were eager to collaborate. Henry Venn, Honorary Secretary of the CMS from 1841 to 1872, 'used to encourage the missionaries to send him samples of dyes, cotton, ginger, arrowroot, pepper, coffee, palm oil, ivory, ebony, etc.'.[86] Like Livingstone's later enterprise on the Zambezi, the Niger expedition was surrounded by high expectations and a blaze of publicity, but proved a failure, largely because of mortality rates among the Europeans involved.

The history of the Niger Mission will always be linked with the name of its leader, Samuel Ajayi Crowther, who was born in about 1806 in a Yoruba town called Osogun. Destroyed by war in 1821, its ruins survive, dominated by a great tree sacred to Obatala, divinity of creativity. For a time, Crowther was a domestic slave in Abeokuta, deterred from escaping by his fear of the shrines that lined the road home.[87] He was sold to a slaver bound for Brazil, freed by the naval squadron, and resettled in Sierra Leone. He became the first student at Fourah Bay College in 1827, and later taught there, catapulted to fame when he took part in the Niger expedition and published his journal. He was ordained in London in 1843—Sierra Leone's first Anglican priest—and returned to Yorubaland as a missionary. He became head of the newly founded all-African Niger Mission in 1857, and was ordained bishop in 1864, 'the symbol of a race on trial'.[88]

The Creoles who volunteered for the Niger Mission were mainly middle-aged men with limited education. In 1870, there were eleven of them, and only four had been to secondary school. The others had been a government messenger, a bricklayer, a carpenter, a farmer, a shingle maker, a shoemaker and a ship's steward.[89]

> I am a descendant of the Ibo tribe, as also my wife, who is more fluent in the language than myself. . . . It has been my desire long ago to become a Missionary to my fatherland.[90]

These humble men and their families endured the hardship and isolation of life on the Niger for decades, creating small churches in a few Niger towns.

The Niger Mission's decline began in 1879, when a European was placed in charge of its 'temporalities', and was complete when Crowther died in 1891, and was replaced by an Englishman. It was destroyed by the attacks of young English missionaries, in the name of Holiness. From the vantage point of inherited money, they condemned their predecessors as worldly, because their wives supplemented by trade the pittance they were paid. There were, indeed, weaknesses in the mission, among them Crowther's protracted absences from his diocese. He did not come from the Niger, or speak local languages, and was fifty-eight when he became Bishop. Not unnaturally, he spent much of the year in Lagos, in activities such as translation.[91]

He was blamed for the preponderance of Creole rather than local personnel, but, of fourteen local boys sent for training, all but four accepted the higher salaries offered by commercial firms. Of those who remained, the gifted Isaac Mba, the first Niger Igbo agent, was forced to resign as a result of European prejudice. Thomas Bako, an Oworro Yoruba who had been enslaved as a child and redeemed by a missionary at Lokoja, endured, although he was denied ordination. He was killed on a missionary journey in 1902.[92] In 1879, a training institute for local youths was established. In 1890, European missionaries sold it to the Royal Niger Company as an army barracks.[93]

By 1883, the mission was in ruins: 'nearly a total clearance of its members . . . by disconnection, dismissal and resignation'.[94] However, the Europeans responsible soon died or left the mission. In 1896, their sole survivor lamented, in vain, the errors of the past:

> I greatly long to see an African Diocese formed . . . I do rejoice to think Archdeacon Henry Johnson is again established. I burn with shame and horror now at the awful charges made against him in 1890 . . . I grieve that such good men as Robinson and Brooke undoubtedly were, should have been so completely misguided and deluded and for a time, I fully believe, lost to all sense of Christian fairness and charity. . . . May God forgive us the bitter slanderous and lying thoughts we had against him and others in those dark days of 1890. We have suffered, no one knows how much, by those rash and hasty actions. We condemned others and we ourselves have done less than they did.[95]

This retraction was of little benefit to the African missionaries whose lives had been blighted, and reputations ruined. They all soon found employment elsewhere, but the pain remained.

Reverend Charles Paul had worked for the CMS for thirty-one years, twenty-five of them on the Niger. He was dismissed, and left dependent on his friends. He worked in the Niger Delta Pastorate until he died, in 1893. In his last illness, 'his trials in the latter years of his service in connection with the CMS had pressed much upon his mind. He was constantly referring to them'.[96]

The Niger churches were small, their members drawn largely from slaves, purported witches, lepers, and mothers of twins, (treasured by the Yoruba, but, in the past, though not now, abhorred by the Igbo). Asaba people spoke of 'a church of backbiters', referred to the slaves' criticisms of the society that, on occasion, offered them in sacrifice. Girls were the first to attend the Onitsha school in 1858, the boys preferred hunting: 'but now and then half a dozen or more of them would rush into the house, and proudly gaze at the alphabet board, and with an air of disdain mimic the names of the letters pronounced by the schoolmaster and repeated by the girls, as if it were a thing only fit for females'.[97] There was nothing to foreshadow the way in which twentieth-century Igbo embraced western education with such passion and resolution.

Sometimes titled men defied the values of the culture that honoured them and became Christians. Ubuechi of Issele-Ukuhad achieved all the distinctions open to him in traditional society: he was a title holder, a blacksmith, a diviner (*dibia*), and a sculptor. By chance, he visited a Catholic church, and was profoundly affected by a sermon on Hell. He dismissed three of his four wives and was baptized as Alexander. He endured much petty persecution, visited the sick, befriended mothers of twins, and held meetings for catechumens. He died in 1903, four years after his conversion.[98]

Similarly, Idigo was a titled man and diviner, wealthy and brave, who turned to Christianity when his arts could not preserve the lives of his own children: 'I perceived above all', said the Catholic priest who baptized him as Joseph, 'that he was religious'. He destroyed his traditional shrines and went to live with witches and slaves on the hilltop Christian village near Aguleri. Christians called the settlement either *Mbito* (Crossroads), or *Nduka* (Life is Supreme).[99]

The Niger Delta

The Niger Mission's greatest success was in the Delta, where a station was established at Bonny in 1865. In a sense, its little states were already attuned to a wider world: they had traded with visiting European merchants for centuries. The Atlantic slave trade made a new elite rich and powerful, and enabled them to supplement their numbers with large accessions of mainly

Igbo slaves. It was a classic case of growth without development, and none realized this more clearly than the people of the coastal states themselves.

In 1842, a letter from a Calabar notable put it all clearly:

> . . . we . . . want something for make work and trade . . . if some man would come teach way for do it, we get plenty sugar too; and then some man must come teach book proper.[100]

They agreed to the establishment of a mission, because centuries of business dealings with Europeans had taught them the value of literacy. They would have preferred secular schools, but this option was not generally open to them, though Ja Ja of Opobo achieved this. In the words of a notable of Elim Kalabari, 'he did not want religious teaching, for that the children have enough at home, they teach them such themselves; that they want them to be taught how to gauge palm oil, and other like mercantile business as soon as possible.'[101]

Bonny was divided into two rival complexes of canoe houses: the Anna and Manilla Pepples—the former opposed Christianity, and the latter welcomed it. Problems developed when slaves refused to go to the oil markets on Sunday, or to take part in the rituals on which each house depended for its survival. Persecution intensified in Bonny in the seventies, at a time of economic crisis. Some of the slaves suffered, and others died for their beliefs, choosing baptismal names such as Daniel and Abednego. When funds were being collected for church repairs, nine-year-old Oparaonyeike Hart said, '*ti aham*', (put down my name).[102] In 1874, Joshua Hart was drowned for his refusal to eat food offered in sacrifice. Later, the Bonny confirmation class prayed, 'Give us the firmness of Joshua'. Asenibiega Hart was deprived of food and water, and took six days to die, while six unnamed women Christians were set adrift in a canoe. Others suffered, but were allowed to live. One of them said, 'Jesus has padlocked my heart'.

As the slaves paddled the great trade canoes to the southern Igbo palm oil markets, they built little chapels, and held church services, inviting local people to join them. The Chiefs were not pleased: 'they never sent their boys to be "Bishops" in Ibo, but to "Trade"'.[103]

> At places sixty, seventy, and eighty miles distant, where they go to buy palm oil for trade they build for themselves rough Prayer-Houses and Chapels. . . . If no missionary is present, two of the leaders will speak, one in the morning and one in the afternoon, and will repeat, perhaps, word for word, sermons heard in Bonny one or two Sundays before. They are also very anxious to read, and eagerly buy up hymn books and easy reading-books.[104]

Bonny traditional religion declined: in 1868, the previously sacred iguanas were killed, and, by the 1880s, the temple of skulls dedicated to the war god, Ikuba, was falling into ruins.

The island kingdom of Opobo was founded in 1869 by Ja Ja, who had originally come to Bonny as a slave and had prospered through his personality and commercial acumen. Although he was an innovator and modernizer, he was not drawn to Christianity: 'Ju Ju is our religion and we must keep it up'.[105] A secular school in Opobo was run by an Afro-American, Emma White (later, Ja Ja), and white visitors compared it favourably with its English counterparts.

Brass (Nembe) was a Delta state further West. Like the other Delta states, it was surrounded by mangrove swamp, where no crops could grow, and its people depended on trade with the lower Niger for their very existence.

The CMS established a mission there in 1868, which won the adherence of the whole community, and not of the slaves alone. In 1879, shortly before he died, King Ockiya gave up all his shrines and divinities, and was baptized as Josiah Constantine. But the Royal Niger Company used its powers to exclude both the Creoles and the Brassmen from their Niger trading partners, and in 1889, King Frederick William Koko renounced Christianity at his coronation. Later, the Brassmen explained it all:

> Some years ago the Christian party was much stronger and more powerful than their opponents; many Chiefs who were brought up as Christians have now gone back to fetishism, among these King Koko, the reason for this being that they had lost faith in the white man's god, which had allowed them to be oppressed, and their trade, their only means of livelihood, to be taken away from them without just cause or reason.[106]

Calabar

The inhabitants of the Niger Delta are Ijo and the 1963 census put their numbers at just over a million. Further East are the Ibibio, who, at that time, numbered just over 2 million, but most scholarly attention has focused on the Efik of Calabar, who speak an Ibibio dialect, and who migrated to the coast at the beginning of the seventeenth century. According to the 1963 census, they number 166 thousand.

In the nineteenth century, they lived in a loose grouping of quasi-independent towns, controlled by oligarchs whom Europeans often called kings. When the United Presbyterians arrived in 1846, there was already an indigenous tradition of literacy in English:

> Many of the natives write English: an art first acquired by some of the traders' sons, who had visited England, and which they have had the sagacity to retain up to the present period. They have established schools and schoolmasters. . . .[107]

When trade declined, it had been the practice to offer a human sacrifice on Parrot Island, facing the open sea, 'to the God of the white man . . .'.[108]

They were torn between their desire for western education and development, and fear at the long-term impact missionaries would have on their political independence and broker role in trade—the latter factor meant that they prevented inland travel. At the end of the century, a Calabar missionary confessed:

> What is sad about the Aro Expedition is that the town names in connection with it are nearly all unknown to those of us who thought we had a passable knowledge of Old Calabar.[109]

Even in Calabar, conversions came slowly: it was seven years before the first Efik was baptized. A school was founded, but, at first, most girls were excluded: 'They no can saby book', it was said, 'They no want go for ship make trade. Suppose they saby book, they saucy book. It no fit they pass boy'.[110] These apprehensions, which were not peculiar to Africa, were overcome. As Waddell noted, the older women were a conservative force, 'the elderly ladies of the town' opposed the missionaries' pleas for the lives of twins.

Mary Slessor joined the mission in 1876, and worked there until her death in 1915. She was to become internationally famous, an eccentric figure, who embodied in her own life the 'preferential option for the poor' among whom she had been born.

Desiring greater independence, she was restive in Calabar and, in 1888, she moved a short distance inland, living among the Okoyong. Her ascendancy among them was such that the British colonial government made her an honorary Vice-Consul, and she was called their White Queen. She was once a child mill hand in Dundee, and this is a good example of the way in which mission work catapulted individuals from obscurity to positions of great influence. However, she made few converts; only eleven had been baptized after fifteen years, and even those were drawn mainly from the circle of her dependants. Nor did the Okoyong prosper; they declined in health and numbers, and observers lamented the prevalence of alcoholism.[111] Late in her missionary career, she wrote:

> I think that it is an open secret that for years the workers here have felt that our methods . . . were far from adequate to overtake the needs of our immense field. . . . Many plans suggest themselves. Church members organised into bands of two or three or four to itinerate for a week over local neighbourhoods; native teachers spending a given number of days in each month in the outlying parts of their districts; trading members of the church undertaking service in any humble capacity on up-river trading stations.[112]

This was exactly what Christians from the Delta and the lower Niger were already doing.

Yoruba and Edo evangelists

In 1893, the complicated conflict known as the Sixteen Years' War came to an end. Many people from eastern Yorubaland and the Edo borderland had been taken as slaves to cities such as Ibadan where missionaries were established. Many became Christians, and, when they were free to return home, they brought their new faith to towns that had never seen an official representative of a missionary society.

One of them, Babamuboni, came from Ekiti. He was enslaved by Ibadan forces, and redeemed by the highly regarded Anglican priest, Daniel Olubi, who, in his turn, had become a Christian while working for David and Anna Hinderer. After twenty years in Ibadan, Babamuboni returned home, and devoted himself to evangelism, 'doing a wonderful work in his own way, neither sparing himself nor his pocket if thereby the kingdom of Christ can be extended and souls saved'.[113]

Shadrach Mogun was another Ekiti man who became a Christian in Ibadan: 'There is not a street, and scarcely a compound in Ibadan, in which he has not preached Christ'. He went home in 1899, supported himself by farming, and preached to his fellow villagers. In a hut hardly big enough to stand upright in, he lived 'all alone with Jesus Christ'.[114]

Samuel Laseinde came from Ora, a town of the Igbomina Yoruba. He was enslaved in 1878, and became a Christian in Abeokuta: 'He was first drawn to Christianity by seeing the Christian Seriki praying morning and evening on war expeditions'.[115] The 'Seriki' was the Balogun, John Okenla, whose example reminds us that not all the converts were slaves. He was a famous warrior, and, when asked about the 'medicine' that underlay his exploits, he showed the enquirer his Yoruba New Testament. Laseinde learned the alphabet from a fellow slave, and began to save up to redeem himself. When he learned that his mother was a slave in Ibadan, he used the money to free her instead. He finally returned home in 1899, introduced the commercial cultivation of cocoa, coffee, and kola, and built up a Christian community. Traditional authorities complained about its members' pugnacity towards the mask cult, *Egungun*, which incarnates the collective dead, and their excessive demands for land. Finally, he was sentenced by the colonial government to six months' hard labour, and many of his followers were driven from their homes.

It was, at this time, common for the agenda of the young to be expressed in religious terms. They found in Christianity, and in cash crop farming, a place on which to stand and move the established order.

Some were willing to make war on whatever aspects of society were perceived as incompatible with the new Evangel; others struggled to reconcile the church's demands with the imperatives of justice and humanity in their own lives, and with deeply entrenched cultural values: 'It may not easily appear to our distant friends with what horror the Ondo mind shrinks from the idea of being buried in the open air'.[116]

In an earlier chapter, we noted the fragmented and transitory beginnings of Christianity in Benin. In the late nineteenth century, a man called Usiokhai was born in a different town, also called Ora, on the western Edo borderland.[117] He was enslaved by the war leader, Ogedengbe, and taken to the Yoruba city of Ilesa. He and his fellow captives were well treated: they married local women, and were sent on long trading journeys, in the course of which he began to attend church. He changed his name to John Alegbeleye, and learned to read in Yoruba. When Ogedengbe was defeated, he returned home, teaching his fellow villagers Yoruba, so that they could read the Yoruba Bible:

> He told us of heaven where the angels paraded with their gracious and merciful wings ready to accept any man who served the Lord. But he told us also of hell with the fires burning for ever where witches, wizards and evil people would go . . . he told us also of the benefits that would accrue to us in form of salaries. We wondered what salary was. It was later on that we started to understand everything.[118]

Alegbeleye was a conciliatory man, who deplored overt attacks on traditional religion, and his personal charm is vividly reflected in modern oral tradition. However, despite this, some converts died for their beliefs, forced by the chiefs to drink sasswood, the poison traditionally given accused witches. In 1898, twenty Ora Christians migrated to Ijero, 'solely for the purpose of receiving Christian instruction'.[119]

Although they lived close to Lagos, the Ijebu resisted Christianity, and strangers in general, for most of the nineteenth century, and even Yoruba traders could not go beyond their boundary markers. They had an intense sense of pride and cultural confidence: the whole world, they said, were slaves, except the white man and the Ijebu.[120]

In 1892, however, the British inflicted a shattering defeat on them. It is likely that they attacked the Ijebu, rather than Abeokuta, because of the latter's standing in missionary circles. The Ijebu turned, with a wholeheartedness that amazed observers, to either Islam or Christianity, a pattern that perplexed the missionaries. It is one of the most convincing illustrations of the thesis that people turn to monotheism when they become part of a wider world. In 1898, it was said:

> It is not possible to say how many churches have been built: the people teach one another and only send for help when their numbers become unmanageable without more disciplined aid. . . . They are a free people: nearly every adherent is a free man or woman . . . nearly all the adherents are young people. Very few exceed 40 years. . . .[121]

The independent churches

It is no coincidence that independent churches of the Ethiopian type flourished in South and West Africa in the late nineteenth century as the largest concentrations of the highly educated were there. They grew out of similar circumstances: white discrimination against black mission agents, disputes over resources, a general feeling, among educated Africans, of being marginalized. There is a sense in which the African churches (as they are known in West Africa) were a form of proto-nationalism, which also found expression, in both South and West Africa, in a vigorous African press.

Nigeria's African churches were founded between 1888 and 1917, and, by then, they were already 'a spent force and an outmoded ideology'.[122] The first was founded by Lagos Baptists, sparked by the grievances of a pastor, Moses Ladejo Stone, and involving major issues of congregational autonomy. Baptist ideals of church polity made both separation and reconciliation easier. Soon, there were twice as many Independent as mission Baptists, a fact that facilitated reunion in 1914.

Independency was in the air in most of the mission churches. In 1886, two years before the Baptists made their move, a layman wrote in the *Lagos Observer*, '. . . a revolution must occur in the Episcopalian church. . . . We cry aloud complainingly . . . and a voice in reply comes to us ringing the word in our ears SECESSION! SECESSION! SECESSION!'[123]

There were many obstacles to secession, not least Anglican concepts of the nature of the Church. Often, the laity were more enthusiastic than the clergy, who were reluctant to depend for financial support on volatile congregations, and a relatively small demographic base. Secession often meant bitter conflicts over property, and the African Baptists admitted that this had caused them initial hesitations. It meant the exclusion of one's children from mission schools, and, when cocoa prices plunged in 1921, the independent churches underwent a financial crisis.

The trials of the Niger Mission in the 1880s gave a focal point to resentments that had previously been relatively inchoate. The flourishing congregations of the Niger Delta became, not an independent church, but an independent Pastorate in the Anglican Church, led by Crowther's youngest son, Dandeson. It was self-supporting, and protected from litigation over property by local land laws, but it experienced financial difficulties when the manilla depreciated.

Two churches seceded from Anglicanism in Lagos: the United Native African Church in 1891, and the African Church (Bethel) in 1901. The United African Methodist Church was founded in 1917.

As their critics pointed out, these churches were not unlike those they had left. A critical white bishop said, in 1936:

179

They call themselves 'African', but their services, the robes and titles of their ministers, their surpliced choirs are all borrowed from England . . . how are they distinctly African?[124]

They were most inculturated in the area of plural marriage, though this was not one of the issues leading to the original separation (with the exception of the Methodists, in 1917).[125] Rather, it was a response to the life situation of their congregations, and, especially, the prosperous cocoa planters whose generosity provided much of their financial support. Their spokesman had a vision in 1900: 'Coker, I want you to go and preach that polygamists become full members of my church'.[126]

Emmanuel Moses Lijadu[127] went to work as a CMS agent in Ondo in 1890, and was ordained six years later. In 1900, he renounced his CMS stipend,[128] and created a self-supporting Evangelists' Band, surviving on offerings from his rural congregations and his own manual labour. However, when his son, Folarin, was due for ordination in 1920, the CMS demanded his little church's property. He refused, ordained Folarin himself, and was disconnected. Litigation followed, and he died in 1926. In an age when mission societies accused their African agents of love of money, he embraced poverty. It was a sad end to a life of heroic devotion and sacrifice.

These churches were often founded in disputes over personalities and leadership, and these factors, as in South Africa, often produced further divisions, such as the split between the African Church, Salem, and the African Church, Bethel. Webster has written perceptively on the way in which different views on theology and church polity were expressed as personal conflict; 'Is it possible to suggest even tentatively that the Yoruba fears an ideological position as being irrevocable? Does he believe that personal animosity . . . can be overcome?'[129]

In a colonial situation, the independent churches created little islands of autonomy. As before, African intellectuals explored the question of their own identity. Some made a symbolic choice of an African name: the fiery, independent Baptist, David Vincent and his wife became Mojola and Adeotan Agbebi. As in many other families, where the husband devoted his energies to the church, whether mission or independent, the wife earned the livelihood. In this case, Adeotan ran the family printing press.

The sense of identity of the African élite remained profoundly paradoxical. They were devoted to the British empire, and believed that British rule was a blessing, but they bitterly resented white racism, and felt a deep need to prove African abilities to a hostile world. The desire for respectability kept them in a western mould. Bethel Cathedral, the tallest building in Lagos when it was constructed, symbolizes their aspirations. Once the passions aroused by the initial crisis had subsided, the élite were inevitably drawn by the resources and prestige, the international linkages and the schools of the mission churches. Despite the sacrifical generosity of their richer members, the African churches could never compete. The issues that concerned them scarcely impinged on the lives of villagers or the new urban poor. These craved, as they had always done, physical and spiritual healing, and protection from the multitude of evils against which the poor are powerless. When African prophets arose who spoke to these needs from the depths of their own religious consciousness, they counted their converts in hundreds of thousands.

Not all 'Ethiopians' founded new churches. The devout and gifted James Johnson (1840–1917, 'Holy Johnson'), was born in Sierra Leone. He was a lecturer at Fourah Bay College, and involved in the agitation that led to the creation of a Native Pastorate in 1861.

In 1874, he was transferred to Yorubaland, and placed in charge of the CMS inland missions. He was regarded as a potential bishop, but soon earned the hostility of white missionaries, as he had done in Sierra Leone. He was removed from the inland missions, in deference to white demands, and placed in charge of Breadfruit Church in Lagos.

In 1891 he was involved in plans for an independent church, but withdrew, for reasons that remain obscure.[130] He refused to be an Assistant Bishop ('half-bishop') when Crowther died, though he accepted such a position later, in 1900.[131]

Bethel Church was founded by a majority of the congregation of Breadfruit at the time, and, although the CMS treatment of Johnson was one of the causes, he refused to side with them, leaving the seceders without a leader, and himself without a following. He stood aloof from the Ethiopian churches, despite the disappointments and rebuffs he suffered, and died an Anglican. The first sermon in the new church was preached from a text from the Song of Solomon: 'Look not upon me, because I am black . . . they made me the keeper of the vineyards; but mine own vineyard have I not kept'.[132]

The African Churches of Nigeria had their counterparts elsewhere. A branch of the African Methodist Episcopal Church (Zion) was founded on the Gold Coast in 1898, by a Jamaican, Bishop B. J. Small, who first came to West Africa as a sergeant in the West India regiment. A number of Methodist dissidents, including Thomas Birch Freeman's son and namesake, joined it. The famous educationalist, J. E. K. Aggrey, studied in America under its auspices, and did not return until 1924. It was, said *The Gold Coast Aborigines* approvingly in 1899, 'an entirely negro church; organized by negroes for negroes, manned, governed, controlled and supported by negro energy, intellect, liberality and contributions'.[133] Many early nationalists joined it. Today, its members consider themselves 'Methodist', rather than 'Independent'.

The Nationalist Baptist Church was founded on the Gold Coast in 1898, and the Nigritian Church in 1907, by Reverend J. B. Anaman—his services were exclusively in Fante. Both were clearly linked with early nationalism, and both were short-lived.[134]

When the Germans took over Kamerun in 1884, the British Baptists handed over their stations to the Basel Mission; there was also a Native Baptist Church, comparable with the Niger Delta Pastorate.[135] When the Germans in Kamerun were defeated, during the First World War, Basel was replaced by the Paris Evangelical Mission. An African Baptist pastor, Lotin Same, defended the autonomy of the Native Baptist Church. 'During 1922–23 the whole town of Douala seethed with this religious "revolt" in which natives paraded up and down the streets singing anti-European hymns'. The Paris missionaries expelled Same, and, in 1938, the administration destroyed the Native Baptist churches. In 1948 the *Église Baptiste du Cameroun*, as it was now called, was recognized, but Same had died two years earlier.

✦ SEVEN ✦

West Central Africa

I was startled to find that Christ could speak Chiluba.

A Shaba Christian in *c.* 1905[1]

The setting

At the heart of West Central Africa lies the Zaire River and its great tributaries, among them the Ubangi, Kasai, and Lualabala. There is a great expanse of rainforest, where settlement was and is sparse, confined to hunter gatherers of small stature ('Pygmies'), and Bantu farmers who cultivate the clearings and the forest edge. Rivers and equatorial forest together symbolized, for late nineteenth-century Europeans, the very essence of Africa as the Other, a perception both shaped by and reflected in Conrad's novella, *Heart of Darkness.* It was largely this idea—that the Congo basin was Africa's dark heart—that led to a massive influx of missionaries between 1880 and 1920; both in their numbers, and in the variety of missionary organizations involved, it was on a scale paralleled only in South Africa.

To the North and to the South and East, the rainforest merges into savanna woodland, where both transport and cultivation are easier, and where most of Central Africa's large states developed. The Kongo kingdom, as we have seen, originally flourished by redistributing tribute from contrasting ecological zones. The majority of Equatorial Africans continued to live in small, decentralized communities. By the late nineteenth century, the copper mines of Shaba and Zambia and the gold mines of Zimbabwe had been exploited by African metallurgists for perhaps a thousand years, and had provided the resources for a succession of major kingdoms.

Population densities were low in the area, and, in some regions, they may have actually declined in the early colonial era. Infertility, and heavy child mortality were particularly prevalent in the Congo[2] and Ogowe basins. These were deeply felt afflictions, as yet imperfectly understood.[3] Perhaps the childless were especially receptive to new movements that promised life, and victory over evil.

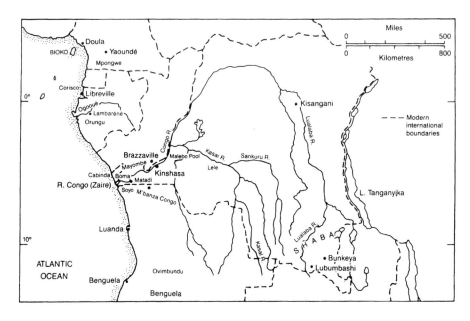

Map 11. Peoples and places in Chapter 7

Gabon

The modern missionary enterprise in West Central Africa began with the arrival of two representatives of the American Board of Commissioners for Foreign Missions in Gabon in 1842.[4] They had had predecessors: Catholic priests from São Thomé visited the area from time to time in the seventeenth century, and Italian Capuchins based on Principe worked in the Gabon estuary in the 1770s, but with no lasting results.

By a strange coincidence both the ABC, and the Holy Ghost Fathers who arrived in 1843, had previously worked in Liberia. The ABC had had a station at Cape Palmas, but did not prosper amid the conflicts of the Grebo and the Americo-Liberians (see pages 165–66) so looked for a new mission field. They found that the Mpongwe of Gabon had already asked the Wesleyans on the Gold Coast for a teacher.

The ABC established a mission at Glass, on the northern shore of the Gabon estuary. The pioneers included a black American printer, B. V. James, and African Christian teachers from Cape Palmas. The mission languished, making few converts, and one of its members complained in 1864, 'The fact is our converts need to be converted over again pretty often'.[5] In 1870 their work was taken over by the American Presbyterians.[6]

The Holy Ghost Fathers[7] had also been at work in Cape Palmas. They set up posts on the Ivory Coast and in Gabon on the basis of an arrangement with the French navy, which had established bases in both areas. In 1848, they were joined by Sisters of the Immaculée Conception des Castres. They had little more success than their Protestant rivals. Converts were drawn from the poor, and often from the enslaved; and the son of a Glass merchant who joined the Protestants was a leper. Women, so often among the first Christians, were hostile in the Gabon, and it took the Protestants twenty years to make one woman convert. Only detailed local knowledge could suggest the reason for these differing responses.

Libreville was founded in 1849. Like Freetown, it was intended as a settlement for slaves liberated on the high seas, but the numbers involved were tiny, and never formed a continuing community comparable with the Creoles of Sierra Leone. The Catholic congregations assumed the pastoral care of the Recaptives, and of 'Black Portuguese' refugees from São Thomé and Principe.

In the 1870s, European traders bypassed the opposition of the Orungu, who had clung to their broker role, and began to trade on the Ogowe. In 1874, the Presbyterians followed them. In 1892, as French control expanded in the interior, they handed over to the Paris Evangelical Missionary Society. It was under its auspices that the thirty-eight-year-old Albert Schweitzer came to Lambarene in 1913, overcoming hesitations about his theology by promising to remain silent on the subject.[8]

Kongo and Angola: continuity and change

In the 1850s, Henrique Nerico Lunga became king of a Kongo that had shrunk to a mini-state in the immediate vicinity of the capital. He ordered the burning of traditional religious emblems on a large scale, and the period that followed was remembered as 'the peace of the royal throne'.[9] In the last two decades of the nineteenth century, a Kongo youth called Nlemvo was a collaborator and language informant of the Baptists, and was one of their first converts. His family was a living bridge with the Kongo Christianity of the past.

> Some old people about the country call themselves *minkwikizi*, 'believers', in some of whom there seems to have lingered some faint glimmerings of such light as had been brought in the old times. At the funeral of a *munkwikizi* there were always some special ceremonies, marks of crosses on the shroud, sprinkling of water, etc. . . . The old uncle of Nlemvo . . . had a small brass crucifix—his Christo—to which he prayed every day, asking a blessing on himself and people. Later on, when he was dying, too weak to raise himself, he had the crucifix stuck up on the wall beside his bed . . . sure in his heart that his Christo would take him safely to heaven.[10]

The first Baptist missionaries landed in the Congo estuary in 1878; they reached San Salvador in 1879, soon to be joined by French Spiritans. To Protestants, the apparent decline of Kongo Catholicism reflected its intrinsic spiritual inadequacies. To the Spiritans, the Kongo kingdom was an ancient Catholic mission field to which they had first claim, and they briefed Pedro V, Henrique's successor, on 'the heresiarchs and chief Heretics' of Protestantism.[11] He was so perplexed by their rival claims, and the political implications of denominational choice, that he evaded the issue by feigning sickness on Sundays: '. . . you white men, you perplex me with your different teachings. I do not know how to choose between you. . . . I shall keep both these palavers in my heart, and when I appear before God, He must decide and judge both . . .'.[12]

In the early nineteenth century, Catholic priests in Angola were few, and accused of inactivity and reluctance to leave Luanda for the interior. When the Portuguese government banned religious orders in 1834, there were two Carmelites and one Capuchin in Angola, together with two dozen African priests; twenty years later, the latter's numbers had shrunk to five.[13] However, for the Luso-Africans of Angola, some form of Catholicism remained a basic dimension of their identity. This was also true of the Creoles of Libreville, who liked to boast that they had been French longer than Nice or Savoy.

West Central Africa
Church and State

The missionary scramble for West Central Africa took place against the background of the rapid spread of colonial jurisdictions, which divided the area into a Belgian Congo, three French colonies (Congo, Gabon, and Oubangui-Chari), a German Kamerun (until the First World War), a Spanish Rio Muni, and a Portuguese Angola. The creation of the Rhodesias frustrated Portugal's long-held ambition to unite Angola with Mozambique.

West Central Africans encountered Christianity through a great variety of denominational and national filters: Flemish Catholics, British Baptists, black Presbyterians from the southern United States, and Scottish Plymouth Brethren among them. Some unlikely alliances developed, notably between Leopold of the Belgians and the British Baptists, but, in general, France favoured French Catholics, Belgium, Belgian Catholics, Portugal, Portuguese Catholics, and so on.

Despite this, a number of Protestant churches were firmly planted in different regions: the Baptist Church flourished among the Kongo in the southern Belgian Congo and in northern Angola. The Ovimbundu of the Benguela Plateau were predominantly Congregationalists, and the Methodist (and Catholic) Churches were strongly established near Luanda. This had the unintended effect of strengthening a sense of monolithic ethnic identity, with tragic consequences for the later liberation struggle in Angola.

The Portuguese government associated Protestantism with political dissent, and it proved a self-fufilling prophecy. Nothing reflects the close links between Church and State more clearly than the way in which missionaries repeatedly abandoned their stations rather than work under a colonial government they perceived as unfavourable. The Baptists' first West African station, founded in 1840 in response to the initiative of liberated slaves in Jamaica, was in Fernando Po, but Spain reoccupied the island, and so they went, in 1858, to Cameroon[14] (the Primitive Methodists stayed longer, and, when they left in 1885, a solitary Protestant missionary, Napoleon Barleycorn, one of the indigenous Bubi, continued their work).

When Cameroon became a German colony, the Baptists withdrew to the Congo, handing over their stations to the Basel Mission, much to the indignation of local Baptists who had not been consulted. Governor Soden refused to allow the French Holy Ghost Fathers to work there, but accepted the Pallotins when they promised to use German personnel.[15]

In 1847, Bremen missionaries looked in vain in West Central Africa for a mission field. On Corisco Island they were told, 'I have promised the Admiral of the Spaniards . . . not to let anyone live on it, except Spaniards'. They hoped to work in Gabon, but were sent away by the local French commandant[16] (they ended up in Togo, only to be dislodged after the First World War).

Church and State: the Belgian Congo

From 1885 until 1908, the vast region that was to become Zaire was a personal fief of Leopold, King of the Belgians. His regime was recognized at the Berlin Conference of 1884–5, on condition that the Congo and its tributaries were open to free trade, and that he practised an 'open door' policy to missions.

Belgium was overwhelmingly Catholic, but Leopold distrusted French and Portuguese missionaries as being likely to further their respective countries' colonial aspirations. In the long run, he encouraged the recruitment of Belgian Catholic missionary personnel. In the short term, he formed a marriage of convenience with the British Baptists, to whom he gave tax concessions and land grants in return for their support. He was well aware of the impact of missionaries on international opinion, and went to the length of inventing a fictitious missionary organization, the Brussels-based West African Missionary Association, as a propaganda exercise. As international attention came to focus on the human cost of Red Rubber, the British (though not the American) Baptists remained silent, as did the Catholics.[17] On the front page of his *Pioneering on the Congo*, published in 1900, Bentley inscribed his Belgian title, *Chevalier de l'Ordre Royal du Lion*. For all his heroism and self-sacrifice, he and many others had become accomplices in an international scandal. Other missionaries were increasingly outspoken in their denunciations of Leopold's regime, and William Morrison and William Sheppard were tried for libel and acquitted.

In 1888, the Governor-General of the Congo Free State wrote, 'the new state is becoming Belgian from the religious point of view as it already is on the political side, and I hope we shall soon have an army of missionaries going to help found a new greater Belgium in that far-off land'.[18] Leopold invited the White Fathers to the Congo on condition that they would employ Belgians where possible, and that the Crown would choose the sites of their missions. In 1906, a Concordat was signed with the Papacy, whereby the Catholic missions obtained state subsidies, and obtained inalienable land grants. Protestants waited until 1946 for the same subsidies. In 1908, the Belgian government annexed the Congo, but the alliance of (Catholic) Church and State continued, even when anti-clerics dominated the home government. The services the missions rendered to the colonial regime were well understood.

Church and State: Angola

Protestant missions were always unwelcome to the Portuguese. Like the Belgians in the Congo, they were forced to practise at least a nominal toleration by the terms of the General Act of the Berlin Conference: 'The free public exercise of all forms of Divine worship, and the right to build edifices for religious purposes, to organize religious Missions belonging to all creeds, shall not be limited or fettered in any way whatsoever'.[19] However, here, too,

Catholic missions were aided by subsidies. Catholic baptism and marriage certificates were legal documents, Protestant ones were not, which was a matter of great practical importance for those who hoped to become *assimilados*.

This alienation was due partly to the attitudes of Protestant missionaries themselves; their contempt for the Portuguese threads its way through their memoirs. They accused the Portuguese of laziness and depravity, the very qualities that the latter saw in Africans! An exception was J. T. Tucker, an American Congregationalist, who reached Angola in 1913. He mastered Portuguese, and deplored the attitudes of his fellow missionaries. In 1921, he pointed out that not only were they ignorant of Portuguese, but that they forbade students to sing a Christmas hymn in it. They had recently produced a geography textbook that showed Washington at the centre of the world, laid emphasis on Guam (a small Pacific island, and a relatively recent American acquisition) but scarcely mentioned Angola.[20]

Missionaries played an active role in drawing international attention to the way in which Angolans were taken to the cocoa plantations of São Thomé in virtual slavery, a scandal comparable with Red Rubber. After 1921, Protestants were obliged to teach in Portuguese—they could publish books in African languages only if there was a parallel text in it.

In 1940, a Concordat was signed between the Vatican and Portugal. The church obtained the right to send non-Portuguese nationals to Portuguese colonies, and considerable financial support for its missions. In return, it accepted a large measure of Portuguese control.

The Catholic Church lost more than it gained by its privileges. Increasingly, in both Angola and Mozambique, it was divided between those who continued to identify with the interests of settlers and metropolis, and those who tried to break away from them—a standpoint that came more easily to non-Portuguese. The hostility to religion, which characterized the MPLA in Angola, and Frelimo in Mozambique, must be understood largely in terms of the close links between the Catholic Church and Portuguese colonialism.

Black missionaries

Many Europeans died in the Congo, often soon after arrival, and so, like West Africa, it was perceived, not without reason, as a white man's grave. Because of this, some missionary societies were eager to employ blacks from the New World, whom they believed (often mistakenly) had greater resistance to tropical diseases. At one point, seven out of twelve Presbyterian missionaries in the Congo were black Americans.[21] The best-known, William and Lucy Sheppard, worked there for twenty years. In 1880, one of the first three representatives of the American Board of Missions in Angola was Samuel T. Miller, a former slave.

The Baptists employed both white and expatriate black missionaries. The

Jamaicans, Joseph Merrick and Alexander Fuller, with his two sons, worked first in Fernando Po, and then in Cameroon, from 1844 on. Merrick died four years later; Joseph Jackson Fuller, who became an ordained minister, was still there when Bentley passed through in 1879: 'In dear old Mr Fuller we could see what the grace of God could do in and through a son of Africa'.[22] The first Baptists to reach the Congo were accompanied by African Christians, among them Misilina, who had been taken as a slave from West Central Africa to São Thomé, and had escaped by canoe to Cameroon with his family.

The role of women

Women were often the first converts, and the most enthusiastic local evangelists. Fourteen years after the Brethren preached their first sermon in the Kundelungu mountains, a man reached the mission with a string with thirty knots in it. Each represented a Christian, and most of them were women. At Lake Mweru, old women were the most successful evangelists.[23] In 1904, Kongo Baptists described a change of marriage customs that had been adopted by the community as a whole in 1897, as a result of mission influence, which they saw as empowering women:

> We lived apart. Many in our town had not been to the river towns. Women married as you might buy a pig; she knew nothing. Then white men brought us the light; great blessing, great cause for thanks. In the dark we did terrible things. Now the change has come thanks to God. You women, you ought to thank God, but you say, what did you give for [us]?[24]

In 1886, Bishop Taylor of the Methodist Episcopal Church attempted to found a mission whose members were to support themselves by their own exertions. Of the thirty to forty volunteers, some died, some returned home, some eked out a difficult livelihood by means such as hippo hunting, but Miss Kildare lived on all alone near the Congo mouth: 'in a wooden shanty, the only one who has carried on any practical mission work'.[25]

The Faith Missions made great use of the abilities of women, and single women sometimes ran mission stations on their own. In the words of the founder of the Heart of Africa Mission:

> Single women go on long evangelizing treks among the villages where there is a shortage of men. Two of the most thriving stations with congregations from five hundred to sometimes as many as fifteen hundred are 'manned' by single women, only.[26]

Missionary nuns are often invisible in general histories,[27] and recent work on the sisters of Our Lady of Namur in Zaire provides a valuable corrective. The oldest Zairois sisters remember how they were insulted when they walked down the road: 'Look at those sterilised cows. Look at those barren women who flee the labour pains of giving others birth! These insults pierced our hearts, they are very strong words for an African woman to hear'. In a society that laid such emphasis on motherhood, even a freely chosen childlessness was an enduring source of pain. African nuns tended to conceptualize their vocation as that of spiritual mothers, and were addressed as *Mama*.[28]

In 1979, there were 4220 professed sisters in Zaire, 2164 of them African; they were divided among 29 diocesan and 126 international, congregations. The former were spared the difficulties of transition from expatriate to Zairois control, but they were rigidly controlled by local bishops and lacked the international contacts, funding, and educational opportunities of their counterparts with branches abroad.[29]

Patterns of missionary expansion

As we have seen, the modern missionary movement in the Belgian Congo began in 1878, with the arrival of two British Baptists in the Zaire estuary. As so often was the case, mission strategies were influenced by spectacular feats of exploration, and the wealth of Robert Arthington.

In 1877, H. M. Stanley completed an epic journey down the Congo River, which made it the focus of international attention. Soon afterwards, he entered the service of Leopold II of Belgium, who aspired to create a personal empire in Central Africa. Even before the news of Stanley's arrival reached London, Arthington had surmised, correctly, that the Lualabala flowed into the Zaire, and not, as Livingstone thought, into the Nile (his geography was not always as reliable as this; when he sent the BMS a thousand pounds to commence work in the forests of the Congo, he foretold that the desert would soon blossom as the rose!) He went on to finance a Baptist river steamer as well. The plan was to join up with the LMS mission on Lake Tanganyika, to which the misnamed Miser of Headingley also contributed.[30] It was the old dream of a chain of stations across Africa that had inspired so many missionaries.

The Baptists' achievements were considerable, despite their high mortality rates. They founded missions along the Zaire River, between Stanley Pool (now Lake Malebo), and Kisangani (formerly Stanleyville), 932 miles upstream. Grenville explored the far-flung tributaries of the Congo River, while Bentley, a humane man who was willing to baptize polygamists without asking them to renounce their supposedly surplus wives, lasted twenty-five years in the mission field. He completed a kiKongo grammar and dictionary with Nlemvo's aid, and died at fifty. Nlemvo's faith was unshaken by the affliction of early blindness:

> As for my eyes, yes, it is true, I cannot even see a very little, but . . . I do not despair. . . . As for my troubles, I am not distressed by them, because I know that God knows the reason and that good will come from these

troubles by and by . . . And if we do not see each other again on earth, in
heaven we shall meet and have happiness evermore.[31]

From 1881, the Congregationalists of the ABC worked among the Ovimbundu of the Benguela plateau in Angola, a mission field selected for its
healthy climate. So successful were they that an anthropologist later found
difficulty in finding 'traditional' Ovimbundu to study.[32] As was so often the
case, the first converts were often the oppressed and enslaved.

The Plymouth Brethren were founded as we have seen in 1830. Their
hostility to existing churches and ordained leadership meant that their mission
work tended to be exceptionally individualistic. Anthony Groves, one of the
founders, went as a missionary to Baghdad. Frederick Stanley Arnot, a former
warehouse clerk who reached Bulozi in 1881, was the first Brethren
missionary in tropical Africa. He had no success among the Lozi, and went on
to work in Bihe, in eastern Angola. In 1886 he reached Shaba, where the
Nyamwezi trader-king, Msiri, had founded a short-lived state. He left after a
year, but others followed, among them, in 1891, Daniel Crawford. These
missionaries lived in evangelical poverty, but made no converts, resisting the
old ruler's willingness to build a giant cathedral, and assemble Christians by
force: 'But all this "Defender of the Faith" role is denied him: it would be
about as appropriate to allow Mushidi to "run the Mission" as it is to see
Bishops in the House of Lords'.[33] They left when Msiri was killed by Leopold's
representative, and Shaba became part of the Congo Free State.

Crawford then founded a new settlement on the western shores of Lake
Mweru. One of those who followed him was a former executioner called
Smish, who became a devoted Christian. However, in general, for twenty
years, the mission had virtually no success. The tide began to turn in 1905,
(remembered as *Mwaka wa Lusa*, the year of Love). In time, the Brethren were
to develop an important network of missions in Shaba, eastern Angola, and
western Zambia.

A thousand Kongo may have been literate by the end of the nineteenth
century. There was a newspaper in kiKongo, also the ubiquitous *Pilgrim's
Progress*.[34] In the early 1920s, a Kongo prophet described his own mystical
experience in these terms: 'I sang the canticles of God and looked at the
images which were open and I saw a great book from which God took various
objects that he gave me in my sleep'.[35]

A number of Faith Missions, that had much in common with the Brethren,
worked in Central Africa. They included the Heart of Africa Mission and the
Africa Inland Mission, which began work in Kenya, and expanded into the
Congo, the Sudan, Uganda, Oubangui-Chari, and Tanganyika.[36] The Living-
stone Inland Mission reached the Congo in 1878, and united with the
American Baptists in 1885, the year in which they experienced a great Revival,
"the Pentecost of the Congo".[37] From 1889 on, the Christian and Missionary
Alliance worked near the Zaire estuary, while yet another Faith Mission, the

Congo Balolo, concentrated on the Lulongo River.[38] The Swedish missionaries of the Svenska Missionsforbundet came to work mainly in the French Congo, and the American Presbyterians reached the Belgian Congo in 1890. The Swiss linguist, Héli Châtelain, founded an interesting independent mission, the *Liga Filafricana*. He reached Luanda in 1885; by 1888 he had not only learned kiMbundu, but also published a translation of St John's Gospel.[39]

The proliferation of fundamentalist missions was a distinctive hallmark of mission work in Central Africa. Because they were often small, and had a great deal in common, they found it easy to work together. Comity arrangements were designed to prevent them competing in the same areas, though the lack of local denominational choice strengthened their control over their converts. The first of many ecumenical conferences was held in 1902, and no fewer than 46 Protestant missions formed the Church of Christ in Zaire in 1970, a number that had almost doubled ten years later.

A variety of men's and women's Catholic congregations came to work in the area. We have already noted the arrival of the Spiritans in the Belgian Congo, in 1880; they were French, and soon found the French Congo a more congenial field in which to work. They had a near monopoly of Catholic mission work in Angola. The White Fathers reached Lake Tanganyika in 1879; the (Belgian) Scheutists arrived in Central Africa in 1888, and worked on the Upper Kasai. The Jesuits concentrated on the area south of Lake Malebo, from 1893 on. In 1894, Trappists settled at Bamania, and in 1898 the Premonstrants did likewise, on the Upper Welle. There were also Portuguese diocesan priests at work in Angola. We have mentioned the Sisters of our Lady of Namur, but White Sisters, Franciscans, and Sisters of Charity of Gand also worked in the Congo. By 1900, there were 150 Catholic men and women missionaries in 17 stations, and 230 Protestants in 40 stations.[40] By 1936, there were 3200 missionaries in the Congo, about a sixth of the total expatriate community (of these, 2475 were Catholics and 725 Protestants). By 1958, the numbers had risen to 5904 and 1652, respectively.[41]

The rapid spread of Christianity in Angola contrasts with the later anti-clericalism of the MPLA. In 1933, less than 10 per cent of the population was thought to be Christian; by 1950, this had risen to 50 per cent, and by 1960, to 49–66 per cent Catholic, and 17 per cent Protestant. In Mozambique, in the same year, only 10 per cent were Christian, a state of affairs that seems to reflect the strength of Islam there.[42]

Despite the attractions of literacy, education lagged far behind conversion. In 1950, less than 1 per cent of the Africans in Portuguese colonies had qualified as *assimilado*. Ten years later, only 6 to 7 per cent of Angola's African children were at school.[43] Many boys in Zaire and Angola went to seminaries, because these were virtually the only avenues to higher education, and there were 706 Zairois priests in 1979.

Anedeto Gaspar came from a family of *assimilados* in northern Angola. He was sent to a seminary against his will, because of the education it provided.

But the *assimilado* paid a price for his privileges: a denial of the heart of his own cultural identity. Gaspar asked, as many others have done, 'Why did we have to study and memorize the names of so many rivers, provinces, mountain ranges and geographical zones in Portugal? Is this kind of curriculum making us better Africans?'[44]

Perceptions

The peoples of West Central Africa glimpsed missionary teachings through a glass, darkly. In the French Congo, far from the area of Swahili speech, children had to learn the catechism in Swahili. An Angolan pupil there was fluent in Portuguese and his native Chokwe; he struggled, not only with French, but also with Swahili.[45] The Scheutists communicated with the Lele in bowdlerized kiKongo, as different from the latter's language as Greek is from English, so that the Lele had to learn it in school.[46] The Luba called European versions of their language 'Bantu of the boots'.[47] When they came to express their own understanding of the Bible in their own language, they gave a missionary new insights, so precious that he called them pearls. The Book of Acts became, 'Words Concerning Deeds', and the Lord's Table, the 'Feast of Memories', or the 'Table of Tears'.[48]

The way in which missionaries were first perceived was clearly shaped by the trans-Atlantic slave trade. At Tungwa:

> The people were alarmed when they learned that the white man would like to come and live among them. They were sure that if they came, every evil under the sun would come with them—drought, famine, pestilence and death. Many believed that if the mysterious strangers settled there, the local witches would have every facility, and would be able to sell everybody to the white men—not as slaves, but that they would sell their spirits. . . .[49]

Nearer the coast, the people believed that the dead were bought by the white men, and that the spirits went to work for the white men under the sea.[50] The kiKongo-speaking Dondo (or 'Bwende') of the French Congo at first believed that schoolchildren were initiated into a book of death, and that they paid for their apprenticeship in sorcery with the life of a relative.[51] Concepts of this kind had an extraordinary vitality. A document written by the Mpadi sect in 1969 explains:

> The Catholics have a kingdom of the blacks, under the earth, the grave. When a black man dies, the whites keep him chained under the earth.[52]

By a strange and terrifying transformation, the real horrors of the slave trade and other forms of white exploitation, are metamorphosed into these supernatural forms.

Often, there were initial fears that the missionary presence would lead to disaster: '. . . wise men . . . were sure that the San Salvador people would die very fast; that there would be no rain'.[53] Fortunately for the missionaries, the rains were abundant, and no one died in their first seven months of residence.

We have noted the tendency to understand Christianity in terms of a traditional high God, so that the Buganda martyrs died with a prayer, not to Christ, but to Katonda. The Kongo called missionaries *ntumwa Nzambi*, ambassadors of (the traditional) God, and Simon Kimbangu was called in visions to be God's *ntumwa*. Some were less than convinced of the identification of the Christian God with *Nzambi*: 'When the catechists preached in the villages and said that Nzambi is our father who loves men, then the old men would not listen. For in their view Nzambi was only "the commander" '.[54] A traditional Dondo priest who became a Christian continued to wrestle with the universal issues that have perplexed believers everywhere: 'Nzambi possesses us, for if he did not exist, we should not be in existence. That is why he is good. Others say that he is wicked, because he is always killing us'.[55]

It was the very veneration for tradition and the past that made the acceptance of a new religion so difficult. Once, when Crawford preached in Shaba, a hearer responded with a song: 'Lombe, you remember, introduced potatoes, and what was reckoned poison is now staple diet'. Crawford was puzzled, but, on reflection, realized that the song was not about potatoes, but about Christianity.[56] Mayimbi, chief of a Dondo village, enjoyed the company of the Swedish missionaries, but refused to join their Church. He did not believe in the Hell of which they warned, and preferred the Dondo version of the life to come: '. . . he did not wish to separate himself from his ancestors, and he did not in the least desire to go to heaven . . . he wanted to go to the underground village where his ancestors lived, especially his mother whom he loved dearly'.[57]

The Christian village

Late nineteenth-century missionaries, like their counterparts elsewhere, tended to found Christian villages, in the belief that converts needed to live apart from traditional society if they were to develop a pure and fervent spiritual life. Often, the village was founded on a hill, because of the view, and to avoid the 'miasmas' thought to cause disease. This meant settlement at a distance from local settlements, which were usually located near sources of water. It also meant that generations of Christians struggled with heavy water containers.

Sometimes, the foundation of new settlements was virtually forced on missionaries by the plight of former slaves and refugees. Daniel Crawford founded such a village near Lake Mweru. He was one of the many missionaries who abhorred round houses and African village layouts, and he prided himself on the straightness of its road! However, his attitude was profoundly ambiguous: he condemned the freed slaves who joined him—'we have a number of redeemed slaves around us, but they are nearly all a bad lot', and, 'the worst type of convert is a redeemed slave'[58]—and he was well aware that it was unsatisfactory for a missionary to become a squire:

> Many a little Protestant Pope in the lonely bush is forced by his self-imposed isolation to be prophet, priest, and king rolled into one—really a very big duck, he, in his own private pond.[59]

The Jesuits and some other Catholic missions, instituted the *ferme chapelle* and the *chapelle école* where children, often redeemed slaves or orphans, grew up outside the structure of their society, ultimately settling in a Christian village. They were ruled by missionaries in the spirit of an autocratic lord of the manor, but, like their Protestant counterparts, they found a haven of security and relative prosperity in a violent and dangerous age.

After 1914, the ideal of the Christian village was gradually abandoned, as it was realized that it was essentially a ghetto, and unlikely to transform society as a whole. Increasingly, the emphasis was on the bush outstation, led by a catechist, and the village school. Boarding schools preserved something of an earlier separateness, as did the practice of keeping catechumens for long periods of instruction (and heavy manual work) at the central mission. Mary Douglas observed the Scheutists in the Kasai in the 1950s; they had worked in the area she studied since 1939. In the beginning, they seized Lele children by force, threatening the parents with prison if they protested. Compulsion soon gave way to attraction, but, in 1950, catechumens still had to spend two years of 'hardship and hunger' working on the mission station without payment: 'They might be abused, struck or whipped for some, to them, obscure misdemeanour'.[60]

In Douglas' view, monogamy, at least among the Lele, was not a deterrent, but an attraction. It enabled a young man to choose and keep a wife, with the full support of the State, provided he restored betrothal gifts already made: 'Not only the young men, but unhappy young wives, childless women, a girl beaten once too often . . . now ran away to marry Christians'.

The Gospel was seen as the source of a new, and radically different order: 'the town has been divided and I am the town spokesman by my boldness; it comes from the gospel'.[61] When young Lele Christians settled in a new village, the elders lost their assistance. When meat was divided, it was all given to cult initiates; Christians, in retaliation, killed and ate forbidden game, such as pangolin. On one occasion, traditionalists sought to punish Christians by telling the missionaries they were practising sorcery.

Individuals wrestled with problems of choice: traditional religion, or Christianity, and the claims of different denominations. A practising Catholic became a convinced Protestant when a Swedish missionary foretold an eclipse: 'The effect was enormous. The village folk were thunderstruck. They drew a quite natural inference. It is the Protestant Mission which is right'.[62]

196

Distances were vast, and European missionaries few. Many did not survive long enough to learn a local language. Successful evangelization was largely the work of Africans, as was the day-to-day pastoral care of the outstations. Early Kimbanguist leaders were often former Baptist deacons, accustomed to running their local church. There was a sense in which the Kimbanguists did not leave the Church at all, rather 'the church broke away from structures it now found alien to its purposes'.[63]

Like their counterparts elsewhere, the missionaries were prone to what Markowitz calls 'rural romanticism': 'The coming of any external influences into Arcadia strikes us as almost indecent'.[64] They often preferred to work in the country rather than among the mineworkers of Shaba, ,or the growing population of the towns. Their ideal was the village Christian, reading the Bible in the vernacular, earning a living in traditional ways. Like colonial administrators, they disliked the *deraciné*, but all Christians were, in a sense, *deraciné*. To encourage just enough literacy to read the Bible, but not enough for a salaried occupation, was to place a ceiling on African aspirations that they would not have accepted for themselves or their children. It sprang, in part, from a horror of attracting Christians to the Church by worldly rather than spiritual motives. The Brethren at Lake Mweru founded an elementary school to give children the modicum of vernacular literacy needed for Bible study, but no more: 'I dread the idea of producing "mission boys" by education which may mean that they are more adept and smarter sinners than raw natives'.[65]

In part, all this reflected a consciousness that Christianity could not be identified with western culture: 'We have to Christianize, not to Anglicise'.[66] But missionaries had themselves instituted the process of change and literacy, and unconscious racism was often an element. When a United Training College for teachers and pastors was mooted for the Upper Congo, one missionary claimed, 'that for the most part even our best and most advanced native teachers and evangelists could not fully appreciate and digest the subjects dealt with in a college curriculum. Why then cast our pearls of knowledge and instruction away in sheer wastage?'[67] Again, the imagery of pearls, but how differently it is used.

Catholics had fewer hesitations about education. While sharing the rural prejudices of the Evangelicals, they did not agonize about the intrinsic desirability of schools, or the motives of those attending: 'The Church will teach in mission lands, just as she will administer the sacraments, because it is her proper function, and in the strictest sense of the word, her monopoly'.[68] Their aim was to build up a large Christian community, and they were not especially concerned to separate the wheat from the tares.

White missionaries tried to choose, on behalf of their converts, what aspects of their lives should be changed. The Church left the missionaries, in part, so that Africans could choose for themselves. However, the issues at stake were complicated: mission education produced, in the long run, a prosperous élite, whose lifestyle, in contrast to that of the rural poor, presents the same challenge to the Christian conscience as does that of the First World *vis-à-vis* the Third and Fourth.

For almost all schoolchildren, education ended at the primary level. In time, however, the missions became more responsive to their discontent. At a conference of Catholic bishops in 1945, one of those present pointed out that 'of 500 children who finished primary school, about 100 are admitted to middle school, about 50 find employment in the region, a number return to their villages, but at least 250 go to the large centres'.[69] The *évolués* became trenchant critics of the missions: 'Europeans, including the missionaries, put us all in the same sack. To them we are all ignorant children'.[70]

In 1948, the government agreed to subsidize five Catholic secondary schools for boys; in 1954, a Catholic university, Lovanium, opened on the outskirts of Léopoldville, despite the opposition of local whites. It is a reflection of Catholic–Protestant hostility that the Protestants later opened their own university, and a sign of post-Vatican II rapprochement that when political troubles delayed this, they used facilities at Lovanium.

Denominational hostility was confusing and disconcerting to new Christians, but it made it clear that there were many possible paths to the Christian God. Africans were empowered to find new paths of their own.

What drew two-thirds of the population of Angola, and over half the population of Zaire to Christianity, despite mission ethnocentricity and racism? The most obvious factor was the missions' near monopoly of education. The fascination with literacy in the late nineteenth century led people to treasure fragments of printed paper, or embark on 'crooked calligraphy'.[71] But there was also a basic congruity between the new religion and changing socio-economic structures: 'the religion of individualism establishing itself alongside the economic individualism of wage-earning and market production'.[72]

The social impact of the missions was various, and went far beyond education, and the advocacy of monogamy. In Angola, as in South Africa, the ox-drawn plough had far-reaching implications, and sanitation seemed an integral part of the new Evangel: 'The message of digging latrines went literally along with the one of Christian faith. It is still quite common to hear a report on how many latrines have been dug during the last quarter when the Methodist Quarterly Conference is in session'.[73]

Christians who went to the new cities and the mines broke free from the rigid hegemony of the rural missionary. Both Simon Kimbangu and Simon Toko spent a period in Kinshasa, at about the time they felt called to found their respective churches. But modernity, urbanization, and labour migration created new difficulties for Christians, themes to which we shall return in a later chapter.

Simon Kimbangu (1889–1951)

In 1880, two Baptist missionaries, Comber and Hartland, were attacked by the Makuta, and fled for their lives. Exhausted and thirsty, they asked a woman working in the Tungwa farms for water. She gave them water and cassava, and refused payment. Fifteen years later, the woman, Madia Kiavevwa, became the first Tungwa Christian. A strikingly similar story is told of Kimbangu's mother.[74]

There is an enormously rich and detailed literature on Kimbanguism, and, more generally, on the relationship between twentieth-century religious movements and traditional African cultures; Africa's prophetic and Zionist churches form a central theme in the later chapters of this book. In West Central Africa, scholars tend to emphasize continuities. The story that Kimbangu's mother gave water to an exhausted missionary is explained by the fact that, in traditional Kongo cosmology, water lies between the worlds of the living and the dead. However, it may be objectively true, and it may reflect a different spiritual reality: 'a cup of cold water given in my Name'. In a sense, the emphasis on continuity is a salutary reaction to the polarities of the early missionaries, but Africans themselves often understood their experience as a radical break with the past: 'Behold I make all things new'.

Kimbangu was a Kongo from what is now the Lower Zaire. He and his wife, Mivilu Marie, destined to be a Mother in Israel to a persecuted church, were baptized in 1915. He hoped to become a teacher and evangelist, but did not read well enough.[75] In 1918, he began to have visions calling him to be a healer and apostle. He resisted this, and went to work in Kinshasa, but did not prosper there. MacGaffey suggests that he and many other prophets were marginal, both in the traditional world (he may have been of slave descent), and in the modern one.[76] When he returned home, he hoped to be appointed to the position of evangelist of his home town, N'kamba, but here, too, he was disappointed.

It is no coincidence that a number of Christian prophetic movements were founded during the 1918 flu pandemic, which made the limitations of both western and traditional medicine painfully apparent. Kimbangu had his first vision at that time, which was the year when, in western Nigeria, the future Christ Apostolic Church was founded. In April, 1921, he healed a critically ill woman called Nkiantondo. Further cures led great crowds to flock to N'Kamba, which is now the Holy Jerusalem of his followers. He laid much emphasis on monogamy, as his church does still. He taught obedience to authority, and forgiveness of enemies: 'Bless all peoples of the earth, great and small, men and women, whites and blacks'.[77] For a time, the mission churches were overflowing. A missionary called it 'the most remarkable movement which the country has ever seen. The prophets only seem to have one goal— the proclamation of the Gospel'.[78]

The Belgian administration was alarmed by the crowds that flocked to

Kimbangu. They were equally alarmed by the reports—sometimes distorted or exaggerated—of the messages of other prophets, *bangunza*, who taught in his name, and who often foretold the overthrow of the white regime. Kimbangu always advocated obedience to the civil authorities, but, when a Belgian official interviewed him, he told him of David and Goliath, and spoke in tongues—a form of critical or subversive discourse that has parallels elsewhere.

In June 1921, an attempt was made to arrest him, but he escaped with some of his followers. In September, in obedience to a message from God, he gave himself up. He was sentenced to 120 strokes of the whip, and to the death penalty. Protestant missionaries protested, and, though the white *commerçants* howled for his death, it was commuted. He and many of his followers were flogged, as was once their Master.

Kimbangu spent thirty years in a prison, far from his home, much of it in solitary confinement. His conduct was so exemplary that both the prison superintendent and the governor of Shaba pressed for his release, but in vain. On his death bed, in 1951, a Zairois Catholic priest tried to convert and baptize him. Kimbangu's followers believe he did not succeed.

The Belgians sacked N'Kamba, outlawed the new movement, and exiled many of Kimbangu's followers to provinces far from their home. This had the unintended result of spreading his message widely, creating a movement that was multi-ethnic, rather than Kongo. The missionaries dissociated themselves from it all; as it was illegal, they could not, perhaps, do otherwise. However, it was felt as a betrayal, and, for a time, the churches emptied again: 'We have been forsaken by both Catholics and Protestants. . . . Kimbangu is the ambassador of God'.[79]

A Catholic priest attacked the Kimbanguists violently, with the result that government measures became harsher. They worshipped in secret, and composed eloquent hymns. In 1923, former Baptist deacons wrote from prison to their quondam pastor, in words that are not unlike those of Paul:

> As for what you say that we are following a 'new teaching', this is not so, our Teacher. . . . As for the sentences given us, some are for 10 years, some 20, others for life: this is the sentence of imprisonment. When these sentences are finished, we cannot go back to our own country, we must die here. But as for us, these tribulations and these sentences 'cannot separate us from the love of Christ and of God, nor can any other tribulation' . . . We assure you we have not broken a single State law, nor been disrespectful to our rulers. 'We give to the Governor that which is due to the Governor'. . . . We are well in body and in spirit. Two deacons died at Thysville in 1921. . . . They died through being much beaten. Others also died, but there is no time to give their names. . . . We get beaten with canes and have other troubles, but Jehovah is our shepherd'.[80]

In 1957, in response to continued arrests and deportations, the Kimbanguists embarked on passive resistance: 600 leading members signed a letter that ran, in part: 'Wherever we meet for prayer we are arrested by your soldiers. In order not to burden the police with added work, we shall all gather, unarmed, in the Stadium, where you can arrest us all at once or massacre us'.[81]

On Christmas day, 1959, Église de Jésus Christ sur la terre par le prophète Simon Kimbangu, (EJCSK) was recognized by the government, and embarked on the difficult transition from underground movement to church. Many left Protestant mission churches to join it, under the headship of Kimbangu's youngest son, Joseph Diangienda. The Church insists on monogamy, on abstinence from alcohol and narcotics, and on a radical renunciation of traditional religion. The ecstatic trembling that characterized Kimbangu and his first followers, and which is still typical of 'Ngunzism', is now discouraged, as is spiritual healing.[82] There was, at first, no baptism, though holy water from N'kamba is of great ritual importance, and is carried to the most remote outposts of the church. Until 1971, there was no communion service, perhaps because witchcraft was thought of as consuming human lives (the Harrists on the Ivory Coast felt the same). Until informed of them by foreign scholars, they knew nothing of the other prophetic churches of Africa.

Kimbanguism is a particularly clear example of what sociologists call 'the routinisation of charisma'. Like other movements that have turned into 'churches', it faces the problem of maintaining a large, centralized organization on the one hand, while keeping the miraculous elements and spiritual power that attracted followers in the first place.

In 1968, Marie-Louise Martin, a Moravian, embarked on a study of the Kimbanguists. She initially believed that as in some South African churches, Kimbangu had replaced Jesus as a Messiah. She became convinced of their orthodoxy ('if you live with the Kimbanguists, you find yourself transferred to the time of the earliest New Testament witnesses'),[83] and became Director of Theological Training at the École de Théologie Kimbanguiste, Kinshasa. In 1970, EJCSK joined the World Council of Churches, and became one of the three churches recognized by the government of independent Zaire.

Bangunza

To some scholars, Kimbangu stood in an indigenous Kongo tradition of *bangunza* prophets. Others, such as Martin, anxious to defend his orthodoxy, stress the gulf that separates the Kimbanguists from what is often called Ngunzism, though this label is unsatisfactory.[84]

Although the modern EJCSK has eschewed Messianism, many groups have, at various times, regarded Kimbangu as an African Saviour, and some still do. Often, the *bangunza* claimed to speak in Kimbangu's name, or even to incarnate him, while other leaders, as we shall see, were also elevated to a quasi-salvific role.

The *bangunza* tended to stress faith healing and ecstatic experience, and often seem closer to cargo cults than to the Zionist churches or the Aladura. They emphasize the Spirit and protection from witchcraft, and stress persistently the idea of the secret teachings of Jesus. All this recalls the gnostics—*plus ça change.* . . . One legend tells how Diangienda, the prophet's son, went to Jerusalem. There, he opened a box, which had another box inside it. When seven boxes had been opened, he found the true Bible, concealed from Africans by the missionaries.[85]

In the 1960s, a man called Bakwafula founded L'Église de la Foi in Zaire, claiming that the power of the whites depended on secret rites conducted in cemeteries by night.[86] Congo independents in the colonial era seemed particularly proccupied with the power of the whites, and the desire to share their prosperity through supernatural means. In the early twentieth century, a coastal branch of the Kongo responded to a drought by destroying their charms, and turning, not to Christianity, but to an ancient healing, divining, and rainmaking cult called Simbi. By 1928, it had been replaced by a movement called *baSantu* (saints), which worshipped *Nzambi a Bantu*, the god of the people. The identity of the chief priest was unchanged. A hostile Catholic missionary said, 'Guess what! The biggest fetisher of the whole district thinks he's a Christian! He knows Jesus Christ, the Virgin Mary, Saint Joseph and Saint Anthony "who carries the baby Jesus on his arm"'.[87] To MacGaffey, this was a Christian veneer, created as a protective screen to shield an ancient cult from the missionaries and the colonial administration. Both hostile missionary, and sympathetic anthropologist concur that the movement was not genuinely Christian, but there is nothing in the data to suggest this, and perhaps they simply chose to practise a new religion in familiar ways.

The eschatological and anti-white element is a recurring one, and in some cases may have been absorbed from Watch Tower, which spread into Shaba from Zambia. However, the French Congo is far from Shaba, and it was there that a missionary said, in 1932, 'the whole movement has at bottom the single aim: we shall ourselves govern and rule our own country. All whites must get out'.[88] Sometimes, they preached a millenial reversal, where the whites became black, and the blacks white.

The Salvation Army reached West Central Africa in 1934. The 'S' on its officers' uniforms led people to flock to them, believing they supported, or even incarnated, Simon Kimbangu. In the French Congo, people treated the Salvation Army as an anti-witchcraft cult, and to shake hands with an officer and survive was to prove one's innocence. It took some time for Army officers to understand all this, and when they did, they disassociated themselves from it.

An independent offshoot of the Army developed in both the Belgian and French Congo, promising health, and protection from witchcraft. Its leader, Simon Mpadi (*b.* 1909), had been a mission teacher with the American Baptists until he was expelled on charges of adultery. He then trained as a Salvationist officer, before founding an independent 'Church of the Blacks' in 1939, and claims to be the 'twin' of Kimbangu. The Church is sometimes called Khakhism, from its uniforms. He was imprisoned from 1944 to 1960, his only crime being the formation of an independent church. During this time, Khakhism generated a large number of prophetic figures, and Mpadi's frequent escapes strengthened his charismatic role.[89] After his release, he headed a church where polygamy is accepted, and ecstatic experience and healing are emphasized. It focuses on Kimbangu, rather than Jesus, who is seen as the saviour of the whites.

His essential concern was with development, and autonomy: 'We want four things, our own government, our own wealth, our own religion, and our own science (*ngangu*)'.[90] However, the way in which they are to be obtained is formulated in a way reminiscent of Melanesian cargo cults: 'Americans' have become supernatural agents, like ancestors and spirits, who will bring the technical expertise necessary for development.[91]

This belief is not peculiar to Mpadi. We have seen how, in the late nineteenth century, there was a prevalent belief that Europeans bought the souls of the dead from witches. When the Congo Free State exported ivory and rubber, it was believed that these were containers for hapless Kongo souls. Some of them were thought to return to the Congo as white 'Americans', with the technical knowledge to contribute to development. MacGaffey himself, in the 1960s, was thought to be such a *revenant*.[92]

If Congo prophets sometimes transmuted Kimbangu into a saviour figure, André Matswa, (1899–1942) went through a still more remarkable transformation. A Kongo from the French Congo, he served in the army, and then lived in Paris. He founded a friendly society for expatriate Congolese, the Amicale, for which he collected donations in the Brazzaville area. It was, on the face of it, an odd project, to collect contributions from a poor peasantry to support the Paris *évolués*. Large sums were collected, and, it seems, the contributors hoped for a variety of benefits. To colonial officials he was clearly a charlatan; perhaps it is more accurate to call him a pioneer political activist.

He and several associates were gaoled in 1930, and he died in prison in 1942. He became the focus of increasingly millenial expectations, the Saviour who, but for his imprisonment, would have transformed his followers' lives. Long after his death, he attracted votes at elections. The *évolué* politician became the founder and saviour figure of a Church: the Religion of the Candle, or the Religion of the Holy Wood (after its characteristic icons).

Perhaps none would have been more startled by these metamorphoses than Matswa himself. They reflect a world where political activity was impossible, so that change must come from millenial dreams:

Father Matswa, free the Congo, the Congo that lies desolate. They can kill it, but they are not able to bury it.[93]

Simon Toko

Prophetic movements flourished in the Congo, but were rare in Angola. Simon Toko (1918–84) began his career as a Baptist mission school teacher in northern Angola.[94] He had close associations with the Kimbanguists, and translated Watch Tower literature. A Kongo, he went to Léopoldville (Kinshasa), where he was a successful artist and choirmaster. In 1949, he underwent a Pentecostal experience that changed his life, and founded an organization that became the World Church of Jesus Christ, often referred to as the Red Star, which was its symbol (replacing the Cross).

His church required monogamy, and women were prominent on church councils. His followers prayed to Father, Toko, and Holy Spirit.[95] He foretold a millenium where white domination would be reversed, or that whites would become black, and blacks, white, and advocated passive submission to white authority. Perhaps this ambiguity of millenial reversal and practical quietism, lies at the movement's heart.

The Belgian authorities deported Toko to Angola, where a Portuguese government, hostile to Protestantism, and doubly so to independency, exiled him to the Azores. He worked there until 1974 as a lighthouse keeper; the symbolism is striking, if unintended.

His is the only independent Church to have spread widely among the different ethnic groups in Angola, largely because the Portuguese exiled his followers to distant provinces. Kimbanguism spread in the same way in Zaire. One remembers the famous words that Gerard Manley Hopkins addressed to a saintly doorkeeper:

> But be the war within, the brand we wield
> Unseen, the heroic breast not outward-steeled,
> Earth hears no hurtle then from fiercest fray.
> Yet God (that hews mountain and continent,
> Earth, all, out, who, with trickling increment,
> Veins violets and tall trees makes more and more)
> Could crowd career with conquest while there went
> Those years and years by of world without event
> That in Majorca Alfonso watched the door.

The Red Star Church survives, but has had a number of clashes with an independent Angolan government.[96] Margarido quotes a very approximate estimate of 10 thousand members in 1963, and Newitt suggests that all the Angolan independent churches together have never had more than 50 thousand members.[97]

Mulele in Kwilu

The Belgian Congo became independent in 1960, and, immediately, the copper-rich province of Katanga (now Shaba) attempted unsuccessfully to secede. From 1963 to 1967 there were a number of revolts in the eastern provinces. Their spontaneity and extent reflect the disappointment felt, when the benefits independence had seemed to promise, did not materialize. One party had campaigned with promises of full employment, free education and medical care, and universal salary increases.[98]

The insurgents relied heavily on 'traditional' magic. In Kwilu, they advanced, invoking Mulele and his magical water.[99] Pierre Mulele was a former cabinet minister who had spent three years as a Jesuit novice.[100] His teachings were an approximation of Marxism, but, to his followers, he became a magician, invulnerable to bullets, and capable of metamorphosis into an animal, or snake. The motif of the magical power of the written word, and of secret knowledge is found here: there were thought to be four books of secret writing, which Mulele would translate.[101]

The world of the educated was a small one, and a number of individuals were prominent in both the independent churches and in politics. Emmanuel Bamba had a long association with the Kimbanguists; after a power struggle with the founder's sons, he established a separate Church, 'The Salvation of Jesus Christ through the Witness Simon Kimbangu'. In 1966, he was involved in an unsuccessful coup and was executed.[102]

Bwiti

Bwiti is a religious movement found among the Fang of Gabon, which grew out of an older ancestral and initiation cult. It began at the turn of the century, and expanded between 1910 and 1930. A classic instance of syncretism, it is abundantly documented in a remarkable ethnographic study by J. Fernandez.[103]

Its members induce mystical experience by the use of local drugs. There are a number of branches. One emphasizes the Holy Spirit, another, called *Sainte Coeur de Marie*, 'arises from a vision of the Virgin with her heart dripping blood'. A third 'considers Christian deities as the Great Gods and focuses principally upon the Sister of God'.[104] These cults promise health and children (infertility is a major problem among the Fang); at most, 20 per cent of the population are members.

They construct buildings, which Fernandez calls 'chapels', that are loaded with symbolic significance. Interestingly, alarm clocks figure prominently in Bwiti ritual life, a symbolic statement of the difference between the seasonal 'eternal return' of traditional culture, and the linear time of the western world. Rituals last from six on Saturday evening until six the following morning, with sermons at midnight.

205

Fernandez writes with great empathy of the circumstances in which Bwiti flourishes; the sense of decline and infertility, disease, poverty, relative deprivation, the terror of witchcraft when traditional means of restraint are forbidden, and the search for spiritual understanding. An elaborate mythology describes the creation of the world, when the sky spider dropped an egg into primordial ocean, and the way in which the principle of evil, Evus, deceived Eve.

Bwiti has a reportoire of 150 songs, and its members search for 'one-heartedness' with ancestors, and the living. Women have a ritual equality denied them in older cults. Through the narcotic *eboga*, members acquire an experiential knowledge of unseen realities, 'the science of the other world'. 'Can Christianity bring the visions or the mingling with the dead that is characteristic of Bwiti?'[105]

Jamaa

Many movements of renewal and indigenization remained within the mission churches. The East African Revival is a famous example, and there was a major, though lesser-known movement among Protestants in the French Congo in 1947.

Jamaa was a new religious movement of a unique kind that evolved in the Catholic Church in Shaba. Its prophetic leader was not an African, but a Flemish Franciscan, Placide Tempels (1906–1977). Working in Shaba, he became increasingly dissatisfied with conventional mission work, with the dominant role customarily claimed by European missionaries, and the disdain of African cultures that too often characterized them.

In 1945, his book, *Bantu Philosophy*, appeared. He analysed Bantu thought with respect and seriousness at a time when whites, missionaries among them, tended to despise all things African. It was welcomed by some African Catholic intellectuals, notably the Tutsi priest, Alexis Kagame, in Rwanda. In retrospect, it forces African world views into the alien and inappropriate categories of scholastic Thomism, but it was important, less for what it achieved, than for what it intended. It was not welcomed by church authorities, and, from 1945 to 1949, Tempels was 'exiled' to Belgium.

In the 1950s, after his return to Shaba, he continued to explore the nature of the Christian dynamic in the local situation, stressing encounter, rather than dominance. *Jamaa* ('family') grew up among the miners of Shaba. Its central focus was on marriage and parenthood, the Baba and Mama. Those who joined were initiated into successive levels, like traditional cult members. The entry to the first is obtained after a dream encounter with Jesus (for the Mama), or Mary (for the Baba).[106] It had many strengths: it deepened and enriched the bonds between spouses and between Jamaa members in general. Although, in a sense, founded by Tempels, it developed a life of its own, which continued when Tempels returned permanently to Europe in 1962.

By making marriage central, it inverted the values of traditional Catholicism, dominated by male celibates, in an extraordinary way, causing much soul-searching for the missionary priests who joined it. A movement within a movement, Katete, developed a strong emphasis on sexuality. There has always been an erotic dimension in mysticism, and it became explicit in Katete, in ways bound to alarm the church authorities.

The Flemish Jamaa priests left Zaire, and, in 1974, the local bishop excommunicated the movement, and a government decree outlawed it, but Jamaa continued a flourishing underground existence among the miners of Shaba. It is likely, in these circumstances, that the Katete element became stronger.

Albert Schweitzer

Albert Schweitzer (1875–1965) was undoubtedly the most famous missionary in twentieth-century Africa. Born in Alsace, he was an extraordinary polymath, who held doctorates in philosophy and theology, made important studies of Bach, and was a world-class organist. Many were drawn to the mission field by an Evangelical theology that led them to believe that the heathens were perishing. Schweitzer adopted a position that many considered post-Christian, and he was accepted as a medical missionary on condition that he remained silent on religious subjects. His most famous book, translated as *The Quest for the Historical Jesus* (1910), criticized the tendency of nineteenth-century scholars to depict Christ in their own liberal image. To Schweitzer, Jesus was a zealot who mistakenly expected the imminent end of the world, but, paradoxically, he respected His ethical teaching, and did far more to follow it than many who, in theory, accepted Christ as Lord. He trained as a doctor, and in 1913, went with his wife to Lambaréné, among the Fang of Gabon.

With a few breaks—including deportation during the First World War—he stayed there until he died. His spectacular sacrifice made him a popular hero, comparable with Livingstone in an earlier age. Many came to Lambaréné as pilgrims. Some stayed to help in his work, but others found much to alarm them, including a racist attitude to Africans, which was typical of many expatriate missionaries, and hospital standards that left much to be desired. 'Life in the African villages as we had known it offers more healthy space and orderly living arrangement than in the hospital'; an African visitor from the interior deplored the absence of sanitary facilities.

He never learned an African language, showed no interest in the culture of those among whom he lived, and often described Africans as unreliable children. He wrote of a missionary who went to live on equal terms in an African village: 'With his abandonment of the social interval between white and black he lost all his influence, his word was no longer taken as the "white man's word" but he had to argue every point with them as if he were merely their equal'.[107] The premise of inequality could scarcely be more clearly stated. Schweitzer embodies, in an extreme form, the paradox of much missionary endeavour: a life of struggle and sacrifice, and of freely chosen exile from one's own culture, coupled with the marginalizing of the African as the perpetually inferior Other.

Tempels and Schweitzer, for very different reasons, are both justly famous, but neither transformed countless African lives, as did the imprisoned Simon Kimbangu.

In late nineteenth-century Shaba, a missionary met 'a dream embassy':

> . . . they had travelled a long way and were afoot on a kind of Missionary journey from one great chief to another. . . . God having spoken to their chief in a great dream . . . he challenged their king as to his dignity; . . . the king responded with his long array of titles . . . the more he vaunted before God the less did his strength become.

In the end, the king said, 'no king am I, but a worthless slave', and then he found that he was made strong in weakness.[108]

·≤§ EIGHT §≥·

Northern Africa

I have been called by some of my priests Frank [that is, a
western Christian]. I am not ashamed of the name, because
both you and myself believe in one Trinity, which is the
foundation of the Christian faith . . . I would rather lose my
head than hold any other faith save that in Christ.[1]

The Emperor Tewedros, shortly before his death

Our aim is not to make Muslims change their religion, but
together to be converted to a greater faithfulness to God.[2]

H. Berlier, the first Catholic Bishop of Niger (1961–1984)

This chapter studies Christianity in Egypt and Ethiopia, and in the Muslim
societies of northern Africa and the western Sudan, where it has undergone a
transition from the triumphalism of a Lavigerie to a spirituality of 'presence'.
Christianity has had very little impact on the Muslim world, whether in Africa
or elsewhere. In contrast, the ancient Christianities of the Copts and the
Ethiopians survive, despite the challenges of an increasingly adverse political
environment, the growth of Islamic fundamentalism in Egypt, and the
establishment of successive Marxist governments in Ethiopia. They have
produced their own charismatic leaders, such as the Copt, Matthew the Poor,
who has renewed the ancient tradition of monasticism, and touched the hearts
of many whose lives lie outside it. In the southern Republic of Sudan, the
mission churches have taken firm root, but at a price. As in Angola, religion
has intensified the consciousness of regional identity, and fuelled a long-
standing and catastrophic civil war.

In 1830, an Armenian Christian told visiting western missionaries that
those who agree on the Trinity, the Atonement, and the divinity of Jesus
should no longer be divided, and that disunity has 'hitherto weakened the
Church and prevented the conversion of the world'.[3] The western missionaries who were to work in northern Africa would have done well to heed his
words.

209

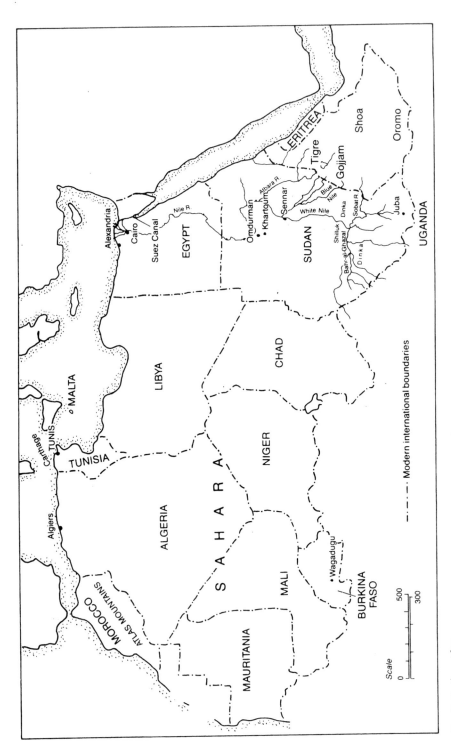

Map 12. Northern Africa

210

Western Christians took it for granted that their own faith and praxis were superior to those of the Copts and Ethiopians, even when, as sometimes happened, they could not answer their theological questions. Protestants and Catholics alike looked on these ancient Christianities, and found them wanting. To Catholics, these churches were schismatic, and, because of ancient christological disputes, heretical. Protestants deplored as superstitious the cult of saints and the Virgin, and had little sympathy with Orthodox liturgies or with confession and fasting. None of this was alien to Catholics, and their Church already embraced a number of Eastern Rites, which a nineteenth-century pope compared with the glorious variety of flowers.

Western missionaries in Egypt, after failing to convert Muslims, often worked among Copts instead. They founded small churches of Uniate Catholics and of Presbyterians, which, in Coptic eyes, weakened the Christian cause in Egypt by dividing it. In the twentieth century, western missionaries in Egypt and Ethiopia came, increasingly, to understand their vocation as one of serving the local church, especially by contributing to theological and general education.

Ethiopia[4]

Here, the modern western missionary enterprise began with the arrival of CMS agents in Tigré, in 1830. Ethiopian tradition speaks of *Zamana Mesafent*, the era of princes, when a *fainéant* emperor at Gondar could do nothing to prevent the interminable struggles of rival warlords. Samuel Gobat, a Basel Mission member in the CMS's employ, who later became Anglican Bishop of Jerusalem, managed to establish a considerable rapport with Ethiopian Christians, with whom he conducted long and complicated theological debates. Habta Sellase, a young aristocrat, 'put several questions to me, on the nature of God—on the manner of the Union of the Divinity with the humanity in the person of Christ, etc., but they were all questions too obscure for me to be able satisfactorily to reply to them'.[5] This and many other such debates reflect an Ethiopian passion for theology rooted in a burning preoccupation with religion, as well as in a narrowly focused educational system.

What united western and Ethiopian Christians was, as both recognized, more important than what divided them:

> *Missionary* 'Do you believe Jesus Christ to be perfect God and perfect Man?' *The Etchegua*: [the *Echage*, Filpos] 'Yes, with all my heart!' *Missionary*: 'Well, we are brothers in this respect, although we express ourselves differently.'[6]

Shortly before he died, in 1838, Sabagadis, *Dajazmach* of northern Ethiopia, said to Gobat:

I love you, not because you are a great man, not because you are a white man; but because you love the Lord whom I wish to love with all my heart. I pray you to be my brother and to consider me as your brother.[7]

Gobat's companion, Christian Kugler, died with prayers in Tigré on his lips.[8] Their successors lacked their flexibility, and were expelled from Tigré. The Ethiopians explained that they had put up with them in the hope of persuading them of their errors: '. . . we had been tolerated only, they . . . had expected us to repent of our heresies and practices . . .'.[9] Deciding to concentrate on non-Christian peoples, especially the Oromo, they moved South, to Shoa, but, within four years, they were expelled from there as well.

Ethiopian princes welcomed missionaries because of a genuine interest in theological dialogue, but they also hoped for access to western technology, and, especially, firearms. They needed the latter, not only in their internal struggles, but because of the danger posed by Muhammad Ali's modernized and militarized Egypt. In 1839, it was said of the Ruler of Shoa, 'He wishes to make use of us as physicians, architects, artists, etc.', but that 'he does not seem to feel the necessity of a reformation of their Church, and endeavours to preserve all things in their old state'.[10]

Protestants were, in principle, willing to 'reform' the Ethiopian and Coptic churches rather than make their members Anglicans or Presbyterians, but Catholics required adherence to Rome. Provided they were willing to make the same concessions to Ethiopian language and culture which had long been embodied in the Uniate churches of the East, they had an easier task.

Two orders reached Ethiopia in 1838, and 1846, respectively: the Lazarists, and the Capuchins. The former, working in the North, sought to establish a Uniate Church with an Ethiopian liturgy, while the latter, in the South, transplanted the Latin rite. Their most famous representative, the Capuchin Bishop, Guglielmo Massaja, who later became a Cardinal, said that, 'the Levantines will never be Catholics in their hearts until they are Latins. . . .' The Lazarist, Justin de Jacobus (1800–1860), felt very differently, adopting the lifestyle of a wandering Ethiopian religious teacher: '. . . he greatly loves the Abyssinian rite and Abyssinia'.[11] The only missionary of the day whose memory is still preserved in oral tradition, Jacobus won a small number of fervent converts, such as the priests Takla Haymanot, and Gabra Mika'el. The latter, when in his sixties, died for his religion, as a result of beatings ordered by Tewodros. When Jacobus died, he left behind him several thousand Catholics, eight parishes and twenty Ethiopian Catholic priests, converts from Orthodoxy.

The Capuchins, for all their insistence on the Latin rite, also succeeded in creating an indigenous clergy. Massaja was criticized for ordaining Oromo ex-slaves, who had little education. However, by 1879, the expatriate Catholic priests in the South had died, or left the mission. When others came, in 1902, the Catholic Church was still alive, sustained by those same indigenous priests.

It has been suggested that, although in itself Catholicism was just as 'hierarchical and sacerdotal' as Orthodoxy, in the Ethiopian context it attracted those 'who temperamentally and sociologically would elsewhere have joined fringe religious movements . . . foreign missionaries, whether fundamentalists or mainline, capture the peripheral protest vote'.[12]

The circulation of British and Foreign Bible Society Bibles led, in about 1860, to a religious movement in Eritrea that was reminiscent of the Reformation in Europe. This group of Orthodox clergy and their followers (who were mainly young, and included many girls), rejected the saying of Mass for the souls in purgatory, and the fasts and feast days so typical of Ethiopian orthodoxy, and taught salvation by faith in Christ alone. Originally intended as a movement of renewal *within* orthodoxy, they were forced into exile, and into the creation of a new Church, in association with Swedish Lutherans, Mekane Yesu.

They embarked on western-style marriages, and willingly worked in mechanical trades (which most Ethiopians shunned because of their caste connotations), and built schools and hospitals.[13]

Missionaries tended to believe that their interests would be furthered by formal or informal colonial expansion. Krapf, who, in another context, was to deplore the mission advocacy of empire, wrote in 1842, '. . . the British must become the guardians of Abyssinia, whatever measures must be applied, whether they are of a forceable or peaceable nature'.[14] The Lazarists looked to France and the Capuchins to Italy. In 1848, Jacobus wrote a letter in the name of Webe, *Dajazmach* of northern Ethiopia, asking for the same kind of Protectorate as France had extended over Tahiti. Later, he supported Negusé, a Tigré-based rebel, against the Emperor, Tewodros.[15]

The Dajazmach, Kasa (1818–68), seized supreme power in 1855, taking the throne name Tewodros (Theodore): there was a widely current belief that a ruler of this name would institute a millenium of peace and prosperity. Tewodros was deeply religious, and often called himself the slave of Christ:

He is persuaded that he is destined to restore the glories of Ethiopian Empire, and to achieve great conquests . . . his faith is signal: without Christ, he says, I am nothing; if he has destined me to purify and reform this distracted kingdom, with His aid who shall stay me: nay, sometimes he is on the point of not caring for human assistance at all, and this is one reason why he will not seek with much avidity for assistance from or alliance with Europe.[16]

He married his consort, Tewabach, in church, and, despite their childlessness, was faithful to her till she died. His great goal was to restore the strength and unity of the Ethiopian State. As he saw Church and State as being inseparable, he could not allow proselytization. However, he was extremely anxious for access to western technology, and, especially, western arms. German missionary artisans of the Pilgrim Mission, trained at Chrischona, responded to his call, and worked for him. Another mission, led by Stern, attempted to convert the Falashas, an enterprise where, for once, they had the backing of the Orthodox Church.

Tewodros came to the throne as a reformer. He allowed missionaries to distribute Amharic (rather than Ge'ez) Bibles, and tried to enforce monogamy, but he spent his reign fighting an unending series of rebellions. The area under his control shrank steadily, and reverses—which included the death of his beloved wife—so distorted his character that he became increasingly violent, and prone to alcoholism. Some believe that he became insane. He forfeited the support of the Church in 1860, when he attempted to reduce the number of clergy, and to give the surplus land to tax-paying peasants.[17]

He had hoped to negotiate with the western powers as an equal, but, when a letter to Queen Victoria, seeking technical aid, went unanswered, he took several missionaries hostage. The British government sent an expedition under Napier, at great expense, to rescue them (it would have cost much less to respond to Tewodros' initial request). On Good Friday, 1868, his army was decimated by British forces. Tewodros sent his hostages away in safety, and, then, on Easter Monday, died by his own hand. It is a bitter irony that the pistol was a gift from Queen Victoria. He had dreamed of uniting Ethiopia, and conquering Jerusalem, and, indeed, the world.

The British expedition was not intended to create a colony and the army soon withdrew. After an interregnum, Tewodros was succeeded by Yohannes IV. His heir, Menelik (1889–1913), united northern and southern Ethiopia. His 'internal colonialism' has been much criticized: 'The fact that Menelik's imperialism was internal or indigenous does not make it any more excusable than Victoria's'.[18]

Ethiopian orthodoxy did not develop a specifically missionary organization until 1963, and it did not, traditionally, feel a calling to preach the Gospel in distant lands. However, as we saw earlier, Christianity spread steadily in Ethiopia itself, albeit as part of a package of Amharic domination and cultural ascendancy.

In 1832, Gobat met a young Oromo who had been enslaved at fourteen, and sold to a master at Gojam. He was baptized, and set free: 'Being free, he might have returned to his country . . . but he was unwilling to be a Christian without knowing the truths of Christianity'. He learned to read and write Ge'ez, returned home, and asked his father to become a Christian:

> His father replied, that he had no kind of objection to embracing Christianity; but that having always been free, he could not bear to be regarded as a slave in the Amhara country. 'But go', added he, 'and bring hither a Christian priest, to teach and baptize us. . . .' He returned to Amhara, but he could not find an intelligent priest willing to accompany him into his country. He resolved, in consequence, to be himself consecrated for the ministry: he became a monk at Gondar. . . .[19]

In the twentieth century, as before, Christianity has continued to spread among the traditionalists of the South. Here, too, a prophet arose who is thought to have foretold the coming of Christianity.

Asa flourished in the Sidama state of Gamo, in southern Ethiopia, after the First World War. He died before the coming of the western missionaries, but foretold their arrival. Sidama was in turmoil, following the invasions by the Christian kingdom in the late nineteenth century, and epidemics that affected both people and cattle. The Sudan Interior Mission reached the area in 1928, and found a 'widespread spirit of expectancy for a fuller revelation from the one true God'; Asa is said to have foretold a Holy Book, and taught the principles of the Ten Commandments. The Capuchins, a little later, found people exhorted to submit to 'Christ and Mary'. Missionaries' enthusiasm for dead prophets, as Singleton points out, contrasts with their persecution of live ones, such as Kimbangu.[20] It is unlikely that Asa specified denominational preferences.

Figures such as Asa, and his many counterparts elsewhere in Africa, haunt us with the questions they suggest. Are these stories examples of the 'invention of tradition', a response, in this case, to Christian/Amharic colonialism? Do they represent an intellectual's response to a changing and enlarging world?

Other vignettes suggest the way in which Christianity was assimilated into the traditional cultures of southern Ethiopia, modern examples of a process that has been going on for centuries. Some Sidama would meet each year on the sacred mountain, Ambaritcho: 'They could be heard crying out "Christos, Christos"'.[21]

The Dorze are another south Ethiopian people, highlanders who seem to have been converted in the fifteenth century. Later, they reverted to an older religion until they were re-Christianized in the twentieth century.[22] They live on the margins between the Christianity of the Amharic heartland, and the 'paganism' of their southern neighbours, and still retain many traditional religious beliefs and practices. In this situation of liminality, they accentuate the traces of their earlier Christian heritage, such as the retention of the word *k'eso*, priest. In a concentrated symbolic statement of these ambiguities, they believe that the leopard, which lives in their mountains, is a Christian, and that it follows the fasts that are at the heart of Ethiopian orthodoxy.[23]

Unlike modern missionary societies, but like the prophetic and Zionist churches, the Ethiopian church has no shortage of vocations. In the 1970s, it had some 250 thousand clergy, (priests, deacons and cantors), 15 thousand churches, 10 million Christians, and 15 thousand monks in 800 monasteries.[24] This ratio of one cleric to every forty Christians may be compared with Dublin, which has one to 947. Priests see their role as being, essentially, a ritual one; and religious teaching and missionary activity have traditionally been the work of monks.

The Ethiopian church evinces striking similarities with the Christian

215

cultures of sub-Saharan Africa. In both cases, canonical marriage tends to be the exception rather than the rule; in Ethiopia, as in the sixteenth-century Kongo, the aristocrats tended to plural marriage. The unions of the peasantry were shifting and unstable, and only the very young and very old went to Communion, few even attended Mass. Tewedros was unusual because he 'partook of the Holy Communion with one woman [wife].'[25] Often, Ethiopian Christians embarked on canonical marriage in old age. None of this meant religious indifference, but, rather, a spirituality that revolved around rigorous and protracted fasts, the keeping of saints' days, and pilgrimages. Many Zionist, and other prophetic churches, share this emphasis on fasting, festivals, and pilgrimages to a holy place.

In Ethiopia, as in many Zionist and Aladura churches, menstrual and post-partum tabus excluded women from Mass. Such rules strike at the very core of a woman's being, which is seen as impure.

Widower priests cannot remarry, nor can married priests make love to their wives on the evening before they celebrate Mass.

As always, these symbolic statements both shape and reflect a wider social reality. An old Sidama man, after a year's catechism, exclaimed, 'God made all things well, except Eve!'[26]

In many respects—its liturgy, drumming, and dancing, its married clergy—Ethiopia is the prototype of a deeply inculturated Christianity. With typical originality and vigour, Singleton has pointed out some of its weaknesses, which are not, of course, peculiar to Ethiopia. They include the identification of Church and State, so that Muslim Ethiopians felt themselves to be non-citizens, and the Revolution, accordingly, a liberation. Casted artisans suffered from much traditional prejudice, which the Revolution attempted to eliminate. After the fall of the Solomonic monarchy, lepers hoped that, for the first time, they would be buried with other Christians in a common cemetery.[27] Ironically, in such respects, the Revolution appeared more Christian than Christianity.

Singleton compares Ethiopia's other-worldly monasteries with farmer Trappists, to the latter's advantage, perhaps overlooking the lilies of the field. He accuses the Ethiopian church of neglecting both the spiritual and temporal welfare of the faithful. He criticizes its esoteric liturgy and obsessive interest in angels and demons. They are unfashionable entities in non-charismatic circles in the western world although it is a preoccupation that Archbishop Milingo shares (see page 6). He criticizes church schools, where 'children, mainly boys, are taught to read, but not to write, religious texts composed in the 231 characters of a long dead language, Ge'ez'.[28] The parish priests' lack of education and training has often attracted adverse comment.

As he points out, much of this was clear to educated Ethiopians before the Revolution. It was Haile Selassie who, in 1959, ended the ancient practice of obtaining the Ethiopian church's head, the *Abuna* from Egypt—Basileos was the first Ethiopian incumbent in 1600 years. A Theological College was founded in 1962 (though few of the clergy have attended it), and a missionary movement the following year. There are a number of strong, lay organizations, such as *Sewasewa Berhan*, 'Spreading the Light'.

In comparison with Orthodoxy's 10 million Christians, the western churches in and near Ethiopia are miniscule: 194 thousand Catholics, with 152 indigenous priests, mainly in Eritrea; Mekane Yesu has 190 thousand adherents, mainly Oromo, and is expanding fast.

As was the case in nineteenth-century Madagascar, some missions have found that they acquired more adherents in the absence of foreign missionaries than when they were present. The Sudan Interior Mission began work in 1927; ten years later, when they had a total of 48 baptized adherents, they were expelled by the Italians. In their absence, the number of Christians expanded dramatically. They returned in 1942, to find 10 thousand Christians.[29] The American United Presbyterians, who began work among the Oromo in 1918, had a similar experience.

The Emperor, Haile Selassie, Lion of Judah, and putative descendant of Solomon, was overthrown in an army coup in 1974, and died a year later. If anything, the crisis of Ethiopia intensified under the Marxist military regime that followed. Its fall, it was claimed, was foretold in a monastic prophecy. The monarchy fell largely because of a rural poverty, which sometimes degenerated into catastrophic famine, and was exacerbated by the exactions of an absentee aristocracy: in the North, 10 per cent of the population owned 90 per cent of the land. The military government dispossessed the landlords, but followed policies of collectivization and compulsory resettlement that the peasants found equally alienating. Ethiopia's 'internal imperialism' in the nineteenth century led to centrifugal tendencies in the late twentieth, and the Dergue was unable to contain some half a dozen liberation movements, or prevent an independent Eritrea.

The Marxism of independent African states has often meant little more than 'radicalism', or 'change', and is by no means always hostile to religion (see pages 350–51), but the close association of the Ethiopian church and the Solomonic kingdom meant that the former was greatly affected by these changes.

Eritrea is equally divided between Christian cultivators, and Muslims. In contrast with Angola and Mozambique, the Eritreans have succeeded in overcoming religious and other differences (including those between agriculturalists and pastoralists), to build a united and successful liberation movement: 'In no other territory . . . has a revolutionary resistance movement proved capable of integrating so diverse a social base'.[30]

The Copts

Coptic religious sensibility has always been dominated by a cluster of core symbols: the tradition that Jesus visited Egypt as an infant during the Flight into Egypt, the belief that the Coptic Church was founded by St Mark, the memory of the martyrs of Diocletian (from whose deaths the Coptic calendar is dated) and reverence for the monastic tradition. Above all, at the heart of Coptic spirituality is the cross, *al-Salib.*

The Coptic cross is woven endlessly on handlooms, and incized, or painted on the outer walls of Coptic homes. Copts wear a cross round their neck, and, in rural areas, tattoo it on the wrists of their children. Coptic Orthodoxy has a distinctive liturgy, marked by its hymns to the Virgin, and by 'simplicity . . . popular character and the unique place given to the reading of holy books'.[31]

The Copts have spoken Arabic as their first language since the twelfth century, and have many practices in common with their Muslim neighbours, but Coptic identity, like Jewishness, is, in a sense, an ethnic quality, independent of religous affiliation, and agnostics remain Copts, members of 'the Coptic nation', and conscious heirs to ancient Egypt.

Individual Copts held high office under the Mameluks, but, when the French invaded Egypt in 1798, they were probably at their lowest ebb, both numerically and in morale. In 1855, the Patriarch of Alexandria put their numbers at 217 thousand in a population of 5 million,[32] and there were only 7 desert monasteries.[33]

Their role in society became more important when, first, Napoleon, and, then, Muhammad Ali drew on their administrative abilities, and gave them leading roles in government. Muhammed Ali freed them from medieval restrictions of dress, and, in 1837, for the first time since the Arab conquest, Christians were allowed to bear arms.[34] They became, increasingly, a prosperous professional and business élite.

Kyrillos IV, the Reformer, Patriarch from 1854 until 1861, founded two schools for girls, and one for boys in Cairo, set up a printing press, and was responsible for a college that taught five languages. He had a great bonfire of religious pictures, which he believed were worshipped idolatrously.[35]

Often, however, the laity were better educated, and more eager for reform than the clergy. In 1874, they fought for the establishment of a Community Council to administer church property, though this led to conflict with successive Patriarchs. Some even joined the American United Presbyterian Church, established in Egypt in 1854, finding it easier to join a western church than to 'modernize' their Coptic heritage. In 1957, it became the Coptic Evangelical Church, and is particularly strong in the Nile Delta; it is by far the largest Protestant church in the Middle East.[36] Its existence has always been a source of great bitterness and division, but, when it applied for membership of the World Council of Churches, the strongly ecumenical Coptic Bishop, Samwil, supported it warmly.

Dubious as the endeavour to 'convert' Copts now appears, and damaging and divisive as Copts themselves have perceived it, Egypt was the chosen field for some notable missionaries, among them the pioneer of ecumenicity, Dr Harpur, founder of the Old Cairo Hospital in 1899, and the Arabist and musician, Temple Gardiner of Cairo (1873–1928), whose Fellowship of Unity did much to lessen the alienation between Copts and Egyptian Protestants. Constance Padwick was one of 'a varied continuity of indefatigable women, who gave as much as half a century of life to obscure corners of the land they had taken for their heritage'.[37] All these were Anglicans, but there were equally remarkable men and women in the Faith Missions. When male missionaries left before the Second World War, Maude Cary and three other single women ran the Gospel Missionary Union stations in Morocco on their own.[38]

Ironically, the position of the Copts improved under a Muslim overlord, and degenerated under an, at least nominally, Christian one. As was so often the case in Africa, the British favoured the Muslim majority, 'a curious instance of the affinity of the British mind for prejudice is the way in which every Englishman I have seen scorns the Eastern Christians'.[39] To Lord Cromer, a Muslim was an Egyptian worshipping in a mosque, and a Copt an Egyptian worshipping in a church. Fearing the revolutionary potential of Islam, they tended to favour Muslims, which caused the Copts the same kind of bewilderment and distress that western missionaries experienced in, for instance, Northern Nigeria.

Copts and Muslims have never been so close as they were during the nationalist movement. It was an alliance scarcely dented by the assassination of Egypt's only Coptic Prime Minister, Pasha Butrus Ghali, by a Muslim in 1910. This kind of co-operation for political purposes came most easily, perhaps, to those whose outlook was predominantly secular. Later, the Copts remembered it as a golden age, when Islamic scholars preached in the churches, and Abuna Sergius spoke on freedom in the mosque of al-Ashar.[40]

In theory, Egypt gained independence in 1922, but, in practice, there was a large, continuing British military presence. It was not until the overthrow of Farouk in 1952, and Nasser's seizure of the Suez Canal four years later, that independence became a reality. By that time, largely as a result of the Palestine conflict, Egyptian nationalism and Islam were tending to become synonymous. Nasser's nationalization of the property of the 600 wealthiest families led to an exodus, both of the richest Copts, and of the large, prosperous, expatriate community of Syrian, Lebanese, and other eastern Christians. The Christian community lost many of its most influential members just at the time when it was imperilled by the rise of a militant Islam. The rapport of the early nationalists was forgotten.

The middle decades of the twentieth century saw both a decline, and a revival in the Coptic Church. The former was very apparent in the state of monasticism, traditionally the very heart of Coptic spirituality. In the late 1960s, there were nine inhabited Coptic monasteries, with a total of some 216 inhabitants,[41] a situation that greatly limited the choice of Patriarch and bishops, who must be monks. When Anba Yusab II was Patriarch, from 1946 to 1956, it was said that sixteen out of nineteen episcopal appointments were sold by his valet. He was exiled by the Coptic community to a remote monastery in Upper Egypt, a year before his death, and was succeeded by a man who was devout and ascetic, but politically inexperienced, Mina the Solitary, who became Kyrillos VI. He had once worked for the firm of Thomas Cook, and was converted by reading the lives of the Desert People. His first action was to build a new monastery. When he died in 1971, he was replaced by Shanuda III, thought to be the 117th Coptic Patriarch of Alexandria.

As in Ethiopia, observers have often lamented the clergy's lack of education and training: only half the Coptic clergy are seminary graduates. The Copts suffered from the growth of Islamic fundamentalism, especially after the 1973 war with Israel, when they appeared to many Muslims, to be a subversive fifth column and threat to national unity. Copts became the sinister Other, and rumours spread. It was said, for instance, that Coptic doctors left Muslim patients to die. Repeatedly, churches were burned, and Coptic property destroyed. In June, 1981, there was a three-day battle between Copts and Muslims in a Cairo suburb.[42] In the same year, Shanuda was exiled to the Libyan desert.

Matta al-Miskin, Matthew the Poor, was once a prosperous pharmacist in Cairo. At the age of twenty-nine, he followed in the footsteps of St Anthony; he sold his goods, gave the proceeds to the poor, and went to the desert. He has become famous as a spiritual teacher and writer, and as a monastic superior. Other university graduates have followed his example, and some have spoken of a monastic revival. A monk who was called from the desert to become a bishop, wrote to a well-wisher, '. . . the Lord . . . on the Last Day, will not ask us for our pastoral grade, but for our purity of heart. . . . I write this letter from my beloved cave.'[43]

There have been efforts to revive the Coptic language and Coptic culture. In 1968, the Virgin was thought to have appeared to thousands on the Coptic Easter, shortly before the consecration of a new cathedral in Cairo. Modern Marian apparitions are a world-wide phenomenon (there are well-known instances at Garabandal in Portugal, and Medjugorje in the former Yugoslavia, and a less famous case in Australia), and are not easy to explain satisfactorily.

Since 1954, the Coptic church has been a member of the World Council of Churches. The Copts are the largest Christian community in the Arab world: it is widely believed that they number 4 million, in a population of 24 million, though estimates vary greatly. They are concentrated in Cairo, Alexandria, and Upper (that is, southern) Egypt. As in Ethiopia, other churches are smaller: there are 200 thousand Protestants, and 100 thousand members of a Uniate church (Coptic in liturgy, but affiliated to Rome), which dates from 1895.[44]

The Copts tend to be more prosperous, and better-educated than their Muslim compatriots: according to the 1960 census, 41.4 per cent of Christians, and 23.8 per cent of Muslims were literate.[45] However, they complain of discrimination in employment, and, perhaps 5 thousand a year become Muslims for this reason, or to facilitate divorce. Only 13 of the 400 members of the 1960 National Assembly were Copts.[46] They continue to regard themselves as the true heirs of Pharaonic Egypt.

The Maghrib

The modern history of Christianity in northern Africa is dominated by the 14 million Christians in the Ethiopian and Coptic traditions. Elsewhere, Islam is dominant, and Christian communities remain very small, consisting mainly of expatriates.

Lavigerie is one of the major figures in nineteenth-century Catholic mission history. It is a paradox that he was Archbishop of Algiers, where there are today scarcely any indigenous Christians. Christianity has fared better among traditionalists, notably among the Nilotic speakers of the southern Republic of Sudan.

Lavigerie's Missionaries of Africa (usually called the White Fathers, after their dress, based on Arab exemplars), were founded in Algiers. They became the largest male congregation established specifically for work in Africa, concentrating not on the Muslim North, but on eastern and central Africa. Their life expectancy, in the nineteenth century, was under forty years. In the late 1980s, there were 2834 White Fathers, 1800 of them at work in Africa.

Charles Martial Allemand Lavigerie (1825–92) influenced the lives of Africans less by his own exertions, than by those of his spiritual sons. He regarded the members of his congregation with parental affection and loyalty, and mourned as sons, the six White Fathers martyred in the Sahara.

He readily identified the interests of the Church with the expansion of France: he displaced the Italian Capuchins from Tunis, and discarded his third name during the Franco-Prussian war. But there was never any doubt as to where his primary loyalty lay. He was a monarchist under the Empire: in 1890, he brought a storm on his head by toasting the Republic at a (royalist) naval banquet. He was not a Vicar of Bray; his overriding aim was always to further the interests of the Church. His irritability was both legendary and understandable; in his latter years, he suffered from chronic ill health, and his authoritarianism was the norm among nineteenth-century founders of religious congregations.

In 1866, given the choice between Lyons—the second-greatest see in France—and Algiers, he chose the latter: 'It would be nicer to live at Lyons, but it would be easier to die at Algiers'.[47] He saw the see of Algiers, created for the benefit of white *colons*, as a springboard for missionary enterprise in black Africa: 'Algeria is only the door opened by Providence on a barbaric continent of two hundred million souls'.[48]

He was an experienced man of affairs when appointed, best-known for his work for the Maronite Christians of Lebanon, who joined Rome *en masse* in the twelfth century, and suffered severe persecution in the mid nineteenth. He had a talent for fundraising, and for influencing those in high places. His crusade against the slave trade brought him close to eminent English Protestants, and he was a friend of Leo XIII, but his work was also supported by anticlericals, such as Ferry and Gambetta, because they believed it helped French colonial expansion. Anticlericalism was not for export, and Lavigerie and Ferry worked together to achieve the French occupation of Tunisia in 1882. Men he sent to a Saharan settlement reported, 'We shall endeavour to hold high the banner of the Sacred Heart and the flag of France . . .'.[49]

Though he spent much of his life working among Muslims, or Eastern Christians, Lavigerie had little respect for the culture of the Other. As a child, he pushed Jewish children into fountains to baptize them. As an adult, he described Islam in the demonic terms others missionaries reserved for African traditional religion: 'The Muslim religion is truly the masterpiece of the spirit of evil.'[50]

His first four years in Algiers were marked by conflict. He declared his goal of converting Algeria in his first pastoral letter in 1867, although it ran counter to the official policy of forbidding proselytization, based on the fear of a Muslim revolt. He and the Governor-General, Patrice MacCahon (later President of the Republic), remained enemies until they died. In a time of famine and plague, he created Christian villages for the orphaned, in the teeth of official hostility. As elsewhere, work among orphans and redeemed slaves never led to the formation of a substantial and enduring Christian community, although it transformed individual lives.

None was more remarkable than that of Dr Adrian Atiman (1866–1956). A Songhai from modern Mali, he was enslaved by the Tuareg as a child, and purchased by a White Father in Algiers. He went to school there, and then was sent to train as a doctor in Malta. After graduating, he walked 700 miles to the White Fathers' station on the shores of Lake Tanganyika, where he became the mission doctor. He married a Bemba woman, and spent the rest of his long life there, as a physican, and teacher of religion. He always wore the costume of Algiers. 'When he died, two thousand people walked in his funeral procession.'[51]

Lavigerie has been called the greatest pluralist of his age. He was Apostolic Delegate to the Sahara and Sudan, and to Equatorial Africa, and Archbishop, not only of Algiers, but, after 1881, of the ancient see of Carthage, and, therefore, Primate of Africa. He was Superior for life of both the White Fathers and the White Sisters, and retained his interest in the Eastern Church; the White Fathers ran a seminary for Uniate clergy in Jerusalem.[52] In 1882, he obtained the cardinal's hat he had long desired.

In 1879, he hoped to uproot the slave trade with a force of papal zouaves, 'for my secret design is really to try to found a Christian kingdom in the centre of equatorial Africa. Two hundred rifles do not seem exaggerated to me'.[53] Shortly before he died, he attempted to found a quasi-military order of Armed

Brothers in the Sahara. In 1888, crippled by rheumatism and sciatica, he founded the *Oeuvrage Antiesclavagiste*, and travelled round Europe to rally support for it. At the end of his life he built a great basilica in Carthage, raising money by real estate dealing, and the sale of canonries. It was dedicated to Saint Louis, the King of France, who died on crusade (this was typical of his patriotism and imperviousness to Muslim sensibilities). In his last weeks, he collected estimates from Italian marble workers for the construction of his own tomb. When he died, the next Superior-General of the White Fathers refused the see of Carthage, hoping to die in the African interior, 'for the Faith and for France'.[54]

In 1889, an agnostic Englishman, while describing missions in North Africa as useless, paid tribute to 'the obstinate goodness and patient teaching of Cardinal Lavigerie's missionaries in Algeria'.[55]

The White Sisters were founded by Lavigerie in 1869. The congregation, at first, made little progress, and he was on the point of disbanding it in 1884 when a suitable leader appeared. Marie Louise de l'Eprevier was drawn to Africa by reading Stanley's account of the finding of Livingstone.[56] When still in her twenties, she became Mother-General. The White Sisters worked wherever the White Fathers went: in the Sahara, the Atlas mountains, the Great Lakes, and the western Sahel.

Several communities of women contemplatives responded to Lavigerie's call: Carmelites from Bayonne came to Tunis and Algiers, in 1872 and 1884, respectively, and Marie Reparatrice Sisters to Uganda in 1913. Totally anonymous, and now forgotten, they persevered in their hidden vocation of prayer.

Charles de Foucault (1858–1916) was an aristocratic French army officer who served in North Africa, and who found himself strongly drawn to its people. Leaving the army, he travelled in Algeria and Morocco, disguised as a Jew. He was converted, in part, through the example of Muslim and Jewish religious devotion. He spent seven years as a Trappist, then left the order, but was still ordained as a priest. He settled in southern Algeria in 1901, and moved deeper into the Sahara four years later. He lived the life of a saint, helping the sick and poor, while he compiled a grammar and dictionary of Tammacheq, the language of the desert Tuareg. He was killed by raiders in 1916, having converted no one. Who is to say that his life was in vain?

Lavigerie's strategies were continental. Protestants in the Maghrib—often Evangelicals—sought individual, fervent Christians. Like the Catholics, they made little progress in the Muslim world, despite the proliferation of missionary societies. A Methodist report on North Africa in 1950 noted that Christians were counted in scores rather than thousands, and that converts tended to migrate to France.[57] In 1962, there were twelve Protestant missionary societies in Morocco, with a total of 575 full members, and 1410 in the 'total Christian community'.[58]

Modern Algeria[59]

Algeria was a French colony from 1830 until 1962. At independence, the Catholic Church there had five bishops, 400 priests, 1400 nuns, over 500 churches, and 1 million baptized Christians; by 1979, the number had fallen to 203 priests, and 549 nuns. Nearly all were foreigners, and over half had been working there since independence. There were 70 to 80 thousand Christians, most of them expatriates working in the country, or students from sub-Saharan Africa.

The church schools and hospitals have been handed over to the government, and most of the churches have been given up. What has happened has been the dismantling of a settler church, which had appropriated to itself the name Algerian, while calling Algerians 'Arabs', or 'natives', and that was associated with social, political, and economic dominance: 'The former Church, while rather poor financially, was rich in buildings, means and activities. Today's Church is poor in terms of specifically ecclesiastical institutions and movements. Whereas the former Church did have a few priests and sisters as well as a couple of thousand faithful of Arabo-Berber stock, today's has next to none'. The Church has survived the departure of most of the French settlers, but, in doing so, has undergone a radical transformation. Surviving church professionals have given up the idea of converting Algeria; they do not wish to replace a church of settlers with one of foreigners, and have moved towards a new calling, 'being for' Muslim Algerians. Some religious, especially women, have embraced a lifestyle of radical poverty. The Benedictine monastery of Toumliline, in the Atlas mountains of Morocco, is another example of the spirituality of 'presence' in the Muslim world.[60]

Other churches have much to learn from this radical and difficult journey from triumphalism.

The Western Sahel[61]

The vast, impoverished nations of the Sahel, which ambitious Frenchmen carved into colonies in the late nineteenth century, are overwhelmingly Muslim. As in Algeria, the Christian community consists largely of expatriates, some of whom are Africans from elsewhere. It is sustained by a declining and ageing band of expatriate missionaries.

Mauritania is an Islamic Republic, Niger a secular state. In the former, there are no indigenous Christians at all. In Niger, with a population of 6.5 million, there are 15 thousand Catholics and 10 thousand Protestants (the latter are either Baptists, or members of the Evangelical Church of the Republic of Niger, formerly the Sudan Interior Mission: 4 thousand of the total are indigenous to Niger). There are no Catholic priests of local origin. The

Catholic mission at Dolbel was founded in 1952 as a result of a long campaign by a local man who had been baptized when a soldier in the Algerian army.

Christianity has made much more progress in Burkina Faso (formerly Upper Volta) because the majority of the population were traditionalists, and remain so. Catholics form 10.6 per cent of the population and the majority of the western-educated élite, Protestants 1.3 per cent, Muslims 30.7 per cent; the rest of the population are traditionalists.

The White Fathers' mission in Burkina Faso dates from 1900, their first convert being Alfred Diban.[62] Diban was born at Toma, north-west of Wagadugu, in the late nineteenth century. He was kidnapped during a time of famine and social disruption caused by the French conquest, and sold, in exchange for salt, to a master living in the Sahara. After repeated attempts to escape, he fled to the Niger, where he chanced to meet a White Father bound for Segu. This was in 1898. For the rest of his long life (he died in 1980), he worked devotedly for the church as mason, cook, and catechist.

By 1913, he had worked in five missions among four different ethno-linguistic groups. Later, he worked among his own people, the Sanan of Toma. In his old age, he said, 'I have always found great comfort in prayer. Prayer is like the breath and the food of a Christian. Without breath and without food, how can we live?'[63] We know of him only because one of his children became a distinguished historian, and wrote his father's biography. He may stand for hundreds of obscure catechists, whose very names are now forgotten.

The Southern Sudan

The peoples of the southern Sudan, the related Dinka, Nuer, and Shilluk, live in one of the most difficult natural habitats in the world. Alternately subject to drought and flood, its people have been decimated in recent times by the combined effects of famine and civil war. Early European visitors, as is so often the case, confused their lack of material possessions with spiritual poverty: 'Without any exception', wrote Sir Samuel Baker, in 1867, 'they are without a belief in a Supreme Being, neither have they any form of worship or idolatry'.[64] Modern research, however, has made the complexity and profundity of their religious systems known to the world.[65]

Earlier, we studied the rise and fall of the Christian civilization of Nubia. The modern history of Christianity began with the establishment of Catholic missions among the Dinka and Bari. Because of the high death rate among the expatriate missionaries, these missions were closed in 1860 and 1861. The Verona Fathers were founded by one of these pioneers, Daniel Comboni, who died at Khartoum in 1880.

The nineteenth-century history of what is now the Republic of Sudan is a complicated one. In 1820–1, it was invaded by Muhammad Ali of Egypt, whose forces penetrated as far as Sennar. In the decades that followed, Egyptians raided for slaves and ivory as far South as northern Uganda (the slave trade was officially banned in 1860). As in Liberia, the independence of nineteenth-century Egypt was increasingly threatened by foreign indebtedness. The construction of the Suez Canal gave the area immense strategic importance, and, in 1882, Egypt became, in fact (though not in name) a British colony.

A year earlier, a Sudanese Muslim who claimed to be the *Mahdi*, the Rightly Guided One of Islamic eschatology, had launched a rising that created a great, though ultimately short-lived, state. In 1898, the Mahdi's supporters were defeated by Anglo-Egyptian forces, and the Sudan became, in effect, a British colony, and the influx of missionaries dates from this time. The death of General Charles Gordon at Khartoum in 1885 had electrified English public opinion, much as Livingstone's had done, twenty-two years earlier. Like the great explorer, he was transformed, albeit posthumously, into a romantic Christian hero. This, and anti-slavery sentiment, led to an upsurge of missionary interest in the Sudan, and CMS representatives, American Presbyterians, Verona Fathers, and representatives of the future Sudan United Mission all arrived in Khartoum.

The British administration was hostile, partly because its officials feared a further Muslim rising, and partly because of a general prejudice, which we have noted in other contexts, against Christian and western-educated Africans: 'a black when converted becomes a scamp, loafer, scoundrel and liar'.[66] But by exercising pressure on the government in London, the missionaries gained access to the southern Sudan.

They followed different strategies: The Presbyterians worked intensively in a limited area on the Sobat, while Catholics and Anglicans covered vast areas to pre-empt their rivals.[67] The teacher-catechists in CMS schools were Ugandan Christians; the first pupils were hostages or the sons of freed slaves.

Christianity spread so rapidly that the southern Sudan was called 'one of the fastest growing churches of the Anglican communion'.[68] Many who became Christians turned into voluntary evangelists. Sheer chance preserves the memory of Petro, who was converted when in the army, and created a congregation of seventy, between Yei and Meridi, which worshipped in the open air: 'He was not a pastor, nor a teacher, and he was not paid'.[69]

In the North, the missions ran schools for, predominantly, Muslim pupils: the Catholic colleges were generically called 'Combonis'. In 1962, shortly before their expulsion from the South, there were 231 Catholic missionaries and 51 Protestants working in the North, and 503 Catholics and 114 Protestants in the South.[70]

Some of the most notable missionaries spent their lives in the Muslim and Arab North. Llewellyn Gwynne, Anglican Bishop of Khartoum, worked there, except for the years of the First World War, from 1899 until 1947. Sophie Zenkovsky, a Russian émigré, was a CMS worker in Omdurman in 1950. Her desire to enter into the lives of local women led her into a profound study of their religious world. A widely travelled visitor wrote, 'nowhere that I have been in Africa have I been so overwhelmed with a sense of the presence of God as in that little oasis in Omdurman'.[71]

Colonial officials oscillated between hostility to missions and mission education, and a desire to separate North and South. They feared that education made the Dinka 'detribalised': 'they became either converts aping Europeans or types of the Effendi class. . . .' In 1930, it was decided to separate North and South. This meant expelling northern traders, and banning Arab dress—the same Arab dress that the White Fathers wore so proudly: 'Shirts should be made short, with a collar . . . and NOT an open neck as worn by the Baggara of Darfur'.[72] The policy had consequences much more serious than the banning of collarless shirts; it contributed to the South's underdevelopment,[73] and to a polarization of North and South, 'Arab' and black, Muslim and Christian/traditionalist, which has meant that, for much of the time since independence in 1956, the Sudan has been ravaged by civil war.

NINE

East and East Central Africa
c. 1900 to c. 1960

The chiefs, the chiefs to whom do they pray?
To the shades! To the shades! . . .
The Europeans, the Europeans to whom do they pray?
To money! To money! . . .
The baptised, the baptised to whom do they pray?
To Jesus! to Jesus!

A song of Nyakusa Christians, in the 1930s[1]

A continental perspective

This chapter and the next are concerned with the fortunes of Christianity during the colonial period, a theme that was briefly adumbrated in the two preceding them. At the time, it seemed to both rulers and ruled that colonialism would last indefinitely. In the event, it proved an episode briefer than the lifetime of a single old man.

One of the best-known hypotheses in African studies suggests that both Christianity and Islam expanded rapidly in the twentieth century because individuals were forced to become part of a wider world, where nature spirits, or ancestor cults seemed inappropriately local (see pages 6, 38, 57). The argument is not wholly convincing as spirit possession cults also expanded during the colonial period, but it sheds light on a complicated phenomenon. There was a widespread feeling that the power and prosperity of the Europeans, and their military success, meant that their religion was likely to be true. A Rwanda royal woman told her daughters, 'My child, we have always believed in the spirits; we have offered them sacrifice and we have followed the customs of our ancestors in everything; what was the use of all that to us?'[2] But many, as before, were brought to the new religion by visions and dreams, like the woman who 'woke up at midnight and said to her husband, "Let us go and worship God".'[3]

The construction of roads and railways, and the increased security of travel,

228

meant that it became easier to spread the Christian message, and often this was done by African laymen in the context of their ordinary avocations, but it was the missions' near monopoly of education that was the single most effective way of attracting new Christians. Governments usually found it cheaper to subsidize mission schools than to run their own, and most, though not all, missions rejoiced in the additional resources.

Where there was a substantial body of white settlers, as in Kenya or the Rhodesias, the clergy were caught in a dilemma as to where their primary loyalty lay: 'It would be better', complained one African Christian, 'to tell us that there are no missionaries in the Copperbelt, but only sometimes a minister from the European church helps us by taking a service. . . . But because they still call themselves missionaries, we are confused and we say we have been deceived . . .'.[4] Where independence was obtained after an armed struggle, as in Angola, Mozambique, and Zimbabwe, these divisions became explicit and acute.

One of the most dramatic new developments was the rapid spread of prophetic or Zionist churches in South Africa, Rhodesia, Kenya, Nigeria, and Ghana. They have attracted a great deal of scholarly attention, for much the same reason that cults, such as Hare Krishna, or the Moonies, have done in the West: they have clearly defined boundaries, and are, at least in western eyes, exotic. However, far more African Christians stayed within the older churches, often creating islands of relative independence within them, what the *Sephiri* of South Africa call 'river pools'. Few generalizations are appropriate for all the prophetic churches. They are often communities of the poor and marginalized, but, in West Africa, they now have many professional people in their ranks, and, on occasion, their leaders advise heads of state (see pages 279, 290). Sometimes independency has articulated a radical political consciousness, but, in 1985, the members of one of South Africa's largest Zionist churches gathered to hear the then Head of State preach a sermon on Romans 13.

White hegemony was only one form of social stratification. It was an enduring paradox of Christian life that mission education created new inequalities. In 1940, a CMS missionary in Kenya lamented this tendency:

> One of the really distressing features of the introduction in African tribal life of the provision of facilities from public taxation is the keenness of the leading Christians to secure for themselves and their circle as large a share of the benefits as they can. . . . They insist on widening ever more and more the economic gap which separates them from their unprivileged countrymen. . . . They attempt, successfully, to extort the very highest price for their services which can be screwed out of the community. . . .[5]

Inequality was often palliated by generosity, but it divided the Christian community at its heart, and the gap tended to widen with every generation.

Nineteenth-century Bulozi exported ivory, and Lewanika once asked

Coillard what his people would do when there were no more elephants. The missionary suggested alternative exports, such as cotton and coffee,[6] but what was in fact exported was human labour. Much of the revenue of Mozambique was earned by its exiled nationals, working on the Rand. The Lozi and other Northern Rhodesians worked in the mines of South Africa, Zimbabwe and Shaba; when the Copperbelt was opened up in the 1920s, their labour was needed there as well. While the missionaries advocated monogamy, social and economic change undermined the stability of any form of marriage. The need to pay taxes, and generate a cash income drove men from their homes. Spouses were separated for long periods, and prostitution flourished. However, despite the many problems it created, geographic mobility weakened a missionary control that depended on a local monopoly. Sometimes the search for a new community led people to join independent churches; it could also lead to the formation of ethnic churches, or, as in the Copperbelt, to new ecumenical initiatives. At a global level, Protestant missionary societies met at Edinburgh in 1910 to plan the evangelization of the world. China was their first priority.

A regional perspective

Here Christianity had made little impact by 1900, and even in Buganda and Madagascar, Christians were in a minority. By 1938, Christians formed 8 per cent of the population of Kenya, 10 per cent of that of Tanganykia, and 25 per cent of Uganda, and the period of greatest expansion still lay in the future. Today, 60 per cent of the people of Uganda and Kenya are Christians, as is a third of Tanzania's mainland population.[7]

Most of the colonies considered in this chapter were British, the exceptions were Portuguese Mozambique, and Rwanda and Burundi, which were German colonies until they became Belgian mandates after the First World War.

The Uganda railway, which was started at Mombasa in December 1895, had reached Lake Victoria by 1901, and had much the same impact on the missionary enterprise as the completion of the Belgian Congo railway had had further West. An enormously difficult and exhausting journey was no longer necessary, and missionary societies became more willing to recruit women. The Indians employed in railway construction added further strands to Kenya's religious pluralism. Hostility to Indians, for different reasons, was something on which most missionaries, and all white settlers agreed.

White settler populations were small compared with South Africa. In 1940, 'whites' comprised 20.9 per cent of the population of South Africa, and 0.5 per cent of that in Mozambique. The percentage in Northern Rhodesia was under 2 per cent and in Southern Rhodesia 4.5 per cent. Post-war European immigration was encouraged, but the white populations remained small. In 1953, a short-lived Federation of the Rhodesias and Nyasaland was created, in the hope of sustaining white settler hegemony. It soon collapsed, and Zambia and Malawi became independent in 1964. In that year, Ian Smith's National Front declared UDI in Rhodesia; in 1980, Zimbabwe achieved black majority rule, after a bitter armed struggle.

There had been a Catholic presence in Mozambique for centuries, but, even at its greatest extent, it was confined to garrisons on the coast, and the *prazos* and trade posts on the Zambezi, and, by the mid nineteenth century, it was vestigial. In the words of Mousinho de Alburquerque, who conquered the Gaza kingdom and, then, in 1902, committed suicide:

> The administrative processes by which our colonies have been governed, or rather, disgraced, may be summed up as conventions and fictions. Vast territories conventionally ours where we exerted absolutely no influence . . . missions without missionaries, priests without churches, and churches without parishioners.[8]

The Jesuits returned to the Zambezi in 1880, and were joined later by Franciscans, and by the White Fathers. Protestant missions were founded in Mozambique from 1879 on, with Methodist ones around Inhambane, and the Swiss Evangelical Mission at Maputo (formerly Lourenço Marques). An Anglican diocese was founded in 1893 to cater to the needs of those who joined the church when they were migrant workers in South Africa, and colonial boundaries left a small, but enduring, Anglican enclave in the northeast. In Mozambique, as in Angola and the Belgian Congo, Protestantism was often perceived as hostile to the State. It proved, as we have seen, a self-fulfilling prophecy.

The extension of colonial rule opened up new possibilities for missionary expansion, and a period of intense rivalry followed. The Catholics, who regarded Protestantism as equally as perilous to the soul as Islam, scattered stations over vast areas to pre-empt their rivals. The Governor of Tanganyika described the situation in the Southern Highlands in 1908, in words which are equally applicable elsewhere:

> The White Fathers and the Herrnhuters [that is, Moravians] . . . no longer fight with fictional occupation of giant stretches of country by means of outposts consisting mostly of a single coloured 'helper' or 'catechist' but through an encroachment upon the established mission sphere of the opposing confession. . . . It is regrettable that many missions, despite all their declarations against Islam, combat the other Christian confessions much more than Islam.[9]

When missions were hundreds of miles apart, a pattern of *cuius regio eius religio* prevailed. As their number increased, they were compelled to work more closely together, and the older Protestant bodies formed comity agreements, to avoid competition. This led to difficulties. For example, an Africa Inland Mission adherent who moved to an Anglican area, found that he was not a member of any local church at all. Local mission monopolies deprived individuals of denominational choice, and left them with no recourse if they were expelled, or refused baptism in the first place. Catholics did not take part in comity agreements, but they attended the Missionary Conference of North-West Rhodesia in 1914, (as did the Plymouth Brethren), and joined the General Missionary Conference of Northern Rhodesia, which succeeded it.[10]

The divisions between the Evangelical CMS and the Anglo-Catholic UMCA were, in some respects, greater than those between the Evangelicals of different churches. In 1913, after an interdenominational Communion service, Frank Weston, the Anglo-Catholic Bishop of Zanzibar, wrote to the Archbishop of Canterbury charging two of his fellow bishops 'with propagating heresy and committing schism'. On another occasion, he posted a notice on his Cathedral door, stating that he was not in communion with John, Bishop of Hereford![11]

Increasingly, different missions and churches were found in close proximity to each other, so that one's denominational adherence was not irrevocably determined by one's place of birth. Urbanization and migrant labour exposed individuals to new experiences and novel forms of religious organization, while separating them, in some cases, from their original church. Many were converted to Watch Tower in the minefields. Labour migration weakened ties to the local shrines and spirits of traditional religion, and, in the unfamiliar wilderness of urban life, new forms of community were precious.

The copper mines of Northern Rhodesia were opened in the 1920s. By 1930, 30 thousand Africans were employed in them, living in extremely grim conditions. Mission-educated men from Nyasaland played a leading role as skilled workers, instructors, and clerks, and they took it upon themselves to create new Christian communities:

> Passing through a compound after dark on almost any night, you could find little groups of people gathered round the light of an underground worker's acetylene lamp, singing Christian hymns. . . . They [built a church] with their own hands, calling it the Union Church of the Copperbelt.[12]

The missionaries, with their strong preference for rural life, were slow to respond to the needs of the Copperbelt. In the end, they followed where Africans had led.

The ecumenism of the Copperbelt Christians was exceptional. Often, the coexistence of rival missions in one area polarized the community, and their rival claims, while providing a dimension of choice, were confusing. The first missionaries to work among the Gusii were the Seventh Day Adventists and the Mill Hill Fathers, whose respective adherents sometimes came to blows.[13] Africans came to internalize these conflicts, which they had played no part in creating. Simeo Ondelo was one of the founders of the Maria Legio among the Luo, in 1962. Like many prophets, he had a near-death experience, and a vision of Heaven and Hell. In it, 'the Anglicans were so close to hell that they could feel the heat'. The Muslims were further away![14]

Missionaries and colonialism

Many British administrators were critical of the missionaries, and hostile to Christian-educated Africans. Uncontrolled missionary activity was worse than rabies, said one exasperated official.[15] The comment should not be taken too seriously, but even committed Christian administrators sometimes consciously fostered Islam, and showed a preference for Muslim soldiers in colonial armies. The common choice of Muslims as domestic servants forced some Christians to conceal their religious affiliation. Officials and settlers often disliked Evangelicals; ' "the puritan tradition" stigmatises many of their pleasures, such as horse racing and the use of alcohol'.[16] Many preferred the company of hospitable Catholic Fathers, who were far from teetotal.

Indirect rule was at its height in the 1930s, a classic case of the reinvention of tradition. Could one bolster up the power of traditional rulers in isolation from rainmaking, or the cult of royal ancestors?

Sometimes, in a bizarre reversal of roles, colonial officials actually found themselves the advocates of traditional religion. In 1935, a district officer suggested that the administration should collaborate with 'good' witch doctors: 'From personal experience . . . I have found that the better-class witch doctor can so co-operate, and is perfectly willing to do so'.[17] As late as 1975, when white rule in Rhodesia was virtually at an end, another told the people of Chiduku, 'The spirit of Mavudzi has not been prayed to for many years. . . . If no rain comes I will not be surprised. . . .'.[18]

Administrators could not rule without clerks and other literate personnel. Commercial enterprises could not exist without them, nor could the railways function, but colonial government relied on Indirect Rule, and the institutions of the past were closely linked with religion. Both officials and missionaries agonized over the evils of detribalization, and, at Malangali school at Tanganyika, the pupils practised spear-throwing and traditional dancing. The experiment was foredoomed. Students did not want to devote time in school to the acquisition of unsaleable skills they could learn better at home.

There was, as we shall see, a tradition of missionary criticism of white administrators and settlers. There have been times when the missionary critic was the only one there was. But, where there is a large settler community, there has always been a tendency for the missionary to turn into a colonial vicar. In 1919, the Anglican bishops of Mombasa and Uganda and the head of the Presbyterian mission to the Kikuyu wrote in support of forced labour: 'for work of national importance'. Soon afterwards, this measure became law. Frank Weston, a fiery Anglo-Catholic, wrote a pamphlet, *The Serfs of Great Britain*, furiously denouncing it and came to England to campaign:

. . . how the Bishops of Mombasa and Uganda have played traitors! It is too horrible for words, and few people get red-hot against it. I am heart-sick with the Christian institutions. . . . My inner mind is to cut myself off from the British, and throw in my lot entirely with the Bantu. . . .[19]

Perhaps it was easier for a celibate bishop based on a Muslim island to distance himself from the values and pressures of settler society, but Weston himself is a good example of the kind of unconscious racism that frustrated African aspirations. He also wrote:

Africans must be encouraged to spend their lives with or near their own tribes for several generations yet. . . . A moving population . . . means . . . a Europeanising of the African . . . the general policy of sweeping away tribal rites is bad. It leaves the Elders with no chance of bringing their young people into the tribal life properly, and makes for Europeanisation. *Education* is in danger of killing Africans, souls and body. I view with great alarm the movement for "educating Africans as quickly as possible". It is a false movement, it is untrue to history, and it is poisonous in its effects.[20]

Officials and settlers feared that mission education would inculcate ideas about equality: 'Are your people taught that all men are equal?', asked the Kenya Director of Education anxiously.[21] In a sense, their fears were groundless; few, indeed, were the white missionaries inclined to regard Africans as their equals. However, literate Africans had direct access to the Bible and worked out its implications for themselves: '. . . there is too much breakage of God's pure law as seen in James' Epistle, v.4'.[22] The verse deals with the defrauding of labourers.

There was a profound ambiguity at the heart of missionary, as of official, attitudes to westernization. There was a tendency to idealize and romanticize rural life, to condemn the 'detribalized', and to see the new cities as dens of vice. A certain anti-intellectualism tended to characterize Evangelicals hostile to new fashions in theology. Those whose entire careers lay in Africa often saw the educated African as a threat. There was no Kikuyu on a CMS committee created to decide on a Kikuyu orthography.

However, white missionaries themselves were the products of a western education, and took the benefits of industrial society for granted. They did not think that education would make their own children worldly. Although often hostile to labour migration and forced labour, the missionaries on the whole supported the colonial regime. During the First World War, an Ngoni chief refused to raise carriers, and sought sanctuary at the mission. The mission did not support him. It was self-evident that God did not want Germans to invade Nyasaland. At Livingstonia, Laws taught theology students the merits of paying taxes, which Africans viewed as oppressive, because so little was given in return: 'Why, this is just like war!' said a Lala princess. The missionaries supported taxation because it would encourage regular paid work, and hence 'improvement'. They did not realize that this was incompatible with the romantic ideal of an undisturbed rural Africa. The missions levied their own taxes, and, in 1910, the Livingstonia missionaries denied baptism to those who had not contributed to church support when catechumens. Two years earlier, they had started charging for medical visits.[23] The Watch Tower leader, Kamwana, left Livingstonia in protest when school fees were introduced. African Christians could make great financial sacrifices for goals of their own choosing: in 1898, some Malawi congregations paid the costs of sending evangelists to Zambia.[24] However, most resented Church taxation, especially when missionaries' standards of living were so much higher than their own.

Missionaries sometimes criticized the upward mobility of African Christians, but there was a great gulf between their own possessions and lifestyle, and those of their congregations. Missionaries were poor in comparison with white officials, but rich in comparison with their flock. In 1892, a Baptist from Australia called Joseph Booth exploded on to the mission scene in Nyasaland. He paid his employees eighteen shillings a month when the other missions paid three, and condemned:

> . . . elegantly robed men, at some hundreds of pounds yearly cost, preaching a gospel of self-denial to men and women . . . compelled to work hard from daylight to dark, six, but more often seven, days in a week for calico costing fivepence per week the men and twopence halfpenny the women. . . . Either we ought to stop spreading the gospel or conform to its teaching amidst such a needy cloud of witnesses as Central Africa presents.[25]

Education

Nineteenth-century rulers were enthusiastic advocates of technical education, but it gradually became clear in the colonial context that artisans were less esteemed and rewarded than teachers or clerks. From this sprang the demand for a literary education, which missionaries and administrators tended to deplore. Ndabaningi Sithole went to a Wesleyan school in Southern Rhodesia in 1932: 'I went to school because I had nothing else to do, and because I thought it was a good thing to do what other children were doing . . . earning and whipping became inseparable'.

> . . . to us education meant reading books, writing and talking English, and doing arithmetic. . . . We resented all forms of manual work. . . . At our homes we had done a lot of ploughing, planting, weeding and harvesting. . . . We knew how to do these things. We had come to school, not for these, but for those things we did not know. What we knew was not education; education was what we did not know. . . . We wanted, as we

said in Ndebele, to learn the book until it remained in our heads, to speak English until we could speak it through our noses.[26]

An African class three teacher told his pupils in Uganda, 'Less study, much work, less pay. Much study, less work, more pay'.[27] It was a formula on which, increasingly, African children and their parents were agreed. Kikuyu children sang:

> Father, mother
> Provide me with pen and slate
> I want to learn.
> Land is gone
> Cattle and Sheep are not there
> Not there any more
> What's left?
> Learning, learning.[28]

To read was synonymous with being a Christian: 'Edward Lwaijumba of Kabale, He "read" and was baptised'.[29]

Many who were drawn to the schools by the desire for education and their sheer novelty later became convinced and fervent Christians. Filipo Njau, a Chagga from Kilimanjaro, went to school because he had little prospects of an inheritance:

> Many boys came to instruction to learn to read and write, things to their advantage. Then behold! In the midst of their craving to read and write, the Word of God in their reading books overwhelmed them. . . . They became Christians, saved by Jesus, children of God. So it was with me.[30]

A pioneer Ganda Christian said, 'But all the time I was called a Christian, or reader, I did not clearly understand what my faith was all about. [Later] I . . . ceased to be a page and became more interested in religion'.[31]

They came from cultures that encouraged obedience, and conformity in the young. In Burundi, a boy who became a priest and an outstanding writer remembered later, 'I contented myself by learning what I was taught "to get marks" and pass for a docile child. But internally I was against anything which opposed my conviction'.[32]

Boarding schools, which were common, were acceptable to parents because of their similarity to traditional childrearing practices where, in the interests of discipline, children were often raised by other relatives (a custom that, paradoxically, the missionaries condemned). However, they both created and symbolized a radical physical and mental separation from traditional culture.

Those who embarked on the long and difficult journey believed that at the end of it they would be part of a commonwealth of educated people. They found instead that white administrators showed a strong preference for Muslims and for chiefs who had no western education at all, and that missionaries looked on them as a threat, rather than as equals: 'Nyasaland white churches are absolutely spoiled, such as the SD Adventist Church, they cannot allow their teachers to use the shoes, suits or even a hat, they say they are only for the whites'.[33]

Change was easier for the young. Like the poor, ill, and marginalized, they had less stake in the status quo. African societies had tended to be dominated by older men, who controlled access to resources, and especially to wives. Christianity gave the young a place on which to stand, a hope of earning an income in the modern sector. They could acquire a wife in mission circles or with their own earnings. The entrepreneur was shielded by the new religion, in part at least, from the witchcraft accusations to which his success might otherwise expose him. In matrilineal societies, it was easier for a Christian to leave property to his own children.[34]

Christianity seemed part and parcel of modernity—just as missionaries in Angola were advocates of the plough, and of latrine construction. In practice, though not in theory, it released individuals from many of the burdensome demands of traditional life. A Bemba elder said in the early 1930s, 'The white man came to teach us not to work except for money'. Paradoxically, the cash nexus swept people in a direction quite different from the Sermon on the Mount: 'A young Bemba asked to help someone in a difficulty [said] "I am a Christian. I don't do things for nothing"'.[35]

The elders seemed suddenly poor, and ignorant, and felt that they were despised. It was observed in Southern Rhodesia, in 1927:

> Any native teacher at a kraal school exercises more influence than all the Chiefs, headmen and Messengers combined. What a teacher says is law, what Chiefs and Messengers say is for heathen only. A wide gulf, as though the country were rent in twain, is separating the old from the young people.[36]

By the 1930s, many Christians were middle-aged, and there is a sense in which the prophetic churches founded then were a revolt of a younger generation against elders who were mission adherents.

The Mission churches

Scholars have tended to focus on new religious movements, to the neglect of the older churches. There is a substantial literature on Dini ya Msambwa, a local movement among the Luhyia of Kenya, which had about 631 members in 1967.[37] According to one estimate, a quarter of Kenya's population are Catholics,[38] but virtually nothing has been written about their history or corporate life. We know far more about the schismatic group, Maria Legio. But in 1972, only 14.6 per cent of Kenya's population—22 per cent of its Christians—belonged to independent churches.[39]

In many respects, the mission outstation was as independent as the prophetic churches. By 1900, a remarkably consistent pattern of Church organization had developed: a central mission, surrounded by a vast network of outstations, run by African teacher-catechists, and only occasionally visited by the expatriate missionary, or African priest. That perceptive Anglican, Bishop John Taylor lamented, in Buganda, a process of 'withdrawal upwards', where white missionaries and the abler African clergy moved into administrative positions, and had ever less personal contact with their flock. From the 1920s, they were often primarily concerned with the administration of Church schools or hospitals, and pastoral care was left to the catechist.[40]

The sheer numbers of African Christians ensured a large measure of autonomy, as there were never enough expatriate missionaries to play much role in their lives. However, the status and income of the catechist declined. From the 1920s, the roles of teacher and catechist were separated; the former's salary was paid by government, with the result that he rose in the social and economic scale. The catechist was chronically underpaid, largely to dissuade the 'worldly' from making a profit from evangelism, so that the abler and better-educated tended to move elsewhere. By the 1950s, a Catholic priest was complaining in Busoga, undoubtedly with some exaggeration, that 'They have too little knowledge of our faith so that they cannot even explain the Sunday Gospel. They have no religious training. There has not been any development since the early beginning'.[41] Belatedly, the training and role of catechists became a central pastoral preoccupation in the churches from about 1970 on.[42]

Some Catholic catechists, debarred from it both by their married state and lack of education, longed for ordination. Marcellianus Orongo, a Luo, was one of them. He founded his own small Church, the African Catholic Legion.[43]

What were African Christians taught, and what did they believe? The religious life of the mission churches, their doctrines, and corporate life have been curiously little studied. In the 1920s, an astute observer commented:

> What is urged upon the convert is an almost purely inward relationship between his conscious self and the God of whom the book tells him. . . . Missionaries have constantly to regret that from candidates for baptism the only answers given to the question, 'How is that Christians should live?' are 'Not having more wives than one, not drinking beer, or joining in dances, nor believing in demons and their power', and that positive rules of conduct are described vaguely or in extravagant terms, as, 'Giving all one's food to the people'.[44]

One tends to write as if the alternatives were 'traditional religion', and various forms of Christianity, but, in reality, each individual created a synthesis of old and new that was uniquely her or his own. Luo ritual specialists would tell potential clients, if they came on Sunday, 'Come tomorrow, for now we are off to Church'.[45] It was the same among the Nyakusa in the 1930s: 'The doctor brought medicine last night, just before dark, and she said to me, "sprinkle the cattle yourself. Perhaps it is taboo for me to do so". I replied, "No, not at all, you sprinkle them; I am going off to church tomorrow, to the catechumen's class" '.[46]

Christians, and their relatives, were faced with a great multiplicity of difficult choices. Each, in a sense, was forced to invent Nyakusa or Luhyia Christianity:

> Once my [betrothed] wife, when she had reached puberty, asked me why I objected to her undergoing the puberty ritual. I said it was forbidden for us Christians to participate in it, and I asked her if she wished to do so. She said, 'Yes', and I asked why. She said, 'See, now I have grown up, but no one sees that I have done so. Only you know.[47]

The *Kazembe* was the king of an eastern Lunda state, founded in what is now western Zambia in the early eighteenth century. In the 1950s, a Catholic Kazembe picked his way between the dictates of Church and tradition. He ate only what the hereditary food taster had tried, and travelled out of his way to avoid, as tradition demanded, the graves of his predecessors, but he stayed in ordinary resthouses, though tradition demanded that he should sleep only where no other had slept.[48]

Many moved easily between two worlds with little conscious reflection, embodying the rituals and attitudes of the past in the churches of the present. Missionaries, when they understood what was going on, did not approve: '. . . the women . . . never learned the difference between the Christian religion and the cult of the ancestral spirits. When they were told to kneel they did so as you would for Lyangombe ceremonies'.[49]

African Christians absorbed terrifying ideas of Heaven and Hell from both Catholic and Evangelical sources. Among the Nyakusa, in southern Tanganyika, African evangelists asked villagers, 'Do you want to burn?' The fears they aroused lingered in the subconscious:

> The fire did not come across the stream. Then I woke up, and discovered with surprise that I had been asleep. Then I thought, 'It is concerning this that the baptised speak'. . . . I thought about this for two months, then I went and repented. That was in the year 1921.[50]

Tonga Christians sang, 'There is a Fountain Filled with Blood', accompanied by a harmonium.[51]

Gender

There is no simple correlation between conversion and gender. Women in polygamous marriages had cause to fear the impact of missionary advocacy of monogamy, and were sometimes hostile (Livingstone described this among Sechele's wives), but, in societies where resources and power were controlled by older men, women, like the young, had less to lose by change. A Kukwe woman, Fiambarema, who had originally come for medical treatment, was the first convert at the Moravian Rungwe Mission in Tanganyika. The missionaries 'responded sceptically, believing that no local person possessed a sense of sin profound enough to make the wish for a saviour genuine. Fiambarema persisted and her open confession during a service released the cautious missionaries from their doubts'.[52] Two women, Nandola and Chipsala, were appointed to positions of authority in the early days of the White Fathers' mission at Chilubula, in Zambia. Both were murdered by their husbands, who then committed suicide.[53] Perhaps Christianity gave them an autonomy that their husbands found, in the most literal sense, impossible to live with.

Increasingly most churchgoers were the product of mission schools, which with very rare exceptions, more boys attended than girls. As the economic advantages of education became apparent, families tended to invest their limited resources in their sons. But although more boys than girls went to mission schools, women comprised the majority of attenders, both in mainstream and independent churches. In the former, it was often because many of the older men had been disconnected for polygamy.[54]

Some women were empowered by church support to refuse an unacceptable marriage, or leave one, especially where polygamy was involved. Young people often found marriage partners in church circles, bypassing the elders and their control of bridewealth. However, to some, church marriage became a prison, leaving them less freedom of choice than they had before. Beidelman recorded a belief among Kaguru men that 'Christian . . . girls cannot divorce men if they tire of them so they must bewitch or poison their husbands if they want new ones'.[55]

Missionaries often opposed bridewealth, but, as a Ganda dignitary pointed out, 'the girl was not forced to go against her wish, but that she liked to see how much the man cared for her, and also that there was a reasonable prospect of her being taken good care of when she had been obtained with some cost to the man'.[56] The Nyakusa made the same point, describing the intergenerational tension that the difference between traditional and Christian courtship practices generated:

> . . . the girl always had power to refuse; no one ever compelled her to agree, even though the man had many cattle. But the custom of wooing in secret first, before a man has been to the father, began among Christians . . . pagan fathers still object, saying, "We will not eat the cattle properly" '.[57]

Very often, women were driven to the churches by suffering and misfortune. They sought help from prophetic prayer in the afflictions of barrenness and child mortality, and in sickness, which, in twentieth-century Africa, as in Biblical times, was both a cause and a result of poverty. They sought protection against witches, whom they often perceived as women. As we have seen, the twentieth century brought new problems to add to the old, and the wife of a labour migrant endured both loneliness and the burden of excessive work. The new cities offered few employment opportunities for women, beyond beer-selling and prostitution.

Colonization undermined the position of titled women and Christianity challenged the women mediums who were sometimes described as 'Queens'.[58]

Royal women had much to lose from changes in the status quo. We have noted the slow conversion, over decades, of a Lozi Queen. Kanjogera, who became the Rwanda Queen Mother in 1889, was implacably hostile, but, by the late 1920s, royal Rwanda women were among the converts, as were both male and female diviners.

In an earlier chapter, we noted the foundation of the Bannabikira, a Ganda order of nuns, in 1910. Another order of African nuns was founded at Karema, in Tanzania, in 1907. When missionary orders of nuns accepted African women, they often expected them to do manual work, such as laundry, cooking, or gardening. They were, therefore, willing to accept candidates with little education, which created problems later. A great number of African women's orders were founded in the 1920s and 1930s, often, though not always, by bishops. They included the Congregation of Sisters of Mary Immaculate, a Kikuyu congregation, the Little Sisters of St Francis in Uganda, and the Holy Cross Sisters in the Rhodesias.[59] Each religious vocation represented the most radical renunciation, in cultures where children are cherished above everything. In West Central Africa, a Kongo woman, who had entered religion forty years earlier, said, 'The fact that I have chosen to live as a celibate woman religious costs me greatly even now in my later years. . . . I will leave no children of my own in this world'.[60]

Revival

Evangelicals sometimes accused their African congregations of a want of spiritual 'life'. In 1923, it was said in Busoga that the people 'have made very little real progress, they are still flat, very heavy . . . a very large number of the baptised Christians have returned to polygamy, devil-possession and drinking'.[61] This kind of comment implied that the missionaries themselves had spiritual qualities their converts lacked, which was an insidious assumption implicit in the strategy followed by the Sudan Party and the first White Fathers, that one converts non-Christians simply by living near them, and manifesting one's superior quality of life. It has often been observed that missionaries demanded a spiritual intensity in Africa that they would not have expected in an English parish. In a sense, this was what they came for, in a flight from modernism, and a worldly and increasingly secular Christendom.

African congregations often made this kind of spirituality their own, an Evangelical emphasis on the conversion experience: an acknowledgement of sin that took the form of public confession, the subsequent close bonding of the 'saved'. White missionaries, as well as Africans, experienced the impulse to create small communities of the righteous. The two doctors who founded the Ruanda [*sic*] Mission broke away from the CMS, as did Mabel Ensor, the founder of the small, and ultimately ephemeral, Mengo Gospel Church in Uganda. The Ruanda Mission was holier than Anglicanism. If parents were not total abstainers, their babies were refused baptism. Ensor was so autocratic that she once burned down the house of a Christian chief who did not help in church construction. She spoke the language of the Revival, but condemned it because it was not hers. It was created by Africans and has endured.

There were Revivals in the 1890s, in both Uganda and Nyasaland. The latter so alarmed the preacher whose eloquence sparked it off that he attempted to subdue its manifestations (which included visions of 'bright angelic forms') with the aid of the contents of the mission dispensary.[62]

A far more famous Revival began in Rwanda and Uganda in the 1930s, and was marked by a conversion experience often associated with visions and dreams, with public testimonies and confession. All of this was very typical of similar movements in Britain and elsewhere, whose members felt, as did a Tanganyika Christian, that 'the church had become worldly and the world churchly'.[63]

Traditional spirit mediumship retreated into the private domain; the Revival took the problem of sinfulness out of the sphere of individual conscience and made it central to society as a whole. It often spoke in the idiom of witchcraft eradication.[64]

The Revival created enduring communities within the Protestant churches of at least six African nations. In 1958, it led to a major schism in the Kenya Church, and the foundation of the Church of Christ in Africa. Paradoxically, its members were not the Revived, but their opponents, who called themselves *Johera*, 'People of Love'.[65]

The Revival, like other rigorist movements in history, had a pronounced fissiparous tendency. Ishmael Noo founded a small Church in 1948, practising free love. This is a recurrent tendency in small, ultra-fervent communities, and is also documented in the Katete movement in Shaba (see page 207), in the Sephiri groups of South Africa, and in some branches of Watch Tower. A section broke away in Busoga in the 1960s, claiming to be 'awakened', it condemned the payment of bridewealth, and life insurance (which is thought to reflect a lack of trust in God).[66]

The Revived were often stricter than the missionaries, more thorough in their rejection of the values of African societies. They condemned much that seems innocuous, such as the consumption of peanuts![67]

Women were often prominent in the evangelizing bands that toured the countryside on foot. Some found in it the support that enabled them to reject polygamous marriages.

Like Evangelical expatriates, the Balokole marginalized the religious experience of other believers. Missionaries often felt threatened by the movement, not least when called on to confess! In the words of the first African pastor in Bukoba:

> They hopped and danced and despised those who had not yet been revived. They refused to eat coffee-beans or groundnuts or to use ornaments and spears. They soon started to have their own services and despised their former friends saying, 'you have not yet been saved'.[68]

African initiatives in the mission churches

The Revival was only one of the many ways in which African Christians created 'pools' of autonomy within the older churches.

In East Africa, as elsewhere, women have often founded powerful organizations within the older churches. Typically, they are dominated by the middle-aged, and wear distinctive costumes. Rukwandzano is a women's organization in the United Methodist Church, in Zimbabwe, which was formed in 1929 in a climate of Revival. The founders, led by Lydia Chimonyo, sought to strengthen their Christian marriages. They excluded those in plural marriages, and opposed infant betrothal. Today, it is the strongest organization in the Church. Like their South African counterparts, and like the members of many prophetic churches, they wear a distinctive uniform. They have come to concentrate on development projects, such as training courses for school-leavers, and they support an African missionary nurse in north-west Botswana.[69]

The place where the Anglican martyr, Bernard Mizeki, died became a place of pilgrimage in Mashonaland, like the tombs of the independent church founders, and his death was encrusted with the miraculous. For example, it was said that a great blaze of light appeared, and that his body disappeared mysteriously, like that of his Master.[70] The shrine is linked with Shona tradition, for its custodian was the youngest son of a famous Shona spirit medium, and it is associated with rainmaking, healing, and medicinal herbs.[71] This is not syncretism; it is the incarnation of Christianity in new cultural forms, which is particularly moving as Mizeki was not a Shona. ·

In Kavirondo (Nyanza) Province in western Kenya, Christianity was spread by catechists from Uganda. By 1916, CMS members there had opted for the distinctive costumes so typical of independency:

> Not all, but some hundreds of them, will be found clothed in a short shirt of white, with dark blue facings . . . the letters, roughly worked C.M.S.K. across the breast . . . A closer inspection will reveal mysterious buttons and stripes showing that, from a corporal to a colonel, every rank is represented.[72]

They had absorbed the concern with uniform so typical of the British armed forces, and copied its forms. This echoing of the externals of a dominant culture can also be seen in the dance societies of the Swahili coast, whose members dressed as 'Scotchi' in kilts, as admirals of the fleet, and even as members of the House of Lords.[73]

By definition, the ordinary members of mission churches tend to remain obscure. Patrick Kwesha (1900–63), was a Shona Catholic who worked as a gardener for a convent in Johannesburg.[74] He did not marry: 'I have lived all my life not for the natural family you think of but for the family of the whole Church'. He taught the catechism to his fellow migrants, and joined the Third Order of St Francis. He longed for the foundation of an order of African Franciscans, 'the order of joy, of gaiety, of mirth and of wonderful riches and pleasures', and for the creation in his homeland of a great shrine to Our Lady of Lourdes. Effortlessly, he bridged the European peasant world of miraculous Marian apparitions and healing shrines, and the world of African rural religion with which it had so much in common. Neither the order nor the shrine eventuated, but, when he returned home in 1947, he established a lay guild of St Francis. His Franciscan spirituality, his lyrical mystical bent, and his total devotion to God have much in common with his Anglican counterpart, Francis Nyabadza (discussed later in this chapter). But he lived and died in the most complete obscurity, and is known now only because a detailed study was made of his homeland in Makoni District.

Mission and society: two case studies

The nature of the encounter between Christianity and the host society was shaped by many variables. The mission itself could be Anglo-Catholic, or Presbyterian, Roman Catholic, or Seventh Day Adventist. The host society might be a kingdom, or comprise a multitude of village democracies, its people involved in migrant labour, like so many in Zambia and Malawi, or peasant cultivators, like the coffee-growers of Buganda or Kilimanjaro. The nature of the encounter was affected by the presence or absence of white settlers, and by whether the colonial government was French, Belgian, or English. It made a great difference whether a specific village was close to a mission centre, or far away from one.

In a general study, it is impossible to examine all these permutations, and so, in the pages that follow, we explore just two contrasting case studies. They have been chosen for the excellence of the secondary literature, but they embody many contrasts which are also found elsewhere. One is the kingdom of Rwanda, in the Belgian-mandated territory of that name. The other is Kikuyuland, traditionally divided into many autonomous ridge settlements, and gravely affected by white settlement in the twentieth century.

THE KIKUYU

The Kikuyu are the largest ethno-linguistic group in Kenya, followed by the Luo.[75] Colonialism in Kenya began with Chartered Company rule in 1887; Kenya became a Protectorate in 1895, and a colony in 1905. By then, white settlement in the Kikuyu highlands was already a clearly defined policy. There were still only 12 510 whites in Kenya in 1925, but their economic and political dominance was quite disproportionate to their numbers. The alienation of land not only affected the livelihood of the African peoples living where they settled, but had profound cultural implications.

The first mission among the Kikuyu was founded in 1898, and others soon followed. The dreadful famines of 1898–1900, and the failure of traditional spiritual remedies to relieve them may have predisposed people to seek the aid of new, and perhaps stronger spiritual powers. Some attached themselves to missions to avoid white demands for labour. The first converts were often the poor, who would, in an earlier time, have cleared land on the edge of Kikuyu settlement, but could no longer do so, because of settler farms. Some Kikuyu notables, the 'New Men' of their time, invited missionaries as a way of cementing closer ties with the administration. Kikuyu clans and villages displayed the same kind of competitive pursuit of modernity that the élite of the Buganda court had shown as individuals. So did the Nyanza Luo.

In the interwar years, proto-nationalist leaders were sharply critical of the divisions Christianity had created: 'The KCA [Kikuyu Central Association] seeks night and day for that which will cause all Kikuyu to be of one mind, educated and uneducated, ceasing to ask each other what school or mission do you belong to or saying to each other, "you are not a reader" '.[76]

In 1929, a conflict broke out in Kikuyuland over what was called, somewhat inaccurately 'female circumcision'.[77] It was abhorrent to the missionaries, both because they saw it as physically dangerous and cruel, and because of the sexually explicit rituals that accompanied it. Some Kikuyu Christians agreed with them, but the operation was the essential prelude to adult social identity and marriage, and in those circumstances most Kikuyu women insisted on it.[78] The issue led to a major crisis in mission churches, and some Kikuyu communities attempted, unsuccessfully, to reclaim mission land, and assert their ownership of local schools. A particularly disgruntled Presbyterian missionary confided to his diary that the KCA leaders, including Kenyatta, should be hanged![79]

More then fifty years later, the story had a sequel. In 1982, President Daniel Arap Moi prohibited female excision in his home area; immediately, the Director of Medical Services extended the ban to the whole country.[80]

The Kikuyu developed a song cycle called *Muthigiru*, which the Government outlawed. It lamented the loss of land, and the way in which Christianity, and western influences had undermined their inherited culture:

> Kurinu I will never be a Christian
> I became a Christian a long time ago
> and I experienced loss rather than gain.[81]

However, while they mourned the past, they were dissatisfied with the quality of western education. By 1931, many Kikuyu had left the missions, setting up independent churches and schools, some of which reached the standard needed to qualify for government grants. By the late 1940s, many of those who had opted to remain had come to have misgivings:

> . . . in the church we have no full [Kikuyu] pastor although you have worked here for over forty years. . . . You annoy us very much because you tell us . . . that you did not come to teach the African education.[82]

The African Christian Church and Schools was formed by disgruntled adherents of the Africa Inland Mission because of well-justified concerns about educational standards, and mission racism. This was the 'Ethiopian' strand, but there was also a prophetic one, whose leaders called themselves seers, or dreamers. They began to experience visions in the late 1920s. One of them said he had felt 'half a Christian in the Africa Inland Mission'. They were disinterested in education, and rejected all things western, including money and shoes, and wore the Muslim *Kanzu*—the gown that, ironically, nineteenth-century missionaries had forced on their converts. While they rejected modernity, their refusal to offer sacrifices or pay bridewealth cut them off from the traditional community. They defined their boundaries by elaborate prohibitions, many of them rooted in the Old Testament.[83] They had invented precisely the other-worldly Christianity the missionaries advocated and did not recognize when Africans discovered it for themselves.

RWANDA

The twentieth-century history of Rwanda is a fascinating case study of the changing relationship between Christianity and African socio-political structures. It was, in the late nineteenth century, exceptionally highly stratified. The Tutsi formed an aristocratic pastoral caste, and created an elaborate oral literature. They were distinguished by their court culture, and their striking height. The agricultural Hutu were in a tributary relationship.

It is possible to exaggerate 'the premise of inequality'. Rich Hutu could acquire cattle and become Tutsi, and not all Tutsi controlled livestock and clients. Much of the elaborate ritual that surrounded the Tutsi King, the *Mwami*, was paralleled in the little courts of Hutu sacred kings.

When the Germans invaded Rwanda in 1897, and the missionaries arrived in their wake, the Mwami had recently come to the throne after a dynastic conflict. The first converts were poor Hutu, and the Tutsi stayed aloof: 'Their salvation does not please', said the Mwami,[84] preferring the more robust pleasures promised to Ryangombe's initiates to an eternity of harps! He perceived, correctly, that Christianity would provide an alternative focus of loyalties: 'They all agree that to frequent the whites is to become their clients and to set up as a rebel against the king; you cannot serve two masters, they think, God and the king'.[85] In time, some of the Hutu converts came to form the nucleus of a new élite, and, in 1919, five were ordained. One of them,

Abbé Donat Leberaho, was famous for his eloquence. He would say 'God [*Imana*] is greater than the *ngabo* [regiments].'[86]

The Tutsi came to realize that Christianity and western education were alternative sources of prestige and authority. Even Musinga, the Mwami whom the Christian salvation did not please, attended classes in literacy, Swahili, and German. Gradually, the tide turned, and there was a mass movement of Tutsi into the Church. In 1931, Musinga was replaced by a catechumen, who was to adhere to the Church's marriage laws despite his childlessness.

An increasing number of Tutsi were ordained as priests. One of them, Alexis Kagamé, ordained in 1941, came from a family of court historians. In a number of books, he perpetuated a triumphalist Tutsi perspective of the Rwanda past. Other Tutsi wrote song cycles on Christian themes in the elaborate language of the court. By 1948, there were 88 White Fathers, 81 Rwandan secular priests, 58 Rwandan teaching brothers, and 155 indigenous nuns in Rwanda. Here, as elsewhere, with very few exceptions, missionary congregations insisted that Africans became diocesan clergy, rather than joining their own ranks.

The White Fathers' attitudes to Rwandan hierarchy were ambivalent. They were well aware of the injustice that so often characterized Tutsi–Hutu relations, but, like their founder, they hoped for great things from the conversion of rulers, and loved to quote the precedent of Charlemagne.

After the Second World War, there was an influx of priests who had been involved in the Christian Workers' Movement, and tended to identify with the Hutu; but, in the event, intergroup relations were soon to move far beyond Church influence or control. In independent Rwanda, the Tutsi were killed or exiled in a Hutu rising; in neighbouring Burundi, the Tutsi slew the Hutu.

New churches

There is an implicit triumphalism in missionary sources, and sometimes in books that are based on them, in that they are more aware of those who joined the churches than of those who left them. However, in Malawi, recruitment to the mission churches declined before the First World War, and recruitment to mask societies expanded, as did witchcraft accusations.[87]

The way in which the position of educated Africans deteriorated from the late nineteenth century on is a tragic theme that recurs in every part of Africa. Many of those affected endured in the mission church until they died, but others formed new churches. These were not the only possible responses, however. They could have rejected religion entirely, become Muslims, or turned to some form of neo-traditionalism. The fact that they chose none of these alternatives reflects the strength of their Christian convictions.

The First World War led to a mass exodus of white missionaries, which created a space in which, for a time, African Church leadership flourished.

Kilimanjaro Christians remembered it later as a golden age; the return to white control was all the more painful later.

It is perhaps surprising that so many independent churches were founded by Catholics.[88] The best-known is Maria Legio [*sic*], founded in 1962. Ironically, it retained at least an approximation of Latin just as the international Church adopted indigenous languages. However, the creation of new churches came more easily to Protestants. The fissiparous tendency of Presbyterianism, for instance, is reflected in mission history; the same belief in the paramount importance of individual religious conviction underlay independency in Africa.

Many of those who joined movements such as Watch Tower had been expelled from a church, or not allowed to join in the first place. In 1929, a village headman said, 'I am a Christian, but I am not a church member'.[89] Like many others, he had been suspended for beer-drinking and polygamy. Would-be Christians waited for years for baptism. To people in these categories, the great attraction of Watch Tower and the prophetic churches was the fact that they baptized all candidates immediately.

The quest for autonomy

The African churches of Lagos and Ethiopian churches of South Africa sprang from resentment at white domination, and a desire for good schools for the young and for better conditions and prospects for Africans in mission employ. The emphasis on education is reflected in the very name of the African Christian Church and Schools.

Often these independent churches sought funding and respectability by affiliating with well-established black churches in America. The initial attempt to establish the African Methodist Episcopal Church in Northern Rhodesia in 1903–4, ended in failure, and the British South Africa Company, like the colonial government in Kenya, prohibited AMEC missionaries. The Church was re-established in Northern Rhodesia in 1930. The growth of copper mining, and the influx both of African workers and of white South Africans, created a situation where the island of autonomy it created was precious.

AMEC expanded in the 1930s and 1940s, but was always handicapped by lack of funds, which made it difficult to run schools to the standard demanded by African aspirations. Government subsidies were not available as it was policy 'to discourage schools belonging to this denomination'. The same lack of funding affected the recruitment and training of the clergy. When Zambia became independent, there were many more attractive outlets for African leadership, and, by 1975, the Church membership was ageing and in decline.[90]

The Ganda, Reuben Spartas,[91] found a place on which to stand in a much older tradition. He was ordained in 1930 by a South African, Daniel Alexander (whose orders derived ultimately from the Jacobite Church of South India), and later attached his movement to the Patriarchate of Alexandria. A political activist, who was gaoled for a time, he established a church independent of Anglicanism by affiliation with one far more ancient, translating the liturgy of St John Chrysostom into luGanda. The path he had chosen seemed confirmed by study: 'Reading history I found there was no Anglican church in the Holy City of Jerusalem'.[92] His church was relatively small, with perhaps 10 thousand adherents by the 1950s, attracted largely by the beauty of holiness, candles, incense, and sacramental oils.

Joseph Booth (1851–1932)

Joseph Booth was a most unusual missionary. He grew up in England as a Unitarian, and was an agnostic for some years before becoming a fundamentalist Christian.[93] For a time, he was a businessman in Australia. He became a missionary when an atheist challenged him to do so, and reached Malawi in 1892. His radical belief in racial equality made him unacceptable to both the colonial government and to the older missions.

He published a document called *Africa for the Africans* to publicize 'the great wrongs inflicted upon the African race in the past and the present and to urge upon those who wish to be clear of African blood in the day of God's judgment, to make restitution for the wrongs of the past and to withstand the appropriation of the African's land in the present'.[94] In 1898, he formulated a petition in the name of African chiefs and others, which was published in the Nyasaland press, and which asked, among other things, that the Protectorate be restored to African rule within twenty-one years.[95]

Booth was a restless spirit, who founded a number of institutions that he soon left, and moved from one denomination to the next. He was, in succession, a Baptist, a Seventh Day Baptist, a Seventh Day Adventist, and what was later called a Jehovah's Witness.

He made several visits to America, in search of financial support. On one of them, in 1897, he was accompanied by John Chilembwe, a Malawian Yao.

John Chilembwe (d. 1915)

Chilembwe joined a black American Church, the National Baptist Convention, and, with its help, founded the Providence Industrial Mission at Chiradzulu, in Nyasaland. There, he devoted himself to schools and agricultural improvement, to hygiene, health, and temperance. He was the archetypal Improver. An asthmatic with failing sight, he was a most unlikely revolutionary, but, in 1915, he led a small-scale rising that was doomed to fail. Three Europeans were killed, as was Chilembwe himself, together with some of his followers.

Why did he embark on a rising that he must have known could not succeed? This question has haunted historians ever since.[96]

He seems to have despaired of Improvement in the colonial situation, especially after the 1913 famine, and the outbreak of war: 'Let the rich men, bankers, titled men, storekeepers, farmers and landlords go to war and get shot. Instead the poor Africans who have nothing to own in this present world . . . are to die in a cause which is not theirs'.[97] He embraced his own death as a protest against injustices that he was powerless to change: 'John said this case stands the same as that of Mr John Brown. Let us then "strike a blow and die" for our blood will surely mean something at last'.[98]

Watch Tower

Booth left Nyasaland in 1903. In 1906, he made contact with the Watch Tower Bible and Tract Society, whose members have, since 1930, called themselves Jehovah's Witnesses. With typical enthusiasm, he revisited America to meet the movement's founder, Charles Taze Russell, and became a Watch Tower missionary in South Africa. His career as a missionary ended when he was deported in 1915.[99]

White missionaries played a role in the origins of Zionism in South Africa, and in the early history of the Christ Apostolic Church in Nigeria, but these churches soon outgrew their mentors, and became powerful indigenous movements. The same was to be true of Watch Tower.

Jehovah's Witnesses believe that the world, including its governments and churches, is ruled by Satan. Jesus will soon return (the precise date has been repeatedly revised) and the Witnesses will reign with him in glory. In the millennium, a new age will dawn on earth, and sickness, death, and war will disappear. This promise of a golden age, and a reversal of present injustices, proved enormously attractive in colonial Central Africa.

News of the First World War suggested that Armageddon was, indeed, at hand. Watch Tower drew most of its recruits from existing missions; one of its great attractions was that it offered immediate baptism. The courses of Bible study appealed to the literate, especially when alternative study materials were lacking. Observers noted the preponderance of women: 'some Witnesses teach that "all women will have children in the Kingdom . . ."'[100] To many mission Christians, it was an acute source of perplexity and anxiety: 'Please am asking you shall this year 1924 the whole world finish?', a Zambian asked a magistrate, reporting the teachings of a certain Shadrack, 'Free Church all of you there is a rock on your heads and you will be smashed up'.[101]

Nyasaland migrant workers in South Africa took Watch Tower doctrines with them when they returned home. Their leader was Elliot Kenani Kamwana, a Tonga, who had studied at the Overtoun Institute.

He returned to Nyasaland in 1908. Within a year he had baptized over 9 thousand. Like so many other independent church leaders, he was to spend much of his life in exile. He was deported to the Seychelles from 1909 to 1914, and again from 1916 to 1937. On his return, undaunted, he promptly founded the Watchman's Society.

Watch Tower was disseminated by Tonga migrant labourers in Southern and Northern Rhodesia; it spread into Angola, Mozambique, and the Belgian Congo, which expelled many adherents. The Seventh Day Adventists had a similar millennial emphasis, and so, indeed, did some traditional religions. Today, 250 thousand of the world's 1.5 million Witnesses live in Africa, 130 thousand of them in Zambia.[102] They have suffered cruel persecution in Banda's Malawi.

In a sense, millenialism was, in Marxist terms, a form of false consciousness, creating an expectation that social and economic problems would be solved by a supernatural intervention, but, in a situation of uncertainty, disappointment, and social malaise, Watch Tower spoke with a clear voice: '[it] provide[d] a vehicle for the critique of industrial conditions and colonial society generally, and it was for this reason that it was regarded with such acute suspicion by the colonial administration'.[103] In 1918, a White Father in Malawi met a man praying in the wilderness: 'Take care, God is great. Pray to God alone'. The White Father arrested and flogged him, and then reported the incident to the colonial authorities.[104]

'It stands out clearly from this book that all men are equal', stated a group of miners in 1936, 'It is not just that the black man who does the work should remain in poverty and misery.'[105] 'The Kenaniites were not against white people, but they believed that the white and the black man would be on the same level when they went to heaven.'[106] 'The Commissioner seems to have disliked the assertion current in Watchtower circles that the races would exchange colour in 1923.'[107] A more alarming prediction was made in 1930, to the effect that Lake Mweru would boil, and the Europeans be thrown into it![108]

Protection from evil

Witchcraft fears became stronger, rather than weaker, in the colonial period. Colonial governments outlawed traditional ways of dealing with witches, such as poison ordeals. Changes in traditional religion itself, paradoxically, often strengthened witchcraft beliefs. Thus, divination virtually disappeared in Ufipa, so that witches could not be identified, and the belief that ancestors caused misfortune declined among the Gwembe Tonga, leaving witchcraft as the only explanation.[109] The gap between rich and poor increased, rather than declined, and Christianity, together with other forms of change, often caused disunity rather than harmony in the village community, as the young and literate challenged the authority of the elders. The departure of young men as migrant labourers deprived the village of their traditional contribution to its labour needs, and imposed burdens on those who remained there. Where married men were forced to leave their wives and children behind, it caused great stress in family life, and in the community as a whole. The witchcraft eradication movement, Mchape (see below), flourished on Likoma Island because of tensions between married women, and women forced to remain single by the exodus of men.[110]

The money the migrants earned empowered them *vis-à-vis* the elders. In particular, it enabled a man to pay bridewealth without the elders' aid. It created a new and enduring dilemma in African life for the wage-earner, which revolved round the conflicting demands and needs of the immediate family and of a much wider circle of kin; to help the one meant to take from the other. A famous study of witchcraft accusations in sixteenth- and seventeenth-century Essex shows that people often accused those *they had failed to aid*.[111]

Would-be converts often found themselves in a quandary. They were expected to relinquish traditional forms of protection against witchcraft, but the mission churches made them wait, often for years, for baptism. Watch Tower's immediate baptism shielded them from the malice of evildoers.

There were many anti-witchcraft movements in East and East Central Africa. One of the most tragic was that begun by Tomo Nyirenda. He came from Nyasaland, and was a product of Livingstonia. He migrated to Northern Rhodesia, was converted to Watch Tower in 1925, and became an itinerant preacher, calling on witches to repent. At first he seemed like an ordinary evangelist, but, soon, he began to detect witches. He settled among the Lala of what is now Zambia, and, by a further sinister metamorphosis, began to kill them. Perhaps 200 died before Tomo himself met his end on the gallows. The Lala, though, called him *Mwana Lesa*, 'Son of God'.

There is a tragic contradiction between the message of love Tomo brought, and the fate of those alleged to be witches. It seems likely that the killings were at the insistence of the Lala themselves. When a chief demurred, 'all the people, the women, who had come and were listening said, "No, let them be killed, they are witches and that is why we are barren"'. One man arrived with the intention of becoming a Watch Tower preacher, and was killed as a witch: 'Tomo said to him, "You have come, Lipereto. Today you are going to die". Lipereto said, "All right, if I am a wizard, I must die. I have a little horn of jealousy"'.[112]

Witch-finding movements often sought to eliminate the *condition* of witchcraft from the community, and sometimes they discerned witches, but purified them by ritual means. Mchape was an anti-witchcraft movement that developed in 1933–4, and spread from Nyasaland to Northern and Southern Rhodesia, Mozambique, and the Congo. The name means washing, and the founder, Kamwende, was thought to have risen from the dead, like so many Christian prophets. Mchape medicine was taken in the context of a village ritual of confession and reintegration. Thereafter, it was promised, God would be in full control of life and death, and no one would suffer or die, save by His will. There would be no more witchcraft or sorcery.[113]

Mchape had a curious modernity, and seemed not unlike a missionary movement. Its advocates were young, and wore western dress; their rituals used imported mirrors, and glass bottles. If Christians refused the medicine, they were in danger of being thought to be witches, but, if they took it, they risked expulsion from the Church:[114] 'A witch doctor . . . sells for one shilling *mushonga* which has the marvellous power to those who keep it a[t] home, perpetual youth, immortality, protection against witches, etc. . . . plenty of our Christians have bought the dirty stuff'.[115] The promises made could not be fulfilled, but the longing for a Golden Age was not easily extinguished. A later version, called *Kamcape*, was documented in southern Tanganyika at various times between the 1940s and the 1960s.[116]

Bwanali, born in 1910, was commissioned by an angel in 1935, and became a famous healer and diviner. He would preach on the goodness of God, and say that witchcraft was a human invention.[117] Scholars tend to distinguish 'anti-witchcraft movements' from Christian evangelism, but the two were often very much the same. New anti-witchcraft movements always found supporters, because the evils that witches were thought to cause—sickness, premature death and barrenness—remained.

Christians who remained in the mission churches grappled with their fear of witchcraft as best they could: 'They say, "See! I am sick, they [the witches] have eaten me!" They say this perhaps to a pagan or to a Christian like themselves, but in public they will deny it. We say that such people are not good Christians. There are some who in the evening will go to the doctors to divine'.[118] This was in Unyakusa. 'I consult magicians and soothsayers, but I do not flinch from the Church of God. I am a Catholic.'[119] These words could well have come from the Nyakusa, too, but, in fact, they are quoted in St Augustine.

The prophetic churches

In 1977, Kenya, with a population of less than 20 million, had 210 independent churches, a number that had risen to over 300 seven years later[120] (the USA, with a population of 200 million, has 700 denominations). Some African independent churches were tiny, others had perhaps half a million members, scattered over half a dozen countries. Some were ephemeral, and others continued to grow. They enriched not only African Christianity, but Christendom as a whole by the richness and creativity of their liturgies, and by their exploration of an insight that the West has often lost sight of but is now rediscovering: the unity of health of mind and body. They found precedents for their emphasis on dreams and visions in both the Bible and traditional religion. Part of their attraction lay in the fact that their prophets took witchcraft seriously, and offered protection against it. Some absorbed other elements from traditional cultures; there are polygamist bishops in Maria Legio.

The prophetic churches defined the perimeters of group identity, often through a distinctive costume and dietary rules, which tended to be based on the Hebrew Bible, and some kept the Sabbath holy. They laid great emphasis on names, including the names of churches: 'when we read in the Bible we never find any Seventh Day Adventist, we only find the Church of God'.[121] Their own churches were named with thought and care, the 'African Israel Nenevah Church' is an example.

Converts were expected to give up all charms and amulets, and the protection against evil they afforded. Some churches renounced western medicine as well. Typically, they abstained from beer, tobacco, and traditional dancing and ceremonies. The implications of all this were far-reaching. Traditional 'beer,' which is more like gruel, is nutritious, and low in alcohol. It is the staple of communal work parties, and brewing is an important economic activity for many women. Like the Revival, the prophetic churches tend to follow tradition in areas where Christianity offers no directives, such as clan exogamy, and the payment of bridewealth.

Some women became famous as founders of prophetic churches. It is clear that what they sought was not power or authority—which they tended to entrust to men—but wholeness, healing, and fertility. Gaudencia was one of the founders of Maria Legio, in Kenya. In Northern Rhodesia, Alice Lenshina founded the Lumpa Church, discussed later in this book.

In Southern Rhodesia, Mai Chaza founded the Guta re Jehovah in 1952, after a vision. She urged her followers to give up all charms, and there was a mass confession of witchcraft. She supplied healing water from her village, which was called 'Zion', and taught in terms of Shona history and tradition. She died in 1961.[122]

Mariam Rogot, and her husband Paul Adika, led an ecstatic millenarian movement that broke away from the Gusii Catholic Mission in the 1950s.[123]

African Christians longed for sources of spiritual power. They found in the Bible, a world of victory over sickness and death, of mastery over evil spirits (it was sometimes suggested that the spirits driven into the Gadarene swine were transferred to Africa!) The emphasis on healing and miracle was not wholly absent from the mission churches, but, typically, they interpreted disease in a rationalist–scientific way, and relied more on hospitals than prayer to solve health problems. African and expatriate Christians in mission churches often experienced the emphasis on miraculous healing as an implied rebuke. In the words of an African Anglican priest:

> People bring and say things in public not because they are really converted but rather . . . they imagine themselves to be in a different world, and they think they can do anything under that imaginary world. . . . Heathen and

Christian brought all sorts of things to Muchapi . . . Vapostori [Apostles] burn a lot of things often. . . . Is there any improvement?[124]

The prophetic tradition tends to assume that suffering is evil, but sanctification through affliction is at the very heart of Christianity.[125] It has even been claimed that the prophetic churches are in the tradition of Simon Magus.[126] Certainly the emphasis on rank and title, the schisms that often follow a founder's death, do reflect a concern for personal recognition and authority, largely because no other avenues to influence and recognition were open to their members.

African 'traditional' religions sometimes embodied a tradition of the Suffering Servant. The Mang'anja people of the Lower Shire Valley worship M'Bona, a diviner slain by an unjust king, who fed the hungry with miraculous rice or pumpkins. His initiates were well aware of the similarities with Christianity, and affirmed them symbolically. Twentieth-century elaborations of the myth state that M'Bona was born of a virgin, and fed his faithful on manna.[127] To the missionaries, his cult was 'a painful manifestation of false religion'.

The Shona prophetic churches

There was a great growth of independent churches among the Shona in the 1930s. As in South Africa and Kenya, this was, at least in part, a reaction to the economic and political dominance of a white settler community, and to the suffering caused by the Depression. There is a natural tendency for scholars to concentrate on the larger movements, but a single, small church that has survived for fifty years is equally notable in its own way. Despite its poverty, it lit a candle that has illumined many lives.

Frances Nyabadza,[128] was a Shona Anglican catechist and teacher. He was totally opposed to the brewing and consumption of beer, and had an explicitly Franciscan emphasis on poverty, which is often a hallmark of Anglo-Catholic spirituality in Africa. He attracted many young people, and founded an order of nuns. In 1942, he was excommunicated.

Despite its poverty and small size, the community survived: 'This is a place of power, a holy place. . . . Who would have believed that there would be water here in this stony place?' When Francis died, he was succeeded by his son Basil, who died in the violence that preceded Zimbabwe's independence.

The prophetic churches often focus on a sacred place, such as Isaiah Shembe's Ekuphakemene, in Natal, but Johane Masowe, John of the Wilderness, (1915–1973), founded a pilgrim Church that worships in the open air.[129] He was a Shona, who, like so many church founders, recovered after a near-death experience, and emerged to a new identity, wearing long white garments, and carrying a staff, and a Bible:

Now I am John the Baptist, I was sent as a messenger to the Africans. I am making a new way amongst black people. . . . I am a teacher of the whole world. I am saying that people should stop practising witchcraft, throw away their medicines, pray to God, and love one another.[130]

The first part of his life was devoted to evangelism, and, in his later years, he embraced a hidden life, a 'secret Messiah'. Shona and Ndebele are dominant in the Church, but it has branches in nine African countries. John died in Tanzania, and there is a congregation in Nairobi, which they see as the heart of Africa, foreshadowed in Isaiah 19.19. They have, perhaps, half a million members.[131] The Apostles worship Jehovah, follow Old Testament dietary rules, and keep the Sabbath. Polygamous marriages are preferred, and John is called the 'Word', 'Spirit', or 'Star of God'.

His followers live in separate communities, distinguished by the women's white gowns and turbans, and the men's beards and shaven heads. They earn their living by various forms of craft activity, such as making tin containers, and avoid working for an employer. There is also a body of Sisters, celibate religious women, who are perceived as a collective Ark.[132] There was a large community in Korsten, a slum area in Port Elizabeth, until the South African Government deported them to Southern Rhodesia, in 1962; they are often called the Korsten Basketmakers.

Above all, John offered spiritual power, against the forces of evil and sickness. As an Apostle put it in 1974:

> When we were in these synagogues [established churches] we used to read about the works of Jesus Christ . . . cripples were made to walk and the dead were brought to life . . . evil spirits were driven out. . . . That was what was being done in Jerusalem. We Africans, however, who were being instructed by white people, never did anything like that. . . . We were taught to read the Bible, but we ourselves never did what the people in the Bible used to do.[133]

One could hardly have a better summary of the wellsprings from which the prophetic churches sprang.

John's first followers were mainly the young, victims of the Depression years. By the time he died, in 1973, his early supporters had grown old, and the movement had turned into a gerontocracy, leading to a secession of some younger members.

The Maranke Vapostori (Apostles) were founded by another Shona, John Maranke, in 1932. They, too, claim half a million adherents in some seven countries. Congregational leaders attend a Passover, held at Umtali, and the leadership of the Church is always Shona. There are four categories of religious specialization: baptists [pastors], evangelists, healers, and prophets, only the last two grades being open to women. The tension between organizational authority and prophetic charisma has caused some divisions. It is a perennial source of difficulty in these churches, especially after the death of the founder, and Shona dominance has been questioned in what has become an international movement.[134] An American scholar, Benetta Jules-Rosette, came to Africa to study the Apostles, and joined them.

The Religion of God

Dini ya Msambwa means the Religion of God. It was founded by Elijah Masinde among the Luhyia of Kenya in the 1940s.[135] Masinde was a remarkable figure, and, perhaps, the only Church founder to have played international football! His followers were active in opposing the colonial Government, and he was imprisoned on several occasions. The movement was proscribed by the Government of independent Kenya in 1968, and Masinde was in gaol when Wipper's study was written, in 1975.

Dini ya Msambwa was founded as a conscious return to the old ways: 'God called Elijah in a vision at night. . . . God informed him that everyone in this world belongs to me, even the polygynist belongs to me', 'God told me to leave Friends [the American Quaker mission] and to follow the religion of my ancestors'. However, it is so full of Christian elements that it could well be called a Church in the usual sense, and it was originally called *Dini ya Israel*. The Dini's Holy Place is a lake high on Mount Elgon, which they call Zion. They wear a cross on their uniforms, and claim that the Trinity was foreshadowed in traditional Luhya thought. The first Luhya progenitors became Mary and Joseph, and ancestors and angels were seen as members of one family of spriritual beings. Members of the Church pray:

> Oh God the Father forgive us and feel pity for us. The foreigners brought the new missions which made us leave our traditional customs which are now lost. We are asking you to bless and give us freedom.

What is explicit is a sense of loss: the loss of land, the loss of the adventure and celebration of the cattle raids that marked young men's entry to adult life, the loss of the unquestioned respect enjoyed by the old.

Esoteric knowledge

Traditional African religions often emphasized secret knowledge. This was the lure that drew the initiate through grade after grade, in cults, such as mask societies. The 'secret' was often trivial, but its possession was a source of power. Christianity was welcomed partly because it seemed to hold the key to modernity, prosperity, and power, yet, those who mastered its secrets, and were able to read the Book often remained as poor as before. An educated Nyakusa in the 1930s was a fisherman, 'and he talks English to the fish as he pulls them out of the Lake'.[136] It was widely believed that there was an inner core of secret knowledge that had not been shared, that parts of the Bible had been suppressed—ideas that are well-documented in the Pacific, and among Native Americans. This enduring hunger for secret knowledge helps explain the success of the Korsten Basketmakers, with their concealed Messiah, and their corpus of secret teaching. John Maranke was given two books in a foreign language, which he was enabled miraculously to understand.

Syncretism

It is important to remember what the very structure of a history of Christianity tends to preclude: recognition of the continuing vitality of traditional religion, and, indeed, the dynamic spread, in many areas, of Islam. The prophetic churches were adamant in their rejection of what they perceived as heathenism, but there were some movements that were clearly syncretistic. Mumbo is a good example.

The cult of Mumbo, a giant water serpent of Lake Victoria, was first recorded among the Gusii in 1913, which makes it, with one exception, the oldest Kenyan independent religious movement. It showed a remarkable capacity for survival, despite repression. It was at its strongest in the 1920s and 1930s, and still survived in the 1950s, and perhaps later.

It was explicitly hostile to European influences and Christianity—'the Christian religion is rotten'—and foretold the same kind of eschatological reversal of black/white relations as Watch Tower's African exponents: 'I will cause cattle, sheep and goats to come up out of the lake in great numbers. . . . All Europeans are your enemies, but the time is shortly coming when they will all disappear from our country'.

However, the movement was full of Biblical echoes, including the belief in an imminent judgement. Mumbo's rhetorical style is much like that of Jehovah: 'I am the God Mumbo . . . go and tell all Africans . . . that henceforth I am their God', and Mumbo swallows and regurgitates a prophet, as the whale did Jonah. The style may derive from the European who reported it, and there are indigenous antecedents for lake serpents that swallow seers, but there can be no doubt about the source of the teaching of Bonairiri, a woman prophet, that woman comes from man's rib.

Traditional religion and revolution

Traditional religion was specifically ethnic; it provided a unifying ideology for Mau Mau, which was a Kikuyu movement. This was both its weakness and its strength. The rising began in 1952, and was effectively defeated by 1954, scholars have attempted to understand it ever since.

It was spearheaded by the squatters on white land, who found their position increasingly intolerable, and there was a dimension of intergenerational conflict. Its ideology lay in a mystical attachment to the land, and in oaths rooted in the sanctions of traditional religion. Because it was specifically Kikuyu, it was unsuited for a national rising. To white settlers and colonial administrators, it was a 'subversive movement based on the lethal mixture of pseudo-religion, nationalism and the evil forms of black magic'.[137] The horrific image of Mau Mau was largely due to the real, or alleged nature of their oathing ceremonies,[138] but, according to official figures, 12 590 Mau Mau and 58 Europeans were killed in the war.

The Kikuyu were profoundly divided, and some fought on the government side. The loyalists have been variously identified as Christians (to whom traditional oaths were unacceptable), and the more prosperous (these were often the same people, and 'Chiefs' tended to be educated Christians). Sandgren points out that Christians themselves were divided: the Independents supported Mau Mau, the adherents of mission churches, the government.

Missionary voices

At the beginning of this chapter, we referred to the way in which missionaries often identified with their fellow Europeans. Not all, of course, made this choice. Missionary criticisms of governmental and settler injustices had a real impact, not least because of their power to influence public opinion in England.

It is no coincidence that far more has been written about white missionaries in twentieth-century Kenya, Rhodesia, and South Africa than in West Africa in the same period, where they remain almost entirely invisible. 'Africanist' scholarship focused on African agency, in religion as elsewhere. In eastern and southern Africa, white Christians clearly have much to gain by emphasizing figures such as Cripps, Huddleston, and the Clutton-Brocks. Modern scholars now tend to stress the limitations of the Christian liberal tradition in South Africa, a theme to which we shall return, and we have already noted the ambiguity, and inconsistency of a 'radical' such as Weston of Zanzibar. This, though, is not to belittle their very real self-sacrifice and idealism.

Arthur Shearly Cripps was an Anglo-Catholic, whose spirituality was cast in a Franciscan mould. He reached Rhodesia in 1901, and died there, over fifty years later, at the age of eighty-three. He lived for decades in an African roundhouse, and was virtually destitute in his last years. He won the hostility of the white community with his defence of African land claims. A minor poet, he paid a tribute to Frank Weston, which can stand as his own epitaph:

> Whence was his Faith? A rushing mighty wind
> First hurled her fierce infections among men.
> But we, innoculating heart and mind
> With spilth of pulpit and with spray of pen,
> Shiver immune from Faith's contagion.

Not so he served. For him Emmanuel glowed
In gleaming Hosts; in faces dark and wild
The Burning Babe of Bethlehem on him smiles.[139]

Cripps was an extreme individualist, but another missionary in Rhodesia, the Methodist, John White, worked effectively for racial justice through administrative structures, and was the architect of the Southern Rhodesia Missionary Congress. As its President, he criticized government policy in 1928; his fellow missionaries did not support him, and he was dropped from it.[140]

Walter Owen was the Anglican Archdeacon of Kavirondo (now Nyanza) in western Kenya from 1918 to 1945, and saw himself as the spokesman of its people's interests. He was criticized at the time, and later, because he did not encourage the people to speak for themselves: 'Owen told the natives to dig *choos*, kill rats and build beds. Meanwhile he translated himself into the native's *alter ego*'.[141] However, 'championing the cause of the native' must be evaluated in the context of his time and environment.

An epistle from the Maasai

The Maasai stood aloof, very largely, from the process of westernization. Warriors and pastoralists, passionately attached to their cattle, they clung, very largely, to their inherited lifestyle. Despite their martial past, they did not fight against the imposition of colonialism. When a colonial government alienated grazing lands that were guaranteed them by treaty, they challenged it, unsuccessfully, in a court of law.

The pure pastoral ideal in a sense, was never fully mirrored in reality. Some Maa speakers were agriculturalists, and even pastoralists relied partly on cultivated products obtained by trade, though they professed to despise farmers, *olmeg*. The Maasai worshipped one God, *Engai*, and feared nothing but evil spirits. They neither consumed nor hunted wild game. They had no structure of government; they were organized in age grades, and charismatic ritual specialists, *laibon*, wielded great influence.

Where most African peoples had a cult of ancestral spirits, and interred the dead with care, the Maasai practised no burial at all, and corpses were abandoned to the hyenas. One might have expected their lack of concern for ancestors to predispose them to religious change, but, in fact, by the 1960s, Christianity had made virtually no impact at all, such was their intense cultural patriotism and conservatism.

In 1966, a Catholic missionary working among the Maasai wrote to his bishop describing a relationship that was 'dismal, time-consuming, wearying, expensive, and materialistic . . . there are no adult Maasai practising Christians from Loliondo mission . . . no Catholic child, on leaving school, has continued to practise his religion. . . .'[142] Missionaries developed warm relationships with the Maasai, but did not try to convert them, much like their counterparts in Muslim lands.

Donovan embarked on direct evangelization, which he believed had fallen into abeyance since the time of Paul! In fact, he was reverting to the 'itinerations' beloved of nineteenth-century missionaries. He was reacting against a missionary lifestyle that had lost sight of direct evangelization, and took it for granted that foreign missionaries were a permanent feature of African religious life; he himself, in due course, returned to America.

He presented the Good News in Maasai cultural terms, stressing the pastoral lifestyle of the Israelites, telling the story of the Good Olmeg. Several Maasai became unpaid evangelists, like so many African Christians before them. No follow-up study has been done, and one cannot know whether his converts persevered, or what pattern their later religious lives took.

In one passage, he describes a group that rejected his message. He took this as definitive, both for the individuals concerned and even for their children: 'I will go elsewhere to find if others want to hear the Christian message. And I do not think that any other Padri will come here after me'.[143] Paternalism takes many forms. Here, Padri not only took it upon himself to deny people the right to change their minds, but also deprived the next generation of the right to choose at all.

The book in which he described his experiment became a best-seller, loved by many who had read nothing else on Africa.

Encounters in the heart

It has been said that the dialogue between Christianity and traditional religion takes place in the hearts of African Christians. We have analysed the corporate responses of churches and new religious movements, but within and beyond these movements, countless individuals invented a Christian lifestyle, and system of beliefs for themselves. It was noted during a revival in southern Zambia, in 1962, that the hallmarks of a Christian were church attendance, and the avoidance of charms, dreams, and sacrifices to ancestors.[144]

The creation of a synthesis between old and new was seldom a major conscious concern for the first generation of Christians. Often, they were more condemnatory of their own society than the missionaries were. To modern African intellectuals, they were 'deluded hybrids', undervaluing their own culture, emulating Europeans who did not accept them as equals. It did not seem like that then: 'Behold, I make all things new'.

There have been curiously few in-depth studies of the actual practice of village Christianity and its relationship with the host culture. Anthropologists have tended to focus on 'traditional' religion, even where this has largely disappeared, seeking out societies that remain relatively unchanged. A study of a village in Buhaya, in north-west Tanzania, provides a corrective to this tendency.

Missionaries have been at work in Buhaya since the 1880s, and the Haya 'are one of the most Christianized populations . . . in East Africa'.[145] In a village survey, 90 per cent identified as Christian, and a Haya of royal descent, Lugambwa, was the first African cardinal. Religious pictures are the only form of decoration in village homes apart from family photographs. Some traditional practices, such as communal sacrifices to the royal ancestors, the Bacwezi, have died out, but a few elderly villagers still make offerings to their own lineage forebears. Public performances by spirit mediums have ended, though mediums are still consulted in private. Women still practise the traditional ritual following a baby's birth, and wedding celebrations have become a composite of traditional elements with exotica, such as a wedding cake and a white bridal costume. Scapulars—understood as amulets, a source of daily protection—are widely worn.

Not all these changes were the result of mission teaching. The decline of royal spirits for instance, can be linked to the abolition of monarchical institutions in independent Tanzania.

The tendency for African Christian spirituality to centre on a traditional God rather than Jesus is too common to be a coincidence. A Rwanda abbé preached of Imana; the Ganda martyrs died for Katonda. The traditional understanding of 'God' developed and changed in the continuing dialectic with Christianity, but it extended, like a bridge, between ancient spiritualities and the new.

Secularization

There is a sense in which the traditional world was profoundly religious; there was no compartmentalized entity perceived as 'religion'. There are sometimes suggestions that the secularization so apparent in the western world can also be discerned in modern Africa. Miller, in a study of the Toba Indians of Argentina, has made the arresting suggestion that western missionaries, by demonstrating a compartmentalized attitude to religion, are actually agents of secularization: 'Christian missionary ideology . . . represents a highly institutionalized operation in which supernaturalism's sphere of influence has been increasingly narrowed and circumscribed in the sending community (western world). . . . Generating few values uniquely its own, mission ideology reflects and even legitimates many of the values being forced at the same time upon the folk society by a colonial administration or a national government'.[146]

It is possible that studies of religious change exaggerate belief, and underestimate the strength of agnosticism and a secular viewpoint. The very presence of a Christian community weakened traditional beliefs: 'We no longer believe in the old rituals', said a young Nyakusa in the 1930s, 'because we see that the Christians do not do these things and nothing happens to them'.[147]

A study of Chezia, a Gwembe Tonga community, suggests that, in the 1950s, several decades after the establishment of an American fundamentalist mission, their attitude was still basically secular. 'Satan' was a term of abuse, and older schoolboys, while not convinced Christians, had lost their confidence in traditional religion, noting that teachers and missionaries made no offerings to the dead, and suffered no apparent consequences.[148]

Jung went to East Africa in 1925, and a Maasai ritual specialist told him, 'In the old days the *Laibons* had dreams, and knew whether there is war or sickness or whether rain comes. But since the whites were in Africa, he said, no one had dreams any more'.[149]

✎§ TEN §✎

West Africa c. 1900 to c. 1960

What their religion means to the women, I could not tell.

A researcher in Nneato in 1934[1]

Contexts: colonial governments

With local and insignificant exceptions, there was little white settlement in West Africa, and nationalists sometimes paid a not entirely jocular tribute to the mosquito. Togo and Kamerun were German colonies until the First World War, and Liberia retained at least a nominal independence. Except for the tiny enclave of Portuguese Guinea, the rest of West Africa was divided between French and British colonies. The Francophone *assimilé*, like the Lusophone *assimilado*, had, in theory, achieved total equality with the colonizers by mastering their language and culture, but very few ever qualified, and those who did, paid the price of alienation from their own cultural inheritance: 'Our ancestors were the Gauls', read West African schoolchildren in their textbooks, 'They had red hair and blue eyes'. It was against this background that Senghor discovered negritude.

British administrators were more likely to express a dislike for the 'detribalized' (that is western-educated) African and a preference for the 'unspoiled' villager or the 'dignified' northern Muslim. In 1912, Edward Lugard denounced 'the civilised trouser-negro of the Coast, who . . . seldom raises his hat to the Governor', and was glad to find his brother acknowledged by prostrations when he reached Ilorin. Frederick Lugard suggested that western education made Africans less fertile, and susceptible to lung disease and tooth decay[2] (the CMS missionary, Walter Miller, had a similar theory about Muslims). A District Officer in eastern Nigeria wrote in 1930, 'Before you know where you are they want to drive you out imagining that they can govern themselves because one or two have been educated. . . . Suppression—not oppression—is the way to treat subject races'.[3] Christianity itself reinforced socio-economic change, in ways that missionaries often did not understand. The need to pay taxes drew people towards a cash economy, a process that began in the nineteenth century, when settlers in a Christian

264

village had to buy windows and doors, and all Christians were expected to wear clothes that did not offend Victorian sensibilities.

Church and State: the Togo example

In Togo, as in Kamerun/Cameroun, the change, after the First World War, from German colony to British and French mandated territories had a peculiarly disruptive impact on local Christians. The Bremen Mission began work among the Ewe in 1847, and used the Ewe language, even in work among other peoples, much as their counterparts in the Gold Coast tended to use Twi. It was, very largely, the missionaries who created 'the Ewe nation' out of 120 separate small peoples.

In 1892, the Divine Word Fathers arrived; they were a Dutch order, able and willing to send Germans to Togo. Togo schoolchildren sang *Deutschland über alles*, and, when there was a crisis in French–German relations in 1911, they drilled with wooden sticks.[4] However, although the Government insisted on instruction in German, many Ewe preferred English, the language of trade.

When the First World War broke out, the German missionaries were interned. The Methodists were willing to take over from the Bremen Mission, but the offer was turned down. This left them free to establish new churches in the wake of the Harris revival in Ivory Coast (see pages 284ff.). The Paris Evangelical Missionary Society, Bremen's preferred successor, was already overburdened, and declined the invitation.

After the war, a painfully acquired knowledge of German was useless to African Christians in Togo. The former colony was divided between British and French mandates, and, with it, the Protestant Church was divided between Anglophone 'Ewe Presbyterian' and an independent Ewe church, which endured great financial difficulties. In the Catholic missions, Germans were replaced by English and French personnel. In 1924, a Catholic dignitary visited the region: 'I closed the meeting amid cries of "Long live the Pope, long live France, long live Togo" '.[5]

Today, Togo Catholics greatly outnumber Protestants, although the latter reached the area forty-five years before them. This reflects, to a large extent, the impact of French colonial policies. In the 1960s, there were 180 thousand Catholics and 45 thousand Protestants in a population of a little over a million.[6]

Rivalry and co-operation

The missionary scramble for newly accessible territory led to bitter rivalries. The older Protestant missions tackled the problem by means of comity agreements. Southern Nigeria, east of the Niger, was divided between four missionary societies and the Niger Delta Pastorate: the CMS in the Onitsha-

Awka area, the Primitive Methodists in three widely separated districts, the Presbyterians, who remained in Calabar and its hinterland, and the Qua Iboe mission which extended from Eket to Aba.[7] Smaller missions, and those that arrived later, such as the Seventh Day Adventists and the Salvation Army, were excluded from these arrangements.[8]

Colonial governments tended to discourage multiple missions in a single community, so rural Africa became a palimpsest of exclusively Methodist, Anglican, or Catholic villages. For a long period, religious pluralism was confined mostly to the towns and cities, although many individuals broke free from this kind of geographical religious determinism. A village schoolmaster recorded his own adventures in comparative religion:

> When I was taking up my scholars in lesson there we read in history about Henry the VIII. How he on account of wife established a new Church on earth which was known to be the C.M.S. After school I call the scholars to my house—that I think we have found out the true Church.[9]

Southern Nigerians and Ghanaians read religious pamphlets avidly, and established contacts with churches abroad. In this way, the Assemblies of God came to Port Harcourt, and the Precious Stone Society made contact with the Philadelphia Faith Tabernacle (see page 280). Ethnic churches were often created to meet the needs of urban migrants, the identification being sometimes formal, and, in other cases, informal. There were twenty such churches in Freetown, in the 1960s. They offered a ready-made community to newly arrived migrants and worship in their own language. However, their impact was divisive, and they did not facilitate integration into the wider urban society.[10]

Catholics and Protestants made no boundary agreements, and their relationships were characterized by great mutual hostility. In part of Togo, the schoolhouse was called the house of battle. 'Hereabouts', wrote a local catechist in 1908, 'the Roman Catholics run about like hungry lions'.[11]

At a 1926 conference, the Sudan United Mission put forward a proposal for a United Church of Africa, to include the Sudan Interior Mission, and three other missions working in northern Nigeria,[12] but the moment passed.

Mission and society

In British colonies, an elaborate ideology of Indirect Rule developed. Where no traditional rulers existed, it was necessary to invent them, and, paradoxically, the British bolstered up 'traditional' rulers (who were not always traditional), and African Christians often challenged them. In 1911, a District Officer in Ekiti reported:

> There is not a single 'Crown Head' who has not complained to me about the behaviour of the Christians, it is always the same complaint: 'the

Christians will not obey me'; the chiefs and old men always complain that
directly their children became Christians they cease to work for them. In
regard to the 'Egungun', the Christians go out of their way to annoy the
followers. . . .[13]

People sought education for their children, not only in the hope that it would
lead to salaried employment, but also in search of protection from oppression:

There was in Ohafia one Vincent, a Seirea [*sic*] Leonian, who was the Native
Court Clerk. He was extremely wicked in his dealings with Ohafia people.
. . . My people wanted a way out of such persecution and my advice to
them was to open a school, educate their children who, knowing what the
clerk knew, could better challenge him and his successors.[14]

They believed, not without reason, that a missionary presence was a
protection against what colonial authorities called 'punitive expeditions'. An
Igbo called Tansi was taken as a hostage by the Royal Niger Company. Later,
he named a son, Iwene, 'let malice not kill me', and sent him to school, so that
he would be able to defend himself against oppression (see page 275).

Sometimes white missionaries seemed xenophobic, and anxious to preserve
white hegemony, while others entered deeply into the study of African
cultures. In 1906, the Divine Word Fathers founded a major ethnographic
journal, *Anthropos*, and Dietrich Westermann, who came to West Africa as a
Bremen missionary, became a famous pioneer of the academic study of African
languages. The Mennonite, A. W. Banfield, translator of the Nupe Bible,
acquired such a degree of language proficiency that he was called the 'white
Nupe'.

However, an understanding and appreciation of African cultures were far
from universal. In 1933, an African teacher who introduced local music into
church services at a Gold Coast Presbyterian Training College was expelled.[15]
It is, moreover, possible for a real knowledge of an African culture to coexist
with attitudes that are very far from respect and mutuality: 'O God teach me
to kill the Western man in me', wrote a missionary, in a book published in
1945; he then went on to compile a catalogue of slanderous racist
stereotypes.[16] 'As often, Christianity is betrayed by Christians'; the words
were intended to apply to Africans.[17]

Many African Christians strove to preserve and defend their cultural
heritage. In 1925, a teacher said in Kumasi, 'To the African the whole universe
breathes of God . . . the extent of his faith . . . is a locked up spiritual capital,
which the Church has to learn to use'.[18]

Others absorbed mission Christianity wholeheartedly, and made war on
mask societies, traditional titles, and polygamy, with little or no apparent
concern for acculturation. In many cases, old and new coexisted, apparently
comfortably. For example, in Freetown, Christianity has been established
since its foundation, in the late eighteenth century, but Yoruba masquerades

are a familiar sight on city streets, and Christians hold traditional funeral ceremonies, and visit the graves of their dead at times of crisis: 'Here is your kola. May whatever we say or do make our hearts cool'.[19]

A brilliant study of Duala, in Cameroon, provides a good example of the complexities of the encounter between the new faith and traditional cultures. Here, missionaries condemned the cult of water spirits, but this created a social vacuum, for many of its functions were no longer filled: 'the *jengu* took care of initiation rites, made peace among various clans, ensured obedience to the law of the clan, apportioned fishing grounds and so on'. The missionaries did not oppose bridewealth, but, when the standing of the elders was eroded by attacks on polygamy and the independence of the educated, they retaliated by raising the bride price. For a time, the Duala internalized the missionary condemnation of their own culture:

> Many traditions were forgotten and not replaced: the impression was that of a cultural vacuum. . . . A bishop could say at this point: 'We manufacture Christians but life takes them away from us. . . . The traditional institutions, more or less maimed, survived. The Christians lived two lives concurrently'.[20]

Accusations of witchcraft became more common, a sure index of social and spiritual malaise, and there was a widespread return to the old rituals.

Marriage

The mission churches' rigid insistence on monogamy led many to join African or prophetic churches, and kept others outside the formal structures of Christianity altogether. An Igbo fourth wife protested in 1924 with justifiable indignation, 'Why fourth wife no fit be good like first wife? Suppose God makes that law, God no do good fashion'.[21] A thoughtful government official suggested that the patriarchal elements in Christianity reinforced similar aspects of traditional Igbo society.[22]

Matrilineal institutions declined in the colonial period, a change that reflects, in part, western and missionary perceptions of 'normal' family and inheritance patterns. Some of the peoples of central Nigeria practised serial polyandry; the initial marriage was usually by exchange, arranged in infancy. Changes of marriage partners did not always represent a woman's free choice, but the general ambience was one where women were courted and sought after. In 1931, it was noted that Christian Kagoro women were rejecting marriages arranged in infancy, and, today, marriage with bridewealth has generally replaced exchange marriage:

> The status of Tiv women is said to have declined after the abolition of sister exchange. . . . Christianity in Nigeria may well reinforce the inequality of women rather than the reverse. The teaching that the first woman was

created from Adam's rib is frequently cited as unassailable proof that woman is inferior to man.[23]

Marriages, which formerly involved long-continued negotiations by two extended families, now often reflected the choices of two individuals. Christianity empowered many (young men, who would otherwise have had a long wait for a wife, and women unwillingly married to elderly polygamists) to choose a spouse freely. However, this led to problems with existing obligations, notably those created by bridewealth payments. Some parents felt that, having made an investment in education, they could not contribute to bridewealth, so that a son married late.

Church marriages were very difficult to leave, and Leith-Ross recorded 'old Christina's spontaneous cry: "Christian marriage is a prison!"' In Igboland, childless Christian widows were often the poorest of the poor, for they were debarred from the system of wife inheritance that had traditionally provided for them: 'Should the husband desert the wife or die, the Christian wife is left far more solitary and unprotected than under the old pagan regime'.[24] Widows were invisible and forgotten victims of social and religious change.

Some paid lip-service to Church teachings on marriage, but evaded them in practice. A view from within of Freetown Christianity reveals a world where divorce is rare, but strict monogamy unusual.[25] In some cases, there was a widespread reversion to polygamy:

> The Foreke people . . . reason that we who marry only one wife have less children and so there is not much progress. This has led the people to go back to taking many wives. There are very few people in Foreke now who are practising Christians. . . . There are more women around than men as the men go to the towns. Women without husbands drift to the towns so that the total population is reduced.[26]

Schools

Colonial governments and commercial firms needed literate employees, and teachers and clerks were the élite of the new age. Children often understood this before their parents did. As early as the 1870s, in Togo, 'All the young folk wanted to go to school; they flocked round the missionaries and begged, "Put me in trousers"'.[27] Parents hesitated at first, largely because they needed their children's help with farm work. As the material benefits of education became evident, their priorities changed.

In French colonies, the limited funds available for education tended to go to government schools, catering for a small number of pupils. In British colonies, subsidies were given to those mission schools that met the required standard. Some Faith Missions, shunning conversions motivated by worldly advancement, did not seek financial assistance, and concentrated on minimal instruction in a vernacular. Their co-operation over education tended to bring the missions that welcomed subsidies closer to the government, though sometimes they were publically critical of government measures, and took the African side. The Wesleyans, for example, actively supported the Aborigines Rights Protection Society in their opposition to the Forest Bill on the Gold Coast in 1912.[28]

In British colonies, the missions had almost a monopoly over education. In 1942, they controlled 99 per cent of Nigeria's schools, and 97 per cent of all students were in mission schools.[29] Only a few primary scholars ever reached a secondary school. Secondary education was usually in boarding schools, mainly in order to be able to accept entrants from a large geographical area.

As we have seen, this isolated children from the wider society, much as the Christian village had done. Those who attended them often suffered greatly. In West Africa, as in Sithole's Rhodesia, it was accepted that learning and whipping were inseparable: 'I remember the day I arrived on campus with my two boxes full of the required items—a broom, cutlass, a hoe, and some books. . . . Nobody could persuade me to go through those three years again'.[30] The words apply to a Presbyterian school in Ghana in the 1950s, where water had to be brought from a river several miles away, and children were woken at three or four in the morning to carry it on their heads. In many West African schools, a self-perpetuating tradition of severity, verging on brutality, and of unnecessarily demanding manual work, still flourishes.

Missions and schools: the South eastern Nigeria example

South eastern Nigeria is a particularly striking example of the way in which Christianity spread through the hunger for education. Bishop Crowther had foreseen the shape of things to come in Igboland:

> . . . the Ibos are very emulative: as in other things, so it will be in book learning. Other towns will not rest satisfied until they have learned the mystery of reading and writing, by which their neighbours may surpass or put them in the shade.[31]

In the words of a researcher in the 1930s, 'The Mission means education and education means a miraculous ladder to fame and fortune'.[32] In old age, one of those early schoolchildren remembered:

> At the beginning it was not all that clear. But some of my mates were in school, so I went to have fun—companionship, to escape the dreariness of farm work, to be like others I admired. It was the thing to do—a necessary step toward becoming like the white man. Then as one grew older one came to see the advantages in more concrete terms.[33]

In the late nineteenth century, Catholic missionaries on the Niger concentrated on redeeming slaves, and providing a refuge for those whom society
marginalized. The Spiritan Léon Lejeune, who died in 1905, and his successor
Joseph Shanahan,[34] concentrated on creating and maintaining a vast network
of State-subsidized schools and, by doing so, acquired a dominant position
among the Igbo that they were never to lose. In 1906, there were 2500
Catholics in the Onitsha-Owerri vicariate; by 1926, the number had risen to
58 thousand; it was 250 thousand by 1946.[35]

For obvious reasons, schoolchildren wanted education in English, not the
vernacular. The CMS favoured African languages, which gave the Catholics a
decisive advantage. Mission bodies that could supply white secondary school
teachers and managers were more popular: 'this partly explains the collapse of
the Garrick Braide churches and the large-scale desertion from the Niger
Delta Pastorate'.[36]

The combative village patriotism that Crowther discerned in the nineteenth
century was very apparent in the twentieth: 'The people of Owerri . . .
though very enthusiastic in the practice of their Religion, are rather
troublesome. . . . Each town wants everything for itself—its own priest,
secondary school, hospital, etc., etc.'.[37]

The French St Joseph of Cluny sisters received nothing but praise as long as
the mission concentrated on charity and care of the sick. The names of Mère
Theonite[38] and Mère Clothilde,[39] albeit names in religion, are rifts in the cloud
of anonymity that so often surrounded missionary nuns. When education
became of central importance, they had to leave the Niger, because of their
imperfect knowledge of Igbo and English.[40]

Families often spent their limited financial resources on the education of
sons, rather than daughters. Many Igbo mothers educated their sons with the
proceeds of petty trade; the sons, in turn, acknowledged their debt by naming
the first granddaughter *Nneka*, Mother is supreme. In Eastern Nigeria and
Cameroon, in 1928, there were 15 thousand boys and 3 thousand girls in
government-assisted mission schools, and 47 thousand boys and 4 thousand
girls in schools that did not attain the standard required for subsidies.[41] Girls'
schools often emphasized domestic training:

> Nor do we think too lowly we must bend
> when taught to wash, to iron and to mend.[42]

In 1924, a solitary Irish Sister of Charity, Magdalene Walker, arrived in
Nigeria. Full of enthusiasm for girls' education and for the Montessori system,
she set up a network of village schools for girls among the Efik and Ibibio,
employing African women teachers. In 1931 she founded a teaching order for
African women, the Handmaids of the Holy Child Jesus.[43] They were joined
by members of an international order. the Holy Child Sisters. The Holy Rosary
Sisters, founded by Shanahan in Ireland in 1924, also ran schools for girls,
despite the misgivings of successive bishops. When the creation of a girls'

secondary school was announced in 1941, Bishop Heerey said, 'the future of educated girls is so uncertain that we feel, and indeed hope, that the numbers will remain low'.[44]

Mission schools required the payment of school fees: 'Nothing is given for nothing', wrote a missionary in 1920,[45] a sad boast for a professional Christian. In 1957, the Government of Eastern Nigeria abolished school fees, but, a year later, they were reintroduced. Igbo and Ibibio mothers rioted in protest: 'thousands of women demonstrators forcibly closed schools in many areas and drove teachers and pupils from school compounds'.[46]

In the 1930s, an educated Igbo was asked why his people became Christians. He replied, 'They become Christian before they get sense', and went on to explain 'that the boy who goes to a Mission school takes it for granted that becoming a Christian is a corollary to becoming a scholar'. When asked 'how many turned to Christianity because they searched for the truth and wanted more than their pagan beliefs could give them', he replied, 'Some old women'.[47]

Church and society: 'the North'

In an earlier chapter, we considered the fortunes of Christianity in the states of the Sahel, and the career of that notable pioneer, Alfred Diban of Burkina Faso. One of the most harmful legacies of colonialism in West Africa was its invention of 'North' and 'South'.

The Muslim North was to be insulated from the disruptive forces of modernity, and from Christian missions. As missions were the main purveyors of western education, northerners were largely excluded from it. By 1951, only one northern Nigerian had received a full university education, and he was a Zaria Christian, educated in Britain by Walter Miller. In 1952, the percentage of the population over the age of seven literate in Roman script was 16 per cent in the Eastern region, 18 per cent in the Western region, 3.3 per cent in what was then called the Middle Belt, and 1.4 per cent in the mainly Muslim North.[48]

Missionary activity was restricted or forbidden in north Togo until 1911, although only 5 to 10 per cent of the population was Muslim.[49] In northern Ghana, the White Fathers secured a foothold in 1907, and the Wesleyans in 1912. But successive Chief Commissioners regarded them with suspicion, and hampered their work. In 1919, only four of a total of 213 government or subsidized mission schools were in the Northern Territories; 194 of them were run by missions.[50] Five years earlier, a Chief Commissioner had written:

> With the Colony enjoying in addition to the Education department, the educational services of the Church Missionary Society, the Roman Catholic, Wesleyan, Basel and Bremen Missions, I respectfully submit that

a few crumbs from this feast of instruction might well be spared for the children of this Dependency.[51]

Like colonial officials, missionaries often felt a real fascination for the North, and tended to regard it as superior to the South. In 1890, Robinson and Brooks set up the Sudan Party to work in Hausaland; they ended up by dismantling the Niger Mission instead (see page 172). Those who went to Hausaland hoping for a spontaneous turning away from Islam were soon disappointed. The expectation that the Hausa would rise against the Fulani, and that 'the whole Hausa world is waiting for Christ'[52] proved groundless. Their access to the North was rigidly restricted by British officials, who often seemed more hostile to western influences than the emirs themselves. The exceptions were Zaria and Nupe, where missionaries were allowed to respond to an emir's invitation. Dr Walter Miller of the CMS settled in Zaria in 1905. He worked for many years in Hausaland, and translated the Bible into Hausa, but remained hostile to Islam and to the Fulani establishment.

In a village 25 miles from Zaria, a small group of Muslims had essentially already converted themselves to Christianity. The Children of the Israelites followed in the footsteps of a scholar called Ibrahim, who was impaled for blasphemy in Kano in 1867. They said, 'our houses are our mosques', and shunned the various public expressions of Islam. They believed that the Qur'an contained a secret meaning, handed down from Ibrahim, and rejected all other books; Ibrahim 'lost all his books of this world and seized this religion inside the Koran'. Muhammad was relegated to a Messenger and Isa (Jesus) became the Spirit of God and Lord of Life and Death, of whom Europeans would bring more knowledge.

By 1913, when they made contact with Miller in Zaria, there were 160 members: 'That day all the disciples did not sleep for happiness'. Not all joined the CMS, and those who did so were made to renounce all their wives but one.

In 1914, the Children of the Israelites founded a new settlement at Gimi, but tragedy lay in store for them. In 1919, two-thirds of them died in an epidemic of sleeping sickness. The colonial government refused Miller's request that they be allowed to resettle on a different site. Most of the survivors gradually became absorbed in the wider Christian community.[53]

Christians from the South worked in northern Nigeria and elsewhere, but were restricted to the *sabon garis*, the ghettos for southerners: 'Thanks to our good Igbo Catholics . . . we have little chapels and schools all along the [railway] line';[54] 'The Ibos are inveterate travellers. There is scarcely a mission in all Nigeria or Cameroons which does not count some Ibos among its church members'.[55] This was equally true of the Yoruba. By 1937, there were 'flourishing Christian churches in the immigrant towns of Jos, Bukuru and Kafanchan'.[56]

These were churches of southerners, with little impact on northern peoples, but, in 1932, Qua Iboe Christians founded a mission among the Igala, and, much later, Reverend Bassey Minso, an Efik, worked with his family as a missionary in Lassa, in North-East Nigeria.[57]

Central Nigeria was to be a much more successful mission field. It is a mosaic of different ethno-linguistic groups, some of which number only a few thousand people. The dominant body was the Sudan Interior Mission, which triumphed over initial disasters and had 550 foreign missionaries and 101 major stations in Nigeria alone by 1958. By this time, it had become Evangelical Churches of the Western Sudan (ECWS). The other major organization in the area was the Sudan United Mission, which became the Church of Christ in Nigeria (COCIN or EKAN, the equivalent in Hausa).

Their initial progress was extremely slow.[58] They sought to convert adults, who acquired only the minimal literacy needed to read the Bible in the vernacular. Their adherents, who were relatively few until the 1960s, often displayed the purely supernatural vision the Faith Missions longed for. Far from leading to material benefits, conversion led to ostracism and isolation. Christian youths pounded their own grain, because no one would marry them, or cook for them. Toma Bot, one of the first two Christians in the Berom town of Forom, married Tin, the first Forom woman convert, in 1921: 'I learnt that my wife suffered a lot but remained in the Christian faith. That was why I married her'. Another Berom Christian, Dajang of Du, converted the first Anaguta Christians and taught them to read the Hausa Bible, but not to write. One of them, Chai, sought safety from hostile masquerades and the sorcery of the elders by moving to Jos. His brother, Nyampi, built a little church in his compound where he held regular services. When I knew him, he was very old and slept with his beloved Hausa Bible under his pillow, although his failing eyes could no longer read. Nyang, the apostle of the Afezerek, sought treatment for leoprosy at a SUM hospital. His case was too far advanced to be helped, but, undeterred, he returned home, and devoted himself to evangelism. Vo Gyang, a Berom, went with her husband, carrying her baby on her back, as an evangelist to the Ganawuri, whom her people regarded as 'cannibals'. She mastered their language, contributed to the Ganawuri Bible, and even pounded her grain in the Ganawuri style.[59]

What drew these pioneers to Christianity was the promise of eternal life. In 1983, in his old age, Chai told me:

> When Christianity came, it said, when somebody dies he does not die, but goes somewhere to stay, that there is a day when God will call him. That is why I became a Christian. For me, before, when you die, you just rot. But when you die you do not rot. Your spirit goes somewhere. If that is the case I will follow, so that when I die my spirit will be taken somewhere and rest.

A Tiv pastor said, 'Just to think of seeing mother again'.[60]

From the late 1940s on, there was a much greater move towards

Christianity, reflecting an awareness of the value of education, and an attraction to the modern world. In 1948, a colonial administrator described, among the Berom, a sudden 'clamorous demand for schools . . . and for wider opportunities'.[61] In the late 1950s, there were still only a dozen Anaguta Christians. The first generation of Anaguta schoolchildren wrote essays in Hausa at the time, which shed a poignant light on their perceptions of their world, and of religion:

> We are very primitive. . . . Then white men invented a better way, that is why Africans started going to school. The use of education is when someone is educated he will get a good job. . . . God created heaven and earth, Adam and Eve, and the whole world.[62]

Central Nigerian Christianity expanded rapidly after independence. In 1960, COCIN had 5644 members, 474 congregations, 452 evangelists, and 18 pastors. By 1980, it had 50 thousand members, 1500 congregations, 1500 evangelists, and 150 pastors,[63] a development all the more striking because the 1960s were a time of intensive Muslim evangelization. The general picture is confirmed by census data which suggests that, between 1953 and 1963, the percentage of Christians in Plateau Province grew from 12.9 to 23.2. The Faith Missions became increasingly involved in education, and, after independence, its rewards were both more abundant and more apparent. The increasing indigenization of the churches may also have made them more attractive.

Consistency

The devoted witness of Central Nigerian Christians has many parallels elsewhere. Sometimes it was easier for celibates to walk on the narrow road the missionaries advocated. Not for them the justified reproaches of abandoned wives, nor the conflicts that arose when education brought prosperity, and the church prohibited the multiple wives and abundant children that were its hallmark in the eyes of their fellow villagers.

   Michael Iwene Tansi died in an English Trappist monastery in 1964. Until 1950, he was a rural priest in Igboland, one of the small minority of those, in any culture, who take Christianity as an exact map by which to walk. He was a man of tiny stature, with a blind eye, and his Irish bishop thought him 'not very bright'. Once, there was a smallpox epidemic:

> Catholics, CMS and pagans were affected, in this very village. Only Father Tansi went to the actual place where they were staying in isolation. . . . Whenever Father came here on trek he visited the houses of the poor and gave them gifts; the lepers, the blind, the lame, the crippled. . . . Whatever little thing he had, he gave them.[64]

In Mount Saint Bernard, he suffered greatly from the cold. His health deteriorated, and he was often marginalized, and misunderstood by middle-class English monks. He suffered from the mysterious inner trials that St John of the Cross called the Dark Night of the Soul. Nothing deflected him from his chosen path: 'If you are going to be a Christian', he said in his Nigerian days, 'You might as well live entirely for God'.

Tansi, like Diban, lived in the framework of generally recognized Church structures: catechist, priest, monk.

Ignatius Bamah also hoped to be a priest, but was sent away from the seminary because of his defective sight. Other ex-seminarians married, and had careers, but Ignatius worked, unpaid, for the mission at Asaba for forty years, until he was killed in a massacre during the Nigerian civil war: 'He decided that since he couldn't be a priest he would be a "Brother". He refused to marry. He refused to have riches. He turned his back on the world and lived for God alone'.[65]

Scholars working on Christianity in West Africa (including the author), have tended to focus on indigenous Christians, rather than expatriate missionaries. Unlike their counterparts elsewhere in Africa, the latter are virtually invisible. But there were remarkable lives among them, and Christianity was not always betrayed by Christians. The SMA priest, Père Coquard, for example, worked at Abeokuta for many years. His true avocation was to medicine and surgery, but in the end the colonial government prohibited their practice by the unqualified. Sadly, he packed his shining instruments away.

Eliza Davis George was a black Baptist from Texas. In 1945, when she was sixty-five and had spent thirty-two years in Liberia, the Baptists insisted she retire. Instead, she raised her own financial support through Eliza Davis George clubs, founded the Elizabeth Native Interior Mission, and worked on in Liberia until she was in her nineties.

In the 1930s, a colonial official paid warm tribute to:

> . . . the admirable record of Bishop and Mrs Melville Jones, of Lagos. She has served with exhaustless energy for fifty years in Nigeria, and is still at her post at the age of eighty-one. The Bishop, with an almost equally long career to his credit, still tours tirelessly his diocese . . . and can give men a third his age a really good game of tennis.[66]

Prophetic churches: some parallels

There were many parallels to the prophetic churches in mission congregations. In 1912, distinctive costumes were described among the Basel Mission Christians of Togo; at much the same time, as we have seen, they were popular among the Anglicans of western Kenya:

> In nearly every larger town [Christian] societies have been formed; all the members of the individual societies wore not only the society's badge but quite distinctive clothing.[67]

Quasi-autonomous movements often flourished in the mission churches. In the early part of this century Lijadu's Evangelists Band in Ondo (see page 180) was such a body.

Women's organizations are often powerful and independent. It has been suggested that one of the reasons independency has few attractions in Freetown is the strength of women's groups, such as the Emmanuel Association and the Martha Davies Confidential Benevolent Association (which, despite its name, is a prayer group). They hold revivalist-type meetings at times scheduled not to compete with the older churches, engage in extempore prayer and faith healing, and often raise funds for the churches, and for charity.[68] Like South Africa's Manyaro, they tend to be dominated by the middle-aged, and they wear a distinctive uniform. They insist on a rigid standard of sexual morality for their members, and, by doing so, as Steady points out, unconsciously reinforce the dual moral code already prevalent in Freetown society (see page 269). When Leith-Ross worked among the Igbo in the 1930s, she lamented the tedium of mission church services, enlivened only at the offertory. Fasholé-Luke, writing of the services in English held by Freetown Creoles said, 'even the so-called "Western Services" in the Creole churches have a distinctive quality of their own'.[69]

Prophetic churches

The most dramatic aspect of the growth of Christianity in twentieth-century West Africa was the growth of the prophetic churches, a trend which dates, for the most part, from the 1920s onwards. However, the majority of Christians remained attached to the older churches. Statistics are especially unreliable in this area as much depends on how a Christian is defined, but they do suggest relative orders of magnitude. In 1958, in the Aladura heartland of western Nigeria, there were thought to be 370 thousand Anglicans and 280 thousand Catholics. The number of Baptist, Methodist and African Church members was estimated to be 50 to 60 thousand each. Of the prophetic churches, the Christ Apostolic Church had some 83 thousand adherents, and the different branches of the Cherubim and Seraphim a total of 50 thousand.[70] A different source suggests that the Church of the Lord (Aladura) had, at about the same time, some 10 thousand members, less than a third of them in Nigeria.[71] The much disputed census of 1963 put the total population of the area at over 11 million.

In an earlier chapter, we noted that independency flourished in Kenya, but not in Uganda or Tanganyika. The prophetic churches abound in Nigeria and, to a lesser extent, in Ghana, but have never been popular in Sierra Leone. When a Nigerian evangelist from the Church of the Lord came to Freetown, he was ridiculed: 'Adejobi is my shepherd, I shall not want; he makes me to lie down on prayer mats'. It is to Islam that the poor in Freetown turn.[72]

Both the number of prophetic churches and their total membership have expanded since Independence. According to the World Council of Churches, there were 800 independent religious movements in Nigeria in 1971. Hackett suggests that there were 1500 in the mid 1980s.[73] They have had a transforming effect on the religious landscape of West Africa. Far from advocating a conscious syncretism, their founders preached a radical rejection of traditional religion. A young Seraphim in 1931 said, 'that the heathens are only deceiving the people by putting on rags, voicing ho ho ho, and saying there is Egungun inside'.[74] But they accepted the reality of witchcraft, and attracted recruits by the offer of protection from evil and its many manifestations.

William Wade Harris preached to non-Christians, and was, undoubtedly, the most successful evangelist West Africa has ever known. Garrick Sokari Braide and the Aladura prophets, on the other hand, attracted mostly those who were members of mission churches, but whose deepest needs were unsatisfied. The Christ Apostolic Church renounced western medicine, and disassociated itself from white missionaries when they used anti-malarials. In their fervour, their all-night prayer sessions and their fasting, the Aladura evince a radical dependence on God. And yet there is much in their praxis that mirrors the traditional world.

Prayer sometimes becomes a form of technology, like traditional rituals; if the right words are pronounced at the right place and time, very specific consequences will follow:

> If an elder or a superior man is angry with you and wants to do you evil, go to the farm or wayside where you can secludedly pray at 6.30 o'clock a.m. before sunrise. Read Psalm 38 seven times with Psalm 39. Pronounce the following Holy names as you are reading it. . . .[75]

To some extent, this attitude has permeated the mission churches. Nigerian Catholics have recommended to me combinations of efficacious psalms to be recited at specific times, and used in conjunction with green scapulars.

In Nyasaland and the Belgian Congo, prophets often foretold an eschatological reversal of present society. Such voices were not entirely absent in West Africa:

> I have heard Jehovah's Witnesses deliver, by means of loudspeakers in the market-places, terrible prophesies of the impending fall of the white man's Government in a Universal War, and the destruction of all kings, both black and white, and ministers of religion. Rather than risk trouble by censoring these outpourings, the Government follow the line of least resistance by adopting the 'Hyde Park' policy. . . .[76]

However, on the whole, West Africa's prophets showed little interest in a kingdom of this world. Harris was a political prisoner, but lost interest in such matters after his conversion.

Where prophets ran foul of colonial governments, it was not because of their involvement in politics, in which, very often, they had little interest, but because of their popularity, their attacks on witchcraft, and, often, because of their followers' attacks on traditional shrines.

Aladura

Aladura is a Yoruba word, meaning 'owners of prayer'. Long ago, Weber described a basic pattern whereby a sect turns into a denomination. It begins by appealing to the poor and disinherited. Gradually, its members move up the social scale, and it adjusts its behaviour to the norms of the wider society.

The churches that became known as Aladura were founded by members of the élite, not by the very poor. Isaac Akinyele became the traditional ruler of Ibadan and Christianah Olatunrinle was a wealthy woman. Both she and Akinyele were siblings of Anglican bishops. J. B. Sadare was one of the founders of the Ijebu Ode Grammar School, and Captain Abiodun was born into the Lagos middle class.

There was an influx of the poor and uneducated during the Revival of the 1930s, and there was, for a long time, a tendency for the élite to gravitate towards the older churches, regarding the Aladura as unsophisticated. Wole Soyinka's Brother Jero plays depict them as churches of the disinherited: 'Make you no forget those of us who dey struggle daily. Those who be clerk today, make them Chief Clerk tomorrow. . . . Those who dey sweep street today, give them their own big office tomorrow'.[77] Nor did the Aladura resent these stereotypes. In the words of a Cherubim leader in 1974:

> We Aladuras in Nigeria are a peculiar church. We want to remain peculiar. We want to remain indigenous . . . many people who do not understand us ridicule us. They say that we are not sophisticated, that we are not educated. We know these things, but we are happy that we are an indigenous church, practising Christianity in the indigenous way . . . God does hear us in this indigenous way and has been doing marvellous work through our hands. Halleluiah![78]

But the Aladuras pray, not only for prosperity, but for healing and children; sickness and infertility are not peculiar to the poor.

It became common for members of the élite to consult prophets secretly, while remaining members of the more socially acceptable older churches. A Nigerian scholar writes of the 'secret admirers' of prophetic churches, 'such as State governors, university professors and civil servants of varying rank', and of the visits of 'a particular top Nigerian Politician' to the head of the Brotherhood of the Cross and Star.[79] Increasingly, élite West Africans, especially among the Yoruba, have become open adherents of these churches. At one Nigerian university, in the 1980s, both the Deputy Vice-Chancellor and the Director of Works were enthusiastic Aladura converts. The Christ

Apostolic Church, in particular, takes education very seriously, and its members' children grow up taking their church affiliation for granted, regardless of their socio-economic status. John Wesley, in his old age, lamented the same process of upward mobility among Britain's Methodists.

People are drawn to prophetic churches by the desire for mental and physical health, fertility, and prosperity. Their supporters are drawn largely from those who believe such prayers have been answered. A former Baptist schoolteacher told an enquirer how holy water from a Seraphim prophet saved his wife when she was near death in childbirth: 'Just as she finished it, she delivered. I am not leaving this church again'.[80]

The first Aladura churches began as prayer groups within older churches. They were a response to a society in crisis, afflicted by epidemics (influenza, smallpox, and plague), famine and a world depression: 'Scores of people collapsed on the roads; many chose shady trees under which to lie down and die. I visited some houses where every member was lying dead'.[81] In the words of a Seraphim prayer, 'Mighty dangers hang over the world . . . all the people of the world suffer from lack of trade, shortage of money and unemployment. . . . Famine, Epidemic and Death are abundant'.[82]

The Precious Stone Society was founded in 1920 by a group of Ijebu Anglicans, led by a goldsmith, Joseph Sadare and by a schoolteacher, Sophia Odunlami, whose visions played a decisive role in the church's early development. The imagery of the jewel came less from Sadare's avocation than from *Revelations*; it was also a core symbol in a Zionist church in South Africa (see page 316). Their rejection of infant baptism, and of both western and traditional medicine, led to a breach with the CMS in 1922.

An Ijebu clerk, David Odubanjo, founded a branch in Lagos. For a time, they were attached to an American sect, Faith Tabernacle. When this fell into crisis and schism, they formed links with the British Apostolic Church, which lasted from 1931 to 1941. They were to break away from their British mentors largely because of the latter's use of quinine, taking the name, Christ Apostolic Church.

One of the first Ibadan converts was Isaac Akinyele, an educated man, who, untypically for the time in which he lived, became not a teacher or clerk, but a successful cocoa planter. He was to become *Olubadan*, ruler, of Ibadan, his brother, Alexander, was its first Anglican bishop. Countless stories are told of Isaac's kindness and generosity. He put large sums into the church collection, using coins of low denominations to disguise the fact that the money came from one donor, and sent anonymous gifts to other Ibadan churches. It was only after his death in 1964, when funds dried up, that people realized where they came from.[83]

With its emphasis on Bible study, the new Church appealed especially to clerks and young men working away from home. Most of the converts were already Christians, especially Anglicans, and some lost their jobs as a result. By 1930, the Church had perhaps a thousand members.[84]

Its fortunes were transformed by a great revival, led by a road-grader driver, Joseph Babalola, who reluctantly adopted a prophetic role after a series of visions. He led a great revival in Ilesa and Ekiti, destined to be among the most thoroughly Christianized parts of Yorubaland. Thousands of non-Christians joined either the Aladura or the older churches, burning their traditional religious images and charms. Babalola was briefly imprisoned on charges of witch accusation.

The ruler of Efon was baptized as Solomon, and a local forest spirit said that 'her pot of indigo dye had been broken by the new road, and that she was leaving Efon to return no more'.[85] The price of bottles sky-rocketed, so anxious were people to obtain water he had blessed; he made no personal profit from all this.[86] After a time, his prophetic gifts left him, and he died in obscurity in 1959.

Of the major Aladura churches, it is the Christ Apostolic Church which comes closest to the older denominations, and many of its members prefer to be called Pentecostals, rather than Aladura. They eschew many ritual practices common to Aladura churches, and are much less concerned with witchcraft. They differ from the older churches in their insistence on healing by faith alone, and on adult baptism.

In 1925, Moses Orimolade, and Christiana Abiodun Akinsowon, ('Captain Abiodun'), founded the Cherubim and Seraphim society. Orimolade suffered from illness as a child, which left him lame. He embarked on a prophetic career from an early age, coming to Lagos in 1920. Christiana was an Anglican from a prosperous Lagos family. In 1925, during the Corpus Christi procession, she entered a trance from which only Orimolade was able to awaken her. Like the Precious Stone Society, they began as a prayer group within Anglicanism, but had withdrawn from it by 1928. Orimolade, 'challenged witches openly. In previous years we were very afraid of them. There were thousands in Lagos'.[87] Abiodun and others embarked on extended missionary journeys, founding new branches of the young Church.

The Seraphim, as they are usually known, divided into a large number of different branches, a process which began soon after the movement's foundation.[88] Orimolade, while he lived, was the recognized *Baba*, Father, Aladura. When he died in 1933, Abiodun, who had been estranged from him for some time, tried unsuccessfully to assert her own right to lead the movement, citing the precedent of the women prophets in the Bible and of Queen Victoria.[89]

Christianah Olatunrinle ('Mama Ondo'), was a wealthy, influential member of the Cherubim and Seraphim. After her marriage failed, and her only child died young, she poured her affections and energies into the new Church. In 1935, she had a vision that she should be Lady Bishop; another vision modified this to Lady Superintendent.[90] Aladura prophets have sometimes been accused of profiteering, but Olatunrinle, like Akinyele, gave money *to* the Church, rather than deriving an income *from* it. In her old age, she embarked on the long missionary journeys so typical of the Seraphim. Shortly before she died, in 1941, she had a vision of a hen with many chickens; a hawk swooped down, and carried away not the chickens, but the hen.[91]

The Seraphim wear distinctive white robes, which also characterize some other Aladura churches, including the Celestial Church of Christ. Just as Anglicans in western Kenya imitated army uniforms, Aladura copy the white soutane of the priest, the habit of religious orders. Office holders in the Church of the Lord (Aladura) include Reverend Mother General, Reverend Mother Superior and Reverend Mother; the 'Cele' robe is specifically called a soutane.

The Church of the Lord (Aladura) was founded by Josiah Ositelu, another Ijebu. He was Anglican teacher-catechist when, in 1925, he had a vision of an eye, shining like the sun, and 'as big as the head of a cow'. He believed himself to be haunted by witches, but a Christian prophet showed him how to overcome them by prayer and fasting. He had a series of visions; he recorded 10 thousand over nine years and, predictably, was dismissed by the CMS. 'The instruction came that I should never eat pork and other unclean things. . . . I was shown the blunders of other denominations. . . .'[92]

At first he joined what was then the Faith Tabernacle, but founded a separate Church in 1930. Other Aladura prophets felt uneasy about his use of revealed Holy Names and Seals, which may reflect the influence of occult texts, such as *The Sixth and Seventh Books of Moses*.[93]

Ositelu, who kept a journal in a secret, revealed script, married seven wives (the traditional hallmark of a powerful man), and died in 1966. He was succeeded by Adeleki Adejobi, a former teacher, who had studied at a British Bible College. Adejobi attended meetings of the World Council of Churches, and, when he died, was succeeded by the prophet's son, Segun, the head of an Ibadan research institute—an interesting example of the upward social mobility of Aladura churches.[94]

The Aladuras are well aware that strength lies in unity. There is a National Association of Aladura Churches, and forty-nine out of fifty-two Seraphim branches have reunited.[95] They are aware of the need for theological training, too. The Church of the Lord has an Aladura Theological Seminary and a Prophets and Prophetesses Training Institute (the latter's title reflects a conscious concern with gender issues).

The central conviction of the Aladura, which they share with many other prophetic churches elsewhere, is the belief that fervent prayer attains specific goals, such as good health, or children. In some cases, their confidence in prayer is so great that they reject both traditional and western medicine. They believe that God speaks to the faithful in dreams and visions, and that blessings are often won by fasting, and have retained from traditional religion a belief in the reality of witchcraft. They are probably much closer to the world of the New Testament than many middle-class congregations in the western world.

Power, Life and Victory—these concepts are at the very heart of Aladura Christianity. But in the nature of things, even the most devoted prayer and fasting cannot always give victory over temporal evils. When this happens, the Owners of Prayer, like other Christians, grope towards an understanding of suffering and the theology of the cross. Turner quotes a childless Aladura, 'I do everything by God, with no native medicine. . . . I pray, Give me pickin. . . . But God knows his own duty and stops this thing to you'.[96]

Aiyetoro

Wole Soyinka's novel, *Season of Anomy* is set in a village called Aiyero, which practises neo-traditional religion. Aiyero is Aiyetoro, and Ofeyi and Irisyise, Orpheus and Eurydice. But the historic Aiyetoro, founded in 1947, was one of a number of small settlements created in the western Niger Delta by offshoots of the Seraphim.

They left their villages because of conflicts with Oro cult members, from 1942 on, over twin-killing. They originally believed that members of the community would not die—a belief that experience weakened as time went on.

Aiyetoro, despite having what would seem to be an inappropriate ideology to inspire modernization, embarked on an amazing programme of development under a remarkable leader. Sturdy homes were built on stilts above the swamps, supported by boardwalks strong enough to carry a car. They built a fleet of motorized fishing launches and ferries, training technical staff in Lagos and Europe, and founded a technical college. They excavated a stupendous seven-mile canal to link the village with inland waterways. All but the Oba lived in great simplicity, and profits were ploughed back into production. *Aiyetoro* means 'happy city'.

But gradually, things fell apart as members aspired to a share of the wealth their efforts had created. Private property was introduced in 1968, and class distinctions began to evolve. The settlement's prosperity declined, and members began to leave.[97]

The Celestial Church of Christ

Until the 1960s, the Seraphim, Christ Apostolic Church, and the Church of the Lord were by far the largest Aladura churches. Since then, they have been overtaken by a relative newcomer, founded in 1947 by a humble carpenter in Porto Novo. 'Cele' has been called 'easily the most popular, the most attractive and the most influential Aladura church today'.[98]

Its founder, Samuel Oschoffa (1909–1985), began his career as a prophet with visions, 'suddenly a peacock, a snake and another bird appeared to me. . . . I spent three months in the bush without seeing anybody. . . . I constantly heard a voice which said, "Grace to God" '.[99]

The new Church was originally called *Le Christianisme Céleste* in French, the Holy Assembly of Heaven in Gun, and the Holy Assembly of Christ from Heaven in Yoruba. Significantly, the word 'church' came later.

Its following was quite small until, in 1952, Gun fishermen founded a branch in Lagos, near the sea, and it began to attract an urban clientele. From 1962, under the leadership of Alexander Bada, Oschoffa's ultimate successor, it spread rapidly, and by 1975, had 150 branches in Nigeria, as well as a steady influx of new members in Benin, where it began. Like other prophetic movements, it seems to have gone through a process of 'routinization of charisma', and has developed a complicated hierarchy: 'In 1967 . . . the aspect of the church began to change. Civil servants of middle and higher grades rallied round the church and it started to spread within an urban context and develop a more bureaucratic structure'.[100]

Much of Cele's success has been due to the singularly attractive personality of Papa Oschoffa. Shortly before his death after a road accident, he gently consoled his distressed followers: 'Why should people think that Oschoffa cannot die? Jesus Christ died. He was only 33. Why shouldn't I die? I'm 76'.[101]

William Wade Harris

In 1910, a forty-five-year-old Grebo called William Wade Harris had a vision in a Liberian prison, to which he had been consigned for his political activities.[102] As his name suggests, he had spent his life on the edge of the Americo-Liberian sphere of cultural influence. He had been brought up in a Methodist minister's household, and was literate. Like so many 'Kru', he had travelled as a seaman, before working, first as a teacher, and later, as an interpreter. He lost his job because of his political involvement, and earned a prison sentence by hoisting the Union Jack. It was a profoundly ironic choice of symbol, but the Grebo preferred British to Americo-Liberian rule.

His vision led to a quantum leap in his own religious experience, and in that of hundreds of thousands of others. He was to be, without doubt, the most successful missionary who has ever worked in West Africa.

On leaving prison, he made an unsuccessful attempt to preach in Liberia, and then went to the Ivory Coast, which had become a French colony in 1895, and had then endured a long period of violent 'pacification'. After several decades of work in that area, the missions had made only a few hundred converts, although they enjoyed the strong support of the colonial government. Some local people had become Christians, feeling that their conquest proved that the stranger's God was stronger, but they reverted to their original faith when their own lives remained unchanged.

All observers testified to Harris' striking appearance, and personality: 'God made the soul of Harris a soul of fire'. Like so many other African prophets, he adopted an outward change as a symbol of an inner transformation. He wore a white gown with black bands, and carried a Bible, a cross, a gourd rattle, and a bowl for the water of baptism. His wife thought he had gone mad, and died of grief. From time to time, he destroyed the cross, and replaced it, so that people would not worship it. The gourd rattle became of crucial importance to one group of his spiritual descendants, the Church of the Twelve Apostles. They ended an association with the British Apostolic Church when the latter's representatives asked them to use tambourines instead.[103]

Harris baptized between 100 thousand, and 120 thousand in a year, and permanently rewrote the religious geography of the Ivory Coast. In a modern population of some 5 million, there are 100 thousand Harrists, 200 thousand Protestants, 500 thousand Catholics, and a million Muslims.[104] All of the first group, and many of the second and third, are his spiritual descendants. He told people to turn away completely from traditional religion, and burn its icons. He baptized them immediately, tolerated, but did not advocate, plural marriage, and added God's name to traditional songs. Most converts went on to a permanent commitment to Christianity.

Harris travelled with two women associates, one of them an educated widow, called Helen Valentine. He claimed to be the last prophet of God. A penumbra of miracles grew up around him: traditional priests who opposed him died mysteriously, and shrines burst into flames. The legends reflect his charisma and eloquence. He made a brief, but successful, foray into the western Gold Coast, where the Church of the Twelve Disciples, founded by Grace Thannie, still flourishes. She had been the medium of a traditional divinity.

French colonial officials were alarmed, not so much by his message, as by his influence, especially after the commencement of the First World War. At the end of 1914, he was deported, and never allowed to return. A prophet without honour in his own country, he had little success in Liberia, and led a relatively quiet life until his death in 1929. Like the Master he served, he had a brief period of remarkable public ministry, and long, hidden years.

Most of Harris' ministry was to the peoples of the coastal lagoons, but his message spread far inland, to regions where he had never been. Distant villages sent delegates to listen to his teaching, and bring it home. Some of the educated clerks from Sierra Leone and the Gold Coast, often Methodists, became his disciples, and spread his message further.

Harris told his converts to await 'teachers with Bibles'. The Catholic missions (the only ones in Ivory Coast at the time) were overwhelmed with new recruits, but some villages were far from a Catholic mission, and the Catholicism of the day did not focus on the Bible. When Protestant missionaries reached Ivory Coast in 1924, they were astonished at the influx of Harris Christians. The Methodist Church there dates its official beginning, not from 1924, when the first Methodists reached Ivory Coast, but from 1914, when Harris did.

Not all the converts found a spiritual home in the mission churches.[105] Some were alienated by their condemnation of plural marriage, their financial demands, and their western style of worship. Several Harrist churches were founded, and, ultimately, amalgamated. They are strongest among the Ebrié, near Abidjan.

Each church has, as well as ministers, Elders, middle-aged Apostles, and a youthful choir, an approximation of the traditional age grade system. They have added to the customary corpus of Christian teaching prohibitions on sexual intercourse in the open air, taken over from traditional societies, and 'eating human flesh', the reference being to witchcraft. The absence of a communion service is rooted in the same perception.

There are other churches that owe their genesis to Harris, and are marked by a concern with healing, and witchcraft eradication. One of these, the Deima Church, founded by Marie Lalou (d. 1952) grew out of her own religious experiences in dreams. She stood explicitly in the Harris tradition, but had moved towards syncretism. When she died she appointed a woman successor. Lalou believed that European missionaries were powerless over local witches, which Harris had expelled, and which had later returned. She prohibited the Bible, and invented her own songs and rituals, centering on holy water and ashes, effective protections against witchcraft.

Walker suggests that Harris' verbal message was close to that of mission churches, while his behavioural message was closer to tradition. The Harrist Church began as a church of uneducated villagers. When individual members rose in the social scale, they tended to join a mission church. The Church has shown an increasing awareness of the value of western education, and, like the Christ Apostolic Church or the Kimbanguists, has gone through a process of upward social mobility.

Garrick Sokari Braide

Braide's career as a prophet was strikingly like that of Harris. He, too, had a visionary experience, followed by a brief and spectacularly successful period of public ministry, brought to an end by a colonial government. His influence led to the creation of new churches, but he never became their institutional head, just as Harris did not lead the Harrist churches.

Garrick Sokari Braide grew up in Bakana, one of a cluster of Kalabari settlements founded on the northern edge of the Niger Delta in the late nineteenth century.[106] His mother belonged to a Kalabari family, and his father was an Igbo in humble circumstances, perhaps a slave.[107] It has been suggested that prophets were often drawn from those who were marginal in the traditional, as well as the modern, world.[108] Until he was thirty, Braide was a paddler on the great trade canoes, but later he earned a living from fishing, and petty trade.

As we saw earlier, Christianity had been well established in the Niger Delta since the mid-nineteenth century. Braide became a Christian, and was baptized in 1910 in the Niger Delta Pastorate, becoming an active and involved church member. He went through a visionary experience as he knelt at communion in 1912, after which he gradually adopted a prophetic and healing role.

Why was this simple fisherman more successful than the Anglicans who had worked in the Delta for half a century? Ijo speakers may have been alienated by the fact that the church used Igbo as the medium of religous instruction,[109] and that its clergy were Sierra Leonian, or Yoruba, but, essentially, Braide won Christians by appealing to their deepest needs, and, especially, by his success as a healer. Crowds flocked to his services, and converts carried his message far into the Igbo interior, sometimes destroying local shrines, against the wishes of their devotees.

The 'Annual Report for Owerri Province' in 1915 paid considerable attention to Braide:

> His extraordinarily great influence is seen by the fact that his followers, professing Christians and pagans alike, have destroyed their jujus and ancestral shrines, and by the equally important fact that there has been practically no sale of trade spirits locally since he began his crusade. Large numbers of natives who are sick have been brought to him and he is reputed to have had very striking cures. . . .[110]

By 1916, he had reached the pinnacle of his influence, and was known as Elijah II. The Niger Delta Pastorate, under Bishop James Johnson, had, at first, acclaimed his work, but later came to regard it with suspicion and hostility. In 1916, Braide and his followers broke with the church. Braide's popularity aroused anxieties in the colonial administration, especially in time of war. He was arrested by the local colonial administrator, the distinguished scholar, P. Amaury Talbot, largely because some of his followers were plundering traditional shrines. He was imprisoned, and died soon afterwards, in 1918, perhaps a victim of the influenza pandemic.

Some of his supporters founded the Christ Army Church, but many, originally drawn to Christianity through his preaching, joined the older churches. Several African church leaders, such as J. G. Campbell, sought to take over his converts, but with little success: 'Lack of money, dearth of personnel, poor organization and lack of schools forced the Ethiopian churches and the Garrick Braide churches to collapse'.[111] Why these factors were operative here, but not where independency flourished elsewhere, is far from clear. Perhaps it was because in south-east Nigeria, schools were all-important.

Like Harris, Braide made war on traditional religion, and urged the destruction of its shrines and charms, though he supported an indigenized liturgy, and the adaptation of traditional song and dance. He made war on the liquor trade, a major source of revenue for the colonial government, and remained silent on plural marriage, which excluded so many from mission church membership.

The Spirit Movement

The Spirit Movement broke out in 1927, among the Ibibio of south-eastern Nigeria, and was very similar, in many ways, to East Africa's Revival. It began in the Qua Iboe Mission, an interdenominational Faith Mission with its headquarters in Belfast.

Unlike most of the movements studied in this chapter, it began, not with a single charismatic prophet, but with a spontaneous movement among church members—the confession of sins, speaking in tongues, and ecstatic phenomena—but without the healing so characteristic of other independent church movements. The local Qua Iboe missionary saw it as the work of the Holy Spirit, but it came to develop the characteristics of a witch-finding movement: 'groups of women or of younger people roamed the countryside extorting confessions, torturing those who refused, attacking traditional shrines . . . and defying the chiefs and elders'. Some were executed for murder.[112] There were further manifestations of the Spirit Movement, such as the small Oberi Okaime church, which has attracted much interest because of its invention of a script and language, both of which are still in use.

British Apostolic Church members visited south-eastern Nigeria in 1932, when they were joined by some congregations influenced by the Spirit Movement. The Apostolic Church in this area remains affiliated to its British counterpart, not to the Aladura CAC, part of a substantial body of Pentecostal churches that retain their western affiliations.[113] This is also true of the Assemblies of God. They have much in common with the Aladuras, including their acceptance of the reality of witchcraft, and their rejection of traditional religion. It was an Assemblies of God convert from Obudu who said:

> Traditional worshippers are foolish. . . . It is likely that they are heading towards hell. I burnt my own shrines immediately I heard of the new religion.[114]

The Apostolic Church uses drums and clapping, emphasizes visions, and practises faith healing. Both flourish in modern West Africa, where the Apostolic Church has forty-three branches in modern Calabar. The academic neglect of these churches contrasts with the attention paid the Aladura.

There were many similar Pentecostal churches with British or American affiliations elsewhere. The Lighthouse Full Gospel Church was founded in Monrovia in 1936 by a black American woman, Leila January, and continued on by a Kru, Mother Frances Blatch. It attracted many Americo-Liberians, especially women, because of its lively services. In a different way, it has been suggested that they were marginalized, too.[115]

The Catholics reached the Obudu plateau on the Nigerian–Cameroon border in 1921. Catholicism is now the majority religion, and very much the establishment. The Assemblies of God arrived in 1950. They regard themselves as a band of spiritual athletes, and look on Catholics with disapproval:[116]

> I still see baptised Catholics accept the fortune-tellers and some still sacrifice to idols. They drink alcoholic drinks, they confess to their priests and come back to do the same thing again.

Both Catholics and traditionalists tend to marginalize Assemblies of God members: 'We listen to them from our own church and laugh at them'. A dream taught a traditional diviner to see things differently:

> When I saw Jesus in a dream . . . he told me that all these churches are one and the same. He said that it is only those of us here that think the churches are different.

Some scholars describe the rise of fundamentalist, Evangelical, and Pentecostal churches in the 1980s as an innovation. The scale of their impact and their close links to New Right American Evangelicals are, indeed, new, but this tradition is much older in West African Christianity.

Musama Disco Christo

Whereas Harris adopted the life of a wandering evangelist, Joseph Appiah was led in visions to become a king, and found a new city. The Musama Disco Christo Church began as a Methodist prayer group, in the Winneba area of what is now Ghana, becoming an independent Church in 1922. Its founder, Joseph Appiah, adopted the name of Jemisimiham Jehu-Appiah, with the title of *Akaboha*, king. Another visionary in the Church, who was given the heavenly name *Nathalomoa*, Queen Mother, became his wife. Their son, Matapoly, succeeded when the Akaboa died in 1948.

Nathalomoa had much the same spiritual powers as Jemisimiham, she was caught up to heaven repeatedly, and had a special gift for reading the hearts of those she encountered. Her visions contributed greatly to Appiah's success. He renamed her Hannah Barnes, but seven angels told her she was Nathalomoa. It has often been said that the power to name reflects control, and it is a power that she appropriated. When she was still single, angels foretold her marriage to Appiah and the birth of Matapoly.

The Church was 'our humble present—a "Myrrh" from Africa to Christ, which is our divine and precious gift, not caring whether others are offering "Gold" or "Frankincense" '.[117]

Church members carved the Holy City of Mozano out of the bush, later moving to New Mozano. The Prophet and his successor were surrounded with the paraphernalia of Akan kings—linguists, drummers, ceremonial umbrellas, and so on. The Church retained some Methodist elements, such as camp meetings, which were combined with rosaries, an Ark, and burnt offerings.

Each member has a heavenly name, peculiar to the recipient. There is no prohibition of plural marriage, and there is an elaborate structure of office-holders. The Church emphasizes faith healing, and has a 'rich and complicated angelology and demonology'.[118] Church members wear copper crosses and rings as a badge of identity.

Baeta's account, written in the 1950s, well reflects the miraculous patina that surrounds events in this and other prophetic churches. When Matapoly was crowned:

> . . . everyone saw a crystal ball the size of an ordinary football, descending gently from heaven. It lighted on Matapoly's head and broke, wetting him and his clothes completely from head to foot . . . Many people rushed to collect this heavenly water [from the cement floor]. . . . The 'heavenly' water collected by those fortunate ones who managed to get some was used for healing with wonderful effect.[119]

By 1958, the Church claimed 150 branches, and a membership of 18 thousand; Baeta called it the largest and best-organized indigenous church in Ghana. Like other prophetic churches, it rose gradually in the social scale, so that by 1975, 'the high and the low, rich and poor, educated and uneducated . . . head of state and politicians all belong to, or come to the church for assistance.'[120]

'Healing homes'

The larger prophetic churches have spread world-wide, with branches in other West African countries, Britain, and America. A woman Seraphim prophet who lives in Tottenham advertises regularly in *West Africa*. There were many less famous religious leaders, whose influence was ephemeral. One of these caused an exodus from Lagos in 1919, when he foretold a tidal wave.[121] Many have been content to supply the spiritual needs of a single small congregation, often meeting in a house church, called in Nigeria, a 'healing home', a name which reflects the paramount importance of the quest for mental and physical health.

Until the Nigerian Civil War, prophetic churches were of minor importance in eastern Nigeria.[122] There was a tendency to look down on them as superstitious and unsophisticated.[123] All this has changed since 1970. During the war, many turned to prophetic movements for protection, and vowed to remain in them if they survived.[124] In Nigeria, and elsewhere in Africa, the strains caused by increasing unemployment, inflation and other ills have led many to turn to churches that offer concrete and specific protection, and answers to prayer. One possible response to unemployment is to found and lead a church. In a small university town of Nsukka, there were nine independent churches in the 1960s; five new ones were recorded in the 1970s, and no fewer than twenty-two additions in the 1980s.[125]

A survey conducted in Calabar in 1983 showed that there were 248 religious institutions in a city of 200 thousand; half of these were of local origin.[126] It has been said that churches are the main form of local industry in south eastern Nigeria!

The small congregations that cluster round a healer/prophet are often short-lived. Prophetic churches have a tendency to divide, because there is a tension between the prophetic personality of the founder and the organizational structure of the church, which tends to acquire a momentum of its own. Those who fail to obtain the blessing they hope for tend to seek it elsewhere, from other healers.

In West Africa, as elsewhere, women have often played a leading role in major prophetic churches. We have already noted some examples, such as Captain Abiodun, Christianah Olatunrinle, Grace Thannie, Marie Lalou, and Nathalomoa, but there are vast numbers of women healers and prophets, each with a single congregation, who inevitably fall through the cracks of academic analysis. A valuable study by Hackett provides a corrective.[127]

In Calabar, in the early 1980s, 12 per cent of the churches of local origin had been founded by women. They included the Church of Christ the Good Shepherd, established in 1946 by an Efik widow, Mrs Lucy Harrison, a former Catholic. 'Big Mamma Prayer' died in 1981, but a small church survives, with a few hundred members. The much smaller Holy Chapel of Miracles was founded in 1947 by another Catholic Efik, Mrs Theresa Effiong, a former midwife. The Church of God Lamentation of Jehovah was set up in 1976 by Mrs Theresa Inyang, who 'believes firmly that only women can see visions and prophesy clearly'. She has a congregation of fifty, and supports herself by trade. These, and other women church-founders, are brought to their calling by dreams and visions, but are content to minister to a small following.

Purity and gender

Baeta's *Prophetism in Ghana* stressed a variable that, until recently, was almost invisible in other studies of independent churches: the frequency of menstrual and post-partum tabus derived from traditional society and from the Hebrew Bible. They tend to be found together with food prohibitions, partly based on Leviticus. Pork is often forbidden, a practice reinforced by the case of the Gadarene swine. To this are added other prohibitions that differ from one church to the next: one forbids eating shark, because it may have consumed human flesh; another prohibits turkey, thought to resemble a vulture.

Baeta recorded menstrual tabus in Musama Disco Christo.[128] Frank Do, the founder of The Prayer and Healing Group of the Evangelical Presbyterian Church at Etodrome, told him, 'Long ago once my wife cooked for me during her period, and I had dreams of seeing the most revolting abominations and filth, things altogether so repugnant that I was not able to bear the sight of them. I learnt from this experience once for all that a woman in this condition is in fact unclean'.[129]

The details of these rules on purity vary from one prophetic church to the next,[130] and are most severe in the Celestial Church of Christ, where menstruating women cannot attend church or put on the white soutane, symbol of holiness and purity. Sometimes they do not prepare the husband's food. As Crumbley points out, 'Cele' is strongest among the south-west Yoruba, where Gelede (a mask cult to placate the 'Mothers', (witches), flourishes. But Cele women sometimes welcome the respite from church attendance, and, perhaps, from cooking as well!

The Brotherhood of the Cross and Star

The Brotherhood of the Cross and Star was founded by Olumba Olumba Obu, born in 1918 in Biakpan, on the Cross River. It began as a Christian church, and was registered in 1964 with the aim 'To advance Christian religion by spreading the Gospel of our lord Jesus Christ'.[131] It has become a messianic movement, focusing on the salvific figure of Obu himself. The celebrated BCS choirs sing, 'I am safe, safe, surely safe in Obu'. The Brotherhood had 600 thousand members by 1980, and some estimates claim a much higher total today.

Obu was originally a cloth trader, operating a small 'healing home' in Calabar, and he founded the Brotherhood after a vision in 1958. OOO, as he is universally called, claims to be the eighth, and final, One in a series of incarnations of God. His first precursor was Adam, and his seventh, Jesus. The letters OOO are thought to be a protection, and are painted on homes and cars. He lives an ascetic life, sleeping and eating little, and dressing simply. He is credited with miraculous healing and psychic powers.

The Brotherhood runs healing and prayer centres (called bethels), and has won many converts in other West African countries, Britain, and America. It claims to be, not a church, but 'the New Kingdom, the New Age, moving towards an apocalyptic fulfilment in the year 2001'.[132] The first issue of the BCS journal begins:

> Hail, All Bow,
> Behold Olumba Olumba Obu
> King of Kings
> The Conqueror and Vanisher
> Sole Spiritual Head of the universe.[133]

Not suprisingly, it has met with much hostility from both mission and prophetic churches (there was a violent clash with the Apostolic Church in 1977), and has increasingly developed links with other religious bodies, including several Indian gurus, the Rosicrucians, the Unification Church, and a local 'spiritual science' group whose leader claims to have met Obu on his astral travels.

Syncretistic and neo-traditional movements

BCS is only one, though probably the most dynamic and successful, of West Africa's syncretistic movements. Syncretism takes two main forms: movements founded by the educated in the name of cultural patriotism, and the neo-traditional ritual groups, comparable with Mumbo in East Africa, which incorporate Christian elements in an older world view and praxis.

Reformed Ogboni, founded by a Yoruba Archdeacon of Lagos in 1914, is an example of the first phenomenon, an attempt to reshape a traditional cult (in this case, of the sacred Earth) to make it compatible with Christianity. It has become a movement much like Freemasonry. Many Christians have joined it, while others are violently opposed.[134] They are equally divided about Rosicrucianism, Freemasonry, and traditional secret societies.

In 1943, A. F. Beyioku published a book called *Orunmilaism, the Basis of Jesuism*:

> Scrap the imported religions . . . I believe we have had enough of these multifarious imported religions. . . . We shall begin on the hypothesis that the Bible is an Ifa book.[135]

Several small churches were founded on these lines. The National Church of Nigeria was a wing of a political party, the NCNC (National Council of Nigerian Citizens), and Mbonu Ojike one of its chief proponents. It was essentially an expression of cultural patriotism, and of hostility to the ethnocentricity of foreign missionaries, and the power they wielded through the church schools. Parrinder called it 'a Church without a religion'.[136]

Godianism was an attempt to found a modern inter-ethnic religion on the basis of the traditional African Supreme God. Founded by an Igbo, Chief K. O. Onyioha, it incorporated both Aruosa,[137] and the National Church of Nigeria. Although it attracted considerable publicity in the 1970s, its membership has always been small.

Movements like Godianism or the National Church of Nigeria were consciously created by the educated, and were shallow-rooted. They have never attracted the mass followings of the prophetic churches. 'Neo-traditional' cults that incorporate Christian elements tend to be confined to one ethnic group and locality, although they have often demonstrated greater vitality and powers of survival. The Igbe cult in the western Niger Delta incorporates the traditional symbolism of kaolin and a secret language; its cult objects include a Bible. Christian influence is also reflected in regular congregational worship, which was not characteristic of earlier ritual behaviour. Like many other such movements, it is mainly concerned with witchcraft eradication.[138]

The Mbula are a small people in what is now Adamawa State, in north-eastern Nigeria. Kulibwui was a prophet who had a considerable, but short-lived impact among them in the late 1920s and early 1930s.[139] He was an epileptic, skilled in traditional medicine. Like many other prophets, he went through a near-death experience, and believed that he was sent back to earth to teach a new religion. It was a time of epidemics and of cattle disease. He practised healing, divination, and rainmaking; creating a composite of Muslim, Christian, and traditional elements. Friday was kept holy, but beer-drinking was permitted, and prayers were offered in the name of Christ. He composed a prayer in a secret language, drawn from a number of local languages, which his followers memorized.

For a brief period he attracted many followers. However, the Sudan United Mission opened a station among the Mbula in 1929, and Kulibwui lost ground steadily, living on in obscurity until 1968.

Literacy

Ositelu's experiments with a new script, and Appiah's invention of new given names reflect a perception that both language and literacy are a means of social control: 'the holy Book of the white man [was] a means of political and religious domination'.[140]

Christianity was a distinctively literate culture, and this modified perceptions of religion in far-reaching ways. The pamphleteering among twentieth-century Nigerian Christians has been aptly compared with that in seventeenth-century England: 'Print it in books', an illiterate Seraphim prophet was told in a vision, 'effect complete circulation, and I will make you a holy Apostle for the whole world!'[141] Another illiterate Christian gave himself a new name, 'I understand Jesus, but not English'.

The power and fascination of literacy are mirrored in the invention of new scripts. There are a number of instances of this in West Africa, the most famous being that developed by the Vai of Liberia in the mid nineteenth century. Josiah Ositelu, as we have seen, wrote his journal in a 'holy script' that had been revealed to him.[142] The Oberi Okaime Church was founded among the Ibibio of south-east Nigeria in the 1920s, and its members invented a script, language, and numerical system that still survive.[143] Until forbidden by the colonial government, they taught them in their own schools. In 1920, an Asante lay preacher, Sampson Opon, held a Revival that attracted thousands to the Methodist Church, he had 'a wonderful stone' where he could 'read the whole Bible from Genesis to Revelation thanks to the holy Spirit, being by nature an illiterate'.[144] There are parallels to this in the history of European mysticism.

Secret knowledge and the hidden Bible

There is a strand in the West African religious sensibility that has been variously labelled spiritual science, gnosticism, or occultism. This can take many forms, and is reflected in the popularity of literature such as the *Gospel of Thomas*, and of books on the *Kabbala* or magic. Such themes are sometimes pursued as an individual interest by church members unperturbed by 'cognitive dissonance'. The tradition of secret knowledge makes Rosicrucianism attractive; the Ancient and Mystical Order of the Rosae Crucis (AMORC) has been established in Nigeria since 1925. In the Nigerian press, in the mid 1920s, there were regular advertisements for the *Sixth and Seventh Books of Moses* and other occult literature.[145] *The Sixth and Seventh Books of Moses* is a collection of spells, magical seals, and incantations to conjure up spirits. It was banned by colonial governments, apparently because it was thought to cause madness. A young patient at an Asante shrine, in 1956, said, 'I have ordered the *Sixth and Seventh Books of Moses*, because with it you can work wonders and without it you can't go to England'.[146]

It has been denounced by Aladura leaders as magical and pagan, but there is, within some prophetic churches, an enduring attraction towards 'gnosis'.[147] Ositelu's Seals and secret writing seem to be influenced by the *Sixth and Seventh Books of Moses*, and early in his career, Appiah 'was denounced to the circuit superintendent . . . for practising curious magical rites and customs, and indulging in the use of secret medicine and special drugs obtained from India'.[148]

The quest for hidden knowledge and its association with power, are rooted in traditional religion, especially in the cults that lead their initiates ever more deeply into the realm of the secret-sacred. Freemasonry flourishes in many African states. Shanahan described its popularity among Nigerians in government service in 1924: 'It displays an activity unknown ten years ago.'[149] In Gabon, where President Omar Bongo is the grand master of the *Grande Rite Equatorial*, membership is essential for the élite.[150]

A recurrent theme, found in the Pacific as well as in Africa, as we have seen, is the belief that Europeans have kept secret those parts of the Bible that provide the key to their wealth and technology. This belief seemed confirmed by the discovery that the Apocrypha are omitted in Protestant Bibles, and by gnostic texts with titles such as the *Gospel of Thomas*. However obscure they are in the West, they are widely studied in Africa.

Among the many case studies recorded by Field among the Brong of Ghana in the late 1950s, was that of a man who 'told me he was a Christian and gave me some tracts. He was the secretary of a society called The Society of the Secret Power of Jesus, whose aim was to find out the wonder-working secret magics by means of which Jesus wrought miracles'.[151] At Aviara, in the western Niger Delta, there is 'a legend, still extant, of a lost Bible, far fuller and richer in content than the usual version in use, which was

originally given (even miraculously disclosed as a bound volume) to Isoko
Christians, but was then taken away and either lost or destroyed by the
missionaries'.[152]

An Ijebu king joined the Seraphim:

> . . . because, as he pointed out, 'Jesus is quicker'. The king explained that
> he knows 'the secret names of Jesus' and can therefore call him at any time
> and 'Jesus will answer.' He does not have to go through a priest, wait for
> divination or offer a sacrifice. Quicker yes, and less expensive.[153]

New Age spiritualities often absorb insights and rituals from primal, (especially
Native American) religions. There is a unity of spirit between New Age and
African traditional religions that has manifested itself in many ways. Among
the commercial firms of Calabar is Okopedi Enterprises (Mystic Division),
'Merchants, Mystic Adepts and Master Occultists'; it retails Indian amulets
and talismans, books on Kabbalism and astrology, love potions and so on, and
its owner studied 'astro-science' in India.[154] Some West Africans have joined
Eckanckar, Subud, the Aetherius Society, the Superet Light Mission, or the
Grail Mission;[155] all these exotica are also found in New Zealand. Bahai and
the Unification Church also maintain a presence in West Africa, but have had
little success.

Miniatures

At a high level of generality, traditional religion recedes, and Christianity
advances. However, many of the inner realities of an older religion are still
found in the hearts of Christians, including the belief in witchcraft. In the
Yoruba town of Okuku in the late 1970s, 10 per cent practised traditional
religion, over half were Christians, and the rest were Muslims. The traditional
cults were so short of members, that a devotee who died was sometimes
replaced with a baby.[156] In the riverain Igbo town of Asaba, virtually everyone
is now a Christian. There are two main categories of titled men, *alo* and *eze*;
Christians take the alo title, and celebrate traditional burials without a qualm,
but do not take the eze title, which is surrounded by ritual restrictions. In
1879, there were 500 ezes in Asaba; by 1985, there were about four in each of
the five quarters. All were old, and the title had not been conferred for five
years.

The greatest divinity was the river goddess, Onishe. Her priests were
ecstatic figures, given to trance and prophecy. Although the last priest of
Onishe died in the 1950s, Asaba people still speak of Onishe as a reality. It is
said that she appeared during the Nigerian civil war, uttering the words, 'You
have killed all my children'. The fear of witchcraft and poison are deeply
ingrained, especially, perhaps, among the successful.[157]

In Calabar, as in Asaba, very few would define themselves as traditionalists
and there are now few cult specialists, or shrines, but drownings are readily

attributed to water spirits, who are then placated with offerings, and even the Nigerian Port Authority performed sacrifices to the water goddess, Anansa, when accidents occurred during port construction in the late 1970s. Another divinity is thought to have delayed Nigerian troops' occupation of the city during the civil war. Some Christians oppose the secret society, Ekpe, while others regard it as a club for gentlemen.[158]

The continuing vitality of witchcraft beliefs was shown in 1978–9, when a young man led a large-scale anti-witchcraft movement among the Ibibio in which some were seriously injured, and others lost their lives. When he was arrested, twenty lawyers offered to defend him free of charge.[159]

In Akuropon, in southern Ghana, in the late 1970s, three-quarters of the population were baptized Presbyterians, and there was an increasing proliferation of independent churches. Two kings had abdicated on their conversion to Christianity, and, although the current incumbent had been educated at a Presbyterian Training College, he still performed the rituals that went with his position. Christians often went to traditional shrines surreptitiously, to be cleansed after a death in the family: 'There are in Akuropon many highly devout members of each faith who would never have anything to do with others; but many, perhaps most, people prefer to go from one to another practitioner seeking cures for their afflictions'.[160]

Cultural revival presents a problem, because so much of traditional culture is linked with religion. Masquerades often are performed at Christmas, with many Christians having no more difficulty with this than modern Catholics have with fireworks on Guy Fawkes day, but others are opposed to it.

These ambiguities are reflected in the 'true fictions' of literature. Gabriel Okara's poem, *One Night at Victoria Beach*, juxtaposes the traditional *babalawo*, ('father of secrets' that is, diviner) the exuberance of the Aladura, and the writer's own loss of faith:

> They pray, the Aladuras pray
> to what only hearts can see . . .
> And standing dead on dead sands,
> I felt my knees touch living sands—
> but the rushing wind killed the budding words.[161]

'Cultures do not hold still for their portraits. Attempts to make them do so always involved simplification and exclusion.'[162]

In the Yoruba town of Ikirun, in the 1930s, a British official encountered a procession:

> I asked what the procession represented. 'We are members of the "African Church"' replied the young man. . . . Before we parted I asked of the leader: 'Why are you members of the "African Church?"', thinking he might air his views on the marriage question. But his reply was simple and brief. 'Because we are Africans', he said.[163]

Christianity and a new élite

As education led to relative prosperity, Christians achieved élite status, if not for themselves, for their children. Nowhere was this more apparent than in Liberia, where Christianity, the True Whig Party, and Freemasonry were the three pillars of Americo-Liberian hegemony. In the government that was overthrown in 1980, President William Tolbert was Chairman of the Baptist Convention, and Vice-President Bennie Warner was a Methodist Bishop. Reginald Townsend, the Chairman of the True Whig Party, was both Moderator of the Presbyterian Church and Masonic Grand Master.[164]

In Liberia, the élite tended to be Episcopalians. Poorer Christians frequented one of the Pentecostal-type churches that grew up from the 1930s on. In these churches, dreams often focused on the suffering in store for the rich and powerful:

> There I saw a man with a light skin inside the coffin groaning very uneasy—I asked, 'What has this man done so much on earth?' He answered, 'I ate one poor boy's money the other day. . . .'[165]

The association of Christianity with an economic and political élite was not peculiar to Liberia. In a book published in 1944, the pioneer Nigerian nationalist, Nwafor Orizu, complained:

> The educated class became a privileged class. . . . This educated class now exploits the masses. It has no use for the poor and underprivileged millions of the country. All that its members care about is to have a beautiful mansion and many servants. . . .[166]

Influenced by the example of South India, Nigeria's Methodists, Presbyterians, and Anglicans moved towards church unity in the 1960s. A date was actually set for the celebrations when a group of Methodists, led by Bolaji Idowu, Professor of Religious Studies at Ibadan, withdrew, and the project foundered.[167] It was not easy to move towards unity when Nigeria seemed to be breaking apart. Ironically, in 1975, Nigeria's Methodists adopted bishops and archbishops, Idowu becoming Life Patriarch.

ELEVEN

South Africa and Its Neighbours since 1900

> . . . South Africa is at the same time among the most 'Christian' and the most oppressive countries in the world.
>
> Charles Villa-Vicencio[1]

South Africa

PRELUDE: DIVERSE PERSPECTIVES

South Africa is a nation of black Christians. According to the 1980 census, 77 per cent of South Africans belonged to a church, and 88 per cent of these were black.[2] The South African experience is of particular interest to the historian of Christianity, for public debate has been couched, to a remarkable extent, in Christian terms. South Africa, moreover, is the only place on the African continent where Liberation Theology—called Contextual Theology locally—has had a major impact. This, of course, reflects the uniquely oppressive situation in which the black majority has found itself.

It has become fashionable, among radicals, to analyse South African society in terms of class rather than race. The two variables are, in fact, inseparable. One cannot write intelligibly about South Africa without using the language of race, 'Coloured', 'Afrikaner', 'Black', but to use these labels, as if they had a self-evident meaning, is itself a victory for racism. Inter-ethnic unions were common until the late eighteenth century, and many Afrikaners are of partly 'non-white' descent. More fundamentally, it has been shown that 84 per cent of all genetic difference is *within* ethnic groups, and only 10 per cent *between* them.[3]

Christians responded to the injustice and oppression of South African society in a number of different ways. Outstanding black Christians, such as chief Albert Luthuli, continued to believe in Improvement and education as the way to attain it. Late in life, he remembered that when he was a young teacher:

299

. . . the world seemed to be opening out for Africans. It seemed mainly a matter of proving our ability and worth as citizens, and that did not seem impossible. We were, of course, aware of the existence of colour prejudice, but we did not dream that it would endure and intensify as it has. There seemed point, in my youth, in striving after the values of the Western world.[4]

A second strand has been called 'Civil Religion'. Afrikaner identity was defined largely in Christian terms, successive governments using the rhetoric of religion in many contexts, including the justification of apartheid.

Many, both in South Africa and elsewhere, opposed the injustices of apartheid and of white dominance. Trevor Huddleston's ministry in Sophiatown, and Michael Scott's long fight at the United Nations for the cause of Namibia are especially famous instances, but there are many others. Until recently, there was a tendency among English-speaking Christians to linger on their achievements, and cast responsibility for South Africa's problems on the Afrikaners. Recent scholarship has pointed to the limitations of the English-speaking church tradition, a theme to which we shall return. There was a

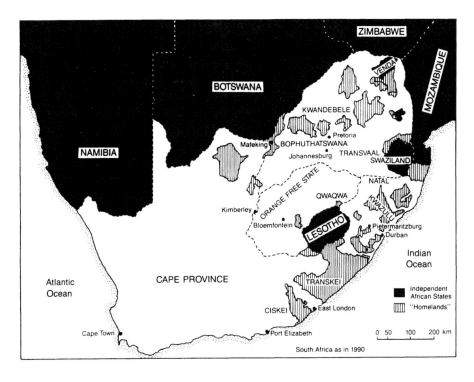

Map 13. South Africa in 1990

300

profound radicalization of black thought from the mid 1970s on, reflecting both an increase in government oppression, and the influence of Black Theology, Liberation Theology, and Steve Biko's Black Consciousness movement. Increasingly, African Christians, such as Desmond Tutu or Alan Boesak, spoke with their own voice, in words that won international attention.

Millions of South African Christians have joined the Zionist churches. Like their counterparts elsewhere, they offer an alternative community, and individual healing. They enrich the lives of many, with their hymns and liturgies, but they could not heal the sickness of a society at war with itself, and many Africans, especially the young, have condemned their political quietism.

THE HISTORICAL CONTEXT

Two former colonies, Cape Colony and Natal, and the two former Afrikaner republics formed the Union of South Africa in 1910. Each of them had a distinctive history that was to do much to shape the future. South Africa's gold and diamonds remained of crucial importance to international capitalism, and the mines continued to exact their human sacrifices, the victims of accidents and of silicosis, pneumonia, and other diseases. In seTswana, the words for money and blood are the same.

Although the war of 1899–1902 ended the independence of the Afrikaner Republics, white hegemony remained, and would intensify. The Cape Colony had, until 1936, a colour-blind franchise, but property qualifications and other factors restricted the number of black voters, and no African was ever elected to Parliament. The 1910 Act of Union confirmed the whites-only franchise of Natal, Transvaal, and Orange Free State, and excluded Africans from standing for Parliament. To educated Africans, this was a betrayal. A delegation went to England to protest, but in vain.

The Afrikaners saw the South African War as an unequal struggle with the forces of imperialism and capitalism. The experience of the war, and especially the memory of those who died in British concentration camps became, like the Great Trek and the battle of Blood River, part of a mythology that fostered the Afrikaner sense of separate identity. It was after the war that Afrikaans was recognized as a language in its own right, and the vehicle of important literature, rather than as a local dialect of Dutch.

In the years that followed, the white minority used its political hegemony to strengthen its economic privileges. A series of laws formalized the white monopoly of skilled work in the mines, with black miners earning less than a tenth of the pay of the whites. The Natives Land Act of 1913 limited the black 70 per cent of the population to 7 per cent (later 13 per cent) of the land. Women, children, and the old struggled to wrest a living from overcrowded and eroded Reserves, while African men went as labour migrants to the mines and cities. Because they could not take their families with them, prostitution and venereal disease spread.

The education of a black child cost one tenth or less of that of a white child.

In the 1930s, half of all African children did not go to school at all, and only 0.6 per cent of those that did went beyond Standard Six. Virtually all African schools were run by missions.

Many Africans lived in appalling conditions in the shanty towns that grew up around the cities. For all their poverty, these 'black spots' in white South Africa developed a vibrant community life of their own: 'Look your last on all things lovely' said Trevor Huddleston, leaving Sophiatown.

The longing for an earthly Zion springs partly from the hunger for land. The Bulhoek massacre of 1921, when 117 of Enoch Mgijima's Israelites were shot, reflects this; they were anxious to settle on their chosen Holy Place, and would not move. Rigid restrictions on freedom of movement were embodied in Pass laws, and urban blacks without a white employer could be deported to a distant Reserve. In 1936, the black voters of Cape Province were disenfranchized.

APARTHEID 1948–1990

Although much was done before 1948 to entrench the privileges of the white minority, the process was expanded and systematized after 1948. In that year, the National Party came to power, committed to a system of apartheid, separateness, an essay in social engineering without precedent in its scale and thoroughness.

Inter-racial marriage, and even sexual relations, became criminal offences, driving some to exile, and others to suicide. The Population Registration Act of 1950 authorized officials to categorize people by their 'race'. The population was divided into white and non-white; the non-whites into Coloured, Indian, and Bantu; Bantu and Coloured into still further subgroups. This policy of 'divide and rule', and the ethnic consciousness it engendered was one of the long-term causes of the black on black violence that was to tear South Africa apart.

The Coloured community had no 'Homeland', and, in religion, language and culture was indistinguishable from the whites. The erratic (because meaningless) line of demarcation between 'light' Coloured and 'dark' whites divided families. It became a catastrophe for 'white' parents to have a dark-skinned child. The Group Areas Act of 1950 determined where each 'race' should live. The Coloured community were deported *en masse* from District Six, their historic home in the Centre of Cape Town. Its churches were left empty, their people expelled to an area without churches. The late Richard Rive's *District Six* is its memorial.[5]

Older pass laws were systematized, the aim being that only those Africans employed by whites should live in towns, while the rest lived as virtual prisoners on the Reserves. Between 1962 and 1985, 3.5 million people were forcibly relocated. The Bantu Education Act removed education from missionary control, and organized it in a way designed to keep the black population in perpetual servitude. The Suppression of Communism Act of

1950 enabled the government to crush political dissent, whether Communist or not. Apartheid created elaborate separateness in every area of life, and was sustained, like Stalin's Russia, by inflated armed forces and vast numbers of bureaucrats. The Coloured poet, Arthur Nortje, studied at Oxford, where he killed himself in 1970, rather than return to South Africa. Many, both black and white, chose political exile. Thousands were imprisoned or kept under house arrest or were tortured or died mysteriously in prison.

To radical Christians of the 1980s, apartheid was demonic. But although its effects were destructive, it was justified in biblical terms, and its architects, at least in theory, did not set out to oppress, but to maintain the uniqueness of peoples, giving to each group the right to determine its destiny in its own separate sphere. The fatal flaw was that resources and freedoms were not equally shared. In the words of one of an increasing number of creative writers in both Afrikaans and English, who eloquently denounced the world in which they found themselves:

> We have proclaimed ourselves the heirs
> To all the richest and most pleasant places
> In this productive land . . .[6]

The system that finally resulted has been called 'internal colonialism'. The Reserves became Homelands, small Third World countries, where 80 per cent of the people lived on 13 per cent of the land.

Beginning with the Transvaal in 1976, ten Bantustans were created. Their sovereignty was fictitious, and, because their passports were useless internationally, their peoples were, in effect, stateless. They served as pools of cheap labour for the First World country, white South Africa.

In 1976, it was estimated that there were 18 629 000 blacks, 746 000 Asians, 2 434 000 Coloured, and 4 320 000 Europeans in South Africa.[7] No white could forget the vulnerability these figures implied. An artificially high standard of living was no compensation, and the incidence of suicide and of mental breakdown was among the highest in the world.[8] A number of Christian leaders, such as the Lutheran, Manas Buthelezi, pointed out that a just society would liberate whites as well as blacks—the poor from oppression and the prosperous from fear.

AFRICANS IN MAINSTREAM CHURCHES

We have repeatedly noted in this study, the strength and autonomy of women's church organizations. In South Africa, *Manyano* enrich the difficult lives of African women in the big cities, often working as domestic servants.[9] Like the Zionists, they rejoice in elaborate uniforms, and structures of authority. They are organizations of church women in good standing, and are dominated by the middle-aged. They prohibit both alcohol and plural marriage, and bear a disproportionate share of the Church's financial burdens, sometimes paying the clergyman's salary.

Their corporate strength is often perceived as a threat, Brandel-Syrier discerned 'a tone of profound antagonism and wrath' in their relations with African clergy. In 1922, in a district that lay between Orange Free State and Basutoland, a Methodist teacher reported that 'some women of our church, including women of our women's association . . . went to Makobeni's homestead and held a prayer meeting'. They opposed land registration, which favoured male applicants, and 'even challenged the men to take off their pairs of trousers and wear frocks as the men were such cowards and were afraid of another man (meaning the magistrate)'.[10]

In an earlier chapter, we considered the African Improvers, some of whom founded Ethiopian churches. What is remarkable is that their dream endured so long. Men such as Chief Albert Luthuli, Professor Z. K. Matthew, and the physician A. B. Xuma were its heirs. Christians, they clung for decades to a dream of a multiracial democracy, and a just society, to be attained by non-violent means.

Charlotte Maxexe was a bridge between the earlier Improvers, and those who came later. As we have seen, she studied in America and played a decisive role in the introduction of the AME Church to South Africa. She was the leading woman member of the South African Native Congress, and founder of its Women's League, that by passive resistance ended women's Pass laws in 1920.[11] In 1958, they were reintroduced, and a later generation of women fought the same battle.[12]

Xuma, President of the ANC from 1940–9, said 'the liberation movement is not anti-white in seeking full scope for African progress'; it was 'working for the good of all South Africans, working to promote the ideals of Christianity, human decency and democracy'.[13] Luthuli, like Tutu after him, won the Nobel Peace Prize. He stood trial for treason, and was deposed from his position as chief of the small town of Groutsville. Later, he was imprisoned for a time, and then confined to his home. He said, 'I do not remember my cell as a place of boredom. It became, in fact, a place of sanctuary, a place where I could make up for the neglect of religious meditation occasioned by the hurly-burly of public life'.[14]

Both White Liberals and Black Improvers were often unconsciously élitist, writing as if a voice in the political process was a reward to be earned by the educated. Because the Improvers saw education as the path to equality, they were especially strongly opposed to the Bantu Education Act. Matthews resigned his position at Fort Hare in protest against the Separate Universities Act; he was two years from retirement, and sacrificed his pension.[15]

When Luthuli died in 1967, Dennis Brutus paid him tribute, from his own political exile:

> . . . he who sustained a faith in grace
> believing men crippled could still walk tall
> in the thorn-thickets of corrupting power . . .[16]

Many of the poor left the mainstream churches to follow one of the Zionist prophets. Over the last twenty years, many, especially among the urban young, have abandoned Christianity altogether, but millions of black Christians have remained in the older churches, despite the alienation and marginalization they have often experienced there. Boesak pointed out the gulf between Calvin's teaching, and Dutch Reformed Church praxis, citing an article in the Church Order of the (Coloured) *Sendung-Kerk*, which lists among the purposes of the Church 'to foster submissiveness to the government and the Law'. He described a situation where:

> Reformed tradition in time became a curious mixture of 'safe' reformed truths and a strange, pietistic, other-worldly religiosity. . . . It was like going to a doctor for a pain-remover for the wounds inflicted during the week.[17]

In 1970, the total membership of all South Africa's independent black churches was 3.5 million. In the same year, there were 1.5 million black Methodists, 1 million 330 thousand black Catholics, 940 thousand black Anglicans and 900 thousand members of the African branch of the Dutch Reformed Church.[18]

THE AFRIKANERS AND CIVIC RELIGION

The insistence of the Afrikaners on their unique identity and destiny was, in part, a reflection of their own marginality. They had been defeated in the South African war, and were outnumbered by English settlers. Their language and culture were often despised, and few were university graduates, professionals, or major figures in business. At the beginning of this century, they were overwhelmingly farmers, hence 'Boer'. By the 1930s, an increasing population, and other factors, were forcing many off the land. Some became landless rural dwellers, *Bywoners*, while others searched for employment in the towns and minefields. It was the poor Afrikaners who saw blacks as an economic threat and as potential competitors.

The Broederbond was founded in 1918, to help Afrikaners newly arrived in the cities. It was a secret society, like Freemasonry, with its own rituals, its membership limited to white Afrikaner males who were members of the Dutch Reformed Church. It came to be an élite organization of politically minded intellectuals. Its members, among them D. F. Malan, a Dutch Reformed Church minister who became Prime Minister in 1948, were the creators of apartheid. He said:

> Our history is the greatest masterpiece of the centuries. We hold this nationhood as our due for it was given to us by the Architect of the universe . . . the history of the Afrikaner reveals a will and a determination which makes one feel that Afrikanerdom is not the work of men but the creation of God.[19]

But when he became Prime Minister, Malan was already old. The architect of apartheid was, above all, H. F. Verwoerd, who became Minister for Native Affairs in 1950 and Premier in 1958. In 1965, he was assassinated by a Parliamentary messenger who had been employed as white; another of the terrible ironies of South African history.

It has been said the Dutch Reformed Church was the National Party at prayer. The two were never coterminous, though many Dutch Reformed Church theologians wrote in apartheid's defence. Apartheid has been called a heresy by its opponents, but it is perhaps more meaningful to call what developed in South Africa a form of civil religion.[20]

Apartheid was justified by citing Biblical texts that speak of the boundaries of peoples.[21] 'Afrikaner politics was slowly but fatally being theologized . . . the National Party was itself becoming, if not a church, then a party imbued with religion—a secular religion—at its very roots.'[22] The preamble of the 1983 Constitution ran:

> In humble submission to Almighty God, who controls the destinies of nations and the history of peoples; who gathered our forebears together from many nations . . . who has guided them from generation to generation.[23]

The authors of the *Kairos Document* commented, 'This God is an idol. It is as mischievous, sinister and evil as any of the idols that the prophets of Israel had to contend with. . . . It is the god of the casspirs and hippos, the god of tear gas, rubber bullets, sjamboks, prison cells and death sentences'.[24]

Afrikaners deeply resented criticism from the outside world and from English-speaking churchmen in South Africa. The attacks of secular radicals, especially Communists, were easily disregarded, but condemnation from a Christian viewpoint was deeply felt. They resented the fact that their critics seldom learned Afrikaans, and were often English nationals, free to leave South Africa. In the end, many of them did leave, or were deported. For the Afrikaners, there was nowhere else to go.

Not all Afrikaners and not all Dutch Reformed churchmen supported apartheid. The late Professor B. B. Keet, a little-known figure, was one of those who spoke against it, describing the actual relationship between white and black Christians as 'Brothers in Christ, Limited'. He said, 'The more one examines the case for complete, permanent apartheid the less can one avoid the conclusion that its supporters are labouring under a delusion that belongs to a world of make-believe'.[25]

The Sharpeville massacre took place in March, 1960. Police fired on a crowd, mainly women, protesting against the Pass laws: 69 were killed and 186 wounded. Thousands were arrested, and both the ANC and Pan-Africanist Congress outlawed. International opinion was outraged, and the ANC decided, reluctantly, to embark on an armed struggle. An Afrikaans poet whose life ended in suicide wrote of a murdered Sharpeville child:

The child has become a man and travels through all Africa
The child has become a giant and travels through all the world
Without a pass.[26]

In 1961, representatives of the World Council of Churches met their eight
South African member churches, including the Dutch Reformed Church, at
Cottesloe. They issued a declaration that defended mixed marriages, attacked
the evils of labour migration, and said:

> We recognise that all racial groups who permanently inhabit our country
> are a part of our total population, and we regard them as indigenous.
> Members of all these groups have an equal right to make their contribution
> towards the enrichment of the life of their country and to share in the
> ensuing responsibilities, rewards and privileges. . . . No one who believes in
> Jesus Christ may be excluded from any church on the grounds of his colour
> or race.[27]

It was a unique moment of rapprochement. The Dutch Reformed Church
delegates, though not the Hervormde Kerk, agreed to sign, but Verwoerd
denounced it and the Dutch Reformed Church Synods not only refused to
ratify it, but withdrew from the World Council of Churches. The moment
passed.

Dr Beyers Naudé was acting Moderator of the Transvaal Dutch Reformed
Church. He resigned both as Moderator and Minister, left the Broederbond,
and became Director of a new Christian Institute, which played a crucial role
both in the radicalization of theology and in the development of links between
the older churches and the Zionists. It was declared illegal in 1977, and Naudé
endured both imprisonment and a banning order that lasted for seven years.[28]
Later, he became a minister of the (black) Kerk van Afrika.

In 1978, the white Dutch Reformed Church rejected an invitation from its
black, Coloured, and Indian daughter churches to form a single, united
denomination. In 1982, the World Alliance of Reformed Churches declared
apartheid a heresy, and excluded the white, but not the black and Coloured
Dutch Reformed Churches in South Africa, electing Alan Boesak leader of the
Sendung-Kerk as its President.

LIBERALISM IN THE ENGLISH-SPEAKING CHURCHES
In South Africa, liberalism is an ambiguous word. It is denounced both by
Afrikaners, who equate it with unbelief, and by modern neo-Marxists, who
tend to identify it with capitalism and free enterprise. Radical analysis
concentrates on capitalism and the class struggle, from which, indeed,
questions of race cannot be separated. In radical circles, 'liberal' is a term of
opprobrium. It has, however, in South Africa, and, indeed, elsewhere, a
history that is often inconsistent, sometimes muted, frequently anguished,
and, occasionally, heroic.

As a recent study by James Cochrane points out, the churches were often unconscious servants of the status quo. The *Methodist Churchman* said in 1914, 'The Native is, we firmly believe, one of the best assets this country possesses. We need him to assist us to develop its vast resources, and he will help us, if we allow him, to make it *a country in which an ever-increasing number of Europeans will live in comfort*'[29] Sometimes, church leaders denounced various forms of oppression, while maintaining a high degree of inequality within their own organization. There was only one black Anglican canon in 1934, and no black Anglican bishop until 1960, when Alpheus Zulu became a Suffragan (that is, assistant) Bishop. African clerical salaries were a third or less those of their white counterparts. Some were embittered by this, to an extent that destroyed their sense of calling and their joy in it.[30] The Catholic Bishops' Statement on Apartheid (1957) said it 'was a blasphemy to attribute to God the sins against charity and justice which are the necessary accompaniment of apartheid'.[31] However, Catholic seminaries were not integrated until 1979.

When a prophetic voice was heard, it came often from celibate Anglo-Catholics. There was a sense in which they were accustomed to marginality. Geoffrey Clayton came to the see of Johannesburg from Rugby and Cambridge, and an Archdeaconry in Chesterfield. He was Archbishop of Cape Town from 1948 until his death in 1957. Although he was authoritarian, and something of a *bon viveur*, in 1941 he set up a Commission that presented its report two years later, and recommended the extension of the (limited) Cape franchise to all men and women in South Africa, and 'a gradual removal of the colour-bar'. For many white South Africans, the Report was too radical. For others, it was not radical enough—why should the removal of the colour-bar be gradual?

For Alan Paton, service on the Commission changed his life. Like many others after him, his consciousness was raised to injustices he had been brought up to take for granted.

> To yield the idea of a continuing white supremacy was in those days an intensely difficult thing for a white South African to do. . . . One loved what was right and good and just, but one did not yet understand that these things could not be had except at the cost of a change in one's whole life and situation . . . being a member of the Bishop's Commission was one of the seminal events of my life, after which I was never the same again.[32]

In 1957, when Clayton was seventy-two, the government introduced the Native Laws Amendment Bill, which made it possible to exclude Africans from white churches. Six churches protested, and Clayton believed that his own opposition to it would land him in prison, but, the next day, on an Ash Wednesday, he died.[33]

Trevor Huddleston became internationally famous for his work in the slums of Sophiatown, but the mission was pioneered by Dorothy Maud. The daughter of the Bishop of Kensington, she lived in Sophiatown from 1928 until 1943 in a house called *Ekutuleni*, 'the place of peace'. She and three women associates ran a host of activities for children, including boxing: 'Everyone who knew Ekutuleni at this time speaks of the gaiety and energy of it'.[34] She returned to England in the end, with the hope of becoming a nun. The Community of the Resurrection, who had previously run a public school for white boys, reconsidered their calling, and followed her to Sophiatown. Father Raymond Raynes built a church and swimming pool, with funds from a retired baker called Mr Smith, who died in 1947, and who was 'a perpetual fairy godfather'. Raynes left South Africa in 1942 to become the congregation's Superior-General.

Trevor Huddleston spent twelve years in Sophiatown, and was recalled to England in 1955 to become Novice Guardian. His *Naught for Your Comfort* shook hearts around the world.

Michael Scott was another Anglican priest who, despite wretched health, was so active in opposing apartheid that he was imprisoned, and then deported in 1950. The people of Namibia, not free to travel themselves, then deputed him to represent them at the United Nations. He did so, to good effect, for years.[35]

The central weakness of Christian concern in these years was that Africans were its objects, not participants. Its heroes are Europeans, with a concern for 'Race Relations'. There was, both then and later, a gulf between the attitudes of, for instance, Anglo-Catholic priests whose life's work lay in African, or English slums, and a laity who enjoyed the material benefits of internal colonialism, and who shared many white supremacist attitudes. The English community as a whole was far from Liberal; Helen Suzman's years as a solitary Liberal member of Parliament reflect this, and it was not unknown for cynics to suggest that English-speakers 'speak with a Progressive tongue, vote with the United Party and thank God for the Nationalists'.[36] Some of the most dedicated white opponents of racism were not Christians at all.

The Christian Liberal critique of racial injustice had a distinguished ancestry, going back to Philip, but, except at the local level, it had little impact on events: 'The charge that liberalism has achieved little in South Africa is, broadly speaking, well founded. . . .'[37] A Presbyterian minister told his General Assembly in 1963, that its recommendations and statements on political events 'have had less effect than the rattling of tin cans tied to a cat's tail'.[38]

RADICALIZATION AND DIVISION

When Trevor Huddleston left Sophiatown in 1955, there were headlines in the African press, 'Do not leave us, Father Huddleston'.[39] A few years later, Steve Biko was speaking with a very different voice, 'They [white Liberals] vacillate between the two worlds, verbalising all the complaints of the blacks beautifully while skilfully extracting what suits them from the exclusive pool of white privileges'.[40] The charge reflected an intense radicalization, which was to affect religious sensibility in many ways.

Black Consciousness, founded by Biko, was a movement of the young and urbanized who sought, with partial success, to submerge the divisions of African, Coloured, and Indian in a common Black consciousness. South Africa's neighbours won their independence—Angola and Mozambique in 1975, Zimbabwe in 1980—and South African blacks were empowered by the realization that their own hopes were not impossible to attain.

The South African government responded with repression. In 1976, hundreds of schoolchildren were killed and hundreds more imprisoned, after riots that began as a protest against the use of Afrikaans in education. Suddenly, Soweto became a familiar name to millions internationally who could not have located it on a map, and thought it was an African word.[41] In 1977, the year of Biko's violent death, many anti-apartheid organizations were banned, among them the Christian Institute and the South African Students Organisation.

Increasingly, African Christians spoke for themselves, among them the Coloured Reformed Churchman, Allan Boesak, Manas Buthelezi, who became a Lutheran bishop, and Desmond Tutu, who won the Nobel Peace prize, and became Archbishop of Cape Town. They were critical of an 'African theology', propounded elsewhere in Africa, that was more concerned with the vindication of traditional religions than with contemporary social and political realities.[42] To those born in the cities, rural eco-religions were of marginal relevance, anyway.

Not all the advocates of contextual theology, as it was called, were black; they included the white South African Dominican, Albert Nolan, and the Afrikaner Reformed Churchman, Beyers Naudé.

South Africa's increasing international isolation, and the threat of economic sanctions led both to increased government brutality and to what was at first largely cosmetic change. There was a growing awareness that it was physically impossible to relocate the black population on the scale planned by apartheid's architects, or to contain the growing volume of black urban opposition. The 'petty' apartheid that imposed segregation on beaches and in restaurants, sport and public transport was given up, without major structural changes. A more important move legalized African trade unions. The Constitution of 1983 introduced a tri-cameral legislature, but no black suffrage. It was largely boycotted by the Indians and Coloured people entitled to vote under it.

The Government came increasingly to realize that it needed black allies. These were the nascent bourgeoisie who were willing to collaborate on township councils, or in the government of the Bantustans. Some of the black unemployed were taken on as temporary police, or *kitskonstabels*. The bitter resentment all this engendered, however, led to an increase of black on black violence. Those perceived (sometimes wrongly) as collaborators sometimes met a cruel death. The openly ethnic Inkatha, a Zulu party led by Chief

Buthelezi, the Chief Minister of the KwaZulu Homeland, introduced an overt ethnic dimension into black politics. Bitter clashes between Inkatha and the ANC, perceived as Xhosa-dominated, became commonplace. Government repression of dissidents continued: between 1985 and 1989, at least 50 thousand were detained without trial and over 5 thousand killed.[43]

> All one attempts is talk in the absence
> of others who spoke and vanished
> without so much as an echo.
> I have seen men with haunted voices
> turned into ghosts by a piece of white paper
> as if their eloquence had been black magic.[44]

In 1985, 150 signatories produced the *Kairos Document*. It stands in the tradition of Liberation Theology, which developed in South America in the 1960s as a response to a situation in which Christianity was traditionally allied with the rich and powerful, and the poor and idealistic were drawn to Marxism. It emphasizes the 'preferential option for the poor', and those biblical passages that proclaim social justice, and denounce oppression, such as the book of Amos and the Magnificat.

The *Kairos Document* distinguishes three theological strands, which it calls State, Church, and Prophetic. It is most assured when it diagnoses the nation's ills, weakest when it comes to suggesting solutions.

To its critics—to be found in milieux as different as the Vatican and Evangelical churches—there is a profound secularity at the heart of Liberation and contextual theology. They believe that its advocates, in their hatred of oppression, have invented a Christianity as instrumental as that of traditional religions, and forgotten that the Kingdom is not of this world. 'Holy Scripture . . . cannot be misused to absolutize and sacralize a theory concerning the socio-political order . . . that order is always contingent'.[45]

Radical Christianity is ecumenical, and the likeminded of different faith traditions worked together without difficulty. The Institute for Contextual Theology, founded in 1981, was interdenominational.

The South African Council of Churches (SACC), which was deeply involved in the liberation struggle, worked closely with the South African Catholic Bishops' Conference. Denis Hurley, Catholic Archbishop of Durban, ordained in 1939, gave public support to white conscientious objectors. Radical black priests, nuns, and seminarians, such as Sister Bernard Ncube, did the same. Father Smangaliso Mkhatshwa, the Bishops' Conference Secretary, was imprisoned, tortured, and banned. In 1988, the Johannesburg head-quarters of the SACC was bombed, and that of the Catholic Bishops' Conference in Pretoria was destroyed by arson. Prominent Christians supported the United Democratic Front, formed to oppose the 1983 Constitution, and participated in what became the Mass Democratic Movement. Boesak said, 'It is not a Christian struggle I am pleading for, it is for a Christian presence in the struggle that I plead'.[46] One of the factors that influenced church leaders was the fear that black Christians would come to reject Christianity altogether.

But individual churches were polarized. In the words of the *Kairos Document*, '*the Church is divided* . . . there are Christians (or at least, people who profess to be Christians) on both sides of the conflict'.[47] There are, of course, many possible degrees of Christian commitment, 'I believe but I'm not a *fanatic*', said someone, 'I don't practise it'.[48] But the devout were also divided.

Frank Chikane was ordained a pastor of the (Pentecostal) Apostolic Faith Mission in 1980. As in the Dutch Reformed Church, the white church has refused to unite with its Black, Coloured, and Indian Missions, despite their urging. Because of his political activism, Chikane was repeatedly imprisoned, and tortured. His church repudiated him, and drove his family from their church-owned home when he was in gaol. He refused to leave South Africa, or change his denomination. In 1988, he succeeded Tutu and Naudé as General Secretary of the South African Council of Churches.

Peter Walshe describes the years that followed the military occupation of the townships in 1985:

> . . . hundreds of clergy and church workers were detained; many were tortured. Others were banned and severely restricted. . . . Death squads assassinated Christian activists. . . . Vigilantes and *kitskonstabels* intimidated, terrorised and killed.[49]

Tutu was protected from all this by his international standing, although his advocacy of economic sanctions was illegal. His enemies, though, pointed to his frequent foreign travel, expensively educated children, and comfortable lifestyle, and said he had made a career of apartheid.[50]

There is a strand in American Evangelicalism that suggests that the righteous are rewarded by prosperity (see page 335). It has tended to identify with government and big business, and to demonize Communism; it has sometimes been accused of racism. Some American Christians, such as Ronald Sider, and the Quaker, Richard Foster, have denounced this doctrine of 'gluttonous prosperity'.[51] Chikane describes the way in which his white fellow Pentecostals identified Liberation movements with 'Communism'. The tele-evangelists, Jimmy Swaggart and Jerry Falwell, both endorsed the South African government, and the South African and American flags flew over the Rhema Centre in Johannesburg.[52] A document issued in 1986 by a group of South Africa's 'Concerned Evangelicals' took a different stand:

> Evangelicalism, being rooted in the USA and Europe, is blind to western domination and exploitation of the peoples of the Third World. What they see is more of winning souls for Christ rather than the pain and suffering the people are going through. Because of this insensitivity and lack of awareness on the part of these white missionaries about the oppressive

nature of their tradition and culture, they have transplanted this oppressive culture into the Church.[53]

The Concerned Evangelicals, who include Naudé and many less famous names, have distanced themselves from the rhetoric of much missionary endeavour, and written a telling critique of a hundred years of European mission. The document's eloquence and effectiveness spring from this very fact, that it comes from *within* the Evangelical tradition.

ZION

At least two thousand churches in South Africa have a name that includes Zion. It derives ultimately from the Christian Catholic Apostolic Church, with its headquarters in Zion City, near Chicago, founded by John Alexander Dowie (d. 1907), a church which catered especially to the urban poor.

In South Africa, in 1903, a young Dutch Reformed Church missionary called Petrus Louis Le Roux joined it, with many of his African congregation, renouncing his home, church, and livelihood: 'I must cut off from all my family and friends. I am in heart and soul Afrikaner and this makes it that much harder'.[54] In time, Le Roux left Zion, and spent the rest of his life as a Pentecostal. He did not want people to have contact with their ancestors or to wear white garments or to carry staffs. But the Zionist churches proliferated, developing rich, distinctive lives of their own, quite independent of European influences. They have their own way of categorizing churches—churches of the (black) people, spiritual churches, and institutional churches of the whites.[55]

The Zionist churches in South Africa are much like their counterparts elsewhere, such as the Aladura churches of Nigeria. Like them, they wear distinctive robes and insignia, and practise various avoidances that are often based on the Hebrew Bible. The robes are often white, blue, or green—the colours of purity, water, and vegetation. Both costumes and tabus mark the perimeters of group identity in the wilderness of urban life, and define an alternative order and system of values. They offer a model of holistic healing, which the western world is now beginning to rediscover, and community, in the dislocations caused by urbanization and labour migration.

Like prophetic churches elsewhere, they are usually founded by a man or woman who adopts a role of religious leadership after a visionary experience, and who is a healer rather than a preacher. Their services focus on hymn singing and liturgies; like the Aladura, they are profoundly indigenized and self-supporting churches. Like some, but not all, prophetic churches elsewhere, they aspire to have an earthly Zion, a 'Holy City'.

Much academic attention has focused on these churches, making it easy to forget that the majority of the black Christian population adhere to the older churches.

It is no coincidence that prophetic movements were particularly successful among the Zulu, who had suffered repeated crushing defeats, most recently in

1906, though not all Zionists were Zulu, and some were Tswana or Swazi. MacGaffey has suggested that prophets were sometimes marginal in both the traditional and modern worlds (see page 199), but, in South Africa, some Zionist leaders had links to the Zulu royal family. Paul Mabilitsa, founder of the Christian Apostolic Church in Zion, was the son of a Tswana chief who renounced his right of succession, for 'I am serving a greater Chief'.

But church leadership and an elaborate structure of office holders often gave authority to the powerless. A Sotho Zionist called Edward Lion, who established a Zion City in Lesotho in 1917, called himself 'General Oversear of the World'. In *Speaking for Ourselves*, a group of Zionist leaders said, 'The members of our Churches are the poorest of the poor . . . when people become highly educated and begin to earn big salaries they usually leave our Church'.[56]

Prophetic leaders created a new kind of leadership role, and, often, like their counterparts elsewhere in Africa, they founded a dynasty. The second generation was usually better-educated, but less charismatic. When Mabilitsa died in 1942, he was succeeded by his son, Philip, (*d.* 1965) a teacher with a B.Sc., while Isaiah Shembe was followed in 1935 by his son, Johannes Galilee Shembe, also a graduate teacher.

Certain symbols are pervasive; one is the Holy Mountain. Prayer on a mountain top has Biblical precedents, and it is a place that is felt to be closer to Heaven. Water, too, is so important as a symbol of cleansing and purification—Sundkler writes of 'water mysticism'. These same symbols are important among Nigeria's Aladura.

The Zionist churches are profoundly indigenized, so much so that some have chosen to regard them as the first local exponents of Black theology. They enrich the lives of believers with their liturgies and community life, and often, they restore them to health, but they cannot heal the society in which they live.

As we have seen elsewhere, women often predominate in these churches. The first Swazi Zionist, for example, was a woman, Johanna Nxumalo, who joined in 1913. Some churches were founded by women, such as Ma Christina Nku, and Ma Mbele. Typically, they concentrate on prayer and healing, while a husband, often with the title of bishop, organizes the church. Bishop Lazarus Nku (Christina's husband) died in 1949; her son, Bishop Johannes Nku, succeeded him, though a rival led a successful breakaway movement. Succession struggles between the prophet's son and his older and more charismatic associates are common. Ma Mbele's husband, also a bishop, rules the church she founded, while she takes refuge in seclusion and silence.[57] Grace Tshabalala (*b.* 1904) was concerned at the great proliferation of different Zionist churches, and devoted herself to uniting them. She founded a movement for Zionist women, which drew its members from thirty-two churches.

The Swazi King, Sobhaza II, who was also the first Head of State of independent Swaziland, worked persistently for church unity. One of his nineteenth-century predecessors had foretold the coming of strangers, with a Book in one hand and money in the other. He told his people to welcome the first, and shun the second. At interchurch meetings on Good Friday, the Swazi sing:

> We are simply Christians, nothing but Christians;
> And Jesus is in his Kingdom above.
> Let us not part then; Let us not hate, then
> For that is not done in heaven.

The most famous Zulu Zion is Isaiah Shembe's *Ekuphakameni*, the Elevated Place, 10 miles north of Durban. Of his 250 hymns, 50 sing its praises:

> I remember Ekuphakameni
> where is assembled
> the saintly congregation
> of the Nazarites.

> I remember Ekuphakameni,
> where the springs are
> springs of living water
> lasting for ever.[58]

In 1937 Ma Nku had a vision of a church on a particular site near Johannesburg. She would go there to pray, although it did not seem promising as it was European land. Then, the area was redesignated for African housing, and in 1952 she built the church with twelve doors that she had seen in her vision.

Shembe learned to write at the age of forty in order to record his hymns, which came to him in visions. The prophets often had a powerful imagination and a fascination with language and symbolism that, had the circumstances of their lives been different, might have made them great poets or artists, but they created churches, for which they composed hymns and complicated liturgies. The deeply traditional belief that words have an intrinsic power of their own is seen in the elaborate names of many of these churches: The Holy Catholic Apostolic Church in Zion of South Africa, The Star Nazaretha Church in Zion of Sabbath, Holy Spirit Jerusalem Church in Zion.

Edward Lekganyane's Zion Christian Church, founded by his father, has perhaps 2 million members, but many Zionist churches were small and ephemeral, although they were just as much achievements of the creative imagination as those that were large.

One of the most distinctive was founded by George Khambule in 1919, and died thirty years later with him.[59] He was fascinated by secret languages, and by stones, especially the gemstones of Revelations. He looked for holy stones in the streams of Natal, which were known by their alphabet-type markings, and kept them in an Ark in the Holy of Holies. The markings on the stones were the key to a secret language, which reflects the joy and wonder of literacy to a man of little education: 'You God have grace and goodness *m r m ſ m r d d ı d*'.

He called himself Saint Nazar and listened to God on a celestial telephone. He invented elaborate liturgies, which were sung antiphonally in Zulu. His congregation lived in isolation, surrounded by complicated prohibitions, and all his followers underwent the Marriage of the Lamb.

Once or twice, Khambule, like other mystics, had doubts about it all: 'You may say I may see heaven. No more did I listen to what is said there. Thy eyes did not thrive. . . . Why is it that [what is sung] in the hymns does not happen? Today there are questions which I cannot answer because I have been speaking on my own behalf. If I can give the answer at all'.[60]

For Timothy Cekwane (1873–1949), the sight of Halley's Comet, in 1910, was the formative experience of his life. The place where he saw it, on a mountain slope in the Drakensbergs, became the Place of the Light, and the Church he founded, the Church of the Light. Its members wear red, the colour of blood, a core symbol. Timothy was a stigmatic; in ecstasy, blood would flow from his mouth and hands, a gift (if we can call it such) that was transmitted to several followers. There is a liturgical use of brooms, a symbol of cleansing from pollution. Like the followers of Saint Nazar, they withdrew from the wider world.

The Zionist churches have a constant tendency to divide. The quest for healing can never be fully satisfied, and the afflicted tend to go from one religious leader to the next. Where roles of power and influence were unattainable in the wider society, it is not suprising that Zionists often had fierce disputes over the leadership of their church, and, as Weber pointed out long ago, the institutionalization of charisma is a perennial problem in religious movements.

Are the prophetic churches a profoundly Biblical, deeply indigenized form of Christianity, or are they syncretistic and post-Christian? The key issue is whether or not the African prophet is regarded as a Saviour, comparable with Christ. Martin, staunch defender of the Kimbanguists, regards many Zionist churches as 'messianic sects'. To Oosthuizen, the Zionists are post-Christian. In his *Bantu Prophets*, published in 1948, Sundkler distinguished a 'messianic' strand. In his *Zulu Zion*, published nearly thirty years later, he had changed his mind, and indignantly refuted Oosthuizen.

Central to these debates is the figure of Isaiah Shembe. Some of Shembe's followers, like some followers of Kimbangu, regard their prophet as divine. Shembe saw himself as a chosen Servant of God. His son, Johannes Galilee Shembe, said, 'Some of our people say "Shembe is God". But no, Isaiah never wanted to accept that'.[61] We shall let the great Zulu poet himself have the last word, as he sings of the universal tragedy of death, of the sufferings of his people, of the Paradise that was lost and can be regained, of the enduring love of God for His people. He walks, as we all do, alone to a solitary grave.

> Give me then
> that courage of Japhet's daughter
> Alone I shall enter
> into my own grave.

He grieves for his people's burdens.

> You lass of Nazaretha,
> cry like a flowing stream
> because of the shame which is yours
> in your own country.

But he hopes for forgiveness, and for Paradise Regained.

> I am in need, my Lord,
> of soap to wash me
> Return me in haste
> to the bliss that was mine.[62]

To many educated black Christians, Zionism is a form of false consciousness, and the Zion Christian Church was conspicuous for its rapprochement with white South African governments. Zionists, in general, had little political awareness, and, in a sense, their energies were deflected by the quest for supernatural explanations and remedies, the search for a heavenly kingdom. Partly because their leaders were uneducated, but partly because there seemed little prospect of changing South Africa anyway, they tended to retreat into a rich world of their own, focused on a home in Zion.

SEPHIRI

Secret prayer groups, whose members belong to one of the mainstream churches are very common.[63] Called *Thapelo ya sephiri* (secret prayers) in Sotho, they are communities of affliction. Those who join tend to do so because they suffer from health problems, and to rise in the organization when they are healed. They have the elaborate offices and the distinctive robes of Zionist churches. They feel a strong sense of identity with the hidden and persecuted early Church, and include the ancestors, with Christ, saints and angels, in a spiritual community. They believe that they know the secret teaching of the Bible, they recognize each other by a coded language, and they call each prayer group a pool of salvation. They are accused of having sexual relations with each other, accusations that, as we have seen, are also levelled at a branch of Jamaa in Zaire. This may reflect the tendency to demonize the Other, but such tendencies have often been documented in small, intense, withdrawn religious groups.

CHRISTIANITY REJECTED

The advocates of radical theology are motivated both by their abhorrence of
injustice, and by their awareness that religion is decreasingly relevant to a
whole generation of black urban youth.

When Chikane visited schools on behalf of the Student Christian
Movement:

> They confronted me with the history of Christianity here and elsewhere, its
> collaboration with oppressive colonial systems, and the usual argument of
> how the missionaries gave us the Bible and took our land. . . . One of the
> students climbed on a chair and called me a non-white. That was the name
> of collaborators then, blacks with no consciousness of their own. . . .[64]

Luthuli, a devout Christian, asked in the early 1960s, 'How do they [the
churches] stand for an ethic which the whites have brought, preached and
refused to practise? . . . White paternalistic Christianity—as though the
whites had invented the Christian Faith—estranges my people from Christ'.[65]
Nolan writes:

> While the majority of the people involved in the struggle are believers . . .
> and some of them are very staunch believers, there is a visible shift away
> from any regular attendance at church services, especially where black
> youth are concerned. Most church services these days are attended by
> women, children, and elderly men. The African Independent Churches can
> still attract middle-aged men but the youth are definitely drifting away
> from all the churches.[66]

The Soweto poet, Oswald Mtshali, writes of Christianity with biting satire:

> Then she came in—
> my woman neighbour:
> 'Have you heard? they've killed your brother.'
> 'O! no! I heard nothing. I've been to church.'[67]

South Africa's neighbours: wars and liberation

Histories of twentieth-century Africa often distinguish between colonies with
a substantial white settler component, and what are sometimes called 'colonies
of exploitation', where the economy depended on the export of primary
produce, such as cotton and palm oil, produced by an African peasantry.
Where the demand for independence ran counter to the interests of an
entrenched white settler class, war often resulted. Kenya became independent
in 1963, but settler hegemony and confidence had been greatly undermined
by the Mau Mau war of 1952–4. In Algeria, there were a million *colons*, and a
war of liberation began in 1954 that, ultimately, led to the fall of the Fourth
Republic in France, to a mass exodus of the settlers and to independence in

1962. Mau Mau derived its core symbolism from Kikuyu traditional religion, Algeria from Islam. Muslim status was enshrined in the Algerian Code of Nationality of 1962, and a triumphalist Church was dismantled forever.[68]

In Zimbabwe and the former Portuguese colonies, as in South Africa, the independence struggle created many dilemmas for the Christian conscience. Church leaders had to choose between supporting Smith's Rhodesia Front or the Portuguese forces on the one hand, or the African guerilla fighters on the other. Smith's regime, like successive South African governments, justified itself in the rhetoric of civic religion. There are equivalents to Huddleston or Scott in South Africa, such as the Clutton-Brocks in Rhodesia. Like them, they bore a striking individual witness, but could not change the general pattern of events. Independence was fought for, and won by Africans. In the Portuguese colonies, the close association of Church and State turned some to atheism and Marxism.

RHODESIA TO ZIMBABWE[69]

In 1953, the Central African Federation was created out of the Rhodesias and Nyasaland. In Northern Rhodesia and Nyasaland, the white settler population was very small, despite a rapid influx in the post-war years, and Africans perceived, correctly, that Federation meant the entrenchment of white power, and carried with it the danger of further land alienation. A highly effective nationalist movement developed, and in 1964, Northern Rhodesia and Nyasaland became independent Zambia and Malawi.

The collapse of the Federation was furthered by the fact that many whites in Southern Rhodesia preferred national autonomy. In 1965, a right-wing settler government, led by Ian Smith's Rhodesian Front, issued a Unilateral Declaration of Independence. Fifteen years of increasingly bitter conflict lay ahead, until Rhodesia became Zimbabwe in 1980.

Garfield Todd, a New Zealander, was a Church of Christ missionary in Rhodesia from 1934 to 1946 and then a United Party MP until 1958. He became Prime Minister in 1953, at the time of Federation.

Uneasily balanced between settler pressures and African needs, he satisfied neither,[70] and, in 1972, he was imprisoned, and then detained on his farm. He was not the only missionary to take an active part in politics. Louis Aujoulat was the founder of a Catholic lay missionary organization, *Ad Lucem*. From 1951 onwards, he represented a black Cameroun constituency in the French Chamber of Deputies.

The Anglicans, Guy and Molly Clutton-Brock, came to Rhodesia in 1949, inspired by Michael Scott. They ran an agricultural settlement called St Faith's Farm, on interracial lines, and were among the few white members of the ANC. In 1970, they were deported. Cedric Widman, who joined them at St Faith's, 'was the first white man, as far as I know, to work under an African farm manager and to accept an African farm labourer's wage'.[71] He died at the age of twenty-nine.

A Methodist, Colin Morris, came to Zambia after reading *Naught for Your Comfort*. He identified closely with the nationalist cause, and became a close friend of Kenneth Kaunda. In December, 1957, a group of nationalists were contemplating a boycott of the churches, and one of their leaders said, 'Let us leave the church of Colin Morris alone'.[72]

Bishop Ralph Dodge of the United Methodist Church, the first President of the Christian Council of Rhodesia, was deported for his opposition to the Smith regime in 1964, and was replaced by Bishop Abel Muzorewa. Bishop Donal Lamont, an Irish Carmelite, was the Bishop of Umtali, and he, too, was deported for his opposition to Smith. A hundred African women demonstrated when he stood trial.

There was a sense in which it was easier for Catholic missionaries, who were celibate, and, in many cases, foreigners, to distance themselves from the settler community. Some clergy, such as the Anglican, Arthur Lewis, preferred to identify with the white settlers. When the archbishop of Canterbury suggested that armed force might be the appropriate response to UDI, some whites burned their Bibles. Lamont was called the Red Bishop, and a Catholic MP spoke for his class when he said, 'As I saw it, the trend was to hand over the country to irresponsible people, with the end result that no people of my race would be prepared to stay, and therefore everything that I owned was at stake'. Like the rulers of South Africa, Ian Smith justified his stand in the rhetoric of civil religion. The unilateral Declaration of Independence of 1965 states:

> We have struck a blow for the preservation of justice, civilisation and Christianity. . . . God bless you all.

Church leaders were influenced, in part, by the perceived danger of alienating African Christians for ever: 'Mr Munangatira stressed the place of Christianity in Nationalism, but also emphasised that if asked to choose between the Church and Nationalism, almost all Africans would choose the latter'.[73]

When Mozambique and Angola gained independence in 1975, most Rhodesians came to see the writing on the wall. The late 1970s was a period of increasingly bloody, and desperate conflict, with African clergy playing a notable role in the freedom struggle. Reverend Canaan Banana, a Methodist, was to be the first president of the Republic. Ndabaningi Sithole, founder of the Zimbabwe African National Union (ZANU), was a Methodist minister, and Joshua Nkomo, founder of the Zimbabwe African People's Union (ZAPU), a Methodist layman. Bishop Muzorewa became politically prominent when other nationalists were in detention or exile. He was part of the government of 'Zimbabwe–Rhodesia', but all real power stayed in white hands, and he was discredited by the association. When elections were held in 1980, ZANU, under Robert Mugabe, had fifty-seven seats, Nkomo's ZAPU, twenty, and Muzorewa's party, three.

Mugabe, originally a Catholic, was theoretically a Marxist, but he was, essentially, a pragmatist, and took pains to work in harmony with the Church and with white farmers.

ANGOLA AND MOZAMBIQUE

The conflicts in Algeria and Rhodesia reflected the fears and entrenched interests of a large body of white settlers. In the Portuguese colonies, it grew primarily out of the policies of the metropolitan power. Guinea-Bissau, Angola, and Mozambique were seen as overseas provinces of Portugal, an essential dimension of national identity. The movements that won independence began as peaceful political parties, but were forced to adopt violent means, by Portuguese intransigence, in Angola in 1961, in Guinea-Bissau in 1962, and in Mozambique in 1964. The increasing cost of the colonial struggle led to a change of government in Portugal itself in 1974, with independence following in 1975.

Because of the traditionally close association between Portuguese colonialism and Catholicism, those from a Protestant background were disproportionately prominent in the independence movement. In Angola, Agostinho Neto, who led the MPLA (Popular Movement for the Liberation of Angola) until his death in 1979, was the son of a Methodist minister and studied medicine in Portugal on a Methodist scholarship.[74] With typical integrity, he informed church authorities when he ceased to be a Christian. Holden Roberto, the leader of the FNLA (National Front for the Liberation of Angola), was named after a Baptist missionary and attended a Baptist school.[75] Jonas Savimbi, the leader of UNITA (National Union for the Total Independence of Angola), had strong links with the Congregationalists; he was the son of Lot Savimbi, the Director of the Chilesso Mission. FNLA support was largely Baptist and Kongo, while that for UNITA was Congregationalist and Ovimbundu. Much MPLA support came from Catholics and Methodists near Luanda, but its ideology was secular, socialist, and opposed to ethnic divisions.

Many humble Christians suffered from the identification of Protestantism with opposition to Portugal. Luisa Caetano, an Mbundu MPLA leader, explained her political commitment:

> My father was killed in 1961 by the Portuguese because he was a Protestant pastor. Before killing him, they tortured him by cutting off his limbs.[76]

Not all the nationalists were of Protestant stock. Mario Pinto de Andrade, a *mestizo*, was the younger brother of Father Joaquim Pinto de Andrade, a prominent figure in the Luanda diocese.

Catholic priests were increasingly divided between those who identified with the government and the Settler community, and those who condemned them. A statement signed by twenty-two Holy Ghost Fathers in 1975 asked:

> How can . . . a society [of Christians] witness to brotherly love and poverty when it parades a style of life which shows an imposing, impressive, official and intimate connection with the powers of this world, and is conditioned by these powers? . . . How can people believe in the disinterestedness and full freedom of the bishops when public opinion can see them only as State officials with the same privileges as these high officials in matters of salary, housing . . . and even retirement pension?[77]

321

These events were closely paralleled in Mozambique. As elsewhere, it was to be easier for foreigners to distance themselves from the colonial power and, in 1971, the White Fathers left the country in protest against the 'grave ambiguity' of Church–State relations.

As in Angola, the Portuguese tended to equate Protestantism with political opposition. Eduardo Mondhlane, who led Frelimo until his assassination in 1969, was the product of Protestant mission schools; the head of the Presbyterian Church, Zedequias Manghela, was imprisoned, and later found dead in his cell, in December, 1972.[78] In April, 1974, in a reaction against colonial wars, the government in Portugal was overthrown.

The late Samora Machel, the first President of independent Mozambique, was a Marxist who made no secret of his hostility to Christianity. In 1975, the Bishop of Nampula, Manuel Vieira Pinto, reflected:

> The Church has actively collaborated with the colonial regime . . . because it willingly lent itself to the spreading of national Portuguese culture, because it showed itself openly on the side of the colonial rulers.

A group of Black Mozambiquan priests went further, 'this colonialist, bourgeois, imperialist church is false'.[79] The 'opaque reality' of the Church's relationship with these and other Marxist governments, and the role of American and other Evangelicals in supporting their opponents is considered in the chapter that follows.

A NEW SOUTH AFRICA 1990–1994

Early in 1990, in a dramatic reversal of policy, President F. W. de Klerk began to dismantle the structure of apartheid. It reflected, perhaps, less a conversion to multiracial democracy than a shrewd acceptance of the fact that change was inevitable. The veteran ANC leader, Nelson Mandela, was released from prison. White right-wing groups regarded de Klerk as a traitor, and the elections of May 1994 were almost aborted by Inkatha's intransigeance. But in the end, agreement was reached, and for the first time in history, black, white, and brown South Africans voted together for black, white, and brown candidates. Mandela was sworn in as the nation's President, de Klerk as Vice President.

Mandela, who has spent twenty-seven years in prison, astonished the world by his magnanimity, inviting his former gaoler to his inauguration. There were to be no reprisals for the crimes which had sustained apartheid, and his central message was reconciliation.

The story of the Rise and Fall of the South African Reich has had, in a sense, a happy ending. But as we shall see in the next chapter, the attainment of independence in black Africa has always led to an outburst of optimism, and in many cases these hopes have been disappointed. Black South Africans aspire to better education, housing, and social services; more and better jobs; and the return of their alienated land. The new government of South Africa faces a task of enormous difficulty if it is to meet these aspirations.

TWELVE

Independent Black Africa since 1960: Church, State, and Society

Before Independence, we dreamed that it would bring us masses of marvellous things. All of that was to descend upon us from the sky . . . deliverance and salvation. . . . But here it is more than two years that we have been waiting, and nothing has come. On the contrary, our life is more difficult, we are more poor than before.

Kwilu villagers, 1962[1]

Contexts

In the early 1950s, the approaching demise of colonialism in Africa was still far from apparent, and young Englishmen still went to the colonies expecting to make a career there. The end, when it came, did so with a speed that often surprised both colonizer and colonized.

In 1958, Chinua Achebe chose the title and epigraph of his first novel, from a poem by Yeats. Ever since, they have been part of educated African consciousness, familiar to many who have read nothing else by the Irish poet.

> Things fall apart, the centre cannot hold,
> Mere anarchy is loosed upon the world.

Paradoxically, his novel was published at a time of tremendous hope and expectancy. Between 1958 and 1964, much of Africa regained independence, in what has been called a conspiracy of optimism. There was a keen awareness of the errors and injustices of colonialism, a confident expectation that political freedom would lead to economic development: 'We must run while others walk', said President Nyerere of Tanzania. It was only later that things fell apart.

Parliamentary democracy did not last, and it was assumed that this particular exotic plant was unsuited to African soil. An increasing number of

323

states had military rulers and, as a body, their record was neither better nor worse than that of their civilian counterparts. Some newly independent nations fell prey to bloodthirsty tyrants, among them, Amin's Uganda, and Nguema's Equatorial Guinea. In much of Africa, corruption became commonplace, and political commentators coined the term 'Kleptocracy'. When the unjust flourished so visibly, at least for most of the time, it was difficult to avoid cynicism and despair.

Some states were torn apart by regional and ethnic conflict, often, though not always, with religious dimensions: Ethiopia, Sudan, Rwanda, Burundi, Chad, Angola, Nigeria, Liberia, Somalia.

International economic forces imposed narrow parameters on African statesmen's freedom of choice. A general decline in the prices of exports nipped many development projects in the bud. The oil crisis plunged many nations into catastrophic indebtedness, and even the oil giant, Nigeria, was caught in a downward economic spiral. Outside observers, and often Africans themselves, may have swung from an excessive optimism to an excessive cynicism. It is easy to focus on the problems, and lose sight of all that has been achieved in Africa since 1960.

Ex Africa semper aliquid novi 'there is always something new from Africa'. In 1990, there was a return (or planned return) on a large scale, to multiparty democracy. Various factors paved the way, not least the dramatic changes occurring in the erstwhile USSR. Western governments, and aid agencies began to exercise insistent economic pressure, and domestic opposition became more difficult to contain. Cynics pointed out that there were now fewer spoils to divide, and suggested that recent converts to democracy were anxious to share responsibility for economic, and other problems.

How many Christians?

There is no doubt that Christianity has expanded enormously since the 1950s, and that traditional religion has declined. The interpretation of the statistical data is a task of enormous difficulty, in part because there is a gap between the statistics filed by churches and the numbers of Christians listed in census returns. Barrett fills the gap with the labels 'nominal', or crypto-Christians, that is, those who, as elsewhere in the world, describe themselves as Christian, but are not active church members. In Nigeria, the percentage of Christians increased from 22 per cent to 34.5 per cent between the 1953 and 1963 censuses. By the mid 1970s, it had risen to 44.9 per cent.[2] Because of Nigeria's enormous population, the absolute number was far larger than that of many smaller countries, where the percentages of Christians were higher. These included Burundi (74 per cent), Congo (92 per cent), and Equatorial Guinea (81 per cent). In Sierra Leone and Liberia, despite generations of a black Christian presence, the percentages of Christians in the 1970s were 8.2 per cent, and 31 per cent, respectively.

Missionaries and moratorium

In the 1940s and 1950s, the missionary enterprise was still flourishing and unquestioned. There was a proliferation of Protestant missionary societies, and of Catholic congregations working in Africa. In 1950, there were four Catholic bishops in Rhodesia: an English Jesuit, an Irish Carmelite, a Swiss Bethlehem Father, and a German Mariannhill Father, as well as a Spanish Prefect Apostolic (a Burgos priest).[3] A 'foreign' identity, and, in some cases, linkages to Latin America, made it easier to avoid the identification with the white settlers that came so readily to the English Jesuits.[4]

At much the same time, a number of missionaries, consciously reacting against the racism of the past, published sympathetic accounts both of African traditional religions, and of new religious movements. A book by the Swedish Lutheran missionary bishop, Bengt Sundkler, led a generation of scholars into a deeper and more appreciative understanding of Zulu independency and the prophetic churches in general. An Anglican bishop, John Taylor, explored traditional religion as the African Old Testament, as did African theologians such as Bolaji Idowu in Nigeria and John Mbiti in Kenya. Their work has been much criticized, as it sees through distorting Christian spectacles, and, in the process, invents an African traditional religion that never existed, in a salutary reaction against a hundred years of missionary Eurocentricity.

The number of foreign missionaries increased in the 1950s, and, when independence came, the older churches were still overwhelmingly dominated by expatriates. There were 5502 expatriate Catholic priests in Black Africa in 1949, and 8703 ten years later.

The approach of independence created something of a crisis for many white missionaries: 'Few of them had really wanted independence to come, and when it had, many of them had lost their nerve, their sense of direction and purpose'.[5] It was transparently obvious that African autonomy in government must be paralleled in church affairs, and church leadership roles were Africanized rapidly in the years that followed. A successful transition presupposed a generosity that was sometimes lacking. In the words of a Kenyan nun:

> The Teresian sisters of Malawi have grateful memories of their transition period, because the White Sister who helped to prepare them for their first chapter worked with them very co-operatively. . . . There were other sad incidents whereby houses were emptied and goods sold by the trustees.[6]

In the older churches, it became increasingly difficult to recruit missionaries. In Catholic circles, this reflected a general decline in priestly and religious vocations in the western world. As changes in religious understanding affirmed the value of other faith traditions, and undermined the triumphalist understanding of Christianity, there seemed to be no compelling reason for being a missionary at all. In the early 1970s, some expatriate nuns were asked what their response would be if they were asked to seek new recruits. Less than half felt able to do so without misgivings, while 18.8 felt unable to do so at all: recruiting is 'the one thing I could not do'.[7] A Holy Ghost Father in East Africa wrote that those who remain in the mission field are 'chronic optimists'.[8]

Although the older missionary societies have declined, there has been a massive influx of missionaries of an Evangelical/Faith Mission persuasion, often with American connections.

State takeovers of mission schools removed what had become a traditional missionary activity, and it was not always clear what should take its place. And to be a missionary, or, indeed, an expatriate lay worker in independent Africa, demanded a very special calling, a willingness to follow in the steps of the Baptist: 'He must become more and more, I must become less and less'. Theo van Asten, Superior General of the White Fathers, acquired a wife, and a secular career. Marcel Lefebvre, Superior General of the Spiritans, led a conservative movement that rejected post-Vatican II changes, and drifted gradually into schism. There was no problem of recruitment in the African prophetic churches, or Ethiopian Orthodoxy.

Looking for new directions, missionaries found them, to a considerable extent, in the words of Christian statesmen such as Nyerere, who urged them to devote themselves to nation building, and the struggle against poverty and disease.[9] Many did so with enthusiasm, while others felt this could be better done by the laity. In a famous speech, Nyerere told the Maryknoll sisters:

> . . . kindness is not enough; piety is not enough; and charity is not enough
> . . . the Church must work with the people in the positive tasks of building
> a future based on social justice . . . it is important that we should stress the
> working *with*, not the working *for*.[10]

They were not easy words to act on, or even, perhaps, to understand.

In 1971, at a Mission festival in Milwaukee, an East African Presbyterian, Reverend John Gatu, called for a moratorium on expatriate finance and personnel to Africa: 'It is certainly not a New Testament idea, but an emanation of the thinking of the industrial society that can see value only in money and statistics'.[11] In 1974, a Cameroon Jesuit, Fabien Boulaga, wrote an article called '*La dé-mission*', 'Let Europe and America give priority to their own evangelization. Let us plan the orderly departure of missionaries from Africa'.[12] The remarkable response to this call, at least in theory, reflected a growing awareness of the fact that much of the money given by western churches to mission fields went on the upkeep of their own personnel (funds that might better be donated to African churches). There was a feeling that people became missionaries as much to meet their own subjective needs as to serve Africa. The church in Madagascar flourished in the nineteenth century when foreign missionaries withdrew, as, in the twentieth, did the Methodists of Inhambane.[13]

Significantly, African church leaders did not endorse the call for a moratorium. Bishop Patrick Kalilombe pointed out that, in his own diocese, Lilongwe, in Malawi, 66 out of 76 priests, 19 out of 20 Brothers, and 61 out of 132 Sisters were expatriates. Although K16 400 of diocesan revenues were generated locally, K80 300 came from abroad.[14] With great perception, he realized that to run the diocese in the style he had inherited would always need foreign financial inputs, and that what was needed was to rethink the whole way in which the church was run, and, in particular, to develop the local Christian community.

Twenty years later, some 30 to 40 thousand Catholic and Protestant missionaries are still at work in sub-Saharan Africa. Traditional recruiting grounds for the former, such as Ireland, Holland, and France, have declined, but there are now more than a thousand Polish missionaries in Africa. Many observers have expressed anxiety about this input from a notably rigid and authoritarian church.[15]

A case study of the Baptists of Kivu, in Zaire, sheds light on the economic problems of contemporary African churches. The pastor's income, derived from local contributions, is small and eroded by inflation, sometimes as little as the equivalent of $20 a month. American churches contribute $40 thousand a year to keep an expatriate missionary and his family in the field. He normally stays only for five years, several of which are spent in language study. But American churches are not willing to subsidize African clergy, who know the language already.[16]

Kalilombe himself, sadly, has long been resident in Birmingham.[17] In the nineteenth century, Colenso's wife wrote from Natal:

> Did you see what Lord Shaftesbury said about the last not least danger to the Eng. Ch. from the Zulu Mission which has just come over from Africa for the conversion of the people of Grt. Britain (hear, hear, & a laugh).[18]

Catholicism: dilemmas and directions

The changes that followed Vatican II, such as the adoption of a vernacular liturgy, and a diminished emphasis on Mary and the saints, defused the hostility that had deformed Catholic–Protestant relations in Africa and elsewhere. Vatican II encouraged a contextualized theology, and a more positive approach to other faith traditions. Hinduism and Buddhism, but not African religions, were specified in the relevant document.[19] However, as elsewhere in the world, the 'demystification' of folk Catholicism left many troubled and alienated. It was precisely elements such as healing shrines, protective scapulars, statues, candles, and holy water, that were closest to traditional religions. To some extent, the vacuum was filled by organizations such as the Block Rosary, the Blue Army of Fatima, and innumerable St Jude Societies.[20] None of this is peculiar to Africa.

Since 1960, there has been a world-wide proliferation of Marian visions. Sometimes these are linked with a conservative message, and threats of an approaching End. Those who dislike changes in the post-Vatican II Church sometimes seek external support in the messages of seers.[21] Some of these encounters, such as Garabandal in Portugal in the 1960s, and Medjugorje in the then Yugoslavia in the 1980s, are internationally famous, while other visionaries are more obscure, such as the Australian lay seer who calls himself the Little Pebble, and expects to be the next Pope.[22]

We have noted the Marian visions seen at Zeitoun in Egypt (1968–71), and their acceptance by the Coptic patriarch,[23] but there have been others. An Igbo seer and stigmatic called Veronica had a vision in 1963, founding a little Church that endured for a time.[24] Marian visions have been described in southern Rwanda, from 1985 on: 'spontaneous assemblies of believers claiming or seeking miracles and apparitions are commonplace, particularly around Kibeho'.[25] In 1986, Marian visions were recorded in Nsimalen, in Cameroon, and there was something of a rift between enthusiastic pilgrims and clergy 'rather embarrassed by the affair'.[26] There were similar happenings in the late 1980s in Nairobi: 'a wave of Marian apparitions and other mystical phenomena which are strongly opposed by a large section of the clergy and which largely escapes their control'.[27]

The modern efflorescence of Marian apparitions is not easy to explain. Some scholars stress psychological factors; to others it is a manifestation of dislocating social change, anomy, poverty, and deprivation. Shorter attributes the Kenyan manifestations to the failure of the Church to become fully indigenized, and to the vacuum left when popular devotional practices are given up. He and others have warned of 'the tyranny of good taste', where Catholic intellectuals have removed loved statues because they are bad art, and popular devotions because they are of relatively recent origin.[28]

For Catholics, the limits of possible inculturation are imposed by Rome. At the 1974 Synod, Bishop Joachim M'dayen of Central African Republic pleaded for the ordination of married men; some African bishops supported him, while others opposed him. The White Fathers' Superior General asked ' "What is the meaning of the witness of celibacy . . . in someone who has given up neither wealth, nor ambition, nor honours . . . ?" To these questions he received no answer'.[29] 'Christian marriage works badly in Africa', writes Cardinal Malula, and, again, 'we deny anyone the right to say, in our place, what are the problems we encounter in our faith.'[30] African theologians pressed for an African Council. In 1994, as this book went to press, there was a Synod of African bishops in Rome. There were prayers in Ge'ez and Swahili, but little likelihood of radical change.

Some radical expatriate Catholic priests also reflected on the content of Church teaching in Africa, and found it wanting. Eugene Hillman and Adrian

Hastings criticized the Church's rigid insistence on monogamy. Hastings, for two decades, questioned obligatory clerical celibacy, and finally married—one of many who, at least in the eyes of the orthodox, radicalized themselves out of the Church altogether.[31]

As foreign bishops and superiors were replaced by Africans, other problems became apparent, at least to some. A Nigerian Holy Ghost Father reflected on the contradictions between a vow of poverty and a relatively comfortable lifestyle, inherited from European predecessors:

> Our vow of poverty is not obvious to the public. To all appearances the Nigerian religious is a rich man or woman as the case might be. He or she had access to the private car, the radio set, the tape recorder . . . magnificent lodgings, superb diet. . . . These are signs of affluence in this country.[32]

An East African nun said, 'African sisters . . . are confounded by the problem of "how to become poor" with so much at their use'.[33] Those who recognized the problem had travelled part of the way towards solving it, but it was easier to absorb the standards of the prosperous. When a survey was conducted in Nigeria, 80 per cent of the seminarians questioned said that they would accept a Mercedes if offered one, and 68 per cent said that Christ would![34]

Priests and religious enjoy a respect and deference that are fast eroding in the western church, epitomized in the way in which Nigerians speak of 'Reverend Fathers', and 'Reverend Sisters', and in the prophetic churches' adoption of such titles, and of the white soutane.[35]

The highly educated sometimes chose to leave priestly or religious life.[36] In the southern Sudan, against a background of immense suffering and social dislocation, 40 per cent of indigenous priests have left the ministry. Even so, indigenous religious societies flourish in Juba, such as the Priests and Brothers of the Apostles of Jesus, the Brothers of St Martin de Porres, and the Sisters of the Sacred Heart.[37]

The profound attraction to prayer, which led some women to be prophets in independent churches, drew others to the contemplative way. In 1934, Belgians founded a Carmel in the Congo, and a daughter house was established in Rwanda in 1962. There is a house of Cistercian nuns (and one of monks) in Uganda, and of Benedictine nuns in Igboland. In 1960, a Poor Clare from a *colon* family in Algeria founded a monastery in Lilongwe, Malawi, where African and foreign nuns lived in extreme poverty, and only Chewa was spoken. In 1975, an African abbess was appointed, and the foundress left for a hermitage in France.[38] There are also male contemplative communities, such as the Trappist monasteries in Uganda, Cameroun, Senegal, and eastern Nigeria.

The number of African priests exanded rapidly, from 3700 in 1975 to over 7000 in 1987[39]—the greatest concentrations being in eastern Nigeria, Zaire, Rwanda, Uganda, and Tanzania—but, in general, a rapidly growing population, combined with the shortage of expatriate clergy, left many areas virtually without priests.

The shortage of clergy converted some bishops to the value of 'base communities', pioneered in Latin America. In the eight dioceses of Kenya, the ratio between priests and people ranges from 1 to 3 thousand to 1 to 7 thousand (in the diocese of Dublin it is 1 to 974, and in Liverpool 1 to 1174).[40] Since 1979, small Christian communities of perhaps forty families have become common in the seven member countries of AMECEA and in Zaire, Mozambique, and Algeria.[41] Members are encouraged to study the Bible, and to apply it to their local situation, which presupposes a certain level of literacy. To what extent these communities can replace the clerically-led sacramentally-orientated parish, remains to be seen. They have sometimes created something of a crisis of identity for local clergy.[42]

Expatriates were often pioneers in the creation of indigenized liturgies and in the reclamation of the African past in Christian tradition. The White Father anthropologist Aylward Shorter, who worked for decades in Uganda and Kenya, is an outstanding example. Some experimented with a radicalized and indigenized lifestyle; one expatriate priest attempted to live as a nomad among the Pokot.

Not all welcomed inculturation. Another missionary in northern Kenya said, '"Africans have no culture, so they must accept Christianity in its Western form completely." Others were ambivalent. Most were inarticulate'.[43]

Missionaries who applauded spirit possession as 'client-centred therapy' took it for granted that these spirits had no ontological reality. An earlier generation of missionaries had seen the spiritual entities in African religion as 'real', but demonic. Archbishop Milingo was overtly hostile to 'the priest-graduates and post-graduates of African Anthropology', claiming that they were incapable of responding to African needs, because they did not accept the objective reality of witchcraft or of *mashavi* spirits: 'One wonders as to whether they intend to convert an African to his own culture or to teach him what he is'.[44] 'I have never come across any Western Missionary who has accepted what I have written about the spirit world . . .' 'I have talked with the witches and I have dealt with the dead'.[45] The effectiveness of his ministry, and that of some less famous African clergy, reflected the fact that he shared a belief in their objective reality with his flock.

Rome is often torn between a theoretical appreciation of the need for inculturation, and a fear of where it might lead to. No less a figure than Cardinal Joseph Ratzinger condemns Liberation Theology, and has publicly expressed his misgivings about African theology: '. . . *African theology* is at present more a project than a reality. . . . We cannot exclude the possibility that the common awareness of what is regarded as "African" may put the common awareness of what is Catholic in the shade'.[46]

Increasingly, complaints are heard that at least some African Catholic clergy have moved away from celibacy. In 1992, the *Kenya Times* claimed that, 'There are numerous Roman Catholic priests with girlfriends, children and even entire families'.[47] There is, of course, a widespread rejection of clerical celibacy in the western world,[48] but many African priests have persevered with their calling, including the commitment to celibacy, until death.

Prosperity and poverty

Those who were in a position to seize the many opportunities independence offered were often the products of mission schools. Their salaries were based on the incomes and perquisites of expatriates, while manual workers' incomes were geared to those of the rural sector. The typical élite Christian was generous, sustaining a considerable number of dependants, but church attendance was a forum for conspicuous consumption, and the need for expensive clothes and substantial offerings often excluded the poor altogether. In Zambia, Archbishop Milingo condemned the élite when other bishops often courted them, as their natural supporters:

> The flattery that goes on in the Church in relation to those who hold high offices in Government or business has to disappear. . . . They are so high that they cannot reduce themselves to the grassroots level of the parish. . . . Surely they enjoy being considered Christians, but as a matter of fact they are not.[49]

A Nigerian wrote, 'The hope for Africa is that Mercedes-Benz cars, large bank balances, political power, large and well-furnished houses and all the other outer trappings of materialism may not . . . choke the spread of the Gospel. . . .'[50]

Although in South Africa, as we have seen, Liberation Theology is well-established, the main concern elsewhere is inculturation, the incarnation of Christianity in African cultures. A practical problem in the indigenization of liturgy lies in the fact that this must necessarily take place in terms of a specific language and culture, and is not easy to apply to the polyglot cities. More fundamentally, in the light of the deepening crisis in Africa, concern about indigenization seems a luxury: 'There are so many problems which the people truly experience: witchcraft, health, healing, military regimes, one-party states . . . social justice. . . . Besides such problems as these, the need to compose African canons for the mass, or to reform the sacrament of confession, pales into insignificance'.[51]

Not all take this view. Shorter points out that socio-cultural factors are important, both for development, and for less tangible indices of well-being. The Camerounian, Jean-Marc Ela, has suggested that, 'Africans themselves cannot carry out inculturation, as long as they are in cultural and socio-economic bondage to non-Africans'.[52]

Why is Liberation Theology, so strongly established in South America, virtually confined in Africa to South Africa? Various factors have been suggested, among these the fact that the colonial era in Africa ended recently, whereas, in Latin America, nominal political independence was achieved long ago, and the contradictions of continuing external economic control and of poverty in a context of apparent autonomy are more apparent. The 'Religious Right' is active in South America as well, while, 'African Christianity's growth and vitality come from the evangelical revival'.[53]

African Christendom, like Africa in general, is divided by language barriers. Indeed, one of the most lasting and pernicious results of colonialism is its division of Africa into English-, French-, and Portuguese-speaking countries. These divisions go deeper than language.

African priests have a formation in philosophy, and indeed, some have gone on to develop a professional involvement in this field. But both philosophy and theology are on the margins of African studies as a whole. Many Africanists would question the whole concept of 'African philosophy'.

There is a band of brilliant Francophone intellectuals, who often are or have been Catholic priests, and who studied in French or Belgian universities. With a few exceptions, such as the Cameroon Jesuit, Engelbert Mveng, their work is little known to Anglophone Christians, or to the international Africanist community. One of their most distinguished representatives is the Cameroonian, F. Eboussi Boulaga. He was a Jesuit professor of theology until he returned to his village to rethink the whole Christian enterprise in Africa, after which he left the priesthood, and the Jesuits. His book, *Christianisme sans fétiches*, is vigorously critical of 'middle-class Christianity', and of missionary discourse, 'The language of derision . . . of refutation'.[54] He has little enthusiasm for Liberation Theology, an attitude shared by the remarkable Zairois intellectual, Mudimbe, whose work, more than perhaps any other, bridges these disparate intellectual worlds: 'It joins in the service of new political chauvinisms and idols, repeating the missionary's dream of conciliating God's glory and Caesar's power.'[55]

Alienation and art

A Zairois writer describes a continuing alienation in Catholic schools: 'the images, symbols, the places mentioned and moreover the language used do not correspond to the creative imagination and feelings of Zairian pupils'. He complains that school-leavers feel more at home with Charlemagne and Abraham Lincoln than with their own culture:[56] 'Alienated. This is what the African has been. Alienated from himself. Because of a complexity of factors— some too painful to enumerate here . . .'.[57]

Modern African literature often describes Christian missions as a source of division and alienation, and this is reflected in the very titles of some of its most famous examples: *Things Fall Apart*, and *The River Between*.

Some escape from these conflicts to a traditional world that perhaps, never was, but is invented in the poems of Senghor, the prose of Camera Laye, and

332

Michel Kayoya. The Nobel Prize winner, Wole Soyinka, writes, with immense affection, of his Christian childhood, but it is a world full of traditional presences, where Uncle Sanya is an *Oro* or forest spirit.

Perhaps the most successful incarnation of Christianity in African cultural life is found in the hymns and liturgies of the prophetic churches, and in art. Mveng suggests, 'We are on the verge of a golden age in Christian art'. It flourishes throughout black Africa, especially, perhaps, in Zaire. Artists are often forced to use cheap materials, cement instead of marble, resin on glass instead of stained glass. Some art is anonymous, some collectively signed, some the work of individuals, such as Pap'Nemma's Christ walking to Calvary through an African city street.[58]

Women

Hastings makes the arresting suggestion that the churches in Africa began as, and have returned to being, 'feminine alternative societies to the male-dominated secular world'; that when the Church was marginal to society, women were central to it, and that they have returned to that centrality. In the colonial period, the Church became less marginal, and women more so.[59]

This is not entirely convincing since most African sisterhoods were founded in the colonial period, and African nuns outnumber African priests today largely because the priesthood requires a long and very demanding course of study. However, there is a sense in which the churches are, in his words, 'feminine alternative societies' that take many forms, the Manyano-style women's organizations, the innumerable women prophets and healers.

Women dominate many church congregations; they also provide the bulk of church attendance in Mediterranean Europe. To Hillman, describing the phenomenon among the Kenya nomads, it is part of 'the feminisation of Christianity', which he deplores.[60]

Despite the immense importance African cultures attach to motherhood, large numbers of women still choose to become nuns. In 1979, there were 33 678 women religious in Africa; 12 thousand of these were Africans (of these, 10 thousand were members of African congregations).[61] In Kenya in 1982, there were 865 priests (214 of them Kenyans), 200 brothers, and 1927 sisters.[62] In Zaire, in 1977, there were 2595 priests (675 of them Zairois) and 4109 professed sisters (1891 of them Zairois). Relatively few African men opt for religious life, partly because of the historic reluctance of missionary congregations to admit them, and partly because they wish to be able to help family members materially, which at least, in theory, a vow of poverty precludes.

The sisters in Zaire alone belonged to 29 diocesan and 126 international congregations,[63] a good example of the extreme fragmentation of women's religious life. Inculturation was easier in African congregations, but they lacked the overseas contacts and financial resources of their international counterparts. Sometimes, they are totally dominated by the bishop, and perform domestic tasks for priests, such as cooking, cleaning, and laundry.[64]

The Protestant Churches

The divisions evident in the Milingo affair have parallels in other churches. In a comparable conflict among the Ewe Presbyterians of Ghana, it is the African church leader who rejects evil spirits as imaginary. Professor Noah Dzobo, Moderator since 1981, is in the tradition of African Christian theologians such as Mbiti and Idowu. He has developed a theology called, in Ewe, *Mele agbe*, I am alive, emphasizing the positive and life-affirming elements in Ewe and Christian tradition. The majority of the Church's members are shocked by his lack of belief in the Devil and traditional spirits, and grassroots prayer groups, dominated by women, hold weekly services, practising healing and exorcism.[65]

Both Catholics and Protestants were gravely affected by the nationalization of mission schools that often followed independence. The relationship between missions and the colonial state was often a cosy one, as missions provided educational and health services in return for government subsidies.

In 1957, the newly independent government of Sudan nationalized mission schools, and many other independent African states were soon to do likewise, including Tanzania, under a devout Catholic President. Mission schools were nationalized in eastern Nigeria, but not in the rest of the country, after the civil war.

The older churches lost an important part of their power base, the patronage, which the control of many salaried posts provided and a captive audience of impressionable children. In Malawi, Presbyterianism was dominant before independence, but is now weakened by government control of schools and health facilities.[66] The decline of external financial aid, the exodus of foreign personnel, the loss of African Christians to prophetic churches—all these factors have undermined the role of the older churches: A perceptive observer of the contemporary Nigerian religious scene writes of 'a considerable erosion of their prestige' and of 'a reduction in commitment and allegiances of many of their members'.[67] Another notes; 'While attendances at the orthodox churches are falling, spiritual churches are swelling in numbers . . . the Celestial and the Cherubim and Seraphim churches show a massive increase in membership.'[68]

The proliferation of new churches

As we have seen, there has been a huge proliferation of new churches in the 1980s, and they undoubtedly represent, to some extent, an attempt to derive a livelihood in an age of unemployment. The founding of churches is a career open to talent, for which no formal qualifications are needed. In 1988, the Nigerian Ministry for Home Affairs received applications to open 33 new churches, and many more were founded without formal approval.[69]

Many of these churches, and many of the new foreign missions being founded, are in the Evangelical and/or Pentecostal tradition, and emphasize the need for a specific conversion experience, and the literal inerrancy of the Bible. Those who choose Jesus have an eternity in heaven; those who do not, an eternity in hell.

Whereas most of the great prophetic figures in the past were people of limited education, many of the new churches are being founded by graduates. In Nigeria, Pastor Chris Okotie is a former lawyer, while the Deeper Life Ministry was founded by William Kumuyi in 1973; at the time, he was a lecturer in mathematics at the University of Lagos.[70]

Many of the new churches bear the imprint of a particular complex of ideas originating in America, but they do not form one, unified corpus of thought. They are divided over pentecostalism, and the merits and demerits of the 'gospel of prosperity'. What may be called, for convenience, the 'New Religious Right' emphasizes the necessity of making a decision for Christ, and the verbal inspiration of the Bible.[71]

Sometimes the latter leads to bizarre exegesis. Pamphlets by Gordon Lindsay, on sale at the Harare 'Fire' Conference of 1986, for example, suggested that the world will end in 3001, and that the Bible predicts both television and the motor car.[72] It has much support in the southern United States, and is often associated with racism, homophobia, sexism, and extreme hostility to Communism, even though these are not the elements that are of paramount concern in Black Africa. There is a widespread belief that the End is near, so that catastrophes such as famines are regarded not as human problems needing human solutions, but as signals of its approach. There is a tendency to interpret social problems in demonic terms, too. It has been suggested that Liberia is afflicted by the demon of rice shortages. There is often an emphasis on miraculous healing.

The 'Gospel of Prosperity' is a remarkable strand in much of this thinking.[73] However bizarre these ideas appear to many Christians (what has happened to 'Blessed are the Poor', or Dives and Lazarus?), they have become enormously influential in American business circles, among white South Africans, and in black Africa generally. The 'Gospel of Prosperity' teaches that God intends His followers to prosper, and that the way to riches is by giving, or, more specifically, tithing. Partly because of the enormous costs of their ministry, these ideas were widely disseminated in America by tele-Evangelists, some of whom are now in eclipse, Jerry Falwell, Jimmy Swaggart, Jim and Tammy Bakker, being some prominent examples.

Benson Idahosa of Nigeria is founder of the Church of God Mission International, which has 1 thousand branches, and is a notable African

335

example. He was one of the African speakers at the 'Fire' Conference in Harare in 1986. The Conference was dominated by American Evangelists, and attracted delegates from forty-one African countries. He said 'The Church can stop marxism, communism and bad politicians', and that South Africa's problems could be solved by 'signs and wonders'. He summarizes his own teaching as the baptism in the Holy Spirit, and the casting out of demons.[74] He is cited by American exponents of the 'Gospel of Prosperity' as a prime example of its effectiveness,[75] as is the Deeper Life Ministry, said to collect at least 20 thousand naira each Sunday.[76]

There is a whole network of large, international organizations, the religious equivalent of the giant oil corporations, including Campus Crusade for Christ, Youth with a Mission, the Full Gospel Businessmen's Fellowship, and many more. Bonnke's Christ for All Nations, based in Frankfurt (until 1986, in Johannesburg), was founded specifically to work in Africa.

These organizations offer support and funds to local collaborators. There is even an independent church in Calabar that is called the Crystal Cathedral after Robert Schuller's church in a Los Angeles suburb (which is neither crystal, nor a cathedral).

The success of all this in Black Africa is not surprising. The 'Gospel of Prosperity' promises a miraculous escape from unemployment and poverty. Also, its exponents, and other Evangelicals offer study courses and reading material, both of which are often in short supply. Gifford points out that the Living Waters ministry, specifically committed to the 'Gospel of Prosperity', has enrolled more students in Liberia than all the mainstream seminaries combined.[77] It fits in well, too, with the values of traditional cultures, where religious rituals ensure health and prosperity and protection against the forces of evil.

The 'Gospel of Prosperity' is popular among white Christians in South Africa, as it seems to bless their privileged position, and guarantee its continuance. Kenneth Hagan, founder of the Rhema Bible Church in Tulsa, is one of its main gurus, and there are a number of flourishing Rhema Bible Church groups in South Africa. Its effect, as Gifford points out, is to defend the status quo, diverting attention from the structural causes of poverty, and defusing dissatisfaction by proferring the hope of a magical transformation. We noted in the preceding chapter how this tendency was repudiated in a document issued by 'Concerned Evangelicals' in South Africa, in 1986: 'We wish to confess that our evangelical family has a track record of supporting and legitimating oppressive regimes here and elsewhere'.[78]

There has been an influx of extreme right wing Protestant missionary societies in Africa. Two of them, the Summer Institute of Linguistics (alias the Wycliffe Bible Translators), and the New Tribes Mission have been fiercely criticized for their role in South America.[79] They have 3500 and 2500 personnel, respectively, world-wide.[80] They are fiercely exclusivist: 'We are not ecumenical, charismatic or neo-evangelical',[81] states a manifesto of the

New Tribes Mission, who have stations in four West African countries, and, 'We believe in the unending punishment of unsaved'.[82] A peculiarity of both the New Tribes Mission and the Summer Institute is that they concentrate so much on language study—often languages spoken only by a tiny community—that this greatly limits their outreach. Lewis described a South American missionary who had spent ten years translating Galatians into Kadiweu, while the Kadiweu themselves died out around him.[83] The New Tribes Mission developed a novel version of the Gospel:

The Panare killed Jesus Christ
because they were wicked
Let's kill Jesus Christ
said the Panare
. . . God will exterminate the Panare by throwing them on the fire. . . .[84]

The Baptist Mid-Missions share this kind of exclusivist outlook, Billy Graham being among the 'neo-Evangelicals' whose fellowship they shun. Exclusivist missions avoid dealings with members of the World Council of Churches, and feel closer to the Faith Missions, especially the Sudan Interior Mission, the Worldwide Evangelization Crusade, and the churches that have grown out of them. In their emphasis on the approach of the End, hostility to Communism, and disregard for social issues, they have much in common with the Catholic, conservative, visionary tradition.

It is possible to exaggerate the novelty of all this. Nineteenth-century Evangelicals believed that the heathen were perishing, and that Britain had an empire because it was blessed by God, and Robert Arthington wanted the Gospel preached to all nations to hasten the millenium. Evangelicalism has always been the core ideology of the Faith Missions, and Pentecostal missionaries founded branches of the Assemblies of God and the Apostolic Church in Africa, and contributed to the growth of one of the leading Aladura churches. However, this said, there is a difference, compounded, essentially, by the sophistication of the information technology used, and the extreme lack of sophistication of the modern vision of the message. Earlier Evangelicals did not think the Lord's children were entitled to the equivalent of a Mercedes-Benz, nor did they make reference to the demon of rice shortages. More than ever before, technological developments make it increasingly possible to change the environment, but, in America, still one of the most powerful nations in the world, an ideology has been widely adopted that despairs of social and economic improvement, and looks to the millenium.

The Born Again divide African Christianity by questioning the religious credentials of other believers. In 1988, a Nigerian self-styled 'Christian fundamentalist' attacked Catholics, Methodists, Presbyterians, and Anglicans, as being 'bent on not conforming to the teachings of Christ'. He was responding to an article by a Nigerian Catholic priest, asking that 'ordinary Christians' should not be treated as unbelievers, and enemies.[85]

Alternatives

In earlier chapters, we documented the survival of traditional religions. Male and female spirit mediums played an important role in the guerilla struggle against white domination in Zimbabwe in the years before independence in the 1970s, for example, and the spirit of Grandmother Nehanda protected the fighters in their hour of peril. Her medium, an old woman, died in Mozambique in self-chosen political exile, and 'When we crossed into Zimbabwe we put our weapons there [on her grave] and praised the ancestors'.[86] Poetry honours the dead in a fusion of traditional and Christian idioms:

> Yet not in death they lie
> But in immortal love of Nehanda,
> Anointed of Chaminuka . . .
> Et lux perpetua
> Luceat eis.[87]

Traditional religion still survives in many forms, not least in the sensibility of African Christians. 'Does your God really want us to climb to the top of a tall palm tree, then take off our hands and let ourselves fall?' questioned an Ijo asked to abandon his traditional gods.[88] Belief in traditional healing and spirit possession is so widespread in post-Independence Zambia that some have spoken of a revival.[89]

Some, especially among the élite, have moved to a post-Christian position, adopting 'scientific socialism', or, more commonly, absorbing the general secularity so common in the western world. Ethiopian students, with whom Singleton conversed in the late 1970s, proved 'resolutely anti-religious if not downright atheist'.[90]

Given the stress and difficulty of life in contemporary Africa, and in the absence of an adequate health system, people frequently explore a number of different sources of spiritual power at the same time. Soyinka satirizes this in his *Requiem for a Futurologist*, but there are many real-life examples. General Ignatius Acheampong ruled Ghana from 1972 to 1978. Born a Catholic, he was, at the time of his coup, a member of the Nazirite Healing Church. He rechristened the many organizations that bore the name Black Star, including the national shipping line, in the belief that it was sinister. An independent church leader, Brother Korie, founder of the F'Eden Church, was one of his ardent supporters, as were the prophetic churches in general; the older churches were more critical. A Californian woman called Mother Prophet, a member of 'a fellowship of ascended Masters' visited Ghana and spoke in support of the government.[91] This panoply of spiritual forces, however, did him little good, and he was executed in 1979.

It is important to realize that many of the developments we have examined are African manifestations of trends that are worldwide, such as the concern for inculturation in mainstream churches, and the rise of the 'Religious Right'. The tendency to 'magical' and instrumental religion, and to syncretism, with an attendant emphasis on benefits in this world, tends to be labelled 'New Age' in the western world.

Church and State: some political leaders

The missions' near-monopoly of education meant that many of Africa's new rulers came from Christian backgrounds. 'Seek ye first the political kingdom and all other things shall be added to you' are the words inscribed on Nkrumah's statue, erected in 1958 and his party adopted 'Lead Kindly Light' as their theme song. The Christian Council of Ghana objected to the inscription, terming it 'an irreverent parody'[92] What it reflects is optimism, and the way in which Christian idioms had become part and parcel of much educated thought.

The leaders of the new states were often acclaimed in quasi-Messianic terms. Nkrumah was called *Osagyefo*, 'Deliverer', a word used for God in Fante Methodist services.[93] Azikiwe's followers were sometimes equally hyperbolic. Zik himself said, 'I will publicly admit that I have never claimed to be a New Messiah, although for reasons best known to a section of the West African Press I have been elevated to that creditable and immortal position'.[94] In the heady days before independence, enthusiasts spoke of 'Dr Kaunda the Son of God who was sent to liberate the Black Zambia'.[95] All this was essentially rhetorical, like traditional praise-singing.

Leopold Senghor, the President of Senegal until a peaceful transfer of power to a Muslim, Abdou Diouf, in 1981, was an ex-seminarian. He had left the seminary reluctantly, and always spoke of his departure with regret. Despite his experience of 'the divorce existing between the doctrine and the life of European Christians, between Christ's word and Christian acts',[96] he remained a Catholic intellectual, much influenced, first, by Maritain, and, later, by Teilhard de Chardin. One of the leading exponents of négritude, he spent many years in Paris, and, in 1960, became President of an independent Senegal. He had a knowledge of Catholic social teachings that had few parallels among world statesmen, and a great capacity for political survival—86 per cent of the population of Senegal is Muslim, 5 per cent Christian—but his socialism was purely rhetorical, a position not peculiar to Senegal.

The President of the Ivory Coast, Félix Houphouet-Boigny (*d.* 1993), was another survivor. He made no secret of his vast fortune,[97] some of which was used to build an enormous basilica modelled on St Peters, and capable of seating 300 thousand. One of the stained glass windows shows him as a pilgrim, the only African image in the vast edifice.[98] It has been interpreted as a symbol of 'a society alienated from its own people'.[99] In 1990, Pope John Paul II opened it in person, despite the opposition of the Ivorian clergy.[100] To most observers, this profligate expenditure in the midst of poverty was a scandal,[101] and the long-term future of the edifice is uncertain as only a tenth of the population is Catholic.

Julius Nyerere began his career as a teacher in a Catholic mission school, and guided Tanzania's fortunes from independence in 1961 until his retirement in 1985. He was committed to what he called African socialism, rooted in Christianity, and in the communal sharing he believed characteristic of African societies in the past. Both by precept and example, he opposed corruption and the pursuit of individual wealth, and committed himself to the bettering of the conditions of the poor. He worked closely with Muslims, and was strikingly successful in avoiding the ethnic and religious divisions that devastated so much of newly independent Africa.

His policies were not always successful, and compulsory resettlement in Ujamaa villages left many families poorer than before. The petroleum crisis, the decline in the demand for sisal (Tanzania's main export), and drought created a catastrophic indebtedness, and narrowly circumscribed Tanzanians' freedom of choice. But the Arusha Declaration speaks to us still, and Nyerere's idealism and altruism have never been seriously questioned. Few have contributed more to the international image of Africa.

Kenneth Kaunda of Zambia was, in some ways, Nyerere's Presbyterian counterpart. Like him, he played a leading role in opposing white domination, a costly and, ultimately, unsustainable policy as Zambia was virtually surrounded by the last bastions of European rule. He developed his own political philosophy, which he called Humanism. However, the dramatic fall in the price of copper in 1975 undermined his popularity, and, in 1990, Zambians rioted for food, and rejoiced at the news of a non-existent coup. In 1991, he acceded to the growing demand for multiparty democracy, and contested an election, which he lost. He was the first African statesman since independence to lose an election, and relinquish power. Nothing in his career became him like the leaving of it.

When one of his sons died of AIDS, he publicly acknowledged the fact, splintering the disastrous denial that had contributed so much to its spread in Africa. Much earlier in his career, he said, 'Christ cuts right through the artificial cloaks with which we surround ourselves and by which we endeavour to give meaning and status to our lives. He uncovers the ultimate truth behind it all and, though often costly and painfully, liberates man from his self-made prison and makes him available to God'.[102]

CHRISTIANS AND MUSLIMS: THE SUDAN

A bitter struggle between the Muslim and Arab 'North' and the Nilotic 'South' began in 1955, and lasted until 1972. After nearly a decade of uneasy peace, war broke out again in 1983. The South is thought to be 70 per cent traditionalist, 17 per cent Catholic and 10 per cent Protestant in contrast with the overwhelmingly Muslim North.[103]

Christian–Muslim tensions, while not the sole cause of civil war, have greatly exacerbated it. Christians are dominant in the southern élite, and their sense of identity, and their grievances sprang largely from legislation that affected religion, such as the State's takeover of mission schools, the replacement of Sunday by Friday as a public holiday, and the expulsion of foreign missionaries in 1964:[104]

> Our problem arose with red people.
> We have no forgiveness.
> They kill us day by day
> Yet they say we are brothers.[105]

The reason for the renewed outbreak of war in 1983 was Nimeiri's introduction of Sharia (Islamic) law. War and drought (and, ironically, floods) have decimated the peoples of the South, but the war continues. The first war was between government soldiers and those of the independence movement, Any-nya. In the second war, the South is itself divided, and has come to experience 'a war of all against all'.[106]

CHRISTIANS AND MUSLIMS: NIGERIA

The Nigerian civil war was not primarily a war about religion. Many perceived it as such, including many Biafrans and church sympathizers abroad, but this was deeply resented by the many Christians on the Nigerian side, including Yakubu Gowon, the Head of the Military Government.

The immediate origins of the war lay in a military coup, in January 1966. Its leaders hoped to end corruption and tribalism, and to establish a unitary and reforming government. Partly through chance, it bore the unintended appearance of an Igbo and Christian takeover. This was the spark that ignited the smouldering resentment at injustices that were rooted largely in colonial policies, which gave the Igbo and other Christian southerners much earlier access to western education, and all the prizes associated with it. All this led to mob violence in the North. The Igbo became scapegoats, the Other, whom the mob pursued, instead of their real enemy, poverty, which was less easily routed. Twice in 1966, Igbo living in the North were attacked; 7 to 9 thousand lost their lives, and, perhaps, a million refugees returned home. Many of their assailants were not Muslims, but Christians from the so-called Middle Belt.

In May, 1967, after unsuccessful attempts at negotiation, Ojukwu proclaimed the secession of the Republic of Biafra. To the Igbo, the justification for their action was self-evident; they were leaving a state in which they had not been permitted to live. Much has been written by scholars (including the author) on the war that followed. After it ended, I recorded a series of conversations with one of the most famous Nigerian Christians, Sir Francis Akanu Ibiam, who renounced his knighthood, dropped his first name during the war, and had acted as a roving Biafran ambassador:

When the war broke out I went to all the most dangerous war areas. I didn't carry arms—I just wore my Biafran cap. Ojukwu asked me to go on missions overseas . . . I refused. I said people say in nine weeks all will be overrun and everyone be killed. I must stay and be killed with my brothers. Then a message came from the World Council of Churches . . . I agreed then, that was the call of the church. . . . I told them—the churches—the Biafran side. I told them to use their influence to stop the war. If they can't get that, to get recognition. If they can't get that, to send clothes, medicine, food. We were completely blockaded. That was the beginning of the most wonderful Christian witness. Otherwise, we would all have been dead.[107]

When the war was over, the genocide the Igbo dreaded did not happen, and the world marvelled at the speed and thoroughness of the reconciliation: 'While the black man has little to teach us about making war he has a real contribution to offer in making peace'.[108]

Ibiam was abroad at the time, and was advised to stay there. He returned, expecting to be imprisoned or shot: 'Everyone was so kind, looking for my bags. . . . Then I found my brother-in-law waiting for me, and we went home'.[109]

On another occasion he told me:

After the war a young man came to me and said, 'We fought in the name of God. Why has he turned against us? I won't go to church again'. I said, 'Who are you to judge God? We put our trust in God. I still don't see to today what we did to the rest of Nigeria. But Christ died on a tree. He went around doing good and they put him to death. That's your answer'.[110]

The Igbo rebuilt their lives with the same courage and determination they had shown in war. The Irish Holy Ghost Fathers had identified strongly with the Igbo cause, finding in it echoes of their own history, but they were not allowed to return, and the church schools in the East were nationalized. There were so many Igbo priests, however, that the absence of expatriates was scarcely noticed. Some of the Spiritans turned to another mission field, often in Zambia. Many did not. It was a striking example of the way in which mission often filled the needs of the missionary.

Christian–Muslim conflict became much more of a reality in the two decades that followed. Many Christians in the South accepted Muslim political dominance, preferring this to the risk of further bloodshed, but there was always an underlying tension. The issue that attracted most impassioned debate at the Constituent Assembly of 1977–8 was the membership of the Sharia Court of Appeal. In 1982, a number of churches were burned by a Muslim crowd in Kano.[111] In 1986, Nigeria was widely believed to have joined the Islamic Conference Organisation,[112] and it was this issue, and the revived question of the Sharia Court of Appeal, that led Christians in the North to a new militancy.

The focus of conflict now became clashes between bodies of fundamentalist Christian and Muslim students in the North.

What became known as the Kafanchan crisis began at a College of Education in central Nigeria. The Muslim Students Society, understandably enough, objected to a banner erected by the Fellowship of Christian Students that read, 'Welcome to Mission '87 in Jesus Campus'. The banner was removed, but a talk during the Mission by a northern Christian was felt to misinterpret the Qur'an. In the days that followed, Christians in Kafanchan attacked Muslims, with swift reprisals following in a number of northern cities. A total of 19 people were killed, and 152 churches and five mosques destroyed.[113]

The following year, Christian and Muslim students fought each other at Ahmadu Bello University; 1 was killed and over 100 injured.

There was an unsuccessful coup attempt in 1990, led by Christians in the North, who sought to excise the five northern states from Nigeria.[114] It was essentially a protest against Muslim dominance in the central government and army. The Kano riots in the same year, in which hundreds died, were sparked by a mission from Reinhard Bonnke. Observers called it 'a microcosm of a crisis waiting to happen across the country'.[115]

In April 1991, hundreds were killed in Muslim–Christian violence in Bauchi State.[116] In February 1992, Muslim Hausa fought Christian Katab in Kaduna.[117]

Religion was only one of many components in the Nigerian civil war, which was caused, largely, by interethnic resentments and stereotypes, and by social and economic problems. Ethnic hostility was recognized as an evil, and, although the conflict produced some atrocities, it was lamented as a brothers' war. Although more recent clashes have exacted lower casualties, they are rooted in religious bigotry. They cast a frightening shadow over Nigeria's future.

UGANDA

In Amin's Uganda, Christians died under a government headed by a Muslim, but the phenomenon was not religious persecution, and probably just as many died under his successor, Milton Obote. In 1959, 28.5 per cent of Uganda's population was thought to be Catholic, 27.7 per cent Protestant, and 4.7 per cent Muslim.[118] Milton Obote's Uganda People's Congress was overwhelmingly Protestant, and the Democratic Party predominantly Catholic.[119] The Ganda movement, *Kabaka Yekka*, 'King Alone', showed a tendency to revive traditional religion.

Idi Amin seized power in 1971, and kept it until 1979. He was a Kukwa Muslim, who relied heavily on traditionally 'Nubian' elements in the army.[120] Thousands died in those years, a number of prominent Christians among them, the victims of ethnic phobia and paranoia rather than of religous persecution. They included the Chief Justice, Benedicto Kiwanuka, who was

A History of Christianity in Africa

the former head of the Democratic Party, and Father Clement Kiggundu, editor of a Catholic daily. Many Christians in the southern Sudan supported Amin, to whom they were ethnically linked.

Amin's overthrow was followed by 'Obote II', seven years of bloodshed and misrule.[121] It came to an end in 1986, when Yoweri Museveni, an ethnic Tutsi, generally regarded as Uganda's most satisfactory ruler to date, led a successful coup. The main rising against his government was led by a woman prophet (see page 349).

Central Africa

CHURCH AND STATE IN ZAIRE

The Catholic church in Zaire displays a striking vitality, reflected in the steady increase in the numbers of priests, nuns, and seminarians, and in the creativity of its religious thought and praxis, exemplified in the Zaire Rite.[122] Its thinkers (together with those of Cameroon and South Africa), provide the cutting edge of African theology. Cardinal Malula has borne a prophetic witness for many years, as an advocate of inculturation and a critic of unjust governments, and, more recently, of his own clergy.[123]

Joseph-Désiré Mobutu seized power in 1965, and has retained it ever since, relying heavily on the support of the western powers, which enabled him to survive the insurrections of 1977 and 1978. From the early 1970s, he developed a policy of 'authenticity' (later, 'Mobutism'),[124] an assertion of traditional African values that, in the eyes of his critics, was a smokescreen designed to distract attention from his pro-western tendencies on the one hand, and his lack of development policies on the other.

In 1972, Christian names were compulsorily replaced with African ones, the President becoming Mobutu Sese Seko. Religious broadcasting, church youth groups, and religious publications were banned, and the Catholic university, the Lovanium, was nationalized. Like Constantine, he sought to unify Christianity in the interests of political unity.

After 1972, only three Christian churches were allowed: the Protestants (who became the United Church of Christ in Zaire, ECZ), the Catholics, and the Kimbanguists. Some small prophetic churches sought admission to ECZ, but without success.[125]

As reports of corruption and human rights violations slowly alienated his external supporters, and his allies—the FNLA—were defeated in Angola, Mobutu, conscious of his own vulnerability, sought a rapprochement with the churches. In 1990 he, too, announced his conversion to multiparty democracy.

By the early 1990s, Zaire was virtually ungoverned, and crushed by its billions of dollars of indebtedness. Mobutu was popularly known as Noah, because he spent so much time on a yacht.[126]

344

A Zairois speaks of the growth of anti-clericalism among the élite: 'A good number of intellectuals . . . prefer to keep at a distance. . . . It could be that they wait for a total "decolonization" of the Church and of the image of the Church'.[127]

CENTRAL AFRICAN REPUBLIC

Jean-Bedel Bokassa, the then head of the gendarmerie, seized power in a military coup in Central African Republic in 1966. He ruled with profligate extravagance and brutality, earning the ridicule of the world when he was crowned as Emperor in 1977.

Some of his shortcomings may have been due to the traumas of his childhood. His father was killed by the French, his mother committed suicide, and he was raised by Catholic missionaries.[128]

He was overthrown in 1979, as a result of street demonstrations by schoolchildren, many of whom were killed (commentators have drawn parallels with Soweto).[129] Today, his palace is overgrown with weeds. Bokassa, his life spared as a result of greater humanity than he showed to others, serves a life sentence. He spends much of the time studying the Bible, signing his letters 'the 73rd disciple of Jesus Christ'.[130]

EQUATORIAL GUINEA

It is sometimes suggested that more Christians have died by Christian hands than by Muslim ones in independent Africa. Those who say this are thinking especially of Equatorial Guinea, and of Burundi.

In 1968, Francisco Macias Nguéma, a former clerk, became the first President of the tiny state of Equatorial Guinea, comprising Fernando Po (now Bioko), and a coastal enclave. He developed a paranoid fear of conspiracy, which caused him to be violently hostile both to the Church and to the nation's tiny élite. Of those who held office at the time, ten out of the twelve ministers and two-thirds of the Assembly had disappeared ten years later. In a population of 280 thousand, some 50 thousand were killed, and the same number escaped into exile.

Macias modified church services: 'God created Equatorial Guinea thanks to Macias'. In 1975, Christian names and Christian funerals were prohibited, and, in 1978, he declared the country 'atheistical' and banned the Catholic Church, to which 70 per cent or more of the population belonged.[131] He fostered a popular belief in his own supernatural powers, and, when he was overthrown in 1979, it was Moroccan mercenaries who shot him.[132]

RWANDA AND BURUNDI

In both of these states, the Hutu formed 80 per cent or more of the population. In both, a consiousness of 'racial' divisions hardened during the colonial period, and, in 1959–62, there was a Hutu revolution in Rwanda. The Tutsi monarchy was abolished, many Tutsi were killed, or went into exile, and

Rwanda became a Republic under a Hutu government. In 1963, 5 to 8 thousand were killed in reprisals after an unsuccessful Tutsi coup.

The atrocities in neighbouring Burundi were due largely to fear, and an awareness of events in Rwanda. Here, the Tutsi minority kept power by a slaughter of the educated Hutu so extensive that it has been called genocide. In 1973, the Tutsi massacred the Hutu on a vast scale, estimates of the number of victims varying between 100 thousand and 200 thousand, while 150 thousand were exiled (the total population is 4.5 million). The dead included 'Hutu civil servants, students, schoolchildren, priests, skilled workers and successful peasants, in what has been rightly termed a "selective genocide" '.[133] Among seventeen murdered priests was the poet, Michel Kayoya.[134]

In the years that followed, the Hutu were largely excluded from schools and universities. The regime came into increasing conflict with the Catholic Church from 1984 on and, in 1986, the Government stopped a literacy and religious education programme attended by 300 thousand Hutu children, and imprisoned a seventy-three-year-old Jesuit, Gabriel Barakana. The Pope, not noted for his rebukes of oppressive African governments, wrote an open letter to the bishops of Burundi, deploring 'the expulsion of missionaries, the imprisonment of several priests, the nationalisation of secondary schools and seminaries, the closure of catechists' training centres and the suppression of the *Action Catholique* movement'.

The predominantly Tutsi hierarchy were often criticized for their silence, and Rose Ndayahozé, the widow of a Hutu minister murdered in 1972, criticized the Bishop of Bujumbura in an open letter.

There was an interesting growth of grass roots Christian communities, *Sahwanyas*, influenced by Liberation Theology, while another movement was dedicated to the Virgin Mary.

In 1988, 20 thousand Hutu were slaughtered in Burundi, and over 50 thousand exiled; commentators compared it with South Africa, to the latter's advantage. In 1994, Rwanda was convulsed by an ethnic bloodletting which may have killed as many as half a million—mainly Tutsi— in massacres explained, though not excused, by a state of civil war (Rwanda was invaded by the (Tutsi) Rwanda Patriotic Front), the holocausts of the past, and the assassination of the Hutu Presidents of Rwanda and Burundi. The victims included the Catholic Archbishop of Kigali and twelve of his priests, and a journalist reported, 'Most of Rwanda's churches are stained with the blood of people who hoped to find safety'.[135]

Malawi

President Hastings Kamuzu Banda was educated in America, with the support of the African Methodist Episcopal Church. He obtained medical qualifications in both America and England, and practised as a doctor for many years in London. He returned to Malawi in 1958 to imprisonment, and led his country to freedom amid tumultuous acclaim. Who would have predicted that he would still be in power in the 1990s aged over ninety, or that he would join the ranks of Africa's dictators (albeit with some peculiarities of his own, such as his protective attitude to the university teaching of classics). He agreed to elections when mortally ill, and was defeated in 1994.

The shortcomings of rulers such as Amin and Bokassa are at least partly due to their lack of education, whereas Banda was better educated than most of the world's leading statesmen. Malawi has been compared with an old African kingdom, without the checks and balances:

> Banda . . . cultivates a supernatural connection. He blesses the farmers' crops. He exploits traditional cults like the *nyau* secret society of the Chewa people.[136]

The Jehovah's Witnesses endured savage persecution, and political opponents were killed, imprisoned, or exiled. In March 1992, the Catholic bishops issued a pastoral letter condemning his government, somewhat belatedly, for its oppression.[137] In the face of increasing popular unrest, the withdrawal of foreign aid, and reminders of his own mortality Banda, too, moved grudgingly towards democracy.

Banda and Macias were not the only African rulers to bolster their position by claiming magical powers. President Gnassingbé Eyadéma, who seized power in Togo in 1965 and has retained it ever since, has a 'mystical cult which he has built around himself and which is vital to his hold on power'.[138]

Liberia

In Liberia, as we have previously seen, Christianity was one of the pillars of Americo-Liberian hegemony. The True Whig Party ruled Liberia from 1869 until 1980, when army forces, led by Samuel Doe, seized power. The preceding government had left much to be desired—a classic instance of a neo-colonial economy, and of 'growth without development'. Doe was pledged to end corruption, and to empower the non-Settler majority, and the coup was greeted with initial jubilation. However, the next decade saw the development of a bloodthirsty tyranny, and a detailed study shows how his regime, like that which preceded it, was defended by the rhetoric of Christianity.

Three very different church leaders, all Liberians, had the courage to condemn it: the Catholic Archbishop, Michael Francis, the Baptist, Reverend Walter Richard, and Abba Karnga, the head of a relatively small church, founded in 1961 by a break with the Baptist Mid-Mission[139] (Karnga also advocates inculturation, in a way untypical of Evangelicals.) They have parallels elsewhere, such as Cardinal Malula in Zaire, noted earlier, and Olubunmi Okogie, Catholic Archbishop of Lagos, who was 'a constant thorn in the government flesh' in Babangida's Nigeria.[140]

In 1990, having lived by the sword, Doe perished by it in dreadful circumstances, and his fall was followed by a protracted civil war.

Nation states and the independent churches

We have seen how colonial governments sometimes supressed independent churches and imprisoned their leaders. Acheompong relied on prophetic church support, and Mobutu recognized the Kimbanguists, but not other prophetic churches. However, often, independent African nations have shown themselves to be less tolerant towards independency than their predecessors: Togo banned thirty sects, Kenya legislated against fringe religious movements, the Tanzanian Ministry of Home Affairs condemned a church called Christ the Light of the World, and, in 1978, the People's Republic of Congo banned all but seven religious bodies.[141]

One-of the most tragic conflicts between Church and State took place in Zambia, soon after Independence. The Lumpa Church was founded in 1955, and, in its aim and origins, was much like innumerable other prophetic churches.[142] Its founder, Alice Lenshina (c. 1919–1978), attended primary school with Kenneth Kaunda. She went through a near-death experience while still a catechumen and was given a special mission:

> I saw a brilliant Light
> I wanted to go forward
> But I heard a voice
> that said:
> No, I send you back to the village
> You have been given a task
> to build on the rock.[143]

She became a baptized member of the Church at Lubwa, which Kaunda's father had founded, but her teachings soon took her outside its fold, as she called on witches to repent, offered protection against witchcraft, and began to baptize. She opposed polygamy, beer, sorcery, divination, and protective charms as well as harmful ones. Her spirituality centred on the sanctity of the home, and the mutual love of husband and wife:

> Look at your happy friends,
> called by the Lord.
> Their marriage sparkles,
> sparkles like a star.[144]

Like Shembe, she was an inspired composer of hymns, in her case in Bemba:

> You who love the land of darkness,
> let us break through, be saved.
> He will help us in everything,
> he will take us out of evil,
> when, when?[145]

She left the administration of the Church to her husband, Petros Mulenga, though, in general, women and men played an equal role in church affairs.

Pilgrims came to her village, Kasomo, from far afield, carrying her teachings back to their homes. A large brick temple was built, and, by 1959, she may have had between 50 and 100 thousand followers, among them Robert Kaunda, Kenneth's brother. 'Lumpa' in Bemba means both to excel, and to go far. It was said that God had given her 'a book specially for Africans, since the Europeans had hidden the book that the Africans should have seen'.[146]

The estrangement that developed between the Church and Kaunda's United National Independence Party (UNIP) was intended by neither. The Lumpa believed that the End of all things was at hand, and, increasingly, sought to withdraw from a sinful world. Their need for land for separate villages led to conflict with Bemba chiefs. Fighting broke out, during which 700 were killed. Many Lumpa went into exile for a time, and the conflict was a great embarrassment to a newly independent Zambia. Petros and Alice died in detention, in 1972 and 1978, respectively, and the great church in Kasomo was razed to the ground. Towards the end of her life, Alice complained that political concerns had obscured her original message of conversion.

The Jehovah's Witnesses have often found themselves at odds with government as their refusal to vote, sing a national anthem, or salute the flag seemed an affront to newly acquired national sovereignty. We have noted their persecution under Banda; 36 thousand fled to Mozambique in 1973, only to be repatriated, to further persecution, two years later.[147]

The Witnesses are the largest Church in Zambia, and are concentrated in Luapula Province. A survey in 1971 listed 130 thousand Witnesses, followed by 85 800 Catholics and 50 thousand African Methodist Episcopalians.[148] They were persecuted by UNIP activists in the late 1960s, until Kaunda asserted his authority in the interests of toleration.[149]

In 1986, 296 people were on trial in Rwanda, including Witnesses, and members of three other independent religious bodies: the *Tempérants d'Afrique Centrale*, the *Abantu Bahimana*, 'the people of God who repent', and the *Abarokoré* (that is, the *Balokolé*, Revival). Charges included their opposition to compulsory Saturday work, and to Party levies. Sects were also blamed for destroying statues of the Virgin Mary.[150]

In 1988, there was a rising among the Acholi of northern Uganda, led by a twenty-seven-year-old woman prophet from Gulu, Alice Lakwena (Lakwena, 'messenger', is a word sometimes used for Christ). She provided magic potions, thought to offer protection against bullets:

> Rebel religious beliefs seem to be a mixture of local rituals and Roman Catholicism, a legacy of the Verona Fathers' 70 year presence in Acholi. One observer thought that the use of magic may have been confined to the Holy Spirit Battalion, but several rebel attacks have been led by charges of men singing Christian hymns. . . . The battle field at Corner Kilak was littered with magical objects made from wire including models of helicopters, tanks and artillery.[151]

Alice Lakwena's forces came within 62 miles of the capital, and then suffered a crushing defeat. She fled to Kenya, where she was detained, but the Acholi rising continued, with the same permutations of religious ideology, reminiscent of eastern Zaire in the early 1960s. One group was led by Joseph Kony, a young man who claimed to be an incarnation of the Holy Spirit. Another was led by Lakwena's father, Severino Lokoya, who called himself God the Father, declared Wednesday a holy day, appointed a bishop, and promised a variety of benefits, including raising the dead.[152]

Many educated Acholi were killed by Amin, and many more live in exile.[153] This type of syncretism fills the vacuum. It reflects political goals that are both passionately held and impossible to attain.

Gender

In some ways, Christianity has empowered women. We have noted the strength of women's organizations in the older churches, and the role of women as healers and founders in the prophetic ones. Some churches have become more aware of gender issues, partly because this is perceived as a dimension of modernity. We have noted the Aladura training institute for 'prophets and prophetesses'.

As elsewhere in the world, many pressures militate against the monogamous and permanent family. An increasing number of urban women are single, or divorced mothers. A study in Cameroon showed that 65 per cent of women whose marriages had broken down remarried, and 42 per cent of men married polygamously.[154] In some cases, Christian forms of marriage gave women fewer rights than they had before. A prominent Catholic laywoman in Tanzania reflected:

> In Africa, the woman as a human being . . . is often puzzled and even confused by Christianity as presented to her. What is puzzling is not the Bible as a whole. . . . The problem for the women . . . is the set-up of the Church as brought to Africa. . . . The woman often finds herself a second, if not a third-class citizen in the Church.[155]

Christians and Marxists: the 'opaque reality'[156]

The reality of Church–State relations in professedly Marxist states in Africa is a complex one. The 'Religious Right' has often transmuted them into Godless Governments, much to the benefit of those who seek to overthrow them. In the mid 1970s, some idealists, such as Basil Davidson, believed that states that won their independence through an armed struggle (such as Angola and Mozambique), and that were, it seemed, committed to socialism, would create the just society, the grass roots participation, that seemed so patently lacking elsewhere. Now he writes of the state itself as being 'the black man's burden'. Similar hopes, perhaps more securely founded, now focus on Eritrea.

The stereotype of Godless Communism can have grave practical implications. In Mozambique, Renamo was virtually defeated by 1980, its
resurgence being due to external (specifically South African and American)
aid,[157] warmly endorsed by the Religious Right. The President of Shekinah
ministries wrote, 'Mozambique is under legal control of an anti-Christian
government; the RENAMO (or MNR) forces are fighting Communism;
Dhlakama, their President, says, 'we need God, we want Jesus'.[158]

In Angola, UNITA enjoys similar 'New Right' support; the result is a
country plunged in war, and banditry costing tens of thousands of lives.[159]

What, if anything, did the rulers of Mozambique, Zimbabwe, Angola,
Benin, Madagascar, Congo, and Ethiopia mean by their Marxism? There is no
single answer. Often it meant little more than the desire for internal reform,
an aspiration to social justice. Cynics claimed that it was intended to justify
autocracy, or win aid and military hardware from the Communist bloc. In
Benin, Marxism was officially adopted in 1974, and given up in 1989, with
scarcely a ripple. In Ethiopia, the government of Haile Mengistu Mariam was
replaced by one more democratically inclined, though still 'socialist'. In an age
of *glasnost*, one hears less of Marxism in Africa.

The freedom of action of these governments has been narrowly circumscribed. Ethiopia has been torn by separatist movements, and wracked with
famine, Angola and Mozambique ravaged by civil war. Zimbabwe is clearly not
hostile to religion at all; many leading politicans are church members, or even
ordained clergy; and there are daily prayers on state-owned television. In
Benin, in the 1970s, schools were nationalized, as they were in many other
non-socialist contexts, some missionaries were expelled, and the celebration
of Christmas was prohibited, but there was no real suppression or persecution.

In Mozambique and Angola, hostility to the church reflected its long-
continued association with Portuguese rule. The late President, Samora
Machel, in particular, made no secret of his dislike of both Islam and
Christianity: 'The seminary emptied during the euphoria of liberation and
independence . . .', and a priest reflected 'I believe that, in the past, the
Church's attitude towards socialism and Marxism was too antagonistic, too
stubborn, and often too absolute and too self-confident. . . . There was no
oppression of religion but repression of reactionary forces'.[160]

The Burundi priest, Michel Kayoya, was killed before these governments
came to power, but he wrote, with prophetic insight, of the intellectual
adventures of his friends:

> The African politician, hard-pressed by action will
> perhaps be able to say with Marx: 'Let us suppress God,
> and man will be happy . . .'.
> After so much trouble I was disillusioned.
> Communism was not only incapable of granting what I
> dreamed. But it was capable of taking it away.

He ended thinking of his people's 'self-construction':

> I felt powerless in front of this task
> But acknowledging my greatness as a man
> I decided to move
> Man is a being who falls as he walks
> Who walks as he falls
> His greatness lies in the strength he has to get up again![161]

A body of superiors of religious orders asked, 'In situations where a Marxist ideology prevails can we not relinquish our security, so often based on esteem, possessions, power, foreign connections, for the sake of the kingdom of God?'[162]

The picture we have painted in this chapter is a sombre one, one of a continent in crisis, where Christianity has sometimes endorsed the forces of oppression and division. But it is possible that upheavals and crises might have a liberating effect, fracturing the institutional Church, so that, through the cracks, living local communities might grow and flourish. This process has been discerned in Zimbabwe:

> Missionary activity in the rural areas along structural ecclesiastical lines was almost totally strangled during the difficult years of war and destruction. Yet the number of the faithful has continued to increase. . . . Priests were no longer in a position to inspire the local communities in the usual manner. . . . Local lay leaders stepped forward and took it upon themselves to keep the community's faith alive.[163]

Postscript

One day, sitting down and reading, I heard humming and chanting. Under a tree there were three men and three women and a child. One of the men was obviously the leader, and one of the women held the young child in her arms. The leader was shaking pebbles in a gourd and chanting a litany. He sprinkled water from the gourd on both child and mother, and gave the child a piece of charcoal. Later on I asked him, 'What were you doing there?' He answered 'We Pokot were talking to God, asking him to cure a sick child'. I asked him 'Were you talking to the Pokot God, or to the European God?' The leader smiled and said 'There is only one God'. Then I said to him, 'Now we have a word for religion, which is "talking to God".' 'What was' I asked him, 'the name of your prayer:' He said 'the blessing of a sick child'.[1]

Notes

Prelude

1 J. O. Mills, 'Comment', *New Blackfriars*, Jan., 1984, p. 3.
2 J. Peel, 'The Christianization of African Society', in E. Fasholé-Luke *et al.*, *Christianity in Independent Africa* (Rex Collings, London, 1978) p. 445. This expression includes expansion elsewhere in the Third World.
3 David B. Barrett (ed), *World Christian Encyclopedia: A comparative survey of churches and religions in the modern world*, AD 1900–2000 (Oxford University Press, Nairobi, 1982) p. 4, Global Table 2. I have rounded the figures, which, in the Table, stand at 9 938 448, 142 962 732, and 393 326 210 respectively. The impression of precision they give, is, of course, misleading.
4 One source suggests that there were 130 million African Christians in 1982 (58 million Catholics, 47 million Protestants, and 25 million Orthodox); another suggests 150 million Christians (48 million Catholics, 69 million Protestants and 13 million Orthodox). Cf. A. Mbembe, 'Rome and the African Churches', *Pro Mundi Vita*, Africa Dossier 37–8, (1986), pp. 3–6, quoting *Encyclopaedia Brittanica* (Book of the year, 1982) and *Missi* (Lyons, 1982,) p. 200.
5 Barrett, *World Christian Encyclopedia* p. 436.
6 A. F. Walls, 'Towards Understanding Africa's Place in Christian History', in J. S. Pobee (ed.), *Religion in a Pluralistic Society* (E. J. Brill, London, 1976) p. 180.
7 Quoted in Peel, 'The Christianization of African Society', p. 450 n. 14.
8 Mbembe, 'Rome and the African Churches', p. 20.
9 Psalm 68.31.
10 A. Shorter, *Towards a Theology of Inculturation* (Orbis, Maryknoll, New York, 1988) pp. 193–4.
11 These are the Igbo names of four of my own children; the fifth is Nkemnacho, which means 'what I have desired is my own', an expression of welcome for an eagerly awaited child. Modern Igbo Christians take it for granted that these are 'traditional' names, referring to a 'traditional' high God, whose attributes are much the same as those of God the Father. Several Igbo scholars have questioned these equations, in important debates we cannot discuss here (cf. n. 30 below).
12 T. O. Ranger, *The African Churches of Tanzania*, (Historical Association of Tanzania, Paper 5, E. Africa Publishing House, Nairobi, n.d.) p. 4.
13 P. Gifford, 'Prosperity: a new and foreign element in African Christianity', *Religion*, 1990, pp. 373–88.
14 Walls, 'Towards Understanding Africa's Place in Christian History', p. 188.
15 Quoted in H. Turner, 'A Typology for African Religious Movements', in his *Religious Innovation in Africa* (G. K. Hall, Boston, 1979) p. 87.

354

Notes

16 A. Shorter, *African Christian Theology: Adaptation or Incarnation?* (Chapman, London, 1975) p. 6.

17 Peel, 'The Christianization of African Society', pp. 448–9.

18 F. Eboussi Boulaga, *Christianity Without Fetishes* (Eng. trans., Orbis, New York, 1984), p. 71.

19 J. V. Taylor and D. Lehmann, *Christians of the Copperbelt* (SCM, London, 1961) p. 287.

20 O. Kalu, 'Broken Covenants: Religious Change in Igbo Historiography', *Neue Zeitschrift für Missionswissenschaft*, 1990, p. 307. Similar reservations were expressed by another Nigerian, the late Byang Kato, and, in South Africa, by C. G. Oosthuizen.

21 L. Gilkey, 'Plurality and its Theological Implications', in J. Hick and P. Knitter, eds, *The Myth of Christian Uniqueness. Towards a Pluralistic Theology of Religions* (Orbis, Maryknoll, New York, 1987) p. 47.

22 I. Hamnett, ed., *Religious Pluralism and Unbelief* (Routledge, London and New York, 1990); E. Isichei, 'Some Ambiguities in the Academic Study of Religion', *Religion*, 1993, pp. 384–5.

23 P. Gifford, *The Religious Right in Southern Africa* (Baobab, Harare, 1988) p. 87.

24 S. Sykes, *The Identity of Christianity* (SPCK, London, 1984) p. 254.

25 Peel, 'The Christianization of African Society', pp. 451–2.

26 Tai Solarin, 'The Christian Church in Nigeria', paper given to the conference on Christianity in Independent Africa, Jos, 1975.

27 Peel, 'The Christianization of African Society', pp. 451–2.

28 T. O. Ranger and I. Kimambo, *The Historical Study of African Religion* (Heinemann, London, 1972); R. Horton, 'African Conversion', *Africa*, 1971, pp. 85 ff., and 'A 100 Years of Change in Kalabari religion', in J. Middleton, ed., *'Black Africa, Its Peoples and their Cultures Today'*, (Macmillan, London, 1970). For a brilliant essay on anthropology and time, cf. J. Fabian, *Time and the Other: How anthropology makes its object* (Columbia University Press, New York, 1983).

29 M. Wilson, *Communal Rituals of the Nyakusa* (Oxford University Press, London, 1959) pp. 157–9.

30 Cf. W. van Binsbergen, 'Regional and non-regional cults of affliction in western Zambia', in R. Werbner, ed., *Regional Cults* (Academic Press, London, 1977) pp. 141ff., and other contributions to this symposium; also M. Daneel, *The God of the Matopo Hills* (Mouton, The Hague, 1970). For a reconsideration of Chukwu, cf. C. N. Ubah, 'The Supreme Being: divinities and ancestors in Igbo Traditional religion: Evidence from Otanchara and Otanzu', *Africa*, 1982, pp. 102ff., and R. Shaw, 'The Invention of "African Traditional Religion"' *Religion*, 1990, pp. 347–9.

31 R. Willis, *There Was a Certain Man: Spoken art of the Fipa* (Oxford University Press, London, 1978) p. 98. The 'God of the Door' is a traditional name, meaning the God who preserves us through the night, so that we can open the door in the morning.

32 R. Gray, *Black Christians White Missionaries* (Yale University Press, New Haven, 1990), p. 1. cf. p. 205–6.

33 James Fernandez, 'African Religious Movements', *Annual Review of Anthropology*, 1978, p. 200.

34 W. MacGaffey, *Modern Kongo Prophets* (Indiana University Press), Bloomington, 1983), pp. 3–4.

35 Cf. N. H. Ngada, *et al.*, *Speaking for Ourselves* (Institute for Contextual Theology, Braamfontein, 1985) p. 5. V. Mudimbe, *The Invention of Africa: Gnosis, philosophy and the order of knowledge* (Indiana University Press, Bloomington, 1988).

36 E. Isichei, 'Introduction', *Varieties of Christian Experience in Nigeria* (Macmillan, London, 1982) p. 8.

Notes

37 Cf., for instance, the section on religion in R. Rotberg and A. Mazrui, *Protest and Power in Black Africa* (Oxford University Press, London, 1970). There are many other examples, often valuable and excellent in themselves.

38 Ngada, *et al.*, *Speaking for Ourselves*, p. 16.

39 For instance, Dr Ayo Ogunranti's work on the Christ Apostolic Church, in which he is a pastor.

40 S. Marks and R. Rathbone, eds, *Industrialisation and Social Change in South Africa* (Longman, Harlow, 1982).

41 Fernandez, 'African Religious Movements', p. 215.

42 E. Evans-Pritchard, *Witchcraft, Oracles and Magic Among the Azande* (Clarendon Press, Oxford, 1937) pp. xviii and 195. In the first passage, Evans-Pritchard is cited during a Foreword by C. G. Seligman.

43 Fernandez, 'African Religious Movements', pp. 220, 225.

44 J. Janzen, 'The consequences of literacy in African religion' in W. van Binsbergen and M. Schoffeleers, *Theoretical Explorations in African Religions* (KPI, London, 1985) pp. 226–7; the seminal study here was J. Goody, ed., *Literacy in Traditional Societies* (Cambridge University Press, Cambridge, 1968).

45 For the comments of a notable architect of typologies to this effect, cf. Fernandez, 'African Religious Movements', pp. 201–4.

46 Dini ya Msambwa, discussed on p. 257.

47 V. Lanternari, 'Revolution and/or Integration in African Socio-Religious Movements', in B. Lincoln, ed., *Religion, Rebellion, Revolution* (Macmillan, London, 1985) p. 129ff.

48 Jean Comaroff, *Body of Power, Spirit of Resistance* (University of Chicago Press, Chicago, 1985) p. 254.

49 Boulaga, *Christianity Without Fetishes*, pp. 30–2; pp. 57ff.

Chapter 1

1 Quoted in J. D. Y. Peel, 'Syncretism and Religious Change', *Comparative Studies in Society and History*, 1967–8, p. 125. Map 3, illustrating this chapter, is not synchronic; it shows the location of the places listed in the text, without reflecting the fact that, for instance, Constantinople/Byzantium was founded in 330, long after the fall of Phoenician Carthage.

2 Herodotus, *The Histories*, (Penguin, Harmondsworth, 1954) p. 294.

3 Isaiah 11.11; 18.1–2; Jeremiah 44, Zephanaiah 3.10.

4 This is argued in H. A. Green, 'The Socio-Economic Background of Christianity in Egypt', in B. A. Pearson and J. E. Goehring, eds, *The Roots of Egyptian Christianity* (Fortress Press, Philadelphia, 1986) pp. 110–111.

5 Mark 15.21; Acts, 2, 5–12; 11, 20, 13.1; 18.24.

6 For this distinctive community, cf. S. Goiten, 'The Jews of Yemen', in A. Arberry, ed., *Religion in the Middle East*, I (Cambridge University Press, Cambridge, 1969) pp. 226ff.

7 J. Quirin, 'The Process of Caste Formation in Ethiopia: A Study of the Beta Israel (Falasha) 1270–1868', *International Journal of African Historical Studies*, 1979, p. 236, n. 3, and *passim*. There are strong Judaic elements in Ethiopian Christianity that seem to have evolved in the middle ages, and one view suggests that the Falashas developed their distinctive identity and beliefs at the same time.

8 D. Kessler, *The Falashas. The Forgotten Jews of Ethiopia* (Allen & Unwin, London, 1982) pp. 161–2.

Notes

9 Quoted in A. S. Atiya, *A History of Eastern Christianity* (Methuen, London, 1968) p. 22.

10 The Children of the Sacred Heart in Northern Rhodesia, in 1958, quoted in J. Taylor and D. Lehmann, *Christians of the Copperbelt* (SCM, London, 1961) p. 167.

11 Eusebius, *Ecclesiastical History*, II, 16.

12 The city of Constantinople was founded in 330. Its position as second see after Rome was affirmed by the Councils of Constantinople (381) and of Chalcedon (451). That of Jerusalem was in abeyance after its fall to Titus (AD 70). After the First Council of Ephesus in 431, the sees of Rome, Constantinople, Alexandria, and Antioch were known as patriarchates. Jerusalem was made a patriarchate at the Second Council of Ephesus, in 449.

13 Cf., for instance. Irenaeus, *Against Heresies*, I, XXIII. Except where otherwise stated, I have read and quote patristic texts in the translations in the Ante-Nicene Christian Library (T & T Clark, Edinburgh, 1967–, 25 vols). This ends in 325. Translations of later patristic texts are to be found in *A Select Library of the Nicene and Post-Nicene Fathers* (Christian Literature Co., New York, 1986–90, 14 vols). A ten-volume new edition of the Ante-Nicene Fathers was issued by W. B. Eerdmans, Grand Rapids, 1986–9. They also issued a fourteen-volume edition of the Nicene and Post-Nicene Fathers, 1983–88 (1st series). Augustine's *Confessions* and *City of God*, and Eusebius' *Ecclesiastical History* are available in paperback as Penguin Classics. Cf. also n. 36 and n. 61 of this chapter, for important collections of primary source material by women.

14 Clement, *Excerpts from Theodotus*, 78, 2, quoted in E. Pagels, *The Gnostic Gospels* (Penguin, Harmondsworth, 1982) p. 18. The perennial fascination of Indian mysticism for Christians in the ancient and medieval world forms the theme of my 'Passages to India: Western Images of Indian Spirituality in the Ancient and Medieval World', *Dialogue and Alliance*, 1991, pp. 66–75.

15 Irenaeus, *Against Heresies*. There is a different account of Basilides in Hippolytus, *The Refutation of all Heresies*, VII, 8–15. Clement of Alexandria (*The Miscellanies*, III, 1) is concerned with his teaching on marriage and chastity. The Victorian translator of Clement in the Ante-Nicene Christian Library (Edinburgh, 1869) translated Book III into Latin!

16 Jerome, *Commentary on Hosea*, 11.10, quoted in W. H. C. Frend, *The Rise of Christianity* (Darton, Longman and Todd, London, 1986 p. 207. I am glad to express my indebtedness to this magisterial work, and other studies from the same hand, and to remember his generous critique of the manuscript of my first book, *Political Thinking and Social Experience: Some Christian Interpretations of the Roman Empire* (University of Canterbury Publications, Christchurch, 1964).

17 Pagels, *The Gnostic Gospels*, p. 62.

18 Hippolytus, *The Refutation of all Heresies*, VI, 37.

19 The account that follows is based on Irenaeus, *Against Heresies*, I, 1–5. Hippolytus gives a different version (*The Refutation of all Heresies*, VI, 25ff.)

20 Quoted in Pagels, *The Gnostic Gospels*, pp. 16–17.

21 Irenaeus, *Against Heresies*, I, 13, 1 and 2.

22 Irenaeus, *Against Heresies*, I, 14, 1.

23 Tertullian, *On Proscription Against Heretics*, 41.

24 Clement, *The Miscellanies*, I.

25 Eusebius, *Ecclesiastical History*, V, 10. He states that he met Jewish Christians there, with the Hebrew text of Matthew's Gospel. On this Hebrew Gospel, cf. Irenaeus, *Against Heresies*, III, 1.

357

Notes

26 Clement, *Misc.*, I, 5.

27 Clement, *Misc.*, VI, 10.

28 Quoted in Frend, *The Rise of Christianity*, p. 372. This, like Clement's *Excerpts from Theodotus*, is not included in the two-volume translation of Clement in the Ante-Nicene Christian Library (Edinburgh, 1868).

29 My main source for Origen is J. W. Trigg's useful study, *Origen: The Bible and philosophy in the third-century Church* (John Knox, Atlanta, 1983).

30 Eusebius, *Ecclesiastical History*, VI, 4–5.

31 This was routinely done by the priests of Cybele, and there are other instances in the early Church, and Alexandria.

32 Quoted in Frend, *The Rise of Christianity*, p. 382.

33 E. Gibbon, *The Decline and Fall of the Roman Empire*. Abridged ed., (Book Club Associates, London, 1960) pp. 315–16.

34 A. H. M. Jones, 'Were ancient heresies national or social movements in disguise?', *Journal of Theological Studies*, 1959, p. 296, n. 2: 'the surviving verses are not very inspiring'.

35 Augustine, *Confessions*, I, 13.

36 Rescued from near oblivion by P. Wilson-Kastner, *et al.*, *A lost Tradition: Women writers of the early Church* (University Press of America, Washington, D.C., 1981). For Perpetua, one of the four, cf pp. 34–5.

37 The standard account is W. H. C. Frend, *The Rise of the Monophysite Movement* (Cambridge University Press, Cambridge, 1972).

38 R. Horton, 'African Conversion', *Africa*, 1971, pp. 85–108; 'On the rationality of conversion', Parts 1 and 2, *Africa*, 1975, pp. 219–35, and 373–99.
    Cf. H. J. Fisher, 'Conversion Reconsidered: Some Historical Aspects of Religious Conversion in Black Africa', *Africa*, 1973, pp. 27–40.
    Cf. also the review article by L. R. Rambo, 'Current Research on Religious Conversion', *Religious Studies Review*, 1982, pp. 146–159.

39 Eusebius, *Ecclesiastical History*, VII, 6–9. He also describes Egyptian martyrs in Tyre.

40 For a recent corrective, cf. Margot King, *The Desert Mothers: A survey of the female anchoretical tradition* (Saskatoon, 1983), the impact of which is reduced by the obscurity of its imprint. This was not available to me.

41 Helen Waddell, *The Desert Fathers* (Constable, London, 1977 pp. 73–4.

42 Waddell, *The Desert Fathers*, pp. 145–7.

43 Waddell, *The Desert Fathers*, pp. 52, 65, 154, 97.

44 Augustine, *Confessions*, VIII, 5.

45 Rutilius, *De Reditu Suo*, II 439ff, quoted in Waddell, *The Desert Fathers*, p. 12.

46 E. Gibbon, *The Decline and Fall of the Roman Empire*, Ch. 37, 'Origin of the Monks'.

47 Hermitages, used for short periods of time, in the Russian Orthodox tradition.

48 This, and what follows, is based on Frend, *The Rise of Christianity*.

49 The account that follows is based primarily on W. Y. Adams, *Nubia: Corridor to Africa* (Princeton University Press, Princeton, 1977), Ch. 13ff.

50 Frend, *The Rise of Christianity*, p. 847.

51 Adams, *Nubia*, p. 467.

52 Extract in G. S. Trimingham, *Islam in the Sudan* (Cass, London, 1965) p. 65.

53 F. L. Griffith, in *University of Liverpool Annals of Archaeology and Anthropology*, 1927, 81–91, extract in Adams, *Nubia*, p. 487. The literal meaning of this palindromic square, which has also been found at Pompeii in Italy and in Cirencester, England, is 'Arepo the sower holds the wheels with care.' Like the fish sign it began as a hidden symbol of Christian identity in an age of persecution. TENET forms a cross; the

Notes

letters can be rearranged to form PATERNOSTER in the form of a cross; the left over letters are AOOA, possibly Alpha and Omega. The letters can also be arranged to read, 'Oro Te Pater, Oro Te Pater, sanas'. 'I pray to Thee, Father; Thou healest.' This formula easily became a magical amulet, with its orginal meanings lost; Theophilus thought the words were 'the names of the nails of Christ'.

54 Quoted in Adams, *Nubia*, p. 539.
55 It should be noted that 'India' and 'Ethiopia' are often used interchangeably in the ancient world.
56 S. Kaplan, 'Ezana's Conversion Reconsidered', *Journal of Religion in Africa*, 1982, p. 102; this article is my main source for Ezana's conversion.
57 Kaplan, 'Ezana's Conversion'. Cf. p. 27.
58 According to the *Historia Augusta*, quoted in F. Millar, 'Local cultures in the Roman empire', *Journal of Roman Studies*, 1968–9, (58–9), p. 127 (*'Afrum quiddam usque ad senectutem sonans'*).
59 Josephus, *The Jewish War*, II, 383, 386. (A modern translation, ed. G. Cornfeld, was issued by Zondervan, Grand Rapids, Michigan 1982).
60 Quoted in P. Brown, *Augustine of Hippo: A biography* (Faber and Faber, London, 1967) p. 22.
61 The text I have used is that in E. Petroff, *Medieval Women's Visionary Literature* (Oxford University Press, New York, 1986) pp. 70–77.
62 Cf. M. Lefkowitz, 'The Motivations for St. Perpetua's Martyrdom', *Journal of the American Academy of Religion*, 1976, pp. 417–21; R. Rader, 'The Martyrdom of Perpetua: A Protest Account of Third-Century Christianity', in P. Wilson-Kastner, ed., *A Lost Tradition*, pp. 1–18.
63 Jerome, *De Viribus Illustribis*, 53 given *in extenso* in T. D. Barnes, *Tertullian: A Historical and Literary Study* (Clarendon Press, Oxford, 1971) p. 3. Barnes, however, rejects the detail concerning Tertullian's father, and also the suggestion that he was a priest (pp. 11ff). He also rejects the statement, found in Eusebius, that he was a lawyer, and the generally accepted belief that he founded the Tertullianistae (pp. 258–9). I find all this unconvincing.
64 Jerome, *Ad Uxorem*, II, 8.
65 I explored this theme in some detail in my *Political Thinking and Social Experience*, Ch. 3, pp. 27–40, 'Tertullian, The Politics of Isolation'.
66 Tertullian, *De cultu feminarum*, 8.
67 Tertullian, *Apologeticus*, 37.
68 Cyprian, *To Donatus* (Ep. I) 4.
69 Cyprian, *On the dress of Virgins*, 14.
70 Tertullian, *De cultu feminarum*, II, 13.
71 Pontius, *The Life and Passion of Cyprian, Bishop and Martyr.*
72 Cyprian, *On the Lapsed*, 6.
73 Tertullian, *Apologeticus*, 9.
74 P. Brown, 'Christianity and local culture in late Roman Africa', *Journal of Roman Studies*, 1968, p. 95.
75 Cf. P. Brown, 'Religious coercion in the later Roman empire: the case of North Africa', *History*, 1963, p. 288.
76 W. H. C. Frend, 'The Christian Period in Mediterranean Africa', *The Cambridge History of Africa* (Cambridge University Press, Cambridge, 1978) p. 469.
77 Quoted in Brown, 'Christianity and local culture', p. 89.
78 W. H. C. Frend, *The Donatist Church*. (2nd ed., Clarendon Press, Oxford 1971). Both the nationalist and socio-economic aspects of the theory have been much criticized.

Notes

Cf. A. H. M. Jones, 'Were ancient heresies national or social movements in disguise?', *Journal of Theological Studies*, 1959, pp. 280–98, and Brown, 'Christianity and local culture', for two examples among many. For a postscript by Frend, cf. his 'The Donatist Church—forty years on' in C. Landman and D. Whitelaw, eds, *Windows on Origins* (Universiteit van Sud-Afrika, Pretoria, 1985) pp. 71ff.

79 Optatus of Milevis, quoted in C. Frend, *The Rise of Christianity*, p. 723.
80 Ep. 185 in Frend, *The Rise of Christianity*, p. 723.
81 *Song of Solomon*, 4.12.
82 Brown, 'Religious coercion in the later Roman Empire', pp. 283–305.
83 Brown, 'Religious Coercion in the later Roman Empire', pp. 285ff.
84 The account that follows is based on the *Confessions*, and, especially, on Peter Brown's superb biography, *Augustine of Hippo* (Faber and Faber, London, 1967).
85 C. R. Allberry, *A Manichaean Psalm Book*, II, (Stuttgart, 1938). Cited from Frend, *The Rise of Christianity*, p. 568.
86 H. Z. Hirschberg, 'The Problem of the Judaized Berbers', *The Journal of African History*, 1963, pp. 313ff.
87 Quoted in Brown, *Augustine of Hippo*, p. 387. (Brown's profound sympathy for Augustine leads him to be less than sympathetic to Pelagians. There is a large and growing literature on Pelagianism: Cf. J. N. L. Myres, 'Pelagius and the end of Roman rule in Britain', *Journal of Roman Studies*, 1960, pp. 21ff—an interesting paper that has not won general acceptance; J. Morris, 'Pelagian Literature', *Journal of Theological Studies*, 1965, pp. 26ff; R. F. Evans, *Pelagius: Inquiries and Reappraisals* (Seabury Press, New York, 1968), and two chapters on the Pelagian circle in P. Brown, *Religion and Society in the Age of Saint Augustine* (Faber and Faber, New York, 1972).
88 Socrates, *Ecclesiastical History*, vii.
89 Tertullian, *Apologeticus*, 40.
90 Cf. 'Lactantius, the Difficulties of Transition' in my *Political Thinking and Social Experience*, pp. 58–71.
91 Lactantius, *Divine Institutes*, VI, 9 and 6.
92 Augustine, *City of God*, XIV, 28, and XIX, 26.
93 Frend, in *The Cambridge History of Africa*, II, p. 479, and n. 3. This is the main source for what follows.
94 Frend, 'The Christian period', p. 488.
95 It has been suggested that 'Donatist' here refers only to North African intransigence; they are, however, referred to as *rebaptizati*. Cf. R. A. Markus, 'Donatism the Last Phase', *Studies in Church History* I, (Nelson, London, 1964), pp. 118–126, (papers read at the Ecclesiastical History Society), and 'Reflections on religious dissent in North Africa in the Byzantine period', *Studies in Church History*, III, 1966, pp. 140–149.
96 I. Hrbek, 'Egypt Nubia and the Eastern deserts', *The Cambridge History of Africa*, III, 23, 38–9.
97 M. Singleton, 'Ethiopia: A Tale of Two Revolutions', *Pro Mundi Vita*, Africa Dossier 5 (Jan.–Feb., 1978) p. 21.
98 M. Brett, 'The Arab Conquest and the Rise of Islam in North Africa', *The Cambridge History of Africa*, II, p. 509.
99 On this obscure last phase, cf. W. H. C. Frend, 'Christianity in the Middle East: Survey down to AD 1800', in A. J. Arberry, ed., *Religion in the Middle East* (Cambridge University Press, Cambridge, 1969) pp. 280–283, and Brett, 'The Arab Conquest', pp. 509–11.

Notes

100 R. Goodchild, 'Byzantines, Berbers and Arabs in 7th century Libya', *Antiquity*, 1967, p. 123.
101 Hirschberg, 'The Problem of the Judaized Berbers', p. 323.
102 Quoted in Brown, *Augustine of Hippo*, p. 190. They mistook the ruined baths for the remains of a church.

Chapter 2

1 Jeronimo Lobo, trans., Samuel Johnson, ed. J. Gold, *A Voyage to Abysinnia*, (Yale University Press, New Haven, 1985) p. 4.
2 Quoted in T. Tamrat, *Church and State in Ethiopia 1270–1527* (Clarendon Press, Oxford, 1972) p. 249. For Coptic Christianity in the Middle Years, cf. pp. 217–18. The word Abyssinia comes from 'Habershat,' which refers to the Semitic speakers of Ethiopia only. This is why the name was inappropriate for the modern nation.
3 S. Kaplan, *The Monastic Holy Man and the Christianization of Early Solomonic Ethiopia* (Franz Steiner Verlag, Wiesbaden, 1984) p. 31. The account of monasticism that follows is based on this study.
4 Alvarez, quoted in Kaplan, *The Monastic Holy Man*, p. 79.
5 Kaplan, *The Monastic Holy Man*, p. 70.
6 J. Iliffe, *The African Poor: A history* (Cambridge University Press, Cambridge, 1987) p. 10.
7 G. Haile, 'A Christ for the Gentiles: the case of zä-Krestos of Ethiopia', *Journal of Religion in Africa*, 1985, p. 89.
8 D. Donham, 'Old Abyssinia and the New Ethiopian Empire: Themes in Social History', in D. Donham and W. James, eds., *The Southern Marches of Imperial Ethiopia* (Cambridge University Press, Cambridge, 1986) p. 12.
9 Donham, 'Old Abyssinia and the New Ethiopian Empire', p. 6.
10 J. Quirin, 'The Process of Caste Formation in Ethiopia: A Study of the Beta Israel (Falasha) 1270–1868', *International Journal of African Historical Studies*, 1979, pp. 238 and 250.
11 Quoted in Tadesse Tamrat, 'Processes of Ethnic Interaction and Integration in Ethiopian History: The Case of the Agaw', *The Journal of African History*, 1988, p. 14.
12 Jeronimo Lobo, trans. Samuel Johnson, pp. 41–2.
13 Jeronimo Lobo, pp. 53–4.
14 C. F. Beckingham and G. W. B. Huntingford, (trans. and ed.), *Some Records of Ethiopia 1593–1646* (Hakluyt Series II, CVII, 1954) p. xxiv.
15 W. C. Atkinson, *A History of Spain and Portugal* (Penguin, Harmondsworth, 1961) p. 109.
16 The unification of Spain was achieved by the marriage of Ferdinand of Aragon, and Isabella of Castile in 1469. Had Isabella married an alternative suitor, Alfonso V of Portugal, Aragon, not Portugal, would have retained a separate identity.
17 *The Voyages of Diogo Gomes* (Hakluyt, Series II, LXXX, 1937) p. 102. The alleged crime was selling arms to the Moors.
18 A. Cadamosto, trans. G. R. Crone, *Voyages*, (Hakluyt, Series II, LXXXX, 1937) pp. 2–3.
19 Tadesse Tamrat, 'Ethiopia, the Red Sea and the Horn', in *The Cambridge History of Africa*, III, (Cambridge University Press, Cambridge, 1977) pp. 177–180.
20 Ian Linden, *Catholics, Peasants and Chewa Resistance in Nyasaland 1889–1939* (Berkeley, 1974) p. 4.

Notes

21 Balthasar Barreira, quoted in G. Brooks, 'The Observance of All Souls' Day in the Guinea-Bissau Region', *History in Africa*, 1984, p. 18.

22 J. Delumeau, 'La Legende du Moyen Age chrétien', in *Le Catholicisme entre Luther et Voltaire* (Paris, 1971), cited in P. Biller, 'The Common Woman in the Western Church in the thirteenth and early fourteenth centuries', in W. J. Sheils and D. Wood, eds, *Women in the Church* (Basil Blackwell, Oxford, 1990) p. 131. Biller also cites a study of a healing cult, centred on a holy dog, near Lyons.

23 These examples come from Brooks' interesting analysis of this theme, 'The Observance of All Souls' Day', pp. 3ff.

24 John Barbot, *A Description of the Coasts of North and South Guinea* (Lintoit and Osborn, London, 1746) p. 157.

25 Balthasar Barreira, quoted in Brooks, 'The Observance of All Souls' Day', p. 18.

26 Richard Gray, 'Christian traces and a Franciscan mission in the Central Sudan 1700–1711', *The Journal of African History*, 1967, pp. 383–7.

27 There are many different versions of his name—Lull, Lully— but this is the most accurate in modern Catalan. The account that follows is based on A. Bonner, 'Historical Background and Life', in his *Selected Works of Ramon Llull* (Princeton University Press, Princeton, 1985) 1, 3–52. This gives, *in extenso*, Llull's autobiography, *Vita Coaetanea*, written in 1311.

28 Llull, *Vita Coaetanea*, 5.

29 Llull, *Vita Coaetanea*, 35.

30 Llull, *Vita Coaetanea*, 20.

31 Gomes Eannes de Azuraza, *The Chronicle of the Discovery and Conquest of Guinea*, Series I, XCV, (Hakluyt, 1896) p. 80.

32 C. R. Boxer, *The Church Militant and Iberian Expansion 1440–1770* (Johns Hopkins University Press, Baltimore, 1978) p. 3.

33 Quoted in M. J. Bane, *Catholic Pioneers in West Africa* (Clonmore and Reynolds, Dublin, 1956) p. 105.

34 J. Atkins, *A Voyage to Guinea, Brazil and the West Indies* (Cass, London, 1735/1970) pp. 93–5.

35 John Barbot, *A Description of the Coasts of North and South Guinea*, p. 252.

36 Cacegas and de Souza, in G. M. Theal, *Records of South-Eastern Africa*, I, (Struick, Cape Town, 1964) p. 402.

37 The Cape Verde writer, Manuel Ferreira, quoted in T. B. Duncan, *Atlantic Islands Madeira the Azores and the Cape Verdes in Seventeenth-Century Commerce and Navigation* (University of Chicago Press, Chicago, 1972) p. 196.

38 Boxer, *The Church Militant*, p. 8.

39 Antonio Vieira, quoted in Duncan, *Atlantic Islands*, p. 233.

40 W. Bosman, *A New and Accurate Description of the Coast of Guinea* (Cass, London, 1704/1967) pp. 417–8.

41 João de Barros, *Da Asia*, Series II, LXXX, (Hakluyt, 1937) pp. 142ff. Jelen was the *Bumi* of Jolof. Cf. P. Curtin, *Economic Change in Precolonial Africa* (University of Wisconsin, Madison, 1975), p. 9

42 Quoted in P. Clarke, *West Africa and Christianity*, (Arnold, London, 1986) p. 14.

43 Brooks, 'The Observance of All Souls' Day', pp. 18–20.

44 E. Hamelberg, 'The Jesuits in Sierra Leone 1605–17: A whirlwind of grace', *The Sierra Leone Bulletin of Religion*, 1964, pp. 1–8.

45 Cf. C. Fyfe, *Sierra Leone Inheritance* (Oxford University Press, London, 1964) pp. 49ff. Both Bane and Groves erroneously identify him with the Oba of Benin (cf.

Notes

Bane, *Catholic Pioneers in West Africa* pp. 77–8; C. P. Groves, *The Planting of Christianity in Africa* (Lutterworth, London, 1948) I, p. 127).

46 F. de L. Coelho (a Portuguese merchant), quoted in A. P. Kup, 'Jesuit and Capuchin missions of the seventeenth century', *The Sierra Leone Bulletin of Religion*, 1963, pp. 31–2.

47 Atkins, *A Voyage to Guinea, Brazil and the West Indies*, p. 54. His local origin is suggested by several references on p. 55.

48 Atkins, *A Voyage to Guinea, Brazil and the West Indies*, pp. 51 and 55.

49 João de Barros, *Da Asia*, p. 121.

50 Barbot, *A Description of the Coasts of North and South Guinea*, p. 183.

51 Barbot, *A Description of the Coasts of North and South Guinea*, p. 157.

52 F. L. Bartels, *The Roots of Ghana Methodism* (Cambridge University Press, Cambridge, 1965), p. 6.

53 H. Debrunner, *A Church between Colonial Powers: A Study of the Church in Togo* (Lutterworth, London, 1965) p. 26. Like Svane (who took his patron's name) he was taken to Denmark by a Danish chaplain, Pastor Elias Svane.

54 H. Labouret and P. Rivet, *Le Royaume d'Ardra*, quoted in H. Debrunner, *The Church in Togo*, p. 22. A Belgian Capuchin, Célestin, received a warmer welcome in 1681–4.

55 P. E. H. Hair, 'Ethnolinguistic continuity on the Guinea coast', *The Journal of African History*, 1967, p. 261.

56 They were contemporaries (*flor.* 1670s). R. Law, 'Religion, Trade and Politics on the "Slave Coast" ', *Journal of Religion in Africa*, 1991, pp. 42ff.

57 P. C. Lloyd, *The Itsekiri* (with R. E. Bradbury, *The Benin Kingdom*, XIII (Ethnographic Survey of Africa, Western Africa, London, 1970); Obaro Ikime, 'The Peoples and Kingdoms of the Delta Province', in O. Ikime, ed., *Groundwork of Nigerian History* (Heinemann, for Historical Society of Nigeria, Ibadan, 1980), especially pp. 99–100).

58 The bishop of São Thomé in 1597, quoted in A. F. C. Ryder, 'Missionary Activity in the Kingdom of Warri to the early nineteenth century', *Journal of the Historical Society of Nigeria*, 1960, p. 3.

59 Quoted in Ryder, 'Kingdom of Warri', p. 8.

60 Olfert Dapper, *Naukeurige Beschijvinge der Afrikaensche Gewesen*, extract in T. Hodgkin, *Nigerian Perspectives*. 2nd ed., (Oxford University Press, London, 1975), p. 173. Dapper was a compiler, who did not visit Africa, but much of his material comes from first-hand sources.

61 Quoted in Brooks, 'The Observance of All Souls' Day', p. 10.

62 J. Adams, *Remarks on the Country Extending From Cape Palmas to the River Congo* (Whittaker, London, 1823), pp. 124–5. (This book was reprinted by Cass, London, in 1966.)

63 Public Record Office, FO/84/858, Beecroft to Palmerston 19 April, 1851, recalling a visit eleven years earlier.

64 De Barros, *Da Asia*, p. 126. The identity of the Ogane is obscure and disputed. The Bini still call the Oni of Ife the Ogene, but Ife is West not East of Benin. It is possible that this sacred figure was in central Nigeria, possibly Nupe. Cf. A Ryder, 'A Reconsideration of the Ife-Benin relationship', *The Journal of African History*, 1965, pp. 25ff. Pereira's account refers to 'a king called Licasaguou', whom one scholar has located in north-east Nigeria. (Duarte Pacheco Pereira, *Esmeraldo de Situ Orbis* (Hakluyt, Series II, LXXIX 1937) p. 126.

65 Pereira, p. 126.

Notes

66 The Voyage of M. Thomas Windham to Guinea and the Kingdom of Benin, extract in Hodgkin, Nigerian Perspectives, p. 136.

67 A. Ryder, Benin and the Europeans 1485–1897 (Longman, London, 1969) p. 71.

68 A missionary account from 1652, in A. F. C. Ryder, 'The Benin Missions', Journal of the Historical Society of Nigeria, p. 247. The devotion of modern Bini to the Oba is well-attested.

69 Ryder, 'Benin Mission', p. 246.

70 H. L. Ward Price, Dark Subjects (London, 1939) p. 238. Ward Price served in Nigeria from 1912 to 1936.

71 For which, see the remarkable study by J. Miller, Way of Death: Merchant capitalism and the Angolan slave trade 1730–1830 (James Currey, London, 1988).

72 D. Birmingham, 'Central Africa from Cameroun to the Zambezi', The Cambridge History of Africa (Cambridge.University Press, Cambridge, 1975) IV, p. 332.

73 J. Thornton, 'The development of an African Catholic Church in the Kingdom of Kongo, 1491–1750', The Journal of African History, 1984, pp. 147–167; also his The Kingdom of Kongo, Civil War and Transition 1641–1718, (University of Wisconsin Press, Madison, 1983) Ch. 5; A. Hilton, The Kingdom of Kongo (Clarendon Press, Oxford, 1985); R. Gray, Come Vero Principe Catolico: the Capuchins and the rulers of Soyo in the late seventeenth century', Africa, 1983, pp. 39ff, reprinted in his Black Christians and White Missionaries (New Haven and London, 1990).

74 Rui de Aguiar, in Sigbert Axelson, Culture Confrontation in the Lower Congo (Gunmessons, Uppsala, 1970) p. 66. Studia Missionalia Upsaliensia XIV which is the major source for what follows.

75 Texts in B. Davidson, The African Past: Chronicles from Antiquity to Modern Times (Penguin, Harmondsworth, 1964) pp. 194–7.

76 Hilton, The Kingdom of Kongo, p. 65. Afonso was the King's eldest son by his principal wife, and the Portuguese took it for granted that he was the heir, but the King was selected from an aristocratic clan, the Mwissikongo. As his mother was not a member, he had, in a matrilineal society, no right to the throne.

77 F. Pigafetta, A Report of the Kingdom of Congo (Cass, London, 1970) p. 82. The 1591 original, in Italian, records information from Duarte Lopez.

78 L. Cacegas and L. de Sousa, History of the Order of St. Dominic, extract in G. M. Theal, Records of South-Eastern Africa (Struick, Cape Town, 1964) I, 399.

79 Cf. R. Gray, 'Come Vero Principe Catolico: The Capuchins and the Rulers of Soyo in the late seventeenth century', Africa, 1983, p. 43.

80 Quoted in Gerald Bender, Angola under the Portuguese: The Myth and the Reality (Heinemann, London 1978) p. 17.

81 For contrasting perspectives on Dona Beatrice, cf. Hilton, The Kingdom of Kongo, pp. 208–10, Thornton, pp. 106–113, and Axelson, Culture Confrontation in the Lower Congo, pp. 136–141.

82 Quoted in Thornton, The Kingdom of Kongo, p. 96.

83 The Tuckey expedition, described in Axelson, Culture Confrontation in the Lower Congo, p. 174.

84 Adolf Bastian, in Axelson, Culture Confrontation in the Lower Congo, p. 191.

85 Thornton, 'The development of an African Catholic Church', pp. 165–6. Grey, 'Come Vero Principe Catolico', also stresses the role of lay interpreters, and lay confraternities.

86 J. Miller, 'Queen Nzinga in a new Perspective', The Journal of African History, 1975, pp. 201–16. J. Thornton, 'Legitimacy and Political Power', The Journal of African History, 1991, pp. 25–40.

Notes

87 There is a large body of literature on the Imbangala, as there is on the Jaga, with whom they have sometimes been identified. Practices such as infanticide symbolized their rejection of the mores of ordinary life. It is likely that they were refugees from drought and enslavement (cf. J. Miller, 'The paradoxes of impoverishment in the Atlantic zone', in D. Birmingham and P. Martin, eds, *History of Central Africa* (Longman, London, 1983) I, pp. 139–40.

88 J. Thornton, 'Legitimacy and Political Power: Queen Nzinga 1624–1663', *The Journal of African History*, 1991, pp. 31–4 and n. 37.

89 There is a large and complicated literature on Zimbabwe. On the Shona kingdoms in general, cf. D. N. Beach, *The Shona and Zimbabwe 900–1850*, (Heinemann, London, 1980).

90 This however is questioned by Beach, *The Shona and Zimbabwe*, pp. 355–6, n. 1.

91 Cacegas and de Souza, in Theal, *Records of South-Eastern Africa*, I, 392, citing João dos Santos.

92 Theal, *Records of South-Eastern Africa*, I, 386.

93 On Pombal's expulsion of the Jesuits, cf p. 84. For this period in Zambezia, cf. W. F. Rea, 'The Economics of the Zambezi Missions 1580–1759' and H. Bhila, 'Trade and the Early Missionaries in Southern Zambezia', in M. Bourdillon, ed., *Christianity South of the Zambezi* (Salisbury, 1977) II, 13–42.

94 Quoted in Beach, *The Shona and Zimbabwe*, p. 107.

95 He was blind in one eye; Africa's sacred kings were supposed to be without physical blemish.

96 Cacegas and de Souza, in Theal, *Records of South-Eastern Africa*, I, 402.

97 André Fernandes in Theal, *Records of South-Eastern Africa*, II, 88.

98 Quoted in Boxer, *The Church Militant*, p. 11.

99 Cacegas and de Souza, in Theal, *Records of South-Eastern Africa*, I, 405.

100 The Viceroy of Goa in 1694, quoted in Axelson, *Portuguese in South-East Africa 1600–1700* (Witwatersrand University Press, Johannesburg, 1960), p. 184.

101 Francisco de Sousa, quoted in *The Cambridge History of Africa*, IV, (Cambridge University Press, Cambridge, 1975) p. 396.

102 Quoted in A. and B. Isaacman, *Mozambique: From Colonialism to Revolution 1900–1982* (Westview, Boulder, 1983) p. 15.

103 Linden, *Catholics, Peasants and Chewa Resistance in Nyasaland*, (University of California Press, Berkeley, 1974) p. 5.

104 M. D. Newitt, *Portuguese Settlement on the Zambezi* (Longman, London, 1973) pp. 78–9.

105 David Livingstone, *A Popular Account of Missionary Travels and Researches in South Africa* (J. Murray, London, 1875) p. 415.

106 Linden, *Catholics, Peasants and Chewa Resistance in Nyasaland*, p. 5. This song was recorded early this century.

107 Eric Axelson, *Portuguese in South-East Africa 1600–1700*, pp. 10, 79–80.

108 Axelson, *Portuguese in South-East Africa*, pp. 84–94. For a Mombasa perspective on him, cf. G. S. P. Freeman-Grenville, *The East African Coast*. 2nd edn, (Collings, London, 1975), pp. 218–9.

109 William Snelgrave, *A New Account of Some parts of Guinea and the Slave Trade* (Cass, London, 1734/1967) p. 46.

110 Groves, *The Planting of Christianity in Africa*, I, 163.

111 Paul Edwards, ed., *The Life of Olaudah Equiano, or Gustavus Vassa the African* (Longman, Harlow, 1988) p. 170.

112 R. Gray, 'The Papacy and the Atlantic Slave Trade: Lourenço da Silva, the Capuchins

Notes

and the decisions of the Holy Office', in *Black Christians and White Missionaries* (New Haven and London, 1990) pp. 11ff, is the source for what follows. Thornton, *The Kingdom of Kongo*, p. 91, locates him in Luanda.

113 W. Bosman, *A New and Accurate Description of the Coast of Guinea*, p. 385.
114 Bosman, *A New and Accurate Description of the Coast of Guinea*, pp. 385–6.
115 C. R. Boxer, *The Church Militant*, p. 10.
116 *The Voyages of Cadamosto*, p. 41.

Chapter 3

1 K. Cragg, 'The Anglican Church', in A. Arberry, ed., *Religion in the Middle East* (Cambridge University Press, Cambridge, 1969) I, 591.
2 J. F. A. Ajayi, *Christian Missions in Nigeria 1841–1891* (Longman, London, 1965), and E. Ayandele, *The Missionary Impact on Modern Nigeria 1842–1914* (Longman, London, 1966). N. Grubb, *C. T. Studd: Cricketer and Pioneer* (Lutterworth, London, 1933, 1953 reprint) is a typical example of the older genre. Many more examples could be cited.
3 Cf. T. Beidelman, *Colonial Evangelism: A Socio-Historical Study of an East African Mission at the Grassroots* (Indiana University Press, Bloomington, 1982). This study, however, has been much criticized.
4 This historiography, in its turn, has been strongly criticized, not least by neo-Marxists, but these debates lie beyond the scope of this book.
5 Sir Samuel Baker, in 1867, cited in B. Ray, *African Religions, Symbol, Ritual, and Community* (Prentice-Hall, Englewood Cliffs, New Jersey, 1976) p. 3.
6 R. G. Lienhardt, *Divinity and Experience: The Religion of the Dinka* (Clarendon Press, Oxford, 1961); E. Evans-Pritchard, *Nuer Religion* (Clarendon Press, Oxford, 1956). Cf. J. Burton, 'The Wave is my Mother's Husband: A Piscatorial Theme in Pastoral Nilotic Ethnology', *Cahiers d'Etudes Africaines* (1982) pp. 459ff, and S. Hutchinson, 'Relations between the sexes among the Nuer: 1930', *Africa*, (1980) pp. 370ff.
7 R. Hackett, 'African Religions: Images and I-glasses', *Religion*, 1990, pp. 303ff.
8 E. Benz, 'Pietist and Puritan Sources of Early Protestant World Missions', *Church History*, 1951, pp. 28ff.
9 For a solitary exception, cf. p. 59.
10 M. Horne, *Letters on Missions Addressed to the Protestant Ministers of the British Churches* (1794), pp. 21–2, quoted in B. Stanley, *The Bible and the Flag* (Appollos, Leicester, 1990), p. 56.
11 Eugene Stock, *The History of the Church Missionary Society* (Church Missionary Society, London, 1899) I, pp. 59–60.
12 In this book, for clarity's sake, I refer, for instance, to the Bremen Mission, rather than to the *Norddeutsche Missionsgesellschaft*, and so on.
13 Quoted in H. Debrunner, *The Church in Togo* (Lutterworth, London, 1965) p. 66; this study is the main source for this paragraph.
14 N. Etherington, 'South African Missionary Ideologies 1880–1920 Retrospect and Prospect', in T. Christensen and W. R. Hutchison, eds, *Missionary Ideologies in the Imperialist Era: 1880–1920* (Aros, Aarhus, 1982) p. 194.
15 N. Leys, *Kenya*, 2nd ed., (Hogarth Press, London, 1925), pp. 230–1.
16 Helen Roseveare, *Give Me This Mountain* (Inter-Varsity Fellowship, London, 1966) p. 92.
17 Bishop Steere in 1881, quoted in R. Oliver, *The Missionary Factor in East Africa* (Longmans, Green, London, 1952) p. 12, n. 2.

Notes

18 Stock, *The History of the Church Missionary Society*, I, pp. 89–90.

19 Captain Sir John C. Willoughby, *East Africa and its Big Game* (London, 1889), quoted in R. W. Strayer, *The Making of Mission Communities in East Africa: Anglicans and Africans in Colonial Kenya 1875–1935* (Heinemann, London, 1978) p. 5.

20 A letter of *c.* 1881, quoted in W. H. Bentley, *Pioneering on the Congo* (Religious Tract Society, London, 1900) I, 372. Cf. p. 84 for the Association for the Propagation of the Faith.

21 S. Potter, 'The Making of Missionaries in the Nineteenth Century: Conversion and Convention', in M. Hill, ed., *A Sociological Yearbook of Religion in Britain* (SCM, London, 1975) VIII, p. 105.

22 Max Warren, quoted in Strayer, *The Making of Mission Communities*, p. 5.

23 Stanley, *The Bible and the Flag*, pp. 80–1.

24 Cf. P. Hichliff, 'Voluntary Absolutism: British Missionary Societies in the nineteenth Century', in W. J. Sheils and D. Wood, *Voluntary Religion* (B. Blackwell, Oxford, 1986) pp. 368–9.

25 Carl Nauhaus, quoted in M. Wright, *German Missions in Tanganyika 1891–1941* (Oxford, 1971) p. 98.

26 Quoted in C. P. Groves, *The Planting of Christianity in Africa* (Lutterworth, London, 1948) I, p. 210, n. 3.

27 Holy Ghost Fathers Archives, Paris (henceforward C. S. Sp.), 191/A/6, Lutz to Sainte Enfance, Alsace, 13 Mar., 1886.

28 Quoted in G. Prins, *The Hidden Hippopotamus* (Cambridge University Press, Cambridge, 1980) p. 205.

29 Bentley, *Pioneering on the Congo* I, 130–1.

30 Bentley, *Pioneering on the Congo*, I, 354.

31 Daniel Crawford in Shaba, quoted in R. Rotberg, 'Plymouth Brethren and the occupation of Katanga, 1886–1907', *Journal of African History*, 1964, pp. 285–297.

32 Stock, *The History of the Church Missionary Society*, IV, 464.

33 J. Buchan, *The Expendable Mary Slessor* (Saint Andrew Press, Edinburgh, 1980) p. 238. They were engaged in 1891, when Mary Slessor was forty-three, and Charles Morrison twenty-five.

34 Roseveare, *Give Me This Mountain*, pp. 70 and 118–9. She left the mission on her first furlough, hoping to marry, and rejoined it when the man concerned did not respond. Cf. A. Burgess, *Daylight Must Come: The Story of Dr Helen Roseveare* (M. Joseph, London, 1975) pp. 136–8. She was a medical missionary for the Heart of Africa mission in Zaire, from 1953. This was part of the Worldwide Evangelization Crusade.

35 J. L. Krapf, *Travels, Researches, and Missionary Labours During an Eighteen Years' Residence in Eastern Africa* (first pub. 1860, 2nd ed. Cass, London, 1968), p. 86.

36 Owen Chadwick, *Mackenzie's Grave* (Hodder and Stoughton, London, 1959) p. 83.

37 Grubb, *C. T. Studd*, p. 140. After a period of invalidism she recovered, and devoted herself to publicizing the new mission, travelling widely in the process. It is possible she recovered when she accepted Studd's departure as a *fait accompli*, which her illness would not change.

38 Stock, *The History of the Church Missionary Society*, IV, p. 465.

39 Strayer, *The Making of Mission Communities*, p. 6.

40 P. Williams, 'The Missing Link: The Recruitment of Women Missionaries in some English Evangelical Missionary Societies in the Nineteenth Century', in F. Bowie, *et al.*, eds, *Women and Missions: Past and present* (Berg, Oxford, 1993) p. 59.

41 Stock, *The History of the Church Missionary Society*, I, p. 75. The separate seating of men

Notes

and women at an Anti-Slavery Convention was a decisive experience for that redoubtable American feminist, Elizabeth Cady Stanton.

42 Quoted in Williams, 'The Missing Link', p. 65.

43 Quoted in D. W. Bebbington, *Evangelicalism in Modern Britain: A History from the 1730s to the 1980s* (Unwin Hyman, London, 1989) pp. 1–2.

44 Henry Venn, Secretary of the CMS, quoted in Bebbington, *Evangelicalism in Modern Britain*, p. 3.

45 Quoted in Bebbington, *Evangelicalism in Modern Britain*, p. 12.

46 Cf. p. 72 for the dialogue between a seventeenth-century Augustinian and a Whydah notable on this subject.

47 J. Campbell, ed., *The Farewell Services of Robert Moffat in Edinburgh, Manchester, and London* (London, 1843) p. 109, quoted in Stanley, *The Bible and the Flag*, p. 65.

48 Edward Ash, *Seven Letters to a Member of the Society of Friends* (Norwich, London, 1855) p. 7.

49 David Livingstone, *A Popular Account of Missionary Travels and Researches* (John Murray, London, 1875) p. 63.

50 T. E. Slater, *Philosophy of Missions: A present-day plea* (London, 1882) p. 26, quoted in G. A. Oddie, 'India and Missionary Motives, c. 1850–1900', *Journal of Ecclesiastical History*, 1974, p. 68. Oddie illustrates the same point with an analysis of the changing content of LMS candidates' applications.

51 Quoted in A. Shorter, *Jesus and the Witchdoctor* (Geoffrey Chapman, London, 1985) p. 196.

52 Beidelman, *Colonial Evangelism*, p. 56. However, this was not always the case. George Grenfell was a pioneer BMS missionary in the Congo, and his second wife was of African descent. In South Africa, both van der Kemp and James Read married Khoi wives. The hymn stanza comes from 'From Greenland's icy mountains,' which also refers specifically to Africa. Its author was Bishop Heber, 1782–1826.

53 J. C. Taylor, in Samuel Crowther and J. C. Taylor, *The Gospel on the Banks of the Niger* (Church Missionary House, London, 1859), p. 325.

54 C. S. Sp. 191/A/5, MS. biography of Father Lutz by Father Ebenrecht, f. 35.

55 Beidelman, *Colonial Evangelism*, p. 135.

56 Quoted in M. Louise Pirouet, 'Women Missionaries of the Church Missionary Society in Uganda 1896–1920', in Christensen and Hutchison, eds, *Missionary Ideologies in the Imperialist Era*, p. 236.

57 An unpublished paper by Kate Crechan, cited in C. Bundy, *The Rise and Fall of the South African Peasantry* (Heinemann, London, 1979) p. 37, unnumbered footnote.

58 D. Crawford, *Thinking Black* (Morgan & Scott, London, 1913) p. 115.

59 U. Long, ed., *The Journals of Elizabeth Lees Price* (E. Arnold, London, 1956) p. 373.

60 The title of a chapter in Charles Dickens' *Bleak House*.

61 Charles Buxton, *Memoires of Sir Thomas Fowell Buxton* (Dent, London, 1925) p. 169.

62 J. McCracken, *Politics and Christianity in Malawi 1875–1940* (Cambridge University Press, Cambridge, 1977) p. 30.

63 *The African Times*, 23 Jan., 1863, p. 79.

64 Krapf, *Travels, Researches and Missionary Labours*, p. 89.

65 Mhala's Great Son, quoted in J. B. Peires, 'The Central Beliefs of the Xhosa Cattle-Killing', *The Journal of African History*, 28, 1987, p. 61.

66 R. Hostie *The Life and Death of Religious Orders*, (1983), cited in P. Collins, *Mixed Blessings: John Paul II and the Church of the eighties* (Penguin, Harmondsworth, 1986) pp. 83–4.

67 They were dioceses, in fact, but not in name, and were called Vicariates.

Notes

68 *Illustrated Catholic Missions*, 1900, 169.

69 For an excellent summary, cf. R. Gray, 'Christianity', in *The Cambridge History of Africa*, VII, pp. 158–162.

70 M. Markowitz, *Cross and Sword: The Political Role of Christian Missions in the Belgian Congo, 1908–1960* (Stanford, 1973) pp. 21–2.

71 'We Who Are about to Die Salute You', Cf. Maurice Briault, *La Réprise des Missions d'Afrique au dix-neuvième siècle Le Vénérable Père F.-M.-P. Libermann* (Paris, 1946) p. 243.

72 *Annals of the Propagation of the Faith*, 1904, p. 256.

73 F. Bowie, 'Missionary Attempts to Define Women's roles', in Bowie, *et al.*, *Women and Missions*, p. 147.

74 *Annals of the Propagation of the Faith*, 1905, pp. 98, 100, 105. The other was in the Nile delta.

75 *Annals of the Propagation of the Faith*, 1905, p. 99.

76 *Illustrated Catholic Missions*, 1900, p. 27.

77 F. Aupiais, SMA, *Le Missionaire* (Paris, 1938) p. 36.

78 N. Etherington, 'Social Theory and the Study of Christian Missions in Africa: A South African Case Study', *Africa*, 1977, p. 34.

79 J. F. Faupel, *African Holocaust* (New York, 1962) p. 15.

80 F. Schimlek, *Mariannhill: A study in Bantu life and missionary effort* (Mariannhill, 1953). Their members are sometimes, inaccurately, referred to as Cistercians.

81 *Les Missions Catholiques*, 1917, p. 204, in an approving review of Le Floch, *Les Elites sociales et le Sacerdoce* (Paris, 1916).

82 D. J. Sullivan, *The Land of the Pyramids and 'the White Man's Grave'* (1919) p. 12. Class distinctions among religious orders continue, and are not confined to Ireland.

83 I. Linden, *The Catholic Church and the Struggle for Zimbabwe* (London, 1980) p. 12.

84 C. S. Sp. 191/A/5, Father Ebenrecht, biography of Reverend Joseph Lutz.

85 SMA Archives, Rome. N. Douau, *Mission en Afrique*, Cahier I, (French original) p. 176.

86 Schimlek, *Mariannhill*, pp. 62–4.

87 Quoted in E. Isichei, *Entirely for God: A Life of Michael Iwene Tansi* (Macmillan, London, 1980) p. 76. He was later accepted by Mount St Bernard Abbey. Cf. p. 275.

88 G. Anawati, 'The Roman Catholic Church', in A. Arberry, *Religion in the Middle East*, p. 407.

89 Quoted in Joan Burke, 'These Catholic sisters are all Mamas! Celibacy and the Metaphor of Maternity', in Bowie, *et al.*, eds, *Women and Missions*, p. 261.

90 Bowie, *et al.*, *Women and Missions*.

91 This account is based on C. Oliver, 'Mother Kevin Missionary and Foundress', in her *Western Women in Colonial Africa* (Greenwood Press, Wesport, 1982) pp. 145ff.

92 J. De Benoist, 'The Church in Senegal', in 'The Church in the Sahel', *Pro Mundi Vita*, Africa Dossier 43 (4/1987) p. 20.

93 'Religous Life for Women in Zaire', *Pro Mundi Vita*, Africa Dossier 14 (May, 1980) p. 8, n. 5. For more on African women religious, cf. pp. 333–4.

94 Quoted in T. Ranger, 'Medical Science and Pentecost: the Dilemma of Anglicanism in Africa', in W. J. Sheils, ed., *The Church and Healing* (Blackwell for the Ecclesiastical History Society, Oxford, 1982) p. 349. His discussion of this theme is invaluable.

95 Ranger, 'Medical Science', p. 353.

96 I. Linden, *Church and Revolution in Rwanda* (Manchester University Press, Manchester, 1977) p. 91, n. 55.

97 Bebbington, *Evangelicalism in Modern Britain*, p. 175.

Notes

98 C. T. Studd's last appeal, in 1915, in Grubb, *C. T. Studd*, p. 163.

99 J. H. Boer, *Missionary Messengers of Liberation in a Colonial Context: A case study of the Sudan United Mission* (Rodopi, Amsterdam, 1979) p. 131.

100 Boer, *Missionary Messengers of Liberation*, p. 124.

101 Grubb, *C. T. Studd*, p. 126. Cf. also p. 80.

102 R. Rotberg, *Christian Missionaries and the Creation of Northern Rhodesia 1880–1924* (Princeton, 1965) p. 160.

103 Crawford, *Thinking Black*, p. 213. This book speaks warmly of European missionaries, but tends to depict African cultures in extremely unfavourable ways.

104 This account is based on D. P. Sandgren, *Christianity and the Kikuyu Religious Divisions and Social Conflict* (New York, 1989) pp. 17ff.

105 Sandgren, *Christianity and the Kikuyu*, pp. 17–25.

106 Quoted in Pirouet, 'Women Missionaries of the Church Missionary Society', p. 238.

107 J. V. Taylor, *The Growth of the Church in Buganda* (London, 1958) p. 87.

108 A. Porter, 'Evangelical Enthusiasm, Missionary Motivation and West Africa in the late Nineteenth Century: the Career of G. W. Brooke', *The Journal of Imperial and Commonwealth History*, 1977–8, p. 31.

109 Porter, 'Evangelical Enthusiasm', p. 38.

110 Stanley, 'The Miser of Headingley: Robert Arthington and the Baptist Missionary Society, 1877–1900', in W. J. Shiels and D. Wood, eds, *The Church and Wealth* (Blackwell for the Ecclesiastical History Society, Oxford, 1987) pp. 371–82.

111 R. N. Cust, *An Essay on the prevailing methods of evangelising the non-Christian world* (1894), quoted in Oliver, *The Missionary Factor in East Africa*, p. 25.

112 Tissa Balasuriya, quoted in Stanley, *The Bible and the Flag*, p. 11. Stanley's work is a useful survey of the relationship between mission and imperialism in general.

113 Krapf, *Travels, Researches*, pp. 512–13. However, at an earlier stage in his career, he influenced the ruler of Shoa, endeavouring 'to rouse up in a prudent manner in his mind the desire of coming in some closer connexion with the English government'. Cf. D. Crummey, *Priest and Politicians* (London, 1972) p. 47.

114 'We must raise German Christians in Kamerun', quoted in K. Rennstick, 'The Understanding of Mission Civilization and Colonialism in the Basel Mission', in Christensen and Hutchison, *Missionary Ideologies in the Imperialist Era*, p. 99.

115 N. Etherington, *Preachers, Peasants and Politics in Southeast Africa, 1835–1880* (London, 1978) p. 28.

116 Cf. R. H. Martin, *Evangelicals United: Ecumenical Stirrings in Pre-Victorian Britain* (London, 1983).

117 R. F. Wylie, 'Some Contradictions in Missionizing', *Africa*, 1976, p. 199, with reference to Ghana Methodism.

118 C. S. Sp. 191/ɞ/II, L. Lejeune, historical account based on community journals, Onitsha, 1902.

119 J. W. Harrison, *A. M. MacKay: Pioneer Missionary to the Church Missionary Society to Uganda by His Sister* (London, 1890) p. 121.

120 Cf. Elizabeth Isichei, *The Ibo People and the Europeans* (Faber and Faber, London, 1973) pp. 95–6.

121 Quoted in J. V. Taylor, *The Growth of the Church in Buganda* (London, 1958) p. 44.

122 Etherington, *Preachers, Peasants and Politics*, p. 43.

123 Which is why the majority church is called the Church of the Province.

124 Etherington, *Preachers, Peasants and Politics*, p. 34.

125 Quoted in Etherington, *Preachers, Peasants and Politics*, p. 57.

126 Markowitz, *Cross and Sword*, p. 13.

Notes

127 Etherington, *Preachers, Peasants and Politics*, pp. 31–32.
128 Leys, *Kenya*, pp. 210–11.
129 For a critique, cf. Okot pBitek, *African Religions in Western Scholarship* (East African Literature Bureau, Nairobi, 1970). For examples of the genre criticized, cf. E. B. Idowu, *African Traditional Religion: A definition* (S.C.M. Press, London, 1973), J. Mbiti, *African Religions and Philosophy* (Heinemann, London, 1969), J. Parrinder, *African Traditional Religions* (SPCK, London, 1962).
130 The division of labour by gender varied. In many Bantu societies, in particular, the women were mainly responsible for cultivation.
131 J. W. Colenso, *A Letter to His Grace the Archbishop of Canterbury, upon the question of the proper treatment of cases of polygamy*, quoted in J. Guy, *The Heretic: A Study of the Life of John William Colenso 1814–1883* (Ravan Press/University of Natal Press, Johannesburg and Pietermaritzburg, 1983) p. 76.
132 Quoted in C. Fyfe, *A History of Sierra Leone* (Oxford University Press, London, 1962) p. 43, the source on which this account is based.

Chapter 4

1 Robert Moffat, *Missionary Labours and Scenes in Southern Africa* (first pub. 1842, Johnson Reprint Corporation, New York, 1969 p. 184. Map 7, which illustrates this chapter is not synchronic. It includes events from different periods, such as the Great Trek, and the arrival of the Ndebele in the Bulawayo region.
2 J. du Plessis, *A History of Christian Missions in South Africa* (1911, Struik, Cape Town, 1965 reprint) p. 404.
3 N. Etherington, 'Mission station melting pots as a factor in the rise of South African black Nationalism', *International Journal of African Theological Studies*, 1976, p. 603.
4 Thomas Pringle on the San, quoted in A. Ross, *John Philip 1775–1851: Missions, Race and Politics in South Africa* (Aberdeen University Press, Aberdeen, 1986) p. 122. Pringle had recently fought against San raids.
5 Moffat, *Missionary Labours*, p. 69. The '-qua' suffix is a plural form.
6 The term and the whole concept have been questioned by scholars such as Julian Cobbing, but these controversies lie beyond the scope of this book.
7 Anders Sparrman, quoted in R. Elphick and R. Shell, 'Intergroup Relations: Khoikhoi, settlers, slaves and free blacks, 1652–1795', in R. Elphick and H. Giliomee, *The Shaping of South African Society 1652–1820* (Longman, Cape Town, 1979) p. 122.
8 Leonard Thompson, *A History of South Africa* (Yale University Press, New Haven and London, 1990) p. 45.
9 Dirk van Reenen, in 1803, in connection with land alienation, extract in J. Sales, *Mission Stations and the Coloured Communities of the Eastern Cape 1800–1852* (Balkema, Cape Town and Rotterdam, 1975) p. 23.
10 I. H. Enklaar, *Life and Work of Dr. I. Th. Van der Kemp* (Balkema, Cape Town and Rotterdam, 1988) p. 84.
11 Quoted in J. B. Peires, *The House of Phalo: A history of the Xhosa people in the days of their independence* (University of California Press, Berkeley, 1982) p. 75.
12 C. Northcott, *Robert Moffat: Pioneer in Africa 1817–1870* (Lutterworth, London, 1961) p. 122.
13 For his career in South Africa, cf. du Plessis, *A History of Christian Missions*, pp. 50–60.

Notes

14 J. E. Hutton, *A History of Moravian Missions* (Moravian Publications Office, London, n.d., *c*. 1922) p. 129.
15 Hutton, *A History of Moravian Missions*, p. 130.
16 Moffat, *Missionary Labours*, pp. 73–80, 83–9, 111–3, 173–86.
17 Moffat, *Missionary Labours*, pp. 185–6.
18 Moffat, *Missionary Labours*, pp. 192ff.
19 Moffat, *Missionary Labours*, p. 200.
20 Enklaar, *Life and Work of Dr. J. Th. Van der Kemp*, p. 149.
21 C. Bundy, *The Rise and Fall of the South African Peasantry* (Heinemann, London, 1979) p. 40.
22 Enklaar, *Life and Work of Dr. J. Th. Van der Kemp*, is the source for what follows.
23 Enklaar, *Life and Work of Dr. J. Th. Van der Kemp*, p. 118.
24 His choice of wife has been variously interpreted, and need not detain us here. His first wife was of working-class origins, as were his earlier partners.
25 V. C. Malherbe, 'The Life and Times of Cupido Kakkerlak', *The Journal of African History*, 1979, pp. 365–378.
26 du Plessis, *A History of Christian Missions*, p. 248.
27 Philip in 1833, quoted in Ross, *John Philip*, p. 95.
28 Not all the charges were substantiated, and he lost a libel case. Philip remains a controversial figure among historians, and he was, understandably, criticized by those sympathetic to the settler viewpoint. Contemporary Marxist historians find other defects in his belief in free enterprise. Ross' biography provides a balanced view.
29 Philip in 1820, quoted in Bundy, *The Rise and Fall of the South African Peasantry*, p. 39.
30 Nxele, quoted in Peires, *The House of Phalo*, p. 66.
31 The account that follows is based on Peires, *The House of Phalo*, pp. 69ff
32 Peires, *The House of Phalo*, p. 73.
33 B. A. Pauw, *Christianity and Xhosa Tradition: Belief and ritual among Xhosa-speaking Christians* (Oxford University Press, Cape Town, 1975) p. 19.
34 Quoted in Thompson, *A History of South Africa*, p. 77.
35 W. W. Gqoba, in 1888, quoted in J. B. Peires, 'The Central Beliefs of the Xhosa Cattle-Killing', *The Journal of African History*, 1987, p. 43.
36 This theme is elaborated in Peires, 'The Central Beliefs', pp. 50–62.
37 J. B. Peires, ' "Soft" Believers and "Hard" Unbelievers in the Xhosa Cattle-Killing', *The Journal of African History*, 1986, p. 453.
38 The roots of the cattle-killing are complicated, and well-explored by Peires: earlier land alienation had made it impossible to abandon the homestead of the deceased, and other mortuary rituals had been given up in the smallpox epidemic of 1770. When customary rites of separation were abandoned, ancestors impinged more closely on daily life. There are many parallels with Melanesian cargo cults.
39 D. Williams, 'Tiyo Soga 1829–71', in C. Saunders, ed., *Black Leaders in Southern African History* (Heinemann, London, 1979) pp. 127–141.
40 Williams, 'Tiyo Soga', p. 136.
41 P. Retief, *Manifesto*, text in A. du Toit, and H. Giliomee, *Afrikaner Political Thought, Analysis and Documents, I, 1780–1850* (University of California Press, Berkeley, 1983) p. 214.
42 Quoted in J. W. de Gruchy, *The Church Struggle in South Africa* (Collins, London, 1986) p. 19.
43 D. Livingstone, *A Popular Account of Missionary Travels and Researches in South Africa* (J. Murray, London, 1875) p. 24.

Notes

44 N. Etherington, *Preachers, Peasants and Politics in Southeast Africa 1835–1880* (Royal Historical Society, London, 1978) pp. 90–100.

45 Bundy, *The Rise and Fall of the South African Peasantry*; the argument is summarized in his, 'The Emergence and Decline of a South African Peasantry', *African Affairs*, 1972, pp. 369–88.

46 Bundy, 'The Emergence and Decline of a South African Peasantry', p. 377, quoting a traveller's account of Glen Grey.

47 Bundy, *The Rise and Fall of the South African Peasantry*, p. 55; Moffat, *Missionary Labours*, pp. 251–3.

48 Etherington, *Preachers, Peasants and Politics*, pp. 55, 57, 64, 90.

49 Etherington, *Preachers, Peasants and Politics*, p. 75.

50 N. Bhebe, *Christianity and Traditional Religion in Western Zimbabwe 1859–1923* (Longman, London, 1979) p. 18. This study is the main source for what follows. The original word for God used by the people who became the Ndebele was *Nkulunkulu*.

51 F. Coillard, *On the Threshold of Central Africa* (London, 1897) p. 44.

52 Bhebe, *Christianity and Traditional Religion*, pp. 30, 31, 53, 61.

53 Bhebe, *Christianity and Traditional Religion*, pp. 114, 117–9, 148, 149.

54 R. Rotberg, *Christian Missionaries and the Creation of Northern Rhodesia, 1880–1924* (Princeton University Press, Princeton, 1965), p. 20.

55 The history, and historiography, of these risings lie beyond the scope of this book. The role of spirit mediums was emphasized in T. Ranger, *Revolt in Southern Rhodesia 1896–7* (Heinemann, London, 1967); for a corrective, cf. J. Cobbing, 'The Absent Priesthood: Another look at the Rhodesian risings of 1896–1897', *The Journal of African History*, 1977, pp. 61ff.

56 For Makua cases, cf. p. 136.

57 J. Farrant, *Mashonaland Martyr: Bernard Mizeki and the Pioneer Church* (Oxford University Press, Cape Town, 1966) p. 64.

58 Livingstone, *Popular Account of Missionary Travels*, p. 23.

59 Livingstone, *Popular Account of Missionary Travels*, p. 25.

60 Quoted in A. J. Dachs, 'Missionary Imperialism—the case of Bechuanaland', *The Journal of African History*, 1972, p. 648.

61 Quoted in Dachs, 'Missionary Imperialism', p. 648. The kaross was the traditional garment of leather.

62 Livingstone, *Popular Account of Missionary Travels*, p. 20.

63 Quoted in Dachs, 'Functional Aspects of Religious Conversion Among the Sotho-Tswana', in M. F. C. Bourdillon, *Christianity South of the Zambezi* (Salisbury, 1977) II, p. 151.

64 Dachs, 'Functional Aspects', p. 156.

65 I. Schapera, ed., *David Livingstone: Family Letters 1841–1856* (Chatto and Windus, London, 1959) I, p. 132.

66 I. Schapera, ed., *Livingstone's Missionary Correspondence 1841–1856* (Chatto and Windus, London, 1961) pp. 14–15, 81.

67 *Livingstone's Missionary Correspondence* p. 225. He had not at the time, he said, felt as if he was sinning!

68 Dachs, 'Functional Aspects', p. 650.

69 Dachs, 'Functional Aspects', p. 156.

70 I. Schapera, *Tribal Innovators: Tswana Chiefs and Social Change, 1795–1940* (London, 1970) pp. 122, 129–30, 135, 165, 168, 245.

71 A. Dachs, 'Functional Aspects', p. 148.

Notes

72 L. Thompson, *Survival in Two Worlds: Moshoeshoe of Lesotho, 1786–1870* (Clarendon Press, Oxford, 1975) pp. 24–7.

73 M.–L. Martin, *Kimbangu: An African prophet and his church* (B. Blackwell, Oxford, 1975) p. 17.

74 Thompson, *Survival in Two Worlds*, p. 63. For West African parallels, cf. E. Isichei, 'The quest for social reform in the context of traditional religion: a neglected theme of West African History', *African Affairs*, 1978, pp. 463–78.

75 Thompson, *Survival in Two Worlds*, p. 75.

76 Thompson, *Survival in Two Worlds*, p. 80.

77 Epigraph to the main source for the account which follows: Thompson, *Survival in Two Worlds*.

78 MacKenzie in Aug. 1876, quoted in Dachs, 'Functional Aspects' p. 650.

79 MacKenzie, 29 Mar. 1868, in Dachs, 'Functional Aspects' p. 650.

80 J. Guy, *The Heretic: A study of the life of John William Colenso 1814–1883*, (Ravan/ University of Natal Press, Johannesburg and Pietermaritzburg, 1983) p. 345.

81 Shula Marks, *Reluctant Rebellion: The 1906–8 disturbances in Natal* (Clarendon Press, Oxford, 1970) p. 357.

82 Marks, *Reluctant Rebellion*, pp. 180–1.

83 Northcott, *Robert Moffat*, p. 73.

84 Quoted in G. M. Setiloane, 'Where are we in African Theology?', in K. Appiah-Kubi, and S. Torres, eds., *African Theology en route* (New York, 1979) p. 63.

85 Josiah Tyler quoted in Etherington, *Preachers, Peasants and Politics* p. 88. Tyler worked for the American Board of Missions for forty years in Natal.

86 L. Switzer, 'The African Christian Community and its Press in Victorian South Africa', *Cahiers d'Etudes Africaines*, 1984, p. 458.

87 Etherington, 'Mission stations melting pots', p. 599.

88 Thomas Arbousset, *Voyage d'exploration aux Montagnes Bleues*, extract in H. Davies and R. W. H. Shepherd, eds, *South African Missions 1880–1950: An anthology* (Nelson, London, 1954) p. 29.

89 The Xhosa ruler Mhala, quoted in J. B. Peires, 'The Central Beliefs of the Xhosa Cattle-Killing', p. 60.

90 Quoted in Peires, *The House of Phalo*, p. 68.

91 Etherington, *Preachers, Peasants and Politics*, pp. 82–3.

92 Livingstone, *Popular Account of Missionary Travels*, p. 14.

93 For a Sotho example, cf. Davies and Shepherd, eds., *South African Missions*, p. 30.

94 Thompson, *Survival in Two Worlds*, p. 320.

95 J. L. Krapf, *Travels, Researches and Missionary Labours*. 2nd ed., Cass, London, 1968, p. 190.

96 A Xhosa question, in Peires, *The House of Phalo*, p. 76.

97 J. W. Colenso, *The Pentateuch and Book of Joshua Critically Examined* (1862), extract in Guy, *The Heretic*, pp. 90–1.

98 The American missionary Aldin Grout, reporting questions he encountered at Mvoti, in Natal in 1855; N. Etherington, *Preachers, Peasants and Politics*, p. 56.

99 Peires, *The House of Phalo*, p. 76.

100 In Daniel Defoe's *Robinson Crusoe*, Man Friday suggested that the devil be killed, rather than converted.

101 N. Bhebe, *Christianity and Traditional Religion in Western Zimbabwe*, p. 42.

102 Van der Kemp, in 1800, quoted in Enklaar, *Life and Work of Dr. J. Th. Van der Kemp*, p. 102.

Notes

103 Reverend Gwayi Tyamzashe. Cf. S. Marks, and R. Rathbone, eds, *Industrialisation and Social change in South Africa* (Longman, Harlow, 1982), 'Introduction', p. 29.
104 Switzer, 'The African Christian Community and its Press', p. 469.
105 D. Chanaiwa, 'African Humanism in Southern Africa: the Utopian, traditionalist, and colonialist worlds of mission-educated élites', in A. T. Mugomba and M. Nyaggah, eds, *Independence Without Freedom: The political economy of colonial education in southern Africa* (A. B. C.-Clio, Santa Barbara, 1980) p. 11. This article is an excellent analysis of these dilemmas.
106 M. Marable, 'John L. Dube and the Politics of Segregated Education in South Africa', in Mugomba and Nyaggah, *Independence Without Freedom*, pp. 113–128.
107 D. D. T. Jabavu, *The Black Problem: Papers and addresses on various native problems* (Lovedale, 1920) p. 16, quoted in Chanaiwa, 'African Humanism in Southern Africa', p. 10.
108 Chanaiwa, 'African Humanism in Southern Africa', p. 13.
109 Quoted in Switzer, 'The African Christian Community and its Press' p. 455.
110 P. Hinchliff, 'African Separatists: Heresy, Schism or Protest Movement?', in D. Baker, ed., *Schism Heresy and Religious Protest* (Cambridge University Press, Cambridge, 1972) p. 394.
111 G. M. Theal in 1908, quoted in G. Shepperson, 'Ethiopianism Past and Present', in C. G. Baeta, ed., *Christianity in Tropical Africa* (Oxford University Press for the International African Institute, London, 1968) p. 250.
112 C. Saunders, 'Tile and the Thembu Church', *Journal of African History*, 1970, pp. 553ff.
113 Reverend Chubbs, quoted in E. Roux, *Time Longer Than Rope: A history of the black man's struggle for freedom in South Africa* (University of Wisconsin Press, Madison, 1948, 1966), p. 78. The classic, first published in 1948, is of enduring value.
114 W. Beinart and C. Bundy, *Hidden Struggles in South Africa* (James Currey, London, 1987) pp. 114–5.
115 Quoted in J. de Gruchy, *The Church Struggle in South Africa* (2nd ed., Collins, London, 1986) pp. 43–4.
116 B. Sundkler, *Zulu Zion and some Swazizionists* (Gleerups with Oxford University Press, Uppsala, 1976), *Studia Missionalia Upsaliensia XXIX* p. 88.
117 W. Johnson, 'The Africanization of a Mission Church: The African Methodist Episcopal Church in Zambia', in G. Bond, *et al.*, *African Christianity Patterns of Religious Continuity* (Academic Press, New York, 1979) p. 95.
118 Quoted in M. Brandel-Syrier, *Black Woman in Search of God* (Lutterworth, London, 1962) p. 137.

Chapter 5

1 This chapter covers the area north of the Zambezi, to Uganda and Kenya.
2 Quoted in G. Prins, *The Hidden Hippopotamus* (Cambridge University Press, Cambridge, 1980) p. 119.
3 J. L. Krapf, *Travels, Researches and Missionary Labours* (first pub. 1860, 2nd ed. Cass, London, 1968) p. 157.
4 Abdullah ben Nadir, in B. Davidson, *The African Past* (Penguin, Harmondsworth, 1964) pp. 303–4.
5 Quoted in S. Feierman, *The Shambaa Kingdom* (University of Wisconsin Press, Madison, 1974) p. 20.

Notes

6   J. Iliffe, *A Modern History of Tanganyika* (Cambridge University Press, Cambridge, 1979) pp. 47–50.

7   J. McCracken, *Politics and Christianity in Malawi 1875–1940* (Cambridge University Press, Cambridge, 1977) p. 55.

8   Krapf, *Travels, Researches and Missionary Labours*, p. 150.

9   An Acoli funeral song quoted in Okot pBitek, *African Religions in Western Scholarship* (East Africa Publishing House, Nairobi, 1970) p. 100.

10 M. Wright, *German Missions in Tanganyika: Lutherans and Moravians in the Southern Highlands 1891–1941* (Clarendon Press, Oxford, 1971), p. 86.

11 T. O. Ranger, *The African Churches of Tanzania* (Historical Association of Tanzania, 5, Nairobi, n.d.) pp. 8–9. For a different view of Kaswa, cf. R. G. Willis, in 'Kaswa: Oral Tradition of a Fipa Prophet', *Africa*, 1970, pp. 248–55. It is not intended to imply that these prophets necessarily spoke the words now attributed to them.

12 Bishop Knight Bruce, quoted in Prins, *The Hidden Hippopotamus*, p. 237.

13 I. Schapera, ed., *David Livingstone: Family Letters 1841–1856* (Chatto and Windus, London, 1959) I, p. 204.

14 pBitek, *African Religions in Western Scholarship*, p. 85. and I. Linden *Church and Revolution in Rwanda* (Manchester University Press, Manchester, 1977) pp. 34, 90n51.

15 M. Wright, *German Missions in Tanganyika*, p. 58.

16 G. S. Haule, 'The entrepreneur', in J. Iliffe, ed., *Modern Tanzanians* (Historical Association of Tanzania, 1973) p. 159.

17 Quoted in Prins, *The Hidden Hippopotamus*, p. 195.

18 Prins, *The Hidden Hippopotamus*, p. 193.

19 Prins, *The Hidden Hippopotamus*, p. 194.

20 Krapf, *Travels, Researches and Missionary Labours*, p. 186.

21 Quoted in Margaret Read, 'The Ngoni and Western Education' in V. Turner, ed., *Colonialism in Africa 1870–1960: III Profiles of Change: African Society and Colonial Rule* (Cambridge University Press, Cambridge, 1971) p. 355.

22 Krapf, *Travels, Researches and Missionary Labours*, p. 140.

23 The Ngoni war leader, Ngonomo, quoted in Read, 'The Ngoni and Western Education', p. 355.

24 J. Farrant, *Mashonaland Martyr Bernard Mizeki and the Pioneer Church* (Oxford University Press, Cape Town, 1966) p. 127.

25 Quoted in R. W. Strayer, *The Making of Mission Communities in East Africa* (Heinemann and State University of New York, London and New York, 1978) p. 34. For Swema, cf. E. Alpers, "The Story of Swema', in C. Robertson and M. Klein (eds) *Women and Slavery in Africa* (University of Wisconsin Press, Madison, 1983), pp. 185ff.

26 Kolumba Msigala, quoted in T. Ranger, 'Missionary Adaptation of African Religious Institutions: The Masasi Case', in T. Ranger and I. Kimambo, eds, *The Historical Study of African Religion* (Heinemann, London, 1972) p. 223. For a collection of valuable studies of modern regional cults, cf. R. Werber, ed., *Regional Cults* (Association of Social Anthropologists, 16, (Academic Press, London, 1977).

27 Quoted in R. Rotberg, *Christian Missionaries and the Creation of Northern Rhodesia 1880–1924* (Princeton University Press, Princeton, 1965) p. 38.

28 Ranger, 'Missionary Adaptation of African Religious Institutions', pp. 232, 233.

29 Quoted in I. Linden, *Church and Revolution in Rwanda* (Manchester University Press, Manchester, 1977) p. 41.

30 Quoted in Rotberg, *Christian Missionaries*, p. 60.

Notes

31 F. B. Welbourn, *East African Rebels* (Oxford University Press, Oxford, 1961) p. 111.

32 Strayer, *The Making of Mission Communities*, pp. 18–20.

33 Strayer, *The Making of Mission Communities*, p. 26.

34 Krapf, *Travels, Researches and Missionary Labours*, p. 122.

35 There is a rich literature on the Mijikenda, cf. F. Morton, 'The Shungwaya Myth of Mijikenda Origins: A Problem of Late Nineteenth Century Kenya Coastal History' *International Journal of African Historical Studies*, 1973, pp. 397–423; T. Spear, 'Traditional Myths and Historians' Myths: Variations on the Singwaya Theme of Mijikenda Origins' *History in Africa*, 1974, pp. 67–84, and T. Spear, 'Traditional Myths and linguistic Analysis: Singwaya Revisited' *History in Africa*, 1976, pp. 229–46.

36 There is a vast body of literature on Livingstone. A good starting point is to be found in his voluminous published writings, and in the collection of essays edited by B. Pachai, *Livingstone: Man of Africa, Memorial Essays 1873–1973* (Longman, London, 1973); cf. also G. Seaver, *David Livingstone: His life and letters* (Harper & Row, New York, 1957).

37 I. Schapera, ed., *Livingstone's Missionary Correspondence 1841–1856* (London, 1961), p. 108. 'Bakwain' was a common name in the mid-nineteenth century, for the Tswana.

38 I. Schapera, ed., *David Livingstone: Family Letters*, II, pp. 191–2.

39 David and Charles Livingstone, *Narrative of an Expedition to the Zambesi and its Tributaries* (J. Murray, London 1865) p. 77.

40 McCracken, *Politics and Christianity in Malawi*, p. 20.

41 O. Chadwick, *MacKenzie's Grave* (Hodder and Stoughton, London, 1959) p. 171. This is the standard account; it focuses on the missionary personalities concerned.

42 Chadwick, *MacKenzies Grave*, p. 221.

43 D. and C. Livingstone, *Narrative of an Expedition to the Zambesi*, p. 571.

44 McCracken, *Politics and Christianity in Malawi*, p. 25.

45 McCracken, *Politics and Christianity in Malawi*, p. 28.

46 For reasons explored in McCracken, *Politics and Christianity in Malawi*, pp. 44–6.

47 D. Crawford, *Thinking Black* (Morgan and Scott, London, 1913) p. 204.

48 The United Presbyterian Church was formed in 1847 by the union of the Secession Church (1733) and Relief Church (1761). The history of Presbyterian divisions and reunions lies beyond the scope of this book.

49 Riddel, in 1878, quoted in McCracken, *Politics and Christianity in Malawi*, p. 89.

50 Quoted in McCracken, *Politics and Christianity in Malawi*, p. 193.

51 F. Macpherson, *Kenneth Kaunda of Zambia: The times and the man* (Oxford University Press, London, 1974) pp. 37 and 42.

52 Domingo to Booth, 1911, quoted in McCracken, *Politics and Christianity in Malawi*, p. 216.

53 Caroline Neale, *Writing 'Independent History' African Historiography 1960–1980* (Greenwood Press, Westport, 1985).

54 Jeanmairet, 25 Aug., 1885, quoted in Prins, *The Hidden Hippopotamus*, p. 206.

55 Prins, *The Hidden Hippopotamus*, p. 199, citing a missionary journal, 1886.

56 Prins, *The Hidden Hippopotamus*, p. 193.

57 Prins, *The Hidden Hippopotamus*, pp. 179ff.

58 Quoted in T. Ranger, 'African attempts to control education in East and Central Africa 1900–1939', *Past and Present*, 1965, p. 60.

59 T. Ranger, 'The "Ethiopian" Episode in Barosteland, 1900–1905', in *Rhodes-Livingstone Journal*, 1965, p. 31. This is the source for this account.

Notes

60 Prins, *The Hidden Hippopotamus*, p. 201.

61 Prins, *The Hidden Hippopotamus*, pp. 230–2. He explains both her decision and Lewanika's acquiescence in terms of kin group power politics, but she does not speak in the records for herself. This is a good example of the way in which many historians seek to explain conversion in economic, social, and political terms. They are part of the story, but not the whole of it.

62 This account comes from M. Jarrett-Kerr, *Patterns of Christian Acceptance* (Oxford University Press, London, 1972) pp. 78–86.

63 Edwin Smith, quoted in Rotberg, *Christian Missionaries*, p. 74. Rotberg's study is the main source for the preceding account.

64 H. M. Stanley, *Through the Dark Continent* (Sampson Law, Marston, Searle, and Rivington, London, 1890) p. 204–6. Cf. also R. Oliver, *The Missionary Factor in East Africa* (Longman, London, 1952) p. 40, n. 2. Maftaa's later reputation was overshadowed by the fact that, in Oliver's words, he 'afterwards became corrupted by riches and power, and fell away from his former zeal, living as an ordinary Arab resident in Buganda'.

65 For this wealthy recluse, cf. p. 97.

66 This is partly because of the martyrs, partly because the British felt the same kind of sympathetic admiration for Buganda as they did, for instance, for the emirates in North Nigeria. The very name of Uganda is the Swahili version of Buganda. For a long time, the history of North Uganda was neglected; the balance was redressed largely through the efforts of J. B. Webster and his associates.

67 C. S. Nason, 'Proverbs of the Baganda', *Uganda Journal*, 1936, p. 250.

68 D. A. Low, *Religion and Society in Buganda 1875–1900* (East African Studies 8, n.d., but 1957) p. 2, quoting J. Roscoe, *The Baganda* (London, 1911) p. 220.

69 D. A. Low, 'Converts and Martyrs in Buganda', in C. G. Baeta, ed., *Christianity in Tropical Africa* (Oxford University Press, London, 1968) p. 157.

70 Stanley, *Through the Dark Continent*, p. 204.

71 Michael Wright, *Buganda in the Heroic Age* (Oxford University Press, Nairobi, 1971) pp. 4–6.

72 Low, *Religion and Society in Buganda*, p. 2.

73 Stanley, *Through the Dark Continent*, p. 204.

74 Low, *Religion and Society in Buganda*, p. 4.

75 J. A. Rowe, 'The Purge of Christians at Mwanga's Court', *Journal of African History*, 1964, p. 68. Some versions say 40.

76 Low, *Religion and Society in Buganda*, p. 7.

77 J. F. Faupel, *African Holocaust* (P. J. Kenedy and Sons, New York, 1972) p. 30.

78 Quoted in Wright, *Buganda in the Heroic Age*, p. 20, referring to a Catholic mission attacked by Protestants in the civil wars.

79 J. V. Taylor, *The Growth of the Church in Buganda* (SCM, London, 1958) p. 46.

80 Faupel, *African Holocaust*, pp. 177–8.

81 Faupel, *African Holocaust*, pp. 180–1.

82 A. Hastings, *African Catholicism: Essays in discovery* (SCM, London, 1989) pp. 13–15.

83 Faupel, *African Holocaust*, p. 193.

84 Faupel, *African Holocaust*, p. 197.

85 Faupel, *African Holocaust*, pp. 129, 226. Her mother claimed she was killed for her religion; Mwanga may have feared that the Christians would claim the throne for her, on the analogy of Queen Victoria.

86 Bartolomayo Zimbe, quoted in Rowe, 'The Purge of Christians at Mwanga's Court', p. 71.

Notes

87 James Miti, quoted in Faupel, *African Holocaust*, p. 137.
88 Oliver, *The Missionary Factor*, p. 184. He aptly compares this with Gregory Nazianzen's description of Christological controversy in Constantinople.
89 A. R. Tucker, *Eighteen Years in Uganda and East Africa* (Arnold, London, 1908) II, 92.
90 Oliver, *The Missionary Factor in East Africa*, p. 186.
91 Taylor, *The Growth of the Church in Buganda*, pp. 192–3.
92 Tucker, *Eighteen Years in Uganda and East Africa*, II, 76–7.
93 Taylor, *The Growth of the Church in Buganda*, pp. 190–1.
94 Taylor, *The Growth of the Church in Buganda*, pp. 61–2.
95 Taylor, *The Growth of the Church in Buganda*, p. 81.
96 J. Bouniol, *The White Fathers and Their Missions* (Sands, London, 1929) pp. 117, 125.
97 F. B. Welbourn, *East African Rebels* (SCM, London, 1961) pp. 31–58.
98 The account that follows is based on H. Deschamps, 'Tradition and change in Madagascar 1790–1870', *The Cambridge History of Africa*, V, (Cambridge University Press, Cambridge, 1976), pp. 393–418, and Jarrett-Kerr, pp. 16–22.
99 Cf. A. Southall, 'The problem of Malagasy origins', in H. N. Chittick, and R. I. Rotberg, eds, *East Africa and the Orient* (Africana Publishing Co., New York, 1975), also 'Introduction', pp. 4–6.
100 'The Church and Christians in Madagascar Today', *Pro Mundi Vita*, Africa Dossier 6, July–Aug. 1978.

Chapter 6

1 C[hurch] M[issionary] S[ociety Archives] (Consulted in London, now at the University of Birmingham), (henceforth CMS) G3/A2/1905/119, E. M. Lijadu, Journal, 10–28 Feb., 1905.
2 E. W. Bovill, ed. *Mission to the Niger: The Bornu Mission 1822–5* (Hakluyt, Series II, CXXX, 1966) part 3, Clapperton's narrative, p. 677.
3 N. Levtzion, *Muslims and Chiefs in West Africa* (Clarendon Press, Oxford, 1968) p. 109.
4 The controversies surrounding Nigeria's successive censuses make all such figures guesstimates. The 1963 Census put them at 9 246 000 in a population of 55.7 million; the national population is now widely assessed at 100 million.
5 CMS G3A3/1897, Bennett to Baylis, 27 Mar., 1897.
6 A. Birtwhistle, *Thomas Birch Freeman* (Cargate Press, London, 1950) p. 4.
7 CMS G3A3/1895/148, Tugwell to Baylis, 16 Oct, 1895.
8 CMS CA3/035, F. Smart, Journal, 2 Jan., 1870.
9 CMS G3A2/177, E. M. Lijadu, Journal, 11 Feb., 1892.
10 O. Ikime, *The Isoko People: An historical survey* (Ibadan University Press, Ibadan, 1972) p. 64. Patani is a village in the Niger Delta. In Calabar 'the matrons or dowagers of great families' opposed the end of twin-killing. H. M. Waddell, *Twenty-Nine Years in the West Indies and Central Africa* (Nelson, London, 1863) p. 484.
11 CMS G3A3/1886/33, encl. Boler to Hamilton, on Bonny.
12 CMS G3/A3/1883, D. C. Crowther to CMS, London, 10 May, 1883, on Bonny.
13 I. Akinjogbin, *Dahomey and its Neighbours 1708–1818* (Cambridge University Press, Cambridge, 1967) pp. 185–6. The context was his anxiety to increase trade with Portugal, at a time of economic depression.
14 N. Smith, *The Presbyterian Church of Ghana 1835–1960* (Ghana University Press, Accra, 1966), p. 235.

379

Notes

15 CMS CA3/04, John to Crowther, 22 Mar., 1879.

16 CMS CA3/04 (b) Crowther, Journal, 12 Aug., 1868.

17 J. Smith, *Trade and Travels in the Gulph of Guinea* (Simpkin and Marshall, London, 1851) pp. 89–95.

18 S. Crowther and J. C. Taylor, *The Gospel on the Banks of the Niger* (London, 1859; 1968 reprint, Dawsons, London) I, p. 250.

19 Crowther and Taylor, *The Gospel on the Banks of the Niger*, I, 269.

20 Anna Maria Falconbridge, *Narrative of Two Voyages to the River: Sierra Leone during the years 1791–2–3* (London, 1794; Cass, London 1967 reprint) pp. 199–200. Horne was a chaplain in Sierra Leone.

21 CMS CA3/030, S. Perry, undated Journal, received London, Jan., 1874.

22 CMS G3A3/1884, D. C. Crowther to Lang, 30 June, 1884.

23 H. M. Waddell, *Twenty-Nine Years in the West Indies and Central Africa*, (London, 1863; 1970 reprint, Cass, London) p. 469.

24 This has been variously interpreted as the result of the revolt of the slaves themselves, organized as the Blood Men, and of an Ekpe law 'as a result of pressure from the Mission and the Captains'. Cf. A. J. H. Latham, *Old Calabar 1600–1891* (Clarendon Press, Oxford, 1973) pp. 93–5 for the latter view. The former is suggested by Waddell's account of these events: *Twenty-Nine Years in the West Indies and Central Africa*, p. 476. Nair attributes it to the work of supercargoes and missionaries: K. Nair, *Politics and Society in South-Eastern Nigeria 1841–1906* (Cass, London, 1972) p. 49.

25 CMS G3/A2/187, E. M. Lijadu, Journal, 22 Sept. 1892. This may have been a response to the conquest of Ijebu.

26 Cf. E. Isichei, 'The quest for social reform in the context of traditional religion: A neglected theme of West African history', *African Affairs*, 1978, pp. 463ff.

27 'A remarkable conversion', *The African Missionary*, 1925, p. 13.

28 M. Easterfield and E. K. Uku, 'Seeds in the palm of your hand', *West African Review*, 1953, p. 50.

29 *Letters of Henry Hughes Dobinson* (Seeley & Co., London, 1899) p. 123. These letters were edited anonymously by his sister.

30 CMS G3/A3/1898/146, Tugwell to Baylis, 20 Aug., 1898.

31 CMS G3/A2/1892/32, Lijadu, Journal, 1 July, 1891.

32 J. B. Webster, *The African Churches Among the Yoruba* (Clarendon Press, Oxford, 1964) pp. 89–90.

33 I. C. Ward, quoted in F. L. Bartels, *The Roots of Ghana Methodism* (Cambridge University Press, Cambridge, 1965) p. 73.

34 N. Omenka, *The School in the Service of Evangelization* (Brill, Leiden, 1989) p. 190.

35 R. Wyllie, *Spiritism in Ghana: A study of new religious movements* (American Academy of Religion, Studies in Religion and Scholars Press, Missoula, 1980) p. 9. This book has different titles on the front cover—as given here—and title page, which reads *The Spirit-Seekers: New Religious Movements in Southern Ghana*.

36 E. Isichei, *Igbo Worlds* (Macmillan, London, 1978) p. 198; R. Horton, 'A Hundred Years of Change in Kalabari Religion', in J. Middleton, ed., *Black Africa: Its peoples and their cultures today* (Macmillan, New York, 1970) p. 204.

37 F. E. Forbes, *Dahomey and the Dahomans* (Longman, Brown, Green and Longman, London, 1851) pp. 119, and 151.

38 A Curé in Gorée in 1841, quoted in D. H. Jones, 'The Catholic Mission and some aspects of assimilation in Senegal, 1817–1852', *The Journal of African History*, 1980, p. 328.

Notes

39 According to a source written in 1880. Traditions collected in Lagos in 1928 state that he came from Angola, and that his masters in Brazil were Franciscan Tertiaries. For his life in general, cf. E. Isichei, 'An Obscure Man: Pa Antonio in Lagos', in E. Isichei, *Varieties of Christian Experience in Nigeria* (Macmillan, London, 1982) pp. 28ff.

40 Different sources suggest dates of 1838 and 1858.

41 C. Fyfe, *A History of Sierra Leone* (Oxford University Press, London, 1962) p. 151.

42 M. Bane, *Catholic Pioneers in West Africa* (Clonmare and Reynolds, Dublin, 1956) pp. 206–9.

43 Lejeune on Aguleri, Holy Ghost Fathers Archives, Paris, 191/A/3, General Report . . . on the Lower Niger.

44 H. Debrunner, *A Church between Colonial Powers: The Church in Togo*, (Lutterworth, London, 1967) p. 84–7.

45 P. D. Boilat, *Esquisses Sénégalaises* (P. Bertrand, Paris, 1853).

46 This account is based on Jones, 'The Catholic Mission in Senegal', *passim*.

47 Falconbridge, *Narrative of Two Voyages to the River*, p. 148.

48 C. Fyfe, *Sierra Leone Inheritance* (Oxford University Press, London, 1964) p. 119. Cf. A. F. Walls, 'The Nova Scotia Settlers and Their Religion', *Sierra Leone Bulletin of Religion*, 1959, pp. 19ff.

49 Falconbridge, *Narrative of Two Voyages to the River*, p. 201.

50 J. F. Ade Ajayi, 'Henry Venn and the Policy of Development', *Journal of the Historical Society of Nigeria*, 1959, p. 338.

51 *Lagos Times*, 9 Aug. 1882, quoted in E. Ayandele, *The Educated Elite in the Nigerian Society* (Ibadan University Press, Ibadan, 1974) p. 15.

52 Quoted in J. Peterson, *Province of Freedom: A history of Sierra Leone 1787–1870* (Faber and Faber, London, 1969) p. 237. Oro was a powerful Yoruba secret cult. Cf. S. S. Farrow, *Faith, Fancies and Fetish or Yoruba Paganism* (SPCK, London, 1926) pp. 73–8; A. B. Ellis, *The Yoruba-Speaking Peoples of the Slave Coast of West Africa* (Curzon, London, 1974) pp. 109–11.

53 C. Fyfe, *A History of Sierra Leone* (Oxford University Press, London, 1962) p. 389. The absentee bishop was E. H. Beckles.

54 The introduction of quinine was one reason, but life expectancy improved before this in some cases, and many of the determining factors are still obscure.

55 Editorial, *Sierra Leone Weekly News*, 8 April, 1916, quoted in L. Spitzer, 'The Sierra Leone Creoles, 1870–1900', in P. Curtin, ed., *Africa and the West* (University of Wisconsin, Madison, 1972) p. 100.

56 M. Kingsley, *Travels in West Africa*. 3rd ed., Cass, London, 1965, p. 660.

57 David Walker in 1829, quoted in T. Shick, *Behold the Promised Land: A history of Afro-American settler society in nineteenth-century Liberia* (John Hopkins University Press, Baltimore, 1977) p. 6.

58 P. Gifford, *Christianity and Politics in Doe's Liberia* (Cambridge University Press, Cambridge, 1993) p. 12.

59 W. Williams, *Black Americans and the Evangelization of Africa 1877–1900* (University of Wisconsin Press, Madison, 1982) p. 106.

60 H. R. Lynch, *Edward Wilmot Blyden: Pan-negro patriot 1832–1912* (Oxford University Press, London, 1967).

61 C. P. Groves, *The Planting of Christianity in Africa* (Lutterworth, London, 1954) II, p. 28. It is possible that 'Keith' and 'Keats' are the same man.

62 Quoted in Williams, *Black Americans*, p. 89.

63 Kingsley, *Travels in West Africa*, p. 657.

64 Williams, *Black Americans*, p. 38.

Notes

65 E. Atieno-Odhiambo, 'A Portrait of the Missionaries in Kenya before 1939', *Kenya Historical Review*, 1973, p. 11.
66 Quoted in Smith, *The Presbyterian Church of Ghana*, p. 91.
67 Debrunner, *The Church in Togo*, p. 209.
68 J. Middleton, 'One hundred and fifty years of Christianity in a Ghanaian town', *Africa*, 1983, p. 4.
69 Smith, *The Presbyterian Church of Ghana*, p. 102, n. 1.
70 Smith, *The Presbyterian Church of Ghana*, pp. 90–1.
71 Quoted in Smith, *The Presbyterian Church of Ghana*, p. 102.
72 Bartels, *The Roots of Ghana Methodism*, p. 8. This study is the main source for this account.
73 F. D. Walker, *Thomas Birch Freeman* (Student Christian Movement, London, 1929), and A. Birtwhistle, *Thomas Birch Freeman* (London, 1950).
74 Quoted in Smith, *The Presbyterian Church of Ghana*, p. 105. The various Akan peoples of Ghana, such as the Fante and Asante, speak Twi languages.
75 Quoted in D. Kimble, *A Political History of Ghana 1850–1928* (Clarendon Press, Oxford, 1963) pp. 152–3.
76 Wyllie, *Spiritism in Ghana*, pp. 5–6.
77 Bartels, *The Roots of Ghana Methodism*, p. 188; Kimble, *A Political History of Ghana*, p. 165.
78 Crowther, quoted in P. McKenzie, *Inter-religious Encounters in West Africa* (Leicester Studies in Religion, University of Leicester, Leicester, 1976) p. 30.
79 E. A. Ayandele, *The Missionary Impact on Modern Nigeria 1842–1914* (Longman, London, 1966) p. 15. On Ogboni, cf. P. Morton-Williams, 'The Yoruba Ogboni cult in Oyo', *Africa*, 1960. On the Saros, cf. J. Herskovitz, 'The Sierra Leonians of Yorubaland', in P. Curtin, ed., *Africa and the West*, pp. 82ff.
80 According to Ayandele, *The Missionary Impact on Modern Nigeria*, p. 270, but it seems unlikely, and it may have been the Reformed Ogboni that they joined.
81 M. Echeruo, *Victorian Lagos: Aspects of nineteenth-century Lagos life* (Macmillan, London, 1977) p. 16.
82 Quoted in Echeruo, *Victorian Lagos*, p. 39.
82 Quoted in Echeruo, *Victorian Lagos*, p. 80.
84 The title of a book by Miss Tucker, published in 1858.
85 *Church Missionary Intelligence*, 1878, p. 165.
86 W. Knight, *Memoir of the Rev. Henry Venn* (Seeley, Jackson & Halliday, London, 1882) p. 540. This may be compared with the disparaging remarks of Cust, in the 1890s, on 'Low Church breeder[s] of cattle or raisers of turnips'.
87 Crowther to Jowett, 22 Feb., 1837, *in extenso* in P. Curtin, ed., *Africa Remembered* (University of Wisconsin Press, Madison, 1967) pp. 298ff.
88 Ajayi, 'Henry Venn', p. 208.
89 CMS consulted in London, now at the University of Birmingham, CA3/04 (b), Crowther, 'Suggestions for the parent Committee', 30 Mar., 1870.
90 CMS CA3/030, Berry to Crowther, 16 Sept., 1872.
91 The reputation of the mission was also blackened by a crime of violence, comparable with the Blantyre case (cf. p. 136). A Sierra Leonian agent, W. F. John, flogged two runaway servant girls, and one died as a result. P[ublic] R[ecord] O[ffice, London] (henceforth PRO) FO 84/1508, Hopkins to FO, 18 Nov., 1878; CMS G3A3, Mba, deposition, encl. in Gollmer to CMS, 26 May, 1882.
92 For Mba, cf. CMS G3A3/1890/132, memo by Mba. For Bako, cf. G3A3/1896/132 Bako to Robinson, 30 Sept., 1896; G3A3/1902/65, Aitken to Tugwell, 5 June, 1902.

Notes

93 CMS G3A3/1884/54, Eden to Lang, 24 April, 1890, (original missing, summary in Precis Book).

94 CMS G3A3/1884/20, Crowther to Lang, 14 Dec., 1883.

95 CMS G3A3/1896/54, Dobinson to Baylis, 30 Mar., 1896.

96 *Lagos Weekly Record*, 3 June, 1893.

97 Quoted in F. Ekechi, *Missionary Enterprise and Rivalry in Igboland 1857–1914* (Cass, London, 1972) p. 24.

98 *L'Echo des Missions Africaines de Lyon*, 1905, pp. 21–29.

99 For a vignette of Idigo, and Aguleri, cf. E. Isichei, *Entirely for God: A life of Michael Iwene Tansi* (Macmillan, London, 1981).

100 PRO FO84/1001, letter from King Eyamba of Calabar, 1 Dec., 1842, encl. in Hutchinson to Clarendon, 24 June, 1856.

101 CMS CA3/04/479, S. Crowther, 'Brief statements exhibiting the characters . . . of the Natives of the Bight of Biafra', 31 Mar., 1875.

102 The words, and the child's first name, are Igbo, reflecting the influx of slaves, which meant that the original Bonny language, Ibani, almost died out. For the Bonny persecutions, cf. E. Isichei, 'Christians and Martyrs in Bonny, Ora and Lokoja', in Isichei, ed., *Varieties of Christian Experience in Nigeria*, pp. 62–8.

103 CMS G3/A3/1884/129, D. C. Crowther to Lang, 30 June, 1884.

104 A letter of 1894, in *Letters of Henry Hughes Dobinson* (London, 1899), pp. 183–4.

105 PRO FO 403/73, Ja Ja to Salisbury, 5 May, 1887 (FO Confidential Print).

106 PRO FO 403/216, 'Statement made by Chiefs, after the Meeting of June, 10, 1895' (FO Confidential Print). S. Crowther in *Church Missionary Intelligencer*, 1881, pp. 420–2.

107 J. Adams, *Remarks on the Country extending from Cape Palmas to the River Congo* (G. & W. B. Whittaker, London, 1823) p.144. For an eighteenth-century Efik diary in trade English, cf. Antera Duke's journal, in D. Forde *Efik Traders of Old Calabar* (Oxford University Press, London, 1956).

108 T. Hutchinson, *Impressions of West Africa*, (Longman, Brown, Green, London, 1858; Cass, London, 1970 reprint) p. 112.

109 Quoted in J. Buchan, *The Expendable Mary Slessor* (Saint Andrew Press, Edinburgh, 1980) p. 170. This is the main source for this account.

110 Waddell, *Twenty-Nine Years in the West Indies and Central Africa*, p. 346.

111 A government report on the Okoyong, cited in J. Buchan, *The Expendable Mary Slessor*, p. 85.

112 Quoted in Buchan, *The Expendable Mary Slessor*, p. 178.

113 CMS G3/A2/1911/72, T. Harding, 'Report of a Visit to the Ekiti Country'.

114 T. Harding, Journal, 12 Dec., 1899, in *Church Missionary Intelligencer*, 1900, p. 444.

115 CMS G3/A2/1900/89, Phillips, Report on Ondo Mission District; T. Harding, 'In Yorubaland', *Church Missionary Intelligencer*, May, 1900, pp. 366ff.

116 CMS G3/A2/1898, Lijadu, Annual Letter, 22 Nov., 1898. This passage refers to the practice of burying the dead person under the clay floor of her or his home; a symbol of the continuing links between the living and the ancestors.

117 The people of Benin are Bini, and they and other peoples speaking related languages are known collectively as the Edo. The account which follows is based on Isichei 'Christians and Martyrs', pp. 72–6.

118 Oral text translated in J. Eboreime, 'Christian Missions in Ora . . .' (University of Nigeria, Nsukka, Special Project in History, 1975).

119 CMS G3A2/1900/139, Phillips, Report on Ondo District.

Notes

120 The son of the Balogun, quoted in S. Johnson, *The History of the Yorubas* (C.S.S. Bookshops, Lagos, 1973) p. 610.

121 CMS G3/A2/1898/146, Tugwell to Baylis, 20 Aug., 1898.

122 Ayandele, *The Missionary Impact on Modern Nigeria*, p. 237. The standard account is Webster, *The African Churches Among the Yoruba*.

123 Quoted in Ayandele, *The Missionary Impact on Modern Nigeria*, p. 198.

124 Melville Jones, quoted in Webster, *The African Churches Among the Yoruba*, p. 125.

125 In general, they accepted polygamy among the laity; whether it was also permissible for the clergy was debated. On this issue, cf. J. B. Webster, 'Attitudes and Policies of the Yoruba Christian Churches towards Polygamy', in C. Baeta, ed., *Christianity in Tropical Africa* (Oxford University Press, London, 1968) pp. 224ff.

126 Quoted in J. D. Y. Peel, *Aladura: A religious movement among the Yoruba* (Published for the International African Institute by Oxford University Press, London, 1968) p. 296.

127 The story of Lijadu's heroic years of missionary work and financial independence is reflected in the CMS Archives, and especially Lijadu's Journals and Annual Letters. For the creation of the Evangelists Band, and the opposition he encountered, cf. CMS/G3A2/190085, Phillips to Melville Jones, 20 Apr., 1900, 87A, copies of Phillips-Lijadu correspondence, and 117, Lijadu to Melville Jones, 7 June, 1900.

128 CMS G3A2/1900/49 xxxi, letters from Lijadu. His stated aim was to come closer to the lifestyle of those to whom he ministered.

129 Webster, *The African Churches Among the Yoruba*, p. 196.

130 Cf. Webster, *The African Churches Among the Yoruba*, p. 66.

131 He was placed in charge of the Niger Delta Pastorate, and accepted the position in the hope that he would be able to raise funds to make it an independent bishopric. For the standard life of Johnson, cf. E. Ayandele, *Holy Johnson: Pioneer of African Nationalism* (Cass, London, 1970).

132 For these complicated events, cf. Webster, *The African Churches Among the Yoruba*, pp. 74–8.

133 Quoted in Kimble, *A Political History of Ghana*, p. 163.

134 'Independent Churches in Ghana', *Pro Mundi Vita*, Africa Dossier 32 (1985/1) pp. 7, n. 13 and 9–10; Kimble, *A Political History of Ghana*, pp. 163–4.

135 The account that follows is based on R. Joseph, 'Church, State and Society in Colonial Cameroun', *International Journal of African Historical Studies*, 1980, pp. 5ff.

Chapter 7

1 Quoted in D. Crawford, *Thinking Black* (Morgan and Scott, London, 1913) p. 480. Cf. p. 473. Chapters 7 and 8 do not follow the chronological division at c. 1900 of the other, regional, chapters, because of the relatively more restricted subject matter. This chapter ends with national independence, a considerably different point in time in Angola and in the other countries covered.

2 'Kongo' is the spelling when one is referring to the people of this name, and to the African kingdom they created, studied earlier, and located in what is now southern Zaire and northern Angola. Congo Free State, the personal fief of Leopold of Belgium, was internationally recognized at the Berlin Conference, in 1884–5; it was taken over by the Belgian Government in 1908, and became independent in 1960 as the Democratic Republic of Congo, usually called Congo-Kinshasa to distinguish it from the former French colony, Congo-Brazzaville. In 1967, the state and the Congo

384

Notes

River were renamed Zaire, Katanga became Shaba, and a number of other places were renamed as well.

3 They are conventionally attributed to venereal disease, but why is its impact greater here than elsewhere?

4 The account that follows is based on K. D. Patterson, *The Northern Gabon Coast to 1875* (Clarendon Press, Oxford, 1975) pp. 17, 93–4, 116ff.

5 Quoted in Patterson, *The Northern Gabon Coast*, p. 119.

6 The American Presbyterians had been working in the area since 1850. Most ABC missionaries were Congregationalists, but there were some 'New School' Presbyterians, members of a liberal schism. When the division ended, they were able to work for the main American Presbyterian mission.

7 In 1843, when they arrived in Gabon, they were members of the order of the Sacred Heart of Mary; it was soon to amalgamate with the Congregation of the Holy Ghost.

8 G. Marshall and D. Poling, *Schweitzer: A biography* (Bles, London, 1971) p. 90.

9 J. Janzen, 'The Tradition of Renewal in Kongo Religion', in N. Booth, ed., *African Religions* (NOK Publishers, New York, 1977) p. 81; also W. Holman Bentley, *Pioneering on the Congo* (Religious Tract Society, London, 1900) I, 32–3.

10 Bentley, *Pioneering on the Congo* (Religious Tract Society, London, 1900) I, 35. Cf. also p. 67.

11 Bentley, *Pioneering on the Congo*, I, 161.

12 Bentley, *Pioneering on the Congo*, I, 194.

13 F. Soremekun, 'Religion and Politics in Angola', *Cahiers d'Etudes Africaines*, 1971, p. 344.

14 Bentley, *Pioneering on the Congo*, I, 101–2 for details.

15 H. Rudin, *Germans in the Cameroons 1884–1914* (Jonathan Cape, London, 1938) pp. 370–1.

16 H. Debrunner, *A Church between Colonial Powers: A Study of the Church in Togo* (Lutterworth, London, 1967) pp. 67–8. Corisco Island is near the Rio Muni estuary.

17 M. D. Markowitz, *Cross and Sword: The political role of Christian missions in the Belgian Congo 1908–1960* (Hoover Institution Press, Stanford, 1973) p. 7.

18 Quoted in M.–L. Martin, *An African Prophet and His Church* (trans. D. L. Moore) (Blackwell, Oxford, 1975) p. 27.

19 L. Henderson, *Angola: Five centuries of conflict* (Cornell University Press, Ithaca and London, 1979), p. 111.

20 Quoted in Soremekun, 'Religion and Politics in Angola', p. 373.

21 Bentley, *Pioneering on the Congo*, II, 418.

22 Bentley, *Pioneering on the Congo*, I, 102.

23 Crawford, *Thinking Black*, pp. 354–5.

24 Quoted in D. J. Mackay, 'Simon Kimbangu and the B.M.S. tradition', *Journal of Religion in Africa*, 1987, p. 119.

25 Bentley, *Pioneering on the Congo*, II, 415.

26 N. Grubb, *C. T. Studd: Cricketer and Pioneer* (first published 1933, Lutterworth, London, 1953) pp. 210–11.

27 Cf. Bentley, *Pioneering on the Congo*, II, 420–1. He lists men's congregations, and mentions the presence of missionary nuns, but does not list them.

28 J. Burke, 'These Catholic Sisters are all Mamas', in F. Bowie, *et al.*, eds., *Women and Missions: Past and Present* (Berg, Oxford, 1993), pp. 251–266.

29 'Religious Life for Women in Zaire', *Pro Mundi Vita*, Africa Dossier 14 (May, 1980).

30 B. Stanley, 'The Miser of Headingly: Robert Arthington and the Baptist Missionary Society, 1877–1900', in W. J. Sheils and D. Wood, *The Church and Wealth* (Blackwell

385

Notes

for Ecclesiastical History Society, Oxford, 1987) pp. 371ff. The BMS and LMS were the main beneficiaries of his will. Cf. pp. 91 and 144.

31 Nlemvo in 1907, quoted in Mackay, 'Simon Kimbangu', pp. 117, 122–3. Cf. Bentley, *Pioneering on the Congo*, I, 242.

32 G. Clarence-Smith, 'Capital accumulation and class formation in Angola', in D. Birmingham and P. Martin, *History of Central Africa* (Longman, London, 1983) II, 197.

33 Crawford, *Thinking Black*, p. 242. 'Mushidi' is one of a number of alternative versions of Msiri.

34 J. Janzen, 'The consequences of literacy in African religion: the Kongo case', in W. van Binsbergen and M. Schoffeleers, *Theoretical Explorations in African Religion* (KPI, Monographs from the African Studies Centre, Leiden; London, 1985) pp. 228ff.

35 W. MacGaffey, *Modern Kongo Prophets* (Indiana University Press, Bloomington, 1983) p. 40.

36 Cf. pp. 89–90.

37 MacGaffey, *Modern Kongo Prophets*, p. 29.

38 Bentley, *Pioneering on the Congo*, I, 411–7.

39 Henderson, *Angola*, p. 148.

40 Bentley, *Pioneering on the Congo*, I, 420–1.

41 Markowitz, *Cross and Sword*, p. 26 n.

42 M. Newitt, *Portugal in Africa: The last hundred years* (C. Hurst, London, 1981) pp. 124–5.

43 Clarence-Smith, 'Capital accumulation and class formation in Angola', p. 197.

44 Anedeto Gaspar, in E. Berman, *African Reactions to Missionary Education* (Teachers College Press, New York, 1975) p. 72.

45 Gaspar, in Berman, *African Reactions to Missionary Education*, p. 63.

46 M. Douglas, *The Lele of the Kasai* (Oxford University Press, London, 1963) p. 264 (referring to 1950).

47 Crawford, *Thinking Black*, p. 61.

48 Crawford, *Thinking Black*, pp. 480–1.

49 Bentley, *Pioneering on the Congo*, I, 82.

50 Bentley, *Pioneering on the Congo*, I, 252.

51 E. Andersson, *Churches at the Grass-Roots: A study in Congo-Brazzaville* (Lutterworth Press, London, 1968) pp. 47–8.

52 MacGaffey, *Modern Kongo Prophets*, p. 135.

53 Bentley, *Pioneering on the Congo*, I, 137.

54 A Dondo informant, quoted in Andersson, *Churches at the Grass-Roots*, p. 46.

55 Quoted in Andersson, *Churches at the Grass-Roots*, p. 113.

56 Crawford, *Thinking Black*, p. 413.

57 Andersson, *Churches at the Grass-Roots*, p. 46.

58 Crawford, *Thinking Black*, pp. 195, 219. The references are to the sojourn in Bunkeya, in Shaba.

59 Crawford, *Thinking Black*, pp. 324–5.

60 This account of the Lele is based on Douglas, *The Lele of the Kasai* pp. 266–9. The traditional system where older men controlled women was palliated by the 'village wife', shared by a younger age grade.

61 Quoted in Mackay, 'Simon Kimbangu', p. 120.

62 Andersson, *Churches at the Grass-Roots*, p. 51.

63 Cf. Mackay, 'Simon Kimbangu', p. 156.

64 Quoted in Markowitz, *Cross and Sword*, p. 13.

65 Quoted in Rotberg, p. 295.

Notes

66 Bentley, *Pioneering on the Congo*, II, 188.
67 Quoted in Markowitz, *Cross and Sword*, p. 53.
68 Quoted in Markowitz, *Cross and Sword*, p. 53.
69 Quoted in Markowitz, *Cross and Sword*, p. 69.
70 Quoted in Markowitz, *Cross and Sword*, p. 107.
71 Crawford, *Thinking Black* p. 172. He assumed this was 'pretend writing', and it may have been, but the invention of scripts is well-attested elsewhere in nineteenth-century Africa.
72 Newitt, *Portugal in Africa*, p. 124.
73 Newitt, *Portugal in Africa*, p. 128.
74 C. Irvine, 'The birth of the Kimbanguist movement in the Bas-Zaire 1921', *Journal of Religion in Africa*, 1974, p. 36. Here it becomes 'the occasion when Cameron fled from the attack at Kimbonza to N'kamba' and the woman is either Kimbangu's mother, Luezi, or the aunt who brought him up, Kinzembo.
75 In this paragraph, I follow Mackay, 'Simon Kimbangu', pp. 124–7.
76 MacGaffey, *Modern Kongo Prophets*, pp. 18, 104–5.
77 Martin, *An African Prophet and His Church*, p. 49.
78 Martin, *An African Prophet and His Church*, p. 51.
79 Martin, *An African Prophet and His Church*, pp. 68, 71.
80 Text in C. Irvine, 'The birth of the Kimbanguist movement in the Bas-Zaire', pp. 73–6.
81 Martin, *An African Prophet and His Church*, p. 106.
82 Janzen, 'The Tradition of Renewal', p. 109.
83 Martin, *An African Prophet and His Church*, p. xi.
84 It lumps together a large number of heterogenous movements, and obscures their links with other forms of Christian independency. For anthropologists' critiques of 'orthodox' or 'syncretist' as relevant criteria, cf. p. 7.
85 An unpublished paper by J. Janzen, cited in H. Turner, 'The Hidden Power of the Whites: The Secret Religion Withheld From the Primal Peoples', in his *Religious Innovation in Africa* (G. K. Hall, Boston, 1979) p. 281.
86 Turner, 'The Hidden Power of the Whites', p. 278.
87 L. Bittremieux, 'Een hiedensche Godsdienst' (1929), quoted in W. MacGaffey, 'Cultural Roots of Kongo Prophetism', *History of Religions* 1977, p. 191, my source for this movement.
88 Quoted in R. Anstey, *King Leopold's Legacy: the Congo under Belgian Rule* (Oxford University Press, London, 1966) p. 131.
89 E. Andersson, *Messianic Popular Movements in the Lower Congo* (Studia Ethnographica Upsaliensia XIV and Kegan Paul, Uppsala and London, 1958) pp. 138ff.
90 Quoted in MacGaffey, 'Cultural Roots of Kongo Prophetism', p. 197; this is the fullest and most sympathetic account of Mpadi.
91 MacGaffey, 'Cultural Roots of Kongo Prophetism', p. 196.
92 MacGaffey, 'Cultural Roots of Kongo Prophetism', pp. 132–9.
93 Quoted in Anderson, *Messianic Popular Movements*, p. 198. For Matswa, cf. also pp. 117ff.
94 For his career, see, J. Marcum, *The Angolan Revolution* (Harvard University Press, Cambridge, Mass., 1969) I, pp., 76ff, and A. Margarido, 'The Tokoist Church and Portuguese Colonialism in Angola', in R. Chilcote ed., *Protest and Resistance in Angola and Brazil* (University of California Press, Berkeley, 1972) pp. 38ff.
95 Marcum, *The Angolan Revolution*, p. 81.
96 *Africa Confidential*, 4 Mar., 1987 (28/5).

Notes

97 Newitt, *Portugal in Africa*, p. 133; Margarido, 'The Tokoist Church and Portuguese Colonialism in Angola', p. 52.

98 M. C. Young, 'Rebellion and the Congo', in R. Rotberg and A. Mazrui, *Protest and Power in Black Africa* (Oxford University Press, New York, 1970) p. 977.

99 Young, in Rotberg and Mazrui, *Protest and Power in Black Africa*, p. 987. Cf. R. Fox, W. de Craemer, and J.-M. Ribeaucourt, ' "The Second Independence": A case study of the Kwilu rebellion in the Congo', *Comparative Studies in Society and History*, 1965, p. 100.

100 Fox, *et al.*, ' "The Second Independence" ', p. 85.

101 Fox, *et al.*, ' "The Second Independence" ', p. 99.

102 Martin, *An African Prophet and His Church*, pp. 126–7.

103 J. Fernandez, *Bwiti: An ethnography of the religious imagination* (Princeton University Press, Princeton, 1982). This study is 700 pages long, and the general reader may do better to start with his articles: Cf. his 'Alar Ayong and Bwiti as movements of protest', in R. Rotberg and A. Mazrui, eds, *Protest and Power in Black Africa*, pp. 427ff. This account is based on these sources.

104 Fernandez, *Bwiti*, pp. 363–4.

105 Fernandez, 'Alar Ayong and Bwiti', p. 451.

106 It is interesting to compare the main studies of Jamaa. W. de Craemer, a Belgian Jesuit, wrote, *The Jamaa and the Church: a Bantu Catholic Movement in Zaire* (Clarendon Press, Oxford, 1977); and cf. his, 'A sociologist's encounter with the Jamaa', *Journal of Religion in Africa*, 1976, pp. 153ff. Cf. the wide-ranging semantic questions raised in J. Fabian, *Jamaa a Charismatic Movement in Katanga* (Northwestern University Press, Evanston, Illinois, 1971).

107 J. Fernandez, 'The Sound of Bells in a Christian Country: In quest of the historical Schweitzer', *Massachusetts Review*, 1964, p. 544, 556.

108 Crawford, *Thinking Black*, pp. 57–8.

Chapter 8

1 Quoted in D. Crummey, *Priests and Politicians: Protestant and Catholic missions in orthodox Ethiopia 1830–1868* (Clarendon Press, Oxford, 1972) p. 143.

2 'The Church in the Sahel', *Pro Mundi Vita*, Africa Dossier 43 (4/1987) p. 13.

3 Pasteur Jean-Michel Hornus, 'The Lutheran and Reformed Churches', in A. Arberry, ed., *Religion in the Middle East* (Cambridge University Press, Cambridge, 1969) I, 533.

4 For Ethiopian Christianity before the nineteenth century, cf. Chapter 3.

5 S. Gobat, *Journal of a Three Years' Residence in Abyssinia*. (2nd ed., Seeley, Burnside & Seeley, J. Hatchard, London, 1847), pp. 82–3.

6 Gobat, *Journal of a Three Years' Residence in Abyssinia*, pp. 75–6. The *Echage* were the abbots of Dabra Libanos, and heads of Ethiopian monasticism; they were second in rank to the *Abuna*.

7 Quoted in Crummey, *Priests and Politicians*, p. 36.

8 Gobat, *Journal of a Three Years' Residence in Abyssinia*, p. 220.

9 Quoted in Crummey, *Priests and Politicians*, p. 45.

10 Quoted in Crummey, *Priests and Politicians*, p. 46.

11 Quoted in Crummey, *Priests and Politicians*, p. 80.

12 M. Singleton, 'Explorations in Ecumenical Topography', *Pro Mundi Vita*, Africa Dossier 10 (Nov. 1979) p. 35, n. 5.

Notes

13 G. Arén, *Evangelical Pioneers in Ethiopia: Origins of the Evangelical Church Mekane Yesu* (Stockholm, 1978); summary in Singleton, 'Explorations', p. 35.

14 Quoted in Crummey, *Priests and Politicians*, p 53; cf. p. 92.

15 Crummey, *Priests and Politicians*, pp. 63, 68, 101–8.

16 Quoted in S. Rubenson, 'Ethiopia and the Horn', in J. Flint, ed., *The Cambridge History of Africa* (Cambridge University Press, Cambridge, 1977), p. 72. Cf. his *King of Kings: Tewodros of Ethiopia* (Addis Ababa, 1966).

17 P. Verghese, 'The Ethiopian and Syrian Orthodox Churches', in Arberry, ed., *Religion in the Middle East*, I, 462.

18 M. Singleton, 'Ethiopia: A tale of two revolutions', *Pro Mundi Vita*, Africa Dossier 5 (Jan.–Feb. 1978) p. 15.

19 Gobat, *Journal of a Three Years' Residence in Abyssinia*, pp. 267–8. He was awaiting the arrival of a new Abuna, so that he could be ordained.

30 M. Singleton, 'Asa—Pagan Prophet or Providential Precursor?', *African Ecclesiastical Review*, 1978, pp. 82ff.

21 Singleton, 'Asa', p. '85.

22 For the ease with which people joined and left the Ethiopian Church in the fourteenth and fifteenth centuries, cf. S. Kaplan, *The Monastic Holy Man and the Christianization of Early Solomonic Ethiopia* (F. Steiner, Wiesbaden, 1984) p. 132.

23 D. Sperber, *Rethinking Symbolism* (Cambridge University Press, Cambridge, 1975) pp. 129–139.

24 Singleton, 'Ethiopia', p. 22 calls these often-cited figures 'slightly exaggerated . . . not far from the numerical truth'.

25 Zeneb, quoted in Rubenson, *King of Kings*, p. 56.

26 Singleton, 'Ethiopia', p. 17.

27 Singleton, 'Ethiopia', p. 16.

28 Singleton, 'Ethiopia', p. 31, n. 11.

29 Singleton, 'Ethiopia', p. 33.

30 C. Clapham, 'How Many Ethiopias?', *Africa*, 1993, p. 123.

31 G. Anwati, 'Christians of Egypt', *Pro Mundi Vita*, Africa Dossier 21, (April, 1982) p. 9.

32 E. L. Butcher, *The Story of the Church of Egypt* (Smith, Elder, London, 1897) II, 393.

33 O. Meinardus, 'The Coptic Church in Egypt', in Arberry, ed., *Religion in the Middle East*, p. 428.

34 R. B. Betts, *Christians in the Arab East* (John Knox Press, Atlanta, Georgia, 1978) pp. 19–20, 26–7.

35 Butcher, *The Story of the Church of Egypt*, II, 398; Anwati, 'Christians of Egypt', p. 11; Meinardus, 'The Coptic Church in Egypt', p. 429.

36 J.–M. Hornus, 'The Lutheran and Reformed Churches', in Arberry, ed., *Religion in the Middle East* I, 569.

37 Cragg, 'The Anglican Church', in Arberry, ed., *Religion in the Middle East*, p. 590.

38 R. Tucker, and W. Liefeld, *Daughters of the Church* (Academie Books, Grand Rapids, Michigan, 1987) p. 318.

39 Lady Duff-Gordon, quoted in Betts, *Christians in the Arab East*, p. 27.

40 E. Wakin, *A Lonely Minority: The modern story of Egypt's Copts* (William Morrow, New York, 1963) pp. 19–20.

41 Details in Meinardus, 'The Coptic Church in Egypt', pp. 442–3.

42 R. Israeli, *Man of Defiance: A political biography of Anwar Sadat* (Weidenfeld & Nicolson, London, 1985) pp. 262–4.

43 Quoted in Meinardus, 'The Coptic Church in Egypt', p. 441.

44 Betts, *Christians in the Arab East*, p. 50.

Notes

45 Betts, *Christians in the Arab East*, p. 123.
46 Wakin, *A Lonely Minority*, pp. 43, 49.
47 Quoted in J. D. O'Donnell, *Lavigerie in Tunisia* (University of Georgia Press, Athens, Georgia, 1979) pp. 3–4. This is the main source for what follows.
48 Quoted in O'Donnell, *Lavigerie in Tunisia*, p. 3.
49 Quoted in C. P. Groves, *The Planting of Christianity in Africa* (Lutterworth, London, 1955) III, p. 157.
50 Quoted in O'Donnell, *Lavigerie in Tunisia*, p.19.
51 Aylward Shorter, *Jesus and the Witchdoctor* (Geoffrey Chapman, London, 1985) p. 134. His account is based on a biography in Swahili.
52 J. Bouniol, *The White Fathers and Their Missions* (Sands, London, 1929) pp. 49–51.
53 Quoted in O'Donnell, *Lavigerie in Tunisia*, p. 211, n. 38.
54 O'Donnell, *Lavigerie in Tunisia*, pp. 195, 196.
55 H. Johnston, 'Are Our Foreign Missions a Success?', *Fortnightly Review*, 1889, p. 487.
56 There is a short account of her in W. Burridge, *Destiny Africa: Cardinal Lavigerie and the making of the White Fathers* (Geoffrey Chapman, London, 1966), p. 163, used to illustrate Lavigerie's work as spiritual director!
57 'A Survey of the Year 1950', *International Review of Missions*, 1951, pp. 36–7.
58 *World Christian Handbook*, 1962, p. 75. Two of the missions had no membership data available, but this would have made little difference to the general picture. Most of them were small Faith Missions.
59 The account that follows is based on J. Déjeux and H. Sanson, 'Algeria 1980: A Church in the midst of Islam', *Pro Mundi Vita*, Africa Dossier 13, (Mar. 1980).
60 K. Cragg, 'The Anglican Church', in Arberry, ed., *Religion in the Middle East*, I, 591.
61 The countries of the western Sahel, such as Niger, are usually treated as part of West Africa, but their religious situation has, of course, much more in common with that of North Africa. The following account is based on 'The Church in the Sahel'.
62 J. Ki Zerbo, *Alfred Diban: Premier chrétien de Haute-Volta* (Cerf, Paris, 1983).
63 Ki Zerbo *Alfred Diban*, p. 60.
64 Quoted in B. Ray, *African Religions: Symbol, ritual, continuity* (Prentice-Hall, Englewood Cliffs, New Jersey, 1976) p. 3.
65 E. Evans-Pritchard, *Nuer Religion* (Clarendon Press, Oxford, 1956), and R. G. Lienhardt, *Divinity and Experience: The religion of the Dinka* (Clarendon Press, Oxford, 1961).
66 Quoted in M. O. Beshir, *The Southern Sudan* (C. Hurst & Co., London, 1968), p. 25.
67 R. Collins, 'The Establishment of Christian Missions and Their Rivalry in the Southern Sudan', *Tarikh*, 1969, III, 1, pp. 38–47.
68 Cragg, 'The Anglican Church', p. 586.
69 Max Warren, *Crowded Canvas: Some experiences of a life-time* (Hodder and Stoughton, London, 1974) p. 197, describing a visit in 1950.
70 Beshir, *The Southern Sudan*, p. 82.
71 Warren, *Crowded Canvas*, p. 144.
72 Beshir, *The Southern Sudan*, pp. 45, 52.
73 Beshir, *The Southern Sudan*, p. 55.

Chapter 9

1 M. Wilson, *Communal Rituals of the Nyakusa* (Oxford University Press for the International African Institute, London, 1959), epigraph.

Notes

2 Ian Linden, *Church and Revolution in Rwanda* (Manchester University Press, Manchester, 1977) p. 173.

3 Linden, *Church and Revolution in Rwanda*, p. 302.

4 Quoted in J. V. Taylor and D. A. Lehmann, *Christians of the Copperbelt* (SCM Press, London, 1961) p. 193.

5 T. O. Ranger, 'African Attempts to Control Education in East and Central Africa', *Past and Present*, 1965, p. 84. This chapter is greatly indebted to Ranger's work as is apparent from the footnotes.

6 A. Roberts, *A History of Zambia* (Heinemann, London, 1976) p. 172.

7 *Africa South of the Sahara*, (Europa, London, 1993) pp. 456, 872, and 912.

8 Mousinho de Albuquerque, *Mozambique*, quoted in A. Hastings, *Wiriyamu*, (Search Press, London, 1974) pp. 16–17.

9 von Rechenberg, quoted in M. Wright, *German Missions in Tanganyika 1891–1941* (Clarendon Press, Oxford, 1971) p. 120.

10 Taylor, and Lehmann, *Christians of the Copperbelt*, p. 18.

11 H. Maynard Smith, *Frank, Bishop of Zanzibar: Life of Frank Weston D. D.* (SPCK, London, 1926) pp. 149, 153, 179.

12 Taylor, and Lehmann, *Christians of the Copperbelt*, p. 34.

13 A. Wipper, *Rural Rebels: A study of two protest movements in Kenya* (Oxford University Press, Nairobi, 1977) pp. 31–2.

14 M. F. Perrin-Jassy, *Basic Community in the African Churches* (Orbis Books, Maryknoll, New York, 1973) pp. 107–8.

15 A District Commissioner in Northern Rhodesia in 1925, cited in J. R. Hooker, 'Witnesses and Watch Tower in the Rhodesias and Nyasaland', *Journal of African History*, 1965, p. 92.

16 A perceptive analysis in Norman Leys, *Kenya*. (2nd ed., Hogarth Press, London, 1925), p. 211.

17 Quoted in K. Fields, 'Political Contingencies of Witchcraft in Colonial Central Africa', *Canadian Journal of African Studies*, 1982, p. 580.

18 T. Ranger, 'Tradition and Travesty: Chiefs and the administration in Makoni District, Zimbabwe, 1960–1980', *Africa*, 1982, p. 35.

19 Smith, *Frank, Bishop of Zanzibar*, pp. 247–251.

20 Quoted in Smith, *Frank, Bishop of Zanzibar*, p. 257.

21 R. W. Strayer, *The Making of Mission Communities in East Africa* (State University of New York Press, London/New York, 1978) p. 102.

22 Charles Domingo, quoted in G. Shepperson, 'The Politics of African Church Separatist Movements in British Central Africa, 1892–1916', *Africa*, 1954, p. 241. This is a continuation of the famous 'too cheaty, too thefty, too mockery' passage, quoted on p. 142.

23 K. Fields, *Revival and Rebellion in Colonial Central Africa* (Princeton University Press, Princeton, 1985) pp. 107, 109, 111, 114.

24 Fields, *Revival and Rebellion in Colonial Central Africa*, p. 110.

25 Quoted in Shepperson, p. 234. Cf. p. 249.

26 Ndabaningi Sithole, *African Nationalism*. 2nd ed., Oxford University Press, London, 1968, pp. 12–14.

27 P. Walakira, 'Part of the Establishment: Catholicsm in Uganda', in E. Berman, ed., *African Reactions to Missionary Education* (Teachers College Press, New York, 1975) p. 149.

28 Ngugi wa Thiong'o, *The River Between* (Heinemann, London, 1975) p. 93.

391

Notes

29 A baptismal song for a Haya king, quoted in L. Stevens, 'Religious Change in a Haya village, Tanzania', *Journal of Religion in Africa*, 1991, p. 4.

30 Filip Njau, *Aus meinem Leben*, quoted in J. Iliffe, *A Modern History of Tanganyika* (Cambridge University Press, Cambridge, 1979) p. 225; cf. pp. 222–223.

31 Toswa Kabine, interview in F. B. Welbourn, *East African Rebels* (SCM Press, London, 1961) p. 107.

32 M. Kayoya, *My Father's Footprints: A search for values* (Eng. trans. East African Publishing House, Nairobi, 1973) p. 53.

33 Quoted in J. R. Hooker, 'Witnesses and Watch Tower in the Rhodesias and Nyasaland', *The Journal of African History*, 1965, p. 93.

34 Sholto Cross, 'Independent Churches and independent States: Jehovah's Witnesses in East and Central Africa', in Fasholé-Luke, *et al.*, eds, *Christianity in Independent Africa* (Rex Collings, London, 1978) p. 307.

35 A. Richards, *Land, Labour and Diet in Northern Rhodesia* (Oxford University Press, London, 1939) p. 258.

36 Quoted in T. O. Ranger, 'Poverty and Prophetism: Religious Movements in the Makoni District, 1929–1940', (paper read at SOAS African History seminar, October, 1981).

37 Cf. p. 257.

38 *Africa South of the Sahara*, p. 456.

39 Strayer, *The Making of Mission Communities in East Africa*, p. 157.

40 J. V. Taylor, *The Growth of the Church in Buganda* (SCM Press, London, 1958) pp. 89ff.

41 Quoted in Tom Tuma, 'Major changes and developments in Christian leadership in Busoga Province, Uganda, 1960–74', in E. Fasholé-Luke, *et al*, eds, *Christianity in Independent Africa*, p. 71.

42 The teaching and writing of Aylward Shorter, a White Father, have been especially influential. Cf. A. Shorter, and E. Kataza, *Missionaries to Yourselves: African catechists today* (Geoffrey Chapman, London, 1972).

43 Perrin-Jassy, *Basic Community in the African Churches*, p. 86. This happened in the 1960s.

44 Leys, *Kenya*, pp. 227–8.

45 Wipper, *Rural Rebels*, p. 51, citing an unpublished study by H. Owuor (n.d.).

46 M. Wilson, *Rituals of Kinship Among the Nyakusa* (Oxford University Press, London, 1957) p. 161. A study, based on her 1930s research, but published twenty years later.

47 Wilson, *Rituals of Kinship*, p. 110.

48 Taylor, and Lehmann, *Christians of the Copperbelt*, p. 103.

49 Linden, *Church and Revolution in Rwanda*, p. 41.

50 M. Hunter, [Wilson] 'An African Christian Morality', *Africa*, 1937, p. 284.

51 Fields, *Revival and Rebellion in Colonial Central Africa*, p. 111.

52 Wright, *German Missions in Tanganyika*, p. 89.

53 A. Hastings, 'Were Women a Special Case?', in F. Bowie, *et al.*, eds., *Women and Missions: Past and Present* (Berg, Oxford, 1993) p. 113, quoting the research of B. Garvey.

54 Hunter, 'An African Christian Morality', p. 271.

55 T. Beidelman, 'Witchcraft in Ukaguru' in J. Middleton and E. H. Winter, eds., *Witchcraft and Sorcery in East Africa* (Routledge & Kegan Paul, London, 1963) p. 87.

Notes

This sheds more light on men's anxieties than women's practice, but that such fears were possible is illuminating.

56 M. L. Pirouet, 'Women Missionaries of the Church Missionary Society in Uganda 1896–1920', in T. Christensen and W. R. Hutchinson, eds., *Missionary Ideologies in the Imperialist Era: 1880–1920* (Aros, Aarhus, 1982) p. 237.

57 Quoted in Wilson, *Rituals of Kinship*, p. 251.

58 Linden, *Church and Revolution in Rwanda*, pp. 19–21.

59 This paragraph is based on A. Kupalo, 'African sisters' congregations: realities of the present situation', in Fasholé-Luke, *et al.*, eds, *Christianity in Independent Africa*, p. 124.

60 Quoted in J. Burke, 'These Catholic Sisters are all Mamas!', in F. Bowie, *et al.*, eds., *Women and Missions*, p. 263.

61 Mabel Ensor, in F. B. Welbourn, *East African Rebels* (SCM, London, 1961) p. 62. This is the source for the account of Ensor that follows.

62 J. McCracken, *Politics and Christianity in Malawi: The impact of the Livingstonia mission in the Northern Province* (Cambridge University Press, Cambridge, 1977) pp. 122–3.

63 Josiah Kibira, quoted in Iliffe, *A Modern History of Tanganyika*, p. 364.

64 Linden, *Church and Revolution in Rwanda*, pp. 204–5.

65 F. B. Welbourn and B. A. Ogot, *A Place to Feel at Home* (Oxford University Press, London, 1966) pp. 21–70.

66 T. Tuma in Fasholé-Luke, *et al.*, eds., *Christianity in Independent Africa*, pp. 74–7.

67 Catherine Robins, 'Conversion, Life Crises, and Stability Among Women in the East African Revival', in B. Jules-Rosette, ed., *The New Religions of Africa* (Ablex Pub. Corp., Norwood, 1979) pp. 185ff.

68 Andrea Kajerero, quoted in Iliffe, *A Modern History of Tanganyika*, p. 365.

69 F. D. Muzorewa, 'Through Prayer to Action: The Rukwadzano Women of Rhodesia', in Ranger and Weller, eds., *Themes in the Christian History of Central Africa* (Heinemann, London, 1975) pp. 256–268.

70 J. Farrant, *Mashonaland Martyr Bernard Mizeki and the Pioneer Church* (Oxford University Press, Cape Town, 1966). Cf. p. 116.

71 T. Ranger, 'Territorial Cults in the History of Central Africa', *Journal of African History*, 1973, p. 595.

72 Quoted in Welbourn, and Ogot, *A Place to Feel at Home*, p. 25.

73 T. Ranger, 'The Invention of Tradition in Colonial Africa', in E. Hobsbawm and T. Ranger, *The Invention of Tradition* (Cambridge University Press, Cambridge, 1983) pp. 244–5.

74 Ranger, 'Poverty and Prophetism', pp. 16–19.

75 According to the Census of 1969, there were 2.2 million Kikuyu, 1.5 million Luo, 1.4 million Luhyia, 1.1 million Kamba and 761 thousand Gusii in a population of just under 11 million (Wipper, *Rural Rebels*, p. 18, n. 1).

76 J. Kenyatta, quoted in Strayer, *The Making of Mission Communities in East Africa*, p. 131.

77 Strayer, *The Making of Mission Communities in East Africa*, pp. 136ff. (A chapter jointly written with J. Murray).

78 Ngugi wa Thiong'o (formerly James Ngugi) classic novel, *The River Between*, (Heinemann, London, 1965), tells of Muthoni, who defies her Christian father, Joshua, to be 'beautiful in the way of the tribe', but dies as a result of the operation.

79 J. Lonsdale, 'European Attitudes and African Pressures: Missions and government in Kenya between the wars', *Race*, 1968, pp. 141–151.

393

Notes

80 S. Clements, 'The Catholic Church in Kenya: A centre of hope', *Pro Mundi Vita*, Africa Dossier 22 (July, 1982) p. 17.

81 Quoted in D. Sandgren, *Christianity and the Kikuyu* (P. Lang, New York, 1989) p. 93. Complete texts, pp. 174ff.

82 Address to the Africa Inland Mission, quoted in Sandgren, *Christianity and the Kikuyu*, pp. 144–5.

83 Sandgren, *Christianity and the Kikuyu*, pp. 121–133.

84 Linden, *Church and Revolution in Rwanda*, p. 64. The account that follows is based on this source.

85 Linden, *Church and Revolution in Rwanda*, p. 61, cf. pp. 83, 135.

86 Linden, *Church and Revolution in Rwanda*, p. 138.

87 J. and I. Linden, 'John Chilembwe and the New Jerusalem', *Journal of African History*, 1971, p. 633 and n. 31. On the antagonism between the Nyau mask society and missions, cf. M. Schoffeleers and I. Linden, 'The Resistance of the Nyau Societies to the Roman Catholic Missions in Colonial Malawi', in T. Ranger and I. Kimambo, eds, *The Historical Study of African Religion* (Heinemann, London, 1972) pp. 252ff.

88 Cf. H. Turner, 'African Religious Movements and Roman Catholicism', in *Religious Innovation in Africa* (G. K. Hall, Boston, 1979) pp. 147ff.

89 Fields, *Revival and Rebellion in Colonial Central Africa*, p. 112.

90 Cf. 127.

91 The account that follows is based on Welbourn, *East African Rebels*, pp. 77–102.

92 Yoswa Kabine, quoted in Welbourn, *East African Rebels*, p. 108.

93 H. Langworthy, 'Joseph Booth: Prophet of Radical Change in Central and South Africa 1891–1915', *Journal of Religion in Africa*, 1986, pp. 22–43.

94 Quoted in Langworthy, 'Joseph Booth', pp. 29–30.

95 Langworthy, 'Joseph Booth', p. 32.

96 The classic account is G. Shepperson and T. Price, *Independent African: John Chilembwe and the origins, setting and significance of the Nyasaland native rising of 1915* (Edinburgh University Press, Edinburgh, 1958).

97 Chilembwe, quoted in Shepperson and Price, *Independent African*, p. 235.

98 George Mwase, *A Dialogue of Nyasaland: Record of past events*, (1932), published as *Strike a Blow and Die*, R. Rotberg, ed., (Harvard University Press, Cambridge, Mass., 1967). On the question of motivation, cf. Robert Rotberg, 'Psychological Stress and the Question of Identity: Chilembwe's Revolt Reconsidered' in R. Rotberg, and A. Mazrui, eds, *Protest and Power in Black Africa* (Oxford University Press, New York, 1970) pp. 336–373. For a different interpretation (from which Mwase is here cited), stressing millenial elements, cf. I., and J. Linden, 'John Chilembwe', p. 632.

99 He returned to South Africa in 1919, but lived in retirement.

100 Taylor and Lehmann, *Christians of the Copperbelt*, p. 236, quoting Ian Cunnison.

101 Fields, *Revival and Rebellion in Colonial Central Africa*, p. 7.

102 Fields, *Revival and Rebellion in Colonial Central Africa*, pp. 114ff.; S. Cross, 'Independent Churches and Independent States: Jehovah's Witnesses in East and Central Africa', in Fasholé-Luke, *et al.*, eds, *Christianity in Independent Africa*, p. 304ff; Hooker, 'Witnesses and Watch Tower' pp. 91ff; N. Long, 'Religion and Socio-Economic Action Among the Serenje-Lala of Zambia', in C. G. Baeta, ed., *Christianity in Tropical Africa* (Oxford University Press for International Africa Institute, London, 1968) pp. 396ff.

103 C. Perrings, 'Consciousness, Conflict and Proletarianisation: An assessment of the

394

Notes

1935 mineworkers' strike on the Northern Rhodesian Copperbelt', *Journal of Southern African Studies*, 1977, p. 49.

104 Fields, *Revival and Rebellion in Colonial Central Africa*, pp. 3–4.

105 Watch Tower supporters at Likasi mine, Katanga, quoted in Perrings, 'Consciousness, Conflict and Proletarianisation' p. 50.

106 A 1923 convert, quoted in Hooker, 'Witnesses and Watch Tower', p. 95.

107 Hooker, 'Witnesses and Watch Tower', p. 96.

108 Taylor, and Lehmann, *Christians of the Copperbelt*, p. 230.

109 R. G. Willis, 'Changes in Mystical Concepts and Practices among the Fipa', *Ethnology*, 1968, p. 145; E. Colson, 'Converts and Tradition: The impact of Christianity on Valley Tonga Religion', *Southwestern Journal of Anthropology*, 1970, pp. 147, 152.

110 R. Stuart, 'Anglican Missionaries and the Problem of Evil: Mchape and the U.M.C.A. 1933', unpublished paper, cited in C. Neale, *Writing 'Independent' History* (Greenwood Press, Westport, 1985) p. 78.

111 A. D. Macfarlane, *Witchcraft in Tudor and Stuart England: A regional and comparative study* (Routledge & Kegan Paul, London, 1970).

112 T. Ranger, 'The Mwana Lesa Movement of 1925', in Ranger and Weller, eds., *Themes*, pp. 58, 59.

113 T. Ranger, 'Medical Science and Pentecost: The Dilemma of Anglicanism in Africa', in W. J. Sheils, ed., *The Church and Healing* (Blackwell for the Ecclesiastical Society, Oxford, 1982) p. 340.

114 Fields, *Revival and Rebellion in Colonial Central Africa*, pp. 79ff.

115 A Jesuit in Southern Rhodesia in 1934, quoted in Ranger, 'Medical Science and Pentecost', p. 349, n. 26.

116 R. G. Willis, 'Kamcape: an anti-sorcery movement in south-west Tanzania', *Africa*, 1968, pp. 1–15.

117 J. C. Chakanza, 'Provisional annotated chronological list of witch-finding movements in Malawi, 1850–1980', *Journal of Religion in Africa*, 1985, p. 232.

118 M. Hunter, [Wilson] 'An African Christian Morality', *Africa*, 1937, p. 271.

119 W. H. C. Frend, *The Donatist Church* (Clarendon Press, Oxford, 1952) pp. 103–4.

120 A. Shorter, *Jesus and the Witchdoctor* (Geoffrey Chapman, London, 1985) p. 167. Cf. Wipper, *Rural Rebels*, p. 2, which suggests that in 1971 there were 157 independent denominations, with 1 694 840 members.

121 Quoted in Ranger, 'Poverty and Prophetism', p. 40.

122 A. Roberts, 'The Lumpa Church of Alice Lenshina', in R. Rotberg and A. Mazrui, eds., *Protest and Power in Black Africa* (Oxford University Press, New York, 1970) p. 566.

123 Wipper, *Rural Rebels*, pp. 73–4; her leadership is reflected in the movement's name, Dini ya Mariam.

124 I. Machika, quoted in Ranger, 'Medical Science and Pentecost', p. 359.

125 Shorter, *Jesus and the Witchdoctor*, pp. 169–70.

126 H. Bucher, *Spirits and Power: An analysis of Shona cosmology* (Oxford University Press, Cape Town, 1980) p. 205.

127 M. Schoffeleers, 'The Interraction of the M'Bona Cult and Christianity, 1859–1963', in T. Ranger and J. Weller, eds, *Themes*, pp. 14–29.

128 This account is based on Ranger, 'Poverty and Prophetism', pp. 34–9.

129 C. M. Dillon-Malone, *The Korsten Basketmakers* (Manchester University Press, Lusaka and Manchester, 1978). Cf. C. Kileff and M. Kileff, 'The Masowe Vapostori of Seki:

Notes

'Utopianism and Tradition in an African Church', in B. Jules-Rosette, ed., *The New Religions of Africa*, pp. 151ff.

130 From a Shona account attributed to Onias Bvuma, given *in extenso* in Dillon-Malone, *The Korsten Basketmakers*, pp. 146–151.

131 Dillon-Malone, *The Korsten Basketmakers*, p. 43.

132 On the symbolic meanings of 'ark', 'wilderness' and 'pilgrimage', cf. R. Werbner, 'The argument of images: from Zion to the Wilderness in African churches', in W. van Binsbergen and M. Schoffeleers, *Theoretical Explorations in African Religion* (KPI monographs from African Studies Centre, Leiden, 1985) pp. 253ff.

133 Quoted in Dillon-Malone, *The Korsten Basketmakers*, p. 26.

134 B. Jules-Rosette, *African Apostles: Aspects of ritual and conversion in the Church of John Maranke* (Cornell University Press, Ithaca, 1975). Cf. her 'Prophecy and leadership in the Maranke Church', in G. Bond, *et al.*, eds., *African Christianity: Patterns of religious continuity* (Academic Press, New York, 1979) pp. 109–136.

135 Wipper, *Rural Rebels*, pp. 124ff. My account of Mumbo (p. 258 below) is also based in Wipper, pp. 35ff. On Dini ya Msambwa, cf. J. de Wolf, 'Dini ya Msambwa: Militant Protest or Millenarian Promise?', and A. Wipper, 'Lofty Visions and Militant Action: A Reply to Jan de Wolf', in *Canadian Journal of African Studies*, 1983, pp. 265–294; R. Buijtenhuijs, 'Dini ya Msambwa: rural rebellion or counter-society?', in W. van Binsbergen and M. Schoffeleers, *Theoretical Explorations in African Religion*, pp. 322ff.

136 Hunter, [Wilson], 'An African Christian Morality', p. 272.

137 Quoted in B. Ray, *African Religions: Symbol, Ritual and Community* (Prentice–Hall, Englewood Cliffs, New Jersey, 1976) p. 165.

138 There were two levels of oathing; it was the more advanced level, for fighters, that is said to have included components such as bestiality. If true, this was a way of bonding the fighters, and defining their identity *vis-à-vis* a Kikuyu society to which such practices were abhorrent. Cf. J. Lonsdale, 'Mau Maus of the Mind: Making Mau Mau and Remaking Kenya', *Journal of African History*, 1990, pp. 393ff. Cf. M. Green, 'Mau Mau oathing rituals and political ideology in Kenya: a re-analysis', *Africa*, 1990, pp. 69ff. Scholars' fascination with Mau Mau is significant in itself.

139 Quoted in D. V. Steere, *God's Irregular: Arthur Shearly Cripps* (SPCK, London, 1973) p. 109.

140 N. Thomas, 'Church and State in Zimbabwe', *Journal of Church and State*, 1985, pp. 118–121.

141 E. S. Atieno-Odhiambo, 'A Portrait of the Missionaries in Kenya before 1939', *Kenya Historical Review*, 1973, p. 8.

142 V. Donovan, *Christianity Rediscovered: An epistle from the Maasai* (SCM Press, London, 1982) p. 15. This is the source for what follows.

143 Donovan, *Christianity Rediscovered*, p. 108.

144 Colson, 'Converts and Tradition', p. 150.

145 L. Stevens 'Religious Change in a Haya Village, Tanzania', *Journal of Religion in Africa*, 1991, p. 4. This is the source for what follows.

146 E. S. Miller, 'The Christian Missionary: Agent of Secularization', *Missiology: An International Review*, 1973, p. 106.

147 Quoted in Wilson, *Rituals of Kinship*, p. 18.

148 Colson, 'Converts and tradition', p. 147. She goes on to describe a short-lived revival.

149 C. G. Jung, *Memories, Dreams, Reflections* (Fontana, London, 1983) pp. 294.

Notes

Chapter 10

1 S. Leith-Ross, *African Women* (Faber and Faber, London, 1939) p. 120.
2 Rhodes House, Oxford, MSS Br. Emp s. 73, Edward Lugard, 'Journal Jottings', 7 Oct., 1912. F. D. Lugard, *The Dual Mandate in Tropical Africa*. 5th ed., Cass, London, 1965, pp. 79–80.
3 Rhodes House, MSS Afr. s. 1152, Bain to Rena Bain, 29 March 1930.
4 H. Debrunner, *A Church between Colonial Powers: A Study of the Church in Togo* (Lutterworth, London, 1967) pp. 119, 122, 143.
5 Debrunner, *The Church in Togo*, p. 161.
6 Debrunner, *The Church in Togo*, p. 1. The modern nation of Togo is the former French mandate; the British mandate became part of Ghana, so these figures exclude the Ewe Presbyterians.
7 E. Udo, 'The missionary scramble for spheres of influence in south-eastern Nigeria 1900–52', in O. Kalu, *The History of Christianity in West Africa* (Longman, London, 1980) pp. 159ff.
8 Leith-Ross, *African Women*, p. 299.
9 *The African Missionary*, Nov.–Dec., 1921, p. 116.
10 E. Fasholé-Luke, 'Religion in Freetown', C. Fyfe, and E. Jones, eds., *Freetown: A symposium* (Sierra Leone University Press, Freetown, 1968) p. 130.
11 Debrunner, *The Church in Togo*, p. 112.
12 J. Grimley and G. Robinson, *Church Growth in Central and Southern Nigeria* (W. B. Eerdmans, Grand Rapids, 1966) p. 78.
13 Church Missionary Society Archives G3/A2/1911, Report by A. H. Blair, 15 Sept., 1911. Ekiti is in eastern Yorubaland.
14 *Autobiography of an Illustrious Son: Chief Eke Kalu of Elu Ohafia* (privately published, Lagos, 1954) p. 8.
15 D. Kimble, *A Political History of Ghana* (Clarendon Press, Oxford, 1963) p. 160, n. 4.
16 J. Faure, *Togo Champs de Mission*, (1945) quoted in Debrunner, *The Church in Togo*, p. 173: 'Enable me to understand why they are so dirty . . . the fat chief who stinks of palm wine . . . the bearded Hausa dignified in his filthy gown, but greedy for money . . .'.
17 Leith-Ross, *African Women*, p. 292.
18 Quoted in Kimble, *A Political History of Ghana*, p. 161.
19 Fasholé-Luke, 'Religion in Freetown', p. 127; J. Nunley, 'The Fancy and the Fierce', *African Arts*, 1881, pp. 52ff.
20 R. Bureau, 'Influence de la Christianisation sur les institutions traditionelles des ethnies cotières du Cameroun', in C. Baeta, ed., *Christianity in Tropical Africa*, (Oxford University Press for International African Institute, London, 1966) pp. 180–1. For a different view of Cameroun water spirits, cf. E. Ardener, 'Belief and the Problem of Women', in S. Ardener, ed., *Perceiving Women*, (Malaby Press, London, 1975) pp. 1ff.
21 *The African Missionary*, 1924, p. 132.
22 For the account that follows, cf. E. Isichei, 'Does Christianity Empower Women?', in F. Bowie, *et al.*, eds., *Women and Missions: Past and Present* (Berg, Oxford, 1993) pp. 209ff.
23 A. Collett, 'The Making of a Patrilineal Ideology: A Study of Continuity and Change in Social Organisation Among the Anaguta of Central Nigeria', (Ph.D. SOAS, 1984), p. 279.
24 Leith-Ross, *African Women*, pp. 103, 153, 309.

Notes

25 Fasholé-Luke, 'Religion in Freetown', p. 127.
26 A Cameroon catechist, quoted in F. Bowie, 'The Elusive Christian Family: Missionary Attempts to Define Women's Roles: Case studies from Cameroon', in Bowie, *et al.* eds., p. 160.
27 Quoted in Debrunner, *The Church in Togo*, p. 89.
28 Kimble, *A Political History of Ghana*, p. 82, n. 5. The point at issue was land alienation.
29 J. Coleman, *Nigeria: Background to nationalism* (University of California Press, Berkeley, 1958) p. 113.
30 F. Yao Boateng, 'The Catechism and the Rod: Presbyterian Education in Ghana', in E. Berman, ed., *African Reactions to Missionary Education* (Teachers College Press, New York and London, 1975) p. 83.
31 S. Crowther and J. Taylor, *The Gospel on the Banks of the Niger* (London, 1859; Dawsons, London, 1968) p. 432.
32 Leith-Ross, *African Women*, p. 132.
33 Quoted in P. A. C. Isichei, 'Ex-seminarian, Ignatius Bameh in Asaba', in E. Isichei, ed., *Varieties of Christian Experience in Nigeria* (Macmillan, London, 1982) p. 179.
34 Holy Ghost Fathers Archives, Paris (henceforward C. S. Sp.) 192/II/B, Lejeune to Superior General, 25 Dec., 1902, and much other correspondence.
35 C. S. Sp. 556/A, anon. ms., 'The Vicariate of Onitsha-Owerri 1939–1946'.
36 O. Kalu, 'Color and Conversion: The White Missionary Factor in the Christianization of Igboland, 1857–1967', *Missiology*, 1990, p. 69.
37 C. S. Sp., 555/VII, Heerey to Hunsec, 26 Mar., 1948.
38 C. S. Sp., *Bulletin de la Congrégation*, 1892, pp. 332–3.
39 C. S. Sp., Lejeune to Superior General, 1 Oct., 1900.
40 C. S. Sp., 192/B/III, Shanahan to Superior General, 18 Apr., 1907.
41 Totals compiled from N. I. Omenka, *The School in the Service of Evangelization* (E. J. Brill, Leiden, 1989) Table 3, p. 110, and rounded to the nearest thousand.
42 An address by the girls of St Joseph's Convent, Calabar, to Lady Egerton, in 1906, quoted in Omenka, *The School in the Service of Evangelization*, p. 208.
43 Omenka, *The School in the Service of Evangelization*, pp. 209–11. Also C. S. Sp., Nigeria Méridionale, Joseph Soul, Report of Visitation, Aug.–Nov. 1929.
44 Quoted in Omenka, *The School in the Service of Evangelization*, p. 215. The order was founded by his famous predecessor, Bishop Joseph Shanahan.
45 C. S. Sp., 191/A/8, Treich, Report on Nteje, April, 1920.
46 C. S. Sp., 557/A/III, Mohan to O'Brien, 20 Feb., 1958.
47 Leith-Ross, *African Women*, pp. 296–7.
48 Coleman, *Nigeria*, p. 133. The discrepancies were even greater, for many of the literates in the North were southerners.
49 Debrunner, *The Church in Togo*, p. 121.
50 Kimble, *A Political History of Ghana*, pp. 83–4.
51 Quoted in Kimble, *A Political History of Ghana*, p. 83. He was seeking, not an influx of missionaries, but more funds for government schools.
52 A CMS publication in 1899, quoted in E. Ayandele, 'The missionary factor in Northern Nigeria', in Kalu, *The History of Christianity in West Africa*, p. 140.
53 This account is based on I. Linden, 'Between Two Religions of the Book: The Children of the Israelites', in Isichei, ed., *Varieties of Christian Experience in Nigeria*, pp. 79ff.
54 C. S. Sp., Nigeria Méridionale, 1920–37 Report on Eke, (n.d.)
55 C. S. Sp., 556/III, Steigler, memo on state of mission, 24 Sept., 1946.

Notes

56 N[igerian] N[ational] A[rchives] I[badan] (henceforward NNAI), CSO 26/2/12601/ XII, E. Pembleton, Annual Report, Plateau Province, 1937.

57 Grimley and Robinson, *Church Growth*, p. 139.

58 Except where other sources are cited, the account that follows is based on my archival and field research in Nigeria.

59 P. Clarke, 'Birom Woman Evangelist: Vo Gyang of Forum', in Isichei, ed., *Varieties of Christian Experience in Nigeria*, pp. 163ff.

60 Grimley and Robinson, *Church Growth*, p. 129.

61 NNAI, CSO 2/26/12601, T. Farley Smith, Annual Report, Plateau Province, 1948.

62 Texts in S. Diamond, 'The Anaguta of Nigeria, Suburban Primitives', in J. Steward, ed., *Three African Tribes in Transition* (University of Illinois Press, Urbana, 1972) pp. 446–54, 459.

63 Anon. *The Church of Christ in Nigeria* (pamphlet, 1980).

64 Oral text, quoted in E. Isichei, *Entirely for God: A life of Michael Iwene Tansi* (London, 1981) p. 67, the source for this account.

65 Oral text in P. A. C. Isichei, 'Ex-Seminarian, Ignatius Bameh', pp. 177ff.

66 H. L. Ward-Price, *Dark Subjects* (Jarrolds Ltd, London, 1939) p. 245; he pays tribute to Coquard on pp. 243–4. For Coquard's account of his own work, cf. *Annals of the Propagation of the Faith*, 1901, pp. 28ff. For George, cf. R. Tucker and W. Liefeld, *Daughters of the Church* (Academie Books, Grand Rapids, 1987) pp. 318–9.

67 Quoted in Debrunner, *The Church in Togo*, p. 140.

68 Fasholé-Luke, 'Religion in Freetown' p. 128; F. C. Steady, 'The role of women in the churches in Freetown, Sierre Leone', in Fasholé-Luke, *et al.* eds, *Christianity in Independent Africa* (Rex Collings, London, 1978) pp. 151ff.

69 Fasholé-Luke, 'Religion in Freetown', p. 132.

70 J. D. Y. Peel, *Aladura: A religious movement among the Yoruba* (Published for International African Institute by Oxford University Press, London, 1968) p. 113. As he points out, these figures were suggested by the denominations themselves, in connection with religious radio programmes, so are of even more than usual unreliability.

71 H. Turner, *African Independent Church* II, (Clarendon Press, Oxford, 1967) p. 14. This is based on the known number of congregations, and on their average size, which is between 30 and 60 people. Of a total of 153, 72 congregations are in Nigeria, and 55 in Ghana, and there were *c.* 50 secessionist churches.

72 Fasholé-Luke, 'Religion in Freetown', p. 128.

73 R. Hackett, ed., 'Introduction', *New Religious Movements in Nigeria* (Edwin Mellen Press, Lewiston, 1987) p. 2.

74 Quoted in J. D. Y. Peel, 'Syncretism and Religious Change', *Comparative Studies in Society and History*, 1967–8, p. 126.

75 Quoted in Peel, *Aladura*, p. 121.

76 Ward Price, *Dark Subjects*, pp. 240–1.

77 W. Soyinka, *The Trials of Brother Jero*, in *The Jero Plays* (Eyre Methuen, London, 1973) p. 29.

78 Quoted in A. Omoyajowo, 'The Aladura Churches in Nigeria since independence' in E. Fasholé-Luke *et al.*, eds., *Christianity in Independent Africa* (Rex Collings, London, 1978) p. 110.

79 F. Mbon, 'Public Response to New Religious Movements in Contemporary Nigeria', in Hackett, *New Religious Movements*, p. 214.

80 Quoted in H. Callaway, 'Women in Yoruba tradition and in the Cherubim and Seraphim Society', in Kalu, ed., *The History of Christianity in West Africa*, p. 328.

Notes

81 Ward Price, *Dark Subjects*, p. 92. The account refers to influenza in Enugu, but is of wider applicability.

82 Quoted in J. Peel, 'The Aladura Movement in Western Nigeria', *Tarikh*, 3, 1, p. 52.

83 A. Ogunranti, 'Pastor and Politician: Isaac Akinyele, Olubadan of Ibadan', in Isichei, ed., *Varieties of Christian Experience in Nigeria*, pp. 131ff.

84 Peel, *Aladura*, p. 69.

85 Peel, *Aladura*, pp. 94–5; cf. pp. 101, 103.

86 Ward Price, *Dark Subjects*, pp. 241–2.

87 Quoted in R. C. Mitchell, 'Religious Protest and Social Change: The Origins of the Aladura Movement in Western Nigeria', in R. Rotberg, and A. Mazrui, eds, *Protest and Power in Black Africa* (Oxford University Press, New York, 1970) p. 481.

88 Peel, *Aladura*, pp. 272ff.

89 Peel, *Aladura*, p. 108.

90 Peel, *Aladura*, pp. 108, 126.

91 A. Omoyajowo, 'Mother in Israel: Christianah Olatunrinle in Ondo' (*c.* 1855–1941), in Isichei, *Varieties of Christian Experience in Nigeria*, pp. 141ff.

92 Turner, *African Independent Church*, I, pp. 35–53. This study is the source for my account of Ositelu.

93 Turner, *African Independent Church*, II, 73–6; Mitchell, *Religious Protest and Social Change*, p. 483, n. 68.

94 D. Crumbley, 'Impurity and Power: Women in Aladura Churches', *Africa*, 1992, pp. 516 and 520, n. 8.

95 O. U. Kalu, 'Broken Covenants: Religious Change in Igbo Historiography', *Neue Zeitschrift für Missionswissenschaft*, 1990, p. 310.

96 Turner, *Church of the Lord* II, 76–8.

97 S. Barrett, *The Rise and Fall of an African Utopia: A wealthy theocracy in comparative perspective* (Wilfrid Levrier University Press, Waterloo, Ontario, 1977); also his 'Crisis and Change in a West African Utopia' in E. Harvey, ed., *Perspectives on Modernization* (University of Toronto Press, Toronto, 1972), pp. 160ff. The 1977 (but not the 1972) version disguises the settlement as 'Olowo'.

98 A. Omoyajowo, 'The Aladura Churches in Nigeria since Independence', p. 96. The account that follows is based on this, on Olupona, 'The Celestial Church of Christ in Ondo: A Phenomenological perspective', and on, R. Hackett, 'Thirty Years of Growth and Change in a West African Independent Church: A sociological Perspective', also in Hackett, ed., *New Religious Movements in Nigeria* (Edwin Mellen Press, Lewiston, 1987) pp. 161ff.

99 Oschoffa at an interview in 1980, quoted in J. Olupona, 'The Celestial Church of Christ in Ondo', pp. 46–7.

100 Hackett, 'Thirty Years of Growth and Change in a West African Independent Church', p. 163.

101 Hackett, 'Thirty Years of Growth and Change in a West African Independent Church', p. 176.

102 Wade is a Grebo name, pronounced Wodi. The main source for the account that follows is G. Haliburton, *The Prophet Harris* (Longman, London, 1971). The Grebo are related to the Kru, and were sometimes grouped with them.

103 C. Baeta, *Prophetism in Ghana*, (SCM Press, London, 1962) p. 16.

104 S. S. Walker, 'The Message as Medium: The Harrist Churches of the Ivory Coast and Ghana', in G. Bond, *et al.*, eds, *African Christianity Patterns of Religious Continuity* (Academie Press, New York, 1979) p. 22.

105 The account that follows is based on Walker, 'The Message as Medium', pp. 23ff.

Notes

106 The account that follows is based on materials in the National Archives, Enugu, and on studies by G. O. M. Tasie, 'The Prophetic Calling: Garrick Sokari Braide', in Isichei, ed., *Varieties of Christian Experience in Nigeria*, pp. 99ff, and Tasie's 'Christian Awakening in West Africa 1914–18', in Kalu, ed., *The History of Christianity in West Africa*, pp. 293ff. Braide was born in another Kalabari settlement, Obonoma.

107 Tasie, 'The Prophetic Calling', p. 113, n. 3; 'Christian Awakening', p. 300, in which he calls his father 'a poor serf'.

108 Cf. W. MacGaffey, *Modern Kongo Prophets* (Indiana University Press, Bloomington, 1983) p. 105, in the contexts of similar statements about Kimbangu.

109 Igbo speakers originally came to the Delta as slaves. Because they were so numerous, their language virtually eclipsed Ibani in Bonny, the CMS' most successful centre. The Kalabari used effective cultural devices to preserve their language and culture, and these have been studied in various papers by Robin Horton.

110 Nigerian National Archives, Enugu, CSE 3/8/3, B738/1916.

111 Kalu, 'Color and Conversion', p. 72.

112 H. Turner, 'Pentecostal Movements in Nigeria', in his *Religious Innovation in Africa* (C. K. Hall, Boston, 1979), p. 123.

113 CAC maintains a separate existence in the East. On all this, cf. R. Hackett, *Religion in Calabar: The religious life and history of a Nigerian town* (Mouton de Gruyter, Berlin and New York, 1989) pp. 142ff, 108.

114 Quoted in M. J. Ada, and E. Isichei, 'Perceptions of God and the Churches in Obudu', *Journal of Religion in Africa*, 1976, p. 170.

115 M. Fraenkel, *Tribe and Class in Monrovia*, (Oxford University Press for International African Institute, London, 1964) p. 170; for another perspective, cf. T. Awori, 'The Revolt against the "Civilising Mission": Christian Education in Liberia', in Berman, ed., *African Reactions to Missionary Education*, pp. 130–1.

116 This account is based on Ada and Isichei, 'Perceptions of God and the Churches in Obudu', pp. 165ff.

117 Church Constitution, 1939, quoted in K. Opuku, 'Changes within Christianity: The case of the Musama Disco Christo Church', in E. Fasholé-Luke, *et al.* eds., *Christianity in Independent Africa*, p. 112.

118 Baeta, 'The Musama Disco Christo Church', in his *Prophetism in Ghana*, pp. 43, 44, 60.

119 Baeta, 'The Musama Disco Christo Church', pp. 42–3.

120 Opuku, 'Changes within Christianity', p. 120; for the occupations of members in the 1950s, cf. Baeta, 'The Musama Disco Christo Church', pp. 46–7.

121 Peel, *Aladura*, p. 61.

122 As is pointed out in R. Horton and D. D. Y. Peel, 'Conversion and Confusion: A Rejoinder on Christianity in Eastern Nigeria', *Canadian Journal of African Studies*, 1976, p. 493.

123 Cf. F. Salamone, 'Continuity of Igbo Values After Conversion: A Study in Purity and Prestige', *Missiology*, 1975, p. 41.

124 F. Mbon, 'Public Response to New Religious Movements in Contemporary Nigeria', in Hackett, ed., *New Religious Movements in Nigeria*, p. 220.

125 O. Kalu, 'Broken Covenants: Religious Change in Igbo Historiography', *Neue Zeitschrift für Missionswissenschaft*, 1990, p. 306. It is not clear if these figures are cumulative.

126 Hackett, 'Women as leaders and participants in the Spiritual Churches', in Hackett, ed., *New Religious Movements in Nigeria*, p. 191.

Notes

127 Hackett, 'Women as leaders', pp. 191ff. This is the source for the account that follows.
128 Baeta, 'The Musama Disco Christo Church', p. 54.
129 Quoted in Baeta, 'The Musama Disco Christo Church', p. 99.
130 Crumbley, 'Impurity and Power', pp. 506ff gives a useful account of this theme, and cf. Hackett, 'Women as leaders', p. 201.
131 Hackett, *Religion in Calabar*, p. 107. The account that follows is based on G. Amadi, 'Healing in "The Brotherhood of the Cross and Star" ', in W. Shiels, ed., *The Church and Healing* (Blackwell for the Ecclesiastical Society, Oxford, 1982) pp. 367ff, and E. Offiong, 'Schism and Religious Independency in Nigeria: The Case of the Brotherhood of the Cross and Star', in Hackett, ed., *New Religious Movements in Nigeria*, pp. 179ff, p. 186ff.
132 Hackett, *Religion in Calabar*, p. 191.
133 Quoted in Hackett, *Religion in Calabar*, p. 187. She goes on to point out that Obu is ambiguous about his own divinity.
134 E. Ayandele, *The Missionary Impact on Modern Nigeria 1842–1914* (Longman, London, 1967) pp. 270–8.
135 Quoted in G. Parrinder, *Religion in an African City* (Oxford University Press, London, 1953).
136 Parrinder, *Religion in an African City*, p. 128.
137 A Christian-influenced cult in the palace of the Oba of Benin. Cf. p. 63.
138 E. Akama, 'The emergence of the Igbe cult in Isokoland', in Hackett, ed., *New Religious Movements*, pp. 19ff.
139 N. Kastfelt, 'The Prophetic Calling: Kulibwui and the Mbula', in Isichei, ed., *Varieties of Christian Experience in Nigeria*, pp. 116ff.
140 P. Probst, 'The letter and the spirit: literacy and religious authority in the history of the Aladura movement in western Nigeria', *Africa*, 1989, p. 482.
141 Peel, *Aladura*, p. 115.
142 Turner, *Church of the Lord*, I, 41–3.
143 M. Abasiattai, 'The Oberi Okaime Christian Mission: Towards a History of an Ibibio Independent Church', *Africa*, 1989, pp. 496ff.
144 Kimble, *A Political History of Ghana*, p. 165 n. 5.
145 Mitchell, 'Religious Protest and Social Change', p. 478.
146 M. Field, *Search for Security: An ethno-psychiatric study of rural Ghana* (Faber and Faber, London, 1960) p. 349, and pp. 41–2; Turner, 'Secret Religion', p. 279, calls it a 'hotch-potch of ancient Egyptian and medieval European magic and occult literature'.
147 Peel, *Aladura*, p. 142, he lists other works that appeal to the 'gnostic' strand in Nigerian spirituality, such as H. Blavatsky, *The Secret Doctrine* (Blavatsky was one of the founders of Theosophy), or S. L. MacGregor Mathers, *The Kabbalah Revealed*.
148 Baeta, 'The Musama Disco Christo Church', p. 30.
149 C. S. Sp. 555/II, Shanahan to Lena, 4 Aug., 1924.
150 *Africa Confidential*, 27 May, 1987 (28/11).
151 Field, *Search for Security*, pp. 267–8.
152 S. Barrington-Ward, ' "The centre cannot hold": Spirit possession as redefinition', in Fasholé-Luke *et al.*, eds., *Christianity in Independent Africa*, pp. 463–4. For a different version of this tradition, cf. E. Akama, 'Evangelist Adam Igbudu and His Mass Movement in Nigeria: A Historical Survey', in Hackett, ed., *New Religious Movements in Nigeria*, p. 349, and p. 124.
153 M. T. Drewal, *Yoruba Ritual* (Indiana University Press, Bloomington, 1992) p. 9.

Notes

154 R. Hackett, 'Close Encounters of the Third Kind: Spiritual technology in modern Nigeria', (paper presented to the XVth Congress of the International Association for the History of Religions, Sydney, 1985) p. 21.

155 Outlined in Hackett, 'Close Encounters of the Third Kind'.

156 K. Barber, 'How man makes God in West Africa: Yoruba Attitudes towards the Orisa', *Africa*, 1981, pp. 742–3.

157 E. Isichei, 'Myth, Gender and Society in precolonial Asaba', *Africa*, 1991, pp. 513ff.

158 Hackett, *Religion in Calabar*, pp. 179–83.

159 D. Offiong, 'Social Relations and Witch Beliefs Among the Ibibio', *Africa* 1983, pp. 77ff.

160 J. Middleton, 'One hundred and fifty years of Christianity in a Ghanaian Town', *Africa*, 1983, pp. 2ff.

161 Gabriel Okara, *One Night at Victoria Beach*, in G. Moore and Ulli Beier, eds., *The Penguin Book of Modern African Poetry*, (Penguin, Harmondsworth, 3rd ed., 1984) p. 175.

162 J. Clifford, 'Introduction: Partial Truths', in J. Clifford and G. Marcus, eds., *Writing Culture: The Poetics and Politics of Ethnography* (University of California Press, Berkeley and Los Angeles, 1986) pp. 160–1.

163 Ward Price, *Dark Subjects*, p. 192.

164 Gifford, *Christianity and Politics in Doe's Liberia* (Cambridge University Press, Cambridge, 1993) pp. 57–8.

165 Fraenkel, *Tribe and Class in Monrovia*, pp. 159–164. Cf. also p. 288.

166 Nwafor Orizu, *Without Bitterness*, p. 99, quoted in Grimley and Robinson, *Church Growth*, p. 31. His views are particularly striking as Orizu himself studied in America; the owners of the 'beautiful mansions' were defined as clerks on £300 a year.

167 O. Kalu, 'The Shattered Cross: The Church Union Movement in Nigeria 1905–66', in Kalu, ed., *The History of Christianity in West Africa*, pp. 340ff. The Anglicans of northern Nigeria did not join the negotiations.

168 Kimble, *A Political History of Ghana*, p. 164. Figures rounded to nearest thousand.

169 *World Christian Handbook* (1962) pp. 68–9, 237. These figures exclude indigenous churches and bodies such as the Jehovah's Witnesses.

170 P. A. Talbot, *The Peoples of Southern Nigeria* (Cass, London, 1926) IV, 103, 106. The 1921 Census figures that he cites are notoriously unreliable, because it was only in urban centres that they were based on systematic enumeration.

171 I. Ekanem, *The 1963 Nigerian Census: A critical appraisal* (Ethiope Publishing Co., Benin, 1972) p. 65.

172 P. Gifford, *Christianity and Politics in Doe's Liberia* pp. 56–7.

173 Percentages for the 1990s come from *Africa South of the Sahara*. (Europa, London, 1993), pp. 160, 311, 404, 422, 659, 720, 383. The lower figures tend to reflect a large Muslim population.

Chapter 11

1 Charles Villa-Vicencio, 'The Covenant Restructured: A Shift in Afrikaner Ideology', *International Bulletin of Missionary Research*, Jan., 1985, p. 13.

2 J. de Gruchy, *The Church Struggle in South Africa* (Collins, London, 1986), p. 242.

3 J. S. Jones, 'How different are human races?', *Nature*, 293, 1981, pp. 188–9.

4 A. Luthuli, *Let My People Go* (Collins, London, 1962) p. 46.

5 Richard Rive, *Buckingham Palace District Six* (Heinemann, London, 1986).

Notes

6 Pattie Price, *The Anatomy of Apartheid* (1967), quoted in W. de Klerk, *The Puritans in Africa* (Rex Collings, London, 1975), pp. 337–8.

7 Figures from *A Survey of Race Relations in South Africa*, 1977, in de Gruchy, *The Church Struggle in South Africa*, p. 245.

8 A. Nolan, *God in South Africa: The challenge of the Gospel* (D. Philip, Cape Town, 1988) p. 81.

9 The account that follows is based on Mia Brandel-Syrier, *Black Woman in Search of God* (Lutterworth, London, 1962).

10 W. Beinart and C. Bundy, *Hidden Struggles in Rural South Africa* (University of California Press, London, 1987) pp. 246–7.

11 N. Parsons, *A New History of Southern Africa* (Macmillan Education, London, 1982) pp. 236–7.

12 Cf. Luthuli, *Let My People Go*, pp. 190–7.

13 Quoted in P. Walshe, 'South Africa: Prophetic Christianity and the Liberation Movement', *Journal of Modern African Studies*, 1991, p. 31.

14 Luthuli, *Let My People Go*, p. 225.

15 Luthuli, *Let My People Go*, p. 39.

16 Dennis Brutus, 'For Chief, A Tribute to Albert John Luthuli', in his *A Simple Lust: Collected Poems of South African Jail & Exile* (Heinemann, London, 1973) p. 170.

17 A. Boesak, 'Civil Religion and the Black Community', *Journal of Theology for Southern Africa*, 1977, p. 37, 38.

18 Government Census figures from J. de Gruchy, *The Church Struggle in South Africa*, p. 246.

19 Quoted in C. Villa-Vicencio, 'South African Civil Religion: An Introduction' *Journal of Theology for Southern Africa*, 1977, p. 10.

20 The concept of 'civil religion', first developed by Robert Bellah in a 1967 paper on civil religion in America, has proved extremely useful, and illuminating.

21 Deut. 32.8, Acts 17.26, Gen. 11 (cf. de Klerk *The Puritans in Africa*, pp. 221–2).

22 de Klerk, *The Puritans in Africa*, p. 199.

23 Quoted in *The Kairos Document and Commentaries* (World Council of Churches, Nov., 1985) p. 16.

24 *The Kairos Document*, p. 16. The same passage is denounced in similar terms in 'Concerned Evangelicals', *Evangelical Witness in South Africa* (W. B. Eerdman, Grand Rapids, Michigan, 1986) p. 32.

25 Quoted in de Gruchy, *The Church Struggle in South Africa*, p. 59.

26 Ingrid Jonker, quoted in de Klerk, *The Puritans in Africa* p. 341.

27 Text *in extenso* in J. de Gruchy, *et al.*, eds., *Apartheid is a Heresy* (W. B. Eerdmans Pub. Co., Grand Rapids, Michigan, 1983) pp. 149–150.

28 This prevented the individual concerned from, among other things, speaking in public, meeting more than one person at a time, or travelling beyond a certain limit.

29 Quoted in James Cochrane, *Servants of Power: The role of English-speaking churches 1903–1930* (Raven Press, Johannesburg, 1987) p. 117.

30 A. Paton, *Apartheid and the Archbishop: The Life and Times of Geoffrey Clayton* (Jonathan Cape, London, 1974) pp. 46–7, 65–6.

31 Quoted in P. Walshe, 'South Africa: Prophetic Christianity and the Liberation Movement', *Journal of Modern African Studies*, 1991, p. 32.

32 Paton, *Apartheid and the Archbishop*, pp. 116–117.

33 Paton, *Apartheid and the Archbishop*, pp. 278–81.

34 N. Mosley, *The Life of Raymond Raynes* (Hodder and Stoughton, London, 1963) pp. 67ff., 121.

Notes

35 M. Scott, *A Time to Speak* (Faber and Faber, London, 1958).

36 John Patten, Editor of the *Natal Mercury*, quoted in F. Bridgland, 'Liberals on the Run', *The Sunday Times* (New Zealand) 23 May, 1993.

37 C. R. Hill, *Change in South Africa: Blind alleys or new directions?* (Rex Collings, London, 1983) p. 30.

38 Reverend Robert Orr, quoted in de Gruchy, *The Church Struggle in South Africa*, p. 93.

39 Mosley, *The Life of Raymond Raynes*, p. 255.

40 Quoted in G. Gerhart, *Black Power in South Africa: The evolution of an ideology* (University of California Press, Berkeley, 1978) p. 264.

41 Soweto is the black sister city of Johannesburg, its name being a contraction of 'South West Township'.

42 Cf., for instance, M. Schoffeleers, 'Black and African Theology in Southern Africa: a controversy re-examined', *Journal of Religion in Africa*, 1988, pp. 99ff.

43 Walshe, 'South Africa', p. 37.

44 Arthur Nortje, 'Soliloquy: South Africa', in his posthumous collection, *Dead Roots, Poems* (Heinemann, London, 1973) p. 5. Nortje died in 1970, but his words remained true.

45 Joseph Ratzinger with V. Messori, *The Ratzinger Report* (Ignatius Press, San Francisco, 1985) p. 90.

46 Quoted in Walshe, 'South Africa', p. 53.

47 *The Kairos Document*, p. 11.

48 Cochrane, 'Servants of Power', p. 166.

49 Walshe, 'South Africa', p. 51.

50 S. du Boulay, *Tutu Voice of the Voiceless* (Hodder and Stoughton, London, 1988), points out his weaknesses as well as his strengths.

51 Cf. for instance, R. Sider, *Rich Christians in an Age of Hunger* (Hodder and Stoughton, London, 1978), and his *Living More Simply* (Hodder and Stoughton, London, 1980).

52 J. Deotis Roberts, Foreword, 'Concerned Evangelicals', *Evangelical Witness in South Africa*, p. 11.

53 *Evangelical Witness in South Africa*, p. 33, Cf. P. Gifford, *The Religious Right in Southern Africa* (University of Zimbabwe Publications, Harare, 1988).

54 B. Sundkler, *Zulu Zion and Some Swazi Zionists* (Gleerups, with Oxford University Press, Uppsala, 1976) p. 24. This is the main source for the account that follows. I treasure my copy, a gift from its remarkable author. Cf. also the insightful analysis of Jean Comaroff, *Body of Power, Spirit of Resistance: The culture and history of a South African people* (University of Chicago Press, Chicago, 1985) chapters 6 and 7.

55 Archbishop N. H. Ngada and others, *Speaking for Ourselves*, (Institute for Contextual Theology, Bramfontein, 1985) pp. 6, 17.

56 Sundkler, *Zulu Zion and Some Swazi Zionists*, Ngada, *Speaking for Ourselves*, p. 30. There is a short autobiography by Nku in Ngada, *Speaking for Ourselves*, pp. 18–20.

57 Sundkler, *Zulu Zion and Some Swazi Zionists*, pp. 79ff.

58 Sundkler, *Zulu Zion and Some Swazi Zionists*, p. 198, 237.

59 Sundkler, *Zulu Zion and Some Swazi Zionists*, pp. 119ff. Khambule was influenced by another visionary, the teacher, John Mtanti (d. 1937). Like so many Zionist prophets, the two came, in the end, to a parting of the ways. The story of Ma Nku's church can be found both in Sundkler's study and in Ngada, *Speaking for Ourselves*, pp. 19–20.

60 Journal entry, 25 Oct., 1928, quoted in Sundkler, *Zulu Zion and Some Swazi Zionists*, p. 135.

61 n 1942, quoted in Sundkler, *Zulu Zion and Some Swazi Zionists*, p. 196, in the context of a rebuttal of Oosthuizen. Cf. G. C. Oosthuizen, *Post-Christianity in Africa* (C. Hurst,

Notes

London, 1968), and *The Theology of a South African Messiah: An analysis of the hymnal of The Church of the Nazarites* (E. J. Brill, London, 1967), M. L. Martin, *The Biblical Concept of Messiahs and Messianism in South Africa* (Morija Sesuto Book Depot, Morija, 1964).

62 Sundkler, *Zulu Zion and Some Swazi Zionists*, pp. 186–205.

63 A. G. Scutte, 'Thapelo ya Sephiri: A Study of Secret Prayer Groups in Soweto', *African Studies*, 1972, pp. 245ff. They are called *umthandazo wemfihlakalo* in Zulu, and are documented in North and West Transvaal, Botswana, Kimberley, and elsewhere, as well as Soweto.

64 Frank Chikane, *No Life of My Own: An Autobiography* (Catholic Institute for International Relations, London, 1988) p. 51.

65 Luthuli, *Let My People Go*, p. 131.

66 Nolan, *God in South Africa*, p. 176.

67 'Just a passerby', in K. Senanu and T. Vincent, eds, *A Selection of African Poetry* (Longman, Harlow, 1976) p. 199.

68 For Mau Mau and Algeria, cf. pp. 224, 258–9.

69 The period before the independence struggle in Angola, Mozambique, and Zimbabwe, and the history of their independent churches, are dealt with in Chapters 7 and 9. Their post-independence experience is considered in Chapter 12, with special reference to Marxism.

70 Cf. N. Thomas, 'Church and State in Zimbabwe', *Journal of Church and State*, 1985, p. 120.

71 M. Scott, *A Time to Speak*, p. 188.

72 J. V. Taylor and D. A. Lehmann, *Christians of the Copperbelt* (SCM, London, 1961) p. 158.

73 I. Linden, *The Catholic Church and the Struggle for Zimbabwe* (Longman, London, 1980) pp. 59, 84, 87–8, 231.

74 J. Marcum, *The Angolan Revolution* (Harvard University Press, Cambridge, Mass., 1969) I, 330–1.

75 L. Henderson, *Angola: Five centuries of conflict* (Cornell University Press, New York, 1979) pp. 174, 205–6.

76 B. Davidson, *In the Eye of the Storm: Angola's people* (Penguin Books, Harmondsworth, 1975), p. 188.

77 Henderson, *Angola*, pp. 218–9.

78 T. Henriksen, *Mozambique: A history* (Collings, London and Cape Town, 1978) p. 171, 215.

79 L. Hertsens, 'Mozambique: A church in a Socialist state in time of radical change', *Pro Mundi Vita*, Africa Dossier 33 (Jan.–Feb., 1977) pp. 19, 20.

Chapter 12

1 Quoted in R. Fox, *et al.*, 'The Second Independence: A Case Study of the Kwilu Rebellion in the Congo', *Comparative Studies in Society and History*, 1965, p. 91.

2 D. Barrett, *World Christian Encyclopedia* (Oxford University Press, Nairobi, 1982) p. 527. This study is the source for the percentages that follow.

3 I. Linden, *The Catholic Church and the Struggle for Zimbabwe* (Longman, London, 1980) pp. 32–3, 43.

4 Cf. J. Kerkhofs, 'The Church in Zimbabwe: The trauma of cutting apron strings', *Pro Mundi Vita*, Africa Dossier 20 (Jan., 1982) p. 20. The Bethlehem Fathers reached

Notes

Rhodesia in 1938, the Carmelites in 1947, the Burgos Fathers in 1953. French Canadian Marist Brothers dominated Catholic secondary schools.

5   V. Donovan, *Christianity Rediscovered: An Epistle from the Masai* (SCM Press, London 1978/1982) p. 9.

6   A. Kupalo, 'African Sisters' Congregations', in E. Fasholé-Luke, *et al.*, eds., *Christianity in Independent Africa* (Rex Collings, London, 1978) p. 126.

7   Quoted in M. Singleton and P. Marens, *Let My People Go: A survey of the Catholic Church in Western Nigeria* (Pro Mundi Vita, Brussels, 1974) p. 249.

8   Eugene Hillman, 'The Roman Catholic Apostolate to Nomadic Peoples in Kenya', *Pro Mundi Vita*, Africa Dossier (15 Oct., 1980) p. 32.

9   Donovan, *Christianity Rediscovered* p. 10, points out that guidelines adopted by the Maryknoll Fathers closely followed a speech by Nyerere.

10   J. Nyerere, 'The Church's role in society', in J. Parratt, ed., *African Christian Theology* (SPCK, London, 1987) pp. 122–3.

11   Gatu, quoted in R. E. Kendall, *The End of An Era: Africa and the Missionary* (SPCK, London, 1978) p. 90.

12   A. Mbembe, 'Rome and the African Churches', *Pro Mundi Vita*, Africa Dossiers 37–8 (2–3, 1986) p. 40. He later left the Jesuits, and replaced 'Fabien' with 'Eboussi.' Cf. p. 332.

13   M. Newitt, *Portugal in Africa* (C. Hurst, London, 1981) p. 133.

14   P. A. Kalilombe, 'The African local churches and the world-wide Roman Catholic communion', in E. Fasholé-Luke *et al.*, eds, *Christianity in Independent Africa*, pp. 84–5. Figures rounded.

15   Mbembe, 'Rome and the African Churches', p. 41.

16   J. Nelson, 'Class Formation and the Professionalization of an African Clergy', *Journal of Religion in Africa*, 1992, pp. 133ff.

17   'President Banda forced his departure from Malawi and the Church insisted on his resignation from Lilongwe', A. Hastings, 'The Council came to Africa', in Alberic Stacpoole, ed., *Vatican II Revisited by Those Who Were There* (Minneapolis, 1986) p. 323 n. 2 (editor's footnote). One of the problems was his involvement in faith healing.

18   J. Guy, *The Heretic. A Study of the Life of John William Colenso* (Ravan and University of Natal Press, Johannesburg and Pietermaritzburg, 1983) p. 134.

19   Declaration on the relation of the church to non-Christian religions', in A. Flannery, ed., *Vatican Council II: The Conciliar and Post-Conciliar Documents* (Dominican Publications, Dublin, rev. ed. 1988) I, 738ff.

20   R. Hackett, *Religion in Calabar: The Religious Life and history of a Nigerian Town* (Mouton de Gruyter, Berlin and New York, 1989) p. 140.

21   E. Isichei, 'Visions and Visionaries: The Search for Alternative forms of Authority Among Catholic Conservatives', *Archives de Science Sociale des Religions*, 1991, pp. 113ff.

22   There is an account of him in my 'Visions and Visionaries'. One interesting aspect that this paper discusses is an informal international network of seers, who support the authenticity of each other's visions.

23   Page 220, and cf. C. Maunder, 'Marian Apparitions', in A. Hastings, ed., *Modern Catholicism* (SPCK, London, 1991) pp. 280ff.

24   H. Turner, 'African Religious Movements and Roman Catholicism', in his *Religious Innovation in Africa* (G. K. Hall, Boston, 1979) p. 152.

25   *Africa Confidential*, 15 Oct., 1986, 27/21.

26   *Africa Confidential*, 20 Aug., 1986, 27/17.

Notes

27 Aylward Shorter, *Toward a Theology of Inculturation* (Orbis Books, New York, 1988) pp. 251–2.

28 Aylward Shorter, *Jesus and the Witchdoctor* (Geoffrey Chapman, London, 1985) p. 78.

29 Mbembe, 'Rome and the African Churches', pp. 25–7.

30 Quoted in Mbembe, 'Rome and the African Churches', p. 45.

31 Cf., for instance, Aidan Nichols, 'Professor Hastings' Vade-mecum of Progressive Catholicism', *Priest and People*, May, 1991, pp. 201–5.

32 Raymond Arazu, C. S. Sp., *The Role of the Religious in the Local Church: The Nigerian Situation* (privately published, Thiala, 1975) p. 12.

33 A. Kupalo, 'African Sisters 'Congregations', in Fasholé-Luke, *et al.*, eds., *Christianity in Independent Africa*, p. 129.

34 Singleton and Marens, *Let My People Go.* p. 206.

35 Cf. p. 282.

36 Kupalo, 'African Sisters' Congregations', in Fasholé-Luke, *et al.*, eds., *Christianity in Independent Africa*, pp. 129–30, and Religious Life for Women in Zaire' *Pro Mundi Vita*, Africa Dossier 14 (May, 1980) p. 24.

37 H. Hoeben, 'The Catholic Church in Sudan: A Golden Opportunity Lost', *Pro Mundi Vita*, Africa Dossier 28 (1/1984) pp. 13, 19.

38 This account is based on A. K. Weinrich, 'Western monasticism in independent Africa', in Fasholé-Luke, *et al.*, eds. *Christianity in Independent Africa*, pp. 554ff.

39 A. Hastings, *African Catholicism: Essays in Discovery* (SCM Press, London, 1989) p. 132.

40 S. Clements, 'The Catholic Church in Kenya: a Center of Hope', *Pro Mundi Vita*, Africa Dossier 22 (July, 1982) p. 6.

41 Clements, 'The Catholic Church in Kenya', pp. 6–8, 11–12. The members of the Association of Member Episcopal Conferences of Eastern Africa are Ethiopia, Sudan, Uganda, Kenya, Tanzania, Zambia, and Malawi.

42 Singleton, 'Explorations in Ecumenical Topography', *Pro Mundi Vita*, Africa Dossier 10 (Nov., 1979) p. 25.

43 E. Hillman, 'The Roman Catholic Apostolate to Nomadic Peoples in Kenya', *Pro Mundi Vita*, Africa Dossier 15 (Oct., 1980) p. 17.

44 Quoted in A. Shorter, *Jesus and the Witchdoctor* (London, 1985) p. 190.

45 E. Milingo, *The World in Between: Christian healing and the struggle for spiritual survival* (C. Hurst & Co. London, 1984) pp. 36, 118–9.

46 Joseh Ratzinger with V. Messon, *The Ratzinger Report* (San Francisco, 1985) pp. 193, 194.

47 Reported in *The Otago Daily Times*, 20 Dec., 1992.

48 This tends to take a different form, with priests who wish to marry leaving the priesthood. However, 1992 saw much publicity being given to the case of Bishop Eamon Casey in Ireland.

49 Milingo, *The World in Between*, p. 9.

50 Bankole Timothy, *Missionary Shepherds and African Sheep* (Daystar Press, Ibadan, 1971) pp. 23–4, quoted in Singleton and Marens, *Let My People Go*, p. 209.

51 M. Singleton, 'Obsession with Possession?', *Pro Mundi Vita*, Africa Dossier 4, N.S. (July–Aug., 1977) p. 15.

52 Quoted in Shorter, *Towards a Theology of Inculturation*, p. 247.

53 Paul Gifford, 'Prosperity: a New and Foreign Element in African Christianity', *Religion*, 1990, p. 381.

54 F. Eboussi Boulaga, *Christianity Without Fetishes* (Eng. trans. Orbis Books, New York 1984) pp. 30, 32.

Notes

55 V. Mudimbe, *The Invention of Africa* (Indiana University Press, Bloomington, 1988) p. 63.

56 H. Kabarhuza, 'Christian Intellectuals in Zaire', *Pro Mundi Vita*, Africa Dossiers 30–1, (3–4/1984), pp. 14, 21.

57 Lawrence Magesa, quoted in Hillman, 'The Roman Catholic Apostolate to Nomadic Peoples in Kenya', p. 30.

58 R. Ostling and J. Wilde, 'Africa's Artistic Resurrection', *Time*, 3 April, 1989.

59 A. Hastings, 'Were Women a Special Case?', in F. Bowie, *et al.*, eds., *Women and Missions: Past and Present* (Berg, Oxford, 1993) p. 122–3.

60 Hillman, 'The Roman Catholic Apostolate to Nomadic Peoples in Kenya', pp. 30–31. There is a large literature on the feminization of Christianity. It relies, as does Hillman's brief discussion here, on the selection of supposedly 'feminine' attributes.

61 Anon, 'Religious Life for Women in Zaire', *Pro Mundi Vita*, Africa Dossier 14, (May, 1980), p. 7.

62 S. Clements, 'The Catholic Church in Kenya', p. 5. Unfortunately, these figures do not give the number of expatriates and Kenyans in the latter two categories.

63 'Religious Life for Women in Zaire', p. 7.

64 'Religious Life for Women in Zaire', p. 17.

65 B. Meyer, ' "If you are a devil, you are a witch and, if you are a witch, you are a devil": The integration of "pagan" ideas into the conceptual universe of Ewe Christians in southeastern Ghana', *Journal of Religion in Africa*, 1992, pp. 100–102.

66 A.-L. Quinn, 'The emergence and persistence of the *Umunyano wa Wanakazi* in Malawi', paper presented to the Satterthwaite Colloquium on African religion, April, 1990, p. 16.

67 Hackett, *Religion in Calabar*, p. 136.

68 B. Olowo, 'God or Mammon?', *West Africa* (Aug. 1990) 13–19, p. 2274.

69 Olowo, 'God or Mammon?' p. 2274.

70 M. Ojo, 'Deeper Christian Life Ministry: A Case Study of the Charismatic Movements in Western Nigeria', *Journal of Religion in Africa*, 1988, pp. 141ff.

71 The account that follows is based on the following works by Gifford, 'Prosperity'; *Christianity and Politics in Doe's Liberia* (Cambridge University Press, Cambridge, 1993); *The Religious Right in Southern Africa* (University of Zimbabwe Publications, Harare, 1988). I differ with Gifford on some details of his analysis.

72 P. Gifford, ' "Africa Shall Be Saved": An Appraisal of Reinhard Bonnke's Pan-African Crusade', *Journal of Religion in Africa*, 1987, pp. 79, 80–1. (The prediction of motor traffic is supposedly found in Nahum 2. 3ff!)

73 Gifford expounds the history of these ideas in terms of the work of Kenneth Hagin. Oddly, he overlooks the influence of Norman Vincent Peale, whose works have been very widely read in Africa for decades (as have books such as Napoleon Hill, *Think and Grow Rich*). Peale emphasized positive thinking in a way very similar to contemporary New Age (and other) advocates of visualization techniques. He was also an advocate of giving and tithing as a way of prospering.

74 Gifford, ' "Africa Shall Be Saved" ', pp. 73, 86.

75 Gifford, *Christianity and Politics in Doe's Liberia*, pp. 152–3.

76 J. Ibrahim, 'Religion and political turbulence in Nigeria', *Journal of Modern African Studies*, 1991, p. 125, n. 37.

77 Gifford, *Christianity and Politics in Doe's Liberia*, pp. 154–5.

78 'Concerned Evangelicals', *Evangelical Witness in South Africa* (W. B. Eerdmans Pub. Co., Grand Rapids, Michigan, 1986) p. 20.

409

Notes

79 N. Lewis, *The Missionaries* (Martin Secker & Warburg Ltd., London, 1988) pp. 105ff and *passim*.

80 Lewis, *The Missionaries* p. 105; Gifford, *Christianity and Politics in Doe's Liberia*, p. 114, n. 25.

81 Quoted in Gifford, *Christianity and Politics in Doe's Liberia*, p. 114, n. 25.

82 New Tribes Mission doctrinal statement, quoted in Lewis, 'The Missionaries', p. 111.

83 Lewis, 'The Missionaries', p. 107.

84 Lewis, 'The Missionaries', pp. 210–211. The Panare are another South American Indian group.

85 *New Nigerian* articles, 1988, cited in J. Ibrahim, 'Religion and Politics in Nigeria', *Journal of Modern African Studies*, 1991, pp. 121–2.

86 David Lan, *Guns and Rain* (University of California Press, London, 1985) p. 6.

87 Quoted in T. O. Ranger, 'The Death of Chaminuka: Spirit Mediums, Nationalism and Guerilla War in Zimbabwe', *African Affairs*, 1982, p. 369.

88 Quoted in R. Horton, 'African Traditional Thought and Western Science', *Africa*, 1967, p. 156.

89 Cf. G. ten Haar and S. Ellis, 'Spirit Possession and healing in modern Zambia: an analysis of letters to Archbishop Milingo', *African Affairs*, 1988, pp. 199–200.

90 M. Singleton, 'Ethiopia: A Tale of Two Revolutions', *Pro Mundi Vita*, Africa Dossier 5 (Jan.–Feb., 1978) p. 18. For complaints about the secularized in Zaire, and Rwanda, cf. Kabarhuza, 'Christian Intellectuals in Zaire' p. 15.

91 J. Pobee, 'Religion and Politics in Ghana, 1972–1978', *Journal of Religion in Africa*, 1987, pp. 44ff.

92 J. Pobee, 'Church and State in Ghana, 1949–1966', in J. Pobee, ed., *Religion in a Pluralistic Society* (E. J. Brill, Leiden, 1976) p. 129.

93 Pobee, 'Church and State in Ghana', p. 137.

94 Quoted in J. Coleman, *Nigeria: Background to Nationalism* (University of California Press, Berkeley, 1958) p. 302.

95 F. Macpherson, *Kenneth Kaunda of Zambia: The Times and the Man* (Oxford University Press, London, 1974) p. 455. Mobutu has also been described in Messianic terms, as have other political leaders.

96 J. L. Hymans, *Léopold Sédar Senghor: An intellectual biography* (Edinburgh University Press, Edinburgh, 1971) p. 18.

97 Cf., for instance, 'Accountability and stability', *West Africa*, 26 June–2 July, 1989.

98 R. Ostling and J. Wilde, 'The Basilica in the Bush', *Time*, 3 July, 1989, pp. 54ff.

99 Ismail Serageldin, quoted in *Time*, 7 Sept, 1992, p. 32.

100 *Africa Confidential*, 28 Sept., 1990, 31/19.

101 Cf. 'Accounting for the church', in *Africa Confidential*, 7 Oct., 1988, 29/20.

102 Quoted in Macpherson, *Kenneth Kaunda of Zambia* p. 460.

103 'The Catholic Church in Sudan', p. 4.

104 'The Catholic Church in Sudan', pp. 6–11.

105 A song by the Nuer Singer, Moses Cot, quoted in D. Johnson, 'Foretelling Peace and War . . .' in M. Daly, ed., *Modernization in the Sudan* (L. Barber Press, New York, 1985) p. 129.

106 M. Mohamed Salih, ' "New Wine in Old Bottles": Tribal Militias and the Sudanese State', *Review of African Political Economy*, 1989, p. 169.

107 Dr Akanu Ibiam, at his home in Enugu, 7 Sept, 1976.

108 J. de St. Jorre, *The Nigerian Civil War* (Hodder and Stoughton, London, 1972) p. 407.

109 Ibiam, 7 Sept, 1976.

Notes

110 Notes of a conversation, 22 Aug., 1975.

111 The occasion was a decision to enlarge an Anglican church standing very close to a mosque. Cf. J. Ibrahim 'The Politics of Religion in Nigeria: the Parameters of the 1987 Crisis in Kaduna State', *Review of African Political Economy*, 1989, p. 66.

112 *West Africa*, 3 Feb. 1986; *The Economist*, 3 May, 1986. There remains considerable mystery about this, and it was never made public. Cf. *Africa Confidential*, 9 Mar., 1990, 31/5, p. 6.

113 Ibrahim, 'The Politics of Religion in Nigeria', p. 67; 'Riots in Kaduna State', *West Africa*, 22 March, 1987; Ibrahim 'Religion and political turbulence in Nigeria', pp. 117, 123, 129, 135.

114 *West Africa*, 7–13 May, 1990.

115 *Africa Research Bulletin*, Oct. 1991, p. 10316.

116 *Africa Research Bulletin*, May, 1991, p. 10141. The occasion was a decision to kill pigs as well as cattle and goats at a local abattoir. It was alleged that these riots were fomented by northern politicians, hoping for a Christian exodus. From the 1980s on, there have also been repeated outbreaks of violence between Muslim groups. Cf. E. Isichei, 'The Maitatsine Risings in Nigeria 1980–85: A Revolt of the Disinherited', *Journal of Religion in Africa*, 1988, pp. 42ff.

117 *Africa Research Bulletin*, Feb., 1992, p. 10471.

118 A. Mujaju, 'The Political crisis of Church Institutions in Uganda', *African Affairs*, 1976, p. 67, n. 1. Some estimates put Muslims at 10 per cent.

119 However, cf. M. Twaddle, 'Was the Democratic Party of Uganda a Purely Confessional Party?', in Fasholé-Luke, et al., eds., *Christianity in Independent Africa*, pp. 255ff.

120 The Nubian element in the Army goes back to Emin Pasha and Lugard, in the nineteenth century. This is a good example of the artificiality of colonial boundaries; Nilotes from northern Uganda were kin to peoples in the Sudan. The Army 'Nubians' were often North Ugandans, who had 'become Nubi' to varying extents. On this, cf. A. Southall, as quoted in A. Mazrui, 'Religious Strangers in Uganda: from Emin Pasha to Amin Dada', *African Affairs*, 1977, p. 23.

121 Cf., for instance, 'Uganda: for whom the bell tolls', in *Africa Confidential*, 15 Aug., 1984, 25/17.

122 Cf. A. Mbembe, 'Rome and the African Churches', *Pro Mundi Vita*, Africa Dossiers 37–8 (2–3/1986) p. 8.

123 Ibrahim, 'Religion and Political Turbulence in Nigeria', p. 126.

124 K. Adelman, 'The Church-State Conflict in Zaire: 1969–1974', *African Studies Review*, 1975; Ngindu Mushete, 'Authenticity and Christianity in Zaire', in Fasholé-Luke, et al., eds., *Christianity in Independent Africa*, pp. 228ff.

125 W. MacGaffey, *Modern Kongo Prophets* (Indiana Bloomington Press, Bloomington, 1983) p. 255, n. 2. Islamic, Jewish and Orthodox communities were also recognized, but were of minor significance.

126 'Zaire: Mobutu takes to the water', *Africa Confidential*, 15 June, 1990, 31/12.

127 Kabarhuza, 'Christian Intellectuals in Zaire', pp. 15–16.

128 C. Young, 'The northern republics, 1960–1980', in D. Birmingham and P. Martin, eds., *History of Central Africa* (Harlow, 1983) II, 321–2.

129 The occasion of the rising was the demand that they buy new school uniforms, bearing his name and insignia, and made by a factory his family owned!

130 C. Simon, 'The 73rd Disciple of Jesus Christ takes stock', *Guardian Weekly*, 20 Dec., 1992.

Notes

131 This account is based on an entry for Equatorial Guinea in *African Contemporary Record*, II, 1978–9, pp. B551–3.

132 Young, 'The northern republics', pp. 321–2.

133 F. Loft, 'Background to the Massacres in Burundi', *Review of African Political Economy*, 1988, p. 91 (Original punctuation amended).

134 I. Linden, 'The Roman Catholic Church in social crisis', in Fasholé-Luke, *et al.*, eds., *Christianity in Independent Africa*, pp. 242ff.

135 *Africa Confidential*, 20 Aug., 1986, 27/17, Jan., 1987, 28/1, and 4 Feb., 1987, 28/3. As these accounts point out, several Burundi bishops have been more outspoken in their critique of government. M. Huband in *The Guardian Weekly*, 5 June 1994, p. 1. Before this, prospects in both countries looked brighter. 1993 elections in Burundi ended Tutsi hegemony (though they were soon followed by a coup), and Rwanda had adopted multiparty power sharing, which included the RPF.

136 *Africa Confidential*, 3 Sept, 1986, 27/8. There are positive aspects as well—peace and stability, albeit achieved through repression—and, above all, a peasantry promptly paid for their produce.

137 C. McGreal, 'Poison fears of Banda's opponents', *Guardian Weekly*, 8 Nov., 1992.

138 *Africa Confidential*, 27 May, 1987 28/11.

139 Gifford, *Christianity and Politics in Doe's Liberia*, pp. 107, 71ff, 139, n. 79.

140 *Africa Confidential*, 13 July, 1990, 31/14.

141 M. Singleton, 'Explorations in Ecumenical Topography' pp. 6–7.

142 On Lenshina, cf. A. Roberts, 'The Lumpa Church of Alice Lenshina' in Rotberg and Mazrui, eds. *Protest and Power in Black Africa* (Oxford University Press, New York, 1970) pp. 513ff., and W. van Binsbergen, 'Religious Innovation and Political Conflict in Zambia: A contribution to the interpretation of the Lumpa rising', *African Perspectives*, 1976, pp. 101ff; G. Bond, 'A Prophecy that Failed: The Lumpa Church of Uyombe, Zambia', in S. Walker, *et al.*, eds., *African Christianity* (Academic Press, New York, 1979) pp. 137ff.

143 Quoted in H. Hinfelaar, 'Women's revolt: the Lumpa Church of Lenshina Mulenga in the 1950s', *Journal of Religion in Africa*, 1991, p. 106.

144 Quoted in Hinfelaar, 'Women's revolt', p. 117.

145 Roberts, 'The Lumpa Church of Alice Lenshina', p. 529.

146 Roberts, 'The Lumpa Church of Alice Lenshina', p. 540.

147 A. Hastings, *A History of African Christianity 1950–1975* (Cambridge University Press, Cambridge, 1979) pp. 195–6. These figures exclude the Independent Watch Tower Church founded by Jeremiah Gondwe, said to have 19 thousand members in 1976. The Witnesses, of course, do not call themselves a church and the word is used for convenience.

148 D. Cook, 'Church and State in Zambia: The Case of the African Methodist Episcopal Church', in Fasholé-Luke, *et al.*., eds., *Christianity in Independent Africa*, p. 285.

149 A. Roberts, *A History of Zambia* (Heinemann, London, 1976), p. 250.

150 Rwanda: Sects and security' in *Africa Confidential*, 15 Oct., 1986, 27/21.

151 *Africa Confidential*, 4 Feb., 1987, 28/3. Cf. 'Goodbye, Mama Alice', *Time*, 23 Nov., 1987.

152 *Africa Confidential*, 1 April, 1988, 29/7, and 3 Feb., 1989, 30/3.

153 *Africa Confidential*, 23 Sept, 1988, 29/19.

154 K. Banda, 'Reflections on the Position of African Women', *Pro Mundi Vita*, Africa Dossier 33 (2/1985) pp. 15–16.

155 Bernadette Kunambi, then Member of Parliament and Head of the Tanzanian Union

Notes

of Catholic Women, quoted in 'Reflections on the Position of African Women', p. 28.

156 Cf. H. Hoeben, 'Africa's Opaque Reality: Marxism and Christianity', *Pro Mundi Vita*, Africa Dossier 23 (1982/4).

157 There is much evidence on this: cf, for instance, 'Mozambique: Pretoria has the key', in *Africa Confidential*, 4 Mar., 1988, 29/5.

158 P. Nesbitt, 'Terminators, Crusaders and Gladiators, Western (private and public) support for Renamo and Unita', *Review of African Political Economy*, 1988, p. 120.

159 Cf., for instance, *Africa Confidential*, 4 Mar., 1988, 29/5.

160 Interviews with priests, quoted in Hoeben, 'Africa's Opaque Reality', p. 15.

161 Michel Kayoya, trans., A. Shorter, and M.–A. Baldwin *My Father's Footprints* (East African Publishing House, Nairobi, 1973) pp. 108–9, 129. For Kayoya, cf. pp. 236, 346.

162 Major superiors in 1977, quoted in Hoeben, 'Africa's Opaque Reality', p. 28.

163 Kerkhofs, 'The Church in Zimbabwe', p. 16.

Postscript

1 Reverend McGovern, 21 Jan., 1982, in S. Clements, 'The Catholic Church in Kenya: A Center of Hope,' *Pro Mundi Vita*, Africa Dossier 22 (July, 1982) p. 15.

References

1 *Political Thinking and Social Experience. Some Christian Interpretations of the Roman Empire*, (University of Canterbury Publications, 1964).

2 *Victoria Quakers.* (Oxford University Press, 1970).

3 *The Ibo People and the Europeans*, (Faber in U.K. and St Martins Press in U.S.A., 1973).

4 *A History of the Igbo People*, (Macmillan in U.K. and St Martins Press in U.S.A., 1977).

5 *A History of West Africa since 1800*, (Macmillan Education in U.K. and Africans in U.S.A., 1977).

6 *Igbo Worlds. An Anthology of Oral History and Historical Descriptions*, (Macmillan Education in U.K., Institute for the Study of Human Issues, Philadelphia, in U.S.A., 1977).

7 *Entirely for God. A Life of Michael Iwene Tansi*, (Macmillan Education in U.K., Cistercian Publications in U.S.A., 1980.)

8 *Studies in the History of Plateau State, Nigeria*, (Macmillan Press in U.K., Humanities Press in U.S.A., 1981). Editor and author of three chapters.

9 *Varieties of Christian Experience in Nigeria*, (Macmillan Press 1981). Editor and author of four chapters.

10 *A History of Nigeria*, (Longmans, 1983).

Index

Index

Index

Donatus, 37
Donovan, Vincent, 261
Dutch Reformed Church, 74, 111, 144, 305, 306, 307, 312; and apartheid, 305, 306

education, 45, 229, 235–7, 264, 267, 269–70; and Central Africa, 193–4; and colonialism, 235–7; and Lozi, 143; and missions, 94, 133, 197, 270–2, 339; and Northern Africa, 227; and Overtoun Institution, 141; and South Africa, 301–2
Efik; see Calabar
Egypt, 2, 13, 18, 43; and Copts, 217–21; and gnosticism, 18; and monasticism, 219–20
Equatorial Guinea, 324, 345
Equinao, Olaudah, 71
Eritrea, 217, 350
Ethiopia, 2, 15, 33, 46–52, 211–17, 351
Ethiopian churches, 3, 49, 124, 125–7, 181; and clergy, 49–50; and Judaism, 49; and marriage, 216; in Northern Africa, 215–16; in South and West Africa, 179–82; and Kikuyu, 246
Eusebius, 17; *Church History*, 17
evangelicalism, 75, 81–3, 93, 223, 241, 326, 332, 347, 335, 337; and commerce, 83–4, 91; and culture, 93; and Faith Missions, 89, 90, 337; and Keswick, 89, 91; and slavery, 81; and Revivals, 242, 332

Faith Tabernacle; see Christ Apostolic Church
Faith Missions, 142, 269–70, 274, 275, 326; in Central Africa, 192–3; and women, 190
Falashas, 17, 50
Franciscans, 54, 87
Francis, St, 54
Freeman, Thomas Birch, 77, 156, 159, 168–9, 171
Frelimo; see Mozambique

Gabon, 205; and Bwiti, 205–6

Genadendal (Valley of Grace); see Moravians
Ghana (Gold Coast), 45, 53, 59, 167–70, 285, 297, 334, 338
gnostics, 20; and Nag Hammadi, 18
'Gospel of Prosperity', 335–6
Griqua, 100, 104, 106; see also Khoi
Guinea-Bissau, 45, 321
Guta re Jehovah; see Mai Chaza

Harms, Louis, 76, 85
Harris, William Wade, 3, 166, 170, 265, 284–6, 278
Hausa, 273, 343
Herero, 101
Hermannsburg Missionary Society; see Harms, Louis
Holy Ghost Fathers, 85, 161, 162, 321, 326, 342
Houphouet-Boigny, Felix; see Ivory Coast
Huddleston, Trevor, 300, 302, 308, 309
Hutu, 150, 246, 247, 345, 355

Ibiam, Francis Akanu, 341–2
Idahosa, Benson, 335–6
Idowu, Bolaji, 325
Igbo, 155, 160, 173, 269, 270, 271, 273, 341, 342
Improvers, the, 110, 124, 304
inculturation, 330, 331, 333, 339
Inkatha; see Zulu
Institute for Contexual Theology, 322
Islam, 43, 57, 98, 128, 130, 131, 135, 139, 209, 221, 228, 272; and Algeria, 319; and Buganda, 146, 147; and Children of the Israelites, 273; and colonialism, 233; and Copts, 43, 219; and Ethiopia, 51; in Eritrea, 217; and Lavigerie, 222; and Nigeria, 275, 342–3; and Nubia, 31–2; in Spain and Portugal, 52–3; in Sudan, 224, 226, 340–1; in Uganda, 343; and West Africa, 153, 277
Ivory Coast, 265, 284, 285, 339

Jager, Afrikaner, 106
Jehovah's Witnesses, 202, 232, 235, 248, 250–1, 347; in Zambia, 349

416

Index

Printed in the United States
68133LVS00004B/71

9 780802 808431